THE MURDER OF KING JAMES I

The MURDER of
KING JAMES I

Alastair Bellany & Thomas Cogswell

YALE UNIVERSITY PRESS
NEW HAVEN AND LONDON

For information about this and other Yale University Press publications, please contact:
U.S. Office: sales.press@yale.edu   www.yalebooks.com
Europe Office: sales@yaleup.co.uk   www.yalebooks.co.uk

Typeset in Minion Pro by IDSUK (DataConnection) Ltd
Printed in Great Britain by Gomer Press Ltd, Llandysul, Ceredigion, Wales

Library of Congress Cataloging-in-Publication Data

Bellany, Alastair James, 1968-
   The murder of King James I / Alastair Bellany and Thomas Cogswell.
     pages cm
   ISBN 978-0-300-21496-3 (cl : alk. paper)
1. James I, King of England, 1566-1625—Death and burial. I. Cogswell, Thomas, 1952- II. Title.
   DA391.B45 2015
   941.06′1—dc23
                                                                              2015023635

A catalogue record for this book is available from the British Library.

10 9 8 7 6 5 4 3 2 1

To

Lucy Cogswell Stewart, Ned Cogswell,
David Yaffe-Bellany and Rachel Yaffe-Bellany

Part One | Slavery and Racial Worlds

CONTENTS

ILLUSTRATIONS

Frontispiece

Crispijn de Passe the Elder, *King James VI and I* (c. 1620), with permission of the Huntington Library, San Marino, California.

Plates

Figures   *page*

ACKNOWLEDGEMENTS

COLLABORATIVE RESEARCH PRESENTS daunting logistical difficulties, espe-cially for two busy academics living and teaching three time zones apart. That we finished this book at all owes an incalculable amount to the American Council of Learned Societies (ACLS) whose award of a Collaborative Research Fellowship gave us the precious time to research and write this study. We are extremely grateful too for support from our home institutions, in particular, the Department of History, the Center for Ideas and Society, and the Senate Research Committee at UC Riverside; and the Department of History, the Center for Cultural Analysis, the British Studies Center, and the School of Arts and Sciences at Rutgers. Vital logistical support was also provided by Ed Ford in Dutch Neck and Sandy Solomon in Thanet Street.

We must also thank the numerous scholars and archivists whose assistance over the years has regularly reminded us of the generosity of our fellow citizens of the Republic of Letters. This book owes much to conversations with Susan Amussen, David Como, David Cressy, Richard Cust, Jordan Downs, Lori Anne Ferrell, Ken Fincham, Paul Hammer, Simon Healey, Cynthia Herrup, Ann Hughes, Sean Kelsey, Mark Kishlansky, Chris Kyle, Peter Lake, Jason Peacey, Steve Pincus, Michael Questier, Joad Raymond, Ethan Shagan, Isaac Stephens, Dan Szechi, Nicholas Tyacke, Tim Wales and Michael Young. Portions of this book have been presented to various NACBS (North American Conference on British Studies) and Huntington Library conferences, and to seminars at the Institute of Historical Research in London, the Center for Cultural Analysis and the Center for Historical Analysis at Rutgers, and at Berkeley, Canterbury, Claremont, Colorado-Boulder, Helsinki, Merced, Oxford, Princeton, Wesleyan and Yale. The feedback from audiences at all these presentations has been inval-uable. We owe priceless research advice, references or transcriptions to the generosity of Frederic Clark, Robert Cross, James Delbourgo, Jordan Downs, Antonio Feros, Simon Healey, James Holstun, Siobhan Keenan, Mark Kishlansky, Ed Legon, Anna-Marie Linnell, Leanna McLaughlin, Noah Millstone, Martin

Mulsow, Patrick O'Neill, Jason Peacey, Curtis Perry, Joad Raymond, Jane
Rickard, Gary Shaw, Christopher Thompson and Tim Wales. We are especially
grateful to Noah Millstone and Joad Raymond for directing us towards manuscript sources that proved of tremendous importance in our understanding of
key elements of the history we were trying to tell.

The acquisition and interpretation of some crucial pieces of evidence
was very much a collective effort. Many archivists provided timely expert
help, most notably the staff of the Bodleian Library, the British Library, the
Folger Shakespeare Library, the Huntington Library and the National Archives.
We are particularly grateful to Nico de Brabander and his staff at the Plantin-
Moretus Archive, to Joachim Tepperberg and his colleagues at the Haus-,
Hof- und Staatsarchiv, to Estelle Lambert at the BIUM in Paris, and to the
remarkably efficient and unfailingly kind staff of the Archivo General de
Simancas. Staff at the Advocates Library in Edinburgh, the James Ford Bell
Library of the University of Minnesota, the Library of Trinity College Dublin,
the West Yorkshire Record Office, and the Hertfordshire Archive and Library
Service kindly—and quickly—provided digital images of rare items. Our grad-
uate students Amy Tims (in Indiana), Jennifer Wilson (at the Bodleian) and
Isaac Stephens (in London) were also invaluable sources of digital images. We
are also extremely grateful for expert assistance and advice on translations
from Frederic Clark and Samantha Kelly (Latin), Martin Mulsow (German),
Patrick O'Neill (Spanish) and Arnout van der Meer (Dutch). Anthony Grafton
and Samantha Kelly also helped untangle a particularly knotty piece of Latin
paleography. We would like especially to thank Frederic Clark, whose brilliant
work with complex neo-Latin poetry and prose opened up numerous interpretive doors that would otherwise have remained closed to us.

We are also deeply indebted more generally to Peter Lake and Cynthia
Herrup, who both wrote letters on our behalf for the ACLS. Peter has remained
a constant source of encouragement and inspiration; and Cynthia provided a
typically useful and astute reading of the manuscript for the press. Much-needed
advice also came from two other still anonymous readers. At Yale University
Press in London, Robert Baldock responded with patience and enthusiasm
when we presented him with a manuscript very different from the one he was
expecting from us, and we greatly appreciate his support for the book. We
are grateful too to Candida Brazil, who has overseen this book's production,
and to our copy-editor Richard Mason, who brought an eagle eye to a long and
complicated text. Deborah Yaffe exchanged her customary blue pen for a
multicoloured track-changes font, but her love of clarity, grammatical rigour
and Austenesque economy helped whip an earlier (and even longer) draft of this
book into shape.

One of the sadder signs of this book's long gestation is the loss of colleagues
and mentors whose advice, encouragement and example have shaped one

or both of our careers. Although they would almost certainly have had very different (and not always positive) reactions to its arguments, we greatly regret that Christopher Hill, Maurice Keen, Mark Kishlansky, Conrad Russell, Kevin Sharpe, Lawrence Stone and David Underdown are not here to read this book.

Finally, it is a pleasure to record debts closer to home. Although we cannot adequately express what we owe to Deborah Yaffe and Georgia Warnke for keeping us sane during the long process of researching and writing this book, we know we are very lucky men. The dedicatees of this book have had to endure more than their fair share of stories of early Stuart poison, medicine and libel over the past few years. In return, they have continually reminded us what really matters.

ABBREVIATIONS

Add.	Additional
Akrigg, *Letters*	*The Letters of King James VI and I*, ed. G. P. V. Akrigg (Berkeley and Los Angeles, 1984)
APC	*Acts of the Privy Council of England, 1542–1631*, eds J. R. Dasent et al., 45 vols (London, 1890–1965)
BL	British Library, London
Bellany, "Lambe"	Alastair Bellany, "The Murder of John Lambe: Crowd Violence, Court Scandal and Popular Politics in Early Seventeenth-Century England", *P&P* 200 (2008)
Bellany, *Politics*	Alastair Bellany, *The Politics of Court Scandal in Early Modern England: News Culture and the Overbury Affair, 1603–1660* (Cambridge, 2002)
Bergeron, *Letters*	David W. Bergeron, *James I and Letters of Homoerotic Desire* (Iowa City, 1999)
BIHR	*Bulletin of the Institute for Historical Research*
BIUM	Bibliothèques interuniversitaires de médecine, Paris
Bod.	Bodleian Library, Oxford
C&T Charles	*The Court and Times of Charles I*, ed. R. F. Williams, compiled by Thomas Birch, 2 vols (London, 1849)
C&T James	*The Court and Times of James I*, ed. R. F. Williams, compiled by Thomas Birch, 2 vols (London, 1849)
CCA	Canterbury Cathedral Archive
CD 1621	*Commons Debates 1621*, eds Wallace Notestein, Frances Helen Relf and Hartley Simpson, 7 vols (New Haven, 1935)
Chamberlain	*The Letters of John Chamberlain*, ed. Norman E. McClure, 2 vols (Philadelphia, 1939)
CJ	*Journals of the House of Commons*
Clarendon, *History*	Edward Hyde, Earl of Clarendon, *The History of the Rebellion and Civil Wars in England*, ed. W. Dunn Macray, 6 vols (Oxford, 1888)
Cogswell, *Revolution*	Thomas Cogswell, *The Blessed Revolution: English Politics and the Coming of War, 1621–1624* (Cambridge, 1989)

Cornwallis	*The Private Correspondence of Jane Lady Cornwallis Bacon, 1613–1644*, ed. Joanna Moody (Madison and Teaneck, 2003)
CSPD	*Calendar of State Papers Domestic (James I and Charles I)*, eds Mary Anne Everett Green, John Bruce, William Douglas Hamilton and Sophia Crawford Lomas, 27 vols (London, 1857–93)
CSPV	*Calendar of State Papers and manuscripts, relating to English affairs, existing in the archives and collections of Venice*, eds Horatio F. Brown and Allen B. Hinds, vols 10–28 (London, 1900–27)
CUL	Cambridge University Library, Cambridge
D'Ewes, *Autobiography*	*The Autobiography and Correspondence of Sir Simonds D'Ewes*, ed. J. O. Halliwell, 2 vols (London, 1845)
D'Ewes, *Diary*	*The Diary of Sir Simonds D'Ewes (1622–1624): Journal d'un étudiant londonien sous le règne de Jacques 1er*, ed. Elisabeth Bourcier (Paris, 1974)
EHR	*English Historical Review*
Ellis	*Original Letters, Illustrative of English History*, ed. Henry Ellis, 2nd Series, vol. 3 (London, 1827)
ESL	Alastair Bellany and Andrew McRae (eds), "Early Stuart Libels: An Edition of Poetry from Manuscript Sources", *Early Modern Literary Studies*, Text Series 1 (2005): www.earlystuartlibels.net.
Folger	Folger Shakespeare Library, Washington, D.C.
Forerunner	George Eglisham, *The Forerunner of Revenge Upon the Duke of Buckingham* (Frankfurt [Brussels], 1626)
Fuller, *Church*	Thomas Fuller, *The Church-History of Britain* (London, 1656)
Goodman, *Court*	Godfrey Goodman, *The Court of King James the First*, ed. John S. Brewer, 2 vols (London, 1839)
Hardwicke, *SP*	Philip Yorke, Earl of Hardwicke, *Miscellaneous State Papers from 1501 to 1726*, vol. 1 (London, 1778)
Harl.	Harleian
HHstA	Haus-, Hof und Staatsarchiv, Vienna
HJ	*Historical Journal*
HLQ	*Huntington Library Quarterly*
HMC Cowper	*The Manuscripts of the Earl Cowper. K.G., Preserved at Melbourne Hall, Derbyshire*, Historical Manuscripts Commission Twelfth Report, Appendix, Part 1, vol. 1 (London, 1888)
HMC Salisbury	*Calendar of the Cecil Papers in Hatfield House*, 24 vols (Historical Manuscripts Commission: London, 1883–1976)
HOC	*The House of Commons 1604–1629*, eds Andrew Thrush and John P. Ferris, 6 vols (Cambridge, 2010)
Holles	*The Letters of John Holles 1587–1637*, ed. P. R. Seddon, 3 vols (Thoroton Record Society 31, 35–6: 1975, 1983, 1986)
JBS	*Journal of British Studies*
KHLC	Kent History and Library Centre, Maidstone

Laud	*The Diary* in William Laud, *The Works of the Most Reverend Father in God, William Laud, D.D. Sometime Lord Archbishop of Canterbury*, vol. 3 (Oxford, 1853)
LJ	*Journals of the House of Lords*
Lockyer, *Buckingham*	Roger Lockyer, *Buckingham: The Life and Political Career of George Villiers, First Duke of Buckingham 1592–1628* (London, 1981)
M&K	*Supplementary Report on the Manuscripts of the Earl of Mar and Kellie*, ed. H. Paton (Historical Manuscripts Commission: London, 1930)
Malcolm, *Reason*	Noel Malcolm, *Reason of State, Propaganda and the Thirty Years' War: An Unknown Translation by Thomas Hobbes* (Oxford, 2007)
Mercure François	*Le Mercure François, ou, Suite de L'Histoire de Nostre Temps*, 25 vols (Paris, 1611–48)
NA	The National Archives, Kew
NLS	National Library of Scotland, Edinburgh
NLW	National Library of Wales, Aberystwyth
NRS	National Records of Scotland, Edinburgh
ODNB	*Oxford Dictionary of National Biography* (Oxford, 2004)
P&P	*Past and Present*
Peake	Peter Peake's Diary, BL Add. MS 71446
PP1625	*Proceedings in Parliament 1625*, eds Maija Jansson and William B. Bidwell (New Haven and London, 1987)
PP1626	*Proceedings in Parliament 1626*, eds Maija Jansson and William B. Bidwell, 4 vols (New Haven and London, 1991–96)
PP1628	*Proceedings in Parliament 1628*, eds Mary Frear Keeler, Maija Jansson and William B. Bidwell, 6 vols (New Haven, 1977–83)
Proclamations, Charles I	*Stuart Royal Proclamations: Charles I*, eds James F. Larkin and Paul L. Hughes (Oxford, 1983)
Proclamations, James I	*Stuart Royal Proclamations: James I*, eds James F. Larkin and Paul L. Hughes (Oxford, 1973)
Prodromus	George Eglisham, *Prodromus Vindictae in Ducem Buckinghamiae* (Frankfurt [Brussels], 1626)
Progresses	*The Progresses, Processions and Magnificent Festivities of King James the First*, ed. John Nichols, 4 vols (London, 1826)
RCP	Royal College of Physicians, London
Register PSC	*The Register of the Privy Council of Scotland*, 30 vols (Edinburgh, 1877–1915)
RO	Record Office
Roe	*The Negotiations of Sir Thomas Roe* (London, 1740)
Rous	*Diary of John Rous Incumbent of Santon Downham, Suffolk, from 1625 to 1642*, ed. Mary Anne Everett Green (Camden Society 1st Series, 66: London, 1856)
Rusdorf	J. J. von Rusdorf, *Mémoires et Négociations Secrètes de Mr de Rusdorf*, ed. E. G. Cuhn (Leipzig, 1789)

Rushworth   John Rushworth, *Historical Collections of Private Passages of State, Weighty Matters of Law, Remarkable Proceedings in Five Parliaments, Beginning the Sixteenth Year of King James, Anno 1618 and ending the Fifth Year of King Charles, Anno 1629* (London, 1659)

Salvetti   *Historical Manuscripts Commission Eleventh Report, Appendix, Part 1: Manuscripts of Henry Duncan Skrine, esq.: Salvetti Correspondence* (London, 1887)

Scrinia   John Hacket, *Scrinia Reserata: A Memorial Offer'd to the Great Deservings of John Williams, D.D.* (London, 1693)

Sharpe, *Image Wars*   Kevin Sharpe, *Image Wars: Promoting Kings and Commonwealths in England 1603–1660* (New Haven and London, 2010)

SP   State Papers

Strafford   *The Earle of Strafforde's Letters and Dispatches*, ed. William Knowler, 2 vols (London, 1739)

ST   *Cobbett's Complete Collection of State Trials*, ed. T. B. Howell, 33 vols (London, 1809–26)

TCD   Trinity College Dublin

TRHS   *Transactions of the Royal Historical Society*

TT   Thomason Tracts, British Library

Whiteway   *William Whiteway of Dorchester: His Diary 1618 to 1635*, ed. David Underdown (Dorset Record Society 12, 1991)

Wotton   *The Life and Letters of Sir Henry Wotton*, ed. Logan Pearsall Smith, 2 vols (Oxford, 1907)

Yonge   *The Diary of Walter Yonge, 1604–1628*, ed. George Roberts (Camden Society 1st Series, 41: London, 1848)

CONVENTIONS

ALL DATES ARE Old Style, though we take the New Year as beginning on 1 January. Spelling has been left in its original form, but we have expanded contractions and have occasionally modified spelling and punctuation where clarity is needed.

Whenever possible when citing from contemporary correspondence, we have noted the letter-writer and recipient. We do not do so, however, in cases where either the writer or the recipients are understood. Thus the Florentine agent Salvetti is always writing to the Archduke of Florence, and the Venetian ambassadors to the Doge and Senate of Venice; John Holles and John Chamberlain are understood as authors of the letters cited from *Holles* and *Chamberlain*; and the correspondence in *M&K* is always from the Earl of Kellie to the Earl of Mar.

Items from the Thomason Tracts are typically cited with their TT number, and we have also inserted the date Thomason purchased the item if known.

"SUCH TALES AS GOES HERE OF HIM"

HISTORY, MEDICINE AND THE MURDER OF

KING JAMES I

F EW MEN KNEW King James VI and I better than Thomas Erskine did. He had sat with him as a schoolboy in Scotland, and in 1585, at the age of nineteen, had become a gentleman of James's bedchamber, an office that kept him in frequent attendance on the young king. In 1601, after Erskine had helped save James from would-be assassins, the king appointed him to the Scottish Privy Council, and, on accession to the English throne in 1603, named him Captain of the Guard. James continued to honour his old friend, making him Lord Erskine in 1604 and Viscount Fenton in 1606, adding him to the English Privy Council in 1610, before naming him Earl of Kellie in 1619. But Kellie's most significant office was the one he had acquired back in 1605, when he became James's Groom of the Stool, the bedchamber servant who dressed and undressed the king and assisted him at the toilet. Intimate bodily service at the heart of the English court gave Kellie virtually unmatched access to the king and thus to power itself.[1]

As head of the royal bedchamber, Kellie had plenty of news to fill his letters home to his cousin the Earl of Mar, one of the most powerful politicians in Scotland. As the years passed, Kellie's letters dwelled increasingly on James's health, which by late 1624 had become alarmingly erratic (Plate 1). Late that November, James was "verrye weill in his helthe", though much less active than he had been. Three weeks later, the king was bedridden, "ill trubled with a universall paine in shulders, elboes, knees and feete". Yet by early January 1625, James seemed "weill convalessed"; indeed, after staying up until the early hours at a court masque, he was ready to quit Whitehall for his hunting lodge at Newmarket.[2] By early March the king was at Theobalds, his grand estate a dozen miles north of the capital. But when Kellie next sat down to write, the news was dispiriting: shortly after arriving at Theobalds, James had fallen ill again.

On 9 March, Kellie reported that James had suffered "three fitts of a tertian agew". This was not particularly worrisome: many suspected a mild intermittent fever might actually do the king good, and although James intensely disliked the hot phase of the fever fit, he coped much better with the shivers and sweats that preceded and followed it. A week later, however, Kellie had started to worry. After spending the night nursing James through his seventh fit, he reported that the latest episode had been less intense than the previous three. But James's usual "impatiencye in the tyme of the heate" tended to prolong the fits, and his stubborn refusal to follow his physicians' advice risked complications. "If he wold be rewled or advysed I doe not doubt but it wold doe mutche good," Kellie complained, "utherwayes he is in perrell to fall in a dropsye, whitche I beseitche God to preserve him from." By 22 March, Kellie's worst fears had been realized. For the past two nights, James had been in such "great extremetye" that "it did frycht us all". The fever fits, initially returning every other day, were now daily events, and had intensified alarmingly. "God save the King," Kellie wrote, praying that James would "have noe more sutche fitts as he had this last nycht and the nycht before." If the illness persisted like this, he confessed, "it shall make us all mourne". The Earl of Mar should have no illusions; James was "a seeke man and worss then I love to wret".[3]

A week later, James was dead and Kellie's world lay in ruins. His first letter, scribbled the day after James died, was noticeably terse: "I culd not but wret, thoe my subject dois not weill pleis ather of us". James had died on Sunday, 27 March, Kellie reported. "For this tyme I will saye noe more, but as he leved in pace soe did he dye in pace, and I praye God our [new] King . . . maye follow him in all his good, whitche for my pairt I think was noe small portione." Ten days later, he sent further news of "this sorrowful accident", reassuring Mar that James had died bravely and well. With the future uncertain, Kellie wondered whether it was time to retire "now, when he is gone that I have waitted on theis fyftye yeares". The veteran bedchamber man had faith in the young King Charles, but others were less certain; many worried, in particular, about "my Lord of Bukkingame his power with him".[4] They had reason for concern. A decade earlier, Kellie and several other courtiers had pushed the handsome young George Villiers onto the path to preferment, hoping that he would counter the influence of the king's current favourite, the Scotsman Robert Carr, Earl of Somerset. But after Somerset's shocking fall from grace in 1615, Kellie had witnessed at close hand Villiers's meteoric rise. By the time Villiers became Duke of Buckingham in 1623, he had amassed unprecedented numbers of offices and titles, and acquired levels of wealth and influence that overshadowed all rivals. No court favourite had ever been quite like him, and his power reached deep into the royal administration, even into Kellie's domain in the bedchamber. As James I's health began to decline, Kellie marvelled at Buckingham's canny cultivation of the heir to the throne; in January 1625 he had told Mar that the "affectione betwyxt" Prince Charles and Buckingham was now "Infinite". This new-formed alliance swept all before it. A fervent supporter of peace with Spain, Kellie had been mostly powerless in James's final months, as the prince and the favourite mobilized the regime for war.[5] For men of Kellie's ilk, the certain promise of Buckingham's continued dominance at court made withdrawal an increasingly attractive option.

Back in Scotland, as he pondered this uncertain future, the Earl of Mar doubtless returned to the letter his cousin had written on 22 March, five days before James's death. Along with Kellie's report of James's violent fever had come equally unnerving news. As the king's condition worsened, his attendants began to quarrel, voicing almost unspeakable allegations against the most powerful courtier of all. "Their hes sume thing fallin out heir mutche dislyked, and I for my selfe think mutche mistakkin," Kellie had written. The Duke of Buckingham, "wishing mutche the Kings healthe," had supplied James with medicines, a plaster "applyed to the Kings breeste" and a "drink or syrope"; and he had applied these drugs "without the consent or knowledge of onye of the doctours". This meddling was bad enough, but there was worse—James had become "extremlye seeke" after taking these unprescribed medicines. "This has spreade sutche a busines heir and discontent as you wold wonder," Kellie reported. A few bold attendants accused the favourite of foul play. "Doctoure Craige is now absented from Court, and Henrye Gibb of his Majesties beddchamber is quarreled for it, and my Lord of Bukkinghame soe incensed as your Lordshipe wold wonder." Despite his ambivalent feelings towards the favourite, Kellie sympathized with the duke's anger. "If I was in his plaice", he told Mar, "I wold be soe myselfe, considering what the world sayes, and I protest I think he gets great wrong in saying sutche tealles as goes heir of him."[6]

* * *

This book offers the first modern account of the long and damaging history of those strange "tealles" about Buckingham's potion and plaster and their role in the old king's death. Even before James had breathed his last, rumours of poisoning had begun to spread outside the court. In the spring of 1626 these whispers acquired a far more detailed and compelling form in a remarkable pamphlet published in Latin, English and German editions that spelled out how the duke had systematically poisoned his court rivals and his king. This book, titled in English *The Forerunner of Revenge Upon the Duke of Buckingham*, was the work of George Eglisham, a Scottish physician, polemicist and poet. Eglisham did not consciously model his narrative on Procopius's famous *Secret History* of the court of the Emperor Justinian, written in the sixth century, but his book followed Procopius's pattern, exposing lurid dealings at court and offering his readers a compelling secret history of the crimes of the great and powerful.[7] George Eglisham's secret history of the murder of James I, and the countless variations his contemporaries played upon it, exerted a near-continuous influence on British political culture for the next thirty-five years. In the late 1620s contemporaries scrambled to find printed or handwritten copies of Eglisham's tract, which they read and pondered with unusual care. In 1626 debates over James's death, stimulated in part by *The Forerunner of Revenge*, irreparably damaged an already fragile relationship between Charles I and his Parliament. Libellous poetry and seditious talk continued to target Buckingham as a poisoner, and these allegations fuelled the mounting popular outrage that culminated in the duke's assassination in 1628. When civil war began in England in 1642, Eglisham's pamphlet reappeared in multiple new editions to harden the resolve of those now taking up arms against Charles I. Early in 1648, as many yearned for a negotiated settlement, radicals in the Army and Parliament used variations on the secret history not only to end negotiations with Charles but also to implicate him in his father's death. A few months later, claims about James's murder hung over the debates about his son's trial. Indeed, by the time of Charles's execution in January 1649, James's murder had become a revolutionary shibboleth, and it figured prominently in the foundational mythology of the English Republic, repeatedly invoked by the regime's propagandists to condemn the Stuart monarchy and defend the Free State. During the 1650s historians and polemicists of many political stripes bitterly debated the manner and significance of James's death as they tried to explain the Stuart dynasty's dramatic fall. Indeed, for the next two hundred years, historians as diverse as Gilbert Burnet, Paul de Rapin-Thoyras and George Brodie continued the debate, feeling obliged to consider the allegation even if they eventually dismissed it.

That debate ended in the late nineteenth century. The first generation of professional historians, trained in the latest positivist methods, were embarrassed by their predecessors' fascination with James's supposed murder. S. R. Gardiner, the brilliant, painstaking scholar who published the first modern analytical narrative of early seventeenth-century English politics, knew very well that allegations about James's death had been central to the parliamentary debates of 1626 and 1648, but he thought their prominence an unfortunate distraction from the more serious religious and constitutional issues at stake (Fig. 1). Between 1863 and 1882, Gardiner produced a *History of England* in five two-volume sets, and the first volume of his pair of books on the years 1624–28 patiently reconstructed what had really happened at Theobalds in March 1625. After detailing how Buckingham and his mother Mary Villiers had applied remedies to the king, Gardiner recounted the physicians' annoyance at this meddling and acknowledged that, "it soon became an article of belief with thousands of not usually credulous persons that the King had been poisoned". Gardiner, however, did not share this credulity. "The remedies may have been, and probably were, harmless", he wrote, adding wryly that the ageing Countess of Buckingham had applied them "with all the zeal which elderly ladies are apt to throw into the administration of remedies suggested by themselves". In a footnote Gardiner added that he considered the "evidence" for poisoning "worthless in itself", for the "only ground for supposing it to have any value is cut away" once we realize that "Buckingham had no object [i.e. motive] in poisoning the King".[8] Of George Eglisham and *The Forerunner of Revenge*, Gardiner said nothing. A non-conformist Victorian Liberal fascinated by stern figures of sound moral character, Gardiner had scant historical sympathy for more equivocal men, little tolerance for scurrility, and no time at all for libel. Thus, in his accounts of the political crises of 1626 and 1648, Gardiner persistently minimized any mention of poisoning talk. He failed to explore the House of Commons' hearings into James's death in 1626, and he passed over most of the bitter debates that ensued. Recounting the parliamentary declaration of 1648, in which the death of James I loomed large, he commented with exasperation that "Unfortunately even the scandal of Buckingham's administering physic to James was raked up." Gardiner did not ask why it was raked up, and he never referred to the charge again.[9]

By the time Gardiner published his revised ten-volume edition of the *History of England* in the later 1880s, he had discovered modern medical support for his verdict. In 1856, Norman Chevers, a thirty-eight-year-old British physician, expert on tropical medicine and the Principal of the Calcutta Medical College in India, had published *A Manual of Medical Jurisprudence for*

Figure 1: James Russell & Sons, *Samuel Rawson Gardiner*, c. 1900 (National Portrait Gallery).

Bengal and the North-Western Provinces (Fig. 2). Poisoning was endemic in this part of the subcontinent, and Chevers devoted a third of his manual to the crime. In passing, he glanced in a footnote at "the libellous Eglisham" who, he concluded, had exaggerated the medical evidence for James I's murder. Yet Chevers's interest was piqued, and he soon began a more systematic inquiry into James's death. In 1862 he summarized his findings in a pamphlet, published in both Calcutta and London, which took as its title the stark question *Did James the First of England Die from the Effects of Poison, or from Natural Causes?* After assembling a wide range of printed evidence and subjecting it to scientific scrutiny, Chevers delivered what looked to be a clear-cut verdict: "there is not a vestige of evidence, which would be accepted in the present day, to show that King James was poisoned." As he prepared the revised edition of his *History*, Gardiner added Chevers's verdict to his original footnote on the poisoning allegations: "Dr. Norman Chevers", he reported, "has shown that there is no medical evidence in favour of the theory of poison."[10] Gardiner's work effectively ended serious scholarly consideration of Eglisham's secret history. The great historian had instructed students of the period to ignore this palpable falsehood, and for over a century virtually all of them complied.

Figure 2: G. Jerrard, *Deputy Surgeon-General Norman Chevers* (Wellcome Library).

Professional historians and their students continue to read Gardiner, but few now pay much attention to Norman Chevers. Yet Chevers had grasped aspects of this strange case that Gardiner was unable or unwilling to see. Chevers was convinced that *The Forerunner* was factually wrong, fatally compromised by Eglisham's "personal malice against the Duke of Buckingham". Eglisham's medical reasoning seemed profoundly flawed; and he had wilfully exaggerated the few shreds of solid information he possessed, which "in the report of a physician who wrote with such direct purpose and with so much command of language . . . amounts to absolute falsehood". Still, Eglisham fascinated Chevers. Tantalized by this elusive figure, Chevers thought it vital to know more about him—was he alive during the civil wars, for instance, or was he bribed to write his tract? Chevers was fascinated too by the unknown history of the tract itself. Unable to find a copy of the 1626 *Forerunner*, he speculated about possible differences between the original and the 1642 republication, and he insisted that "a close scrutiny into all that relates to the Eglisham pamphlets is much needed", urging future students to make a "search in foreign libraries, especially in Belgium and Holland" to trace the true history of the book and its author. Most important, unlike Gardiner, Chevers realized that this potently constructed "falsehood" mattered. He believed that in every political conflict, a "circumstance of aggravation" could sting the "combatants to desperation" and render "all compromise impossible". This is what had happened in 1626, when *The Forerunner* apparently "stained" the duke's hands with the late king's blood. This attack on the royal favourite, which a majority in the Commons endorsed, soon rendered impossible any compromise between the king and Parliament. The long-term consequences were devastating. Eglisham's pamphlet, Chevers argued, was nothing less than "the spark igniting that train which exploded in the Great Rebellion and in the death of King Charles the First upon a scaffold at Whitehall".[11]

Chevers understood the power that a widely shared perception, even a palpably false one, could have in early modern political life; in effect, he suggested that since the truth about James's death had now been established, it was time to explore the stories about the king's murder from new and more productive angles. Gardiner recognized the historical existence of the perception, the "article of belief" about James's poisoning. But because this "article of belief" had no basis in fact, and, perhaps more importantly, because it did not conform to his understanding of the political world, the eminent historian, and the generations of scholars who followed in his wake, had little or no interest in the origins, nature and significance of that "article of belief". This lack of interest had steep costs; for, as we hope to show, the secret history of James's murder is not a bizarre aberration disconnected from the great ideological and religious struggles of the early Stuart age that so preoccupied Gardiner and his successors. In fact, it allows us to see their true nature.

* * *

Our book starts from a simple premise: what matters in the history of *The Forerunner* and of the numerous variations upon it, is not whether the poisoning claims were true. What matters is whether, how and why contemporaries claimed or believed them to be true, and the nature and consequences of those claims and beliefs. Drawing on the insights and methods of both traditional political historiography and the new "post-revisionist" cultural history of early modern politics, we have thus written a case study of the making, mutations and manipulations of a potent and destabilizing set of political stories, myths, perceptions and representations.[12] We work on the assumption that historians cannot fully understand the power politics of early Stuart England without understanding the presuppositions and codes, images and representations, symbols and rites, beliefs and perceptions that underpinned action and discourse. Political historians cannot afford to dismiss the strange, the implausible, the fantastic: if our subjects wrote about it, talked about it, debated it, believed it or scoffed at it, then it matters. Political images, myths and perceptions drove political action, they sustained and challenged authority, and they made sense of complex events and confusing realities. Using eyewitness experience, rumour and report, and pursuing personal as well as political goals, George Eglisham crafted a compelling story of James I's court and the poison politics that threatened to destroy it. For complex reasons this story, and the variations played upon it, had real cultural and political traction. It provided anxious contemporaries with a coherent way of explaining an increasingly turbulent and confusing political world; its credibility allowed ambitious men to advance different political causes; and it provided a set of images that were, as the ethnographers like to say, "good to think with", offering ways of wrestling with fundamental political questions about the operation and nature of monarchical power in an age of widening ideological and religious division.[13]

This book thus reconstructs the history of a political myth—what we will call a secret history—and of the various images, adaptations and actions it spawned: how they were made, what they meant, and how they changed meaning as they served various ideological purposes across more than three decades of crisis and unrest. We argue that, far from distracting us from what *really* happened and what *really* matters, a systematic examination of the secret history of James I's murder opens up important new perspectives on the turbulent politics of early and mid-seventeenth-century England, while revealing in often startlingly new detail the complex ideological and political forces that unsettled and eventually destroyed the Stuart monarchy. Some of our interventions contribute directly to important debates about causation and political conflict. It is clear, for instance, that we cannot understand either the calamitous breach between Charles I and his Parliament in 1626, or the emergence of regicidal politics in 1648, without appreciating the centrality to both crises of stories about the murder of James I. Political historians' habit of brushing these stories aside has fundamentally distorted our understanding of these two crucial seventeenth-century crisis points.[14] But the secret history of James's murder can teach us much more. Like a radioactive dye on a medical scan, stories of James's murder reveal the essential features of early seventeenth-century political culture and the fault lines running through it. As we follow these stories, we thus cast new light on the political and cultural dynamics at the heart of the long-term origins of the English Revolution, and on the forces that made that revolution both imaginable and possible.[15] By exploring the media history of James's murder, for instance, we see how an emergent public sphere of increasingly engaged critical readers could fundamentally destabilize a monarchy as yet unprepared to shape publicity to its own ends; and by following this media history across time, we can trace the genealogy of the fully revolutionary public sphere of the 1640s that would permanently remake the practice of politics in England.[16] By analyzing how myths and perceptions sustained or critiqued royal power, we can rethink the nature of the legitimation crisis that weakened monarchical authority in the decades before the Civil War, and, then, more radically, in the years leading up to regicide. By paying attention to the role of politicized memories of James's murder in the 1650s, we can explore too how England's republican regimes engaged in their own quest for legitimate authority.[17] And by listening closely to the anxious, angry and often radical words that contemporaries across the country and the social spectrum used to talk about James's murder, and by opening our eyes to the wide range of texts and idioms they used, we can restore a sense of the simmering ideological conflict long missing from academic discussion of the causes and course of the mid-century Revolution.[18]

Our pursuit of George Eglisham and his secret history of James's murder has also forced us to rethink the geographical and geopolitical units in which we research and write English political history. Since the beginning of the 1990s, the study of early modern England has been framed first by the "British problem", focused on the interactions and interconnections among England, Scotland, Ireland and Wales, and, more recently, by the new Atlantic and global history of the Isles and their politics.[19] The intellectual and methodological significance of these shifts cannot be overestimated. But this broadening of horizons has long suffered from a curious blind spot. As English historians became British and British historians became Atlantic and global, the British archipelago became increasingly unmoored from continental Europe. Indeed, it now seems long past time for English and British historians to consider the benefits of a revived European "turn" to their studies. The story of George Eglisham and his secret history makes clear just how much we lose by uncoupling Britain from Europe, for it is a story that only makes sense in a transnational European context.[20] Eglisham's life and work were shaped by his movements through European cultural, political and ideological networks—Flemish, French, German, Dutch, Spanish and Italian, as well as Scottish and English. The reception of The Forerunner, written and printed in Flanders, also took place across national borders. Copies circulated far beyond English shores in different forms and languages, through different communication networks, acquiring different meanings for different readers of different religious confessions and nationalities. Furthermore, the book's making, meaning and reception can only be understood within a set of diplomatic, military and political contexts that were European rather than simply British in scope.[21] The story of Eglisham's secret history, we suggest, reveals the workings of a densely entangled transnational European political culture in which ideas, people, goods, news and texts were in constant motion across the Continent. Until we begin to explore these transnational mobilities and entanglements, our understanding of English political history will necessarily remain parochial and incomplete.[22]

* * *

To capture the multi-centred and multinational entanglements that shaped the story of James I's murder, we have had to approach our subject from many different vantage points. Our book follows a chronological arc, but includes several abrupt shifts in perspective, source base and narrative strategy that allow us to pursue our quarry from numerous intersecting angles. This multi-faceted approach emphasizes the interconnections between numerous sites of political engagement and maps a political world that stretches from court and Parliament-house to hunting lodge and tavern, from city streets to country houses, from London to Brussels, Uppsala and beyond. And we situate the political events and discourse around these sites within multiple, interlinked social and cultural spheres, from the Latinate republic of letters to the demotic networks of plebeian rumour and news. Our analyses rely on a correspondingly diverse array of archives and evidence: libellous poems, parliamentary speeches, diplomatic correspondence, cheap pamphlets, medical treatises, newsletters, account books, stage plays, criminal depositions and religious polemics. And we depend upon an equally diverse set of methodologies and narrative strategies to bring this evidence to life. Sometimes we play the biographer, hunting clues to the lives and passions of libellers and kings alike; other times we play the historian of mentalités, exploring cultural attitudes to illness, or poison, or the secrets of dead bodies. At times we play the traditional historian of high politics, analyzing factions and politicians, states and institutions; at others, we play the historian of ideas, closely reading texts and textual debates, and situating them in fluid contexts. Furthermore, this diversity of evidence and approaches has required us to engage with interpretive techniques from many different historical sub-disciplines, while all the time maintaining open lines of communication with literary and art historians, ethnographers and historians of the book. This is a book about cultural mobility—the movement of people, ideas and narratives—across time and space; and it deploys an innovative structure to capture this history, deliberately collapsing or bending older paradigms of historical analysis as it does so. At the same time, we have also paid close attention to the nuances and details of our evidence, allowing the dead a chance to speak as we strive to capture something of the sound and feel of passionate political engagement in a long-vanished world.

The book begins by setting out two intersecting contexts that framed the emerging stories of James's illness and death: the interpersonal relationships of king, favourite and prince, and the political and diplomatic crises that placed these relationships under significant strain. Having established these contexts, Part I of the book turns to the "authorized version" of James's death: the official medical reports that explained how and why a usually harmless tertian ague had killed a king; and the narratives of the king's good death that celebrated James's spiritual confidence and confessional orthodoxy. This authorized version of James's death reaffirmed monarchical authority, but within months this version had been challenged by an unsettling secret history of courtly betrayal and poison. Part II reconstructs the making of the secret history by returning first to Theobalds in March 1625, where we situate the initial recriminations over James's medical treatment and death within bitter disputes about foreign and military policy. We then piece together the remarkable career of George Eglisham, following him across northwestern Europe and tracing his precipitous rise and calamitous fall from grace, experiences that shaped the writing of *The Forerunner* and explain its remarkable power.

Eglisham wrote and published in Brussels, and to understand his work we need to understand its European contexts—its place in a long line of Catholic polemical interventions in English affairs, and its central role in the remarkable, transnational Habsburg propaganda campaigns early in the Thirty Years War. Having uncovered the European context, we then explore what *The Forerunner* said, how it said it, and what it meant, analyzing how Eglisham connected his compelling stories of Buckingham's crimes to his portrait of broader political and moral decay, and unpacking the literary and cultural strategies that made his murder narrative so persuasive. We then turn to the political damage *The Forerunner* left in its wake. Part III offers a new account of the 1626 parliamentary impeachment of Buckingham, exploring the Commons' investigation of James's death, the framing of the charge against the duke of "transcendent presumption", and the ensuing battle to define or refute the volatile allegation of murder, a battle that left king and Parliament-men dangerously at odds. Angered by the Commons' claims about his father's death,

Charles dissolved Parliament and struck back at Buckingham's sharpest critics, but he decided against a large-scale campaign to discredit Eglisham. The costs of this inaction were high. The secret history quickly established itself in the English political imagination, and in Part IV we reconstruct the mechanics of the underground publication systems that allowed this to happen, while exploring the politics of the growing belief, articulated in verse libels, manuscript separates, pamphlets, seditious talk and rumour, that Buckingham was a poisoner. We conclude Part IV with an analysis of Thomas Scott of Canterbury's unusually well-documented reading of *The Forerunner*, a reading that led him to the revolutionary conclusion that King Charles must have been complicit in his father's murder.

The consequences of Charles's possible involvement take centre stage in Parts V and VI, which explore the secret history's mutations during the revolutionary crises of the 1640s and 1650s. Hard-line Parliamentarian propagandists repeatedly used Eglisham's allegations to support the case for war against a badly misguided king; and during the opening months of 1648, a radical variation of the secret history was at the heart of the bitter pamphlet debates that would pave and litter the road to regicide. The ghost of the murdered James I that haunted Charles I's trial and execution was not easily exorcized. Throughout the 1650s, the secret history continued to mutate, as defenders of the republican regimes used it to denigrate the Stuart dynasty and to legitimate the Free State and Protectorate, while Royalists tarred Eglisham's allegations as nefarious falsehoods that had helped ambitious traitors turn the world upside down. After the Restoration of monarchy in 1660, the secret history ceased to play a central polemical role, but it only slowly faded from political consciousness. Our epilogue thus explores how later writers kept the debate over the murder of James I alive well into the nineteenth century.

* * *

Was James I poisoned? Unfortunately for readers expecting a footnoted episode of "CSI: Jacobean London", we offer no definitive verdict—far too much evidence has long since turned to dust. This is a book more concerned with the multiple retellings of the event than with the "real history" of the event itself. Still, the question is not an idle one. Retrospective medical diagnosis of long-dead historical figures is, of course, a tricky—possibly futile—endeavour. Yet historians and physicians continue to ask whether James's "tertian ague" was *really* a malarial fever. They have pored over the king's medical history and suggested that he *really* suffered from variegate porphyria or from chronic vascular dementia, hypertension and cardiovascular disease. They have argued that James's medical and emotional history is consistent with mild cerebral palsy. And they have maintained, in the most recent attempt at retrospective diagnosis, that he had a mild (attenuated) variant of the neurological disorder

Lesch-Nyhan disease, along with "associated Asperger traits", and that James died "following a stroke, associated with probable hypertension".[23] None of these modern studies ponders the possibility of poison; for the retrospective diagnosticians, at least, that particular case appears closed. But it is important to acknowledge that something untoward probably did happen in James's sickroom, and that, even as we turn our attention from what happened to how it was re-presented and perceived, the fact remains that Buckingham's medical meddling may have contributed, most likely unintentionally, to James's death. Norman Chevers, for one, thought this a real possibility, concluding that "The medical facts of the case render it, in the highest degree, probable that the king's death resulted from natural disease, *the severity of which appears to have been aggravated by the use of common but inappropriate medicine*".[24]

Yet at this late date, even the most ambitious historical prosecutor would find it difficult to frame a watertight charge of manslaughter or reckless endangerment, still less of wilful murder, against the duke. And given the brutal nature of orthodox early Stuart medical treatment, there is little reason to assume that Buckingham's interventions shortened James's life any more than his physicians' remedies already had. What ultimately matters, however, is not the lack of evidence to establish the truth of James's death, but the survival of evidence, in often astonishing abundance, demonstrating how the secret history of James's murder gripped the imagination of his contemporaries. By tracking that story's making, meanings and mutations, we cannot hope to solve a four-hundred-year-old cold case. But we can cast new light on England's most revolutionary age.

OUT OF THE SPANISH LABYRINTH

THE KING, HIS SON AND HIS FAVOURITE, 1618–24

Dudley Carleton counted himself a very lucky man. The nephew and namesake of the English ambassador to The Hague had only just returned from Holland, when, noticing a crowd milling around Whitehall, he found himself drawn into one of the most compelling pieces of political theatre anyone could remember. On 23 February 1624 the House of Lords had invited the Commons to join them the following afternoon in the Painted Chamber to hear "certain Particulars, of great Consequence". But as excitement mounted, the Lords proposed a last-minute shift: the expected crowds would be "better accommodated" in the Great Hall of the adjoining Palace of Whitehall. The Parliament-men agreed, but anxious about security they ordered that "none be admitted to this Conference, but the members of this House", each of whom had to present the sergeant-at-arms with "his Name, in Writing, and the Place, for which he serves". The Marquis of Hamilton, the Lord Steward, arrived early to help with security, but crowd control proved ineffective, and young Carleton found himself carried along in the crush, getting "entrance among others that had as little to do in the assembly as my self".[1] The crowds had come to witness an unprecedented address on matters of the highest importance, an address that would fundamentally reorient English foreign policy.

Over a decade earlier, James I of England had married his daughter Elizabeth to the Calvinist Frederick V, the Elector Palatine, thus forging an alliance between England and one of the leading German Protestants. In 1619, against his father-in-law's advice, Frederick accepted the crown of Bohemia from the Protestant rebels attempting to throw off the rule of the Catholic Emperor Ferdinand II (Fig. 3). Frederick's decision proved disastrous. The Emperor had powerful allies, most notably his Habsburg cousin, the king of Spain, and imperial troops soon drove Frederick first from Prague and then from the Palatinate. In 1622, as Elizabeth and Frederick took refuge in The Hague, Habsburg forces stormed first Heidelberg and then Mannheim. In March 1623, Frankenthal, the Elector's last town in the Palatinate, surrendered;

the previous month, the Emperor had transferred the title of Elector Palatine to the Catholic Maximilian of Bavaria. The debate about England's response to these events haunted the politics of the 1620s. While many of James's subjects, especially the more godly Protestants, called for full-scale intervention in what was, to their minds, a religious war, the king favoured a primarily diplomatic approach. Conscious of his massive debts and anxious to avoid becoming dependent on parliamentary finance, James had few military options. A major land war would prove inordinately expensive—an army of 20,000 men would cost more than a million pounds annually—and the Exchequer had trouble funding even token English garrisons abroad. The Spaniards had helped finance the Emperor's military operations, and had provided troops for the conquest of the Palatinate; in 1621, moreover, they had resumed their war against the Protestant Dutch. To many English Protestants, Spain was England's natural enemy, committed to crushing the Reformation and establishing a "universal monarchy". James, however, saw Spain as the solution, and renewed efforts to marry his son Charles to the Infanta Maria, sister of Philip IV, the king of Spain since 1621. This alliance, James hoped, would resolve the Palatine situation without the expense of English blood or treasure, and a generous

Figure 3: *Frederick V and Elizabeth, King and Queen of Bohemia*, 1619 (National Portrait Gallery). The image celebrates the ascent of James's daughter and son-in-law to the Bohemian throne, and the expulsion of Romish religion from their new kingdom.

Spanish dowry would bring the cash-strapped Exchequer a massive infusion of ready money (Fig. 4).

Many in England, however, feared the price of the Spanish match. Philip insisted on a formal toleration of English Catholics, not just in the royal household but across the country. And since a Catholic consort would control her children's upbringing, James's grandchildren were likely to be raised in the Roman faith. The match would also bring England into the Spanish diplomatic orbit, forcing James to abandon German (and perhaps Dutch) Protestants to the militant Catholic Reformation. While James was willing, albeit reluctantly, to go ahead with the Spanish match, many of his subjects refused to put either England's independence or the True Religion at risk. Others thought the Spanish were playing false, and deliberately protracting negotiations to immobilize James while the Habsburgs crushed their German opponents. Rather than more diplomacy, then, many in England called for military action. James could strike the Spanish Netherlands, a project sure to win Dutch support and unite the two major European Protestant powers. More tempting still, he could follow his predecessor Elizabeth I's lead, challenging Spanish control of the Atlantic and Caribbean while picking off their treasure ships as they headed home to Seville. But James clung to his strategy, reminding the warmongers of

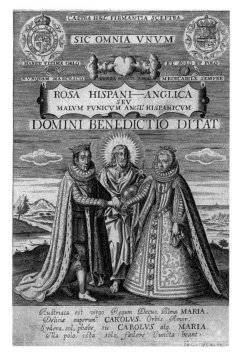

Figure 4: *Prince Charles and the Infanta Maria*, 1622 (National Portrait Gallery). This frontispiece to Michael Duval's Latin tract, eventually translated into English as the *Spanish-English Rose*, praises the planned Spanish match.

the Latin tag, "*dulce bellum inexpertis*"—war is only sweet for those who have never known it.[2]

James's son Charles and his favourite, George Villiers, Marquis and later Duke of Buckingham, publicly supported royal policy, but became increasingly restive. The prince was close to his sister Elizabeth and saw the resolution of the Palatine question as a matter of family honour (Fig. 5). In 1619, Buckingham had declared "that as he had received all he had from His Majesty's most gracious favour and bounty, so he was ready to spend it all in the cause of the King of Bohemia", and in 1620 he had contributed £5,000 to the benevolence for the Palatine cause. Although he continued to follow James's lead, Buckingham also began reaching out to the war party, forging connections with such committed Calvinists as Sir Edward Conway, Sir John Coke, John Packer and the preacher John Preston.[3]

Early in 1623, Charles and Buckingham settled on a bold plan to secure the Spanish match and to restore the Palatinate. Donning false beards, and travelling as Jack and Tom Smith, the two slipped out of England and rode through France to Madrid. Some characterized the journey as a chivalric romance, "an action", explained Sir George Calvert, the Secretary of State, "affected with much passion" by Charles "out of an earnest desire to see his mistres". But, as Calvert also acknowledged, the trip was primarily intended "to give a finall end to that Businesse that had distracted his Maiesties other affaires so long a time".[4]

Figure 5: Willem de Passe, *Triumphus Jacobi Regis Augustaeque ipsius Prolis*, 1622 (British Museum). This Stuart family portrait depicts James VI and I, enthroned above his children and grandchildren, as a symbol of patriarchal, dynastic authority.

Provided the marriage took place in a timely manner and restored the Palatinate to his sister's family, Charles was willing to accept almost any terms, including a formal suspension of the penal laws against English Catholics and even an Anglo-Spanish dismemberment of the Dutch Republic. Domestic reaction to the Madrid venture, however, verged on panic. The Venetian ambassador to London thought the expedition "strange, unexampled and incredible . . . an abyss of marvels, a monster among decisions, a labyrinth without head or way out", while one godly Englishman dubbed the prince's departure a "dolefull day that made everie good Protestant sadd". In Madrid, Charles and Buckingham soon became frustrated, convinced that the Spanish had no intention of sealing the alliance, but only wanted to keep the English dangling, and out of the European war, as long as possible. Extricating themselves proved difficult, but in October 1623 Charles and Buckingham returned to England. They arrived without the Infanta, but with a definitive verdict for James: there never would be "a finall end to that Businesse". The implications were far ranging. Back in March, after informing Charles and Buckingham that the Emperor had transferred the Palatinate to Maximilian of Bavaria, James had warned that "if my baby's credit in Spain mend not these things, I will bid farewell to peace in Christendome".[5] By the time they returned, the question for Charles and Buckingham was whether they could convince James to "bid farewell to peace" and avenge his daughter's humiliation.

The failure of the Madrid trip and the conversion of Buckingham and Charles to the cause of war marked a momentous shift, the beginnings of what one contemporary dubbed a "blessed revolution". The prince and favourite now began working with godly peers and Parliament-men to break the Spanish treaties and to commit England militarily to the Protestant cause. The crowds gathered at the Great Hall on 24 February 1624 had come to hear the prince and the duke set out what had happened in Madrid in 1623 and to map the way forward.

After an hour of rising tension, the two men entered the room. The prince took a seat at the head of a long table while the duke stood behind him, sometimes leaning on his chair. The great lords of the realm sat around the table and on benches set up in the hall, while the Parliament-men crammed in on scaffolds six rows deep. Although a nervous public speaker, Charles made several memorable interventions, and he recalled how, amid fears of his arrest in Spain, he had stoically told James that if "he was deteyned in that State as a Prisoner", then the king should "be pleased (for his sake) never to thinke upon Him any longer as a sonne, but to reflect with all his royall thoughts upon the good of his sister". But it was Buckingham who performed "the longest part" in the day's drama. He noted modestly "how unusuall it was for him to speake in so greate and iudicious an Auditory", and insisted that he spoke only as "a true hearted Englishman". Since Charles "saw his Fathers Negotiation plainely deluded,

Matters of Religion gained upon and extorted, [and] his sister's Case more and more desperate", the Spanish journey had been the means to cut the Gordian knot, "to helpe things of[f], or on". In Madrid the two men had discovered the true nature of the "Spanish labyrinth"—the "juggling" and the brazen attempts to pervert the prince's religion—and now they offered their listeners unprecedented insight into the diplomatic manoeuvring, detailing their conversations with the king of Spain's ministers and their arguments with England's diplomatic representatives, and reciting verbatim the secret letters that revealed Spanish deceit. A mere three years after James had angrily rebuked Parliament for presuming to debate his foreign policy, Charles and Buckingham were opening the secrets of state, the *arcana imperii*, to parliamentary and public scrutiny. And while Buckingham made clear that he had been shrewd enough to find the way out of the Spanish labyrinth, he insisted that, "If the bringing us from Darkness to light did deserve any thankes", then they "must wholly ascribe it to the Prince".[6]

The audience was stunned. "In handling these Matters", one noted, "there have been such things discovered . . . that passed in Spaine which never came hitherto to any men's knowledge out of that sanctuarie." The news quickly spread, and the duke's "Relation" became one of the most widely copied items in contemporary manuscript collections. The "Relation" made Buckingham a patriot hero. As Arthur Wilson recalled, the Parliament-men "with elevated Voices would scarce be contained from acknowledging him the Preserver of the Nation", and for several months the duke became that rarest of creatures, a royal favourite who was also "the Darling of the Multitude". He was "St. George on Horseback", and "could hardly goe or ride or stand in his gates, for press of people to behould him".[7]

It was a remarkable transformation. Half a year earlier Buckingham had been the object of near universal scorn and derision. But now, with Charles's help, he proposed leading the country, and its reluctant king, out of the Spanish labyrinth, and into battle. Never before had a royal minister, much less a royal favourite, organized a broad coalition at court and in the Parliament-house to coax and cajole a monarch towards policies he so visibly disliked. But Buckingham's new status as leader of a popular Protestant war party came at a steep cost; though it brought him closer to the prince, it deeply strained his relationship with King James, the relationship upon which his whole world was built. If we are to understand the circumstances and controversy around James's final illness and death, we need to examine not only the blessed revolution in foreign policy that dominated the king's last months, but also the personal intimacies and political tensions that shaped the relationships between James, Buckingham and Charles.

Dad and his "Sweet Boys"

Charismatic and handsome, "naturally modest, affable, kind and courteous", George Villiers was the second son from the second marriage of a minor Leicestershire knight (Plate 2). He owed everything to royal favour. He had come to James I's attention in 1614, pushed forward by courtiers eager to damage the king's favourite, Robert Carr, Earl of Somerset. The speed of Villiers's subsequent ascent astonished everybody.

By the time of Somerset's scandalous fall following his arrest for the murder of Sir Thomas Overbury late in 1615, Villiers was the king's closest companion, and with this unparalleled access came title, office, reward, and steadily increasing political influence (Fig. 6). James knighted Villiers in 1615 and soon made him a baron, then a viscount, then an earl, then a marquis and finally, in 1623, a duke, one of only two in the kingdom, the other being a royal cousin, the Duke of Lennox. Buckingham also acquired major offices and honours. Appointed gentleman of the bedchamber in 1615, he would later become Lord Admiral and Master of the Horse, a Privy Councillor and a Knight of the Garter. In 1620 he took an illustrious bride, Katherine Manners, the daughter of the Earl of Rutland, who linked him to some of England's oldest noble families. James also promoted the favourite's kin. Buckingham's mother, Mary Villiers, and his sister, Susan Feilding, became countesses; his brother John became Viscount Purbeck, his brother Christopher, Earl of Anglesey. His kinsmen also acquired lucrative royal office. His half-brother became Master of the Mint, his brother became Prince Charles's Master of Robes, and his brother-in-law Master of the Great Wardrobe. Marriage alliances extended Buckingham's power and responsibilities even further. In 1622 his young niece Mary Feilding married the eldest son of the Marquis of Hamilton, cousin to the king, and on Hamilton's death in early 1625 his widow begged the favourite "to become a father" to the boy "and a protector to his wife and remanent children". Other marriages connected Buckingham to key players in the royal administration. One cousin married Lord Treasurer Cranfield, and another Sir James Ley, Lord Chief Justice of the King's Bench. And Buckingham was rarely a disinterested bystander in the wider scramble for promotion. Office-seekers "can obtayne no grace except they vowe and beseeche at the shrine of the greate one", John Castle explained to the diplomat William Trumbull.[8] With title, office and advancement went property and money, first directly by royal grant, later through the highly lucrative sale of royal offices, titles and patents. Irrefutable evidence of the favourite's staggering wealth could be seen in London and the provinces. In addition to great country houses at New Hall in Essex and Burley-on-the-Hill in Rutland, by 1625 Buckingham owned three London properties, including a Thames-side mansion at York House that housed one of the finest art collections of the age.[9]

Figure 6: Simon de Passe, *George Villiers, Marquess of Buckingham*, 1620 (National Portrait Gallery). This early engraving of Buckingham depicts the favourite in an aristocratic pose and lists his already numerous titles and offices.

The prefatory dedication to James I's 1619 meditation on the Lord's Prayer offered his subjects an official portrait of his relationship with Buckingham. James presented himself as his favourite's teacher and mentor, "not onely your politike but also your oeconomicke Father", who had to "dayly take care to better your understanding, to enable you the more for my service in worldly affaires". Buckingham was his pupil, but was also his confidant—the king's initial musings on the Lord's Prayer had been entrusted to "you, and only you", and it was the favourite who had urged James to "put pen to paper". James now dedicated the work to Buckingham "as a token of my love", in testament to his exemplary piety, nurtured by the king's own "godly and virtuous . . . advices". But James also acknowledged the value of Villiers's "service" in the king's "worldy affaires". Explaining why such a brief meditation was ideal for a courtier, James noted that "when I consider of your continuall attendance upon my service . . . and the uncessant swarme of suitors importunately hanging upon you without disrupture, I can find but very litle tyme for you to spare upon meditation".[10]

Buckingham was indeed a skilled man of business whose tedious labours as James's informal secretary insulated the king from work and distraction. While a Secretary of State was often in attendance, James increasingly relied on Buckingham to handle some of the most sensitive matters of state. And since James disliked his capital city, Buckingham was often on the road between the king's hunting retreats and Westminster to see to business requiring royal attention. He also helped the king avoid the "uncessant swarme of suitors" by taking care of patronage requests, and often acted as James's representative to various foreign diplomats in London. Buckingham would sometimes acknowledge the toll this work could take. "To serve you", he once confessed to James, "I have my self nothing but truble and vexation."[11]

Buckingham's constant access to the king troubled contemporaries who worried over the duke's apparent monopoly of power, patronage and influence. Privately they wondered how this obscure younger son of an obscure gentleman had risen so high without blood, virtue or obvious talent to recommend him. Some observers had a disturbing answer.

In August 1622, Simonds D'Ewes, a student at the Inns of Court, spoke with an old Cambridge friend about a particular "secrett" thing—"the sinne of sodomye", and "how frequente it was in this wicked cittye". The signs were everywhere. Boys, "growen to the height of wickedness", painted their faces like women, while a French usher at a London school "had buggered a knights sonne" only for Chief Justice Montague to reprieve him from punishment, reportedly at the king's request. But the real horror for D'Ewes and his friend was that "Wee had probable cause to feare" that the sin of sodomy was "a sinne in the prince as well as the people". This "sinne in the prince" had dire political implications. In other countries "men talked familiarly" of James's unnatural tastes, damaging the kingdom's repute, while D'Ewes thought that James was "wearye enough" of Buckingham, "but for shame would not putt him away". More traumatic still was the thought of what England could expect from an angry God. The sin of sodomy deserved "some horrible punishment", but because it was a "sinne in the prince", only God could impose appropriate justice, for "noe man else indeed dare reprove or tell them of ther faults".[12] According to this providential calculus, the whole realm could soon expect a divine punishment for James's sins.

Modern historians continue to debate the nature of James's relationship with Buckingham, though discussion is often marred by squeamishness or by anachronistic attempts to squeeze early modern desires and modes of personal and physical intimacy into modern categories of sexual identity.[13] Given the fragmentary evidence, it is now very difficult to prove, or disprove, that James had physical sexual relations with his favourite. But their remarkable correspondence does provide invaluable insight into a powerful and sometimes tempestuous intimacy.

That intimacy was forged and marked by a range of experiences, but none more important than the shared pursuit of James's greatest passion—hunting. By the early 1620s, James was in his mid-fifties, his hair was turning white, and heavy drinking had left him with a ruddy complexion. Yet despite his worsening arthritic problems, James remained the "Grand Cazador", the Great Huntsman, never happier than when riding down a country road, surrounded by "Begles, Spaniells, Greyhounds, Sparrowhawkes and Goshawkes".[14] As early as 1613 a Spaniard reported that James had become so "fatt ... that he is not able to followe his violent Hunting without some paine", and a few years later the Venetian ambassador noted that James could no longer hold the reins, "relying chiefly upon the address and dexterity of the grooms, who run on either side of him".[15] Yet in 1623 he still went hunting "almost every day", and in 1624 six days a week. Although he was not particular about his quarry, deer were his favourite sport. James insisted on hunting them with "running hounds", and not that "theevish forme" using "gunnes and bowes". He could not resist, as one contemporary recalled, "to come in at the dethe of the deare, and to heare the commendations of his howndes".[16] The royal deer hunt was an extended, bloodstained homosocial ritual. The king and his small entourage of courtiers, grooms and dogs would chase a stag for miles. Once he brought a deer down, James would personally slit its throat and feed the entrails to his hounds while daubing his companions with blood.[17]

James appreciated the informality of the hunt as much as the sport itself. His hunting lodges were refuges from both the "pomp and gravity" and the swarms of suitors that made court life so burdensome. James "prefers living in the country", the Venetian Foscarini observed, "and dislikes too large a following, preferring to take a few with him". The king was particularly fond of a circuit of parks at Newmarket, Royston and Theobalds. Whereas Theobalds was a major country house, the other two were essentially rustic lodges, so primitive that James's queen, Anne of Denmark, only rarely visited them and some of his small retinue had to board in neighbouring villages. But James thrived there. The Venetian envoy once found him in an Essex park in "narrow, one might say poor quarters"; but the king was exultant "in the midst of his beloved forests, full of great herds of stags and deer, hunting with enthusiasm".[18]

The rituals and homosocial camaraderie of the hunt were essential to James's most important relationships, and both Buckingham and Charles shared his passion for the pleasures of the chase. Talk of hunting filled their letters, and their long days in the parks and forests gave the three men a shared language and set of experiences that helped express their intimacy. Buckingham once hurried to join the king, hoping to "be at the death of a stag with you", and after James arrived in one favourite park, Buckingham told him that "you are now in the place I love". On one occasion Buckingham and Charles wrote to

James that they would await him at Theobalds: "the one will hunt hinds and does, the other survaie the trees walkes ponds and dere", all in hopes that they would "lay our selves at your feet there craving your blessing".[19]

James and Buckingham used their personal correspondence to express and fashion their relationship in a variety of complex ways. They used a range of affectionate nicknames and a language of kinship to express their intimacy. Buckingham's letters invariably began, "Dear Dad and Gossope", acknowledging James as both father and godparent—in 1622 James became godfather to Buckingham's first child, Mary—and inserting the favourite into a familial (and familiar) relationship with the king. James addressed Buckingham by his nickname, "Steenie", a Scots contraction of Stephen that alluded to Buckingham's resemblance to a portrait of the angel-faced saint. But James also styled his favourite as a son, as "My onlie sweete and deare chylde" and (once) as "my bastard brat". His love for his "son" extended to Buckingham's wife Kate, who became "my daughter", and James heartily wished the new husband "all kind of comfort in your sanctified bed" so that "I may have sweet bedchamber boys to play me with". James's love for his hunting dogs could occasionally colour this fascination with Buckingham's marriage bed. The master of the dogs once bred "so fyne a Kennel of yong howndes" that James thought "some of thaime" were "so faire and well shaped and . . . so fyne prettie litle ones as thaye are worthie to lye on steenie and Kates bedde". When Kate became pregnant, James fussed over her and "the sweete litle thing that is in her bellie".[20] During Buckingham's long sojourn in Spain in 1623, James sent him news of Kate's next pregnancy, reporting her "little casting" (vomiting) in the morning and hoping that "I shall shortly be a gossip [godfather] over again". Buckingham's daughter, Mary or Mall, became James's "sweet little grandchild", and he rejoiced when "my little grandchild" was "well weaned".[21]

James's letters also acknowledged the importance of Buckingham's other female relatives. His formidable mother, the Countess of Buckingham, and his sister, Susan Feilding, Countess of Denbigh, joined the king's wife and daughter as part of James's extended family. Resorting to a bawdy pun suited to the masculine space of the hunting lodge, Buckingham and James used a crude contraction of "countesses" when referring to the women. On one occasion James told Buckingham that "I wolde have thee to bring all the cuntis with thee (I mean both thy wyfe, thy mother and thy sister) that oure ioy maye be the more full at oure happie meeting", and on another that "it will be a greate comfort unto me that thow and thy cuntes may see me hunt the buck in the park". Buckingham often presented himself as part of this larger family, informing James once that "Mall, Great Mall [his mother], Kate, Sue and Steenie shall all wait of you on Saturday". James embraced them all, calling for God's blessing on "thee, and my sweet daughter, and my sweet little grandchild, and all thy blessed family".[22]

This familial language was shot through with tensions. The banter about the "cuntis", for instance, recognized the importance of the Villiers women while using a louche jest to distance the two men from the female relatives. Occasionally, the Villiers women became a problem. At one point Kate quarrelled with James, and the favourite had to persuade her that "you are the best man in the world". Following the countess's conversion to Catholicism in 1622, James effectively shunned her for two years, and there are signs that after the 1623 trip to Spain the women's presence caused more frequent irritation. Early in 1625, Buckingham wrote that "I would gladlie know whether it would offend you or not, if I brought the cunts with me", and clearly James sometimes wanted Buckingham to himself.[23]

The letters reveal other modes and styles of intimacy that self-consciously subverted the deference that usually distanced king from subject. Buckingham often displayed a jocular insolence that James prized, and the duke enjoyed parodying the formal codes of address. He signed his letters as the king's "most humble slave and dogg" and referred to himself as "your Dogg Steenie", playfully abasing himself while alluding to the king's love of hounds. "I must be sausie", Buckingham often wrote, but he never forgot his gratitude "for so great a kinge to desend so loe as to his humblest slave and servant to communicate himself in a stile of such goodfellowship".[24] This "goodfellowship", developed among the small knot of "merry boys" who accompanied James on his constant hunting trips, encouraged a vein of bawdy humour. Buckingham wrote in one letter of "shitten mouths", adding "I pray you sir doe not kiss that word", and in another compared his royal master playfully to a "towrd", probably a toad, but also a pun on turd. The letters also reveal the favourite's easy familiarity with his master's body; one letter teased James, who had had difficulty walking since childhood, about his "well shaped legs".[25]

The letters also make clear that the two men sometimes shared a bed. Bedsharing was widely recognized as a sign of friendship, and in at least two letters Buckingham invoked his place in the royal bed as the paramount symbol of his favour. In one, written on the eve of his return from Spain, Buckingham vowed once he got "hold of your bedpost again, never to quit it", and in another he alluded to "the time which I shall never forget at Farnham, where the bed's head could not be found between the master and his dog".[26] The letters also evoked intimate bodily gestures to convey emotional attachment and longing. James told Buckingham that he wore his favourite's portrait in miniature next to his heart while he was away in Spain.[27] Buckingham wrote from Madrid that he looked forward to "getting libertie to make the speedier hast to lay my selfe at your feete for never none longed more to be in the armes of his mistris".[28] As his return grew imminent, Buckingham told James how "my heart and very soul dances for joy", jumping "from trouble to ease, from sadness to mirth, nay from hell to heaven". In his fervour, he confessed, "I cannot now think of giving thanks for friend, wife, or child; my thoughts are only bent on having my dear Dad and master's leg soon in my arms". James's letters, while rarely as effusive, did contain suggestive variants on "god sende me a ioiefull and a happie meeting with my sweete steenie this evening".[29] His most striking letter, however, was written at the end of 1624, the year of greatest strain in the two men's relationship. After expressing the customary wish for "a ioyefull and comfortable meeting with you", James shifted registers, praying:

> that we maye have at this christenmasse a new mariage, ever to be kept hearafter, for god so love me, as I desyre only to live in this worlde for your saike, and that I hadde rather live banished in anie paairte of the earth with you than live a sorrowefull widowes lyfe without you.

James asked God to "blesse you my sweet chyld & wyfe & grawnte you maye ever be a comforte to youre daide and master". James then crossed out "master" and inserted "husbande". Buckingham sometimes echoed this marital language. In one letter he called the king "my pourvier, my goodfellow, my phesition, my maker, my frend, my father, my all". He praised James for taking better care of him than masters did of their servants, or fathers of their children; and thanked the king for giving him "more affection then betweene lovers in the best kinde man and wife".[30]

These letters reveal the depth, intensity and complexity of James and Buckingham's relationship. But they do not definitively prove the two men were lovers. The language is tricky to interpret, and has to be read according to early modern rather than contemporary sensibilities, and with an ear for play as well as passion. Sharing a bed signified, above all, a close friendship; thus Buckingham's reminder of the night at Farnham was a memory of the event, the first sharing of a bed, which had signalled his privileged status as the king's friend. Bedsharing led to physical intimacy, perhaps contributing to the humorous ease between the two men in their discussion of bodies and bodily functions, but it did not necessarily lead to or imply sexual intimacy. Other physical intimacies mentioned in the letters also had complex valences. Buckingham's anticipated embrace of the king's leg was as likely to have been a flamboyantly exaggerated gesture of formal abasement by a "slave and dogg" as a lover's caress. Even James's remarkable anticipation of "a new mariage" is not as transparent as it seems. Reading the letter as part of a culture of ritualized friendship dating from the Middle Ages, Alan Bray has argued that James was offering Buckingham a renewed "covenant of friendship" to be sealed at the Christmas communion. To call Buckingham his "wyfe", Bray suggests, was typical of the "terms in which James and Buckingham characterized their friendship . . . in which different types of kinship terminology overlap and mix together in apparently bewildering profusion".[31] The letters take us to the heart of a powerful, intimate friendship, and reveal a shared, private and playful language, but they are far harder to use to prove a "secrett sinn of sodomye".

The fact that Prince Charles often read, and sometimes wrote, these letters makes their interpretation all the trickier. It is clear that the three men, different in character as they were, shared both the language and the rituals of the homosocial intimacy forged in the hunting lodges. Charles's relationship to Buckingham had been cool at first, but the reserved, soberly dressed prince and the flamboyant, stylish Buckingham soon became close (Fig. 7; Plate 3). The two men shared an enthusiasm for the hunt (which bound them to James); but by the early 1620s they also shared a passion for the visual arts, a cultural enterprise that held little interest for the king. For Charles, the favourite was both friend and older brother, and Buckingham's letters treated Charles with some of the playful insolence he showed the king. One bids farewell to "babie Charles" (his use of the familiar "babie" borrowing James's own name for the prince) adding that "I kiss thie wartie hands". This piece of irreverence delighted James, who praised his "kind drolling letter" celebrating the relationship between baby, Steenie and their dad.[32]

Figure 7: *King Charles I when Prince of Wales*, c. 1620 (National Portrait Gallery).

Outsiders often found these intimacies strange. Shocked at the informality of Buckingham's interactions with Charles in Madrid, the Spaniards complained that the duke did "manie things against the authoritie and reverence due to the most illustrious Prince". Buckingham sat "whilest the Prince stood" and rested "his feete . . . upon another seate after an undercut manner". He performed "divers obscene things" and used "immodest gesticulations", and he dined with Charles "unreverantly". More shocking still, Buckingham was "wont to move into the Princes Chamber with his Cloathes half on" and to call the prince "by ridiculous names".[33] These actions violated princely and aristocratic decorum, especially acute at the rule-bound Spanish court, but they expressed an intimacy bred in the fields and hunting lodges, an intimacy that both displayed and accounted for Buckingham's remarkable power.

Jove and Ganymede

James's relationship with Buckingham confused many of his subjects. Signs of physical intimacy between equals were often read as evidence of unproblematic masculine friendship; but the same signs between a master and his servant raised suspicions of unnatural desires. D'Ewes's diary tracked these signs of Buckingham's remarkable and troubling favour. Early in January 1622, James reportedly declared to Buckingham at a court masque, "Becote George I love thee dearly", an anecdote that "drew" D'Ewes and his friend into "other storyes" about the king and his favourite. In July, D'Ewes heard that James had hugged Buckingham "very seriouslye" and proclaimed "Begott man, never one loved another moore than I doe thee". Surrounding these diary entries was D'Ewes's troubled commentary on the realm and the wider Protestant cause. James had broken the 1621 Parliament, it seemed, only to indulge the papists and appease Spain. Instead of fighting to redeem the Calvinist Palatinate, James cowered at home in "base feare". When news reached D'Ewes that the hunter king had fallen from his horse into a pond, he noted that "some imputed" the fall "to the sudden breach of the parliament, others to his coolness in religion". D'Ewes thought it "certainly . . . a warning from God unto him and I beseech him to sanctify it". These troubling anecdotes repeatedly cast the favourite as a malignant force. His rapacity was legendary. D'Ewes heard that Lord Norris had committed suicide after being extorted for an earldom; and he and his friends talked of how Buckingham used strategic marriage alliances to advance his family. In a time of confessional war the favourite's religion was uncertain. His mother was "reconciled to the Church of Rome" and reportedly "mooved the King to turne papist". When a Buckingham chaplain preached a sermon full of "anabaptisme, poperye and almost atheism", nothing happened to him, for "in truth the Marquesses shadow was not to be trodd upon". Hearing that after Heidelberg's fall the king had brought an injured bird to Buckingham, D'Ewes seethed that "Our King upon his losse of creditt and estimation with other princes, now begann to play with birdes".[34]

D'Ewes grew nervous about these stories and in 1622 began ciphering his diary entries, convinced that the only safe way in such "base times" to "write moore freely ... of the publicke occurrents" was to do so in code. But others vented their discontent with Buckingham in more public forms. In January 1623, D'Ewes noted that "A libell was sett upp at the Court against the Marquesse of B., worse then the song that went abroad, for which hee offered 1,000 pound to know the author". He reported too that a "booke" with the ironic title of *The Chast Matron*, had detailed "all the villanis, witchcrafts and lasciviousness of the olde Countesse, the Marquesses mother". Indeed, as D'Ewes was busy coding his diary entries, dozens of scabrous verse libels—passed from hand to hand, chanted in the street, pinned to walls or copied down into commonplace-books—took aim at Buckingham's misrule. And some of these poems confronted head on the terrifying "secrett thing" that so unnerved D'Ewes.[35]

At least two libels from the early 1620s explicitly accused the king of sodomy, using the mythical figures of Jove and Ganymede as transparent disguises for James and Buckingham. By far the most widely read was a 1623 poem known as the "King's Five Senses", one of the era's most artfully crafted pieces of political writing. Parodying a song from Ben Jonson's *Gypsies Metamorphosed*—a masque commissioned and staged by Buckingham to entertain James—the poem presented the dire threat posed to the king's senses by seductive forms of political, moral and religious corruption. Buckingham appeared in several threatening guises. In the first stanza, "Seeinge", he was "younge Phaeton", the mortal who persuaded his father, Apollo, to let him drive the chariot of the sun, and whose beauty might "captivate my Soveraignes sence". In the fourth stanza, "Feelinge", Buckingham was the owner of the "smooth, and beardless Chinn" and "moyst palme" that might provoke the king to sin. In the fifth stanza, "Smellinge", he was "a Ganimede" whose perfumed "whoreish breath" could lead the king "which way it list". And in the concluding stanza, which asked God to awaken the king to his duties, Buckingham was among those "rascalls" whose "blacke deeds have ecclips't" James's royal worth.

The favourite's handsome face, beardless chin, perfumed breath and moist palm threatened to seduce the royal senses, causing the king to lose control of himself and his kingdom. Instead of governing his passions, the king's reason was now captivated by sensual beauty, while his soul was set "a reeling" by the touch of beardless chin and moist palm. Seduced by Ganymede's "whorish breath", the king was no longer a leader, but was being "led". Besotted by Phaeton/Buckingham, the king subverted the political order by resigning to him "his throne", just as Apollo allowed his son to drive the chariot of the sun. But Phaeton/Buckingham was "skillesse and unsteaddie", unsuited for power. He was socially unfit—a "proud *Usurping* Charioter", an ambitious "upstart"—and too young, a mere beardless boy. The political consequences were disastrous. Surrendering power to Phaeton or Ganymede would, barring divine intervention, "prove the ruine of a land", "Earthes Calamitie".[36]

"The King's Five Senses" figured Buckingham and James as sodomites, symbols of profound moral disorder.[37] And because contemporaries usually imagined sodomy as part of a nexus of sins, the libeller had room to make suggestive connections between the king's sexual and political proclivities. English Protestants imagined sodomy as a particularly "popish", Mediterranean vice, and "The Five Senses" neatly fused the threats of courtly sodomy and Hispanophile Catholicism. Ganymede's touch and smell worked on the royal senses alongside an array of other seductive, popish threats, including the "daingerous fig of Spaine", the Jesuits' "Candied poyson'd baites", "Italian Salletts" and "Romish drugs". Popery—like Ganymede—seduced and disoriented the senses, and the poet suggestively compared the "damn'd perfumes" of myrrh and frankincense thrown upon (popish) "altars built to Gods unknowne" with the favourite's "whoreish breath". The poet's indictment of a royal court polluted by sexual and religious transgression ended by begging God to "take the film away/That keeps my sovereign's eyes from viewing/That thing that will be our undoing". Only God could awaken the king and make him hear "the sounds/As well of men, as of his hounds".

Within months of this poem's composition, popular opinion of Buckingham began to change. Amid the tolling bells, blazing bonfires and drunken revelry that greeted Charles and Buckingham's return from Madrid in October 1623, an astonishing political transformation occurred. The man excoriated as a parasite and a prodigal, as Phaeton and Ganymede, was reborn as a patriot Protestant hero. One poet compared Charles's return with that of Aeneas, "the wandering Prince of Troy/When hee to Carthage went", and ended by declaring "I love the Prince and every name/That honours noble Buckingham". Another poet exclaimed, "Oh for an Ovid or a Homer" who could capture "this dayes joy", for "Charles and George . . . have outstript all story" and "Must want a pen t'imortalize their glory", so "That in record of everlastinge fame/Men still might read great Charles and Georges name". The poet hailed:

> great Buckingham fortunes best child
> On whom both heaven and earth and seas have smil'd
> Live long in that high sphere wherein you move
> In Gods, the Kinges, the princes peoples love.

"Detraction now repeales what she hath spoken", the poet insisted, and "Envy hath drunke her last is swolne and broken".[38]

The conversion of Buckingham and Charles to an aggressive anti-Spanish policy late in 1623 and early in 1624 further fuelled "the peoples love" and helped end (at least temporarily) the libellers' assaults on the duke: Ganymede became St George. Yet the transformation was conditional. Old rumours, charges and images were not forgotten, and if St George stumbled, envy and detraction would be there to explain the fall.

Be Wary with Drugs and Physicians

Buckingham and Charles's new anti-Spanish policies severely strained their relationship with James. Although the Palatinate crises in 1620–22 had occasionally led the prince and favourite to take more aggressive stances than James desired, these tensions were nothing compared to the divisions that opened up in 1624. While Buckingham was in Madrid, Tobie Mathew had warned him that many "great men ar watching very close upon the Kinges hart, to see if they can discover any hayres breath of seperation therein from you". Glimpses of separation became apparent late in the Madrid stay when Buckingham began complaining about the Spanish ministers, while James remained "somewhat unwilling to believe it".[39] The gap widened after Buckingham's return. In mid-October 1623, when a Habsburg diplomat requested Buckingham's assistance to arrange a coach to Dover, the favourite balked, remarking that "he had much adoe to gett a Coche for monie at Madrid to bring him awaye". And when the two Spanish ambassadors came to congratulate the prince and Buckingham on their return, the duke refused even to look at them and "gave them such answeares as made them plainely see that his hart was ulcerated". It soon became clear that while James remained "infinitely desirous to have the match goe forward", Buckingham was "very opposite and much against it".[40] The Earl of Kellie, the old Scottish courtier, marvelled that since his return Buckingham was "more precipitate in his counsells then utherwayes he wold be", while James lamented that his favourite "had (he knew not how many) Devils within him since that Journey". But the trip to Madrid had not only opened a political rift between Buckingham and the king; it had also changed the duke's relationship with Charles. The two had become closer than ever, and Kellie confessed that "I can see the Prince loves him in an extraordinarye degree".[41]

Charles and Buckingham remained devoted to James. But as the continental crisis continued, they found it increasingly impossible to ignore the thorny issues that divided them. Meanwhile the collapse of the Spanish match left James without palatable policy options, and since he could do nothing to redress his daughter's wrongs and he dared not declare war against Spain, serious policy discussions became agony. Rather than allow courtiers and envoys to pester him, James withdrew to Royston and Newmarket, surrounded by his dogs and a few grooms. The king continued to reassure diplomats that he was still in control, declaring that, "he doubted nothing of the Prince, or his own Power, to sever them two [Charles and Buckingham], when he pleased".

But the strains were evident. Buckingham and Charles had taken the political initiative in 1624, forging a patriot coalition of courtiers and Parliament-men to break the treaties with Spain and to ally England with the anti-Habsburg powers, the Dutch Republic, Denmark, Venice, Savoy—and, most importantly, France, with whom they now hoped to conclude a marriage treaty between Charles and Louis XIII's sister Henrietta Maria (Fig. 8). No longer merely the king's "minion", Buckingham was acting the part of chief minister, directing, not just implementing, foreign and domestic policy. This angered James, and in April 1624 he chose to take seriously accusations levelled by the Spanish ambassadors that Charles and Buckingham were planning to confine him to his hunting lodges, assume control of the state, and marry Mall Villiers into the royal family. These allegations precipitated the most severe crisis yet in James and Buckingham's relationship. Charles could not sleep or eat for two days; and the king ostentatiously refused to let Buckingham ride in the royal coach. The duke's health suddenly collapsed, and he remained ill for several months.[42]

Illness had long been an important emotional crucible for the creation, expression and renewal of intimacy between James and his favourites. When

Figure 8: Thomas Scott, *Vox Regis*, 1624 (British Museum). This frontispiece to Scott's pamphlet depicts the remarkable dynastic and parliamentary unity in support of the militant Protestant Cause following the end of negotiations with Spain.

Robert Carr, a groom of the bedchamber, had broken his leg at the 1607 accession-day tilt, James's visits to his convalescing servant helped forge the bonds that soon made Carr the king's acknowledged favourite. The shared experience of illness had also been central to James's relationship with Buckingham. The duke had helped nurse the king through a major medical crisis in early 1619, and when, a couple of months later, the favourite himself fell ill, James and Charles "continuallye visited him". When the convalescing Buckingham fainted after overexerting himself in a foot race, James reportedly "gave him a sharpe kind chiding for adventuring him self so much".[43]

Now in 1624, at the lowest point in their relationship, illness, and the shared intimacies it entailed, helped heal the two men's estrangement. The whole court noticed James's concern. On 10 May, five days after the duke fell ill, Sir John Coke reported that James and Charles had spent almost three hours at Buckingham's house in London and that James had sent his own "barber" to wait on the patient. Coke later noted, "His Majesty hath shewn great tenderness over him and sendeth unto him three or four times every day". After the doctors told James "that unlesse he would please remeddy the continuall visitts that were made (which take away all opportunities of sleep and repose from him) they could not save him with all their arte", he ordered a tight guard around Buckingham's residence to shield the duke from business.[44]

Observers recognized these visits and ostentatious expressions of concern as signals of restored royal favour. But the personal letters written during Buckingham's 1624 illnesses also played a crucial role in expressing and renewing their intimacy. These letters shared news, offered counsel and comfort, traded medical advice, and reinforced affection with compliments and anecdotes. In one, James confessed that the news of the duke's illness "made my heart to bleed" and prayed that "God ever bless thee . . . and send thee health and heart". He reiterated his love using their old familiar language, addressing the ailing duke as "sweet heart" and "my only sweet and dear child" and signing off as "thy dear dad". James also sent medical counsel, warning Buckingham "for God's sake" to "be as wary as thou can with drugs and physicians, for they are but for cases of necessity". The king fussed over Buckingham's convalescence: "Remember now to take the air discreetly . . . and for God's sake and mine, keep thyself very warm, especially thy head and thy shoulders." He set out "diet and journeys" for his favourite to follow, advice "I assure myself thou will punctually observe", and hoped that "God . . . give thee grace to bid the drugs adieu this day". James also cheered Buckingham with news of his recent hunting failures, blaming his ill success on Buckingham's absence. Mustering the jocular tone that James so loved, the duke replied, "I ame verie sorie for this new vaine you have taken of lousing of stags; but ame much rejoyced, that you atribute so much to my good lucke, as to think if I were there your ill fortune would alter: for which caus, to pleas you and manie more to pleas my selfe, I will make all the hast my weaknes will give me leave."[45]

For his part, Buckingham wrote letters to inform and reassure his master. In one, the duke offered a detailed account of his fragile physical condition. "I thanke God", he wrote, that "my grudgings have left me againe; but the hines [highness] of my urin, with the yallowness of my skin, betokens a yallow jandeis; which will be no greate matter to cure, if it prove so." His sickness also gave him a means of expressing his humble love for James. "I ame yett but weake", he confessed, but, although the king might be annoyed that he should exhaust his strength by writing letters, "I must have leave now and then to write you with my one [own] hand".[46] Buckingham also enquired after the king's well-being. In one letter, Buckingham was happy to hear of the king's robust appetite—his "good stumake"—and hoped to hear more "news of your helth and merth". In another, Buckingham's wife told the king that her husband "beseeches your Majestie to send him word, how you speede; and whether your ablenes to ride contunues answerable to the former day: which nwse will be the best cordialle your Majestie can send him in his sicknes." James often shared medical news with the duke. Charles passed on reports of James's arthritic infirmities and reported the king's theories on the shared celestial cause of the two men's sicknesses: "& that ye may see how mischeefes comes by Planets & never one single", the king "has commanded me to tell you, that he is as ill tormented at this tyme in his right elbow & knee, as he was at Cambrig." But the prince went on to report that James hoped the duke's "comming merrilie hither with the Cunts in your companie to be his Nurses will make him a hole man again".[47]

Along with advice and support, James sent food and medicine. In a letter that the weakened duke dictated to his wife, Buckingham thanked the king for his "swett [sweet] cordiall", presumably a medicinal drink to reinvigorate the vital spirits. In another, Buckingham thanked him for his gift of melons, grapes and peaches. On 19 May, Coke reported that "Yesterday hee sent him cheries" and "this day hee sent the eys, the tong, and the dousets [testicles] of the deer hee killed in Eltham parck". On 16 June, James sent more sweetbreads; the next day, strawberries and raspberries; and a week later, yet more fruit. Other courtiers followed the king's lead.[48] The royal gifts of food and game served several purposes. They were intended to restore Buckingham's health—diet was a crucial component of therapeutic as well as preventive medicine—but they were also gestures of friendship, displaying and renewing the deep emotional ties between the two men.

Although the duke's recovery was worryingly slow, his illness brought him closer to the king at the very time when deep political differences had threatened to divide them. When the doctors finally let Buckingham leave his house in late May, still "much discoloured and lean with Sickness", the favourite knelt before James, "his hatt off and his hands upp". Overcome with emotion, James declaimed, "Steeny I pray God either to recover thee of this sicknesse or else (the teares breakin downe upon his cheekes while he was speaking) to transfer the same upon me, as one that would stand in the gapp for thee." Then he showered Buckingham "with one hundred kisses at the lest and continuall hanging about his neck".[49]

After months of uncertainty, these semi-public gestures made clear that Buckingham had retained the king's favour. But the political differences over Spain and the Palatinate remained unresolved. Over the winter of 1624–25, Buckingham and Charles would labour to organize a broader anti-Habsburg military alliance and to secure a French bride for the prince. But James remained deeply sceptical of his sweet boys' efforts.

To Theobalds

Theobalds, the prodigy house created by Lord Burghley and his son, Sir Robert Cecil, was a marvel: expansive yet intimate, free of the insalubrious London air yet only a short ride from the capital, it was one of James's favourite hunting retreats. By the end of 1624 he was moving noticeably slower than usual. His gout was so bad that he had to be carried between two servants, requiring "all the doores betwene his bedchamber and the parke" to be "inlarged".[50] Despite his infirmities, James was eager to begin hunting again. He had his eye on Hinchinbrook House outside Huntingdon, but Charles and Buckingham wanted him at Theobalds. With critical diplomatic negotiations ongoing, they both needed to stay within easy reach of London. Buckingham argued the merits of an extended stay in Hertfordshire. If James agreed to Theobalds, the prince could join them, and without him "we should neither play at cards, golf, nor set up for does". At Theobalds, James would find "young trees to plant, new ridings to make, and for other lesser pleasures, have you not hawking the partridge, the pheasant and river hawking in greater abundance than in any other place?" Besides, "your dogs and horses will be in better breath" there. Hinchinbrook, Buckingham reminded the king, "stands in so ill an air that you seldom go thither that you do not return sick again".[51] James disregarded these pleas and spent most of the winter at Newmarket, requiring the entire French diplomatic delegation to ride to Cambridge to sign the marriage treaty, the cornerstone of the duke's new foreign policy. After a brief stay in Westminster for the holidays, James headed back to East Anglia and then to Newmarket, Chesterford Park and Royston. Eventually, he arrived at Theobalds by 28 February.

He would not leave there alive.

PART I

THE AUTHORIZED VERSION
1625

PROLOGUE

THE KING'S GOOD DEATH

Sɪʀ Wɪʟʟɪᴀᴍ Pᴀᴅᴅʏ had long been James I's personal physician. With a medical degree from Leiden, Paddy had pursued a lucrative practice at court since the early 1590s. He had attended Elizabeth's chief minister, Lord Burghley, during his final years, and had become a fellow of the College of Physicians in 1591, eventually serving four terms as its president.[1] He was in his early seventies when James fell ill in March 1625, and perhaps because of his age was no longer in regular attendance on the king. When he finally came to Theobalds on 26 March, he soon realized that James was beyond his help. "I held it my christian duetie to prepare hym", Paddy recalled, "telling hym that ther was nothing left for me to doe ... butt to pray for his soule." Yet Paddy lingered in the bedchamber as Archbishop George Abbot and Bishop John Williams asked James whether "they shold praye with hym". The king "cheerfullie" consented, and, as Paddy looked on, Williams guided James through his final hours of life.[2]

After the king's death, Paddy copied out into the blank pages of a *Booke of Common Prayer* a series of forty-one "sentences" that Williams had "distinctlie pronounced" to the dying king. Mostly taken from Scripture, these pious phrases and fragments sought to express and encourage the trust in God, in Christ's sacrifice, and in salvation that would allow the dying man to meet his end patiently. "Into thy hands I commend my Spirit, for thou has redeemed me O Lord thou God of Truth," the first sentence ran. "As by Adam all die", read another, "so by Christ shall all be made alive." "I am now readie to be offred", Williams recited to the king, for:

> the time of my departure is at hand. I have fought a good fight. I have fulfilled my course. I have kept the faith. Henceforth there is layd up for me a crowne of Righteousnes, which the Lord, the Righteous Judge shall give to me at that day, & to all that love his Comming.

Twice the bishop repeated the exhortation, "Come Lord Jesu, Come quickly."[3]

Paddy had paid close attention to the king's response, noting how "att the End of every Sentence" James raised his eyes, "the messengers of his Hart", "up unto Heaven", a gesture that gave "godlie Assurance" of the king's "livelie Faith" in the promise of eternal life.[4] For Paddy, this deathbed performance confirmed James's adherence to true religion, "accordinglie as in his godlie Life he had often publiquelie professed". Well aware that he had witnessed an extraordinary moment of religious and political apotheosis, Paddy added his signature to the end of his notes, verifying his eyewitness testimony (Fig. 9). He left the prayer book to St John's College, Oxford, as a precious relic of his friendship with a most pious Protestant king.

Paddy believed he had witnessed a good death that had sacralized James's royal authority. Vivid depictions of good deaths had long been part of the Christian tradition, and narratives of the good deaths of kings played an important role in both Protestant and Catholic mythologies of sacred monarchy.[5] James himself had outlined the essential features in a letter to his brother-in-law, Christian IV of Denmark, following Queen Anne's final illness in 1619. Contemporary reports suggested that Anne had not been able "to prepare herself and set all things in order" until the very end. James, however, rewrote his wife's death for her grieving brother, so that Anne's "sanctity" and "piety" clearly "shone forth". In James's reworking, Anne was reconciled to her fate and had "eagerly entered upon that heavenly journey for which her entire being yearned". James hoped for a similarly edifying end: "May God, the greatest and best, grant us that we conclude the brief drama of this life with an equal felicity of departure, found in meditation upon death before it comes, so

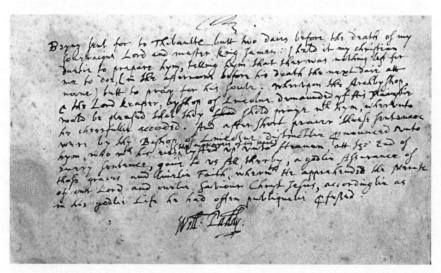

Figure 9: Sir William Paddy's note in his copy of the *Book of Common Prayer* records James I's final hours and bears witness to the king's good death (St John's College, Oxford).

that satiated with earthly pleasure we may in that moment strive for celestial glory that is without satiety".[6]

Almost immediately after James breathed his last, his courtiers and clerics began to tell stories of his exemplary death. In their narratives, James was wholly conscious of his impending mortality and embraced death with a patient confidence in salvation. Bishop Laud noted that James had called continuously for prayers "with an assured confidence in Christ", and that his final act had been "as full of patience as could be found in so strong a death". James "wente out of the worlde", Sir Edward Conway, the Secretary of State, told Dudley Carleton, "like a Christian, that had a stronge hearte and a humble minde". God allowed the king both time and breath to confirm his commitment to Protestantism and to "express a lively faith, and the definition of a pure Christian"; indeed, he had "concluded the verbal Creede with these words 'There is no other beleefe no other hope'". The Earl of Kellie was pleased, he told his cousin the Earl of Mar, that James had died "so weill sattilled in religione". In his report to James's daughter Elizabeth, John Chambermayd stressed that the king's declaration should scotch any rumours the Catholics might spread of deathbed conversion, and added that James had asked the Earl of Pembroke to be his witness "agaynst those scandalls that may be raysed". He also noted James's rousing "confession of his fayth" before receiving the sacrament:

> he was resolved to dye professing the fayth he had allwayes lived in, and in whiche he was more willing (he sayd) to suffer as a martir than to dye his naturall deathe, in any other, charging all ther present to bear true testimony of what he had sayd (as they would answere it at the great day).[7]

Others noted James's exemplary performance during the various deathbed rituals performed in his final days. Secretary Conway reported that James had received clerical absolution, taking care to remind Carleton that this rite was not "popish" in any way: "When the Lord Keeper [Williams] asked him whither hee wolde have the absolution read, hee answered 'As it is practised in the English Church I ever approved it, but in the darke way of the Church of Roome I doe defy it'." Laud highlighted James's "devout receiving of the blessed sacrament", while Conway told the diplomat Isaac Wake that the king's "calling for and receiving the Communion and performing those actions of devotion and pieitie" had given the court "much comfort" in the middle of such "extreame sorrow and greife". "Hee received the communion", Abbot told Sir Thomas Roe, "and made a most christian ende".[8]

Similar reports soon circulated outside the court. The king was "naturallie impatient", Edward Tilman, a Cambridge Fellow, observed, "yet before his death verie patient". In Cambridge, news circulated that James had left "a Confession of faith to be published, to stop the mouthes of Papists". The Florentine agent Salvetti heard that James had made a firm declaration of his Protestantism and had declared himself willing to die a martyr for the faith, while the Venetian ambassador reported James's insistence "that he died in the Protestant faith". "He made a worthy confession of his faith", noted the diarist and Parliament-man William Whiteway in Dorchester, "and gave great testimonys of devotion and piety".[9]

Many of these reports discussed James's supposed final words of advice to his son. Many observers hungered for reports of James's final words to Charles, though some conceded that the king had been unable to say much of substance. Kellie claimed to have never seen "onye bodye keepe his memorye and under-standing soe long and soe weill as he did", but acknowledged that "his speitche failled him sume good tyme before he dyed, whitche if it had not I think he shuld have showin to the King that now is theis derektions and consell whitche I think he shall never have from onye uther". Nevertheless stories of deathbed counsel soon spread. In Cambridge the scholar and avid news collector Joseph Mead heard that before losing his speech the king had had three hours alone with the prince, with everyone else in the sickroom commanded to leave and remain out of earshot. Salvetti reported news that James, although speechless during his last days, had given Charles "a paper, written by his own hand, containing various statements; but of the truth of this there is no information on which we can depend". In Dorchester, Whiteway confidently reported that James had commended the Earls of Pembroke and Montgomery to Charles "as his best servants" and instructed his son "never to suffer a toleration of Popery in England". The official *Mercure François* focused mostly on reports of James's supposed conversations with Charles about England's future role in Europe's ongoing struggles. Conscious that he was "close to the end of his days", James had reminded his son to protect the Church, to reward those who had served his father well, and to cherish the "children of the Electress Palatine". Above all, the *Mercure* claimed, James had urged Charles to "restore the lands and titles" of the Elector. In "his death agony" James spoke again, offering Charles his blessing and asking God to preserve his rule over the "earthly kingdom" that James was exchanging for a heavenly one.[10]

The making of this authorized version of the king's good death, testifying to James's piety, orthodoxy and wisdom, was mostly a top-down process, orchestrated by senior courtiers, physicians and clerics; but others, including foreign ambassadors and the king's own subjects, collaborated in the work. The authorized version of James's death would eventually contain two basic stories: an official medical assessment of what had killed the king, and a far more widely circulated story about the king's spiritual confidence and exem-plary piety. The medical narrative set out the natural causes of James's death; most importantly, it completely effaced any mention of unauthorized medical meddling and closed down any speculation about poison. The religious stories of the "good death", on the other hand, reworked claims about kingly piety and confessional orthodoxy that were central to the legitimating mythologies of early modern monarchy, helping recharge monarchical charisma at the vulnerable moment of transition between reigns.[11]

Much of the authorized version was constructed in writing, but the process culminated in the spectacular multi-part funeral ceremonies held for James in April and May 1625. Commissioned at great expense by Charles I, these rituals celebrated the virtuous life, splendid achievements and pious death of the first Stuart king of England and theatrically proclaimed the promise of Charles's reign. These myths and rituals mattered a great deal, for the power of early modern kings depended on stories and ceremonies that could seize the imagination and subtly compel the obedience of the ruled.

CHAPTER ONE

CRUEL FIRE

THE PHYSICIANS EXPLAIN JAMES I'S DEATH

O N THE DAY James died, 27 March 1625, William Laud was scheduled to preach a mid-Lenten sermon at Whitehall. "I ascended the pulpit", he wrote, in a "much troubled" state of mind. It was a "very melancholy moment, the report then spreading" through the palace "that his Majesty King James, of most sacred memory, was dead". Midway through the sermon, with the Duke of Buckingham's loud wailings now audible above the murmurings of the congregation, Laud abruptly left the pulpit. The bishop was pleased by reports that James had died well. "He breathed forth his blessed soul most religiously", Laud noted, "with great constancy of faith and courage." But he remained troubled by aspects of the king's death, and had his own opinion about what had gone wrong. When James had fallen ill, his disease initially "*appeared* to be a tertian ague", Laud wrote. But the doctors had been deceived. "I fear it was the gout," he noted. This misdiagnosis had unfortunate consequences, for the "wrong application of medicines" had driven the gout from James's "feet to his inward vital parts". Other courtiers had different theories. John Williams, Bishop of Lincoln and Lord Keeper of the Great Seal, had heard a royal doctor say that James "us'd to have a Beneficial Evacuation of Nature, a sweating in his left Arm, as helpful to him as any Fontinel [a natural or medical ulcer for draining off humours] could be". But this natural evacuation "of late had failed", indicating that the king's "former Vigour of Nature was low, and spent". This "might well cause a Tertian Ague, and a Mortal", Williams's chaplain later reflected, "when the Spring had Entred so far, able to make a commotion in the Humours of the Body, and not to expel them, with accustom'd vaporation". Farther from court, interested contemporaries often made do with bald summaries of the medical facts. Edward Tilman in Cambridge heard that "a tertian turn'd into a burning fever hath divorced his soule from his bodie", and William Whiteway in Dorchester noted only that James "died of a burning feaver".[1]

When the king fell ill, early in March, few doubted that he would soon recover. The fatal turn of events later in the month thus caught many by surprise, fuelling speculation about what had gone wrong. The king's doctors, however, quickly produced an authoritative explanation of the medical circumstances of James's illness and death, offering a comprehensive account of the pathological forces that had destroyed him. Their account, written in the language of learned medicine, formed one crucial strand of the authorized version of James's death.

Tertian Agues and the Princes of the Art

On 16 March 1625, nearly two weeks into James's illness, Secretary Conway reported that the royal doctors had diagnosed the king with a "pure intermitting tertian" ague, or fever.[2] The king's physicians were trained in the orthodox, humanist-Galenic medical tradition that dominated contemporary learned thought on fevers and taught that all agues belonged to the category of hot and dry distempers, consisting essentially of "a superfluous, hurtfull, and unhaile heate, that sometimes often, and sometimes more vehement than before commeth againe, and returneth".[3] These agues could take a staggering variety of forms, with different types resulting from the putrefaction, superfluity or excessive heating of different combinations of the four humours present in the human body.[4] Each ague type had its own distinctive symptoms, and each required a specific therapeutic response. Since misdiagnosis could potentially result in dangerously misapplied therapy, it was crucial the physicians had a precise understanding of the ague's exact nature.

The culprit in tertian agues was putrid choler, the quintessentially hot and dry humour also known as yellow bile. Learned physicians explained its putrefaction as the result of a range of factors, including "a hot and dry distemper; hot constitution of ayr, eating of hot meats, and drinking of hot drinks, using of hot medicines, watching, fasting, labour, and too much exercise". The symptoms of a pure tertian ague were highly distinctive. The fever fits followed a three-stage trajectory. They began, noted one physician, "with great shaking, and cold . . . more violent in this tertian than in any other Ague", which could feel as if it were "pricking the flesh". The cold fit was followed by a hot one: the heat was "sharp and biting, and in its vigour . . . extended equally over the body, whence the sick draw their breath much, and are troubled with thirst". Some physicians thought the pricking sensation continued through the hot fit, making the patient feel "as if he were prickt with nailes". The hot fit sometimes included symptoms of mental distress—"great disquietnesse", insomnia, even "Ravings"—and during the fit, alert physicians might identify objective signs of the distemper using pulse and urine analysis. The pulse accelerated at the height of the fit, becoming "strong" and "swift", while urine became markedly discoloured and remained cloudy at the fit's end. At various points in the fit's arc—at the end of the "shaking", for instance, or at the peak of the heat—the patient might vomit, as the body attempted to purge the putrid choler. These tertian symptoms, which could last up to twelve hours, were eventually "terminated by Sweat", the third and final phase, which some thought worked as a beneficial natural purgation that helped expel corrupt humour. The symptoms returned every other day, creating a distinctive day-on, day-off pattern. (The other two intermitting agues—the quotidian and the quartan—followed different timetables, with the quotidian fever fits striking daily and the quartan fits following a one-day-on, two-days-off cycle.) Complicating diagnosis, learned physicians had also identified variants of the tertian ague. These included the "halfe tertian Ague", which partially mimicked the intermitting pattern of the pure tertian fever, being "a very strong Ague that never ceaseth altogether, but hapneth one day gentle, and the other day harder"; and "the spurious" or "the counterfeit and bastard Tertian", which replicated the intermitting pattern of the pure tertian with symptoms that were "not so vehement" yet lasted a great deal longer.[5]

Although practitioners and commentators engaged in advanced medical thought continued to debate certain aspects of the distemper—the physiological location of the putrid humour at different stages of the fits, for instance, or the reasons for the strict periodicity of the symptoms—most physicians saw little danger in a pure tertian ague.[6] Generally speaking, learned commentators thought intermittent fevers much less threatening than continuous ones, in part because the physician could take advantage of the times when the fever abated to strengthen the patient. Hippocrates, one of the two great classical authorities who governed orthodox medical thought, had argued that "Exquisite or exact Tertian Agues last but for seven fits at most" and that "all Intermitting Feavers are void of danger". The pure tertian, one contemporary medical manual affirmed, was "wholy without peril". Some contemporaries believed that tertian agues at certain times of the year might even be beneficial—"an ague in spring is physic to a king", ran one proverb much cited in discussions of James's illness. But the doctors knew of several ways a pure tertian could become dangerously "pernitious" or "Malignant". An elderly or weak patient was always at greater risk. And if either patient or physician made an error in treatment or diet, dangerous complications might ensue. If the disease were prolonged by such errors, then it could mutate into more dangerous forms. Indeed, one medical writer believed that after the Hippocratic seven fits, the pure tertian would either end or inevitably "alter her owne nature into another Ague". The corrupted humour could become unusually dangerous and affect other parts of the body if it was "exceeding thin, putred, [or] filthy", or if it became mixed with other humours, or acquired a "malignant quality", or "if a thick humour poured out by heat, either fall down into some principal part, or cause a dangerous Catarrh, or Asthma, or the Gout". The doctors also knew of particularly dangerous forms of the distemper, "Malignant and

Pestilent Tertians", which, though they might ape the features of the pure tertian, complete with "evident Intermissions", "yet do they often kill the Patient". Putrid choler could also produce more dangerous distempers. In some cases it could cause a "burning Fever", "the hottest of all other Agues" that "proceedeth of a red Cholera, which putrifieth and enflameth in the veines neare the heart, in the lyver, and in the mouth of the stomack". Its symptoms were terrifying—a "never ceasing burning", a blackened tongue, loss of appetite, "fiery" yellow urine, loss of "hearing, seeing and speech", and a "great binding of the body". This ague was particularly "perillous"—in a week, the patient would either recover or die.[7]

James's initial diagnosis did not provoke much concern. If his tertian ague were correctly identified and treated, then it posed little danger. Protocols for the medical treatment of the king were already in place. James's chief physician, the French Huguenot Theodore de Mayerne, was out of the country when the king fell ill, but had left behind two sets of detailed instructions for his

Figure 10: William Elder, *Sir Theodore Turquet de Mayerne*, late seventeenth century (National Portrait Gallery). James I's chief physician, Mayerne was out of the country during the king's final illness, but had left behind detailed protocols for managing a royal medical crisis.

colleagues, one composed in 1623, the other in 1624 (Fig. 10).[8] As far back as 1613, when James had suffered from a serious kidney disorder, Mayerne had insisted that no single physician should be responsible for the king's medical care. Instead, a team of four or five "experienced men", who were "doers not talkers; men who are calm and sociable and committed to the king's wellbeing", would oversee any health crisis.[9] In late August 1624, shortly before he left for the Continent, Mayerne added to his second memorandum on the king's health (written with Henry Atkins) a series of rules—a sickroom protocol—for managing royal illness. Mayerne urged his colleagues to mobilize courtiers and councillors to persuade James "not so much by reasons . . . as by prayers and conjurations" to follow his physicians' advice. But strict limits had to be placed on any other outside interference. Mayerne's protocol gave a select team of learned, skilled and experienced physicians, "the princes of the art", complete and *exclusive* control over the king's diagnosis, care and treatment. "All amateurs, whether laymen or unqualified doctors", including the nostrum peddlers and empirics, "the cranks and triflers, the fraudulent parasites of the great" who hung around the court, must be kept away from the royal sickbed. Mayerne added six further rules to guarantee the best care, prevent divisions among the doctors, and protect the physicians' reputations if anything went wrong:

> [1] There must be free and open deliberation. [2] All others being removed (unless a surgeon is required), only the doctors must decide. [3] Any disagreement among the doctors must be totally and rationally resolved, before they separate, so that no doubt remains to be exploited. . . . [4] Decisions are to be recorded in writing on the spot. [5] Prescriptions are to be signed by all the doctors and handed to the apothecary. [6] Finally, "if you wish to live in peace", nothing must be said in public about their discussions: only the decision should be uttered, as an oracle.[10]

Early in March 1625 the "princes of the art" confidently diagnosed James with an intermitting fever that posed little danger to their patient. So what went wrong?

The King's Sickly State

Shortly after James's death, one or more of his physicians produced a Latin official report on the king's final illness. The report detailed James's symptoms, treatment and sudden turn for the worse and set out the results of the physicians' post-mortem inspection of the king's body. The report was an authoritative statement, conforming to the Mayerne protocol on consensus and transparency. The account of the post-mortem inspection ended by asserting that "all these things were seen and observed by the supervising physicians of the king and the surgeons administering the cutting", that the medical personnel signed the report, and that the report was then shown "to very many others from the chambers of his majesty and the attendants who were present". The document was probably intended as the official record for both the physicians and the court, and in its original form it does not appear to have circulated very broadly beyond those circles—although, as we shall see, summary (and often distorted) descriptions of the post-mortem examination eventually reached metropolitan and provincial newsletter-writers. Only two copies of the full report survive, one collected by a later Bishop of Lincoln, Thomas Barlow, the other by the Jacobean physician Thomas Marwood.[11]

The authorized report told a coherent story of an ageing, sickly man "invaded" by a "malignant" fever that manifested first as an intermittent tertian ague but mutated later into a more dangerous distemper too strong for the weakened patient. The report began by detailing the poor state of James's health even before his final sickness, arguing that his pre-existing bodily condition—his natural complexion, dietary habits and chronic ailments—helped explain the nature and development of his disease. The report described James's long-standing physical problems, drawing extensively from Mayerne's 1623–24 memoranda on the king's health and medical history. James had become seriously weakened by age and poor living, as well as by the "influence of external causes". His major organs, which Mayerne had thought in mixed condition in 1623, were by late 1624 chronically distempered, lacking the moderate "nature and temper" that constituted good health. His brain was too hot and wet and was plagued by catarrh; his liver, lungs, heart and bile were overheated; his belly, though cooler, was afflicted by chronic indigestion. Humoural balance was, at best, precarious. The king's spleen was "swollen" with melancholy, causing "very grave melancholic symptoms", including heart palpitations. And he continued to suffer from the long-standing problems with kidney stones and arthritis that Mayerne's memoranda had emphasized.[12]

The report made clear that James's lifestyle had exacerbated these chronic problems. His diet was disordered, partly because tooth loss left him unable to chew his food, compromising the digestive process so crucial to good health. A healthy diet, the physicians knew, required not only moderation but also attention to the timing and correct "order of receiving of meates and drinke". By these standards, as Mayerne had made clear in 1623, James lived dangerously—he ate at odd hours, consuming fruit constantly and "without order"—and the post-mortem report emphasized that James's bad eating habits persisted until his death. But an even greater problem was the king's drinking. "In drink", Mayerne had noted, James "errs in quality, quantity, frequency, time and order", consuming beer, ale and various French and Spanish sweet wines. Furthermore, James "hates water", the best drink for conserving natural moisture and promoting healthy digestion. The post-mortem report argued that James's "indiscriminate" consumption of beer and wine, and especially of the thick, sweet wines favoured by his household, had generated corrupt humours in his liver, belly and spleen. Lack of exercise compounded these problems: having abandoned what Mayerne called "the vigorous exercise of the hunt", James had become increasingly sedentary and gained significant amounts of weight. The only reason he had avoided serious illness as long as he had, the post-mortem report argued, was because the increased rate and volume of his defecation purged his body of the dangerous humours constantly accumulating inside it.[13]

Over the winter of 1624–25 the king's health worsened. James's prophy-lactic excretions—not only his recently increased defecation but also a regular and beneficial haemorrhoidal bleeding that had begun in 1619—began to taper off, and his body became increasingly unable to purge excessive and pernicious humours. As James became progressively weaker and more sluggish, corrupt humours began to accumulate; it was only a matter of time before serious distemper occurred. The burdens of kingship, the endless preoccupation with affairs of state, also took a toll. "Continuously concerned for the peace and tranquility of the whole Christian world", James suffered from a melancholic depression of the spirits that further weakened his physical constitution. Mayerne, too, had worried about the physiological impact of the king's turbu-lent "affections of the mind", which could easily throw the natural functions into turmoil. Although the king was quick to anger, he was equally quick to calm down; his tendency to melancholy, and to traumatic melancholic ailments, was far more troublesome.[14]

Mayerne's two reports had laid out in detail the major distempers to which James was particularly prone. He had been "subject to diarrhea" his whole life, with poor diet, emotional distress and the change of seasons often acting as trig-gers. But by 1623 his attacks of diarrhea had become increasingly debilitating, often striking in concert with other ailments. For years his vigorous horseback riding had caused "turbid urine, red like Alicante wine", but by the time Mayerne wrote his reports, this painless condition had become a more painful kidney distemper ("nephritis"): James experienced burning on urination, passed bloody urine "with red sand" and "thick sediment", suffered from "pain in the left kidney", and vomited frequently. Sometimes the attacks culminated in the ejec-tion of sandy, loosely congealed kidney stones. James also suffered from arthritic distempers, particularly in the winter. Some of these arthritic conditions had identifiable external causes, and the "atrophy" of James's legs, "which from child-hood were slender and weak", could be explained by his lack of exercise. The king's feet, legs and arms, Mayerne had reported, were riddled with arthritic and gouty pains. His right foot, "which had an odd twist when walking", had become misaligned and chronically painful, particularly around the ankle. "The great toe of the left foot", the knees, the shoulders and the hands were all susceptible to "acute" pains. On three separate occasions, the most recent in the autumn of 1623, the king was "seized with most severe pains of the thigh . . . as if by a spasm of muscles and tendons bending the left leg" (see Plate 1).[15]

Mayerne knew that mental distress and "low spirits" could set off one or more of these conditions. The failure of the 1610 Parliament and the death of Prince Henry in 1612 had triggered "watery bilious, fetid and black" diarrhea, and severe nephritic attacks had dogged James during the politically tense summer of 1613 and autumn of 1615. His most serious illness had come in 1619, when the death of Queen Anne had brought on all three major distempers—arthritic pain, nephritic fits, and "bilious diarrhea, watery and profuse", along with a host of other unnerving symptoms.[16] By March 1625, the post-mortem report concluded, the king was in an increasingly "sickly state", his body choked with "the congested filth of vicious humours".[17] He was highly vulnerable to multiple distempers and plagued with dangerous melancholic cares.

Mayerne's reports had shown little concern with agues: the king "rarely has fever", and when he did, it was typically "short and ephemeral".[18] But when James eventually did fall ill early in March, he became feverish, exhibiting the classic symptoms of what the post-mortem report labelled "an intermittent tertian fever". To begin with, his symptoms were relatively mild. James's tertian ague followed the predictable pattern, with a two-hour shivering fit followed by a hot fever fit that transitioned into a therapeutic sweat. The first couple of paroxysms ended with what the post-mortem report termed a "perfect quiet", suggesting no grave cause for concern. But while the distemper did not seem dangerous, from the start the doctors were confronted with a different problem: their old and sickly patient refused to follow instructions.

"He laughs at medicine"

This came as no surprise; his doctors were well aware of James's attitude towards them and their "art". He had always been an exceptionally difficult patient. "He laughs at medicine", Mayerne had noted in 1623, and "regards physicians as not only unnecessary but positively useless. He says that their art rests on mere conjectures, which are uncertain and therefore invalid." The king reacted badly to ill health. He was "most impatient of pains" and desperate for "relief", Mayerne had written, but he acknowledged neither the underlying causes of his condition nor the rationale that underlay orthodox therapy. The king would never follow the regimen necessary for good health, nor would he ever conform to the "rules of our art". James particularly disliked the physicians' standard therapeutic repertoire. Powerful purgatives, he believed, "destroyed nature", and he would only tolerate milder versions of the drugs. James disliked medicine that caused excessive stomach cramps, and until 1613 he had refused any type of "clyster" (enema), the standard purgative treatment for evacuating noxious humours from the bowels. He was equally opposed to phlebotomy (therapeutic bleeding) and was not bled medicinally until his dangerous health crisis in 1619. Even then, his physicians used leeches (applied to the haemorrhoids) and blistering cups, rather than the knife. In some cases the king's chronic conditions made standard therapies unworkable. His sensitive skin, for instance, made it difficult to treat arthritic pains with the usual plasters, ointments and poultices.[19]

James's attitude to physic and physicians posed a real problem. The physicians knew that the tertian ague was readily amenable to what one expert termed "a regular and methodical cure", which sought to counteract and purge the affected humour, reinvigorate the patient, and tackle the underlying causes of humoural putrefaction. According to Galenic logic, the tertian ague was "hot" and "dry" in both humoural origin and febrile symptoms, and thus was "cured and corrected with contrary things, to wit, with cold moist things". A cooling, purifying and moistening diet was one element of the therapeutic response. Hot and dry food and drink, which stimulated choler, had to be avoided, of course. Environmental adjustments that counteracted the effects of heat—fresh water baths, cool air that "penetrateth to the heart, and other inward parts"—were also beneficial, as were clean linen, pleasant smells, and even the sight of water. But a full cure required the complete purgation of the putrid humour. Partial purgation occurred naturally during the course of the tertian fits, as vapours produced by the corrupted humour made their way to the skin and were "purged away either by Sweats, or by insensible Transpiration, or by Pushes and Pimples". The patient's natural evacuations— urine, faeces and vomit—also expelled corrupt choler. Although some believed that the best response to an ague was to let the body naturally handle the necessary purgation, most physicians argued that this was insufficient. Effective treatment required administering artificial "Medicaments" to prepare corrupt humours for purgation and then drive them out. These medicaments were composed primarily of herbal or mineral ingredients believed not only to produce the correct effect—preparative, purgative or regenerative—but also to work actively against the hot and dry qualities of the putrid humours.[20]

Physicians had a repertoire of tested ague therapies: drinks or juleps to "prepare the humors"; purgative drugs (laxative, emetic, diuretic and sudorific) and surgical phlebotomy to evacuate the humours; medicines to counteract choler, reduce fever and chills, stimulate appetite or quench thirst; and topical applications, like the soft and moist "cooling Epithems" applied externally, over the heart, liver or loins. Correctly timing the therapy was as important as correctly choosing the medicinal ingredients. As they implemented a treatment regime, physicians had to pay close attention both to the patient's age, strength and complexion and to the distinctive periodicity of the tertian ague, the alternation of healthy and feverish days, and the progression of the fever from cold fit to hot fit to sweat. The order in which therapies were given and the timing of their application to different phases of the fits were thus absolutely crucial. Similar rules governed diet: food and drink, important as both counteractive therapy and essential sustenance for a patient weakened by illness, had to be taken at the correct times. Eating just before the fit began was a bad idea, as the body had to focus on "concocting" the "Morbifick Humors" rather than digesting the newly swallowed food, which risked being corrupted by the distemper's "filthy vapor".[21]

James's impatience with the rules of the "regular and Methodical Cure", his contempt for physicians, his dislike of purgatives and phlebotomy, his refusal to moderate and order his diet, all caused immediate problems in March 1625. Indeed, the post-mortem report argued that James's stubbornness had significantly worsened his illness. The report noted that the king would not follow his physicians' instructions about what to consume, and when: he took drink at the start of the fit, against his doctors' recommendations, and he would not stop drinking wine, a dangerous source of heat. James also appears to have refused any drug to encourage sweating. Because the king refused to listen to his physicians, the report concluded, his distemper quickly became "more vehement", straining his already weakened constitution.[22]

The first signs of danger soon appeared. "After the third attack", the report noted, James's pulse became variable and his breathing laboured, melancholy increased in his spleen, and the king became "sad, anxious, full of sighs". The physicians began to fear that putrid combinations with another humour might mutate the tertian ague into something more dangerous. Now positively alarmed at James's intransigence, the doctors turned to Mayerne's protocols. Mayerne knew that neither a direct "harangue" nor deferential cajoling from his physicians would persuade the king to toe the therapeutic line. To deal with James's stubbornness, the doctors had to use other forms of courtly influence, and so Mayerne had urged his colleagues to mobilize courtiers and councillors to persuade James, "not so much by reasons . . . as by prayers and conjurations", to follow his doctors' prescriptions. According to the post-mortem report, after the third fit of the tertian fever and the first signs of melancholic symptoms, the doctors had called on the "humble prayers" of courtiers to persuade the king to follow their orders. The doctors warned the courtiers that:

> although this fever did not seem so dangerous in its nature as a fever, nevertheless . . . every feverish sickness is great and not free from danger, especially in an old man, and that (unless errors might be avoided), it could change its nature from being intermittently single to double or continuous.

In other words, if James did not become more pliable, his fever would turn into something far more dangerous than a pure intermitting tertian ague.[23]

According to the report, the king heeded his courtiers' intensive lobbying and submitted to a more methodical treatment. With James's reluctant consent, the doctors stuck closely to treatments recommended in the orthodox medical literature. They tried to expel noxious humours using herbal purgatives administered in clysters containing, among other things, "tamarind" and "manna", both widely recommended for "cholerike diseases, as burning Fevers, Tertians, and the like". The doctors also bled the king, relying (as they had in 1619) on leeches, "since he altogether abhorred vein-cutting in his arm", and they deployed various cooling, preparative and "opening" medicines, including a syrup of citrus juice and sorrel and a "cooling julep" of barley, chicory, sorrel, hartshorn and marigolds. Some treatments combined herbs with newly fashionable chemical ingredients, creating compounds like the moistening "extract of violets and cloves with the breath of vitriol", or the broth "for cooling and opening" that contained extracts of saltpetre (sal prunella), pearl and coral "dissolved in beer". The physicians also applied a cooling epithem to James's chest and administered a preparation to treat the melancholic symptoms in the king's "left hypochondrium". At this point all they could hope was that the implementation of a regular and methodical cure had not come too late.[24]

Cruel Fire

In spite of his doctors' efforts, the king's fever "overcame all remedies". The report did not specify when James's symptoms began definitively to worsen, but worsen they did. His fits became longer and more brutal, his pulse rapid and weak, and his breathing laboured. The febrile heat caused desperate thirst, but swelling in James's throat made swallowing difficult, and he could not consume enough water to ease his symptoms. The fever's "ferocious internal fire" left scabs on his tongue, while the melancholic vapours, which depressed his breathing and induced loss of consciousness, complicated everything.

As the end neared, the king's symptoms became truly alarming. A twenty-hour fit left the exhausted patient in a deep sleep. But when the fever abated and his pulse slowed at last, the king began to exhibit worrying new symptoms, including an "uncertain change in his urine ... indicating an obscure and hidden malignity". After his eleventh fit the doctors renewed their purgative treatments, only to have a new complication emerge. Over the course of twenty-four hours the king produced more than thirty bowel movements, excreting "burned, bilious, and putrid things" in massive volumes of diarrhea. At first, the doctors thought this prodigious purgation would leave James slightly stronger, and they became cautiously optimistic that, with so much corrupt material purged from the body, the next fit "would be milder". But they were cruelly disappointed:

[A]gainst hope and contrary to reason, [the fit] attacked with great fierce-ness, with both a long and horrible chill and a cruel fire. As his weaker strengths were no match for so unequal an antagonist, after a long and diffi-cult fight they wholly succumbed; his speech failed him and so did his pulse, and with very many black ejections and a diaphoretic sweat—a conflict in which he had endured for almost forty hours, and held on with every aid—finally the most pious soul of the king—the most prudent, the most just, and the most Christian of all kings—flew away from this earthly prison, not without the greatest grief and the most profuse tears of all his people, towards Jesus Christ the redeemer and into eternal joy, on the twenty-seventh day of March in the year of the Lord 1625.[25]

The following day the surgeons opened James's body and his physicians "dili-gently inspected" his major organs. Their inspection corroborated what they already knew of James's medical history—a shrivelled kidney explained his chronic nephritis, for instance—and revealed the cause and course of his final illness. According to the report, many of James's major organs bore the imprint of both his pre-existing distempers and the hot fever that had killed him. Signs of burning and dryness—effects of the fever's heat—were everywhere, along with the telltale signs of corrupt and putrid humours. His liver was "dry and arid"; his spleen was "lax, soft . . . clearly putrid to both the sight and touch . . . replete with black and melancholic blood"; his gall bladder, "scorched with bile", was full of the black, turgid liquid he had excreted in his death throes. Similar marks of burning and putrefaction, as well as pools of "black, liquid, stinking excrement", appeared throughout his lower digestive tract. The black blood in the king's lungs bore witness both to his pre-existing disposition to heat and to the fever that had afflicted him. Signs of heat also appeared in the heart, where the surgeons found the king's pericardium completely dried up.

The post-mortem examination also explained why James's tertian fever had proved fatal. The putrid black liquid around the gall bladder suggested that "alienating and rotting humours" in the body had kindled an "intermittent bastard fever"—that is, they had turned the "pure" tertian fever into a more complex and dangerous variant that had spread to his belly and intestines, causing both the putrid diarrhea and the intense thirst of his later fits. Another clue appeared in the king's heart, where the dried-out pericardium was encased in a deep layer of fatty tissue. The report concluded that this layer of fat had acted as insulation, preventing the "febrile heat inflamed in his heart" from escaping the body.[26]

Thus, the symptoms perceived on the surface of the body during the illness all left traces on the internal organs inspected after death. When the post-mortem report was added to the king's medical history, and to the physicians' account of the early phases of his illness, the diagnosis became straightforward.

An old and already sickly man had fallen prey to a fever that began as a tertian but then mutated into something more dangerous.

Implicitly, the report suggested a number of reasons why the mutation occurred. The king's body was vulnerable to various humoural distempers, which increased the likelihood of a melancholic combination with his putrifying choler. He had failed to follow a regular, methodical course of treatment in the fever's early phases, thus increasing the chances of a mutation. And physiological weaknesses, such as the insulating layer of fat around his heart, had left James unable to cope with the fever's potent heat. The report also hinted that the malign qualities of the fever might have been present from the start. As Mayerne had acknowledged in 1624, it was a pestilent time in England, with "malignant fevers of an evil fashion passing through everywhere", and Mayerne himself had worried that James might fall victim to the current epidemic "purple fever" (probably typhus), a distemper of great virulency with dramatic symptoms and a potent "malignity".[27] The post-mortem report did not suggest James had succumbed to the purple fever, but it clearly linked the mutation of his fever to a "malignancy" peculiar to the season and the time.

In short, the doctors had done their best. They had used their training, their experience and their knowledge of James's medical history to treat the king's fever in orthodox fashion. When stymied by the king's stubbornness, they had followed Mayerne's advice and used courtiers to bring James around. Moreover, the report revealed that the physicians had followed Mayerne's protocols of consensus and transparency: they had all "seen and observed" the royal corpse and "witnessed" the official report "in their own handwriting" before it was "shown to very many others" in the royal bedchamber. The king's death was unfortunate; perhaps a better regimen and an immediate resort to a methodical cure might have saved him. But death, while not inevitable, was not inexplicable—there were natural causes aplenty.

As important as what the report said, was what it did not say. The report made no mention of the conflict in the sickroom that the Earl of Kellie had reported to his cousin the Earl of Mar a week before James's death. It contained no hint of contested diagnoses or debates about therapies among the physicians. More important, it said nothing about unsanctioned medical interventions, about controversial plasters and potions and their possible role in James's abrupt decline and death. In the authorized medical version, we hear no "strange tealles" of the king's final days. Indeed, according to these detailed reports, nothing untoward had happened at all.

Most of the post-mortem report used the dispassionate language of contemporary elite medicine to document the dissolution of the king's frail flesh. But the doctors also had to acknowledge the peculiarly elevated status of this still-royal body. The report introduced James as "the most august king of Britain . . . our most clement lord of most pious memory". The account of his death sang the praises of his "most pious soul" and celebrated James as "the most prudent, the most just, and the most Christian of all kings", at whose demise his loving subjects had shed "profuse tears". His death was a soteriological as well as a physiological event. James had passed from "this earthly prison ... towards Jesus Christ the redeemer", from "this mortal and afflicted life to perennial happiness".[28] Like the court correspondents, the royal doctors were keen to transmute a royal death into the stuff of political myth. In these phrases the authorized medical version of James's death overlapped with the other contemporary narratives that mythologized the king's illness as a test of Protestant devotion and sacred kingship. Unlike the physicians' report, however, the other narratives sanitized the gruesome bodily experience of James's dying. The physiology of death had no place in the poetics of power, and when the physicians of the royal soul told the story of the king's good death to the mourners in Westminster Abbey, they presented a tale free of putrid discharges and vile black excrement. And they made this sanitized story of the king's good death a culminating centrepiece of the spectacular funeral rites that celebrated James's virtues and achievements and presented Charles as the worthy heir to his father's crown.

CHAPTER TWO

THE GREATEST FUNERAL THAT EVER WAS KNOWN

MEMORIALIZING JAMES I

I T IS AN unimpressive sight, little more than a large, crudely fashioned head-less wooden doll (Fig. 11). Its once-magnificent costume has disintegrated, and its arms, originally held in place by canvas sockets, have disappeared. A pair of realistically shaped wooden legs remain, awkwardly yoked to the torso with rudimentary iron strapping, but the feet are gone, leaving behind only a telltale layer of the gypsum plaster from which they were made. Five feet seven inches in length, the figure is topped with a wooden peg, which originally held its long-vanished head. Hard as it is to imagine, this pathetic, dismembered mannequin is all that remains of one of the early seventeenth century's most calculated and most spectacular displays of monarchical splendour. Dressed in robes of state, its lifelike features fashioned by the royal carver himself, this wooden doll once played a leading part in what one seasoned observer considered "the greatest [funeral] . . . that ever was knowne in England".[1]

In the days after James's demise in late March 1625, courtly narratives of his good death had reasserted monarchical claims to sacred and explicitly Protestant kingship while putting in place an authorized version of the king's last weeks and hours. But work on the authorized version was not finished. James had to be buried, and, in one of the most important decisions of his young reign, Charles I chose to invest unprecedented sums of money and significant cultural capital in the rituals that would lay his father to rest. Mobilizing stunning material splendour, theatrical spectacle and eloquent rhetoric, the new regime used these rituals to project a revitalized image of royal authority, celebrating Jacobean rule and Caroline promise, while transforming the tragedy of James I's death into a display of monarchical power. And much of what the funeral had to say about Jacobean virtues and the king's good death would soon be rearticulated in a broad range of printed works, including sermons, elegies and engravings, that would present the authorized version of James's death to an even larger public audience.

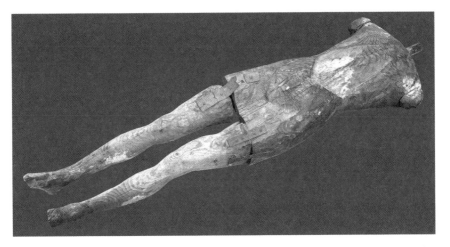

Figure 11: All that remains of the funeral effigy of King James I. This was one of two effigies used in his funeral rituals to symbolize the king's immortal authority (Westminster Abbey).

Walking with His Father

Charles appointed a commission of leading household officers to work alongside the College of Arms in overseeing the series of spectacular ceremonies that would memorialize the dead king's undying fame. The commissioners devised a four-stage funerary ritual that would be performed across various secular and sacred spaces, in and around London. The rites would begin on 4 April with a partially torch-lit procession of James's embalmed and coffined body from Theobalds to Denmark House in the Strand. This would be followed by a month-long ceremonial lying-in-state at Denmark House, during which a lifelike effigy of the dead king was displayed upon his coffin to symbolize his immortal monarchical authority. The drawn-out ritual process would culminate on 7 May with a procession from Denmark House to Westminster Abbey, in which thousands of mourners, dressed in black and precisely ranked according to their status, would escort the royal coffin through the London streets, surrounded by the dynastic and heraldic insignia of the House of Stuart. The procession complete, the rituals would conclude inside the abbey with a funeral ceremony that celebrated James's virtues both symbolically (in a splendidly decorated hearse) and rhetorically (in an eloquent funeral sermon). These interlinked rituals would insistently display power and hierarchy, promulgate various myths of royal and Stuart authority, and tell compelling stories about the life, death and virtues of the late king.[2]

The expense was staggering. The treasury stood at a "low . . . ebbe", and money was needed not only for James's funeral but also for Charles's coronation, his marriage, his royal entry into London, and a war with Spain. A French dowry would help, and the king confidently assumed Parliament would quickly fund the war, but on 15 April the Crown was in such serious straits that it had to ask the City for a £60,000 loan. Despite these fiscal pressures, Charles refused to scale back the funeral plans. Estimates for the final cost vary. The Lord Chamberlain's accounts recorded some £40,000 worth of expenditures, while one report put the total cost at "above £50,000". By contrast, Elizabeth I's funeral *and* tomb monument cost £17,000, while Queen Anne's notoriously expensive 1619 funeral ran to £20,000.[3] Charles's unprecedented outlay for James clearly indicates the importance he placed on the power of public ritual to celebrate and reaffirm his father's—and now his own—monarchical authority.

What did the money buy? Simply put, it bought the magnificence that would display and embody royal power. Some £235 was spent caparisoning horses; a further £72 paid for the funeral chariot to carry James's body to Westminster, while £64 4s covered the cost of the "great Embroydered banner" made of velvet, satin, gold and silver cloth, Naples silk, and pearls. A little over £27 bought the wooden chairs and stools placed around the hearse in the abbey. But by far the biggest expense was cloth: cloth to drape Denmark House and Westminster Abbey, to cover funerary chariots, hearses and coffins, and to garb the thousands of mourners. Nineteen different retailers received more than £28,000 among them for supplying funeral cloth of many types, styles and fabrics. Simply finding that much material was a challenge, and as late as 26 April the Privy Council was still working to negotiate "reasonable prices" for the massive quantities required. Costs could run as high as the 35s 8d a yard paid for the black velvet coffin canopy. But the largest single outlay was for the funeral "blacks" given to the designated mourners. These cloth allocations were finely calibrated to distinguish among the array of noblemen, state officials, clergy and household servants who were to march with James's coffin. At the social apex, the Duke of Buckingham received 16 yards of black cloth, at 40s a yard, for personal use, and a further 32 yards for his nine servants. Earls and foreign ambassadors received 16 yards for personal use, but only 24 for their servants. The royal physicians, many of whom had attended the dying king, had 7 yards for personal and 8 for their servants' use, while the surgeons and the apothecaries, who received 7 yards for themselves, were granted only 4 yards for their servants, the same allocation as the royal jester. At the bottom of the social order, the poor mourners, selected to march at the head of the funeral procession, each received 4 yards of cloth at 11s a yard.[4]

Each stage of the funerary rites deployed visual and material spectacle to symbolize power. James's body entered London from Theobalds at dusk on 4 April and was followed by a procession of carriages, with Charles at their head, which accompanied James through the streets of his capital haloed by torchlight.[5] James's lying-in-state at Denmark House attracted numerous courtly visitors, many of whom marvelled at the royal effigy's "excellent likeness"— representing the physical body that died and the mystical body that did not—

and noted that the royal servants continued to observe "all state" around James "as if the king were living".[6] The great funeral procession on 7 May was one of the most spectacular displays of the Stuart age, presenting thousands of onlookers with an indelible image of royal authority. Sheer scale mattered: the endless parade of mourners signified the old king's standing; material magnificence, the rich cloths, embroidered banners, fine horses and gilt weaponry, the spectacular clash of bright colours and rich black mourning clothes, signalled power and status; crowns, regalia and icons of state represented sacred royal authority, while flags and banners celebrated chivalry, dynasty and nation. With their vivid colours and sombre movements, their chilling soundscapes of silence punctuated by drums, trumpets and sacred song, these rituals brought brilliant political theatre to the streets of early Caroline London; they were the very stuff from which royal authority was made.[7]

Thousands walked in the procession from Denmark House to Westminster. The diplomats Amerigo Salvetti and Zuane Pesaro counted "5,000 persons", while others put the number between eight and nine thousand. The heralds who assigned each participant a specific spot in the procession hoped to turn the parade into a moving hierarchical display with the most privileged men close to the funeral chariot, and with the rank of each cohort of processants visibly marked by their distance from the royal body, by the cut and length of their mourning blacks, and by the flags, standards and banners that surrounded them.[8]

Most eyes were naturally drawn to the rear of the procession where the body and effigy of the late king rested on an elaborate funerary chariot (Fig. 12). The chief heralds led this portion of the procession, each carrying James's chivalric regalia, and accompanied by drums, fifes, trumpets and the great embroidered banner. Behind them was Lord Chamberlain Pembroke, head of the royal household. Six horses decked in black pulled the velvet-draped funeral chariot, while the Gentlemen Pensioners and footmen marched on either side. Six earls served as "Assistants to the Corps", each holding an edge of the pall covering the coffin, while the gentlemen of the privy chamber held the velvet canopy above it. A dozen knights displayed small bannerols celebrating Stuart dynastic history, while a "seigneur" at the rear of the chariot held the effigy's head and crown in place. Behind the chariot marched the kingdom's most powerful men. Although Sir William Segar, Garter King at Arms, walked in front, all eyes were on the next marcher, the "Chief Mourner", King Charles, who processed under a canopy, dressed in a "long black robe with a black hood". Two supporters accompanied the king, while five peers carried his train. In his wake walked the leading bedchamber officers and fourteen noble "Assistants to the Chief Mourner".[9]

Charles's participation in his father's funeral attracted widespread notice. It was his first major public appearance as king, and he had clearly decided that the moment was right to show himself to his new subjects. Not every English

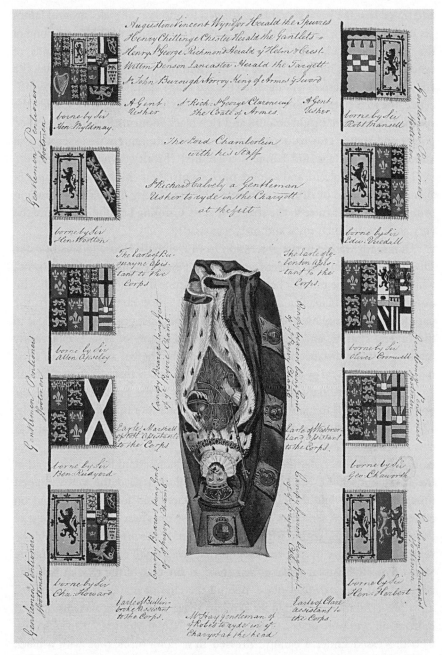

Figure 12: A reconstruction by George Nayler (d. 1831) of James I's coffin and effigy and the heraldic flags carried in the funeral procession to Westminster Abbey on 7 May 1625 (College of Arms).

monarch marched in his predecessor's funeral, and Charles's decision to do so was deliberately eye-catching: he was making a statement of filial love and of political continuity. Many years later, John Rushworth still thought it a powerful display of "piety towards his deceased father" that Charles had "dispense[d] with Majesty" to walk behind James's bier.[10]

The logic of the procession, obvious in most cases, did have some oddities. Political considerations shaped certain decisions about marching order, especially the allocation of positions around the new king. Five peers carried Charles's train, his two young Scottish kinsmen—the Duke of Lennox and the Marquis of Hamilton—and three English earls, including Buckingham's brother-in-law Denbigh, the mix of nationalities symbolizing the union of crowns. Marching on either side of Charles were his two chief supporters, the Earls of Arundel and Rutland, senior peers from old families now singled out by their proximity to the king. Buckingham was conspicuously absent from Charles's immediate entourage. Early drafts of the procession script, however, had placed him alongside Arundel as the second supporter to the chief mourner, but his father-in-law, Rutland, was eventually pencilled in to replace him. Buckingham processed instead in his office as Master of the Horse, following just behind the royal party, dressed in a black robe and hood and leading the "Royal steed . . . caparisoned in black velvet embroidered with silver and pearls". The decision to replace the duke as Charles's "supporter" is interesting. Perhaps he or Charles feared that the duke's presence might stimulate controversy; perhaps Charles wanted to appear as his own man or to surround himself with two nobles of unimpeachably ancient lineage. Yet Buckingham remained a commanding ritual presence. According to Salvetti, he processed at the head of twelve more horses, all draped in black, and an entourage of knights and nobles carrying twelve royal standards.[11]

By all accounts, the crowds lining the streets between Denmark House and Westminster Abbey were impressed by the arresting image of a young king surrounded by his nobility, his bishops and archbishops, his officers and countless functionaries, all draped in rich black cloth, all marching together in an apparently effortless display of power. There was much to catch the eye. Those denied access to Denmark House could now see the old king's effigy, "richly dressed and crowned", placed prominently on the chariot to signal the myth of monarchical immortality. Numerous flags and banners with heraldic and dynastic insignia celebrated James's achievements and virtues. The Rose and Thistle banner hymned the Union of England and Scotland, the message of unity reinforced by a pair of clasped hands. James's "Beati Pacifici" motto appeared on the banner of the "Union of the two Crosses" and the Scottish unicorn standard. His religious virtues, emblematized by the motto "I have made God my helper", adorned the standard of the dragon.[12]

These rituals celebrated social and political hierarchy while simultaneously displaying community and harmony, integrating the social elite with the poor mourners who marched at the procession's head, the court with the City, the English with the Scottish nobility. But there were small ritual blemishes and visible exclusions that compromised the integrative functioning of the ceremonial display. In mid-April, Charles had ruled recusant Catholics ineligible for grants of mourning cloth, which was, Pesaro noted, a cheap way for the king to "show rigour about religion". Salvetti thought this a very "bad omen", but English Protestants warmed to the decision as another sign the new king was "zealous for Gods truth".[13] Religious tensions of another kind forced the leading Scottish churchman, John Spottiswood, Archbishop of St Andrews, to sit out the procession. Having secured the right to march alongside the Archbishop of Canterbury, Spottiswood then "flatlie refuised" Charles's demand that he dress in English-style episcopal vestments. Also missing was the Venetian ambassador, Pesaro. Charles had sent him mourning blacks, but the Master of Ceremonies convinced Pesaro he need not march, since neither the French nor the Habsburg representatives were intending to participate. The ambassador was thus mortified when he spotted the two French representatives walking "in a noble position . . . as I should have been". Pesaro thought "this most prejudicial sight" a great insult to the Serene Republic, and despite English explanations the injury rankled. Pesaro remained convinced that the Master of Ceremonies, a crypto-Catholic Hispanophile, had deliberately sought to sow discord between the Venetians and the French. It was a sign, like the clash between Scottish and English church-styles, that even ritual unity was a fragile commodity in a world of confessional and diplomatic division.[14]

And, of course, not everything went according to script. Rain had dampened the torchlight procession bringing James's body to Denmark House in April, and the heralds found it impossible to keep the main funeral procession on 7 May in strict hierarchical order. But those who recorded their reactions were, on the whole, highly impressed. The news intelligencer John Chamberlain thought the event "the greatest [funeral] indeed that ever was knowne in England", "performed with great magnificence", even if the marching order became "very confused". Pesaro judged the procession "stately", while Edmund Howes noted that James's "corpes" was transported "with all magnificence and state"; "the like number of Mourners", he added, "cannot be said to have beene at any time". James Beaulieu, the French Secretary, thought the funeral "very magnificente and glorious" and "would have appeared more so, if it had been as orderlie carried as it was full and costly". Nevertheless, "the greatest glorie and raritie of the same was King Charles own presence".[15]

Great Britain's Solomon

Once they reached Westminster Abbey, the king's bier and effigy were placed inside a spectacular hearse, designed by Inigo Jones, that Chamberlain considered "the fairest and best fashioned that hath ben seen" (Fig. 13). Built of wood

Figure 13: Inigo Jones's design for James I's catafalque in Westminster Abbey, 7 May 1625 (Worcester College, Oxford).

and draped in black and purple cloth, the neo-classical structure was a bravura exercise in the art of symbolic politics. The royal bier, pall and effigy rested on an elevated platform enclosed by an octagonal colonnade, with the eight columns supporting a domed roof. The royal arms, James's monogram and various heraldic pennants studded the dome, which was topped by a large crown imperial. Twelve statues on the hearse personified the late king's virtues and achievements. At the four corners of the base stood Fame, Dignity, Glory and Public Felicity, while the eight statues around the drum included Liberality, Learning, Religion and Peace. Four inscriptions glossed the visual display. One celebrated James as imperial ruler, the creator of Anglo-Scottish Union, the Ulster Plantation and colonies in America. Another drew on Augustan Golden Age imagery to celebrate James's revival of dormant customs, the expansion of trade and improvement of cities. The third, headed by James's "Beati Pacifici" motto, celebrated royal justice and the love of peace. While the fourth trumpeted the classical virtue of "Pietas", religious piety and familial duty, noting James's support for the Church, respect for his ancestors, and love for his son and his subjects.[16]

Jones's lavish hearse thus lauded James as a king of virtue, a British Augustus, the pious exemplar of good rule, a bringer of peace and prosperity. Many of

Figure 14: John Williams, Bishop of Lincoln and Lord Keeper of the Great Seal, c. 1621–25, supervised the religious rituals around James's deathbed and delivered the king's funeral sermon in Westminster Abbey (National Portrait Gallery).

these themes reappeared in Biblical dress during Bishop John Williams's funeral sermon that portrayed James in one of his favourite monarchic roles, the modern Solomon (Fig. 14). Williams hymned James's pious poetry and eloquent speech-making, and hailed his "actions", every one of them "a Vertue, and a Miracle" without compare. He dwelled on James's remarkable record of providential deliverance from his enemies' plots, which made him a "miracle of kings"; and he reaffirmed James's confessional orthodoxy. James was the ideal Protestant ruler, Williams insisted, "constant, resolute, and settled . . . in point of Doctrine", and a strong champion of episcopacy, "the only Discipline that ever agreed with the Fundamentall Lawes of any Christian Monarchie". James was an exemplar too of the quintessential royal virtue of Justice, and never were the "poore, and rich so aequally righted" as they had been in his courts. Although not warlike, James had played the role of royal shepherd, suppressing revolt in the Highlands and using his strength to shelter his subjects. Jacobean peace had brought pros-perity and power, with colonies settled, and the Anglo-Scottish border, so long a zone of disorder, finally secured. Peace, good governance and books full of "Divinitie, Moralitie, and Humanitie" were all emanations of James's Solomonic wisdom. Like Solomon, James had also overseen the growth and efflorescence of a great capital city and, through the Union of crowns, had created an Empire where none existed before. And like Solomon, James had sealed his reputation with a good death: "as he lived like a King, so he died like a Saint".[17]

Williams offered his audience a thrillingly intimate account of the king's final days, an account that made public the pre-existing courtly narratives of James's good death. "Never", Williams declared, had any king "left this world more resolved, more prepared." James had made a declaration of faith and repeated "the Articles of the Creede" as the English Church defined them. And he had insisted with "a kinde of sprightfulnesse, and vivacitie, that what ever hee had written of this Faith in his life, he was now ready to seale with his Death". James had forgiven all who had offended him and asked forgiveness from those he had offended; he had confessed his sins to God and received ritual absolution, that "heavenly comfort", from his loving bishops. His deathbed rites had culminated in Holy Communion, received with an amazing "Zeale and Devotion, as if hee had not beene a fraile Man, but a Cherubim cloathed with flesh, and blood".[18]

Williams lingered on the miracle of the king's final hours. James became increasingly passive as "sicknesse prevailed", but because his "Sense, and Memory" were "not much impaired", Williams and others had continuously recited "short sentences of Devotion" to "raise, and lift up his Soule into Heaven". The dying king was "so ravished and Comforted" by this that although "he groaned . . . under the pangs of Death, yet was hee ever still, and as quiet, as a Lambe, when these Eiaculations were infused into Him". Enveloped in prayer, James' death became a spiritual consummation:

> his hastning on forward towards his End, hastned us also to that Prayer usually said at the houre of Death; the which was no sooner ended . . . [then] with out any pangs, or Convulsion at all . . . Salomon slept.[19]

Williams closed by looking ahead. The "Magnificence" of James's "Stately Funerals" testified to the filial devotion of "a pious Sonne of a most pious Father". And Williams found the mystery of succession in the myth of the king's many bodies. James had embodied Solomon, had been his "statue". But James's immortal kingly body lived on, not in statues or effigies but in Charles:

> God hath provided another Statue yet to adorne the Exequies of our Late Soveraigne. I doe not meane this Artificiall Repraesentation within the Hearse; for this shews no more then his outward Body. . . . But I meane the Statue which (beyond all former praesidents of Pietie) walk't on foot this day after the Hearse. . . . A breathing Statue of all his Vertues. . . . Though

his Father be dead, yet is he, as though hee were not dead, for he hath left
One behinde him most like himselfe.[20]

Williams ended at around seven o'clock, about nine hours after the procession
had set out from Denmark House. All that remained were the "Offering", a
sacralized chivalric ceremony of succession, and the semi-private interment
according to the burial rite of the *Book of Common Prayer*. James was laid to
rest in the Henry VII chapel where his wife, his mother, his oldest son, his two
youngest daughters and his predecessor lay. But his coffin was not placed in
their vaults. Instead, it was interred underneath the chapel's central monument, next to Henry VII and his wife, Elizabeth of York.[21]

The abbey's keeper of the monuments placed one of James's effigies in a
special "press", probably located in a chamber off the Henry VII chapel, where
"the Representations of the Kings and Queenes, his famous Predecessors" were
housed. Aside from the heraldic "hatchments" left up in the chapel, the effigy
would be the abbey's only monument to the king. Funds remained scarce, but
tomb monuments were relatively inexpensive and so Charles must have felt
little need to further commemorate his father inside the abbey. James had built
monuments for Elizabeth and his mother Mary in part because he was a
foreigner from a new dynasty that needed to make its presence felt. And though
James commissioned modest monuments for his two daughters, Sophia and
Mary, he built nothing for his wife Anne or his son Henry.[22] In the end, Charles
chose to spend £3,000 to memorialize his father not in stone, but in paint,
commissioning Peter Paul Rubens's spectacular canvases for the Banqueting
House ceiling in Whitehall. Rubens produced vivid images of James the
Peacemaker, the Learned and Wise, the Imperial Father of Great Britain, the
Solomonic King of Virtues—James as Williams's sermon and Jones's hearse
had described him. In the centre of the ceiling, in a great oval panel, Rubens
gave James his apotheosis, shepherded by Justice, Faith and Religion to eternal
glory on the back of an imperial eagle. As his painted image soared in the
Banqueting House, James's corpse rested, unmarked, in Henry VII's vault, the
first Stuart king of England alongside the first Tudor, at the physical and
symbolic heart of the most sacred royal space in the kingdom.[23]

Souvenirs

More ephemeral monuments appeared in print. The royal printer issued an
elegant edition of Williams's sermon, complete with a striking frontispiece of the
enthroned king, clearly intended to fix the bishop's image of "Great Britains
Salomon" in the public memory (Fig. 15).[24] Other funeral sermons quickly
followed Williams's into print, including one preached by Daniel Price at Theobalds
the morning of James's death, and one by Phineas Hodson delivered at Denmark

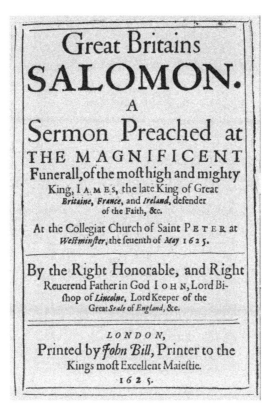

Figure 15: Title page of John Williams, *Great Britains Salomon*, 1625, the king's funeral sermon elegantly printed by the royal printer John Bill (Huntington Library).

House the Tuesday before the funeral. Several poetic elegies and at least one engraved image also appeared. Some publications used visual and typographic effects to enhance their commemorative function. The title page of Hugh Holland's elegy was printed like a tombstone inscription, and the page between dedication and elegy was left as a solid black square (Fig. 16). The title page of Thomas Heywood's poem depicted James's funeral effigy inside his hearse (Fig. 17). While John Taylor's pamphlet was prefaced by drawn curtains revealing the poem's title printed on a tomb-shaped box. Beneath the box a recumbent skeleton symbolized death's dominion over the body natural, while images of time and fame promised that Memory and History would immortalize the dead king (Fig. 18).[25]

These printed texts developed much of the funeral and Williams's portraits of James as pious man of virtue. The preachers searched for appropriate Biblical parallels, with Hodson comparing James to Moses, and Price opting for Hezekiah. But the dominant theme was royal virtue. Religion bulked especially large. James's zeal, Hodson claimed, was the "Crowne of his Crowne". Taylor remembered him as a "most Religious" king, who defended the True Faith against the Popish Antichrist, protected the Church and nurtured the preaching

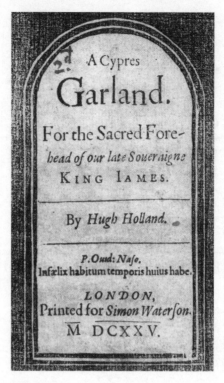

Figure 16: Title page of Hugh Holland's 1625 elegy for James I, *A Cypres Garland*, using typographic layout to create a visual image of mourning (Huntington Library).

ministry. Many dwelt on James's good death. He "Life forsooke,/With Patience", wrote Taylor, and "like a Lambe his Death he tooke", and "That Faith, which in his Life he did expresse,/He in his Death did constantly professe". Price thought that God had granted James "an especiall measure of grace" in "manifesting his heartie and devout profession of the Faith and Protestant truth, which hee had lived in, and maintained, and resolved to dye in". Some emphasized the king's last communion. Price thought it had sealed the king's "resolution" to die a Protestant, and after the "divine repast", James's "soule was setled in so ioyfull a repose, as that all worldly content could not compare". Francis Hamilton noted the ceremony's providential timing—on the twenty-second anniversary of the king's accession to the English throne—and interpreted the rite as a sign of James's confident faith in "The Sacramentall seales of his Salvation". Hamilton also lauded James's responses to his clerics' prayers: as "approching Death did him assaile", the king raised "his eyes, his armes, his hands" in "cleare consent".[26]

James's political virtues complemented his religious ones: bounty and liberality, a "large heart, and a large hand"; an eloquent "tongue . . . prompt and ready"; great "prudence"; Solomonic wisdom; and deep learning. And the poets were convinced that James had ensured Charles would exhibit the same

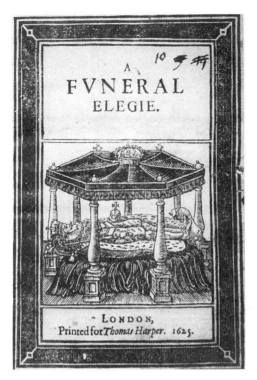

Figure 17: Title page of Thomas Heywood's 1625 *A Funeral Elegie* presenting a stylized image of the royal effigy lying in state under a canopy (Huntington Library).

qualities. Holland described James counselling Charles from his deathbed, giving him advice "at parting" to supplement the admonitions written long ago in his *Basilikon Doron*.[27]

Virtually all the printed texts celebrated the "rex pacificus", the "Peace-full Servant to the God of Peace".[28] Yet the preachers and elegists were highly conscious of the persistent criticism of James's pacifist policies after 1618, and some struggled to praise his pacifism while anticipating Charles's bellicosity. Hodson argued that:

> if Moses were a great Warrior; King Iames was as great a Peace-maker. I would I had not cause to complaine, that the Israelites never murmured more against Moses . . . then Many of us against his Majesty for labouring to keepe the Drum and Cannon from amongst us.

But if James was Moses, then Charles, Hodson affirmed, would be Joshua, sent to avenge the "blood of those Saints, which hath beene so prodigally shed", and to ensure that "Those of his owne Royall blood be delivered from the oppression, which now they suffer". Price prayed that the "spirit of your gracious

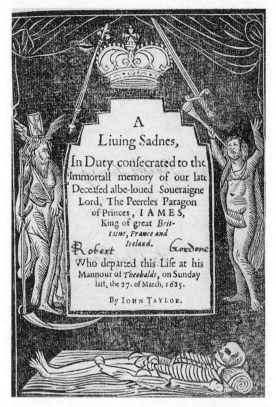

Figure 18: Title page of John Taylor's 1625 *A Living Sadnes*, in which figures of Time and Fame promise some measure of immortality to the dead king (Huntington Library).

Father may be doubled upon your Highnesse" and "that true Religion may florish under you". Charles's return from Spain in 1623 had been a "miraculous" deliverance, just like the miracles that had saved his father. Like David, Charles took the throne knowing that a "dangerous warre was in hand, the Philistins were his deadly enemies, hee had beene among them, and knew them, and was now to make provision against them".[29]

Whether thrilled or troubled by the impending war, poets and preachers alike idealized the monarchical succession as a smooth transition. "Now", wrote Heywood, "in these ominous Ides of March/Is snatcht away, our strong and glorious Arch", which might well have left the realm "crusht beneath his fall". But fortunately, James had left "an Atlas . . . behinde":

Succeeding him in potency of minde,
In vertue, goodnesse, royalty of State,
And all things, that a Sonne may imitate
So great a Father in.[30]

Figure 19: Abraham Darcie and Robert Vaughan, *Maiesties Sacred Monument*, 1625, the most elaborate visual souvenir of James I's good death and funeral (British Museum).

In June 1625 George Humble published an engraved broadsheet designed by Abraham Darcie as a "Sacred Monument" to royal majesty (Fig. 19).[31] Dominating the sheet was a lavish, if awkward, image of a towering funerary monument replete with columns, canopies, heraldic symbols and personified virtues. Dressed in robes of state, James's effigy lay on a plinth from which arose ten columns, supporting a mantel and archway and the heraldic icons of England, Scotland, Ireland and France. Above the archway climbed six ascending platforms, each displaying images of Jacobean virtue, and culminating at the structure's pinnacle in the Pauline trinity of Faith, Hope and Charity. All these virtues, Darcie avowed, "grac'd" the king, and "By these Sublim stepps his rare soule ascended/Up to ye Starry Heav'n".

Peace was conspicuously absent from this list, and Darcie and his engraver Robert Vaughan chose to present the Caroline succession as the consummation of a militaristic turn in which the "brave Succeeding Son" would finish what his father had "left undone". Charles stood by his father's tomb, his sword unsheathed. Upon the blade was inscribed the final part of the Virgilian tag "*Debellare Superbos*"—"to tame the proud". But Charles's sword had clearly come from James's empty scabbard, grasped in the effigy's hand, which bore the first part of the tag, "*et parcere subiectis*"—"to bring peace to the conquered". The imperial sword of war *and* peace had thus been handed from father to son—Charles's actions fulfilled rather than repudiated James's. With this kingly sword and his new French allies, Charles would now restore his sister Elizabeth, who sat mournfully in a corner, surrounded by her "fruitfull progeny", to her lost Bohemian and Palatine crowns. "To Her I heare this second Charlemaine say":

> Ile See thee once more as thou erst hast been
> (As th'art anoynted) reinvested Queene
> Of Bohem.

At the top of the image, the saved souls of James and his queen sat surrounded by a heavenly congregation of Britain's aristocratic dead. Darcie offered a providential gloss on these recent deaths at court, noting they had all occurred between the "blasing starr" of 1618, which foretold Anne's demise, and a "Starr" that "appear'd within the Moone to shine" shortly before "Iames was made Divine".

Other elegists also sought to explain the timing and cause of James's death. Heywood noted the "strange varieties of stormy weather" in March 1625, a providential foreshadowing of the loss to come, and argued that James's death was divine chastisement for his subjects' ingratitude, a point echoed by John Taylor. Others, noting the king's love of peace, suggested that James had been fated to die in March, in part because it was the month of Mars, the god of war. Taylor thought that James's death during the same month in which he had succeeded to the throne marked a providentially determined circuit for his reign.[32]

Some poets pondered the ague that had cut James down. One could hardly believe that a mere fever had killed a king who had escaped so many assassination plots. But even death by fever could be transformed into the stuff of panegyric. Only royal blood, distempered by fever's heat, had sufficient power to kill a king. He:

> whome Spanish craft, Romes cannon shott,
> False Gloryes treason, Catesby's powder plott
> Could not destroy (for heavens did him save)
> A feaver hath now melted to his grave.
> For hee, being mortall, fate could not invent
> His passage by a nobler Instrument

Then his owne bloud, which made him comprehend
Within himselfe, the glory of his end.

Holland found the ague less easy to transfigure. At first he took the illness upon
himself, the shaking of his grief making him feel as if the king's "Ague hath me
whole". But soon he began cursing a disease that, usually, no one feared. It was
a "furious . . . infernall Feaver" that had destroyed such "pretious dust". Holland
asked his patron Buckingham why he did not save the king:

> You of the greatest Isle, no petty piller,
> Who beare the name of George the Dragon-killer;
> Ah! could not you, and could not all the Order
> That Dragon-Fever hunt out of that border?

In the end, Holland cast the blame on faulty medicine and nervous doctors:

> Can vulgars scape the dropsie, scape the Phthisik
> And is there for the Crowned head no physicke?
> Oh subject state of Kings to hard condicions,
> Betwixt our flatteries, and their owne suspicions!
> Whose mindes to practise on the flatterer spares not,
> But on their bodies the Phisition dares not.[33]

Holland and the other elegists were also perturbed by the recent spate of deaths
at court. Price lamented this "fatall Yeare", plaintively asking, "How many noble
and valiant have fallen"? Holland asked, "How many Great ones here not meanly
graced/In thirteen months, the dance of Death have traced"? The names made
sobering reading—two Dukes of Lennox; the Marquis of Hamilton; the Earls of
Dorset, Nottingham and Southampton; Southampton's son, Lord Wriothesley;
and Lord Chichester of Belfast. Some elegists suggested these great men had
died so that they might be ready to receive their master in heaven. For Heywood,
they were "harbingers" sent to view the "place,/Where thou art anchor'd now".
"As in life", John Taylor noted, "they were on him relying,/So many of them
ushered him in dying". But Price worried that these deaths were tokens of God's
displeasure: "is not this an ill boading prodigious time"?[34]

George the Dragon-Killer

As the elegists tried to make sense of James's death, they returned to the authorized version of the king's final weeks—the fever that turned malignant, the
"good death" at Theobalds, the spectacular commemoration and reassertion of
royal authority at Denmark House and Westminster Abbey. Within the

confines of the authorized version, royal authority not only survived the king's death, it was enhanced by it. But another narrative was beginning to take form in these early weeks: a secret, politically subversive, history of James's death that would offer persuasively simple explanations for the losses of this "fatall Yeare". This history would puzzle over a surprisingly deadly tertian fever, and reassess the suspiciously long list of powerful men who had died so suddenly in so short a space of time. It would note, too, a great political shift at court, and would identify the biggest beneficiary of all these deaths and changes. The solemnity of James's funeral, the printed sermons and elegies, and the doctors' official reports left no place for even the faintest whisper of anything unusual about James's death. But less than a year after his burial, contemporaries were to see these eulogies in a different light. They would pause over the Marquis of Hamilton and the Duke of Lennox in the list of departed aristocrats; and would come to find Holland's lavish praise of "George the Dragon-killer" dangerously misplaced. For in the secret history of James I's death, St George had not simply failed to save the king. He had killed him.

PART II

MAKING THE SECRET HISTORY
1625–26

PROLOGUE

THE TRAVAILS OF CHRISTOPHER HOGG

O N 19 NOVEMBER 1625, Christopher Hogg was near the end of a long walk home after a stint driving cattle to the St Martin's Day fair in Hempton, Norfolk. Somewhere in north Yorkshire he overtook "a man cloathed in black seaming to be a minister". The man, a Northumberland clerk called Martin Danby, struck up a conversation, and asked Hogg "what newes there was in the South". Hogg did not have much to offer. He had kept to himself at the fair; he was a "poore labourer . . . hired to drive & looke to the cattell he had in charge", as he later put it, and he spent most of his time in Norfolk taking care of his animals. But he had overheard people talking about "Our greate duke whoe was in Spaine with the king", saying that he was "committed to prison and the Earle of Rutland with him". When Danby asked Hogg whether he knew the reason for their arrest, Hogg answered that "he hard it reported it was for geving the kings Majestie poyson". King Charles had been "sick three daies", Hogg added, "yet God be thanked was recovered".

This conversation nagged at Martin Danby, and a week later he reported the exchange to a Justice of the Peace, William Carr, who ordered Hogg arrested and imprisoned in Newcastle. Under questioning, Hogg confirmed Danby's account, and a few days later Carr sent the evidence to Buckingham and Rutland. What the duke thought, we do not know, but Rutland was furious. On 26 December he wrote to Secretary Conway decrying the aspersions cast on his honour and urging that the case be formally examined. He closed with a vehement protestation of loyalty, calling on Jesus to "damne him perpetually" if "either of us have such a thought any way to hurt his Majestie".

Conway decided the case was worth pursuing and ordered Carr to hand Hogg over to a royal messenger who would escort him to London. Hogg was virtually indigent, with barely enough clothes to keep off the vermin, and his escort later petitioned the Crown to cover the costs of feeding, clothing and lodging his prisoner during the journey south. On 25 February 1626 the ragged and no doubt bewildered drover's man stood before the royal judge, Sir Ranulph

Crewe. Hogg repeated the story he had told Danby and Carr, but when Crewe asked him to identify the men from "whom he hard this sclanderous report", Hogg confessed only that "he hard itt of soome people in the fayre as he was keeping his beasts . . . but he can not tell who they were", nor had he "inquired after the men that used such talke". Hogg also insisted that he had paid no "great heed" to "that which he hard". After consulting several councillors, Crewe recommended that Hogg be returned to Yorkshire, tried at the assizes, and then "whipped by the sentence of the court". Three weeks later, Crewe changed his mind. He told Conway that Hogg was so "base & contemptible" that it would be easiest to "have him whipped in Bridewell" in London. After a good scourging, "the baggage fellowe" could be "descharged."[1]

Stories of the deaths or illnesses of kings were a staple of popular rumour in early modern England, and their proliferation nicely illustrates one of the fundamental anxieties of life in a hereditary monarchy.[2] A whole succession of such stories spread during the early months of Charles I's reign. In mid-June 1625, Justices of the Peace in Wisbech, Cambridgeshire, forwarded several statements accusing a local cordwainer of spreading reports "that our king was deade and that he was made away with within theise three dayes". Such rumours were not only the province of drovers' men and cordwainers. In September 1625 the Cambridge scholar Joseph Mead heard talk that Charles had died of the plague, and then that he had not died but had fallen seriously ill, and that the news had been "kept secret" until some "ill patriots" leaked it to the Spanish to encourage a succession crisis. Mead initially dismissed the talk "as an idle rumour", revised his opinion when several heads of college "averred it as true", and eventually learned that Charles had not been sick at all. A little over a month later, Mead heard new reports, this time of arrests of several men over-heard talking of a popish uprising and boasting of their plan to "kill the king". "The grounds are feeble", Mead commented, and "there goes stranger reports abroad, but all false."[3]

Such talk tapped into specific political anxieties—of Spanish invasion or popish plot, for instance—or even specific hopes. Henry Denne, the Wisbech cordwainer, had allegedly thought the news of Charles's death cause for cele-bration: "I will warrant you", he said, "now the world will mend, we shalbe joviall boyes, we shall have old Cussing, & ffighting, and old men shalbe regarded, for Ritch men have gotten all the goods into their handes, and wilbe gald [galled] to give good recompense."[4] The talk that Christopher Hogg heard in Hempton sprang from a different set of anxieties, centred not only on the vulnerability of the monarch but also on the dangers posed by the royal favourite. The story is an early appearance of what would become, by 1626, a widely held belief: that Buckingham was a poisoner. The precise origins of the 1625 rumour are mysterious, but the drover's tale belongs to a broader story of the manufacture, between March 1625 and March 1626, of a secret history of the late Jacobean court, a secret history of how Buckingham had poisoned his rivals and his king. Rumours that the duke had poisoned James first emerged in the days immediately before and after the king's death in late March 1625. Initially contained within the court, these allegations soon circulated more widely, before appearing to fade away by early summer. In the spring of 1626, as Christopher Hogg made his way back north, his back still smarting from the Bridewell whip, these rumours re-emerged into popular political discourse, this time to spectacular and long-lasting effect. How that happened—how court rumour became secret history, and what that secret history meant—is the story of our next few chapters.

CHAPTER THREE

STRANGE TRAGEDIES

FEVER AND POLITICS AT THEOBALDS, MARCH 1625

A S THE LONDON representative of the Infanta Isabella, governor of the Spanish Netherlands, Jean Baptiste Van Male spent much of his time dealing with aggrieved Flemish merchants and anxious English Catholics. But he was also responsible for gathering intelligence on English affairs. Over the winter of 1624-25, as war between England and Spain began to look increasingly likely, Van Male stepped up his operations. He ran several unusually well-placed secret agents in and around the royal court, including a man who went by the code name "X". On 25 March 1625, two days before James died, X warned his superiors that his latest letters contained explosive new information: "*nous avons icy des estrange tragédies*", he reported: These "strange tragedies" involved "*emplastres et cordialls*"—plasters and potions that had brought King James I to death's door.[1]

Van Male's spies were not the only contemporaries feverishly tracking the course of James's illness, and a stream of rumour and report on the king's health flowed steadily from the court. But the talk during the last weeks of James's life focused not only on his illness and death but also on the illnesses and deaths of other great men, and on the tense power struggle between James, Prince Charles and the Duke of Buckingham over diplomatic and military policy. These political conflicts would profoundly affect how, why and when the seeds of rumour and accusation surrounding James's final days would flower into a secret history of murder and betrayal. This process was highly complex. By approaching it from multiple angles, shifting focus from events to their contested perception, we can see how a sequence of political struggles and diplomatic and military crises intersected with reports about courtly illness and death.

Nothing but Deaths

The bumper crop of melons in the summer of 1624 made Lord Carew nervous. A change in the weather had corresponded with an outbreak of plague on the

Continent and a spike in sudden deaths in England. Carew thought this rise in English mortality was due to "the Aboundance of fruites, whereof there was such a store this last summer as Melons had beene sould every where as ordinarily as Coxcombs". Others drew attention to a similar abundance of cucumbers, possibly corrupted by the putrifying matter pooled in noisome irrigation ditches. Some feared that "these hot and drie sommers" did not suit English constitutions. But no matter what the underlying causes, the consequences were clear: deadly fevers were sweeping inexorably through the kingdom, the most terrifying of which was the "purple" or "spotted fever". The newsmonger John Chamberlain thought it "cousin german" to the plague, adding that it "makes as quicke riddance almost".[2]

These epidemic fevers claimed an astonishing list of victims. In February 1624 the Lord Steward, the Duke of Lennox, died just before Parliament opened (Fig. 20); in April the Earl of Dorset joined him in the grave. Lennox's brother and successor died in July and the Earl of Thomond in September. Two months later, first Lord Wriothesley and then his father, the Earl of Southampton, expired within a week of each other, prompting Princess Elizabeth to warn a correspondent, "I send you nothing but deaths." More were to come: the Earl of Nottingham, who had fought the Spanish Armada in 1588, died in December 1624, and two months later it was the turn of Lord Chichester, a veteran of the Irish campaigns. Men of "suche great vertues", the Earl of Clare observed, "ar out of fashion and rather ey-sores, better to be spared, then our imbrodered Epicurean courtiers".[3] The next shocking death came early in March 1625, when the Marquis of Hamilton succumbed to a powerful fever (Fig. 21; Plate 4). The marquis, noted Owen Wynn, a protégé of Lord Keeper Williams, was "much lamented beeinge generallie reputed to be an honest man and the best conditioned of that nation [Scotland]". The night Hamilton died, Buckingham burst into the French ambassador's bedroom to tell him the news, only to break down weeping. In Scotland this "greevous and unexpected calamitie" reduced the Earl of Roxburgh to "teares and sobs", while the Earl of Melros announced that "I would have rather wished to have beene in Constantinople" than witness the grief of Hamilton's wife, which "can hardlie be conceived by them who have not seene it".[4] "This hath ben a dismall yeare to great men", Chamberlain observed, citing "the losse of two dukes, fowre earles and I know not howe many Lords". Joseph Mead concurred: "What a number of great ones and I think of the best have we lost within a 12 month." Since these men had all been "very sounde for religion", Archbishop Abbot worried that "it pleaseth God to take unto himselfe men whome hee had fitted for himselfe and to leave worse behind".[5]

The steady succession of deaths created a mounting sense of grief and dismay, and as James became feverish in early March, the roll call of the sick ran the gamut, from the Earls of Pembroke and Middlesex and the new Marquis

Figure 20: Johan Bara, *Ludovic Stuart, Duke of Lennox and Richmond*, 1624, after a painting by Paul Van Somer (British Museum). Lennox, the cousin of the king, depicted here in garter robes and carrying the Lord Steward's staff, died suddenly early in 1624.

of Hamilton to the daughter and maidservant of the king's French secretary, "so rife is that kinde of disease nowe in these parts". The fever soon sent the intelligencer John Castle to his bed, and prompted Owen Wynn to caution his brother against coming to London.[6] The high mortality at court frightened the king. In the early days of his ague, James talked of "nothing but deaths", particularly those of his kinsmen, the Lennox brothers and Hamilton. He slept little the night Hamilton died, and the following day was "heard to say to some that sought to comfort him 'when the branches decay the Tree must follow'".[7] Although many sought out natural causes for the heightened mortality—the royal doctor Theodore de Mayerne brooded over how to treat the purple fever—others searched for signs of God's intervention, speculating about providential patterns in the year-long cull of the court elite. But old assumptions and worsening ideological conflict at court encouraged more dangerous speculation during these feverish months, including talk of poison. When Buckingham fell ill in the spring of 1624, contemporaries had quickly made sinister as well as medical diagnoses. A tertian ague was blamed, but his condition worsened, and while his doctors concluded he had jaundice, some

Figure 21: Martin Droeshout, *James, 2nd Marquis of Hamilton*, 1623 (British Museum). Depicted here in armour, Hamilton succeeded Lennox as James I's Lord Steward and served until his own sudden death early in 1625.

observers were convinced he was the target of a plot.[8] Buckingham "is poisoned" by the Spaniards, thought Walter Yonge, because "he was earnest against the match with Spain". Castle recorded the same story, noting that "many pustules and blaines" had "broken out" on the favourite's body. In Paris an anonymous correspondent heard that the Spanish minister, the Count-Duke of Olivares, had ordered "a certaine Irish Captaine", a man who was "the greatest monster for such ill deedes that ever was in this world", to poison the duke.[9] As a succession of leading nobles succumbed to sudden illness in 1624–25, similar anti-Catholic rumours swirled. These reached a climax after Hamilton's death in early March.

Emotions boiled over after Hamilton's corpse began displaying unusual symptoms. The marquis's kinsman, Captain John Hamilton, who had been at his bedside, reported that "15 houres efter expiring, the corps begoude to swell incredeblie great, fumed at the nose 24 hours continually, his skin become livide, blowen up lyke 2 bledders in bothe sides . . . the haere but twitched come out with the skinne". The captain did not mention poison, but newsletter-writers quickly reported the rumours beginning to spread. John Castle noted that Hamilton had died "not without suspicion of poison; his body upon the viewe of it after it was layde out being found fill of blaves and ulcers; his flesh loose and gangrened and with some issues of blood breakinge out upon his body". Chamberlain wrote that the marquis had died "of a pestilent feaver as is supposed, though some suspect poison, because he swelled unmeasurablie after he was dead in his body but specially his head. Upon the opening of both the physicians saw no signes of any such suspicion, but ascribe the swelling to some maligne or venomous humor of the small pocks or such like that might lie hid". One of Joseph Mead's correspondents reported there were suspicions of poison, "because after death his whole body with neck face & head swelled exceedingly, & was strangely spotted". He later described Hamilton's body as "greatly swelled on the head & face, haire & nayles fell of, the skin turned black, blisters & bumps arose, his lyver was all spotted, & the flesh came from the bones". The letter went on to report that "the Physicians are sayd to hold, it was not of poyson given & received, but ex veneno ingenito", an inborn poison, a diagnosis the correspondent thought "A strange Paradox".[10]

These letter-writers all were either in, or on the edge of, the elite. But the disturbing news quickly leaked out into the capital and the provinces. Later in March 1625, Stephen Plunkett, the son of a minor legal official, told an acquaintance that "he had heard Marques Hamilton was poisoned"; when questioned, Plunkett claimed he had heard the story as "common Rumor as he (being a boy) passed to and fro about the streets". Plunkett's acquaintance told the authorities that the boy had also claimed the poison in question had been administered a full year before the marquis's death, though Plunkett himself denied this. In Dorset, William Whiteway noted in his March 1625 diary entry that at "The beginning of this moneth the state of busynesse began to alter at our Court", as the French marriage plans stalled and the Spanish ones revived: "Besides, the marquis Hamilton died at this tyme, and some 10 daies before him Viscount Grandison, not without suspicion. Thearle of Pembroke also and marquis Hameltons sonne are very sicke".[11]

Because Hamilton had died amid bitterly contested rumours of a deathbed conversion to Rome, Protestant contemporaries thought they knew who was responsible for his death. In Cambridge, Edward Tilman wrote that the "Papists" had "given out that Marquesse Hamilton died Roman catholique", adding, " 'Tis thought he was catholiquelie poisoned, and so is his name: but this will bee vindicated". But the person most distraught was Hamilton's friend, Lucy Russell, Countess of Bedford, who was "a maimed body and worse" after the news of his death (Fig. 22). She had been struck by how suddenly and unexpectedly Hamilton had succumbed, especially since "for his years, strength, health and temper" he "was like to have lived to much greater age than any I have left". But it was Hamilton's peculiar post-mortem symptoms that troubled her. At his death, both doctors and servants affirmed that Hamilton's corpse was "as fair . . . as ever their eyes beheld", yet within three hours it had "swelled so strangely and gangrened so generally as it astonished them all". The countess reported various medical explanations for these symptoms, but remained unconvinced. Some physicians claimed to have seen similar symptoms "in pestilential fevers", while others "impute part of the cause" to the hot cloths used to massage Hamilton's body before he died and to keeping him "too close in the bed" afterward. The countess was equally sceptical of the physicians' autopsy reports; "It is true that, when he was opened in his stomach and head, there appeared nothing to confirm this jealousy, which makes the physicians confident it could be no poison they are in these parts acquainted with". Nevertheless, "both myself and many other of his friends rest not clear of doubt". She retained "strong suspicions" that Hamilton had been "unnaturally cut off", perhaps by "the lying papists", who "used means for the shortening of his noble days" because he was "the boldest opposer of their ends". In the end, she agreed that absent "further evidence", the question of his death "is not to be stirred in". But, she avowed "if ever the least light can be gotten, the fear of all mortal men should not hinder our just prosecution of so abominable a fact".[12]

Figure 22: Simon de Passe, *Lucy Russell, Countess of Bedford*, c. 1618, Hamilton's close friend and a supporter of the "honest" party at court (National Portrait Gallery).

Figure 23: Francis Delaram, *Ernst von Mansfeld, Count von Mansfeld*, 1620s, German soldier and commander of the ill-fated Anglo-French expedition that foundered in the Netherlands, early in 1625 (National Portrait Gallery).

These mysterious deaths were only one of the many issues preoccupying the politically and ideologically fragmented court during the winter of 1624-25. After months of intense struggle in 1623–24, it looked as if Prince Charles and Buckingham had secured control of England's foreign policy. They had ended the treaties with Spain, long the centrepiece of James's diplomacy. They had embarked on negotiations for a French match and had sent a large contingent of English troops under Count Mansfelt to intervene in the European land war (Fig. 23). Early in 1625, however, James made it painfully clear that he had not surrendered control of his state. The subsequent wrangles almost ended Buckingham's war before it began, and they cast a long shadow over the illnesses decimating the Anglo-Scots elite.

"A perplexed worke"

Early in February 1625, Sir Francis Nethersole, secretary to Princess Elizabeth in The Hague, wondered how Mansfelt's army, supposedly sent to relieve the Palatinate, had ended up stranded in the Netherlands. Mansfelt's expedition was the first military fruit of Charles and Buckingham's new foreign policy, and it would prove unusually bitter. The enterprise was originally an Anglo-French initiative, but at the last minute the French had insisted that the 12,000 English infantry march to the Palatinate through the Dutch Republic, not through France as initially planned. This abrupt switch triggered a calamitous sequence of events. In January 1625 the English agent accompanying Mansfelt had warned that "If I understand any thing this Army will come to nothing." Secretary Conway pronounced the mission "a perplexed worke", while Buckingham "bemoaned the ill satisfaction the Parlament must receave, the losse of time and the unfruitful expense of money, my industries made vaine, my Judgment infinitly charged ... and the good cause by theis misfortunes put much further back."[13] As the situation worsened, conversations at court centred obsessively on what had gone wrong and who was to blame.

Even by Jacobean standards the arrival of the English troops was chaotic. Whitehall sent neither the Dutch government nor the English ambassador advance warning, and Mansfelt disembarked without weapons or money. Initially, the Dutch provided supplies, and in mid-February Mansfelt ordered his men to march to the relief of Breda, a Dutch frontier town besieged by the Spanish (Fig. 24). At this point the six English colonels led by Lord Cromwell opened their instructions from James, only to discover that the king expressly forbade them to relieve Breda. But when Mansfelt opened a letter from Buckingham, he found orders "to goe whether he wold and in his judgment

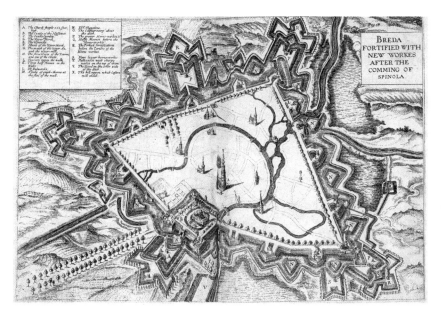

Figure 24: "Breda Fortified With New Workes After the Comming of Spinola", in Herman Hugo, *The Siege of Breda* (1629) (Huntington Library).

thought best". The confusion only increased, Cromwell explained, when "we beheld not with a little amazement both our instructions and the Duke's letter beinge one date and wrighten by one hand", that of Conway's secretary.[14] The frustrated commanders stayed where they were, awaiting clearer orders.

The colonels, along with Sir Dudley Carleton, the English ambassador, barraged Whitehall with letters, begging that the restriction on relieving Breda be lifted. Meanwhile the soldiers, already weakened by their mid-winter voyage, began, as Cromwell put it, to "dye lycke doggs" as food and Dutch patience ran out. "Charity", Carleton predicted, "will grow cold with these people when they shall find that those who have nothing else to live on may not help towards theyr defense". As supplies dwindled, conditions among the troops rapidly deteriorated. One man became so miserable that he "cutt his owne throat" so he would "suffer no more". Death and desertion winnowed the force from 12,000 in mid-February to 9,000 by the end of the month; by early March only 5,000 men were fit for service.[15] The recriminations began immediately. "If they were voluntaries the hurt were the lesse", Carleton warned, "but being prest men, it will breed a great crye in our Countrey to have them exposed" to such suffering. Cromwell insisted that "we live with a great deal of dishonor to our nation", for "such a president never was, for so many men to be prest out of the country . . . in a war by [the king] not owned". He worried that the disaster would incense Parliament. The Earl of Clare agreed: "If this be the issue of so many subsidies . . . my masters of the lower hows can not muche bragg of their wisdome."[16]

As Charles and Buckingham worked desperately to salvage something from the expedition, James remained intransigent. In early March, Conway bemoaned that "time and Money" had been "wasted impertinently, his Majestie discouraged, the Troops despaired and the action blasted in the beginnings". Charles and Buckingham had managed to keep the expedition going after the French unilaterally changed the landing site, but James had made progress impossible by clinging to his prohibition on the relief of Breda. James, Conway reported, suspected his French allies wanted to suck him "into an open warre with Spaine from which the French king would yet be free"; so James wanted Mansfelt to proceed down the Rhine to Heidelberg, and would "by noe meanes . . . lett the Troopes goe to Breda". The colonels regarded this order as military suicide without Dutch or French military support. The Dutch themselves were baffled. "It was a hard measure", Prince Maurice observed, "to send a nessessitous armie unto there Country whome they must feede and not imploy." Yet rather than follow the emphatic advice of his son and his favourite to assist the Dutch, James decided the moment was right to demand reparations for the English merchants murdered by agents of the Dutch East India Company in Amboyna early in 1623. "This short word Amboyna", Conway sighed, "doth breed ill bloud", and will cause "such mischiefes . . . which executed will not easily be redeemed." To further exasperate the Dutch, James requested an immediate loan of £20,000 for Mansfelt's English troops. He conceded that the money "ought in truth to be provided for by the French king who hath brought these troopes into this inconvenience", but absent French aid, James expected the Dutch to cover Mansfelt's expenses. At the same time, James made absolutely clear that the army was neither to help the Dutch nor to provoke Isabella: "to goe to Breda or to make any hostile attempts upon the Archduchesse will not be permitted them at this time".[17]

Buckingham continued to lobby James to lift this restriction. The duke knew that unless he changed the king's mind, he would have to explain to Parliament how England's first major military action in two decades had consumed thousands of lives and nearly £200,000 without accomplishing anything. If the expedition failed, English enthusiasm for war would likely fade, and Anglo-Dutch relations would be ruined. Meanwhile, the number of able-bodied men under Mansfelt's command continued to plummet. On 21 March, Conway assured Carleton that Charles and Buckingham were still eager to unleash Mansfelt, but they could only speak to the king "att such times as his Majesties health would permit". Three days later Conway told his son-in-law that "his Majestie cannot yet be moved, to change his first resolutions".[18] Despite the best efforts of his son and his favourite, despite the dire political and diplomatic repercussions, and despite his own medical decline, James refused to let Mansfelt march to Breda.

Tertian Fits

At the end of February 1625, after weeks at Newmarket and Royston, James moved to Theobalds, eager for his favourite's company. As Charles explained to Buckingham, "if you shall not be ready to go with him to Theobalds . . . he can take no pleasure to be there". The duke, staying nearby at New Hall, asked for a little time; the French ambassador had just left and Mall, the duke's daughter, had been "importunate" with him "to staye". Delighted by Buckingham's "merry letter", James expected him the next day to "make him laugh according to your promise".[19]

Shortly after arriving at Theobalds, James fell ill, and the court intelligencers immediately began reporting and assessing the news. On 8 March, Edward Fotherbye wrote from London that "the Court is settled at Tyballs; our king falne into some Indisposition of body; his Phisitions with some of the bedchamber sent for from hence".[20] By 9 March James had had "three fitts of a tertian agew", but the Earl of Kellie at least hoped "it shall doe him good and noe harme". Others reminded James of the adage that "a Tertian in the spring is physick for a king", but James, plagued "with his owne more then others apprehension of danger" and anxious, as always, about medicine, began "cursing them that should believe or say any physick could be whollsom that was so troublesome". Nevertheless, on 12 March, Chamberlain thought the king in no serious danger, provided "he wold suffer himself to be ordered and governed by phisicall rules".[21]

James's courtiers carefully monitored his illness, counting the fits, measuring their duration and intensity, and assessing how well he withstood them. On 16 March, Conway informed the Earl of Carlisle of "the sharp and smart accesses of his Majesty's fever, though a pure intermitting tertian, whereof this day early he had his seventh fit". Two days later, a London newsletter-writer reported that the king's "tertian is sayd yet to continue, from which God graciously free him", adding in the margin that "Some say he hath fittes of 10 houres long".[22] Agent X reported on 11 March that between attacks, which "have not beene so vehement", James "playeth at cardes with the Duke of Buckingham". Many of these reporters were aware that James was a difficult patient. John Castle heard that the king, racked with fever, had thrown "the clothes from his Armes . . . [and] putt his hands upon the outside of a bason that had cold water in it", and then plunged his hands and arms into cold water, making his fever "much more vehement and intensive". The frustrated king was said to have exclaimed that "it was absurde to have it found hereafter in the Chronicles of England that their kinge was burnt in his bed".[23]

As James sickened, court business slowed. On 11 March the Venetian ambassador had to postpone a royal audience because the king was "ill of a tertian fever". Eager for James's approval of the Maundy Thursday service at St Paul's, the Bishop of London sent up the proposal on 16 March, conceding it might be hard to obtain the king's signature "whilst his Ague holds him". Frederick and Elizabeth's envoy Rusdorf reported on 15 March that, thanks to the king's "*fievre*", James "denies free access to his person and does not want to be troubled with business".[24] Yet the king still followed affairs, albeit intermittently, and the previous day, while James was wrestling with the sixth fit of his ague, the court had received welcome news of a major diplomatic success.

James had signed the marriage treaty between his son Charles and Louis XIII's sister Henrietta Maria three months earlier, but in February the French king had angered English negotiators by requesting several emendations, most notably adding a demand for a formal Catholic toleration. The negotiators denounced "these unworthy false monsieurs" and begged James "to reiect those presumptuous and unseasonable demandes with a sharpe stoute Negative". Sir George Goring cautioned Buckingham that the situation was perilous, considering "how your Grace is interested in these theyre courses and you only ar the man on whome the least miscarriadge of this business thus conveyed must reflect". The French demands infuriated James and Charles, who both rebuked the French ambassador, the Marquis D'Effiat. Buckingham had hoped to conclude negotiations with a feast that everyone could relish "avec bon bouche", but now thought the French would dine with "shitten mouthes".[25] On 1 March,

James made his formal reply, accepting a few minor alterations but rejecting the major ones with a "peremptorie denial". He gave Louis an ultimatum: he had seventy-two hours to agree that his sister would marry Charles by proxy within a month, with or without papal dispensation.[26] On 14 March, Walter Montagu, a minor diplomat, arrived with the news of Louis's capitulation; as the Earl of Holland explained to the prince, "Your mistress is yours in dispight of the Pope." Conway was elated: "the joy in the thing, and the surprise, in time and manner, had been inexpressible." The news prompted celebrations at Theobalds, where everyone "made so merry that they were faine to be carried to bed and remayne there till the next day". James's reaction was more muted; since Montagu arrived during the king's fit, "he could not express what he would have done, if his state of health had answered his affections", Conway said. Nevertheless, James "left not undeclared his contentment".[27]

With the good news from Paris came optimistic bulletins on the king's health. Early on 16 March Conway reported that "thanks be to God" James's latest fit was "less intemperate than the rest, and hath left more clearness and chearfulness in his looks than the former". The intensity of the fever attacks continued to lessen, and on the night of 18–19 March "his fitt was so little as [his doctors] held him cured". D'Effiat certainly thought the news was good, as did Chamberlain, who heard that James's fits "grow lesse and lesse". Conway told Carleton that the court hoped James's fit on 19 March "may be the laste" for he "shewed more cheerefulnes", adding in his postscript that "there appears nothing but lessening of the fittes". The doctors consequently "muche hope that this will be the last, or at the most the next fitt will be as muche lesse then this fitt as this is lesse then the last". Sir Albertus Morton gave thanks for "the blessed news of his Majestyes better health", and James's staff began planning his move to Hampton Court "for better ayre".[28]

Throughout the first fortnight of James's illness, Buckingham had been in constant motion; as D'Effiat reported, the duke "came and went everyday", shuttling back and forth between London and Theobalds. London talk made much of the favourite's concern for his master. Chamberlain reported that although the king was improving, "yet I do not thincke the Duke will leave him till he seem him perfectly recovered".[29] But as James recovered, the duke had other reasons for anxiety; for James not only continued to stand firm on the Breda dispute, he now appeared ready to reopen talks with Spain.

The Two Diegos

In January 1625 news had reached London that Diego Sarmiento de Acuna, the Conde de Gondomar, proposed returning to England (Fig. 25). Buckingham rarely wrote letters himself—since he often forgot to use what he termed "my legable hand", it was better for all concerned that he used a secretary—but on

16 January he personally added a postscript to a dispatch to Sir Walter Aston, ambassador in Madrid. "I must needs tell you", he wrote, that it "was much wondered att here by all that you should use diligences for the coming hether of goundemar," a man who had been "the instrument to a base my master the prince and the state". He warned Aston that "if now by your meanes the kinge should be fetched on againe upon a new tretie the blame would light upon you[,] the state having once advised him from trusting that people who have hether to nor never will doe other then cozen him."[30]

The duke had ample reason for irritation and alarm. After a decade in London, Gondomar knew England unusually well, and his sly wit had won him friends across the ideological spectrum. But his greatest achievement was the close relationship he had built with James I. Indeed, the personal friendship of the "two Diegos" had kept the Anglo-Spanish entente of 1604 alive during the grave tests posed by the Bohemian and Palatinate crises of 1618–23. With Gondomar's support, James had turned aside calls for full-scale English military intervention, even as Spain and her allies drove Frederick and Elizabeth from Prague and Heidelberg, and pursued instead a Spanish match and a negotiated settlement to the continental war. Charles and Buckingham were convinced that Gondomar had used the promise of a marriage alliance to delude the king,

Figure 25: Simon de Passe, *Don Diego de Sarmiento, Conde de Gondomar*, 1622 (British Museum). As Spanish ambassador in London, Gondomar acquired an extraordinary knowledge of English affairs; many English Protestants feared his influence over James I.

and in 1624 they had mobilized a patriot coalition to persuade James to termi-
nate the negotiations and prepare for war. Late in 1624, Buckingham seemed to
have finally broken Gondomar's influence over English policy; but, now, early
in 1625, James was ready to welcome him back.

For Buckingham, the dangers were acute. Gondomar's arrival would rally the
court's moribund Spanish faction, whose members Charles and Buckingham
had systematically isolated over the preceding months. The large, aristocratic
Howard clan, led by the Earl of Arundel, along with Catholic peers like Monteagle,
Vaux, Petre, Worcester, Montagu and Buckingham's father-in-law, Rutland,
would welcome Gondomar's return. Worse still, Gondomar's presence would
require Buckingham to confront the Earl of Bristol, the former English ambassador in Madrid and a leading advocate of Anglo-Spanish entente. The favourite
and the envoy had quarrelled in 1623, and Buckingham had made Bristol the
scapegoat for Spanish perfidy in his lengthy address to the 1624 Parliament. The
earl was currently under house arrest pending a formal investigation, but
Gondomar's arrival could easily lead to Bristol's restoration to royal favour.

James and his entourage had scarcely settled into Theobalds before
Gondomar's secretary arrived to request a passport for his master. Buckingham
"marveled at this coming", and thought Gondomar "very daring". With Thomas
Middleton's recent theatrical satire on Gondomar fresh in the memory, Clare
was astonished at what "a bould man he is, that after declamations in Parlement,
representations in scorne, with a plaudite, upon a publik stage, acted 10 times
together without a sufett[,] will adventure, nay bestow his person, and indevors
among us". But James welcomed the count's offer to help resolve the vexed
Palatinate question. "The coming of Gondomar creates uneasiness in every
direction," the Venetian diplomat Zuane Pesaro noted. "The Duke of Buckingham
more than anyone else ought to take double precautions with his own salvation,
as his fall or discredit would result from any renewal of confidence or relations
with the Spaniards."[31] The French ambassador was equally alarmed to find
people readily lending "an ear to Gondomar's man". Meanwhile, Hispanophile
expectations soared; Owen Wynn reported that "he brings with him fayre
overtures of peace as the restoringe of the palatinate gratis without desire of
recompense towards the chardge of that warr".[32] After the dark farce of the
Mansfelt expedition, many were willing to reconsider a Spanish diplomatic
solution to a conflict that seemed destined only to consume England's treasure
and destroy her honour.

Already stymied on the Breda question, Charles and especially Buckingham
were now powerless to keep Gondomar out of England. Buckingham tried to
make peace with Bristol, but the earl rebuffed his overtures. Conway struggled
to remain optimistic. On 21 March he tried to reassure Carleton that
Gondomar's return "is of doubt and offence to those that iudge of it a farre of,
but those that looke upon it att hand can see no danger". After all, Gondomar

"will not be able to move the king to a daies cessation of Armes or to forbeare any attempt or Act, which is already propounded or shalbe before his coming ... conceived fitt to be done." Nevertheless, apprehension in anti-Spanish circles spread. The London newsmongers made "great talk" of the ambassador, some of them speculating that "there is no bulwark strong enough against him": Gondomar, they worried, "will marre all".[33]

"What an Age doe we live in"

On 22 March, Bishop Williams rushed to Theobalds. He had just heard the alarming news that "his Maiesties Sickness" had suddenly become "dangerous to Death". Two days later, James's perilous condition caused Charles to ask the French to delay the marriage celebrations and allow his kinsman, the Duc de Chevreuse, to replace Buckingham as his wedding proxy. As Conway explained, "it cannot be suteable with the good nature of a Sonne, in so dangerous estate of his Fathers health to entertaine such iollitie and triumph as duely belong to soe acceptable a Marriage." Nor was it "congruous with the thankfulness and faithful love of the Duke of Buckingham to leave his Majestie in such condition as he now is".[34]

Although Conway still clung to hopeful signs, the medical bulletins remained worrying. As he explained to Carlisle, James's fit late on 23 March "exercised much violence upon a weak body" and "struck much sense and fear into the hearts of his servants that looked upon him". The next morning the king drank some broth, "had large benefit of nature" (i.e. purged his bowels), and "slept well". Later in the day, he "did, with life and chearfulness, receive the sacrament in the presence of the Prince, the Duke and many others, and admitted many to take it with him", thus confirming "his writings and his wide and pious profession and did justly produce mixt tears between comfort and grief". On 24 March the king rested quietly, regaining "strength, appetite and digestion", and this "gives us great hope of his amendment". In a letter to his son-in-law written the same day, Conway added that "there are good hopes and probabilities this may be the last fitt and his speedie recovering follow".[35] Others were more pessimistic. On 23 March the Countess of Bedford learned that James "was this morning in so weak state, as there was no hope of his life". She added that "till his 3 last fits there was no doubt of his safety then of every man's that has an ordinary ague, so fatal a year is this to great persons as well as meaner." Anxious to see for himself, Clare rode to Theobalds on 25 March, where he found the prince more eager "to cleere, then to fill the chamber". When Charles went to dinner, Clare peered through a rip in a screen and "saw the King in his bedd" surrounded by doctors. He stayed until four in the afternoon when James "was faling into it, his pulse altering to the wors, and his hands sumwhat colling". The doctors could only pray "the fitt would be less violent". That same day, Sir Allen Apsley reported, "the kinge slept this afternoone from one or two o'clocke till five and then woke being in a great sweate, and as they feared falling into his fit." James subsequently produced no fewer than twenty-seven stools.[36]

On 26 March, Rusdorf found the regime in disarray. James "was unable to speak, and . . . most people thought that barring a miracle the king would not recover"; Archbishop Abbot had ordered the churches to pray for him. The Privy Councillors in London petitioned to come to Theobalds while people on the street, so Rusdorf heard, were convinced "his majesty was already dead". The end came around noon the next day, and Pesaro soon heard reports of the clinical details: three days earlier, James had suffered "an apoplectic fit, which affected his chin, loosening his jawbone and enlarging his tongue, and finally a violent dysentery carried him off, the very bed exuding the excrement".[37]

A week earlier, James had seemed on the brink of recovery, and now contemporaries began speculating about what had gone wrong. Pesaro noted the ill effects of James's "irregularities, his fits of temper, and his lack of care of himself", but others were already pointing to a much more disturbing explanation.[38] Kellie had witnessed James's illness from the start, and on 22 March confessed his uneasiness about the king's deterioration to his cousin the Earl of Mar. Kellie prayed that the king "maye have noe more sutche fitts as he had this last nycht and the nycht before", for James "is a seeke man and worss then I love to wret". Kellie then admitted that "their hes sume thing fallin out heir mutche disliked, and I for my selfe think mutche mistakkin". The problem was that:

> My Lord of Bukkinghame wishing mutche the Kings healthe cawsed splaister to be applied to the Kings breeste, efter which his Majestie was extremely seeke, and with all did give him a drink or syrope to drink; and this was done without the consent or knowledge of onye of the doctours.

This meddling had "spreade sutche a business heir and discontent as you wold wonder, and Doctoure Craige is now absented from Court, and Henrye Gibb of his Majesties bedchamber is quarreled for it, and my Lord of Bukkinghame soe incensed as your Lordshipe wold wonder." Kellie himself protested, "I think he gets great wrong in saying sutche tealles as goes heir of him."[39]

The Habsburg agents soon picked up the story. On 25 March, Van Male wrote to Brussels about "*estrange tragedies*" involving "*les emplastres et cordialls*". The same day an agent codenamed "XX" wrote in great haste "from the courte at theobalds", adding that "the difficulties are greater then I have knowne them". Since "the kinge is still sicke, and his recovery is douted", XX lamented that "I feare to all christendome, for the duke hathe the absolute power and possession of the prince", and Buckingham "will not only endevore the ruin of the hous of Austria but of all the catholice princes."[40] Along with this dispatch came an anonymous letter, bearing startling news written "late at night" from Theobalds. James:

having an ordinarie Ague and his fitts lessening by faire degrees, the D. of Bucq. eyther to post it away or for a worse end, did on munday last [21 March] at night force the king to take a plaster on his stomack and a scurvie drinke inwards without so much as acquainting any one doctor therewith though 8 were in the house.

Consequently "that night he was one hower dead, and two houres more sencelesse, not knowing anny body, and his next accesse [of the fit] was little lese discomfortable then that." All but one of the physicians agreed that "if he have another fitt, itt will kill him or make him past help". The dissenter, Dr. Beton, thought "he will live". For his part, Buckingham:

> is enraged att all that speake of the plaster and came to towne last night onely (as I thinke) to confer with the treasurer [James Ley, former Lord Chief Justice of King's Bench] (who is a cunning man in the law) what course he maye take against them that speakes against him and he hath alredie prevailed with the prince to commit to prison his doctor called Cragge, one of the 8, who sayd he has as good have given the king poison.

The duke had also threatened "Gibb a groome of the Kings bed chamber, for the same occasion". Thus, "you maye see the power he assumes over our Lyves, yea, and over the kings lyfe". Van Male's anonymous correspondent added that the favourite had used the king's stamp to sign a warrant "to staye the Count of Gondomar from coming hither", since the old envoy was trying "to compound all confusions which are threatened". The letter concluded with an outburst: "Fye upon this time what an Age doe we live in."[41]

The Doctor of Dunmow

Sir Sackville Crowe kept accounts of Buckingham's personal expenses, and his entry dated "at my returne to Theobalds", 1 March 1625, recorded payment of £2 to a messenger that "went to fetch the Dr of Dunmoe to the king" and £20 to the doctor himself. Later in the account book, Crowe recorded a second £20 payment "To the Dr of Dunmoe for his iourney to Theobalds the 23 March". Over the years, Crowe had accounted for many similar outlays on medicines and doctors, including the £300 paid to the five learned physicians who had attended the duke during his prolonged 1624 illness. But never before had Buckingham paid a doctor to attend the king.[42]

As we have seen, late in 1624 the king's chief physician Mayerne had established a protocol strictly limiting James's medical care to a small team of elite physicians. No outsiders, neither the great courtiers nor their ragged band of healers, should play any part in the king's treatment. But at the very beginning of March 1625, before James's physicians had diagnosed him but, presumably, after the king had begun to feel ill, Buckingham had brought just such an outsider, the Doctor of Dunmow, to advise on the king's health; and he would bring him again to court three weeks later. For all Mayerne's strictures, there was nothing surprising in Buckingham's initial interference, for, as we have also seen, the sharing of illness—of nursing and consolation, advice and remedies—was a central feature of the intimate relationship between king and favourite. From the moment James felt the initial symptoms of his ague, Buckingham would have been among the first to know; and the two men had almost certainly already discussed the duke's own recent experience with the fever. Feeling aguish in the summer of 1624, Buckingham had returned to his estate at New Hall in Essex, anxious to avoid the press of suitors at court. Aware of the medical importance of climate, the duke also worried that Theobalds was "now verie hot, and hath but few chang of roomes, both inconvenient to a sicke bodie". Moreover, the Earl of Warwick had told him that "Newhall are [air]" was "as good a one to ride away an ague as anie in England; and that latelie he [Warwick] lost [an ague] by the benefit of that are." Warwick had also told Buckingham about a local physician expert in ague cures. Essex was a fever-pestered county—some doctors referred to the "Essex ague" as a distinct illness—and it was hardly surprising that local practitioners specialized in its treatment. Between 22 June and 9 July 1624, Crowe recorded three payments of £10 to "the Doctor of Dunmoe". Buckingham also paid, at his mother's behest, for "herbes & for posset ale", perhaps ingredients for the doctor's favoured ague remedy, a medicinal julep to drink and plasters for the patient's torso and wrists.[43]

The Dunmow doctor was John Remington. Although he apparently lacked formal medical training, he counted several local worthies as patients, including the godly Joan Barrington, wife of Warwick's ally Sir Francis.[44] Remington operated in a medical world more variegated and eclectic than the one governed by the royal doctors, and his ague remedies belonged to a vast contemporary fever pharmacy that extended far beyond the purgative regimes recommended by the learned physicians. The physicians themselves acknowledged that there were alternative treatments whose effects Galenic logic found hard to explain. There were "medicines ... which by a certain *peculiar force* are said to oppugne Tertians"; and an "almost infinite number" of "specifick and Empirick medicaments, both internal and external ... commended by Practitioners, and frequently used by the common people." Many of these popular remedies relied on "cataplasms" or plasters. "Neither are those Medicines wholly to be rejected which the common people are wont to apply unto the Wrists of such as have Agues," one physician conceded, "For not only the Opinion of People is hereby satisfied, who conceive that many are cured with these Remedies; but somewhat they may effect, by communicating their vertues unto the Heart by those notable Arteries which are scituate in the Wrists."[45] But these "specific" remedies made up only a fraction of the early modern ague pharmacy. Sufferers could try newly discovered cures like the Florida sassafras, known in England as the "ague tree", or the native "bastard Rubarb" plant.[46] Wealthy patients might opt for Francis Anthony's panacea "aurum potabile", a drug that procured many testimonials from former ague sufferers.[47] Others could turn to John Gerard's printed *Herball* and its list of sixty "simples" for agues, or to the best-selling medical collection offering no fewer than forty-eight remedies.[48] Contemporaries also tackled agues with magical or spiritual therapies, whether "popish charms" deploying verbal formulae, ritual gestures and sacramental objects, or herbs chosen for their numerological symbolism.[49] Mainstream English religion provided its own therapeutic resources. The Essex Puritan minister Ralph Josselin treated a tertian ague by combining prayer and introspection with several purgative drugs and cooling foods.[50] Josselin, like many of his contemporaries, diagnosed and treated his ague without advice from any doctor. Indeed, a late Henrician statute (34 & 35 Hen. VIII c.8) explicitly allowed ordinary people to give "drinkes for . . . agues", without fear of penalty for violating the medical establishment's closely guarded monopolies.

Many of the Doctor of Dunmow's powerful patients embraced this therapeutic eclecticism. The Duke of Buckingham would have found nothing odd about patronizing an obscure Essex physician: the duke's therapeutic tastes were broad, and he and his family often tried fashionable "new" cures and healers.[51] The madness of his brother John Villiers, Viscount Purbeck, had led Buckingham to the clerical physician Richard Napier, whose blend of magical, astrological, natural, Galenic, chemical and religious medicine set him apart from other learned doctors.[52] Purbeck also brought Buckingham into contact with more heterodox healers. Early in September 1624, Buckingham consulted Bishop Laud "about a man that offered him a strange way of cure for himself and his brother".[53] While we do not know what Laud thought, Buckingham was prepared to deal with healers of clearly dubious repute. From 1624 he was involved with the notorious "Doctor" John Lambe, a convicted witch and rapist who practised a form of magical medicine. And in a remarkable letter to James, Buckingham referred to another heterodox practitioner—he called him only "my divill"—whom he paid over £400 for various services. In addition to claiming that he could find the philosopher's stone, this "divill" had concocted powerful medicines, including one sent to the king "to preserve you from all sicknes ever herafter".[54] Buckingham was sceptical of his devil's claims, but the fact that he paid the man so handsomely and sent his preservative to James suggests both the breadth of his therapeutic tastes and his usual habit of sharing medical talk and treatment with the king.

It was thus only natural for James to discuss his latest sickness and treatment with the duke. And when Buckingham mentioned the Doctor of Dunmow, he was simply passing along Warwick's and his own recommendation about a proven cure for ague. Remington's remedies—a plaster and a drink—no doubt also appealed to James's impatience with his doctors' noxious clysters, purges and leeches. And so, presumably at James's request, Buckingham brought Remington and his medicines to the king at Theobalds. The first application, a plaster, probably used on 8 or 12 March, caused little consternation; indeed, few even noticed that it had happened. Given their relationship, there was nothing odd about Buckingham providing James with medicine, and if James had recovered, nobody would have thought anything of it. But on 20 March, when James received Remington's remedies a second time, something went disastrously wrong. Although Buckingham hastily summoned Remington back to court, within a week James was dead. The familiar story of one friend medicating another with a well-trusted specific remedy now seemed potentially far more sinister, and those who lost materially, politically or ideologically by the king's death would have more than enough motive to recast the duke's interventions in a more dangerous light.

The Court's Great Earthquake

Sir Robert Kerr, one of Prince Charles's servants, had long been dreading it, but as James breathed his last, the "Court's great earthquake" rumbled through Whitehall and Theobalds. The damage was extensive. Initially, Conway insisted that James's death would change nothing, since Charles "in his reverence to so good a Father hath confirmed all his acts and in his favor to his Ministers all his choices". More realistically, Archbishop Abbot predicted that James's death "will alter many proiects", and the Earl of Exeter lamented that "the ould world is done and a new beginning".[55]

Courtiers and bureaucrats were anxious, for all royal appointments ended with the king's death. Four hundred sailors who had been pressed for the fleet knew that much; on news of James's demise, they headed for their homes, as the local magistrates watched helplessly. Reappointments were common but far from automatic. Charles quickly made clear that the Spanish faction had no place on his Privy Council; he removed Lord Baltimore, a crypto-Catholic, when he declined to take the oath of allegiance and supremacy. He also dismissed several pro-Spanish councillors like the Earl of Suffolk, Viscount Wallingford, and Lord Wotton. Agent X noted that "there is noe man in any truste that is thought to have desired the matche with Spayne".[56] Some officials got only conditional reappointments. In early April, when several office-holders surrendered their patents, Charles returned them all except Lord Scrope's. "It is not with an intention to take it from you", Charles told Scrope, the Lord President of the North, "but to tell you that instead of Suppressing the Papists, you doe not onely cary a favorable hand over them, but cherish them." Then the king handed the patent back to the "amased" peer, adding "If you forbeare you may parchance hould it, if not be ridd of it sooner then you are aware." The earthquake's epicentre, however, was in the Household, where James's "familiars and the Scots", as well as the court Catholics, were now marked men. The outcome was so clear that some well-connected courtiers immediately moved into the Whitehall lodgings of their predecessors: Lord Ley took over Bristol's rooms, Sir Henry Vane took Sir Marmaduke Darrell's, and Sir James Fullerton occupied Kellie's.[57]

Amid the turmoil, one old servant remained calm. Although some contemporaries wondered what would happen to Buckingham, better-informed observers knew that his power would likely increase under Charles. X reported at the end of March that the duke "hathe more power in the sonne then he had in the father"; indeed, as "soone as the father was dead the sonne was seenne to kisse the duke with much affection". When Charles left Theobalds for St James's Palace a few hours after his father died, Buckingham travelled "in his coach" and then "lodged in the same house as neere to the king as with conveniency might be". Later that night, after others had retired, the duke attended Charles "very late and continued with him alone in very private and serious discours for more then two howers". Charles's behaviour signalled his extraordinary regard for the duke, "the kinge soe much favoring him as he hath not yeat stirred from him". Pesaro reported that "It is thought that his fortunes are better assured by this new prop than by his former credit with the late king, when he might any day experience some rebuff in the uncertainty about the steps to be taken." These developments also troubled Kellie: "there is sume that dois feare my Lord of Bukkinghame his power with him, and I assure you that it is not pleasing to moste men nather of one degree nor the uther."[58]

Buckingham's control over the regime, which had been tight during James's last years, now tightened further. His anti-Spanish efforts had been regularly rebuffed not only by the king, but also by independent members of the Privy Council and even old bedchamber men like Kellie, who had ushered Buckingham's enemies up the back stairs to visit James without the favourite's knowledge. Buckingham now moved swiftly to insulate Charles by tightening control over the royal bedchamber. "Buckingham first and alone of all the officials took the oath as first gentleman of his Majesty's chamber," Pesaro reported on 8 April. The duke's relatives, Lord Compton and the young Marquis of Hamilton soon joined him in these sensitive posts around the king. Charles's insistence on much stricter court decorum helped seal him off more completely from unwanted influence, for, as X observed, "the pages and groomes shall not come in but when they shalbe called" and consequently "the secrets of the bedchamber shall not be revealed".[59]

Buckingham also bypassed the Council. Since late 1623 he had only rarely attended full Council meetings, preferring instead to secure a direct royal command or use a smaller subcommittee packed with his allies. At Charles's first Council meeting, the Earl of Arundel reportedly moved that "these greate businesses now in hand soe much concerning the honnour and safety of the king and kingdome might be communicated to some of them and not to be managed by soe few as hitherto they had beene."[60] But Buckingham quickly institutionalized the managing of business "by soe few". In early May, the Earl of Clare grumbled that "the same hand governs still court and state, the councell board neither more or less, only a Commity from among them." This committee, consisting of Buckingham, Pembroke, Conway, Ley and Lord Brooke, went by various names—the "quinque-virale", the "cabinet council", the "closet counsel"—but by any name its monopolistic control over major issues was near complete.[61] The only potentially independent member of the group was Pembroke, and Buckingham now tried to tame him by promising to make him Lord Steward and his brother Lord Chamberlain.

Policy changes quickly followed the reshuffling of offices. "Here businesses are in throng", Conway explained, "and are clogged with many distractions and the consultations are not onely what is fitt to be done but how to be done". Almost immediately "the resolution falls upon Money to make all liquid", for the royal finances were "not onelie defective in part but totally", thanks to the expenses of Mansfelt's army, James's funeral and Charles's marriage. But Charles had little time for fiscal caution; with breathtaking confidence, his new regime assumed that "the Parlament will supplie all for the kingdome". And without waiting for this guaranteed flow of money, Charles authorized further military action. On 12 April he released Mansfelt's English troops to relieve Breda; as Conway told Carleton, "the restriction concerning Breda died with our late Soveraigne". Charles also quickly dashed hopes of Gondomar's return and sealed off the Spanish faction from influence and access. With the cabinet council in charge, Charles and Buckingham rapidly moved towards open war. "Now ar we blotting out the motto of 22 years standing, beati pacifici," Clare noted. Late in 1623, after Charles and Buckingham had first adopted their bellicose anti-Spanish position, Kellie had gloomily prophesied to Mar that "it maye cume that young folks shall have their world. I know not if that wilbe fitt for your Lordship and me." By early April 1625 he—and all those who wanted peace—knew that the "young folks" had got their way.[62]

Poisonous Applications

The Duke of Buckingham "is likely to doe all", thought the minor bureaucrat Nathanial Tomkins, provided "his griefe and sicknesse shorten not his dayes as his friends feare it will". James's death had prompted an emotional outpouring at Theobalds, much of it from the favourite, who reportedly "grieved exceedingly and fainted twice".[63] Pesaro heard a similar account: seeing "the tears which the duke shed for the loss of his master, his Majesty comforted him, promising that though he had lost one master he had gained another, who would be even more gracious". Indeed, Charles had to explain to Buckingham that "to grieve more would show a want of confidence in him". Nevertheless, the favourite's health quickly collapsed. On 31 March, Conway found him "sorrowe it selfe".[64] The following day another man noted that "ever since his Majestie died", Buckingham "hath ben ill and this afternoon was brought very sick from the Court to his house". Two days later, Robert Mason observed that the duke and the Earls of Montgomery and Holderness, two earlier royal favourites, "are all sick", adding that Buckingham "sounds [swoons] oft and Holdernes is like to die for greefe". Buckingham was still bedridden several days later.[65] His prolonged sickness made one contemporary worry about poisoning: "I pray God that they have not done some mischief to the Duke of Buckingham", for "me thinks he hath not loked well."[66]

As Buckingham convalesced, expectations of some great action grew: Charles was hailed as "Great Britaines Charlemagne" and the duke as "the Favorite of God, his King, Prince and Country". Conway assured Princess Elizabeth that Buckingham "hath noe other affection appearing in him but the zeale of his Maisters honor and the restauration of their Majesties" to their lands. With James's death the favourite seemed set to complete his reinvention as a Protestant patriot hero. But rumours about the events at Theobalds would not disappear. Charles and Buckingham had tried to stifle talk at court by making examples of Dr Craig and Henry Gibb. But allegations about Buckingham's medical interventions had already begun to spread beyond the court, particularly among those discontented with the new regime. While Pesaro thought that "The assured hope of a proper cause and generous resolution in the new king consoles all right minded men", he admitted that, "the familiars and the Scots [from James's household] . . . and above all the Catholics lament."[67] Here were men ready to believe the worst about Buckingham—and perhaps willing to exploit the peculiar circumstances of James's final illness and death.

By early May 1625 unsettling rumours had reached William Trumbull in Brussels, who in turn began pressing James Beaulieu, a close friend at court, for information about Hamilton and James's deaths, making Beaulieu distinctly uncomfortable. Meanwhile, alarming, though somewhat garbled, stories were already circulating outside official channels. An anonymous letter dated 31 March, fearful that a Catholic poisoning campaign was working its way through Whitehall, concluded with a prayer for divine protection of "all the faythfull ones that waver not", among whom was Buckingham himself. The letter reported that "the Countess of Buckingham and some other women which were about the kinge in his sicknes applied some medecyn unto him which increased his fits".[68] In this rumour Buckingham was not a perpetrator but a potential victim, yet the letter clearly implicated his Catholic mother in the king's death. One of Mead's newsletters levelled a similar allegation:

The Countess of Buckingham, the Tuesday before [James] died, would needs make trial of some receipt she had approved; but being without the privity of the physicians, occasioned so much discontent in Dr. Craig, that he uttered some plain speeches, for which he was commanded out of the Court; the duke himself, as some say, complaining to the sick king of the words he spoke.[69]

Much fuller versions of the rumour also began to circulate. On 27 March, Pesaro maintained that shortly before James's death, Buckingham had refused to take communion with him, and when the king had asked for an explanation, the duke had complained of "internal pains", confessing that "some valet de chambre", no doubt Henry Gibb, "had announced that the duke and his mother in applying some medicaments had taken not the medicine but the poison". James had ordered the man imprisoned, and he "remains in custody by the prince's order as they suspect him of malice, because he was a dependent of Somerset, the former favourite." Ten days later, Pesaro reported that no one was convinced by these official attempts to explain away Gibb's accusation as a factional smear. The ambassador believed that "parliament will want to enquire into the rumours about poisonous applications to the disease of the defunct." Agent X was more direct. On 31 March, so alarmed that he resorted to code, he explained that "there be" those who "will say that the dukes mother hathe poisoned king james and bewitched kinge charles." Although he accused the mother, he had not forgotten about the son: "it were a greate pity but that the Christian world should take notice of these thinges especially in Scotland that the people of that nation mighte drawe from the boasome of there kinge the monster that hath set up his [nest]." It should be "the common care of christendome", X added, "to displante this canserous weede."[70]

As these reports began to spread, George Eglisham was somewhere in England, trying to evade the agents sent by Buckingham and Archbishop Abbot to find him. As a Scottish Catholic and sometime royal doctor, who had served at the dying Hamilton's bedside, Eglisham moved in the right circles to have heard talk about the tensions between James, his son and his favourite over Mansfelt, the French match and Gondomar, as well as the shocked whispers about what had happened at Theobalds. About a year after James's death, Eglisham would produce his own sensational account of events, turning the fractured rumours and anxious whispers of 1625 into a devastating narrative of murder and poison, and mounting a compelling case for why "this canserous weed" had to die.

CHAPTER FOUR

THE KING'S BRAVE WARRIOR

THE MAKING OF GEORGE EGLISHAM, c. 1585–1620

P UBLISHING UNWELCOME TRUTHS about monarchs or their ministers was a
dangerous game, best played beneath the protective cloak of anonymity.
The author of the sensational Elizabethan Catholic libel usually known as
Leicesters Commonwealth (1584) identified himself only as "A Master of Arts at
Cambridge", while the men who composed the infamous anti-episcopal Puritan
libels of the late 1580s selected the witty pseudonym "Martin Marprelate".
Thomas Scott's notorious 1620 anti-Spanish tract, *Vox Populi*, was anonymous;
Scott felt safe enough to put his own name on later works only after relocating
to the Dutch Republic. John Reynolds published his anti-Spanish pamphlets as
S. R. N. I. in the 1620s; while the refugee English Catholic polemicist Richard
Verstegan published his Hispanophile pamphlets in the early 1620s using the
final initials of his name, D. N. Of all these authors, only Reynolds was ever
caught, and then only because a friend betrayed him.

But when *The Forerunner of Revenge* appeared in the spring of 1626, its
author's name proudly adorned the title page: "M. George Eglisham, one of
King Iames his Physitians for his Majesties person above the space of ten
yeares". This was no pseudonym or fake attribution designed to put the authorities off the trail. Indeed, as readers quickly discovered, Eglisham's carefully
fashioned authorial presence—his claims about his personal history, patronage
connections, trustworthiness and expertise—lent a great deal of credibility to
The Forerunner's allegations. George Eglisham was also a known man. During
the 1610s he had established himself as a respected minor figure in the international republic of letters. Wielding a sharp scholarly pen, he had served James
I at home and abroad, and, in return, royal patronage had afforded him a
comfortable living in Jacobean London. By early 1621, far from being a
dangerous malcontent, Eglisham seemed one of the lucky ones, a man with
connections and a secure place in the world. His good fortunes would not last.
Over the course of three or four years, he found himself pushed inexorably
towards the margins of a world where he had once thrived. His secret history

would carry the deep imprint of his tumultuous, cosmopolitan life experience, his making and his unmaking.

Early Years, c. 1585–1605

George Eglisham was born some time around 1585, probably in Hamilton about thirty-five miles southwest of Edinburgh.[1] Of his childhood and family we know little, aside from what he tells in *The Forerunner*. His descent through the Lundies, lairds of Balgonie, and the cadet Hamilton branch of Silvertown Hill gave Eglisham an "interest of bloud" in the senior Hamilton line, and thus in the House of Stuart. Furthermore, the Eglishams had served the Hamiltons since his grandfather's days, with a "friendship established by mutuall obligation of most acceptable offices". This long and honourable connection meant that George grew up alongside James, the future second Marquis of Hamilton. According to *The Forerunner*, John, Lord Hamilton, presented both boys to James VI, instructed them to "kisse his Maiesties hand", and then commended Eglisham "unto his Maiesties favour", declaring that "this young man his father was the best friend that ever I had or ever shall have in this world".[2]

Eglisham spent his early years in powerful Scottish circles. Lord John, first Marquis of Hamilton from 1599, became a Privy Councillor and close friend of the king. Eglisham forged a strong friendship with Hamilton's oldest son, endeavouring, he later wrote, to "deserve of him as much commendation as my father did of his father".[3] In 1603, Hamilton's son followed James to England, assuming his father's title in 1604 and later becoming Earl of Cambridge. Meanwhile, Eglisham had taken a very different path out of Scotland. Some time in his teens he had drifted away from the Hamilton circle, eventually leaving Scotland for the Continent. Whether born into the old faith or a youthful convert, Eglisham was now a Catholic, divided from his staunchly Protestant erstwhile patrons. For the next dozen years he lived as a peripatetic Scots Catholic exile, acquiring an education and fashioning a controversial career as a physician, teacher, philosopher, poet and polemicist, while moving easily through a variety of transnational intellectual, religious and political networks.

He appears to have begun his travels in the Spanish Netherlands. A friend, the expatriate Scots intellectual Thomas Dempster, believed that Eglisham had "studied the arts assiduously at Louvain in Belgium", which suggests (along with other evidence) that he was enrolled at the famed Catholic university. The university matriculation records are lost, but he likely completed the two-year course in philosophy, studying Aristotelian logic, physics and metaphysics, and probably took the baccalaureate and licentiate degrees. A later source suggests that ill health—difficulty breathing and swallowing—may have prevented him completing studies for the masters.[4] Whether before, during or after his time at the university is unclear, but in January 1601, Eglisham was one of three men newly enrolled at The Scots College, the Jesuit seminary temporarily located in Louvain. How long he stayed at the seminary, with its "convenient house, in a good quarter, with gardens and an orchard, capable of accommodating forty persons", is not clear. But there is no evidence that he completed ordination, and Eglisham's subsequent relationship with the Jesuits suggests he might have left on bad terms.[5] In any case, by 1604 he was far from Louvain, working near Rotherham in Yorkshire as tutor to the children of the former Justice of the Peace, Sir Thomas Reresby. Reresby's religion was sufficiently orthodox for him to hold various public offices. But at some point his wife "changed her religion to papist", and thus it is possible Eglisham came to her notice through her Catholic, or the family's Scottish and Flemish, connections.[6] Unfortunately for Eglisham, he also attracted the authorities' attention: "George Egleseme a Scottishe man, a scolemaster wich teacheth the children of Sir Thomas Reresby" was cited as "A recusant" for failing to take Easter communion in 1604.[7] Whether he remained in Yorkshire after this, we cannot tell. But by 1607 at the latest he was back in Catholic Europe.

Eglisham resurfaced in Rouen in Normandy, long a haven for English and Scottish Catholic refugees, where he again found work as a teacher, now specializing in philosophy, with as many as forty students under his direction in one of the city's Benedictine schools.[8] But Eglisham once again found trouble. This time the problem was his former mentors, the Jesuits, who, Eglisham later claimed, tried to force him out of his teaching position late in 1607 as they sought to make Rouen's newly reopened Jesuit College the city's predominant educational institution. The College, which by 1605 already enrolled two thousand students, was too wealthy and well connected for Eglisham to fight off.[9] Whether he left Rouen at this point is unclear, and his movements for the next two or three years are impossible to trace.

"Un Célèbre Philosophe Médecin": Paris, 1610–12

We next catch sight of Eglisham in Paris. His name appears in the University of Paris's registers for 1610, attached to the "German Nation", but with his exact course of study within the faculty of arts unspecified. He also appears in April 1610 in the registers of the university's Faculty of Medicine as a candidate for the baccalaureate that formed the first stage in the qualification as a physician.[10] The registers record three payments from Eglisham associated with the bachelor's degree, but it seems he progressed no further in the course. After taking the baccalaureate, candidates were required to serve a two-year probationary period during which they would present and dispute three theses before receiving a licentiate degree and progressing towards the doctorate. Eglisham presented no thesis, and participated in no disputations; after 1610, he disappears from the Faculty's registers. It is unclear why his progress stalled. A note appended to his first appearance in the registers recorded the Faculty's doubts about Eglisham's qualifications, including questions about his incomplete studies at Louvain, and concerns about his character. Eglisham, it seems, "behaved with very little modesty towards his colleagues". The Faculty Censor was thus at first unwilling to admit him to the degree, and although Eglisham was able to muster supportive documentation to assuage the Faculty's concerns, this uneasy beginning may have discouraged him from taking his studies further.[11]

Soon, however, he was pursuing a different avenue of advancement, one that would put him profoundly at odds with the Parisian medical establishment—and it may have been a profound intellectual disagreement that caused Eglisham to turn his back on formal studies. By 1611 he was known about the city and at court as "a famed physician-philosopher, and teacher of philosophy in Paris". Where he taught is not yet known; a later report claimed he lectured at the "Academia Parisiensi", the university itself, but there were other outlets where he might have pursued a career as what Dempster termed a "professor of philosophy".[12] More significantly, Eglisham had by 1611 become a leading figure in the highly controversial circle of chemical doctors around the court of Louis XIII. French proponents of chemical, or spagyric, medicine were an intellectually diverse group. Some followed Paracelsus, advocating diagnoses and therapies radically different from the traditional Galenic medicine practised by most educated physicians. Others blended Galenic and Paracelsian ideas, or situated themselves in the long tradition of Christian alchemical medicine. The orthodox Galenists who dominated the university's medical faculty derided and harassed the Paracelsians and their fellow travellers, but since the reign of Henri IV the chemical physicians had found protection and patronage at court.[13] Prominent among these courtly chemical practitioners was the royal almoner Gabriel de Castaigne (or Castagne), a Franciscan friar and client of the Duc de Bellegarde. Castaigne was an outspoken advocate for the quintessential alchemical drug *aurum potabile* ("L'or potable"), a gold-infused cordial that he believed could "cure all ills". Many learned contemporaries shared his enthusiasm; one English advocate, for instance, hailed "aurum potabile" as a "Generall or universall Medicine" that "cureth most and the greatest diseases". In 1611, Castaigne published an inflammatory pamphlet in defence of the drug, claiming that not only had the cordial been approved by "the famed intellectuals" of the medieval world—Thomas Aquinas, Albertus Magnus and Raymond Lull—but that its efficacy was also recognized by many contemporary expert and learned philosophers. Castaigne named only two of these learned contemporaries. One was the famed poet and churchman Béroald de Verville; the other was "*le Sieur George Eglissem*", who would also appear, later in the tract, as a witness to the cure of a courtier given up for dead by his doctors but saved by "*l'or potable*".[14]

In November 1611 the university medical faculty denounced Castaigne's book as a tissue of "lies and frauds" and set out to prosecute its author, but

Castaigne continued to argue his case. A second edition of *L'Or Potable* appeared in 1613, incorporating new material previously circulated as a leaflet. Entitled "La Verrification de l'Or potable faict par Messieurs les Medecins de Verville & Eglissem en la presence de Reverend Pere Castagne", the additional material asserted that de Verville and Eglisham had no peers in the difficult art of dissolving gold or other metals in liquids or foods. A "small phial" of their drug, Castaigne boasted, had even been given to the young king, Louis XIII.[15] Castaigne repeated this claim in his 1615 pamphlet, *Le Grand Miracle de Nature Metalique*, in which he added Louis to the list of worthies, dead and alive, who had approved the drug. The king had further signalled his support by appointing as his "Conseiller & Medecin ordinaire" the "famed philosopher, Master Eglisham".[16]

For Castaigne, Eglisham's endorsement gave "*l'or potable*" intellectual credibility, but whether that credibility stemmed from Eglisham's reputation as a philosopher or from his supposed expertise or success as a physician, we cannot tell. It is also unclear whether he had ever received formal medical training beyond whatever courses he attended at the Paris Faculty before taking his baccalaureate; though it is possible he could have acquired some earlier training from the medical faculty at Louvain. Neither institution, however, would have exposed him to Paracelsian ideas.[17] Whatever the source of his medical education, Eglisham's commitment to "*l'or potable*", and his close ties to Castaigne and Verville, put him firmly among the "chemical physicians" in the bitter disputes that wracked the Parisian medical world. Within a year of taking his baccalaureate at the university, Eglisham had placed himself completely beyond the Faculty's pale.

Like many spagyrists, including Castaigne, Eglisham remained eclectic in his approach, and probably did not subscribe to the complete overthrow of the Galenic system. Dempster characterized his friend as "greatly learned in spagyric medicine", but thought his practice "neither too hostile to Galen nor overly committed to chemistry".[18] Eglisham's promotion of "*l'or potable*" does, however, suggest intriguing possibilities about his world view. He almost certainly dabbled in the medieval and Renaissance alchemical literature that first discussed gold's medicinal properties, and he probably knew the writings of Paracelsus and his followers, despite their close ties to reformed religion. But he was probably most comfortable in the Castaigne milieu, in which alchemical medicine was a priestly calling, a work of Christian charity carried out by men who saw themselves as heirs to a long tradition of monkish chemists in the style of Roger Bacon.[19] But Eglisham was not simply interested in medicinal gold as a theoretical possibility; he also had the technical skills to manufacture the drug. According to the most vocal English promoter of *aurum potabile*, Francis Anthony, gold in its normal condition had no medicinal potency; it had to be "Philosophically opened, resolved and made potable", its "latent and hidden virtues" unlocked by the chemist's art. Only distillation and dissolution would transform the "grosse body" of the metal "into a subtile, penetrant and volatile nature", and thus "exalt" it "into the full activitie of a most precious Medicine".[20] How Eglisham did this, we do not know, but the fact that he did it reveals his serious engagement with one form of early modern experimental chemistry.

His Paris years also taught Eglisham valuable political lessons. After dropping out of the Faculty of Medicine, he occupied a marginal place in academic medical culture, but his connections at court gave him both freedom to experiment and access to royal rewards. His years in the capital also exposed him to the complex intra-Catholic and inter-confessional fault lines in regency France, and to the sometimes unpredictable ways in which religious difference shaped contemporary intellectual life. In addition to the disputes over chemical medicine, Eglisham became peripherally involved in the University of Paris's attempt to prevent the Jesuits establishing a teaching presence there. During court hearings late in 1611 the university's advocate attacked the Jesuits as disseminators of poisonous political doctrines and insisted that no state could survive if its youth were exposed to such teachers. Wherever Jesuits had established an educational foothold, the advocate noted, they did not rest until they had driven out all rival forms of instruction. Among the cases he cited was Eglisham's experience in Rouen:

> [T]heir ordinary practises in places where they are established, may make us iudge sufficientlie of their intention, in that they receive no doctrine, nor instruction, but from those of their owne society. Master George Englisemnis [sic] would have read Philosophie at Rouen ... but [was] ... hindered by them.

The Jesuits' lawyer denied the accusation, arguing that Eglisham had taught at Rouen during 1607 without any conflict with the philosophy lecturer at the Jesuit College. Eglisham had maintained a healthy number of students and had even allowed his charges to participate in disputations with the Jesuits' pupils, both at the College and at the Benedictine Church of St Ouen. The Jesuits never tried to prevent Eglisham from teaching, their lawyer claimed; indeed, Eglisham only started complaining about their influence after completing his course, and had stopped teaching "without being solicited by any Jesuit, either directly or indirectly".[21]

How comfortable Eglisham was in this Parisian political, religious and intellectual crossfire is difficult to say; neither the Paris Faculty of Medicine nor the Jesuits were enemies to be taken lightly. By the opening weeks of 1612, as the Faculty bore down on Castaigne, Eglisham may well have been looking for a way out.

Vorstius and Huygens: The Hague, 1612–13

Eglisham's Parisian sojourn ended abruptly, early in 1612, when he headed north to the Dutch Republic.[22] He left to serve the Scottish king who now sat on the English throne, in the final stages of the campaign James had orchestrated against the controversial German theologian Conrad Vorstius (Vorst).[23] In 1611, Vorstius had succeeded Jacob Arminius as professor of divinity at the University of Leiden. Arminius's teachings on predestination had deeply divided the Dutch Republic into Remonstrant (Arminian) and Counter-Remonstrant (Calvinist or Gomarist) parties. Vorstius was the Remonstrant candidate for Arminius's chair, "an irenic liberal" who had clashed with Calvinist scholars in Heidelberg, and whose writings were "marked by Socinian tendencies".[24] Concerned by the appointment's religious and political implications, and convinced that Vorstius's 1610 *Tractatus theologicus de Deo sive De natura et attributis Dei* was riddled with dangerously heretical, indeed atheistical, opinions, James and his ambassador, Sir Ralph Winwood, pressured the Dutch to rescind the appointment and banish Vorstius, lest "the reformed Religion suffer by the Entertainment in the University of Leyden of this Atheist and Heretick". The English campaign against "so Monstrous an Atheist" continued for most of the following year. Winwood continuously lobbied the Dutch authorities and offered support to Counter-Remonstrant polemicists. James composed a declaration against Vorstius, which was presented to the Dutch States General and published in French, Latin, English and Dutch editions early in 1612.[25] The English also recruited various writers for the campaign. In January 1612, Winwood reported that "many Pieces" against Vorstius had appeared in the press, but he wanted more. The previous month he had asked the English agent in Brussels whether he knew of any "smart Jesuite who hath a quick and nimble Spirit" and who might, with appropriate coaching, write "a few Lines agaynst the Atheisms of thys Wretch". Vorstius's writings, he added, provided "Matter enough for a Wit that hath either Spirit or Courage". Satire was particularly welcome; "I look for no solemn Work," Winwood claimed.[26]

In mid-March 1612 the States of Holland decided that Vorstius should be "dislodged from Leyden" and confined to Gouda, where he was ordered to spend the next eighteen months defending himself, in writing, against "all those Heresies wherewith he is charged". James, however, wanted Vorstius's banishment, and continued to apply pressure.[27] The terms of Vorstius's exile in Gouda required that he answer not only "such bookes, and writings" already produced against him, but also any that "shalbe published against him, within these three months next ensuying". If his replies to his critics were deemed acceptable, then Vorstius would be readmitted to the Leiden chair; if not, the States of Holland would "banish him, with shame and ignominy, owt of theyr Province".[28] In the spring of 1612, then, the time was ripe for Vorstius's enemies to unleash a final burst of criticism. It was Eglisham's moment. Constantijn Huygens, who was soon to know Eglisham well, believed that he was "brought with great haste into these parts, more for the sake of his king than for his own religion or conscience". Whether Eglisham took the initiative or whether someone recruited him is not clear. But he headed north primarily to serve James I. Perhaps his track record as a philosopher in Paris made him a particularly appealing candidate to challenge a theologian whose own religious ideas were rooted in rigorous philosophizing.[29] How closely Eglisham worked with English agents is unclear—Winwood's surviving correspondence mentions neither Eglisham nor his publications—but his impact in The Hague was dramatic.

From the start, Eglisham showed a talent for polemical theatre. On his arrival he challenged Vorstius to a public debate, a brash gesture that grabbed attention, and after Vorstius wisely declined the invitation, Eglisham turned to the press. In Delft in the spring and early summer of 1612 he published two learned Latin books, which blended polemical jibes with technical philosophical critique and taunted Vorstius to "appear and defend himself".[30] *Crisis Vorstiani Responsi*, published in April, hyperbolically accused Vorstius of "Atheism, Paganism, Judaism, Turcism, Heresy, Schism, and Ignorance" (Fig. 26). Divided into ten sections, the book subjected Vorstius's opinions to robust critique, including syllogistic analysis; different sections focused on different errors, and tables

Figure 26: Title page of George Eglisham, *Crisis Vorstiani Responsi*, 1612, the first of his two pamphlets supporting James I's campaign against the theologian Conrad Vorstius (Balliol College, Oxford).

clarified the theologian's flawed logic. Eglisham concluded his assault with three polemical epigrams.[31] His brash tone appealed to the Dutch anti-Vorstians. Newsletters to the leading Calvinist Sibrandus Lubbertus alerted him to the book in late April, and reported Eglisham's pledge to expose Vorstius's appalling lack of philosophical rigour. Eglisham, they noted, was a Scottish doctor practising medicine at The Hague and a "most learned man and most skilled philosopher" with years of teaching experience in France. The book also attracted attention from Vorstius's supporters, and Nicolaus Hasius issued a broadside attacking Eglisham and offering to refute him on Vorstius's behalf. Reports circulated that Eglisham had penned a reply to Hasius, but it does not appear to have been printed.[32]

The anti-Vorstians waited expectantly for Eglisham's next move. In mid-May, Abraham Williams alerted William Trumbull in Brussels to the impending appearance of "something out in printe against Vorstius which shallbe as it is expected somewhat extraordinary", but this "booke against Vorstius made by a Scottsman" was continually delayed. On 29 May, Williams thought the book was "now in the presse", but a fortnight later he reported that it was "not yet come owt".[33] The book eventually appeared in July; it incorporated addresses and epistles variously dated from May to July, which suggests that Eglisham delayed publication as he added new material. The *Hypocrisis Apologeticae Orationis Vorstianae* singled out for particular scorn the "apologetical oration" that Vorstius had delivered to the States of Holland in March 1612 (Fig. 27). Again, Eglisham branded the German an atheist and offered a ten-part philosophical critique, this time focusing on controversial claims about God's infinity, immutability, omnipotence and omniscience. As in the *Crisis*, Eglisham concluded with a trio of epigrams, this time augmented by polemical anagrams of Vorstius's name.[34] Rumours circulated that Vorstius had at last been stung into action. In mid-August 1612 an informant notified Trumbull that the much-anticipated Vorstius–Eglisham public debate would occur "in a few days". Whether the debate took place or how it turned out if it did, we do not know. Writing much later in the century, Pierre Bayle implied that Vorstius had wisely "suffered the challenges of this" well-connected "Scotchman to fall to the ground".[35]

Eglisham's theatrics caught the attention of Christiaan Huygens, secretary to the Dutch Council of State. After discreet inquiries, Huygens discovered that Eglisham was a seasoned philosopher with several (now lost) publications on metaphysics and theology. Impressed by Eglisham's knowledge and seemingly straightforward character, Huygens offered him a position tutoring his teenage sons, Maurits and Constantijn, who were being groomed for public service. It is possible that Winwood may have brokered this job offer as the king's "preliminary recompense" for Eglisham's pamphleteering, though Huygens's own anti-Vorstian inclinations might have drawn him to Eglisham in any case. At the very least, Huygens probably consulted the ambassador, with whom he "freely and familiarly conversed", before making the appointment.[36]

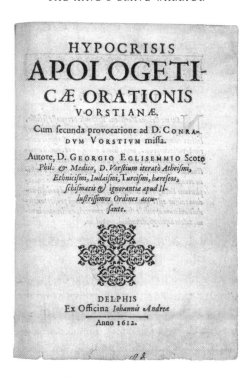

Figure 27: Title page of George Eglisham, *Hypocrisis Apologeticae Orationis Vorstianae*, 1612, his second pamphlet against Vorstius (Bodleian Library).

Between the late spring of 1612 and the autumn of 1613, Eglisham taught the Hugyens sons and two other young men, one Dutch, the other French. The fifteen-year-old Constantijn and his older brother Maurits had already studied Latin, Greek, French, grammar, prosody, rhetoric, mathematics and art. So in July 1612, after working through a "not completely useless" treatise on disputations, Eglisham and his pupils embarked on a rigorous ten-month course in logic. Writing a decade and a half later, his intellectual world now transformed by Baconian natural philosophy, Constantijn recalled only the crushing boredom of Eglisham's antiquated thought, and painted a faintly comical picture of his tutor, flush with enthusiasm, mounting the lectern to torture his pupils with Aristotle and his mind-numbing sixteenth-century commentators. In May 1613, doubtless to the boys' relief, Eglisham switched to geography and astronomy, during which he may have demonstrated his facility with astrological computation. Perhaps in these final weeks, Eglisham also showed off his familiarity with the hermetic ideas popular among the Parisian chemists.[37] Although the logic classes had been hard to stomach, Constantijn Huygens retained a genuine admiration for his teacher. His autobiography claimed that Eglisham was a man "with whom he would have been as readily prepared to live as to die, if he were his companion in travel or study", while a much later poem fondly remembered the "famous Scottish athlete", the die-hard philosophical Aristotelian with a strong, fierce voice.[38]

The Irregular Extraordinary Royal Physician: London, 1614–20

In the summer of 1618, Constantijn Huygens accompanied the English ambassador, Sir Dudley Carleton, back to London, the first of four visits to England that transformed the young Dutchman's thinking and shaped his political career. During this first trip, Huygens met many powerful, cultivated men, but he also found time to call on his old tutor. On 11 June, Huygens told his family that he planned to visit "Eglisemius" the following day. He had teasingly sent word that "a Dutchman wanted to see him", but "he doesn't know it's me".[39]

Eglisham had settled in England some time between late 1613 and the following September. In his letter home, Huygens reported that James had rewarded Eglisham for his anti-Vorstian efforts with "un bon benefice", "a good reward", although Huygens did not specify what it was.[40] The pursuit of further reward would dominate George Eglisham's next six or seven years in England. His work on the Vorstius campaign had taught him how to play the game; now he tried to transmute his continued royal service into gold. By no later than September 1614, Eglisham was actively pursuing a medical practice in or around London where alchemical and Paracelsian medicine had long found favour in courtly circles. The London College of Physicians, which by royal charter attempted to regulate the practice of medicine in and around the City, remained uneasy about the new thinking. It had moderated its militant defence of Galenism and admitted a few notable chemical physicians as fellows, and it would soon incorporate chemical medicines into its official pharmacopoeia.[41] Yet conflicts remained, and one of them may have given Eglisham pause. He undoubtedly knew of the College's harassment of Francis Anthony, England's most outspoken proponent and prescriber of *aurum potabile*. The College had denied Anthony a licence and spent nearly two years trying to prevent him from practising his art. Between 1602 and 1616 the College cited him on at least seventeen occasions; in 1609 it oversaw a public trial of Anthony's concoction; in 1611 it sponsored Matthew Gwinne's printed critique of it; and in 1614 the Censors explored allegations of malpractice following the death of one of Anthony's patients. Although the College eased the harassment in the later 1610s, orthodox Galenists continued to identify *aurum potabile* as a dangerous drug, and to attack Anthony as an unlearned empiric hawking a fraudulent universal remedy for personal profit.[42]

The hounding of Francis Anthony probably worried Eglisham, and may also partially explain his uneasy history with the College. In late September 1614, Eglisham appeared before the College for his "examination"—presumably to get a licence—but the appointment was postponed for a week and apparently never rescheduled. The physicians, however, did not forget him. In May 1618, Francis Herring, a prominent fellow of the College, "made a complaint against Dr. Eglesom, of Scotland", and the College summoned him for questioning. In November 1619 another complaint was lodged, this time concerning "a certain Collison", perhaps a dissatisfied patient. Neither complaint went anywhere. The College Annals record no follow-up proceedings on the Herring charge, and the Fellows deferred further "investigation" of the Collison case and never returned to it.[43] Likewise, since no evidence suggests that either the College or the Church ever licensed Eglisham as physician, he must have practised medicine in London as an unlicensed "irregular", always vulnerable to the College's disciplinary attentions.[44] Why he failed to obtain a licence remains a puzzle. The College records do not specify any intellectual or personal shortcomings. Eglisham was a Scot, a Catholic, the product of foreign education, and a proponent of chemical medicine; perhaps he concluded that even if none of these facts by itself would have prevented the College from denying him a licence, all four of them together were bound to doom his chances. Perhaps, like others, he thought the annual licentiate fees extortionate. But the College's well-publicized pursuit of Francis Anthony may also have convinced Eglisham that he was better off steering clear of such a sceptical audience. His Parisian experience had taught him that with the right patrons and court connections, he could run a lucrative practice without the College's blessing. After all, Anthony had survived in large part because he had well-connected patients willing to vouch for and protect him. Eglisham may have assumed that his chemical expertise could also find patients, and that connections at court would protect him if and when the College took action. The peculiarly abortive nature of the disciplinary attempts of 1618 and 1619 suggest his faith in patronage was not misplaced.[45]

Much about Eglisham's medical practice is difficult to gauge. We know only two of his patients. Nicholas Withington, a hard-drinking merchant, gaoled in the London Compter by the East India Company on his return from India, had developed a "great malladye and sicknesse", which he attributed to his "greife" at the Company's "ungratefull oppression" and his "loathsome imprisonment". Eglisham apparently took "pittye" on Withington and "in charitye" treated and cured him late in 1616.[46] Eglisham's other known patient was his old friend and patron the Marquis of Hamilton, whose final illness in 1625 would inspire *The Forerunner of Revenge*. It is also impossible to determine how lucrative Eglisham's practice was. There was money to be made in London as a chemical physician specializing in *aurum potabile*: by the late 1610s, Francis Anthony, who charged 20 shillings for a 4-ounce dose, was becoming a rich man, but Eglisham does not appear to have been as lucky.[47] Indeed, the difficulties of making a living in London's crowded medical marketplace may have briefly encouraged Eglisham to look elsewhere. In 1616 he published a collection of blank astrological charts designed for medical use (Fig. 28). This type of publication was typically used as advertising, so it may be significant that he had the book printed by Andrew Hart in Edinburgh.[48] However, the publication may have been intended not to mark Eglisham's permanent return home, but to mark a visit, perhaps on family business, or perhaps in anticipation of James VI and I's 1617 progress to Scotland, his first visit north of the border since 1603. For the book also recorded just how far Eglisham had come: according to its title page, George Eglisham was now "Doctoris Medici Regii", the king's physician.

In 1626, *The Forerunner* would make the same claim, introducing Eglisham as "one of King Iames his Physitians for his Majesties person" for the past ten years. Eglisham also laid claim to the title in print in a 1618 work of neo-Latin poetry, and many contemporaries recognized his office. His patient Nicholas Withington termed him "One of His Majesty's doctors of phisicke", while a co-signatory to a loan recalled that Eglisham "alleaged himselfe to be the kinges

Figure 28: Title page of George Eglisham, *Accurata Methodus erigendi thematis natalitii*, a book of blank astrological charts for use in medical practice, printed in Edinburgh in 1616 and advertising Eglisham's title as royal physician (Huntington Library).

Servant", and thus immune to arrest if he defaulted. William Barclay's 1620 critique of his friend's recent work addressed Eglisham as "Medico Regio", and a 1621 petition to Parliament described "Doctor Eglesham" as "one of his Maiesties Phisitians".[49] *The Forerunner* would provoke controversy and critique for over three decades, but none of its legions of critics ever questioned its author's claims to have been the king's physician.

Unfortunately, the exact nature of his office remains mysterious.[50] Records of many appointments to the king's medical staff are lost, and no trace of Eglisham can be found in the Close or Patent Rolls, Exchequer documents, or in the patchy Lord Chamberlain's records.[51] He clearly was not one of the roughly four to six "ordinary" royal doctors who regularly attended the king; the members of this group are all well known, and because they were paid, there was a limit on their number. If Eglisham was a royal doctor, he was most likely one of the heterogeneous group of "extraordinary" royal doctors who had neither a salary nor the right to dine at court. Although the office came with no money, it did offer Eglisham distinct material benefits: he could advertise his appointment to lure in new patients, and use his status as royal servant to keep creditors at arm's length. If Castaigne can be trusted, Eglisham had received a similar office from Louis XIII, and the new title may have proved useful for a physician hoping to make a living in London's furiously competitive medical marketplace while avoiding the unwelcome attentions of the College of Physicians.[52]

Duellum Poeticum, 1618–20

Eglisham practised physic, but continued to write. His second major venture into print was at first glance very different from his work in Holland, but like the attacks on Vorstius, Eglisham's new work was designed primarily to assist James I. The book Eglisham published late in 1618 was an eccentric compilation of neo-Latin poetry and literary criticism in which, styling himself as "the king's doctor", he challenged the late George Buchanan, "the king's tutor", to a *duellum poeticum*, a poetic duel, for the best Latin paraphrase of the 104th Psalm (Fig. 29).[53] Eglisham could not have chosen a more formidable target: Buchanan's psalm paraphrases were widely admired and frequently reprinted, and many considered his version of Psalm 104 a "masterpiece".

Unsurprisingly, Eglisham's hubris created a small sensation; a second edition appeared in London in 1619 and possibly a third in Paris the same year.[54] But the book was much more than a literary critique. *Duellum Poeticum* was also a calculated intervention in Anglo-Scottish ecclesiastical controversy, supporting the king's controversial new policies in the Scottish Kirk by attacking two titans of Scots Reformed Calvinism. In addition, the book presented James with a subtly fashioned portrait of George Eglisham as not only a grateful recipient of past rewards but also a suitor seeking new ones.

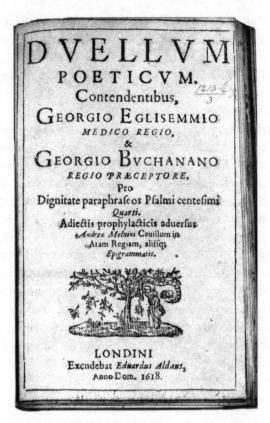

Figure 29: Title page of George Eglisham, *Duellum Poeticum*, a 1618 work of literary criticism, neo-Latin poetry and Stuart panegyric (Huntington Library).

James had long struggled to break the hard-line Calvinists' power in the Scottish Church. Years earlier, he had managed to graft a weak episcopal structure onto the Kirk, but in 1616 he proposed five new canons, or general principles, that would bring the Scottish Church much closer into line with its English counterpart. Even his bishops worried that the proposals, which included requirements on kneeling at communion, might go too far too soon, and after they were forced through the general assembly at Perth in 1618, the hard-line Calvinist reaction was predictably quick. From his billet in London, Eglisham took up the royal cause. His condemnation of George Buchanan mixed highly technical literary critique with an implicit religio-political attack. He conceded that the king's old tutor had written "many things brightly, truly, and politely" and even "rather ingeniously", but Eglisham accused Buchanan of pouring forth "many things falsely, foully, more rudely and more stupidly". Sometimes his style was "grave", but at others it was "puerile"; sometimes he preached truth, but "at others . . . things most alien from the truth". Eglisham accused Buchanan of various crimes against poetic excellence, critiquing his prosody, repetition, rhyming, elision and digression, and systematically contrasting Buchanan's paraphrase not only with Eglisham's own but also with earlier translations by St Jerome, Arias Montanus, Tremellius and Junius. Eglisham's Buchanan was not simply a failed neo-Latinist. The icon of Reformed religious purity and the eloquent apologist for political resistance to wicked monarchs like Mary, Queen of Scots was guilty of "impiety towards God, perfidy to his prince and tyranny to the muses", however much he remained the hero of what Eglisham suggestively dubbed "the impure assembly of the Puritans".[55]

Eglisham attacked other Calvinist heroes. After his psalm paraphrase came a suite of six "epigrammata prophylactica" that savaged the hard-line Presbyterian leader Andrew Melville and his notorious 1606 Latin epigram "on the royal altar". Melville's poem had denounced the "popish" liturgy and furnishings of the English royal chapel as dangerous warning signs of what a king besotted by Anglican ceremonialism might impose on the Scottish Kirk. For Melville, the closed books, unlit candles and empty basins on the royal altar were marks of religious corruption, evidence of a Church "Blind of her sight, and buried in her dross". Garbed in "Romish dress", the king's altar bore witness to a Church subservient to the "purple whore" of popery. James imprisoned Melville for his epigram, which quickly became a target of various poetic ripostes. The furor over the Articles of Perth gave Melville's epigram new currency, and Eglisham seized the chance to attack it anew. His six epigrams played on the real spiritual meanings of the candles, books and basins, exposing Melville's inability to perceive their religious lessons. "With its basins, books, and lights", Eglisham wrote, "the sacred altar instructs you, O England, with royal warnings." He argued that a correctly focused spiritual vision would grasp these objects' metaphoric resonance; by understanding their meaning, the pious worshipper could approach the sacred mysteries of the Christian faith. "Receive the lights not with the eye, but with the mind," he wrote. "Close off the books from profane things, and fill the dry basins with tears." These mysteries, this "worshipful experience" and the "sense of God", were unavailable to poor "Furious", "unclean" Melville, "puffed up" as he was "with self love". But they lay open to the English whom Melville had so misguidedly disdained.[56]

Eglisham supplemented his defence of royal ecclesiastical policy with panegyric verses to the Stuart dynasty. His four poems on Prince Charles drew from the prophetic genealogical researches of the Scots scholar James Maxwell, whom Eglisham called a "most learned antiquary", and who argued that James's reign was the harbinger of a glorious future for an imperial Britain. James and his new British Church would lead Christendom into peaceful reconciliation, while Charles would lead the reunited Christendom in a war of conquest against the Turk. Eglisham's verses rehearsed Maxwell's claims about the prince's auspicious genealogy, including his supposed descent from the house of Austria and from earlier kings named Charles—the Fair, the Hammer, the Great, the Wise, the Bold and the Pious—all of whose virtues the prince now embodied.[57]

Duellum Poeticum was also a careful piece of self-presentation and self-promotion. As loyal servant of the Stuart dynasty, Eglisham denounced Buchanan for denigrating James's mother and preaching the abhorrent doctrine of political resistance. Eglisham extended this political self-fashioning with his prefatory epistles to James, himself a translator of Psalm 104 and in many ways the poet's primary imagined reader. Eglisham signed one epistle as the king's "humble subject, faithful servant, and brave warrior" and another as the king's "*Addictissimus Famulus*"—his "most devoted servant". Two of the shorter poems in the collection spoke directly to Eglisham's relationship with James, highlighting the pattern of service and reward that bound them together. The first imagined what Eglisham had said to James "when he solicited the position of physician to the king". Harkening back to his youth, he recalled how "great your voice has breathed in Hamilton's citadel" and hoped that "royal deeds" continued to "sound so great to me". As he petitioned for his place, Eglisham presented himself as a son beseeching his father. Since his own father was dead, Eglisham had "sworn that I wish that you will be a father to me". "Either raise [my] father from the grave", Eglisham challenged James, "or render yourself as a new father to me." "O time and again my Muses [will be] . . . blessed by you, my father," Eglisham wrote, "if your orders shall establish me as your physician." This petition was followed swiftly by a poem of thanks, which acknowledged that words were not enough to pay his debt: "What thanks shall I pay you, O greatest king of kings? Neither are my words or vows pleasing enough. . . . None of my gifts are worthy of so great a prince, and none of my gifts are equal to your gifts."[58]

Having commemorated his earlier reward, and having once more taken up his pen in the king's defence, Eglisham also highlighted his political and intellectual connections in Britain and across the Continent, perhaps in hopes of demonstrating his qualifications for future royal patronage. Thomas Dempster's commendatory verse alluded to Eglisham's success in Paris. Epitaphs on Thomas Hamilton, Lord Priestfield, a loyal supporter of Mary, Queen of Scots, and the father of James's current Scottish Secretary of State, linked Eglisham to the Scottish political establishment. A poem in praise of Enno III, the Lutheran Count of East Friesland, illustrated Eglisham's contacts across the continental religious divide. His verse commending the Franco-Scots physician Henry Blackwood demonstrated his friendship with a prominent Marian family well established in Parisian intellectual circles. Finally, his lines on the teenage prodigy Bathsua Reginald, daughter of a London schoolmaster and recent author of a multilingual book of royal panegyric, linked Eglisham to another Stuart poetic loyalist at work in his adopted home town.[59]

Although some modern scholars admire Eglisham's literary criticism, his assault on Buchanan's famed paraphrase attracted a mostly hostile contemporary response. Constantijn Huygens's friend Daniel Heinsius was unimpressed, and two prominent Scots leapt to Buchanan's defence. Arthur Johnston, professor of logic, metaphysics and medicine at the Huguenot University of Sedan, was particularly scathing, while William Barclay, an old Paris friend of Eglisham's and a fellow Catholic poet and physician, joined the attack.[60] Johnston's satire diagnosed Eglisham with a dangerous "madness" and mocked him as "Hypermorus Medicaster"—"Idiot Quack". In another poem Johnston dubbed Eglisham "Onopordus", a somewhat opaque Greek pun meaning something like "flatulent ass" or "Ass's Fart". He also mocked Eglisham's medical skills: when, miraculously, the curse of mortality was lifted from the human race, Johnston wrote, Onopordus was sent from Hades to Holland to re-establish death's dominion over the world by killing off countless patients with his incompetence. Although confined to the learned consumers of neo-Latin poetry and literary criticism, this satirical mauling may have damaged Eglisham's reputation. One contemporary reader of *The Forerunner* described Eglisham as "a kind of mad Scottish poet and physician . . . a doctor whom his own countrymen held half frantic before", a characterization that suggests the continued influence of Johnston's hatchet job on Eglisham's domestic fame.[61] Yet this humiliation was a small price to pay for a book so clearly designed to please an audience of one.

The Company of Gold and Silverbeaters

Eglisham would have denied any suggestion that his continued pursuit of royal favour could be reduced to anything so crass as a mercenary desire for material self-advancement. Service to the king had metaphysical rewards—"you are a great part of my soul", he told the king in one of his poems; "you who give laws to the British people give hope, O James, to my muses." But that service also deserved tangible recognition. Another of *Duellum Poeticum*'s poems to James played with the language of gold, the stuff of Eglisham's medical experiments and the quintessential symbol of royal authority and material reward. "A golden love urges on my muses", Eglisham wrote; and he hungered to see "the secrets of ornamented gold . . . revealed". The king's "golden signs rose" at his birth, thanks to his mother, "the golden goddess", and to "the golden lineage of your blood". Just as the gods gave the king his "golden fates", so too James's reign ushered in for "Britons a golden age". The conceit had endless possibilities. James's "mind", the "sweet eloquence" of his "speech", his very "tongue"—all were "golden". His care for his people was "golden" too, and it naturally followed that his wife was "the golden queen", "a golden nymph" who gave birth to "golden progeny". On he went. "Your kingdoms are golden, your vigour is golden, and so is your form; you move golden scepters with golden fingers". Even James's misfortunes were "golden evils". Indeed "Your life is golden, and after you have done so many golden things,/may a golden Fate end your golden days at a late time." The "golden poem" concluded with an audacious plea: "since everything is simultaneously golden for this golden king, will you not bestow golden gifts upon me?"[62] Within months, Eglisham had his "golden gift", one that promised not only significant material benefits but also a place in the power structures of his adopted city.

Eglisham's Catholicism may have compromised his attempts to build a thriving medical practice, but it gave him access to fellow believers, many of whom operated with relative impunity on the fringes of the court. Among these well-connected crypto-Catholics was Sir Henry Britton, a man who kept his religious views quiet, but whose openly Catholic friends and family left him, as a 1621 parliamentary committee noted, widely "suspected for his Religion".[63] During the 1610s, Britton had become unusually skilled in one of the court's most lucrative fiscal games: the granting of royal patents and monopolies to "projectors" peddling inventions and schemes guaranteed to make money for the cash-strapped Crown, while simultaneously filling their own pockets.

Contemporaries generally accepted that those who had developed a new invention or manufacturing process deserved special compensation, but Parliament had long taken a dim view of monopolies over the production or retail of everyday items like starch and soap, or that delegated royal regulatory powers to profit-hungry consortiums of private men. The wholesale privatization of royal powers to regulate industry and commerce seemed an unconscionable betrayal of the common good. But aside from a short and contentious session in 1614, James did not call Parliament between 1610 and 1620–21. In the interim, projectors swarmed Whitehall and the king, desperate for ready money, listened to their schemes. Generally, a substantial share of the profits from these projects went to the king, or to a royal servant, who would take the rewards in lieu of other compensation. To get into the game, a projector needed connections at court. But a projector with both the right connections and a history of uncompensated service to the Crown was in an even better position.

By 1619, Britton had acquired an impressive track record as a projector. In 1614 he had persuaded James to appoint a commission—with Sir Henry in it—to investigate parks and warrens. Owners who failed to secure the necessary royal permissions would have to pay Britton and his associates a fine, a portion of which theoretically went to the Exchequer. In 1618, James named Britton to another commission, this time to investigate, and fine, those landlords who had recently converted arable land into pasture. In addition, Britton also secured a royal patent granting him the sole right to produce and market a type of hard wax. Finally, in 1619, he began talking to George Eglisham about another scheme: this one concerned foliat—gold and silver leaf.[64]

A luxury product, foliat adorned the lavish bindings of expensive books, the exteriors of coaches and cutlery, and the interiors of rich men's homes. Eglisham knew gold—what it could do and how it could be worked—and probably at Britton's urging, he entered into a partnership with a half-dozen other men involved in the trade. One of these, William Spencer, had developed a new method for making foliat that produced better-quality leaf at a lower price. The new technique presented a dazzling business opportunity. Foliat had long been manufactured in England, but the domestic industry had declined greatly in the face of cheaper Dutch imports. Furthermore, the economic crisis then deepening across the Continent and drying up the supply of coin threatened to kill off the trade completely. In February 1619, desperate to prevent "Moneys and Coyne" from being "turned into any dead Masse of Plate" and to forestall "the promiscuous use of Gold and Silver Foliate", James banned the use of foliat in "Building, Seeling, Wainscot, Bedsteads, Chayres, Stooles, Coaches or any other Ornament whatsoever, except it be Armour in weapons, or in Armes and Ensignes of Honour, at funerals or Monuments of the dead". He further ordered that foliat could no longer be produced by melting down English coins; it had to come exclusively from "old plate, forraigne Bullion or Coyne".[65] Eglisham and his partners offered the king an alternative: he should establish a company whose members had the exclusive right to manufacture and sell cheaper and better-quality foliat, using Spencer's new technique. They had in mind a small organization, at most thirty men, and they aimed to elevate these "goldbeaters" to the status of the City's chartered companies, with their attendant monopolies and political and commercial powers.

Britton knew the projecting game, but Eglisham knew how to approach the king and had recently done him a service for which he had not yet been compensated. Although Britton was "coadiutor" and Spencer "the proiector", Eglisham was at the centre of the scheme. When the patent was attacked two years later, it was described as the "Patent of Dr. Eglesham of gold and silver foliatte".[66] It was the king's physician and "brave warrior" who would help broker the goldbeaters' project at court, using his contacts to secure the patent and his own "golden reward" for half a dozen years of loyal service.

The Crown's initial fears that the new company might melt down English coins already in critically short supply were quickly assuaged when the putative company members swore their foliat would come exclusively from imported bullion. More importantly, twelve Master Goldbeaters would each guarantee this promise by depositing a £500 bond in the Exchequer, in effect, a sizeable donation to the cash-starved regime. Once the deal was made—the company offered the Crown a yearly rent of 26s 8d and an annual fee of £7—the Crown issued a patent creating a company with six wardens, twelve Masters, and a maximum fellowship of thirty goldbeaters. The new company would also have a principal Master, appointed for life. The Attorney General, Sir Henry Yelverton, and the Solicitor General, Sir Thomas Coventry, drew up the patent, and on 11 October 1619, James signed it, making George Eglisham Master for Life of the Goldbeaters Company of London.[67]

With the new office came status. In short order, a representative of Eglisham's new company stood before Wardens of the Goldsmiths Company, one of the London's Great Twelve Livery Companies, asking for their advice and acceptance. Eglisham's office also brought in a salary of £3 per week, which, with other emoluments, added up to some £200 a year.[68] It was money he sorely needed, and it made him a man of substance in London.

Bacon House

Walking north from St Paul's Cathedral across Cheapside and along Foster Lane, a Jacobean Londoner would eventually arrive at Noble Street in Aldersgate Ward (Fig. 30). The street stood in the heart of an affluent and socially distinguished neighbourhood: the halls of two of the twelve great livery companies, the Haberdashers and the Goldsmiths, stood close by, and the Guildhall was only a short distance away.[69] At Noble Street's northern end sat another impressive building, one that contemporaries knew as Bacon House. Its west front ran 70 feet along Noble Street, with a gateway leading visitors into a courtyard. Its southern walls ran along Oat Lane, while its back garden stretched eastwards to abut the Parish Church of St Mary Staining. During the 1550s, Sir Nicholas Bacon, Elizabeth I's Lord Keeper, had remodelled the late-medieval building, creating three inhabitable floors built around the central courtyard (Fig. 31). The ground floor boasted kitchens, a washing house and "A Greate Halle with a Chimney", and two cellars underneath. The first floor had nine rooms, some designated as offices or studies, many wainscoted, several quite large, and one that in 1612 was "honge with painted clothes". A chamber, a study and several garrets occupied the floor above, while a 70-foot walkway supporting a first-floor gallery ran along the south side of the garden.[70]

The house had seen various residents and uses since Bacon's remodelling. The Recorder of London, William Fleetwood, had lived there for four years, and in 1579, Christopher Barker, the Queen's printer, took a lease on the property, which he bought outright in 1585. Barker and his son Robert based their extensive printing operations there for many years. Nicholas Goffe (or Geffe) and his son, also called Nicholas, briefly owned the property early in James's reign; one of them was a projector who addressed a 1607 treatise on silkworms "from Bacon House". The property then passed to George Smythes, an influential goldsmith and alderman who served as Sheriff of London in 1611–12. When Smythes died in 1615, his widow Sarah took control of the property. She remarried in 1616, and her new husband, Sir Arthur Savage, an old soldier who now served as Vice-Treasurer and Privy Councillor in Ireland, spent most of his time away from London. Savage's finances were shaky—he would die a debtor in 1632—and Lady Sarah's need for revenue during his long absences may have encouraged her to bring a co-owner and co-resident into Bacon House.[71]

When the property was sold to the scrivener Charles Bostock in 1628 for £810, the deed of conveyance described the house as "late in the occupation of

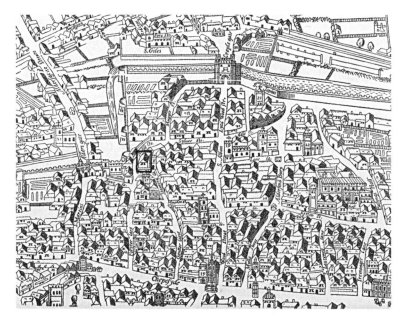

Figure 30: Noble Street and its affluent London neighbourhood, with the location of Bacon House outlined, from the "Agas Map" of the 1560s (London Metropolitan Archives).

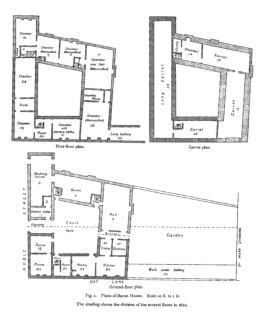

Figure 31: Floor plans of Bacon House on Noble Street where Eglisham lived in the early 1620s; from C. L. Kingsford, "On some London Houses of the Early Tudor Period", *Archaeologia* 71 (1921), fig. 1, p. 34.

Dame Sara Savage and George Eglishawe, Doctour in Physick". Eglisham was in residence by early 1624 at the very latest, and it seems likely that he had moved in some years before. When the property was transferred to the Scriveners Company in 1631, the deeds showed that it had already been subdivided into two residences, which suggests that Eglisham occupied one set of rooms and Lady Sarah the other. More important than the spacious living arrangements, however, was the social status that such a property undoubtedly conferred on the king's physician and new Master of the Goldbeaters Company.[72]

Eglisham's new neighbours made useful additions to his professional networks. A fellow Scotsman, Sir David Foulis, lived across the street in a large property formerly owned by Lord Windsor. With the Goldsmith's Hall nearby on Foster Lane, many gold-traders and gold-workers lived in the vicinity, and any of them could have been useful acquaintances for the purveyor of *aurum potabile* and foliat leaf. Physicians were also thick on the ground. Past Windsor House, up Mugwell Street and north towards Cripple Gate was the Barber Surgeons Hall and garden, a site of anatomical dissections and perhaps a convenient source of medicinal herbs. At least two well-known physicians, Richard Palmer and John Gifford, owned property in the area. John Bannister, surgeon and chemical physician, whose anatomy lectures at Barber Surgeons Hall were commemorated in a 1580 painting, was buried in the church of St Olave, Silver Street, a few yards north of Bacon House.[73] A brief walk would have taken Eglisham from his home to the commercial thoroughfare of Cheapside and the information thoroughfare around St Paul's, where booksellers offered their latest wares and ambitious gentlemen trolled in search of news. Here, a well-connected, curious writer could make contact with the wider world.

The house on Noble Street was that of a successful man, a man of substance. By 1620–21, still in his mid-thirties, George Eglisham was on the cusp of success: service as the king's "brave warrior" had brought significant reward in London, while a decade of travels had left him with cosmopolitan experiences and significant "friendships . . . with many learned men".[74] He would draw on all these as he sat down to write his secret history in 1625–26. But it was to take the collapse of his world to turn the king's brave warrior into the secret historian of the Jacobean court's poison politics.

CHAPTER FIVE

A DOCTOR SUSPECTED OF PAPISTRY

THE UNMAKING OF GEORGE EGLISHAM, 1620–25

"Heaven blesse King James our joy", the song begins, and the poet continues in this loyal vein, calling down heaven's blessings on the king and on "charles his baby" and "Great George our brave viceroy/And his fayre Lady". But already the mask of deference is slipping. Is "baby" the most decorous term for the Prince of Wales? Is "viceroy" a hint that the favourite's power has exceeded its proper bounds? And then, abruptly, the mask drops away, and the poem snarls, scabrous and obscene. The favourite's mother, Mary Villiers, Countess of Buckingham, takes the stage with her former chaplain, John Williams, now Bishop of Lincoln and Lord Keeper of the Great Seal:

Old Bedlame buckingame,
With her Lord Keeper.
Shee loves the fucking game
Hee's her cunt creeper.

Now the poet hits his stride, excoriating the parade of relatives—siblings and cousins, parents and step-parents—who, pulled along on George Villiers's ascent, now "goe so gay,/In court and citty". In the process they consume title, office, power, bodies and booze, hauling riches so great that their weight makes "the wagons crack". This rapacious acquisitiveness is fuelled and expressed by sex: by marriages between Villiers kin and prominent or ambitious families, and by sexual excess—adultery and cuckoldry, sodomy and fornication. The Lord Keeper owes his place to "the fucking game" he plays with Buckingham's mother. The Lord Treasurer, Lionel Cranfield, married the favourite's cousin Anne Brett, but Anne "was us'd you know how,/By the earle Marshall", the Earl of Arundel, who has given Cranfield horns:

These bee they, goe so gay
And keepe the mony,

Which hee can better keepe
Then his wifes cunny.

The countess's "cunt" and Lady Cranfield's "cunny" have become pathways to power and office. Other ambitious courtiers who hitch themselves to the tribe understood the new rule of advancement: "They gett the divell & all" that "swive [fuck] the kindred". This hectic pursuit of power leads to perverse marriages like that of "Old Abbot Anthony"—the septuagenarian Anthony Ashley—who "left sodomy" to marry nineteen-year-old Philippa Sheldon, sister of the woman who married Buckingham's brother. Ashley must now seek sexual solace (if he can keep his "tarse whole", his penis erect) in his wife's "buttocke plumpe" and "black arse hole". The language is cruelly derogatory, using images of sexual excess, bodily transgression and reckless pleasure as metaphors for the broader political corruption of the Villerian age, when to be "of the blood" or to "swive the kindred" is the road to "grace". "Few love" them, "no man cares for them", and yet the tribe continues to "goe so gay" in court, city and kingdom, determined to:

drinke & play,
In court still busy
They will supp at the cupp,
Till there braynes dizy.

Here was England in the early 1620s under "Great George our brave Viceroy": afflicted by a plague of locusts, a swarm of caterpillars, a carnal clan of Villierses and Comptons, Bretts and Beaumonts, Feildings and Sheldons, whose monopolistic pursuit of private advantage had stripped the common weal bare.[1]

The poem was the kind of thing one might find circulating around St Paul's, a short walk south from Noble Street, and clearly it struck a nerve. Buckingham reportedly offered a large reward for the author's name, while contemporaries eagerly sought out copies to add to their collections. George Eglisham probably knew the poem, or others like it. He had no political connections with the Villerian tribe, and until 1621 he had no particular grievances against them. But in the spring of that year Eglisham became ensnared in the first of a series of reversals that were to unmake the comfortable position he had patiently constructed over the previous seven years. He was caught in the crossfire of parliamentary attempts to check Buckingham's rapacity in 1621. Three years later, Eglisham would be left dangerously exposed by the abrupt swings in English religious and diplomatic policy engineered by the royal favourite. By early March 1625, Eglisham had lost nearly everything, and at each stage in his unravelling, he would have become more exquisitely conscious of the Villerian tribe's power. By the time he reached his lowest ebb, in March 1625, George Eglisham knew his enemy.

Doomsday

On 27 April 1621, George Eglisham stood in the Palace of Westminster before a House of Commons committee headed by the great lawyer Sir Edward Coke. The Committee had summoned Eglisham to talk about the new Goldbeaters Company.

The Parliament-men had a mission. For more than a decade they had been unable to check the fiscal abuses that had crept into the state, but now was the time to act: it was, one Parliament-man predicted, "doomsday" for "the Frogs in Egypt", the projectors, patent-seekers and monopolists who had pillaged the common weal. The king would no longer protect them. Determined to help Elector Frederick and Princess Elizabeth defend their lands in the Palatinate, the debt-plagued king could do nothing, diplomatically or militarily, without Parliament; and so, after a seven-year gap, he reluctantly summoned a meeting early in 1621. Most of the Parliament-men sympathized with Frederick and Elizabeth, and quickly voted James money; in return, the king gave them leave to investigate a long list of grievances. By mid-April they were ready for the "Frogs of Egypt".[2]

Eglisham and his fellow Goldbeaters might have hoped their patent would be overlooked. The Commons had dozens of schemes to consider. Some were logical enough, like the French Company's exclusive right to trade in France, or the Company of Ship Carpenters' monopoly on shipbuilding. Others involved inventions—imitation indigo, horseless plows, furnaces that did not use wood—that, no matter their feasibility, might reasonably claim a patent. But many of the schemes fit the model of corrupt private benefit operating at the expense of the public good. Some patents granted exclusive rights to manufacture ordinary items: tobacco pipes, pins, playing cards, paint pigment, pumps, beaver hats, or gold and silver thread. Others conferred the sole right to sell logwood, lampreys, lobsters, hot clothing presses, hard wax, tobacco or Welsh butter. Still others allowed patent-holders to collect fines for violating regulations on markets, fairs, wills, peddling, apprenticeships, tithes, tolls or concealed lands. One gentleman had the right to the "sole packinge of Codd" and another the exclusive licence to show visitors the lions in the Tower.[3]

With more than a hundred patents under scrutiny, the Goldbeaters might have been lucky. The Parliament-men had fun mocking the more ludicrous patents. One member denounced the hot-press patent as but "a Way to spoil our Cloth", and another thought the lamprey monopoly would lead to new ones on "Smelts", "Eels, etc" and then "how shall we do for Fish?" Unfortunately for Eglisham, two things prevented the Goldbeaters from slipping the Commons' net. The first was the patent's connection to Sir Henry Britton, who had already attracted the House's ire. First the Commons nullified his election, in which a Catholic landlord backed Britton and another Catholic candidate against the Protestant inhabitants. The Parliament-men next interrogated him about both his patent to collect fees for improper parks and warrens, and his patent on hard wax. Even in a session full of projectors, Britton's involvement in a *third* patent—the Goldbeaters—was unprecedented.[4] But Britton was not the Goldbeaters' only problem. They were also caught up in the Commons' investigations into the financial dealings of Buckingham's brothers, Edward and Christopher Villiers, who held a patent to produce gold and silver thread. And thread quickly led the Commons to foliat; indeed, earlier complaints to the Privy Council had yoked the two patents together. With the Commons keen to check the Villiers family's corruption, the Goldbeaters had little chance of avoiding exposure. On 17 April, Sir Edward Peyton reported the Committee of Grievances' next wave of investigations, and Eglisham's patent was among the fourteen named. Ten days later, the king's brave warrior stood before the Committee.[5]

In the interim, the interested parties printed breviates to make their case to the Committee. The Goldbeaters' critics—the cutlers, painter-stainers and bookbinders who had been compelled to buy gold and silver leaf from the new company—denounced the cabal controlling foliat manufacture: "Doctor Eglesham, Sir Henry Breton, the sixe Wardens of the Goldbeaters and . . . Norton then Clarke." In two broadsides these critics charged that the new company had "inhaunced the price" of foliat "to the great impoverishment of the Petitioners and other his Maiesties subiects". The increase in the price of silver leaf was especially noticeable. The Cutlers protested that they now had to pay 11s for sheets that had previously cost only 7s 6d, while the Painters objected that the cost of new silver paint had soared from 20s to 30s. To compound the aggravation, the new company's foliat was also "thinner and deceiptfuller then the same was made before" and "doth sooner decay and fade in wearing". If consumers complained, the Company threatened that they "better be content, for if they did finde fault therewith, they should pay more for the same". Anyone who doubted the monopolists' ruthlessness had only to speak with Mr Spencer, whom they had prosecuted in Star Chamber and driven to ruin. Finally, unless it was checked, the Company would deprive the English elite of the means to display their rank, a state of affairs "displeasinge for the Kings Maiestie, the Nobilitie and Gentrie, which needeth or shall need the use of guilding for adorning of their howses, Armes, Bookes and other things."[6]

The Goldbeaters fought back with an astute and forceful *Answer* that may have come from Eglisham's experienced pen. First the Company countered the charge that Eglisham had conjured up the whole enterprise for his own benefit. Since "the mystery of gold-beating hath beene an ancient and setled trade with this kingdome many hundred yeares, as by ancient Recordes ready to be shewed may appeare", it followed that "it was lawfull for them to procure a Charter of incorporation . . . as it hath beene done for other trades". As for any "rewards or gratuities" given to the Master and Wardens "for procuring thereof", the *Answer* reminded readers that "the same hath beene out of theire owne estates, and no more then other trades upon their incorporation have done". The document claimed that the Crown, not the Company, set prices for gold and silver, and the Company flatly denied allegations of shoddy work. Their foliat was "more substantiall, larger and in all points more sufficient, then . . . in former tymes". As for Spencer, he had been a founding Warden, but the Company had sued him when he tried to pass off "base and deceitfull stuffe, mixt with copper" as pure gold, and, when discovered, he urged others to leave the Company. The Company acknowledged that it was a monopoly, but given that dozens of other trades had been incorporated in the past, "every one of them may as well be charged, with savouring of a Monopolie, as this". The *Answer* also neatly parried their opponents' warnings that nobles and gentlemen would soon seek good gold leaf in vain. The complainants were not the social elite but the aggrieved middlemen, who feared that their elite customers would "make their owne provision" directly from the Goldbeaters.[7]

These printed exchanges might set the terms of a debate, but they could not control the outcome of the hearings. On 27 April the Committee heard nine cases, the third of which dealt with the Goldbeaters. A quick glance around the lobby would have told Eglisham that he was in dubious company. Waiting their turn were patent-holders for playing cards and coal, ahead of them were men defending their exclusive right to pack cod and sell lobsters. Coke's participation was also a blow to the Goldbeaters' chances. Late in July 1620, as the first complaints about the new company were aired, the Privy Council had turned to Sir Edward for assistance, naming him to a subcommittee to interview all concerned. His legal expertise qualified him to deal with the complexities posed by a case of an improperly incorporated company. Although the council had never produced an opinion on the charter's legality, Sir Edward had had plenty of time to weigh the case.[8]

Eglisham was the first witness. He admitted that he "himself preferred the Petition to the King", who in turn had sent it to his legal officers Sir Henry Yelverton and Sir Thomas Coventry for comments. Secretary Calvert volunteered the information that "Mr Attorney and Mr Sollicitor" had in fact made "Two several and different Certificates therein", and suggested they be called as witnesses. The Committee declined the suggestion, instead allowing the patent's critics to make their case. Two painters and a bookbinder testified to the various price increases. Other witnesses described the Company's attacks on those who dared complain. If anyone found "Fault either with the Goodness of this Folia, or with the Price of it, they shall have worse, and pay dearer for it". William Spencer's fate exemplified the Goldbeaters' tyranny. Britton, Spencer testified, had "threatened to lay him by the Heels", and the Company had soon followed through on its threats, imprisoning him and then suing him in Star

Chamber for £2,000. Spencer's supposed crime exposed the patent's corrupt nature. Believing the Company "would not hould", Spencer had left them "and wrought privatelie", making higher quality foliat "and better cheape". In reprisal, the Company had seized "his Tools and Instruments". Eventually, the Company had agreed to his release "on Condition that he should come and work with the Patentees", but by then "he was so poor, that he was never after able to buy any more Tools".[9]

After this testimony, Coke outlined his criteria for a viable patent:

1. the commoditie must be as good as before
2. as good cheape
3. it must be a new invention never used before.

While he acknowledged the Company's contention that goldbeating "was an ancient trade before", he followed his tripartite criteria and agreed with the plaintiffs that the company had "not made it as good as before; tis thinner, not of the same scantlinge [i.e. thickness]; [and] they have not sould it as good cheape". After protests that the company paid Eglisham and Britton £200 and £50 each per annum, Eglisham insisted that "he hath out of this Patent only Three Pounds a Week", or about 20 per cent less than reported. An anonymous patentee then seconded Eglisham. After maintaining that the price was effectively set by the royal "Standard of Gold", he explained that "a Reason why it was so cheap heretofore was, that every one then might work and mix what he list with the said Gold Folia, and so making it worse might well sell it cheaper". After Sir Samuel Sandys called for a vote, the Commons committee agreed that in both its creation and its execution, the patent for the Goldbeaters Company was a grievance.[10]

On 2 May the case went to the whole House. Coke explained the Committee's judgement, stressing again that the price of foliat had gone up while the quality went down, before adding two new damning pieces of information. While Coke admitted that English artisans had long produced foliat, his legal opinion was that goldbeating was "no Trade in Lawe" because it was not listed in the 1563 Statute of Artificers (5 Eliz.c.4). Coke's second judgement was equally damaging. The original plaintiffs had been Bookbinders, Cutlers, Paint-Stainers and Stationers—formidable enough, but not among the truly "great" London livery companies. But Coke now argued that the Goldbeaters' patent had infringed on the jurisdiction of the Goldsmiths, one of the greatest livery companies, and thus that the Goldbeaters were, in fact, "within the Government of the Goldsmithes". Finally, Coke reported that the company had not "performed their Covenant to bring in Bulion enough for supply of the worke" and thus had contributed to the dangerous depletion of domestic stocks of precious metals. He concluded that this patent fit the pattern of other destructive grants, illustrating once more that the purpose "of all Monopolies" was "private Gain, though the publick pretended". The Commons agreed and voted "Eglesham's Patent" a grievance.[11]

On 26 June 1621 the Privy Council informed London's Mayor and the Surrey and Middlesex magistrates that in response to parliamentary complaint, James would revoke the Goldbeaters' patent and order their tools confiscated. Early in July a royal proclamation formally withdrew the patent.[12] The Villiers brothers' patent on gold and silver thread was also rescinded. The same day the Commons voted against the Goldbeaters, the Parliament-men angrily debated whether to allow Sir Edward Villiers to attend the sessions while his conduct was under review in the Lords.[13] Coming on the heels of the final decision about "Eglesham's Patent", this episode may have confirmed Eglisham's suspicion that, if not for the Villiers gold- and silver-thread patent, the Goldbeaters might have evaded parliamentary scrutiny. And while the loss of the Goldbeaters patent delivered a serious blow to Eglisham's fortunes, the end of the gold- and silver-thread patent barely dented the Villerian tribe's wealth. Exonerated by the Lords, Sir Edward Villiers took the financial loss in stride. While men like Eglisham scrambled to survive, the Villiers brothers continued to thrive. Sir Edward soon became Master of the Mint and Lord President of Munster, and Christopher the Earl of Anglesey. "They gett the divell & all" that "swive the kindred" was a political credo that would now haunt Eglisham.

Coining Double Pistoles

Eglisham's finances were not sufficiently robust to absorb the loss of the Goldbeaters' patent, as papers from a 1623 lawsuit make clear. In February 1623, Walter Partridge, a joiner and citizen of London, sued Eglisham in Chancery over a series of complex loans and loan guarantees made in 1619 and 1620. In the summer of 1619, Eglisham, Partridge and three other men, including William Spencer, had entered into a bond to guarantee the repayment of a loan from a London tallow-chandler, John Marshall. In their Chancery depositions none of the men involved could agree on the reason for the loan—Partridge alleged that it had been made "at the instance and request and for the only and proper debt of George Eglisham", while Eglisham countered that the money was not "for his owne particuler use and benefitt" but for several men, including Partridge. Simon Borthwick, a London tailor who signed the bond, thought that "the saide money was to be disposed for the use of a certen companye called the Goldbeaters", which, if true, suggests that Eglisham may have been raising capital in the summer of 1619 to help the Goldbeaters cover the costs of securing their charter from the Crown.

But the 1623 suit did not concern the origins and purpose of the original loan. Instead, Partridge alleged that Eglisham and his friends had contrived an elaborate scheme that had left Partridge exposed for their debts if they defaulted on the loan and the various bonds to guarantee its repayment. Eglisham had indeed failed to pay back the loan, and Simon Borthwick, the London tailor who had assumed the responsibility of compensating Marshall if Eglisham failed to do so, sued Partridge for the money to cover the original loan and the various penalties assessed for its default. Partridge alleged Borthwick and Eglisham had plotted to do this from the start, but Borthwick's testimony made it clear that he had had little confidence either in Eglisham or in the doctor's friend and co-signatory, a man called Edward Yates "of the parrish of St Savior in Southwarke". Borthwick had targeted Partridge, because he considered Eglisham and Yates "men . . . of poore and meane estate . . . not likely to secure" him if they defaulted. Nor did he think he had much chance using the law to secure repayment, for "Eglisham alleaged himselfe to be the kinges Servant and was not to be arrested", and Yates could easily disappear as he "lyveth in some partes beyond the Seas".[14]

The surviving documentation contains no verdict in this tangled case. But it makes clear that Eglisham's financial and personal credit had become strained by the late 1610s and early 1620s. He had borrowed money in the summer of 1619 to further the Goldbeaters' ambitions, and he had been unable to pay it back in either January or June of 1620, which suggests that he had yet to receive any income from the Goldbeaters' Company. Eglisham had defaulted on the loan, leaving other men liable for repayment and the penalties that accrued. Eglisham had enough personal credit and connections to persuade four fellow Londoners—two of them identified as citizens—to co-sign various bonds and counter-bonds to secure the original loan from Marshall. But Borthwick, for one, appears to have been sceptical about Eglisham's capacity to pay his debts.

Borthwick had been equally sceptical about Edward Yates, Eglisham's partner in a second round of bonds and counter-bonds. In Borthwick's estimation, Yates was a man "of poore and meane estate" who, while currently resident in Southwark, could not be counted on to remain there, as he "lyveth in some partes beyond the Seas". We have one additional, tantalizing glimpse into Eglisham's relationship with Edward Yates, which may show the learned poet-physician operating much further out on the margins than his career hitherto would suggest. In late May 1627, about a year after Eglisham published *The Forerunner of Revenge*, Andrew Herriott penned an angry letter to Edward Nicholas, Buckingham's secretary. Herriott upbraided Nicholas for taking into his "protection the advancement of one Edward Yeates" who was a "villaine", a "pirotte" who had sailed with "Captaine Herriot, as a private man" and, whatever he might have told Nicholas, had never served as "sowledier by sea or land in his whole lyefe tyme". Yates, Herriott alleged, was a "poore manes sonne" from Kent and a "mere mountebanke" who had deceived "many poore people", who still "verry heavyly feele" their losses. "Besydes", Herriott continued, "this

Yeates was the only companion with doctor Eglesame att bed & att borde for manye yeares together in so muche as they coyened many dublle pistolares to gether. Yett both of them", he pointedly observed, "hethurunto unhanged." Eglisham, Herriott reminded Nicholas, "is the only invective man againste my Lord Dueke of all our nation, and hathe written manye dainegeroues thinges againste hime." How Buckingham's secretary could favour this man's friend was beyond comprehension.[15]

Some of Herriott's allegations have a basis in fact. Eglisham knew an Edward Yates and co-signed a bond with him in 1620. In 1624 an "Edward Yates" sailed with the notorious Scottish pirate George Herriott in the seas off Devon and Cornwall.[16] And in July 1625, Nicholas helped free a "Captaine Edward Yeates" from prison to take command of a company of troops recruited for action overseas.[17] But whether Eglisham's associate, the erstwhile pirate and the long-time soldier of "civill cariadge, and good demeanor" who later claimed to have served in Prince Henry's household, were the same man, or three different men, is now impossible to determine. But it is worth lingering on the rest of Herriott's denunciation, and in particular on his allegations about Edward Yates and George Eglisham's relationship.

Herriot accused Yates of being a "mere mountebank" and claimed that he was "the only companion" with Eglisham "att bed & att borde for many yeares together in so muche as they coyened many dublle pistolares to gether". The language here is suggestive, and it is possible Herriot was insinuating an unnat-ural sexual relationship. Companionship "att bedd & att borde" implied not merely cohabitation but something closer, including the sharing of a bed; in fact, "att bedd & att borde", a phrase used in versions of the pre-Reformation marriage rite, implied marital cohabitation. "Coining" was contemporary bawdy slang for sexual intercourse, while sexual puns and phallic riffing on "pistol"—a "pizzle" was an animal's penis, a "pistol" a phallic object liable to discharge—were legion. But the same language could be read differently. The claim that the two men had shared a bed, for instance, did not necessarily imply anything sexual: bedsharing was usually taken as an unproblematic sign of male friendship.[18] And it seems equally, if not more, likely that the alleged "coining" was in fact the literal counterfeiting of "double pistoles", a Spanish gold coin widely used throughout Europe and valued at between eleven and fifteen English shillings.[19]

Was George Eglisham a counterfeiter? It is possible we are dealing here with a smear or rumour, a projection of stereotypically linked allegations onto a man whose reputation Herriot meant to destroy (Yates) and a man whose reputation was already beyond the pale (Eglisham). The charge of counter-feiting fits neatly with the two men's other offences: Herriott claimed Yates was a "mere mountebank", and the mountebank and coiner were both character-ized by fraud.[20] Eglisham subverted the state not only by forging libels against the king's favourite but also by forging Spanish coins to deceive the people and defraud the king. Coining, after all, was a serious offence, a high treason, one judge asserted, "by which the State is troubled and the people of the King deceived". Henry Peacham included coining in a 1612 emblem depicting "the most wicked of crimes", ranking it alongside sodomy, incest, witchcraft, poisoning and murder.[21]

We cannot know whether Eglisham was a coiner, but the charge, for all its suspicious neatness, seems plausible. His finances were never fully secure. Aside from the brief period in 1620–21 when money from the Goldbeaters patent had begun to roll in, Eglisham may have found that his ambitions stretched farther than his resources. Furthermore, he had long experience manipulating gold— whether making *aurum potabile*, or working with gold leaf. Perhaps, after the collapse of his company in the spring of 1621, Eglisham put his expertise to new, more lucrative uses. In addition to skill, the work of coining required privacy and a properly ventilated workshop where metals could be melted, molded and marked. The spacious premises on Noble Street, hidden in plain sight among the London elite, might have served as a useful base for mixing gold with base metals and then stamping the result, to create a coin that resembled a double pistolet but lacked its full gold content. It is not clear whether Eglisham or Yates could have used forged pistolets for everyday expenditures in London. Foreign coins were frequently used in early modern English cash transactions, but an Elizabethan proclamation had excluded the pistolet from its list of continental coins accepted as "current money". Nevertheless several London traders— including at least one prostitute—accepted counterfeit "pistols & pistoletts" from the French ambassador's entourage early in 1621.[22] Alternatively, given Yates's frequent travels abroad and Eglisham's long-term connections on the Continent, the two men might have counterfeited Spanish coins with the intent of "uttering" them overseas.

The possibility—and it remains only a possibility—that Eglisham collaborated with Edward Yates to counterfeit foreign gold coins offers some intriguing hints about the man, his abilities and his character. The coiner's art demanded not only technical skills but also a talent for deception and a willingness to take risks. We know from Partridge's Chancery suit that Eglisham's finances were straitened, particularly after the Goldbeaters collapse; all this might have given him motive enough to dabble in counterfeiting. On the other hand, if Herriott's information was false, based solely on rumours about Eglisham and Yates, that fact suggests that, at least in some circles, Eglisham had acquired a dangerous reputation years before he wrote *The Forerunner*: he was closely linked to a "mountebank" and thought to be meddling in a crime with potent links to political subversion, religious heterodoxy, and dissimulation.[23] In the end, however, it was religious heterodoxy— "popery"—that would finally unmake the life that Eglisham had fashioned for himself in Protestant London.

"A Scottish-man in Noble Street"

On Sunday, 26 October 1623, John Gee, a curate whose commitment to Protestantism had been weakening for some time, joined a crowd of about three hundred people—open and closeted Catholics, curious onlookers and wavering Protestants—to hear the Jesuit John Drury preach on the upper floor of the French ambassador's gatehouse in Blackfriars, London. About three or four in the afternoon, in "the middle of their sermon", the beams supporting the gatehouse floor gave way, sending the congregation plummeting downwards with such force that they "brake downe a second" floor beneath them. One hundred people died—"battered and bruised, but most part smothered", as one Londoner reported—and many others were "hurt, maymed" or "lost their limmes". Angry Protestants refused to assist the wounded and "insulted upon them with taunts and gibes" as they were taken away. Sixty bodies, left unclaimed, were later buried in two pits dug in the embassy "court and garden". As John Chamberlain reported, commentators immediately rushed to interpret the event. Catholics insisted the victims would bypass the pains of purgatory and go "directly to heaven", while some Protestants pointed to the providentially resonant date of 26 October, which was 5 November in the New Style calendar, and thus the eighteenth anniversary of the Gunpowder Plot, when God had intervened to strike a blow against popery (Fig. 32). For Chamberlain, however, the most disturbing fact was that such a large, semi-public gathering had happened at all: "you may see", he told Dudley Carleton, "how bold and forward they are upon a litle connivence."[24]

John Gee survived. Although "all . . . that stood about mee perished in that calamity", and although he was "involved in the down-fall, and falling, beeing covered with the heaps of rubbish and dead carcases", it nevertheless "pleased God to hasten my Escape, beyond my owne expectation and humane understanding". Gee would come to see his providential deliverance as the moment when God had set him back on the path of true religion. Others, however, saw an opportunity. Archbishop Abbot, who counselled the young curate and talked him back from the "Babylonian pit", encouraged Gee to write a book as a "monument of my thankfulnesse" to God, exposing to the world the cunning deceits of the "ravening brood of Iesuites and Priests".[25]

Much of what Gee wrote was familiar to Protestant readers—tales of Catholic lies, of false miracles and exorcisms, of "dog-tricks, and forgeries" that drew the ignorant and gullible into error. But what made Gee's *Foot out of the Snare* so compelling was its detailed portrait of the thriving Catholic underground that had grown in size, confidence and visibility in the early 1620s. Gee's readers learned names, aliases and descriptions for the 261 priests and Jesuits based in and around London. They could peruse the titles of "the swarmes of their books, which you may heare humming up and downe in every corner".

Figure 32: *No Plot, No Powder*, a Protestant broadside (published by Thomas Jenner) celebrating the providential building collapse at Blackfriars that killed a hundred Catholics attending a clandestine Jesuit sermon in October 1623 (British Museum).

The papists, Gee argued, had sold "more of their Pamphlets within this Twelve-month, then they did in many yeers before". Claiming that Catholic "Printing-presses and Book sellers" could be found almost everywhere, Gee also identified by neighbourhood and street the locations of more than twenty book distributors, printers and sellers.[26]

Committed to "unmasking . . . the vailed fraud of the Iesuits & Priests", Gee apologized for glossing over the dangers posed by an equally corrupt group of papists. Much remained to say about the:

> insinuations & incroachments used by those of that stamp, who professe physick: Who, whatsoever they doe unto the bodies, infuse into the mindes of many the Kings Subiects, bitter distempers; whereby those patients tongues distaste the wholsome food of our Church, and their hearts are stricken with antipathy against our present State.

In lieu of a detailed exposé, Gee produced a "Catalogue of such Popish Physicians in and about the City of London, as the Author knoweth, or by good information heareth of", providing the names, addresses and details for twenty-seven physicians, three surgeons and five apothecaries. All were agents of Roman conversion, Gee claimed. Many had medical degrees from "popish Universities beyond the seas" and had sworn oaths of obedience to Rome; some even had special licence "to exercise the authority of Romish Priests in reconciling or absolving their patients . . . upon point of death or great danger." Some were dubious foreigners: Doctor Iaquinto, "an Italian"; Mr. Lucatelli, "a Mountebanck, lodging without Temple-barre"; and "Monsieur, a French Doctor, lurking about the Strand". A few were unlearned quacks—Mr Covert was "an Empericall man" in Holborn, and Mr Sharpleys "another such"—but many were educated men and some had positions in the medical establishment. Dr Reade, "lodging in Holbourne or Bloomisbury", was a "Doctor of Padua"; Francis Prujean of Silver Street was "a Candidate of the Colledge", and Dr Palmer, "much suspected" of popery, was a Fellow. Some on the list were notorious: Dr Price of Chancery Lane, "a man of very ill behaviour", had spent years in Rome and Brussels, where he had acquired the nickname "Iohn Iesuite". But others had cunning cover stories—Dr Webb of the Old Bailey masqueraded as a language teacher. The sixteenth name on Gee's list also had distinguishing features and extra-curricular activities: he was "a Scottish-man" who lived in Noble Street and who had "made great challenges to dispute with Protestants". His name was "D. Eglestone".[27]

Gee was mostly well informed. Some of the men he named were doctors of repute and apparent religious orthodoxy. Two—Dr Richard Palmer and "D. Gifford in Mugwell-street" (probably John Gifford, who lived on Silver Street, around the corner from Mugwell)—were Eglisham's neighbours; both were long-term Fellows and officers of the College, and both had attended Prince Henry during his final illness in 1612. Gifford, the only one of the two still alive in 1626, did not appear that year on the College's own list of doctors "suspected of papistry". Prujean was indeed only a candidate of the College when Gee wrote in 1624, although he would become a Fellow two years later.[28] But in other cases Gee's accusations had more plausibility, for some on his list did have problematic track records. Joseph Webbe, who taught languages in the Old Bailey, had spent time at the English College in Rome and studied at the Universities of Bologna and Padua. John Price ("Iohn Iesuite") had a degree from Bologna and would confess his Catholicism to the College in 1627. Dr Lodge "dwelling on Lambert Hill" was probably the Catholic writer and physician Thomas Lodge, who read medicine at Avignon and secured a licence from the College only after swearing the Oath of Allegiance.[29]

The publication of Gee's list coincided with the beginning of an anxious time for England's Catholics. Gee had addressed his book to the Parliament that assembled in February 1624, a Parliament widely expected, under Charles and Buckingham's leadership, to reverse the king's pro-Spanish foreign policy and to crack down on Catholics who had enjoyed a de facto toleration while negotiations with Spain continued. Gee's detailed lists provided ammunition for an anti-Catholic manhunt, and they put "Dr. Eglestone" of Noble Street in dubious company and at serious risk.[30]

Eglisham's Catholicism dated back at least to 1601. He had studied at the major Catholic universities of Louvain and Paris; he had enrolled in the Jesuit Scots College at Louvain and had taught for the Benedictines in Rouen; in 1604 he had appeared on an official list of Yorkshire recusants. When he left Catholic France in 1612, travelling first to Calvinist Holland and then to England, Eglisham learned to veil his beliefs. Although he compiled a track record as a religious controversialist in the 1610s, he sublimated his Catholicism into an ardent Stuart loyalism. His attack on Vorstius in 1612 was an attack on atheism, not Arminianism; his attack on Buchanan and Melville six years later came down in support of a Jacobean not a Roman ecclesiology. Hard-line Dutch Calvinists had lionized Eglisham in 1612, and a leading Dutch politician had trusted him with his sons' education. James rewarded his doctor's polemical labours with "un bon bénéfice".

During most of his years in London, Eglisham had concealed his religion. At the unusual (indeed, non-canonical) hour of "eight of the clock at night" on 13 September 1617, he married Elizabeth Downes in a Catholic ceremony performed before two witnesses by the Benedictine monk Thomas Preston. The ceremony took place inside the Clink prison, where Preston and many other priests were imprisoned, and it was performed as secretly as possible. Thirteen years later, when he needed proof of the marriage to draw up a financial settlement for his only surviving child, Eglisham had to write to a Benedictine in England to ask Preston for "testimonie". Eglisham claimed that at the time of the wedding he had secured no documentation partly to protect Preston, since several noblemen had posted bond "to the king that he should not exercise the function of a priest". But secrecy had also suited Eglisham, who was afraid "that the king whose Physitian then I was, should gette notice that I was married by a Priest". Any publicity about his religious beliefs might also have attracted unwelcome attention from the College of Physicians or, more dangerously, from Archbishop Abbot, who supported stricter policing of Catholic doctors lest "they doo ill offices unto those whom in their tyme of sicknes they converse withal".[31]

Beyond the fact of their Clink marriage, we know very little of the Catholic life that Eglisham and his wife lived in London. Since they were never prosecuted for recusancy, they probably attended the official Church frequently enough to avoid suspicion. In any case, zealous Catholic-hunters do not seem to have spent much time trolling Noble Street or its environs; Aldersgate Ward had one of the lowest rates of identified recusancy in London. Unfortunately, gaps in the parish registers for St Mary Staining mean there is no evidence for the baptism of Eglisham's daughter, nor for the baptisms and possible burials of other children. If the Eglishams pursued an active Catholic ritual life, they most likely found it in the western and southern extramural suburbs, around Holborn and the Inns of Court, in the chapels of Catholic embassies or prisons like the Clink.[32] Eglisham's travels may have given him contacts in the embassies and, as we shall see, he was on good terms with at least one Habsburg agent in London. But the only illicit Catholic ritual we know he attended was his marriage. Eglisham's decision to use the Benedictine Preston may have been based on pre-existing ties to the Order whose Rouen church had provided a home for his philosophy lectures.

By the time of Gee's denunciation in 1624, however, Eglisham's confessional allegiances had become more broadly known. Given the doctor's ties to the notorious crypto-Catholic projector Sir Henry Britton, some contemporaries may have suspected Eglisham's religion during the 1621 Goldbeaters hearings.[33] But Eglisham had become increasingly open about his Catholicism in 1622 and 1623 as the king's negotiations for a Spanish marriage temporarily halted enforcement of the penal statutes against recusants and encouraged Catholics to hope for a formal toleration. By early 1623, as news spread of Charles and Buckingham's mission to Madrid, the match began to seem inevitable and Catholics became more assertive. High-profile conversions were both a response to, and a catalyst for, these exalted expectations. The favourite's mother, the Countess of Buckingham, converted in 1622 and his brother Purbeck followed a year later. Meanwhile, the Jesuit mission's annual letter for 1623 claimed an astonishing "2630 converts from heresy to the Catholic faith". Eglisham did not have to travel far to mingle with some of these newly assertive court papists. Sir Arthur and Lady Savage co-owned Bacon House, and Sir Arthur's cousin, Sir Thomas Savage, a financial officer for Charles and Buckingham, was increasingly open about his Catholicism.[34]

With the new religious dispensation, Eglisham cast aside all discretion. Gee noted that he "hath made great challenges to dispute with Protestants", suggesting that the Scotsman had taken advantage of the Hispanophile moment to dust off his skills as a religious polemicist. The wave of high-profile conversions in 1622–23 led to a series of formal and semi-formal disputations between Protestant and Catholic clergy. One series turned on Protestant efforts to win back the Countess of Buckingham; another took place in 1623, after Jesuit attempts to convert the ageing gentleman Edward Buggs.[35] Disputations like these played to Eglisham's strengths, giving him the chance for the kind of public debate that Vorstius had denied him. In April 1623 he was the leading Catholic participant in a notably intemperate debate on transubstantiation held at the College of Physicians on Paternoster Row, during which he traded syllogistic proofs and logical barbs with the Protestant clergymen George Walker and Daniel Featley, Archbishop Abbot's chaplain and a leading licenser for the press. The printed Protestant account of the debate depicted Eglisham as an arrogant fool far out of his depth, and Featley, having outwitted the Scotsman in a bit of Patristic close reading, ended by advising him "hereafter to keepe within your owne element, and dispute in physic". Like the other disputations, the clash on Paternoster Row soon became the subject of further discussion, and a number of "defective" manuscript accounts circulated among interested observers, further publicizing Eglisham's confessional identity.[36]

The general Hispanophile turn at court also encouraged Eglisham to lend his poetic talents to a verse compilation printed in Milan in 1622–23 to honour the late Juan Fernandez de Velasco, Grand Constable of Castile, former Spanish Viceroy in Milan, and Spain's extraordinary ambassador at the 1604 London peace talks that had ended the Elizabethan Anglo-Spanish war. Eglisham contributed two Latin poems to the polyglot collection, hailing the nobly born and virtuous Velasco as the author of a "great friendship" between England and Spain that had banished "the furies of war". "Peoples who have rushed forward into fierce wars have been made friends by your counsels," his epigram concluded; "O Velasco, glory of the Spanish race, with what mouth will we sing your praises?" These hymns to Anglo-Spanish peace and to one of the greatest Spanish potentates of the age made Eglisham's political allegiances and aspirations in 1623 absolutely clear.[37] With the Prince of Wales about to marry the Infanta Maria Ana and workmen putting the finishing touches to the future queen's new Catholic chapel at St James's Palace, Eglisham must have seen little need to continue living a double life. When, at the start of their debate, George Walker asked Eglisham whether he had received ordination, the doctor unabashedly replied, "I am a Romane Catholique, not a Priest, but a Doctor of Physick."[38]

The return of an unmarried Charles from Spain in October 1623 marked the dawn of the "blessed revolution" that would break the peace that James and Velasco had forged in 1604. Most English Protestants greeted this transformation with joy; English Catholics were first stunned and then terrified. At court, Buckingham began systematically to destroy his erstwhile allies in the Spanish faction, toppling Lord Treasurer Middlesex, Secretary Calvert, the Earls of Arundel and Bristol, and eventually Lord Keeper Williams. With them went scores of minor officials, courtiers and poets. Outside Whitehall, Catholics and Hispanophiles also felt the chill as James, grateful for a handsome subsidy, granted Parliament's request for strict enforcement of the penal laws and banishment of the Jesuits. "No more terrible storm", the Jesuits concluded, "has fallen upon the Catholics for the last thirty years".[39] It was possible to survive this sudden reversal of fortunes, but George Eglisham was left exposed; and John Gee had his name.

The Physician's Folly

The coming of the anti-Catholic storm might have encouraged Eglisham to exercise caution. Instead, he gambled. In the relatively tolerant atmosphere of

1623, his reckless action would have been risky; in the newly anti-Catholic climate that followed, it nearly destroyed him. The crisis arrived early in 1625, when Eglisham was called to the bedside of his friend, patron and patient, James, Marquis of Hamilton. The circumstances of Hamilton's illness and death early in March 1625 generated great scandal. As we have seen, some of the marquis's friends believed he had been poisoned. But there was other, equally sensational talk. Immediately on Hamilton's demise, it was reported that he had been reconciled to Rome, and that Eglisham had engineered the conversion.

Real and alleged deathbed conversions were fodder for heated inter-confessional polemic in the early 1620s. In December 1623, Chamberlain had lamented the increasing impudence of the "priests and Jesuits" who "swarme" in London:

> [Whenever] any of qualitie . . . fall sicke and have any frends or kinred that way affected, under that colour they will find accesse to them and use perswasion which whether it prevaile or no, if the partie die, they will find meanes though they be past sense to anoint and crosse them . . . and then geve out they were theirs and won by them.[40]

When Edward Buggs fell ill in 1623, for example, he was "sollicited by some Papists then about him to forsake the Protestant faith", and at his request a Jesuit and two Protestant ministers debated the visibility of the True Church.[41] For John Gee, Catholic physicians were the crucial intermediaries in these attempts at deathbed conversions, and he chronicled various Catholic efforts to claim high-profile deathbed converts even when priestly overtures had been rebuffed or never happened. He pointed to a 1623 Jesuit pamphlet claiming (falsely) that John King, Bishop of London, had been "reconciled to the Church of Rome" on his deathbed "by a certaine Priest there not named", and Gee reported the case of Baron Bromley who received the last rites from a "Mercenary Mountebanke Priest" brought in by "a Popish insinuating companion" after losing consciousness.[42]

The conversion of Hamilton, a man of royal blood and apparently sound anti-Catholic and anti-Spanish convictions, would have been a major propa-ganda coup. The rumours spread quickly. A Catholic newsletter reported that the marquis had "ended his dayes as befitted a good Christian to doe, for soe I am more than credebly informed, and therefore I doe pray for him." Chamberlain noted that Hamilton was "much lamented" but that "the papists will need have him one of theirs, which neither appeared in his life nor in his death that we can any way learne, but it is no new thing with them to raise such scandalls and slaunders."[43] On 9 March, the Earl of Kellie reported the rumour that Hamilton "shuld have dyed a papiste" and insisted flatly that it was "fals". A week later, he lamented, "Their is heir sutche a rumore rissine that my Lord Hammiltone dyed a papiste and that he had a priste with him and reconcealed himselfe to the Pope of Roome". But Kellie insisted that the dead marquis "getts great wrong". Hamilton much preferred "his pleasours and the companye of wemen then to preeests", Kellie noted, and if indeed there "was a preest with him sume two days before he dyed", his purpose was more likely to have been an intermediary on "weemens besines" than to have concerned "preests affairs". Nevertheless, Kellie continued, "you can not believe what is talked of it and how the tryell of it prosecute". By this point, however, Kellie had found someone to blame for the scandal: the marquis's doctor "Ekklingein" was "the cawss that monye believes this matter", for the doctor "is thocht to be a great papiste". Lucy Russell, Countess of Bedford, Hamilton's close friend and ideological ally, who angrily dismissed the "lying" papists' conversion claims, also blamed Eglisham, writing to a friend that "they got some colour to invent this slander" through the "folly or villainy of a physician waited on him (who was Popish)". In his own sickness a few days later, King James took pains to testify publicly to his own faith "least those scandalls might pass of him that passed of some other lately meaning it seemed of my lord Marquis Hamilton whome the Papists give out to have dyed a Romish Catholick."[44]

It is hard to say what Eglisham may have done—whether he manufactured a conversion tale, facilitated a failed conversion attempt, or actually oversaw its completion. Although several doctors were treating the marquis, Eglisham was the only one mentioned in the conversion reports.[45] Some commentators suggested that he had simply spread the story; others argued that he had brought in the priest who had conducted (or attempted to conduct) the reconciliation and last rites. According to Catholic sources, a Jesuit, "one of the padri cauled Wood did the deede", and William Trumbull later reported that Eglisham himself had boasted about bringing "one Wood, a Jesuitt or a Prieste to administer unto [Hamilton] the last Sacrament".[46] A priest called Wood had participated with Eglisham in the disputation on transubstantiation at the College of Physicians in April 1623, but given the frequent use of aliases by English priests and Jesuits, the identity of Father "Wood" is now unclear. Gee's catalogue included a "F[ather] Wood, a very dangerous fellow", whose image also appeared in contemporary woodcuts of secret popish conclaves in the City (Fig. 33). But no English Jesuit called Wood had sufficient seniority to administer the sacraments.[47] Two other men are possible candidates. One is John Wood, a Scotsman who had entered the Order in 1600 and was the son or brother of the Laird of Boniton, a prominent Catholic executed in 1601. Logically, Eglisham might have turned to another Scot to reconcile his fellow countryman, but the evidence is thin.[48] The other candidate is the far more notorious English Jesuit Alexander Baker, described by Gee as a particularly skilled evangelist who used no fewer than eight different aliases, among them "Mr. Wood".[49] Baker had a good track record securing high-profile converts; a decade earlier he had helped persuade the

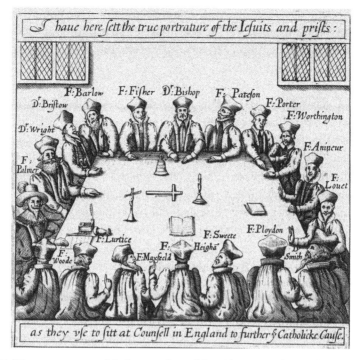

Figure 33: "The true portrature of the Iesuits and prists", from Thomas Scott's 1624 *The Second Part of Vox Populi* (British Museum). This image of a conspiratorial meeting depicts, at bottom left, a "Father Woode" who may be the Jesuit whom Eglisham allegedly brought to Hamilton's deathbed.

fifteen-year-old son of the stridently anti-Catholic Sir Edward Coke to abandon his father's faith. Later in 1625, Baker was imprisoned in Exeter, and when the French ambassador secured him a royal pardon, the Parliament-men decried the release of this "known and notorious Jesuit" whose "conversation will be very dangerous to the perverting of many of his Majesty's subjects". Furthermore, according to Gee, Baker shared Eglisham's interest in "the Chimicall Trade".[50] Although it is impossible to confirm his presence in London in late February and early March 1625, Baker certainly had the status for a high-stakes conversion attempt.

The fallout from the Hamilton scandal left Eglisham dangerously exposed. The Venetian diplomat Zuane Pesaro reported that the ailing king "spoke wrathfully against the Jesuit who administered extreme unction to the marquis . . . and against the physician who assisted there." Although James was reportedly "soon mollified"—indeed, Pesaro thought he was using the controversy to keep pro- and anti-Catholic court factions in check—Archbishop Abbot opened an inquiry to punish those "concerned in the conversion"; and only the French ambassador's lobbying, Pesaro reported, restrained the archbishop from punitive action, lest too vigorous a proceeding "cast a slur on the memory of the deceased". Instead, Abbot focused on redeeming Hamilton's reputation, beginning work on "a book praising the marquis as a Protestant".[51] With James angry, Hamilton's friends aggrieved, and the archbishop on his trail, Eglisham went into hiding.

From his safehouse, Eglisham confronted an increasingly bleak prospect. Hamilton's death had robbed him of his most powerful court patron, and within days he must have heard the news of James's death, and perhaps the first reports of the accusations aired in the sickroom. Eglisham, James's brave warrior, had lost his master, and perhaps his last chance of redemption. He had no relationship with the new king, and Charles, who had been present throughout his father's illness, would have heard James's angry words about Hamilton's conversion. More worrying still were the early signs of the new king's religious and foreign policies. While James had clung stubbornly to his dream of Anglo-Spanish peace, Charles immediately set the realm on a collision course with Philip IV, sending couriers to begin readying an invasion force against Spain. The new marriage treaty with France required Charles to suspend the penal laws, but the new king made it all too clear that English Catholics would find no welcome at court. And it was soon obvious that Buckingham, the architect of the breach with Spain, dominated the son even more completely than he had the father.

In late March 1626 the College of Physicians, responding to a request from the Committee on Religion, informed Parliament that "Dr. Egglesham of Noble Street" was one of thirteen London "Doctors suspected of papistry".[52] By this point, however, Eglisham was long gone from Noble Street. After weeks in hiding, he had slipped out of the country and made his way to Brussels, one of the great gathering-spots for Irish, English and Scottish Catholics. In 1618 he had used his pen to present himself as a loyal servant of the king, a cosmopolitan physician who moved easily among the Scottish and European intellectual and political elites. Now he was a popish projector, an enemy of the Protestant common weal, the associate of shadowy figures like Father Wood, one of the "Black Breed" of priests and Jesuits plotting to undermine the realm.[53] By March 1625, George Eglisham had been unmade. He had no safe place in early Caroline England.

Brave Scipio

The aftermath of the 1624 "blessed revolution" had all but destroyed George Eglisham, yet it had transformed Buckingham into a popular patriot hero. Thomas Scott's *Second Part of Vox Populi* was one among many texts busy reinventing the corrupt, crypto-popish, "Ganymede" as a virtuous Protestant champion (Fig. 34).[54] Scott lauded Buckingham as a "Noble, Wise, and a Generous Prince" whose rich rewards were "deservedly conferred" for "faithfull

Figure 34: Crispijn de Passe the Elder's frontispiece to Thomas Scott's 1624 pamphlet *Vox Dei* depicts Buckingham (in the bottom left of the triangle) in his new role as patriot hero crushing the sins of Faction and Bribery (British Museum).

service" protecting Charles in Madrid. He was the people's favourite, basking in the "generall love" of commoners as well as in the "affection and heart of the King and Prince".[55] Buckingham's popular apotheosis was consummated in his portrayal as the valiant and wise White Duke of Thomas Middleton's *A Game at Chess* that played to sold-out audiences at The Globe in the summer of 1624. But the transformation appears even more striking in the verse libels that had once done so much to revile the favourite.

When the Spanish ambassadors in 1624 demanded Buckingham's head, one poet hailed him as both a new Sir Walter Ralegh, militant anti-Spanish paragon, and as a new Scipio, exemplar of patriotic virtue and imperial might. The libeller warned that James should "Be no wayes guilty of so vilde a thing" as to surrender his favourite to the Spanish:

> Let not that head satisfy the thirst
> Of Morish pride, which was the very first
> Of all thy favourites er'e undertooke

His Countryes Cause and thus did overlooke
Spanish Deceiveings. For he hath done more
Then twenty of thy favourites before.

Instead, James should free Elizabeth and the Elector Palatine from the "bondage" of "Spanish Tyrannie", and let Buckingham head the crusade against Spain and revive English "spirits, which in a womans raigne" had burned Cadiz and "with pale terror strooke all Spayne". "Give him but force", the libeller concluded, "his owne head to maintaine/And like brave Scipio he will sacke proud Spayne". The poem starkly contrasted the heroic, virtuous, and militantly Protestant Buckingham with the commonwealth's enemies, the "Jesuited Englishe drunke with Popery/What veiw your Country with a Spanish eye", those who, deceived by Spanish "bloody damned pollicyes/Maskt in faire shewes of formall fopperyes", compromised their "allegiance" to "prince & land".[56] A year earlier the libellers had thought Buckingham a chief of those "Jesuited Englishe"; but he was now their antithesis. The man once feared as Ganymede had proven to be the man who had awoken the king to his duties.

Buckingham relished his transformation. But his new role carried heavy expectations, and when the duke failed to fulfill them, it was all too easy for old accusations and anxieties to re-emerge. In 1625, George Eglisham was among those "drunke with Popery", left adrift and vulnerable by the breach with Spain. A year later, the disastrous beginning to Buckingham's Spanish war gave Eglisham an opportunity to destroy "brave Scipio". From his refuge in Brussels, drawing upon lessons learned and connections made in a long career of polemical engagement and cosmopolitan mobility, Eglisham would rewrite the recent past, redeem his own battered reputation, and turn the great "White Duke" into a monster blacker than hell. He would do it by writing the secret history of the murder of James I.

CHAPTER SIX

AT THE SIGN OF ST ANNE

PRINTING THE SECRET HISTORY

WHEN THE DUKE of Buckingham went to Paris in May 1625 to collect Charles's new bride, Henrietta Maria, he seized the chance to meet the famed artist Peter Paul Rubens from whom he commissioned several paintings, including a massive equestrian portrait, to hang in his York House collection. While Buckingham sat for him, Rubens drew a quick portrait in ink and chalk that elegantly captured the favourite's commanding gaze, stylishly barbered beard and Parisian curls (Fig. 35). As he worked, Rubens talked about the need for peace between England and Spain, and reported later that he had "perceived in the Duke's conversation a laudable zeal for the interests of Christianity". Rubens hoped Buckingham would "pacify" Charles and halt the drift to open conflict, for "war" would be "a scourge from Heaven" that "we should do our best to avoid".[1] The great painter was to be grievously disappointed in Buckingham. After the duke launched a naval attack on Cadiz later that year, Rubens had little "doubt that war will follow", and privately bemoaned the favourite's "caprice and arrogance", telling a friend that "I pity that young king who, through false counsel, is needlessly throwing himself and his kingdom into such an extremity. For anyone can start a war . . . but he cannot so easily end it." By January 1626, Rubens sensed that Buckingham's arrogance had brought him to "the precipice"; indeed, his rivals now openly rejoiced over the failure of the "utterly foolhardy" Cadiz raid. Mulling the alarming possibility that France would soon join the anti-Spanish coalition, Rubens insisted "it would be better if these young men who govern the world today were willing to maintain friendly relations with one another instead of throwing all Christendom into unrest by their caprices".[2]

Rubens knew that modern wars were fought with ink and paper, as well as blood and iron, and kept a close watch on the pamphlets pouring from the Continent's presses. Some of what he read was little more than scandalous provocation. In late January 1626 he sent a friend a copy of a rare but "highly infamous" pamphlet, whose author should and would be punished "if he were known". Rubens insisted he was fortunate to live in a well-run state where "the

Figure 35: Peter Paul Rubens's drawing of George Villiers, Duke of Buckingham, made in Paris in 1625, and the basis for a series of later painted portraits (Albertina Museum).

Most Serene Infanta, as well as her principal ministers, are very hostile to such libelous publications; that is why they have very little vogue in this Court".[3] But he, like many others, was fascinated with the latest *succès de scandale*. In February, Rubens returned home to Antwerp, where he could once more frequent the famed Plantin-Moretus bookshop, located just a short walk south from the cathedral.[4] Rubens was a close friend and collaborator of the scholarly proprietor Balthasar Moretus and a frequent customer at his shop.[5] Some of the painter's purchases that winter and spring were eminently respectable, but on 18 April he paid 1 florin and 6 stivers—about 4s 4d—for two copies each of a pair of more "infamous" works.[6] One was an eccentric mélange of Latin, French, Italian and Dutch fragments titled *Veritas Odiosa, fragmenta varia colloquii Machiavelli et Mercurii*: "The Hateful Truth: Fragments from the Colloquy of Machiavelli and Mercury" (Fig. 36). Purporting to be the work of "Richard Attonitus" ("Richard Thunderstruck"), the supposed "proto-Chancellor" of the recent English fleet, the pamphlet flaunted its satirical intent, even claiming to have been printed on the Oxford press of the long-deceased churchman "Walter Map". The title of the other book, however, must have immediately grabbed Rubens's attention: *Prodromus Vindictae in Ducem Buckinghamiae, pro viru-*

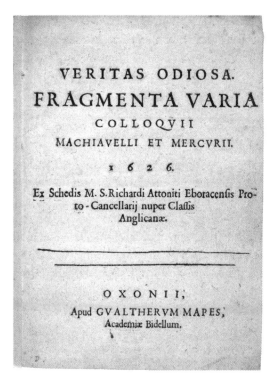

VERITAS ODIOSA.
FRAGMENTA VARIA
COLLOQVII
MACHIAVELLI ET MERCVRII.

1 6 2 6.

Ex Schedis M. S. Richardi Attoniti Eboracenſis Pro-
to - Cancellarij nuper Claſſis
Anglicanæ.

O X O N I I,
Apud GVALTHERVM MAPES,
Academiæ Bidellum.

Figure 36: Title page of "Ricardus Attonitus", *Veritas Odiosa*, 1626, a complex and playful polyglot work of Habsburg disinformation (Bodleian Library).

lenta caede potentissimi Magnae Britanniae Regis IACOBI, nec-non Marchionis Hamiltonii, ac aliorum virorum Principum: "The Forerunner of Revenge Upon the Duke of Buckingham for poisoning the most potent James, King of Great Britain, as well as the Marquis Hamilton and other nobles". The author's name, no clever pseudonym, adorned the title page: "Indice Georgio Eglisham Scoto, Iacobi Regis pro persona Regia supra decennium Doctore Medico": "Discovered by George Eglisham of Scotland, one of King James's physicians for the royal person for over ten years".

Rubens's purchase on 18 April is the earliest recorded appearance of Eglisham's secret history of James's murder. More importantly, Moretus's meticulous ledgers reveal not only when Rubens purchased the book; they also tell us who printed it. With obviously false Frankfurt imprints, the Latin and English versions of Eglisham's work have long confused bibliographers, who have mustered various educated guesses about its origins, ranging from "the Netherlands" to Delft and The Hague. The Plantin-Moretus records, however, allow us to reconstruct for the first time the real printing history of the most infamous book of the early Stuart age. They direct us to a young printer, Jan Van Meerbeeck, and to a specific place, a small Brussels shop at the sign of

St Anne. And from there they allow us to connect a secret history of events at the Jacobean court, written by an angry and arguably desperate man, to the work of various diplomatic agents of the king of Spain and his satellite regime in Flanders, and to the turbulent polemical battles of the early stages of the Thirty Years War.

This chapter presents the hitherto untold history of the making of *The Forerunner of Revenge*. We follow George Eglisham from London to Brussels, from the fringes of the English court to a new circle of friends eager to hear and to use his stories about Buckingham. We then situate Eglisham's book in both short and longer-term polemical contexts—as the latest in a long series of polemical libels and "disinformation" produced in the Spanish Netherlands for English readers, and as a crucial part of a coordinated propaganda campaign designed to sow confusion and mistrust among the Habsburgs' enemies in the mid-1620s. By looking closely at *The Forerunner*'s making—at the men who made it, and the places where it was made—we can finally appreciate the European history of a book that would haunt English and Scottish political culture for decades.

A Person of Great Parts and Letters

Eglisham went into hiding early in March 1625 following the scandal over Hamilton's alleged deathbed conversion; but he was soon on the move. On 20 May, Jean Baptiste Van Male, the Flemish agent in London, wrote to his superior, Charles della Faille, the Infanta Isabella's foreign secretary, informing him of the imminent arrival in Brussels of "Docteur Eglisemius", someone whose conversation della Faille had apparently enjoyed in the past. Van Male offered more details in a letter to the Infanta, explaining that "George Liscmius, Scottish doctor of medicine and physician to the late King", had "resolved at last to retire secretly and place himself" under her care. Eglisham, he reported, had been "persecuted by the Archbishop of Canterbury and others for having caused the conversion of the Marquis of Hamilton" and by Buckingham himself for charging that the duke had poisoned the marquis. Eglisham had "hidden for some time" but had ultimately been unable to find a place of "security" in England. The French had offered Eglisham safe haven "by which he would take residence in Paris" and "occupy the chair in philosophy", in effect returning to his work of 1610–12. But Eglisham had decided on Brussels instead. Van Male urged Isabella to "protect and favour" the doctor, but to do so "secretly". He was potentially a very useful man, "a person of great parts and letters" who could perform all kinds of "useful services due to his great experience" of English affairs. And Van Male had every reason to know, for "I have had correspondence" with him ever "since he came to this kingdom."[7]

After Charles and Buckingham had outmanoeuvred him early in 1624, the Marquis of Hinojosa, the Spanish ambassador in London, retained a series of secret agents to provide a steady flow of information, and following the ambassador's departure in July 1624, Van Male took over running the five informants: X, easily the most prolific, XX, XXX, OOO, and, the only one who rejected a code name, William Sterrell. Eglisham was unlikely to have been one of these spies—each continued writing after the doctor left London—but he had likely been a long-time occasional informant for Van Male. He may very well, for instance, have been the unnamed source behind Van Male's report on 18 March 1625, telling the Infanta that Hamilton's doctors were certain of the marquis's deathbed conversion, and is a plausible source for a late March letter calling on the Scots to avenge James's murder. Van Male's letters of introduction to della Faille and Infanta Isabella were thus partial recompense for services rendered. Eglisham was eager to come in from the cold; he had skills to offer, and Van Male, his old friend, had arranged a warm welcome.

Meanwhile, as war between England and Spain grew ever more likely, William Trumbull, the English agent in Brussels, repeatedly warned Secretary Conway of serious security problems in Whitehall (Fig. 37). "Your Courte and Cittyes are full of Spyes," he had once told his superior, and on another occasion

Figure 37: A late seventeenth- or early eighteenth-century engraving by Simon Gribelin of William Trumbull, the long-serving agent of James I and Charles I in Brussels (Huntington Library).

advised that, in the event of war, the Habsburgs "have alwayes the advantage of you that you can neither thinke, speake nor project any thing, but wee [in Brussels] know it before hande, by Spyes of the English and Scottishe Nations". Trumbull thus paid close attention to the movements of such men through Brussels, and in early June 1625 informed Conway that "one Dr. Eglestone a Scottish man (I suppose)" had "comme hether". He knew that this was the same man who more than a decade earlier "wrote against Vorstius". But now Eglisham was telling "strange tailes of the poverty of our Country and the perversion of the late L. Marquis Hamilton upon his death bedd". Indeed, Eglisham now claimed credit for Hamilton's conversion, bragging that he had "brought one Wood, a Jesuitt or a Prieste to administer unto him the last Sacrament", and that, for his pains, he had been "persecuted by my L Archbishop of Canterbury". According to Trumbull, Eglisham was also "a greate man with our Cardinall", Alfonso de la Cueva, the formidable Marquis of Bedmar and veteran Spanish administrator, who had taken holy orders in 1622 but continued to serve as the Infanta's councillor. Thanks to his Brussels contacts, Trumbull confirmed something else about Eglisham; he had been "an Instrument in matter of spyinge", who had "profitably served" both the Infanta's agent in London, Van Male, and the Spanish one, Bruneau.[8]

Four days later an anonymous Spanish agent confirmed Trumbull's sighting. He reported to Madrid that "a doctor of medicine named Ecelson" had arrived in Brussels full of information. "Ecleson" claimed, for instance, that the crypto-Catholic Earl of Arundel had suffered a providential judgement after taking Protestant communion with the new king, falling from his coach and lying "senseless for six hours". He reported too that the Lord Chancellor of Scotland and various Scottish nobles had warned Charles that he must be crowned in Edinburgh before he was crowned in London. And, most sensationally, "Ecleson" was insisting that "they gave poison to the Marquis of Hamilton", adding that the poison in question was a long-acting drug that "worked in him for more than a year". The Spanish report noted that the doctor had fled England after "words exchanged with Buckingham ... that the Marquis of Hamilton died of poison ... and that not only the Marquis ... but also the Duke of Lennox and that 13 doctors of medicine swore that to be true." Buckingham had threatened that "the Doctor would pay with his head", causing Eglisham to flee the country. The 1625 Parliament had yet to open, but "Ecleson" was confident that "they mean to fight Buckingham in the Parliament, and that many papers are sent against him".[9]

Eglisham had arrived to find Brussels in a celebratory and confident mood that would last well into 1626. A few days before his arrival, the Spanish Army of Flanders had captured the Dutch border fortress at Breda after a year-long siege. The Spanish chief minister, the Count-Duke of Olivares, had already shifted Spain's resources to a naval campaign, establishing a new Admiralty of the North based in Dunkirk. As Flemish warships began to ravage Anglo-Dutch shipping in the North Sea, Olivares seemed on the verge of realizing his dream of expanding Spanish naval power into the Baltic and destroying Dutch commerce. The Spanish also began thinking of using their new-found naval strength to target the British Isles, with invasion sites in Ireland, Essex and Scotland under consideration. A few weeks after Breda fell, news arrived of another triumph in which a Spanish expeditionary force drove Dutch interlopers out of Brazil. Charles and Buckingham provided the final victory in the Habsburg *annus mirabilis* of 1625. By the time Charles's order releasing Count Mansfelt had reached the Netherlands, most of his English troops had either fled or died. But even though the 1625 Parliament had proved uncooperative, that October, just as the weather worsened, Charles dispatched a massive Anglo-Dutch fleet carrying 10,000 infantry to raid Spain. All of Europe watched, while the Spanish waited nervously, wondering how to defend their long coastline. As the fleet approached, some of Olivares's critics began second-guessing his decision to block the marriage of Charles and the Infanta Maria in 1623. But the English attack miscarried calamitously, and apprehensions about England's entry into the war gave way to yet more Habsburg celebrations.[10]

But there were still good reasons for concern in Brussels and Madrid. The Army of Flanders was the largest and best-trained force in Europe, but it had to protect the strategically vulnerable Spanish Netherlands from a daunting array of enemies. Breda had fallen, but the formidable Dutch army, led by the Stadtholder Frederick Henry, was intact, and in spite of the Dunkirkers' best efforts, the maritime power of the United Provinces remained unparalleled. Late in 1625, Charles I and his uncle Christian IV of Denmark had joined the Dutch in alliance against Spain, forming a potentially overwhelming naval force and reopening the land war in northern Germany. The Anglo-Dutch-Danish alliance was ominous enough, but for much of 1625, France also seemed poised to join their ranks. Hitherto reluctant to embark on open war, Louis XIII and Cardinal Richelieu had energetically pursued various anti-Spanish proxy conflicts. In Liguria a French army seconded the Duke of Savoy's efforts to besiege Genoa, a sensitive Spanish financial and logistical hub, while in Switzerland another French army acting on behalf of the Protestant cantons managed to close the Valteline passes, thus cutting the vital "Spanish road" linking Flanders to the Spanish stronghold in Milan. If France itself entered the war, then the Army of Flanders would find itself in a potentially impossible situation, beset on three sides by major military powers.[11]

Eglisham had arrived in Brussels at a remarkable moment, at once exultant and apprehensive, and quickly discovered that he had many friends in the small city. He would likely have found old colleagues from Louvain, and found common cause among the local medical and literary establishment. He was well acquainted with Cardinal de la Cueva, one of the pre-eminent figures at court; and Van Male, his old friend from London, soon joined him in Brussels, where he doubtless introduced Eglisham to the Infanta's inner circle. If he wanted the company of fellow Scots, Eglisham would have found hundreds of clerics, merchants, scholars and soldiers crammed into the Flemish capital. The number of English émigrés was even larger, a fact that doubtless pleased Eglisham's English wife and daughter. Brussels lacked the cosmopolitan flair of Paris or London, but it was an ideal locale for a Scottish scholar and physician looking to repay those responsible for his ignominious flight from Noble Street.

There was another new visitor to Brussels. Early in 1625 the imminent return of Count Gondomar to London had precipitated a crisis at James's court, and, as we have seen, those whispering about James's death maintained that Buckingham had poisoned the king to forestall the envoy's return. Charles had immediately withdrawn Gondomar's invitation, and the ambassador headed instead to Brussels, arriving in the city shortly after Eglisham. Alarmed by Gondomar's arrival, Trumbull warned Whitehall that the count had come to mobilize "his friends and well-wishers in England" to assist Spain by "discoveringe the secret affairs of his Majestie and his kingdomes". But Gondomar soon called on Trumbull with an offer to open negotiations for the restoration of the Palatinate, an offer that Charles ignored. Gondomar remained in Brussels for nearly a year. As Philip IV explained to Isabella, Gondomar had a new mission, one that Trumbull had already suspected: with Charles uninterested in negotiation, the old ambassador was to develop a large-scale intelligence operation, recruiting English allies to the Spanish cause.[12] Clearly, the Spanish planned to meddle in English domestic politics in hopes of undermining the war effort from within. Here then was a chance to put George Eglisham and his poison stories to work.

Eglisham had probably met the ambassador during Gondomar's long stay in London between 1613 and 1622. British Catholics formed a small self-contained world whose religious life in the capital revolved around masses at the ambassadorial residences; either the doctor or his wife may well have attended services under Gondomar's roof. And Gondomar, like Van Male, would have seen the benefits of cultivating the well-connected Eglisham as a useful source of information. Evidence of Gondomar's activities in Brussels has mostly been lost, but we have one precious contemporary report connecting the diplomat and the Scottish doctor in 1626. As part of their speculative invasion planning, the Spaniards maintained contacts with various Scottish agents, one of whom, a priest who went by the name of Father Watson, travelled to Brussels with important information. His contacts in Flanders are illuminating. He went first to "Doctor hekssum", almost certainly Eglisham; and it was Eglisham who then brought Waston to "wan male", who then "did take" Waston "instantlie to the Count of Gondomar, who sent him with Dillegence to

Spaine".[13] This report suggests that after his arrival in Brussels, Eglisham remained well connected to key figures in the Habsburg diplomatic service close to the heart of power in Flanders and Spain. These were the men who would broker the production of *The Forerunner of Revenge*.

Dung-pits of Scandals and Lies

The Forerunner was far from the first commentary on English affairs written and produced in the Spanish Netherlands. English and Scottish Catholic exiles had long published controversial works using commercial printing presses in Antwerp and Brussels or smaller operations in the émigré seminaries at Douai and St Omer. Late in Elizabeth I's reign, Flemish presses had supported the Catholic cause and the English Jesuit mission with scandalous attacks on the queen's ministers and polemics that broached explosive contemporary issues, including the highly vexed question of the royal succession.[14] The Anglo-Spanish peace treaty of 1604 had lowered the ideological temperature, but Flemish presses continued to produce Catholic works for English readers. Most were books of piety and devotion, but some were overtly polemical and libellous, as two vivid examples make clear.

In 1609 a printer in St Omer working with the local Jesuit seminary published the Latin satire *Prurit-Anus*.[15] Ostensibly an attack on Puritans—the scatological title conflated "Puritanus" with "Prurit-anus", or "Itchy Bum"—the pamphlet's real target was the Church of England and the monarchs who governed it. It appeared in at least two issues, both with false imprints. One, published without an author's name, claimed to be a much-admired Oxford manuscript, while the second added an invented author, one Horatio Dalabella of Naples. The satire parodied Protestant hyper-scripturalism by deliberately misusing "the words of holy writ" in response to "various witty and ridiculous questions". It attributed the origins of the English Church to Henry VIII's incestuous lust for Anne Boleyn, and linked Henry to the "great red dragon", a demonic beast with "seven heads and ten horns", and clearly a figure for the king who had had six wives and desired a seventh, and had acquired five sets of cuckold's horns courtesy of his second wife's carnal adventures. *Prurit-anus*'s commentary on Elizabeth I, Sir Henry Wotton noted, implicitly accused the queen of "immodesty, of having given birth to sons and daughters, of having prostituted her body to many different nationalities, of having slept with black-amoors". Meanwhile the tract mocked James's passion for the hunt and his subservience to the Kirk, dismissing the Scots as a "barbarous" "worms" and "locusts" who were consuming England's wealth.[16] "The book is scurrilous without any touch of religion," the Venetian ambassador reported, "foolish, ignorant and witless." Wotton thought it "full of blasphemies", "hideous, horrid, and infamous" in method; it was nothing but a "dung-pit of scandals and lies".[17]

Six years later, a Flemish press issued an even more scandalous attack on James. Written in Latin for continental as well as English audiences, *Corona Regia* was the work of many hands. After years of "restless indeavours", William Trumbull offered the Privy Council an overview of the complex semi-official operation behind the book. The chief author was Cornelius Breda, a "yong Student" at Louvain, later killed fighting for the Habsburgs in Bohemia. His collaborators included Maximilian Pluvier, a Franciscan and former secretary to the Count of East Friesland; and the Louvain academic and Jesuit ally Erycius Puteanus, who corrected Breda's text and added the concluding verses. Under Puteanus's supervision, the Louvain publisher Jean-Christophe Flavius manufactured the libel, Remacle Roberti supplied paper and paid production costs, while Nicolas Damseau oversaw the printing and distribution of the book. Both Roberti and Damseau were Habsburg officials: Roberti, who had close ties to the Jesuits, was a "Comissoner of the Victualls to the Kinge of Spaines Armie" and later worked in the Chambre des Comptes in Brussels; and Damseau, formerly the Infanta's master "des Pages", had since become "one of the Chaplains of her Oratorie". The collaborators knew each other well, with Puteanus the key link between them. Breda was Puteanus's pupil, Roberti and Pluvier were Puteanus's friends, and Flavius owed Puteanus his start as a printer.[18]

The libel adopted satirical masks to conceal its origins and heighten its effects. Its central conceit was that at his death in 1614 the Huguenot scholar Isaac Casaubon had left unfinished a panegyric to James I, now edited by "Euphormio" and published by the royal printer John Bill. Readers quickly saw through these claims, as the book mixed comically exaggerated flattery with patently libellous accusations. The book constructed a complex libellous portrait of the king, linking his vile manners and unnatural sexual tastes to systematic moral, political and religious corruption. It depicted James as a Machiavellian tyrant, mocked his intellectual pretensions, and claimed he was a changeling—the son, not of Mary, Queen of Scots, but of a Calvinist preacher. Like *Prurit-Anus*, *Corona* also ridiculed the Church of England as the bastard offspring of the "incestuous" and "prodigious lust" of Henry VIII and Anne Boleyn, the creation of "the king's salacious tail" and "the queen's wanton conch". Most notoriously, it portrayed James as a physically deformed sodomite, linking his disordered rule to his disorderly bodily desires. James's shins were disproportionately large, his countenance was ugly and "worthy of despotic rule", his gait so peculiar that he walked in circles, and he inhaled food and drink one minute and vomited the next. Like the classical tyrants Sardanapalus and Heliogabalus, James had an insatiable appetite for strong drink and handsome boys. Claiming that the king lavished honours and wealth on courtiers who excelled not in "virtue" but in "beauty", the libeller catalogued James's favourites, culminating with George Villiers, "a young man of incomparable beauty". The king was ruled by his sexual appetites: at courtly banquets, religious debate mixed promiscuously with drunken excess and illicit sexual desire, as James caressed and kissed his favourites, putting his "amorous passions and entice-ments" on public display. "The words of Christ were, 'suffer little children to come unto me'. You summon boys—the very fair ones in particular—and appre-ciate the benefactions and miracles of nature in them." The libel concluded with the striking image of James descending on Rome "to emancipate the Church from superstition" with an entourage of catamites who would prove that the notoriously sodomitical Italians had nothing to teach the British about "the coaxings of pleasure".[19]

Corona posed a real threat to the king's reputation. It was hawked by the chapmen of Louvain and Brussels, and packets of the book made their way to the 1615 Frankfurt book fair. Only a few copies circulated in England, but they were read and anxiously discussed. Early in October 1622, Simonds D'Ewes recorded that he had had "much good discourse" with friends about "some rare bookes", including "*Pruritanus* . . . and . . . *Corona Regia* or *Manes Causaboni*". The former was "sett out 1608 and 1609", D'Ewes noted, and was reckoned to be "infinite profane". Yet *Corona* was much worse, "whollye against the King himselfe, accusing him of athisme, sodomye etc".[20]

To Sow Jealousies and Enmities

With the outbreak of the Thirty Years War in 1618, books and pamphlets began to pour from both Protestant and Catholic presses on the Continent, many of them commenting on England and its ruler. In May 1621, for instance, the Venetian ambassador reported that two books printed in Paris were now "selling freely" in England, one alleging that James had granted English Catholics "free exercise" of religion, the other that Parliament had deposed the king and executed his favourites. While Buckingham and Charles were in Madrid in 1623, D'Ewes and his friends discussed an engraving circulating in Rome that depicted the favourite and the prince in a cage. On one side stood James in "a fooles coate", and on the other the king of Spain carrying the key to the cage. A fool's motley lying on the floor signified that Philip would be a fool if he used the key to free Charles and Buckingham. But for now, the only fool was James, who had put his son and heir into the hands of a foreign monarch.[21]

The Flemish presses joined the debate. Richard Verstegan, a veteran of the Catholic propaganda campaigns of the 1590s, used the Jesuit press at St Omer to laud the Anglo-Spanish alliance and to mock the Dutch. *London's Looking-glasse*, for instance, responded to London apprentices who had taunted Gondomar by deriding their "brutish savagenesse" and xenophobia and bewailing the moral degradation of a people deprived of traditional Catholic religious discipline. Puritan preachers and pamphleteers were cynically using "the London-laddes" as "instruments of their intended endes", sowing disorder and encouraging popular intrusion into the *arcana imperii*, and thus, Verstegan argued, the Puritan was a far greater threat to royal authority than the papist. "Must the King acquaint Puritan-Preachers & Apprentices with his designes," he asked. "Do brainsicke Puritan-Preachers know what belongeth unto matter of State? ... They better know how to stirre up sedition." Spain was not England's enemy, Verstegan insisted; the English should worry instead about the "high & haughty" Dutch so loved by Puritans. Later pamphlets, most notably 1623's *A Toung-Combat*, returned to these anti-Dutch themes, linking radical Dutch "Gomarists" to seditious English Puritans and warning of the anarchic consequences of Dutch-style "liberty of conscience".[22]

Verstegan deployed fictional framing devices. *Londons Looking-Glasse* claimed to come from a moderate Protestant Englishman, while *A Toung-Combat* recorded a debate between two English soldiers of different religions. But the fictions were transparent, and although the author cloaked himself in initials ("D. N.", the last letters of his forename and surname), his Catholic commitments were self-evident. Masks, varying in degrees of opacity and disguise, were a common feature of polemical literature in the war-torn 1620s. Many publications were pseudonymous or anonymous, issued either without imprints or with fake ones, while many texts falsely claimed to be leaked letters, minutes, or intercepted secret instructions. Undoubtedly, some of these fictions deceived some contemporaries, but others learned to read through these devices, appreciating fictive masks as works of a politic art that added to the depth—and pleasure—of a text's political intent.[23]

As Charles and Buckingham pressed for England to enter the war in 1624, the Flemish presses attempted to inflame English anger at the Dutch massacre of English merchants in Amboyna. In October 1624, Trumbull reported plans in Brussels to "animate our nation againste the Hollanders" using a polyglot print campaign to "publishe to the view of the world" the "barbarous ... murthers and crueltyes" of the Dutch. The authorities were seeking "an Englishe Printer" for the job and assessing shops in St Omer, Douai, Louvain, Malines and Antwerp that had "English Presses" already in place. This tactically sophisticated campaign, which produced at least one printed narrative and perhaps a visual depiction of the "tortures", sought to stoke tensions between the English and the Dutch and within England itself, deploying texts originally produced by the rival East India Companies and manipulating them to further Catholic Habsburg interests. As Trumbull noted, the Flemish used a "relation" of the massacre "framed ... in England, a Copye whereof hath ben sente hether by M. Van Male the Infantas Agent". This Amboyna campaign pioneered a Flemish strategy for undercutting Buckingham: identify pre-existing cultural and political tensions in England, resurrect old texts and charges, and exploit English political debates to damage the duke's domestic authority. Trumbull also learned, for instance, of plans to publish "a libell

against my L. Duke of Buckingham, under the Title of Buckinghams Common
Welth in imitation of that (it should seeme) which long since was written and
printed of the Earle of Leicester".[24] Although no copy of this particular libel has
survived, the Flemish plainly remembered *Leicesters Commonwealth*, a 1584
Catholic attack on the great Elizabethan favourite, and they realized how
damaging its stereotyped allegations of ambition, debauchery and poisoning
would be to Leicester's Jacobean successor.

By early 1625, Habsburg propaganda against Buckingham and Charles had
become more intense and more pronounced. A Jesuit working for Maximilian
of Bavaria produced a printed collection of eight letters titled *Mysteria Politica*,
purportedly the "secret correspondence of illustrious men" but actually artful
"impostures" designed to exploit divisions within the anti-Habsburg coalition.
One letter, ostensibly dated from London in mid-July 1624, reacted sceptically
to the proposed Anglo-French marriage alliance; others mocked English military preparedness or hinted at English plans to use military intervention in the
Palatinate to erect a Huguenot enclave in France under English control.
Another letter warned that the English, Dutch and Venetians hoped to embroil
France in a war with the Habsburgs for their own ends. The final letter, wrote
a French critic, contained "an invective against the king of Great Britain, a
reproach on the government of his kingdoms" and a series of lies designed to
"sow jealousies and enmities", dividing James from his children, the Crown
from Parliament, Anglican bishops from "Calvinist puritan ministers". Like
other Habsburg propaganda, *Mysteria Politica* relied on masks and fictions,
forged letters, anonymous authorship, a hidden place of publication, mixing
libel and polemic with disinformation and misdirection. According to one
hostile summary, the book was admired not only by Habsburg partisans but
even by those of the "contrary party" who acknowledged its skilled use of the
political dark arts.[25]

In the Putterye

Before 1626, Jan van Meerbeeck had never sent any books to the Plantin-
Moretus bookshop. But that year he appears in the ledgers as "Jan Meerbeeck a
Brusselles", listed as the producer of three titles for sale in the Antwerp store
(Fig. 38).[26] His printing shop was located at the sign of St Anne in the "Putterye",
the Putenhof or Jardin aux Puits (Garden of Wells) district of Brussels. For
about a decade between 1624 and 1634, Meerbeeck printed and published
books in Latin, Dutch, Spanish, French and perhaps Italian on a range of
subjects; much of his work bore his title-page emblem, a globe resting on a
sword and an open book, with the motto "His Nititur Orbis" ("The world rests
on these") inscribed above (Fig. 39).[27] He published histories and hagiographies,
poetry and political theory, manuals of warfare and treatises on matrimony, as

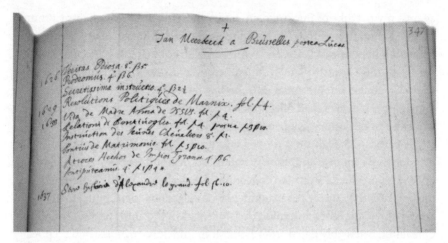

Figure 38: Ledger from the Plantin-Moretus bookshop in Antwerp recording the receipt of copies of Eglisham's *Prodromus Vindictae*, *Veritas Odiosa* and *Secretissima Instructio* from the Brussels printer Jan van Meerbeeck.

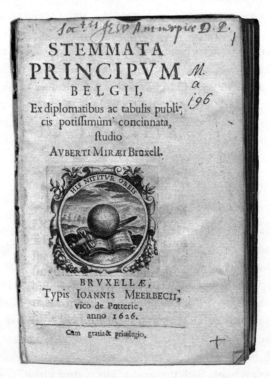

Figure 39: Title page of Jan van Meerbeeck's 1626 publication of Albertus Miraeus's *Stemmata Principum Belgii*, incorporating the printer's emblem "His Nititur Orbis" (The World Rests on These) (Koninklijke Bibliotheek).

well as works on recent and current events. In 1625 he published both Antonio Carnero's Spanish history of the Dutch revolt and his brother Adriaen van Meerbeeck's three-volume *Nederlandtschen Mercvrivs* ("The Netherlands Mercury").[28] In 1626, Meerbeeck issued a Latin panegyric on the celebrated general Ambrogio Spinola and, in 1628, a French account of Spinola's great victory at the 1604 siege of Ostend. In 1629 he helped publish Puteanus's edition of Cardinal Guido Bentivoglio's memoirs of his tenure as papal nuncio in Flanders.[29] A number of Meerbeeck's books were prestige publications by powerful, well-connected authors, issued in expensive folio editions. Among the ten Meerbeeck publications stocked by the Plantin-Moretus bookshop between 1626 and 1633, four were luxury folios costing between 4 and 5½ florins at wholesale. *Prodromus Vindictae* was a significantly cheaper proposition, listed in the bookshop ledgers as a quarto costing 6 stivers, and sold to Rubens at a 1-stiver markup.

The Plantin-Moretus accounts identify Meerbeeck as the man who printed George Eglisham's secret history of James's murder, but how and why Meerbeeck got the job is harder to determine. He certainly had the right technical skills and professional connections. He was based in Brussels, the seat of Isabella's government, and his output was conspicuously orthodox. He owned the typefaces and knew the compositors and proofreaders necessary to publish works in different languages. More important, he had already collaborated with powerful men connected both to the state and to the Flemish propaganda network. In 1624, Meerbeeck published both Verstegan's collection of Dutch epigrams and a Latin work by Aubert Le Mire (Miraeus), an influential Antwerp historian and churchman with multiple ties to the Netherlandish intelligentsia and Brussels regime. Miraeus had served as Archduke Albert's court chaplain and librarian before becoming dean of Antwerp Cathedral, and his pen was frequently in official service: he wrote the Infanta's 1634 funeral oration, a life of Albert and several accounts of Habsburg military campaigns. Miraeus also worked for Spinola, cultivated connections to both Verstegan and a quasi-official newsbook operation in Antwerp, and patronized Meerbeeck's brother, the historian Adriaen. Miraeus was, in Paul Arblaster's words, "just the sort of multifaceted cultural broker . . . one would expect to mediate relations between the authorities and the press".[30] But he was not the only influential man who knew the shop in the Putterye. In 1625, Meerbeeck had published Antonio Carnero's history of the Netherlands' "guerras civiles". Carnero was a central figure in the "Spanish-Flemish connection" that knit Brussels to Madrid. In his youth he had served Don Enrique de Guzman, father of Philip IV's chief minister Olivares. In the 1580s he had worked with his uncle, Alonso Carnero, in the Spanish military administration in Flanders where he returned after political service in Spain and Milan. His cousin—also Antonio Carnero— had served the Spanish minister Baltasar de Zuñiga in Madrid and became

Olivares's "private secretary and . . . right-hand man".[31] No evidence explicitly proves that Miraeus, Verstegan or Carnero encouraged Meerbeeck's 1626 venture into covert propaganda. But Meerbeck had a reputation for skill and reliability, and a set of important connections that might have brought him to the attention of the men who sponsored Eglisham's tract.

The Plantin-Moretus ledgers identify Meerbeeck as the producer of *Prodromus Vindictae*, but they do not tell us which of the two extant Latin versions he printed. To answer that question, we have to resort to the uncertain art of typographic comparison. Contemporary experts believed that typography could betray a printer's identity, but because so many presses used type from the same foundries and shared or traded ornaments, any identification can only be tentative. Yet since we know that Meerbeeck printed a Latin edition of Eglisham's tract, we can scour other Meerbeeck books to see whether his ornaments—capitals, head- and tailpieces, etc.—match either the Latin or the English editions of the *Forerunner*. These comparisons suggest quite clearly that Meerbeeck printed at least two versions of Eglisham's book: the Latin version with the "Frankfurt" imprint and its English translation (Figs 40 and 41). For

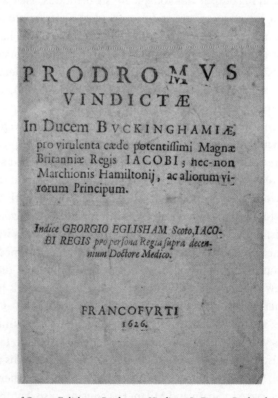

Figure 40: Title page of George Eglisham, *Prodromus Vindictae In Ducem Buckinghamiae*, printed by Jan van Meerbeeck in Brussels in 1626 (Bodleian Library).

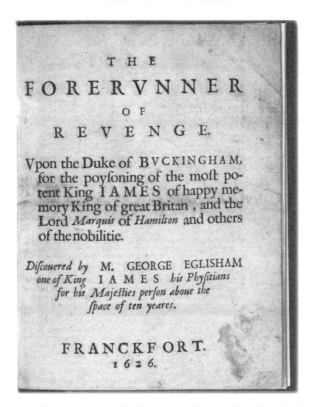

THE
FORERVNNER
OF
REVENGE.

Vpon the Duke of BVCKINGHAM,
for the poyfoning of the moft potent King IAMES of happy memory King of great Britan , and the
Lord *Marquis* of *Hamilton* and others
of the nobilitie.

Difcouered by M. GEORGE EGLISHAM
one of King IAMES *his Phyfitians
for his Majefties perfon aboue the
fpace of ten yeares.*

FRANCKFORT.
1 6 2 6.

Figure 41: Title page of George Eglisham, *The Forerunner of Revenge Upon the Duke of Buckingham*, printed by Jan van Meerbeeck in Brussels in 1626 (Huntington Library).

instance, the ornamental capital "S" used in the opening sections of both the Latin (Frankfurt) and English versions appears in several places in Meerbeeck's 1624 edition of a Jan Ruysbroeck book and at least once in his 1629 edition of Jean de Marnix's *Resolutions Politiques* (Figs 42–45). An ornamental capital "Q" used in Ruysbroeck's book also appears in the "Frankfurt" Latin edition of the *Forerunner*. The tailpiece ornament used in the English *Forerunner* appears throughout Meerbeeck's *Resolutions Politiques* and in at least two places in his 1624 edition of Verstegan's *Nederduytsche Epigrammen*.[32]

The Hateful Truth

The Plantin-Moretus records also cast light on Meerbeeck's other activities in 1626, allowing us to place *The Forerunner* in a more precise propaganda context. In 1626 the shop purchased three titles from Meerbeeck—Eglisham's *Prodromus* and two other works: *Veritas Odiosa*, an octavo pamphlet whole-saling at 5 stivers, and the *Secretissima instructio*, a quarto priced at 2½ stivers. Meerbeeck, it seems, had been commissioned to print not one but three works

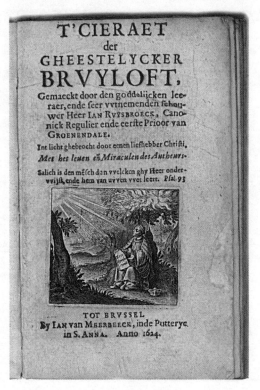

Figure 42: Title page of Jan Ruysbroeck, *T' Cieraet der Gheestelycker Bruyloft*, published by Jan van Meerbeeck in 1624 (University of Ghent).

to advance the Habsburg cause; Eglisham's secret history was one component of a broader multilingual, international propaganda campaign with multiple forms and targets.[33]

Aside from their political agenda, Meerbeeck's three books have very little in common. *Veritas Odiosa* was an eccentric, riddling hybrid of polyglot textual fragments, composed and printed early in 1626, which brazenly challenged its readers. Its language was difficult, but also unusually playful and reflexive. It blurred genres and styles, incorporated large swathes of other texts and constantly (and knowingly) adverted both to its own artifice and to its broader polemical contexts. Built around a colloquy between Mercury, the messenger god and newsmonger, and Machiavelli, the archetypal amoral political thinker, the tract forced the reader to manoeuvre through a fragmentary text punctuated with dashes, gaps and ellipses, designed to create the illusion that these were the unfinished scraps of the pseudonymous Ricardus Attonitus's work. The gaps and redactions required readers to work between the lines to decipher the secrets of state. Folded into the main colloquy was a jumble of other texts: news from Rome; a prose epitaph on the late Dutch stadtholder, Maurice of

Figure 43: An ornamental capital "S" from Jan Ruysbroeck's *T' Cieraet der Gheestelycker Bruyloft*, p. 12, which matches the ornamental 'S' used in the "Frankfurt" Latin and English editions of Eglisham's *Forerunner of Revenge* (University of Ghent).

Figure 44: An ornamental capital "S" from Eglisham's *Prodromus Vindictae In Ducem Buckinghamiae*, sig. A2r (Bodleian Library).

Figure 45: An ornamental capital "S" from Eglisham's *Forerunner of Revenge*, sig. A2r (Huntington Library).

Nassau; a defence of the papacy supposedly taken from a "little book" written by a "certain Frenchman in Rome"; a subtly edited Italian extract from Traiano Boccalini's 1615 *Pietra del Paragone Politico* ("The Political Touchstone"); Latin excerpts titled "Fragmenta Proditionis Gallicanae" ("Fragments of the Gallic Treason"), drawn from *Relatio de Proditione Gallicana*, published the same year; Latin and Dutch inscriptions and poetry on both Maurice and his rival Johan van Oldenbarnevelt; and a mocking inscription to the Elector Palatine followed by a near blasphemous pro-Habsburg parody of the 114th and 115th Psalms.[34] The book concluded with a list of twenty works for further reading, including *Theses 400. super vita Cardinalis Richelieu* ("Four Hundred Theses on the Life of Cardinal Richelieu"), *Lamentatio Hollandiae* ("Holland's Lamentation"), *Palamedes, seu Innocentis Barneveltii Simulachrum* ("Palamedes, the Statue of the Innocent Barnevelt"), and the *Florilegium Nequitiarum Halberstadt* ("A Collection of Halberstadt's Crimes"). These extracts and suggested readings heightened the polemic's reflexive sense of its own role in the pan-European polemical war. The reading list at the back not only contained the *Relatio de Proditione Gallicana*, plundered earlier in the text, and other works, like the *Admonitio ad Ludovicum XIII Regem* of September 1625 that attacked Cardinal Richelieu, but also the French texts *Le Catholique d'Estat* and *Le Miroir du temps passé*, which Richelieu had commissioned to answer his critics.[35]

For all its multifaceted playfulness, *Veritas Odiosa* advanced a straightforward political line. The parodic psalms wittily hymned Catholic military triumphs, converting the psalmist's "Tremble, thou earth, at the presence of the Lord, at the presence of the God of Jacob" into "Germany trembles at the presence of Spinola,

at the presence of the servant of the Emperor". The Biblical image of God transforming rock into water became a panegyric to the general who "changed
Heidelberg from a stagnant pool of Calvinists into the rock of Catholic truth".
Most of the barbs in *Veritas* were aimed at the Dutch and the French. The tract
probed the rifts between Dutch Arminian and Calvinist factions: it attacked
Maurice, Prince of Orange, as a tyrannical "atheist, who believed that no God
ruled in the sky, but fabricated idols of his own ambition on earth", and it praised
the Remonstrant leader Oldenbarnevelt whom Maurice had executed.[36] *Veritas*
supported the French *dévots* who backed militantly Catholic policies and
condemned the *politique* Richelieu whose anti-Spanish alliances with the heretical
"brothers of the Huguenots" betrayed "his Catholic friend of peace" and left
France prey to its unreliable new allies, the "Calvinists, atheists, perfidious ones
and wizards (or poisoners)" that Richelieu now bankrolled. And to what end?
"Four thousand infantrymen and three thousand Gallic cavalrymen", *Veritas*
noted, were "conscripted in the hope of loosening the siege of Breda, and all are
extinguished at once by tempests and sickness: we have covered the sea of
Brabantia with shipwrecks and the cadavers of men and horses". Worse still,
French subsidies had funded the Protestant freebooter Christian of Halberstadt,
whose troops had sacked monasteries, raped "holy virgins", and "mocked,
mangled" and burned Westphalia's churches.[37] These horrors stemmed from the
French "exalting of Reason of State" to justify "robberies, assassinates, and such
slaughters of men" that the "rivers . . . runne with humane bloud".[38]

   Veritas glanced only briefly at English affairs, alleging that Charles mistrusted
Buckingham's ambitions and suspected him of "secret machinations" with the
Elector Palatine, a claim often recycled in Habsburg propaganda. Charles was
so insecure, *Veritas* suggested, that he had pushed forward his own coronation
to stymie Buckingham's plotting and Parliament's plans to deny him the throne.
Meanwhile, Charles's Catholic queen had "rejected the hand of a heretical
prelate" and refused to take part in the coronation ceremony, thus exposing
the unnatural alliance between Protestant England and Catholic France. After
deriding English poverty and Buckingham's humiliating attempt to pawn the
crown jewels in Amsterdam, after cataloguing "fifteen thousand British" deaths
in Mansfelt's army, and after celebrating the "unhappy return of the English
fleet", *Veritas* directed interested readers to a work, apparently now lost, entitled
Excidium Britanniae sub Carolo Infaelice ("The Destruction of Britain Under
the Unfortunate Charles").[39]

   Meerbeeck's third entry in the Plantin-Moretus 1626 ledgers was
"Secretissima Instructio". Most likely, this was a reprint of *Secretissima Instructio
Gallo-Britanno-Batava, Frederico V. Comiti Palatino, Electori Data—The Most
Secret Franco-British-Dutch Advice to Frederick V, Elector Palatine,* a notorious
work of Habsburg disinformation from early in the Bohemian crisis. Ten anon-
ymous Latin editions of the tract, printed without a place of publication,

appeared in 1620, followed by printed German, Dutch and French versions, as well as manuscript translations in English and Italian. Masquerading as counsel to Frederick, the new king of Bohemia, the pamphlet ridiculed him as a Machiavellian dissimulator. This classic work of disinformation was republished in later years, often with a fictitious "Hague" imprint, and the Plantin-Moretus records suggest that Meerbeeck printed at least one of these editions in 1626. But it is also possible that the book he published was the even more ambitious *Altera Secretissima Instructio*, written in August 1626, a clever sequel that, as we shall see, recycled material from Eglisham. Like the original, the *Altera*, which claimed to be friendly advice to Frederick, used the fiction of intercepted "secret" instructions to mock and divide the Habsburgs' enemies. And like the reprinted original, the *Altera* used a fake Hague imprint.[40]

Both *Veritas Odiosa* and the *Secretissima Instructio* used masks—fake imprints with false or missing authors' names—and fictive devices—secret instructions, fragmentary colloquies, "news", and extracts from published and unpublished texts. Some readers were fooled, but others were drawn into a hermeneutic game in which fictions, once peeled away, exposed the hidden "reasons of state" behind the continental conflict. Eglisham's pamphlet shared some, but not all, of these features. Far from being disguised, its author's name appeared on the title page and at the foot of the two petitions in the text. To be sure, the "George Eglisham" of *The Forerunner* was a carefully constructed persona designed to persuade the reader. But for all the artifice involved, the power of his secret history stemmed from his personal credibility, professional expertise and eyewitness testimony. Putting Eglisham's name on the title page was risky; it invited retribution, whether physical or polemical, and ended any hope he had of returning to Britain. Claiming authorship also left Eglisham open to critics who might expose his sometimes unsavoury career. He tried to forestall such attacks by offering a highly sanitized version of his past, finessing the book's foreign origins, and effacing his Catholicism through the use of a fake imprint. Fake imprints could perform many functions. Some were satirical, like the claim that *Veritas* was printed on the Oxford press of Walter Map. Some made a text appear to originate with the person under attack: *Corona Regia* was supposedly printed by James I's printer, while Meerbeeck's edition of the *Secretissima* used a "Hague" imprint to bolster the claim that the secret text was a Protestant work of counsel given to the exiled Elector Palatine. The fake imprint on Meerbeeck's Latin and English editions of *The Forerunner* located production in the Lutheran German city of "Franckfort". It was a clever (and common) choice. Sometimes books marketed at the famed Frankfurt book fair carried the imprint, and other publications used it to "conceal the true place of printing". The Frankfurt imprints on *The Forerunner* functioned as both misdirection and confessional disguise. While a Brussels imprint would have immediately betrayed the pamphlet's Catholic Habsburg origins, a Frankfurt imprint could suggest a Protestant or Protestant-friendly work. Although a few well-informed English readers were not fooled, many more were taken in.[41]

At the Frauen Tor

Meerbeeck produced the two "Frankfurt" editions, one Latin and the other English. But who was responsible for the second Latin edition of *Prodromus* (Fig. 46)? This version presented the same text as the "Frankfurt" edition but compressed Meerbeeck's forty-eight pages into fewer than thirty, thus lowering the printing costs and, possibly, the retail price. This version carried no place name—it read simply "Impressum Anno M DC XXVI"—and thus masked its origins without misdirecting the reader to Lutheran Frankfurt. It is impossible to tell which of the two Latin versions appeared first, although we believe it was almost certainly Meerbeeck's "Frankfurt" edition. Perhaps another enterprising printer sought to capitalize on the original's notoriety. Perhaps the absence of the Frankfurt ruse indicates that this version was directed primarily at Catholic readers, who might have avoided an item from a Lutheran city. In this case, typographic clues are even more treacherous than usual, but they are intriguing. For instance, the ornamental capital "S" at the beginning of the first petition in the alternate Latin edition matches the ornamental "S" in a 1627 "Hague" edition of the *Secretissima Instructio*.[42] Since Meerbeeck was responsible for a 1626 edition of the *Secretissima*, he might have produced a 1627 version; perhaps, then, the alternate Latin Eglisham is his. Even if this 1627 edition was not Meerbeeck's work, the evidence suggests that whoever printed the alternate Latin Eglisham was also involved in the broader campaign to disseminate the *Secretissima* and the *Altera Secretissima* pamphlets. Examining the distinctive printer's ornament on the title page and final page of the alternate *Prodromus* suggests different hypotheses. The same ornament appears on at least two late sixteenth-century books printed by the Commelinus press in Heidelberg. Founded in the late 1580s, the press became famous for its classical and patristic editions, as well as its Calvinist theology. By 1626, however, the Calvinist Elector Palatine no longer controlled Heidelberg; the new governor was the pious Catholic Maximilian of Bavaria. Thus it is just possible that the alternate Latin edition of Eglisham may have been created in a Heidelberg print shop swept clean of heresy by the Bavarian Catholic Reformation.[43]

From Meerbeeck's shop in Brussels, English and Latin copies of Eglisham's tract doubtless followed well-established communication routes into England and across continental Europe.[44] While it is impossible to trace the circulation of his Latin tract, we do know that some Habsburg propagandists hoped to extend its continental readership beyond the Latinate intelligentsia. Early in the eighteenth century, the Scottish physician-historian James Welwood was "prevail'd with to add some Notes and Observations" to a new edition of Arthur

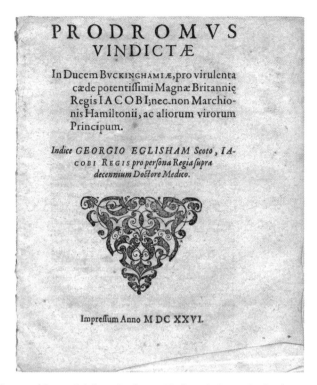

PRODROMVS
VINDICTÆ

In Ducem Bvckinghamiæ,pro virulenta
cæde potentiſſimi Magnæ Britanniȩ
Regis I A C O B I;nec.non Marchionis Hamiltonii, ac aliorum virorum
Principum.

Indice GEORGIO EGLISHAM *Scoto* , IA-
COBI REGIS *pro perſona Regiaſupra*
decennium Doȼlore Medico.

Impreſſum Anno M DC XXVL

Figure 46: Title page of George Eglisham, *Prodromus Vindictae In Ducem Buckinghamiae*, a second 1626 Latin edition of Eglisham's tract, perhaps intended for a European Catholic readership (Folger Library).

Wilson's history of James I, which prompted Welwood to discuss the book that "Dr. Eglisham, one of the King's Physitians" wrote "to prove King James was poyson'd". Some years earlier, Don Pedro Ronquillo, Spain's ambassador to England, had told Welwood that Eglisham had also been "translated into High-Dutch [i.e. German], about the time Gustavus Adolphus was entring into Germany for recovering the Palatinate; and that by a Secret Order of the Court of Brussels, to throw Dust upon the Royal Family of England".[45] Welwood's recollection of Eglisham's text is confused, but Ronquillo, at least, was correct that the "Court of Brussels" had a stake in its publication; and although it pre-dates the Swedes' full-scale intervention in Germany by four years, there was indeed a German translation of *The Forerunner*.

Prodromus Vindictae, Das ist: Vorlauffer oder Vorbott der billichen Raach, a twenty-seven-page quarto pamphlet, was published in 1626 (Fig. 47).[46] Advertised as a translation from the Latin text, the book retained the original's four-part structure, with Eglisham's poems presented in both Latin and German. Yet unlike the Latin and English editions, the German version concealed neither its religious affiliations nor its origins. Its publisher and place of publication—

Figure 47: Title page of George Eglisham, *Prodromus Vindictae. Das ist: Vorlauffer oder Vorbott der billichen Raach*, the 1626 German translation published by Andreas Aperger in Augsburg (Huntington Library).

Andreas Aperger, in the Free Imperial City of Augsburg—appeared openly on the title page. Aperger had started in the printing business in 1617 and by 1619 had established his own premises near Augsburg's "Gate of Our Lady" (the *Frauen Tor*). From the start his business had a distinct confessional bias. He was the only Catholic printer in the bi-confessional city, where Catholics comprised only a quarter of the population. Although he published books by Kepler, medical treatises like Joseph Schmid's *Spiegel der Anatomie* (1646), and a luxury edition of Fugger portraits, the core of Aperger's output was religious. He published numerous broadsheets and pamphlets on miracles and the sacraments, many in collaboration with Augsburg's Jesuit College. He also specialized in ephemeral accounts of political and military affairs, becoming "the most prolific publisher of *Neue Zeitung* (news reports) in Augsburg during the first half of the seventeenth century", with at least one hundred titles to his name. The German wars brought him both opportunities and difficulties. In 1632 his "ardent" Catholicism caused the Swedish army to expel him from the city, and in 1635 he was expelled again, this time for publishing an "unauthorized news report". But in that same year his friends in Augsburg's Jesuit and Catholic elite helped him to the lucrative imperial privilege to print calendars. Six years later he secured a second one for another profitable publication.[47]

The Aperger imprint thus marked the German-language edition of Eglisham as a Catholic book, published by a man close to the Jesuits and committed to publishing Catholic interpretations of the news. It is unclear what role, if any, the Flemish Jesuits had played in the making of *The Forerunner* in Brussels. Eglisham's relationship with the Order had not always been easy: he had quarrelled with them in Rouen, testified against them in Paris, and been married in England by a Benedictine monk thought to be "much hated and persecuted by the Iesuiticall faction".[48] Yet in 1625 he most likely brought a Jesuit to Hamilton's deathbed. In any event, the Jesuits were almost certainly involved with Aperger's German translation, and they had every reason to broadcast Eglisham's charges to the largest possible German audience. Readers were left in no doubt of its Jesuit origins. The decorative headpiece printed over the first page of text depicted two winged putti, or angels, supporting an oval shield bearing the Society of Jesus's distinctive IHS monogram (Fig. 48). If in its Latin and English forms *The Forerunner*'s Catholic origins were masked or muted, the German version proudly carried what the hotter sort of English Protestants would have immediately recognized as "the usuall Badge of Iesuiticall Bookes".[49]

Significantly, the *Vorlauffer* was not Aperger's only work of covert Flemish propaganda in 1626. He also produced the *Holländisch Apocalypsis*, a German translation of a tract by Carolus Scribani, a prominent Flemish Jesuit. Scribani's pamphlet circulated in multiple forms and languages—Latin, Dutch and French as well as German—and a Latin edition (*Apocalypsis Hollandica*) appeared in *Veritas Odiosa*'s catalogue.[50] Scribani wrote under the pseudonym "Pambon Vreimundima", and many editions used a fake publisher's imprint: "Jean Le Vray", for instance, supposedly printed the French edition in "Ville Neuve". Like much of this literature, the tract practised disinformation to exploit pre-existing tensions among the Habsburgs' enemies. The target here was the rivalries within the Dutch Republic after Prince Maurice's death in 1625. Purportedly written by a Dutchman, the book indicted Dutch religious hypocrisy and attacked the provinces' new leaders as irreligious power-seekers who would betray their country to the English and the French. The pamphlet enumerated the Habsburgs' recent military victories, all of them God's handiwork, and lingered over Spinola's triumph at Breda in 1625, a victory attributed in part to Isabella's intense piety. God had inflicted disasters, tempests and diseases on Mansfelt's army and the Cadiz expedition, providential defeats that brought "perpetual dishonour" to the English and Dutch. Scribani catalogued the Dutch and their allies' offences against God—piracies and oppression in the East Indies, the seizure of the Bohemian Crown, the execution of Oldenbarnevelt, the persecution of Arminians, the taking of Spanish ships.

Figure 48: The Jesuit emblem in the headpiece of the first page of Aperger's German version of George Eglisham's *Prodromus Vindictae* (Huntington Library).

And he also tried to sow Dutch suspicions about their English allies. After the death of Oldenbarnevelt, a man who had freed the Dutch from the "English slavery imposed on us by the Earl of Leicester", the Prince of Orange ruled, but only, Scribani suggested, "under English heels". Buckingham meanwhile threatened the Dutch by conspiring with the Elector Palatine in "secret plots" against "the freedom of our country". Aperger's edition of the *Hollandisch Apocalypsis* further underscored Habsburg hostility to Anglo-Dutch rapprochement by appending a copy of the September 1625 Anglo-Dutch treaty of Southampton.[51]

When set against this backdrop, it becomes clear that George Eglisham's *Prodromus Vindictae* has to be understood as one paper bullet in the much broader polemical fusillade unleashed from Flemish and other Habsburg presses in 1625–26. The French, not the English, took the brunt of this onslaught. In Paris the officially sponsored *Mercure François* noticed the unusually large number of "libelles" in print:

There have been sent out this year from the Spanish Netherlands—either those which they brought from Germany or those that were printed there—

more *libelles* against England and France than have been made for over twenty years. Those against England were directed ostensibly against the Duke of Buckingham, favourite of the king of Great Britain: but were in effect against the king himself.

The *Mercure* listed eighteen libels "which they sell in the Catholic towns of Flanders and Germany", noting that there were "many others" in circulation "of the same quality". *Prodromus Vindictae* failed to make this particular list, which understandably focused on anti-French items. But other works associated with Eglisham's tract did appear: *Veritas Odiosa* and the republished *Secretissima Instructio*, printed by Meerbeeck and sold to Plantin-Moretus; Scribani's *Veredicus Belgicus*, which reprinted the "Dutch Apocalypse" that appeared in German from Eglisham's Augsburg printer; and the *Relatio de Proditione Gallicana* excerpted in *Veritas*.[52] George Eglisham's secret history thus belonged not just to the political culture and literary underground of early Stuart England but also to the major propaganda and disinformation campaign, centred in the Spanish Netherlands and broadcast across the Continent, promoting the Habsburg cause against its legions of enemies.

As we follow Eglisham's book across the sea and into the hands of its English and Scottish readers, we will begin to track its long and damaging influence on the British political imagination. But it is vital to acknowledge that, like Eglisham himself, *The Forerunner* was fashioned by broader European contexts. It was made and consumed in a world of cultural, geographical and confessional mobility. In Latin, German and English, whether claiming a "Frankfurt" or an Augsburg origin, or no origin at all, whether speaking to Protestant or Catholic readers, masked or unmasked, *Prodromus Vindictae*, *The Forerunner of Revenge* and *Vorlauffer oder Vorbott der billichen Raach* meant different things to different people, and played different roles in varied European contexts. Its history underscores the fact that events and actors in Brussels, Madrid and Augsburg, as well as in London and Edinburgh, could shape the turbulent course of early modern British politics. The story of *The Forerunner* reminds us that early modern England was embedded in trans-national European contexts and networks. And in the end, only a European history can fully capture the remarkable story of the political damage wrought by a small book first printed on an otherwise obscure Flemish press at the sign of St Anne.

CHAPTER SEVEN

"WHAT CAN BE FULLER OF WONDER?"

THE FORERUNNER MAKES ITS CASE

A BOUT A MONTH after Rubens bought his copies of *Prodromus Vindictae* in Antwerp, an English Catholic wrote to a priest in Spain. Gabriel Browne considered himself a loyal Englishman, but was dismayed at the "blast of perse-cution . . . as vehement as [it was] causeless" that had afflicted English Catholics since 1624. There were, however, remarkable new developments to report, particularly about the Duke of Buckingham. In 1624 the duke had been the people's hero, the man who "had the art to overreach all the wits of Spain"; but now he was "the most distasted man alive"; "Let him guard his head", for they have "so covered him with the filth" of numerous "foul crimes" that the stain of suspicion "will not be washed off in haste with all the water in the Thames or ocean". This sudden change was most evident in Westminster, where the Parliament-men were trying "to tear . . . piecemeal and eat . . . raw with salt" the man "whom so little a while since they did so measurably extol". And near the centre of this storm was a book, come over from the Continent, "printed in English, under the name of a kind of mad Scottish poet and physician called George Eglisham". This book "bravely" accused "the Duke that he poisoned no fewer or meaner persons than King James, the Dukes of Richmond and Lennox, the Lord Marquis Hamilton, and the Earl of Southampton". What is more, it "lays sorcery to his charge and combination with infernal fiends and witches". "Lord God", Browne concluded, "what can be fuller of wonder?"[1]

Jan van Meerbeeck's "Frankfurt" editions of Eglisham's secret history were indeed full of wonder. With its Flemish origins masked but its author's identity freely exposed, *The Forerunner of Revenge* began its long and eventful political life in England late in April 1626. Later chapters will explore the book's reception and circulation. But we must begin with the book itself and under-stand why its stories gained such an attentive domestic audience. *The Forerunner* was an undeniably skilful piece of writing—vivid, detailed and dramatic. It used elements from a variety of well-known genres—the petition, the provi-dentialist murder pamphlet, even the revenge tragedy—to frame its compelling narratives. It fashioned an authorial persona that neutralized George Eglisham's problematic personal story. It reworked the whispers around the "strange tragedies" of 1624–25 into a powerful secret history that finally explained the traumatic succession of mysterious deaths. And it spoke convincingly to multiple anxieties, echoing critiques of Buckingham found in earlier verse libels and tapping into deeply embedded fears about poison and court politics. The courtly poisoner, the quintessence of political corruption, was a stock figure on the Elizabethan and Jacobean stage and in widely read histories of imperial Rome, and haunted contemporary political memory. Catholic libels against the Earl of Leicester had memorably depicted Elizabeth I's favourite as an assiduous student of the arts of poison, but far fresher in the mind was the scandal around James's earlier favourite, the Earl of Somerset, who had been arrested and convicted in 1615–16 for poisoning Sir Thomas Overbury. The widespread commentary on the Overbury scandal had reinforced all kinds of contemporary anxieties, linking courtly poisoning to deep-rooted political, gender and religious disorder.[2]

The Forerunner derived much of its energy and plausibility from these memories and anxieties. But it also made unusually systematic use of forensic evidence to provide credible "proof" of Buckingham's guilt. In 1616 prosecuting lawyers in the Overbury case had argued that poisoning was a "most secreat" crime, difficult to prove using normal standards of evidence; and contemporary poisoning allegations were often accompanied by intense debates about the material and medical proofs that might sustain a prosecution.[3] But Eglisham did not rely on vague allegations; he used circumstantial evidence, eyewitness testimony and expert knowledge of poisons and poisoned bodies to support his case. His charges certainly played to stereotypes, but he framed those charges in ways that could not be easily dismissed.

Eglisham's problematic past complicated his assignment. Although *The Forerunner*'s title page trumpeted James's poisoning, Eglisham lavished much greater attention on Hamilton's murder, and his account drew considerable force from earlier rumours about the marquis's death. But those same rumours had left Eglisham himself dangerously exposed. Hamilton's friends had feared that the marquis was "catholiquelie poisoned", and they had bitterly blamed Eglisham for the marquis's alleged deathbed conversion. Any story Eglisham now told about Hamilton's death had to rework the poison rumours into a different narrative frame. He obviously had to cut any mention of the conversion; but he also had to subvert the story, promoted by the marquis's Protestant friends, that Hamilton was the victim of a Catholic poisoning. Other complications arose from the fact that Eglisham was writing to order. His Habsburg backers in Brussels wanted a story that would exploit English political divisions, damage Buckingham, and undermine the English war effort. If Eglisham's narrative were too obviously Catholic, it would alienate English readers; thus his religious allegiances had to be masked. On the other hand, a virulently anti-Catholic pamphlet, playing on long-established English stereotypes of poison as a popish crime, would be equally counter-productive. Finally, the Brussels regime's need to accuse Buckingham of James's poisoning brought Eglisham additional difficulties. Eglisham had been in hiding during James's illness, and he could not muster the same level of eyewitness detail that enlivened his telling of Hamilton's story. Indeed, Eglisham's relatively brief narrative of James's death looks and reads like an afterthought, appended to an original draft focused on the marquis. Eglisham probably had heard stories of the Theobalds sickroom from Scottish and medical colleagues, and his friend Van Male had sensational reports from agents X and XX safely filed away. Eglisham could construct a compelling account of Buckingham's assault on the king from these sources, but he had to work carefully to tie the separate parts of the pamphlet together. The fit was not quite perfect, but he established enough thematic and forensic continuity to conceal most of the joints. Work like this demanded significant literary skill and audacity. A lifetime of polemical conflict, frequent disguise and constant reinvention had left Eglisham ideally suited to the task.

To Die like Asses in Ditches

Eglisham's tract opened with a daring meditation on justice addressed to Charles I. The "severe and exact iustice of God" demanded eternal rewards for the righteous and everlasting torment for the wicked. Sometimes evil deeds went unpunished on earth, but God saw all, and never forgot. "Wilfull and secret murder", however, "hath seldome bene observed to escape undiscovered or unpunished even in this life." And in this world, it was the king's duty to emulate God and punish the crime. Such ideas were commonplaces. But as he reminded Charles of a king's duty to "honestie" and justice, Eglisham adopted an unusually bold tone. Kings are bound by their coronation oaths to perform justice, Eglisham told Charles; failure to do so made a king "false and periured". Indeed, justice was the very essence of kingship. "What need hath mankinde of Kinges, but for iustice?" he asked. "It is iustice that maketh Kings, iustice that maintaineth Kings". And so, from the outset, Eglisham made clear his expectations. If the king exercised justice in this case of "secret murder", it would "yeeld a most glorious field for your Majestie to walke in, and display the banner of your Royall vertues". But if the king failed to perform justice, he would pay an awful price. Injustice, Eglisham insisted, "bringeth both Kingdomes and Kings to destruction to fall in miserie, to die like asses in ditches or more beastly deathes, with eternal infamie after death, as all histories from time to time doe clearly testifie".[4]

It was a breathtaking opening. Having warned of the destruction of "Kingdomes and Kings", and having reminded Charles of his obligations, Eglisham introduced himself as the man who would reveal the "secret murder" to the world. He acted out of unavoidable duty, for no other man was "so much obliged to stirre" in this case. Not only did Eglisham know the truth of the murders, he was bound to the murdered men by ties of "humane obligation". "Interest of bloud" through the "house of Balgony Lundy or by the house of Silvertonhill" as well as three generations of family service to the Hamiltons gave him motive enough to act, but it was "the interest of receaved courtesies and the heape of infallible tokens of true affections" that really bound him "to stirre . . . therto". Eglisham fondly recalled the "Royall celebration of our friend-ship" when Hamilton's father had presented him and the future marquis to James, and he noted the motto inscribed in all his books: "Always the King, and Hamilton,/Within thy breast conserve./Whatever be thy action/Let Princes two deserve." Hamilton had long protected Eglisham, even offering to "hasard his life in combat" for his friend. "Our loves", Eglisham declared, "increased with our age"; Hamilton had "put trust in me, and I fully to addict myuselfe [*sic*] unto him". Eglisham was equally bound to King James who "from the third yeare of my age, did practise honourable tokens of singular favor towards me" and "with giftes, patents, offices, recommendations, both in privat and in publicke, at home and abroad, graced me so farre that I could scarce have asked him any thing which I could not also obtaine." The deaths of Hamilton and the king had injured Eglisham, "for who hath killed King Iames and the Marquis of Hamilton in that parte of the iniurie which is done to me, therein he hath done as much as robbed me of my life and of all my fortunes."[5]

Honour thus compelled Eglisham to seek revenge. He had rather a "dolefull day/Set me in cruell fate", he added in verse, than leave Hamilton's "death strange, without revenge". Private obligation was also a public duty. "Who . . . can iustly blame me for demanding iustice . . . seinge I knowe whome to accuse", and nothing could "hinder me from undertaking the hardiest enterprise that ever any Roman undertooke." This claim to Roman-style civic virtue was central to Eglisham's self-portrait as a fearless plain-speaker. Most contemporaries did not know the details of these murders, and "others albeit they know as well as I, and ar obliged as deeply as I, yet dare not complaine" of Buckingham's power. But Eglisham could speak "boldly" because he was not dependent on the favourite and because he had reached a place of safety, "ultramarin unto these dominions" where the duke "raigneth and rageth". Although he had "retired . . . amongst Buckingham his enemies", Eglisham insisted that he did not write for "any entertainement here present". Rather, he had fled to Buckingham's enemies because they alone would allow him to write what he had to write. Eglisham knew he was a marked man, and that the murderous duke wanted no "discov-erer or revenger" of his crimes left alive, "for . . . the dead can not bite". And Eglisham assumed his pamphlet would inevitably "provoke the Duke to send forth a poysoner, or other murtherer to dispetch him and send him after his dead freinds". He faced the danger with stoic contempt: "let the event be what it will, come whatsoever can come, the losse of his owne life your petitioner valueth not", for he reckoned "his life can not be better bestowed then upon the discovery of so haynous murthers."⁶

Having presented himself as a man of honour, Eglisham began to paint a startling portrait of his monstrous antithesis, the Duke of Buckingham. Eglisham urged Charles to consider how Buckingham "hath tyrannised over his Lord, and master, King James, the worldly creator of his fortunes, how insolent, how ingrat an oppressor, what a murtherer and treator he hath proved himselfe towards him, how treacherous to his upholding friend the Marquis of Hamilton and others." Buckingham's power corrupted the state, holding kings in thrall. "Your Majestie suffereth your selfe so farre to be led", Eglisham warned, "that your best subiects ar in doubt, whether he is your King or you his." Indeed, "so farre hath his ambitious practises gone", Eglisham added in his petition to Parliament, "that what he wold have done should have been performed whether the king would or not." Buckingham, not Charles, governed, and his grip on the state was "so powerfull that unlesse the whole body of a parliament lay hold upon him, no iustice can be had of him". Eglisham asked the Lords and Commons to acknowledge that "all the Iudges of the kingdome, all the officers of the state ar his bound vassals, or allies, or afeared to become his outcasts." There was no place of justice, no "degree of honor in the kingdome" that the duke "hath not sold, and sold in such craft that he can shake the buyers out of them and intrude others at his Pleasure." Parliament itself had experienced Buckingham's "violent pleasure" and "ambitious villanie". Alluding to the sudden dissolutions of 1621 and 1625, Eglisham insisted that it was the duke alone who "procureth the calling, breaking or continuing of parliament". Through means "lawfull or unlawfull, humane or diabolicke", Buckingham now "tortereth the kingdom"; only by surrendering Buckingham to justice, Eglisham insisted, would the king "deliver your selfe, and your Kingedoomes from the captivitie in which he holdeth them and your Majestie oppressed".⁷

The extent of Buckingham's tyrannical power left Eglisham little hope that Charles would heed his plea or that Parliament could act. But he knew the political costs of inaction: Charles would "incurre such a censure amongst all vertuouse men . . . that your Maiestie will be loath to heare of. . . . No other way there is to be found to save your honor, but to give way to iustice against that traitor Buckingham, by whom manifest damage apphroacheth [sic] unto your Maiestie no otherwayes then death approached unto King Iames". Whether that "damage" would be political or mortal, Eglisham left provocatively unclear.⁸

Base Brood Risen Aloft

Having established his unimpeachable motives for writing, Eglisham turned to Hamilton's murder, framing the story as the collision of the traditional aristocratic ethos with low-born "upstart" ambition. He began with the crucial explanatory fact. Buckingham was a low-born ingrate suddenly "raised from the bottome to the top of fortunes wheele". Like all such upstarts, Buckingham had become arrogant and ambitious: "No thing more proud", Eglisham quoted "the proverb", "then baser broud [sic] when it doth rise aloft". Sidestepping the question of James's role in Buckingham's ascent—"by what desert" he rose, "by what right or wrong" was "no matter"—Eglisham immediately turned to the conflicts that ended in Hamilton's death. Restless ambition drove Buckingham to aspire to ally his "meane" family with Scotland's royal blood. Knowing that Hamilton, "next to [James's] owne line in his propre season might claime an hereditarie title to the Kingdome of Scotland", Buckingham proposed that his niece Mary Feilding marry Hamilton's eldest son; and he "never suffered the King to be at rest" until the alliance was concluded. To tempt Hamilton, Buckingham offered a massive dowry of £50,000, the title of Earl of Orkney, and even the chance to become "the first Duke of Britane". But Hamilton stood firm, for "the matter of money was no motive" for him to "match his sonne so unequally to his degree". Buckingham, "the chief of his kindred", was "but a novice in nobilitie, his father obscure among gentlemen, his mother a serving woman". Worse still, Buckingham himself was "infamous" for the debased company he kept, and particularly for "his frequent consultation with the ringleaders of witches, principally that false Doctor Lamb publikly condemned for witchcraft". But Hamilton had little freedom of manoeuvre. Since James "was so farre bewitched to Buckingham" that he would do whatever the favourite wanted, the marquis understood that he would face "the kings deadly hatred" if he refused the alliance. His only option was to concede and play a longer game. Buckingham's niece was "not yet nubile in yeares", and until the marriage was consummated, an annulment remained a possibility. But the favourite would not be outplayed. "Fearing that delayes Wold breed lets", Buckingham hurried the marriage. One Sunday morning, James invited Hamilton's son to Greenwich "where never a word was spoken of marriage to the young lord" until "a little before supper", when Buckingham pounced:

> [this marriage was] made before the king after supper and to make it more authentike Buckingham caused his neece be layd a bed with the Marquis his sonne for a short tyme in the kings chamber and in his Majesties presence, albeit the brid [sic] was yet innubile.[9]

News of this abrupt, unseemly marriage "astonished" the court and left "the Marquis friends fretting". But the marriage remained unconsummated. To buy time to "untye that knot", Hamilton planned to send the boy "beyond the seas" to France and Italy. But once again he was outflanked. Buckingham persuaded James to appoint the young man as a Gentleman of the prince's bedchamber, thus keeping him "within the Kingdome untill the bride was of yeares ripe for mariage". When the girl became "ripe", Buckingham pressed to have the marriage consummated. Hamilton "scorned the notion", and soon the two men exchanged heated words. Buckingham charged Hamilton with slandering his family, Hamilton rebuked the favourite's insolent tone; Buckingham threatened "revenge", and Hamilton offered "defiance". The French ambassador intervened to reconcile them, but no reconciliation would last. The "ambitious matching of his neece" thwarted, Buckingham's "anger and furie" became "inextinguible", his "malice insatiable". Hamilton soon "fell sicke".[10]

Eglisham was Hamilton's physician, and from this point in the narrative, he became a uniquely privileged eyewitness, testifying to Hamilton's fears and suspicions as well as to Buckingham's "vindictive" cruelty and dissimulation. From the beginning, Hamilton was convinced he would be poisoned, and "his suspicion of Buckingham, he expressed by name" both to Eglisham and to others. Fearful of continued assault, the marquis "wold not tast of any thing that was sent to him by any of Buckinghams freinds", unless a servant tasted it first—and, Eglisham noted, two of his staff eventually died "with manifest signs and symptomes of poyson". Meanwhile, Hamilton clung to Eglisham "whom he wold never suffer to go out of his sight", and Eglisham, "for the love that was mutuall" between them, also "tasted of all that he tooke at that time". Hamilton begged Eglisham "not to suffer my Lord of Buckingham to come neere him", and when the duke finally forced his way in, Hamilton told the doctor to "gett him away quikly".[11]

Yet in spite of these precautions, the marquis's health steadily declined. Four days before Hamilton's death, Eglisham had to tell his friend "to dispose of his estate and of his conscience because his sicknes was not without danger", though he urged him not to despair, for "howsoever he had gotten wrong abroad, he should get none in the cure of his disease". Eglisham struggled to save his patient, trying various antidotes, but the "poyson was such and [so] farre gone that none could helpe". As the marquis sickened, Buckingham cruelly blocked the son from coming to his father's side, lest Hamilton give "some privat instruction to shun the mariage of Buckinghams neece or to signifie unto him the suspicion that he had of poyson". After Eglisham warned him to prepare for death, Hamilton berated William Feilding, Earl of Denbigh, his son's new father-in-law, saying "it is a greate crueltie in you that you will not suffer my soone to come to me when I am a dying that I may see him and speake to him before I die". Only when Hamilton's "agonie of death was neere" did Buckingham permit his son to see him. By then it was much too late for deathbed speeches.[12]

After Hamilton's death, Eglisham instructed the servants "to suffer no man to touch his body" until he returned to see it being "opened". This post-mortem inspection was crucial, for Hamilton's corpse contained material evidence of the cause of death. But "to have the matter concealed", Buckingham's "folks" pressed for an immediate burial in Westminster Abbey, "saying that such delicate bodyes as his could not be long kept". Heeding Eglisham's instructions, Hamilton's friends insisted that the marquis had to be buried in Scotland "in his owne Chappell where his ancestours" lay, and that his corpse "must be first visited by his Physitians".[13]

But even a hasty burial could not have prevented Hamilton's body from revealing the truth. Eglisham's lengthy description of the corpse formed the core of *The Forerunner*'s forensic evidence:

> No sooner was he dead, when the force of the poyson had overcome the forces of his body, but it begoud [sic] to swell in such sort that his thighes were as big as six tymes there naturall proportion, his belly became as big as the belly of an oxe, his armes as big as the naturall quantitie of his thighes, his necke so broad as his shoulders, his cheekes over the tope of his nose, that his nose could not be seene or distinguished, the skinne of his forehead over his eyes, and the same skinne, with all the rest of the skinne of his head two finger high swelled, his haire of his beard, eyebrowes, and head, so farre distant one from an other, as if an hundreth had beene taken out betwixt every one, and when one did toutch his haire it came away with the skin as easily as if one had pulled hay out of an heape of hay.

This monstrous swelling and loosening of the hair was accompanied by vivid blistering on the skin. Hamilton's corpse was "all over his breast, necke, shoulders, and armes, blistered with blisters so big as ones fist . . . blisters . . . of six divers colours, full of waters of the same coulours, some white, some blacke, some red, some yeallow, some greene, some blew". After opening the body, the physicians found "the cavities of his liver greene, his stomake in some places a little purpurated with a blewish clammie matter adhaeringe to the sides of it". Meanwhile "his mouth and nose" haemorrhaged "blood mixt with froth of divers coulors a yard highe". All the marquis's servants agreed; the signs were clear that "he was poysoned".[14]

To make the truth "manifest", Eglisham told the servants, he needed a "jury of physicians". Some wanted to call in the duke's doctors, but Eglisham rejected the idea, insisting they needed "indifferent", that is impartial, men. However, Captain Hamilton, the marquis's cousin, thought they might test the duke's guilty conscience by watching his reaction when they informed him that "all who see the Marquis his body both Physitians and Chirurgians and others think he is poysoned". If Buckingham had been innocent, Eglisham now claimed, he would have sent his own doctors to help inquire after the truth. But instead, the duke summoned his doctors and told them "there is a brute spred abroad that the Marquis of Hamilton is poysoned". "Go and see", he instructed them, adding "in a threatning forme of delivery" that they should "beware what you speake of poyson".[15]

The duke's men joined the other physicians assembled to view "this pitifull spectacle". They were all impressive individuals. Some were Fellows of the College of Physicians, some held court appointments, and many had extensive clinical experience. But they were unprepared for what they saw. So shocking was "the sight of my lords body", that all the doctors, duke's men or no, were stunned. "Doctor Moore" (John More) lifted up his hands and eyes to heaven, saying "Iesus blisse me, I never sawe the like". Hamilton's body was unrecognizable; "I can not distinguish a face upon him", More exclaimed. Most of the others had never seen anything like it, "albeit they had traveled and practiced through the greatest part of Europe". Significantly, the one exception was a doctor who had witnessed, in Holland in 1624, the opening of the Earl of Southampton that found him also "blistered all within the breast", and the earl, Eglisham noted, "was also one of my L. of Buckinghams opposits". But Buckingham's influence quickly disrupted the doctors' initial consensus that something was amiss. The duke's "creature", "Doctor Leaster" (Matthew Lister), took the amazed physicians aside "and whispered them in the eare to silence them, whereupon many went away without speaking one worde". Those who remained agreed that the bizarre symptoms—"those accidents of the dead body"—could only have been the result of poison. The evidence, however, was so unusual that the doctors "could not know how such a subtil art of poysoning could be brought into England". Eglisham assured them (and his readers) that "money could bring both the art and the artist from the furthest part of the world". The remaining physicians had seen enough, and they "were willing to certifie" in writing "that my L. Marquis was poysoned". But Eglisham "tould them it was not needfull, seing we must attend Gods leasure to discover the author, the matter being so apparent, and so many hundreds having seene his body to witnesse it".[16]

But courtly dissimulation could obscure even self-evident truths. Immediately after Hamilton's death, Buckingham feigned inconsolable grief, "making some counterfeited show of sorrow to men of great qualitie". When the body was moved from Whitehall to the marquis's house in Bishopsgate, "Buckingham came out muffed and furred in his coach, giving out that he was sick for sorrow". Among his own friends, however, the duke rejoiced, and as "soone as he went to his house out of London", at New Hall in Essex, "he triumphed and dominired with his faction so excessively, as if he had gayned some greate victorie". Yet the very next day when he saw the king, Buckingham again "put on a most lamentable and mournefull countenance". This dissimulation was accompanied by a more audacious action. To shield himself from accusation, he "found no other shift to divert the suspicion of the poysoning of the Marquis from him selfe, but to lay it upon his Master the King". And so

Buckingham praised Hamilton as a man "borne worthy to reigne", and let it be known that James "hated [Hamilton] to death, because he had a spirit too much for the commonwealth". Appalled at this unconscionable attempt to paint the king as a "bloodthirstie murtherer", Eglisham declared that "If any dissimulation be greater then Buckinghams, let any man iudge."[17]

Eglisham made clear that he had continued to gather evidence of Hamilton's poisoning even after fleeing England. Since the plague was poised to return to London when Hamilton died, Eglisham wanted to rule out the possibility that the marquis had died of "the venime of the pest". He had thus consulted "the skilfullest pestmasters that could be found", who assured him that they had never known the bodies of plague victims to exhibit the blistering and swelling of Hamilton's corpse. Eglisham also talked to men who had tested poisons on dogs and "found that some poysons have made the dogges sicke for a fortnight or more, without any swelling until they were dead, and then they swelled above measure, and became blistered with waters of divers colours, and the haire came away with the skin when it was touched." The testimony of skilled "pestmasters" and the tests on dogs thus proved that Hamilton's symptoms were best explained by what Eglisham termed a "subtil art of poysoning". And Eglisham knew the appropriate suspect—a "poysonmunger mountibanck" "greatly countenanced" by Buckingham, who obtained, by the duke's influence, "letters patents and recommendation from the King, to practise his skill through all England", and "who coming to London offered to sell poysons to kill men or beasts within a yeere, or halfe a yeare, or two yeares, or a moneth, or two, or what tyme praefixed any man desired, in such sort that they could not be helped nor yet discovered".[18]

Eglisham then turned to additional evidence, this time from the London streets. He recalled "the bruit" that "went through London long before my L. Duke of Richmonds [Lennox's] death, or his brothers, or my lord of Southamptons, or of the Marquis, that all the noblemen that were not of Buckingham's faction should be poysoned, and so removed out of his way." He remembered too that over Christmas 1624 "one of the Prince his footemen sayd that some of the greate ones at court had gotten poyson in his belly but he could not tell who it was." Finally, there was the evidence of "a paper . . . founde in kingstreete" around the time of Lennox's death in February 1624. It contained "the names of all these noblemen" who had died, and had been shown to Hamilton by his cousin "lord Oldbarres dawghter". Eglisham had seen his own name next to Hamilton's on the list, with the words, "to embaume him" written alongside. Initially, Eglisham had thought nothing of the paper, but when he saw "the Marquis poysoned, and remembered that the rest therin noted were dead", he realized that this was a "roll . . . of those that were to be murdered" and that the list "next pointed" at him. When, after Hamilton's death, both D'Effiat, the French ambassador, and Buckingham's mother, the countess "sent on every side to seeke me", Eglisham knew that the duke wanted "to silence me with death".[19]

With the old marquis removed, Buckingham concluded his plans for Hamilton's son whose "captivitie" began the day of his father's death. Buckingham sent the young man "out of the towne, keeping him as a prisoner that none could have privat conference with" until he consummated his marriage to the duke's niece. Kept constantly under surveillance by his Villiers in-laws, the young marquis was prevented from hearing "how his father was murthered". Eglisham claimed, however, that he did get to see the boy, but decided "not to speake to him of the poysoning . . . because there sorrow was too recent". There would be no second visit. Anxious lest the "intended marriage . . . be over throwne", the duke would not let the new marquis attend his father's funeral in Scotland or even talk with advisors about his new estate. This confinement only ended after a private conference in St James's Park where Charles persuaded young Hamilton to consummate the marriage "without any more delay". Once that was done, the duke thought he was safe. Even if "the young lord" should come to "understand how his father was poysoned", his marriage to the duke's niece would ensure he would "not sturre to revenge it".[20]

Having provided such bountiful circumstantial and forensic evidence, Eglisham pleaded with Parliament to act. Buckingham had committed treason by murdering a Privy Councillor. Legal proceedings should be opened, inter-rogatories framed and witnesses examined. There was more than enough evidence to "take him and torture him, if he were a private man". Indeed, far "more is discovered to beginne with all, then was layd open at the beginning of the discovery of the poysoning of sir Thomas Overbury".[21]

White Powder

Eglisham explained that Buckingham had murdered Hamilton in order to ally the favourite's "meane" family to royal blood. But when discussing Buckingham's dissimulated grief for Hamilton, Eglisham had introduced another motive. The duke could have obtained "No greater victorie . . . then to have destroyed that man who could and would have fetched his head of his shoulders if he had outlived King James to have knowen his cariage in the poysoning him [i.e. James] in his sicknes, wherfore he thought it necessary to remove the Marquis before hand". In other words, Buckingham had to kill Hamilton in order to proceed to his next, and greatest, crime.[22] The bulk of *The Forerunner* consists of two petitions, one to Charles and the other to Parliament, the latter containing the case on Hamilton. Appended to this second petition is a three-page section, "Concerning the poysoning of King Iames". The section looks like a late addition, and it lacks the eyewitness testimony that made Eglisham's account of the Hamilton case so vivid. But it built on themes already established in the Hamilton narrative to set out a chilling account of the king's murder.

Eglisham had disentangled Hamilton's death from the controversial politics of 1625 by casting the marquis as the noble victim of upstart ambition, not the Protestant victim of popish malice. But Eglisham's account of James's murder was set squarely within the contested politics surrounding the collapse of the Spanish match and the push for war in 1623–24. While in Madrid in 1623, Buckingham heard disturbing reports that James had begun "to censure him in his absence freely and that many spoke boldly to the King against him". Among these critics was Hamilton, who "nobley reprehended the King, for sending the Prince with such a young man without experience, and in such a privat and suddain manner, without acquainting the nobilitie or counsell." In response, Buckingham "wrote a very bitter letter" to Hamilton; but, more importantly, he "conceived new ambitious courses of his owne". He began by destroying the Anglo-Spanish marriage, using "all the devises he could to disgust the Prince his minde of the match with Spayne". Returning to England, Buckingham attempted to control foreign policy; "whatsoever the King commanded in his bedchamber", Buckingham now "controlled in the next chamber". He inter-cepted dispatches "from forraine Princes", answered them "without acquainting" James, and told him only "a great time thereafter". James was "highly offended", and his "mind" began to "alter towards" the duke. He took very seriously Hinojosa's 1624 accusation that Buckingham had plotted to retire the "old man" and confine him "to some parke to passe the rest of his tyme in hunting". James's cooling favour meant that for the first time Buckingham was "quar-relled and effronted in his Maiesties presence". The favourite's anxiety grew as James urged him to leave for Paris to conclude the French match. It deepened further when he saw that James had "reserved my Lord Bristow to be a rod for him" and was set to welcome Gondomar back to England during the duke's absence in France. Bristol was a serious problem, but Gondomar was the mortal danger. Buckingham "feared" the old ambassador and knew how much the Spaniard was "estemed and . . . credited by the King". Once back in Whitehall, Gondomar would not only "second" Bristol's "accusations against" the duke, but would also reverse Buckingham's anti-Spanish foreign policy. Although Parliament had emphatically recommended an immediate end to the Spanish treaties in 1624, James had complied with obvious reluctance, vowing to "bring the Spanish match about againe", even if "all the devils in hell" stood against him. In short, "the more the King urged him to be gone to France the more shiftes he made to staye, for he did evidently see that the King was fully resolved to rid him selfe of the oppression wherein he held him".[23]

Buckingham decided to strike first. When James came down with an ague in the spring, which, as the proverb put it, "was of it selfe never found deadly", the duke poisoned him. He first took the opportunity when "all the Kings Doctors . . . were at Dinner" to offer James "a white powder" as medicine. James initially balked, but "overcome by [Buckingham's] flattering importunitie at length", drank it down in a glass of wine. The king "immediately became worse and worse, falling into many soundings and paynes, and violent fluxes of the belly", crying out "o this white powder, this white powder! wold to God I had never taken it, it will cost me my life." A few days later, with the doctors again at dinner, the favourite's mother, the former "serving woman", "applyed a plaster to the Kings harte and breast, wherupon his Maiestie grew fainte, short breathed and in great agonie". Returning to the sickroom, the doctors detected the plaster's "offensive smell" and "exclamed that the King was poysoned". The duke immediately tried to silence the outcry, commanding "the Physitians out of the roome", confining one of them to his chamber and expelling another from court. Buckingham also clashed with "others of the Kings servants in the sick Kings owne presence, so farre that he offered to draw against them in the Kings sight". The countess then complained to James that some had had the gall to say that "my sonne and I have poysoned your Maiestie". All James could say to that was "Poysoned me", before turning away in a faint. A few days later, he was dead.[24]

Again Buckingham attempted to conceal his crimes. He demanded that the king's doctors "signe with there handwrits a testimonie that the poweder which he gave the King was a goode and safe medicin, which", Eglisham added, "they refused to do". The physician who had been confined to his room was set free "with a caveat to hold his peace", while the other doctors were "threatned if they kept not good tongues in there heades". Buckingham put on his usual "counterfeit" show of excessive grief, and his "creatures" started a rumour "that Buckingham was so sory at the Kings death, that he wold have dyed, that he wold have killed him self, if they had not hindered him". But Eglisham again unmasked the duke's performance. Those close to Buckingham confessed that, in fact, he had been unmoved by James's illness and death. One day, when James was "in great extremitie", Buckingham had ridden posthaste to London to ensure his sister-in-law's punishment for adultery; and he was "bussy contriving and concluding a mariage for one of his cousins" during "the Kings agonie". All the duke's efforts at dissimulation were once more given the lie by the testimony of the poisoned corpse: "the Kings body and head swelled above measure, his haire with the skin of his head stucke to the pillow his nayles became loose upon his fingers and toes." After the vivid description of Hamilton's post-mortem, Eglisham only added here that he "needeth to say no more to understanding men". He closed his secret history with one last set of requests: that the "traitor" should be taken "without any feare of his greatnes", that "the other matters be examined", and that "the accessories with the guilty" be "punished".[25]

Masks

Eglisham's startling allegations were heady stuff, reshaping confused whispers into coherent secret history. Much of his own problematic past remained masked, and he presented himself throughout as a trustworthy man: an honour-bound harbinger of revenge, a loyal friend and servant, a credible eyewitness, a fearless speaker and an expert judge. But while no hint remained of Hamilton's scandalous deathbed conversion, Eglisham's mask was not entirely secure. The Frankfurt imprint might have diverted many readers away from Meerbeeck's shop in the Putterye, but close attention to the text would have allowed them to place Eglisham in the Spanish Netherlands. Eglisham confessed that he had taken refuge among Buckingham's enemies, which meant, in 1626, he had to be somewhere in Habsburg territory. Flanders, home to so many Scottish exiles, was the obvious locale. Furthermore, by linking James's poisoning to a revived Spanish match, by reminding Charles of his "most kind usage in Spaine", and by lamenting the "bloudy warre" that had "buried with King Iames the glorious title of a peacemaker Kinge", Eglisham replicated arguments usually associated with Spanish and Catholic sympathizers.[26]

But Eglisham's accusations did not depend on Catholic or Hispanophile sympathies. His attacks on Buckingham's cruelty, insatiable ambition, relentless matchmaking, and near total domination of James and Charles, all echoed earlier Protestant critiques of the duke that had often been strongly anti-Catholic in tone. Nor did Eglisham's pamphlet pursue a clear Catholic confessional or political agenda; to the limited degree that Eglisham relied on religious arguments or imagery at all, he drew from a shared Christian theology of divine justice and providence. Above all, *The Forerunner* demanded justice against a wicked murderer—and who, Papist or Puritan, could deny the importance of justice?

Eglisham did not explicitly evoke well-worn English images equating poison with "popery", though there was nothing in the pamphlet that would stop a reader making those connections. But Eglisham did successfully mobilize several other stereotypes of the crime that helped enhance the power of the stories he had to tell. Poison was the cowardly weapon of the weak and the base; and Eglisham told of how a social upstart and his low-born mother had poisoned Hamilton and James. Poison at court was often seen as a crime of the restlessly ambitious man, with neither blood nor virtue to sustain him; Eglisham's tales thus replicated a central feature of contemporary narratives of such infamous "low-born" courtly poisoners as the Earls of Leicester and Somerset.[27] Poison was feared as a crime of deception that betrayed intimacy; Eglisham made distressingly clear the ease with which the favourite and his mother had attained intimate access to the king's body, delivering death in the guise of medicine. Contemporaries found the poisoning of friends particularly chilling, and Somerset's murder of his friend Overbury had provoked real horror. Eglisham presented Buckingham as a double betrayer of friendship; killing James was an act of treacherous ingratitude for the king's love; while murdering Hamilton had betrayed an "upholding friend". Of all kinds of murder, Eglisham wrote, "the poysoning under trust and profession of freind-ship, is the most haynous". If left unpunished, poisoning rendered everyone a potential victim: "let no man thinke him selfe so secure to live amongst you . . . for by vigilancie and industrie meanes may be had to resist, or evite the most violent beast that ever nature bred, but from false and treacherous hartes, from poysoing murtherers what wit or wisdom can defend?"[28]

Eglisham's frank political talk also offered much to fascinate his readers. He was a self-proclaimed Stuart loyalist, but that loyalism was strained by his recognition of the Stuart kings' complicity in Buckingham's misrule. His portrait of James I teetered uneasily between criticism and compliment. Eglisham praised James's virtues; indeed, he reminded Parliament that James "hath often publickly protested, even in the presence of his apparent heire, that if his owne sonne should commit murther or any such execrable act of inius-tice, he would not spare him, but would have him die for it, and wold have him more severely punished then any other."[29] Yet at the same time he painted a troubling portrait of James's inability to control the monster he had created. James had been complicit in the Hamilton–Denbigh match, and it had taken him far too long to see through Buckingham's manipulation. But James had, in the end, seen the light, a comforting thought, even though this political redemp-tion cost the king his life. Eglisham was tougher on Charles, and his threatening language in the opening paean to justice was unusually frank, arguing a radical conception of kingship as contractual obligation, and insisting that unjust kings faced destruction at the hands of God or man. In 1618, Eglisham had mocked George Buchanan's politics as well as his poetry; in 1626 he was broadcasting the old royal tutor's justifications for political resistance.

Eglisham offered more than fearless speech. His pamphlet was also a powerful work of political demystification, dedicated to exposing political secrets and uncovering the hidden mechanisms of courtly power. He presented himself throughout the book as a shrewd analyst of courtly life, and his recur-ring discussions of the practice and politics of courtly dissimulation added a Tacitean resonance to *The Forerunner* that might have appealed to the growing numbers of contemporary readers fascinated by the political dark arts.[30]

The Forensics of Poison

Eglisham claimed to see through the courtly mystifications masking ambition and murder. But at the core of his credibility was an ability to identify and interpret the forensic evidence of poisoning on its victims' corpses. And here Eglisham could play on widespread contemporary fascination with the "manifest" signs that poisons left on the outside and inside of bodies.[31]

Educated contemporaries would have known that Galen thought it possible to diagnose a poisoned corpse from external signs, and throughout the Middle Ages such signs—hair loss, swelling, skin discoloration and loose nails—were commonly cited as proofs of poisoning. By the early modern period, expert medical treatises had begun to explore the signs and symptoms of poisoning more systematically. Eglisham's German contemporary, Daniel Sennert, cited Galen to prove that "one killed by poyson" could "be discovered certainly". The first sign was when a healthy man "abounding with good humors" died suddenly; then, "if his body be blew or blackish, or of divers colours, or stink, they say he is poisoned". Sennert agreed that sudden afflictions with violent symptoms were always suspicious since the symptoms of natural disease developed incrementally. Sennert thus advised physicians to pay particular attention to "Cold sweats, and chilness, swollen tongue, black and inflamed lips, swollen belly, and body often, with spots".[32]

The sixteenth-century French surgeon Ambroise Paré also argued that "certaine signes and notes" indicated "such as are poysoned or hurt by poysonous meanes".[33] But these "signes and notes" had to be carefully distinguished. Some poisons worked because of "manifest and elementary qualities"—they were "too immoderately hot, cold, dry [or] moist"—whereas others worked by a "specifick and occult propertie" of venomousness intrinsic to the substance and drawn from "the stars and coelestiall influence".[34] Paré thought there were some general signs of poisoning, such as when "the colour of the face changeth suddenly", but he insisted that "every kinde of Poyson hath its proper and peculiar Signes and Effects". According to Paré's schema, the spectacular external signs on Hamilton's corpse might have suggested specific poisons: salamander bites, for instance, caused "white spots over the body, then red, afterwards blacke with putrefaction, and the falling away of the haires"; snake bites produced dangerous bodily swelling; while the toad's "cursed venom" caused victims to "turn yellow, swell over all their bodies", suffer "difficultie of breathing, a Vertigo, convulsion, sowning [swooning], and lastly ... death". Sennert noted that mercury poisoning made "the whole body swell" and turn a "lead blew", while mercury sublimate or precipitate intensified these symptoms.[35]

While elite physicians debated classificatory distinctions, less skilled contemporaries followed a simpler, metaphorical logic that treated a swollen, discoloured body, loose hair and nails as evident signs of all kinds of poison, the body's distortion matching the monstrousness of the crime. Images of the externally distorted body thus appear in many types of poison narrative. The catalogue of the Elizabethan earl's poison victims listed in *Leicester's Commonwealth* included Alice Draycott, whose corpse was "swollen unto a monstrous bigness and deformity". Schoolboys encountered similar claims about "presumptive proof" in Cicero's *Rhetorica ad Herennium*: "if the body of the deceased is swollen and black and blue it signifies that the man was killed by poison".[36] The unnamed poison in Barnabe Barnes's 1607 play *The Divils Charter* caused victims to "puff up" and "swell"; a cardinal, assessing a dead pope who had ingested the poison by mistake, concluded "Even as his spirit was inflate with pride,/Behold his bodie puffed up with poison." So common was the emphasis on swelling that ballads could comically link the symptoms of poisoning and pregnancy. In "The famous Ratketcher" an expert with poisons gets a girl pregnant: "on the Baite she nibled,/so pleasing in her taste,/She lickt so long, that the Poyson strong,/did make her swell i'th waste." The link reappeared in more sober works. John Bale's dramatization of the murder of King John had the king, poisoned with toad venom, complain that "My body me vexeth: I doubt much of a tympany", a medical condition in which the stomach swells. The illustration of John's murder in John Foxe's *Book of Martyrs* depicted the monk who had poisoned the king lying dead, killed by the same poison, with a conspicuously swollen abdomen (Fig. 49). Swelling, unsurprisingly, also appeared in mundane criminal accusations of poisoning.[37]

Discoloured, blistered or spotted skin was also a culturally recognized sign of poisoning. Eglisham's readers might have recalled the evidence of discolouration and blisters presented in the Overbury trials of 1615–16. The prosecution emphasized "the excellent constitution of [Overbury's] bodie, when he lived, and the cleanenesse of his skinn, and with what strange blisters and botches it was filled after his death". The Middlesex coroner recalled "on the belly of him two or three blisters of the bigness of a pea as yellow as amber"; the woman who helped lay out Overbury's body remembered "his belly full of yellow blisters"; while the apothecary Paul Lobell had been shocked to find his corpse "full of yellowe blysters, and so consumed away that he never sawe the lyke bodie". A contemporary narrative of Overbury's murder alleged his "unnaturall death" was revealed by his "disfigured and discolored" corpse, "lothsome to the eye and noysome to the smell, his belly full of boches, his reines and other partes blackish yellow".[38]

Evidence of poisoning was also believed to hide beneath the skin. External signs were useful, Sennert argued, but "the best way to make [poison] manifest, is to open the body, and have an expert and wise Physitian" inspect it, for poisons left telltale marks. Paré recounted a case in which he had opened a poison victim and "found the botome of his stomacke blacke and dry, as if it had been burnt with a Cautery", clear proof that the victim "had [mercury] sublimate given him".[39] While the dissection of corpses to acquire anatomical knowledge was well known, what we would call an autopsy—opening dead bodies in search of interpretable signs of cause of death—was still comparatively rare in England. But Eglisham's English readers were increasingly aware

Figure 49: "The description of the poisoning of king Iohn" (from John Foxe, *Actes and Monuments* [1610], p. 233) depicts (in the top left panel) the telltale swollen belly of the monk who had shared the poisoned wine with his royal victim (Huntington Library).

of the practice.[40] Funerary embalming, for instance, encouraged an emergent practice of impromptu autopsy. By the 1610s, surgeons routinely opened elite corpses to prepare them for the embalmer, and this allowed the attending physicians to look for pathological symptoms. In 1619, John Chamberlain reported that at Queen Anne's "opening she was found much wasted within, specially her liver as it were quite consumed", and in 1621 news of the stones found in the late Bishop of Exeter's bladder likely derived from observations made during his embalming.[41]

Forensic autopsies—the opening of bodies in search of criminal evidence—were also becoming more common.[42] Coroners and their juries were supposed to examine the outside of dead bodies for signs of violent death, including poison. In the late 1580s a Sussex jury "viewed" the body of Mary Butcher, poisoned by a friend.[43] But allegedly poisoned bodies were also being opened. Cheap printed murder pamphlets, for instance, sometimes included details of forensic autopsy, the "ripping" of poisoned bodies, and their accounts reveal that surgeons expected not only to find the marks left by a poison, but also traces of the poison itself.[44]

Autopsy evidence was far more controversial when the political stakes were high.[45] By far the most important and vexed early seventeenth-century post-mortem came after the death of Prince Henry in 1612.[46] As Eglisham's readers assessed his autopsy reports on the exterior and interior of Hamilton's and James's corpses, they had Henry's case as a compelling precedent of what autopsy could, and could not, prove. Baffled by his illness, Henry's physicians had good medical reasons to open his corpse, but it was widely believed that the body was "opened being suspected of Poyson". Reports of Henry's autopsy—initially in manuscript, but eventually also in print—circulated in England and abroad to counter these damaging rumours, for "the times are full of evil deeds and men's tongues prone to wag".[47]

The most sustained contemporary narrative of Henry's autopsy argued unambiguously that the bodily evidence, examined by learned courtly physicians, disproved "vaine rumors" of poison. The examination began on the surface, observing the prince's skin, which was pale but bore no traces of poison, no spots, no evidence of violence or "contagious or pestilential Venome". Although Henry's stomach was "somewhat swollen and stretched out", once the surgeons opened the belly, it rapidly deflated. The report then documented the state of Henry's major internal organs: some bore no visible sign of disease or distemper, and none bore the marks of poison. His stomach, for instance, contained no sign that it "had received any secret wrong". Other organs bore positive traces of disease. The prince's lungs were almost completely black or spotted with black, and full of burned blood of "a corrupt and thicke ferocitie". The colour of Henry's arterial blood and the state of his lungs were part of a network of legible signs left by humours out of place, burnt or corrupted. Some signs were left by the "Fever maligne", some "by reason of the convulsions, resoundings and benummings" that "conveyed his Highnesse to the grave"; and all, the autopsy insisted, "without any token or accident of poyson".[48]

The evidence convinced some contemporaries. "There wanted not suspicion of poyson", Chamberlain noted, "but upon the opening of him . . . there was nothing found. His heart was sound and goode, his stomacke cleane, his liver a litle perished, his lunges somwhat more and spotted, his gall was cleane gon . . . his spleene very blacke, his head full of cleere water, and all the veynes of the head full of clotted blood." "The body was opened", reported the Venetian ambassador, "and a careful examination showed that this blow came solely from the hand of God." Yet the examination did not convince everybody. The abbreviated versions of the autopsy report that listed pathological signs without explaining them only encouraged suspicions, and some contemporaries clearly found the report less persuasive than the culturally familiar notion of a nefarious popish poison plot against the godly prince.[49]

The wide discussion of Henry's autopsy indicates contemporary familiarity with forensic medical evidence in a highly politicized case of suspected poisoning. The official report on Henry, like other evidence we have explored, rested on the assumption that the dead body could, if read correctly, supply proof, and that poisons left legible traces. Thus, Eglisham's use of forensic autopsy evidence had real cultural traction. His detailed enumeration of the signs of poisoning on and inside Hamilton's body conformed both to the presuppositions of elite medical discourse and to the broader belief that evidence of poison would be made visible by the corpse's swelling, blistering and discolouration. Eglisham's status as a physician mattered too, for it gave him the authority to interpret post-mortem evidence. But such evidence was rarely sufficient on its own to prove a poisoning; it was typically assessed along-side a variety of other kinds of medical and circumstantial clues.[50] In Henry's case an unambiguous and detailed autopsy finding failed to convince those who found the stereotyped narrative of a godly, virtuous prince felled by popish malice more comprehensible than details of burnt humours and dangerous plenitudes. By contrast, Eglisham's powerful medical and autopsy evidence reinforced, and was reinforced by, the cultural expectations that made Buckingham a most credible poisoner.

In the Hamilton case, Eglisham repeated forensic evidence that had circu-lated at the marquis's death. With his extended account of Hamilton's autopsy as background, Eglisham also made daring claims about the evidence of poison on James's body, alleging post-mortem swelling, as well as loosening of the hair and nails. This claim directly contradicted medical reports on James's death circulating in March 1625. The king had been embalmed, and during the process his physicians made the observations later summarized in the author-ized medical report. Although never publicly released in full, brief accounts of post-mortem observations did circulate in the weeks after James's death. They were a curious mix: some interpreted pathology, glossing what the king's internal organs revealed about his fatal illness; but others proceeded analogi-cally, assessing bodily clues as signs of the king's moral character. Joseph Mead learned that when James's "body was opened" his physicians "found his heart of an extraordinary bignes, all his vitalls sound, as also his head, which was very full of braines; but his blood was wonderfully tainted with melancholy & the corruption thereof supposed the cause of his death." "His harte was found to be great but soft", noted another account, and Simonds D'Ewes, thinking back on James's failure to take up arms to defend the Palatinate, added that this "argued him to be as very considerate" but also "so extraordinary fearful, which hindered him from attempting any great actions". The king's liver, it was reported, was like a young man's, but one of his kidneys contained two stones and was so shrunken it was difficult to find. The king's head, so hard to open it could hardly be breached "with a chissell and a sawe", was found "so full of braynes as they could not, upon the openninge, keepe them from spillinge". William Neve interpreted this cerebral superabundance as "a great marke of his infinite judgement": the autopsy evidence thus confirming James's self-proclaimed role as "Great Britain's Solomon".[51] Eglisham's account of the telltale signs of poison on the king's corpse thus not only challenged the author-ized medical interpretation of the autopsy evidence; it also undercut this broader attempt to locate signs of royal virtue or weakness in his physical remains.

Poison Artists and "infernall ffiends"

Eglisham refused to specify which poison had caused the telltale signs on the corpses, but he did make two further important diagnostic claims. He asserted that experimental knowledge of poisons—tested on animals—could partly explain Hamilton's distinctive post-mortem symptoms.[52] And he also strongly implied that Hamilton had been murdered by a peculiarly "subtil art" of poison, a slow-working drug designed by a foreign "artist" and "mountebank". Eglisham suspected Hamilton was poisoned during "all the tyme of his sicknes", but that "this poyson was such and *so farre gone*" that he was powerless to help. Furthermore, he cited a court servant who had said three months before Hamilton fell ill, "some of the great ones at court had gotte poyson in his belly".[53] The impli-cation was clear: Hamilton had been given poison sometime before he began to show symptoms. These claims about "subtil" poisoning were crucial parts of the pamphlet, and would allow Eglisham literally to demonize Buckingham. They also had significant cultural traction with contemporary readers.

Many expert medical writers were sceptical about delayed-action poisons designed to kill at a specific time. Paré acknowledged that different poisons killed at different speeds, but insisted that the variable "tempers and complex-ions" of victims meant that "you may finde no such as will kill in set limits of time, according to the will and desire of men".[54] But contemporaries were fasci-nated by the fantasy of the slow-acting designer poison. Most early modern English poisoning was far more mundane, involving a few well-known toxic substances, all quite easy to find and to slip into food or drink. But everyday poisoning coexisted with a widely shared cultural fantasy around figures like Eglisham's mountebank, the ingenious maker of designer drugs that killed in cruel and subtle ways. These poison artists made drugs whose bodily effects would mimic natural diseases, making discovery yet more difficult. Their poisons penetrated the body through multiple points—mouth, skin, eyes, nose, ears, even clothes—and in the course of everyday activities—eating, praying, riding, dressing, socializing or making love. Popular fantasy often heightened these anxieties by connecting poison artistry to a foreign Other: Italians and Spaniards, in particular, were supposed masters of this subtle art. Cultural ster-eotypes of "drug-damned Italy", and of courts plagued by venomous Spanish figs and Italian "sallets", were omnipresent in English culture.[55] It was a "slow poison which would leave no trace", procured from an Italian supplier, that reportedly killed Catherine of Aragon, while *Leicester's Commonwealth* featured a doctor who by "the excellency of the Italian art" devised poisons that "might be so tempered and given as it should not appear presently, and yet should kill the party afterward at what time should be appointed". A commentator on the Overbury murder thought to "kill lingeringly" was to be "like the Italian".[56] Eglisham could not link Buckingham's "poysonmunger mountibanck" to the Catholic Mediterranean, but when the doctors examining Hamilton's corpse "could not know how such a subtil art of poysoning could be brought into England", Eglisham told them "that money could bring both the art and the artist from the furthest part of the world".[57]

Other sources legitimated popular fears of designer poisons. Theophrastus, an influential classical authority, described how a special compound of aconite could "prove fatal at a certain moment", and early modern writers used astrology to explain how it did so. Tacitus told how the emperor Tiberius's favourite Sejanus used "a poison the gradual working of which might be mistaken for a natural disorder", while the Empress Agrippina killed her husband Claudius with a "rare compound" that was "slow and lingering" yet immediately "derange[d] his mind".[58] In Shakespeare's *Cymbeline* the wicked queen experimented with "strange ling'ring poisons", the "movers of a languishing death", while the discovery of potent new poisons in America, Africa and Asia further stoked early modern poison fantasies, leaving virtually no claim too outlandish.[59]

Medical specialists offered plausible natural explanations, where possible, for poisons that might work by touch, vapour, scent and even sight, but they debated the degree to which human art could manipulate poisons to act in ways that stretched nature's laws.[60] Eglisham's evocation of an "art" of poisoning that potentially violated the laws of nature thus sat awkwardly with some strains of learned medical literature, but it resonated powerfully with the fantasies and fears articulated in other contemporary discourses around the crime.

Nature's laws, however, did not always apply to witchcraft. During the Overbury trials, Sir Edward Coke had asserted that men could do little to thwart poisoners, because "the devill hath brought manye to be verie cunninge in itt, soe that they can poyson in what distance or space of tyme they please . . . in 1 month or 2 or 3 or more as they liste." The deeply rooted cultural link between witchcraft and poisoning was evident in Latin usage of the same words for both witch and poisoner (*veneficus/venefica*), and for witchcraft and poisoning (*veneficium*), as well as in classical literary depictions of women like Medea and Canidia who combined the two crimes. The connection would have been particularly vivid for Eglisham's contemporaries, many of whom remembered the explicit allegations of witchcraft against those accused of poisoning Overbury.[61] Readers may thus have assumed that Buckingham's mountebank was not merely a poison artist but a witch, wielding demonic power to devise poisons that violated nature's laws. Although Eglisham never

named the mountebank, his charge drew on the duke's well-known relationships with occult practitioners operating in the ambiguous zones between
illicit demonic witchcraft and licit natural medicine. Buckingham may have
sought out these practitioners for magical protection against his enemies or for
medical help for himself and his mentally unstable brother, and he certainly felt
uneasy about the company he was keeping. By early 1625, the duke was genuinely concerned that he himself was a target of witchcraft. Chamberlain
reported allegations that the Buckingham's adulterous sister-in-law, Lady
Purbeck, "did intoxicate her husbands braines" using "powders and potions"
and had "practised somwhat in that kinde upon the Duke of Buckingham".[62]

Eglisham scattered hints about Buckingham's use of witchcraft and witches
throughout *The Forerunner*. He played with a metaphorical language of
bewitchment to depict the favourite's corrupt hold over others: the duke's allies
were "inseparable from him by his enchantments", while the king consented to
the Denbigh–Hamilton match because he was "so far bewitched to Buckingham".
At another point, Eglisham wondered whether Buckingham's control over the
state was the result of "meanes . . . humane or diabolike". More importantly,
Hamilton had disdained the Villiers marriage partly because the duke held
"frequent consultations with the ring-leaders of witches, principally that false
Doctor Lambe, publicly condemned for witchcraft". John Lambe was a figure
of unusual notoriety, a well-known astrological and magical healer dismissed
by some as a charlatan but feared by others as a witch. In 1622, Lambe was
convicted of witchcraft, and two years later, was condemned for raping a young
girl, yet somehow he managed to escape the hangman. Lambe had been linked
to Buckingham since at least 1624, when the duke allegedly helped him evade
execution on the rape charge. But Lambe had also been among the "sorcerers"
allegedly employed by Lady Purbeck, and early in 1625 Buckingham had him
thoroughly interrogated. Whatever the truth of their relationship, rumour and
libel had by 1626 begun to link the two men. While Eglisham never identified
Lambe as the "poysonmunger mountibanck", he supplied enough evidence for
others to make that deduction and to link Buckingham's poisonings to demonic
witchcraft. As we have seen, these links made a considerable impression on at
least one of Eglisham's early readers, the Catholic Gabriel Browne who marveled
at how *The Forerunner* "lays sorcery to his charge, and combination with
infernal fiends and Witches".[63]

Again and again, Eglisham insisted that imposing justice on Buckingham
was imperative. It was the only way to punish murder and stem the corrosive
crime of poisoning. And it was the only way, Eglisham told the king, to "deliver
your selfe, and your Kingedoomes from the captivitie in which he holdeth
them and your Majestie oppressed". So great was Buckingham's power that it
was difficult even to speak of his crimes, let alone prosecute them; indeed,
Eglisham had had to fly the country in order to speak when so many held their

tongues. Yet in spite of these dangers, *The Forerunner* had made its case, and it did so plausibly, with skill and force. But in a polity so thoroughly corrupted, Eglisham recognized that there was little hope of securing justice. At Westminster, however, determined, angry men stood ready and willing to bring the duke to account. The secret history had been perfectly timed.[64]

PART III

IMPEACHING BUCKINGHAM
1626

PROLOGUE

"THE FIRE IN THE LOWER HOUSE"

THE NEW SESSION of Parliament that opened in February 1626 almost immediately began airing bitter grievances about the Duke of Buckingham's incompetence and corruption (Fig. 50). By mid-March 1626, Arthur Brett was lamenting that "the fire in the lower house ... against my lorde Duke groeth into a greater flame every day", and soon the Parliament-men began to assemble the scattered complaints into a formal bill of impeachment. The political atmosphere was toxic, and contemporaries lamented the endless "hot Skirmishes" and "hot wars" between the duke's supporters and critics.[1] Owen Wynn likened the turbulent session "to a tertian fever, everie third day it hath a shroad fit ... then there wilbe a Altum Sylentium in the house for a day or two until the Commons fall anew agayne upon the duke". Desperate for taxation to fund the ailing war effort against Spain, Buckingham and Charles I repeatedly tried to dampen the blaze, but only succeeded in fanning the flames. As the assault on the duke burned out of control, Charles abruptly dissolved Parliament, a decision that cost him over £300,000 in revenue and an incalculable amount of political capital. Buckingham's ally, Secretary Edward Conway, ended the session with "so little grounde to builde any hope upon as if I did not defy it dispaire wolde take upon every corner of mee". Indeed, "I cannot see any other helpe then that which they use to say in the plague time every man for himselfe Lord have mercy upon us". John Hacket would later conclude that the 1626 Parliament "brought forth nothing but a Tympany of swelling Faction, and abrupt Dissolution".[2]

Scholars have long acknowledged the significance of parliamentary turmoil and Buckingham's impeachment in 1626, and have variously attributed the difficulties to sharp factional division within the court, uneasiness over the conduct of the Spanish war, the Earl of Bristol's impeachment, and the arrest and confinement of the Earl of Arundel. These various explanations all have considerable validity. Yet scholars have given only glancing attention to the political significance of the stunning parliamentary decision to investigate

Figure 50: An image of the early Stuart lower house of Parliament (Huntington Library).

Buckingham's role in James I's death. Conrad Russell's detailed examination of the session noted that Sir John Eliot and Sir Dudley Digges both gave lengthy addresses suggesting that "Buckingham was responsible for the death of James" and intimating "that they regarded Charles as an accessory".[3] But Russell failed to situate these speeches in their proper parliamentary and political contexts, and neither Russell nor any other scholar of the session has explored the coincidence of Parliament's investigations with the publication of George Eglisham's secret history.

The following chapters reorient our understanding of this crucial parliament, one whose failure opened a rift between the king and the House of Commons that, to a significant extent, never healed. We do so by placing the murder of King James I at the heart of the parliamentary story. However indifferent modern scholars have been to accusations about James's murder, the Parliament-men of 1626 took them very seriously indeed, devoting three days in late April to investigating what had happened in James's sickroom, and then adding a charge on James's death to Buckingham's impeachment. Although it did not accuse the duke of wilful poisoning, this last-minute addition to the indictment proved incredibly volatile, triggering fraught debate and escalating clashes between the Crown and the Parliament-men. Lurking in the background all the while was George Eglisham's little book. The first copies of *The Forerunner* probably reached London just before Parliament took up the case in late April, and it quickly became the talk of the town, looming over the remainder of the impeachment proceedings.

The decision to investigate James's death proved to be the critical accelerant in the conflagration that consumed that 1626 session, and marked a dramatic turning point in the politics of the 1620s. It wrecked all hopes of a generous parliamentary subsidy, which in turn tipped the regime into profound fiscal crisis. More importantly, the open, albeit muted, parliamentary discussion of James's death also ensured that the secret history of the king's murder would play a long and destabilizing role in an increasingly turbulent political culture.

CHAPTER EIGHT

WHALE FISHING IN WESTMINSTER

THE FAVOURITE AND HIS CRITICS

W HEN CHARLES I neglected to send Bishop John Williams a summons to the 1626 Parliament, Williams shrugged off the slight with a quip. He was happy to have missed the session, for "as the Voyagers to Greenland say, When the Whale-fishing begins, it is better to be on the Shore, and Look on . . . than to be employed in the Ships to strike them, and hale them to land". In 1626 there was little doubt about the identity of the whale in question. In 1624 the Duke of Buckingham had been acclaimed by Parliament-men and the people alike, hymned by Thomas Scott and Thomas Middleton, and celebrated by the libellous poets who for so long had mocked him. But in 1626, as one Catholic marvelled, the Commons "fiercely assailed" the duke as "the grievance itself of all grievances whom but as it were the other day, they did not only seem to carry upon their shoulders in triumph, but even in their eyes alas as the redeemer forsooth of our country . . . and the author thereupon of a war with Spain".[1]

To understand Buckingham's transformation from "redeemer" to reprobate, we must begin with the policies and failures that initiated the great Westminster whale hunt.

Buckingham's War

The Anglo-Spanish entente, the centrepiece of James's foreign policy, finally ended late in 1625 when thousands of English troops waded ashore in Andalusia. This attack, Secretary Conway explained, was designed "to move those that have disposest his Maiesties deare Sister [Elizabeth] of her inheritance [in the Palatinate] to loose that prize" and to restore "our gratious Master's Sister and Nephewes, for the publique good, for the honour of our nation, and the glorie of our Gracious King and master". Eager for support from Venice, Savoy, and, most important, France, the English insisted their goals were not confessional. Buckingham assured Cardinal Richelieu that his sole intent was "to be a good Instrument in the peace of Christendome which will never bee if theis twoe

Crownes doe not ioyne constantly and hartely together".[2] Buckingham took charge of organizing the war effort. In September 1625, England and the Dutch Republic signed a military alliance, which quickly expanded to include Denmark. Although this alliance set armies marching, Buckingham never forgot the importance of the traditional blue-water policy that focussed on disrupting Spanish shipping. He explained to the Swedes that the Spaniards had risen with "the wealth of the Indies". Consequently:

> itt is ... a necessitie that those mynes bee ether wholly taken from them or they soe continually weakenned by spoyling their Tresures or sharing with them, or by troubling their Commerce att sea as that they may be rendered in a measure impotent.[3]

Buckingham's strategy initially centred on a massive amphibious expedition of over a hundred vessels, some Dutch but mostly English, carrying 10,000 English soldiers. Certain of success, the duke recruited men eager "to measure gold by there hatts and other spoyles by shippes lading". With confidence soaring, the time seemed ripe to make the new king "Great Britaines Charlemagne" (Fig. 51).[4]

Figure 51: Willem de Passe's 1625 engraved equestrian portrait of the Duke of Buckingham portrays him as a virtuous and victorious military commander, a depiction that became increasingly controversial after a string of military failures (British Museum).

Despite these lofty hopes, disenchantment with Buckingham's war was swift to emerge. English Catholics loathed the idea of war against Spain, especially as it prompted Charles to begin strictly enforcing the penal laws against them. And some moderate Protestants, especially in the merchant community, were equally cool to a Spanish war, fearful of trade disruptions abroad and of a Puritan resurgence at home. Their ambivalence turned to anger once things went awry. Catholic and mercantile opposition was expected, but more surprisingly, Buckingham's war also alienated some of the godly who had long dreamed of a crusade against Spain. For them, war with Spain abroad should have inaugurated further religious reformation at home, purging England of its sins. Instead, the godly could only marvel as, thanks to the terms of the French marriage treaty, a French bishop and a dozen priests paraded through London in clerical garb in the summer of 1625. Parliament eventually persuaded Charles to enforce the anti-Catholic penal laws, but any godly satisfaction was offset by the king's reluctance to discipline the cleric Richard Montagu for his anti-Calvinist publications. Fears of a growing "Arminian" faction in the Church were only heightened in February 1626 when Buckingham's attempt to resolve the theological rift at a York House conference left many convinced that the duke shared Montagu's anti-Calvinism.[5]

Equally unsettling was the duke's lavish lifestyle. In both 1625 and 1626 Buckingham's parliamentary clients pressed for a generous subsidy bill to fund the war. But many Parliament-men suspected that these funds would simply underwrite the duke's staggering prodigality, already amply and publicly displayed at York House, with its lavish gardens and spectacular artwork. The duke was a work of art in his own right (Fig. 52 and Plate 5). He planned to travel to Paris to collect Henrietta Maria in a coach with "ritch velvet" inside and "gould lace all over", accompanied by "eight score" musicians, forty-five labourers, forty-four yeomen, twenty-seven cooks, twenty-four footmen, twenty gentlemen, nineteen grooms, twelve pages, six huntsmen, all in "ritch suits", and twenty-two watermen "suited with skycollared taffaty all gilded with anchors and my lordes Armes". Buckingham himself planned to wear a "ritch white satten uncut velvet suite sett all over ... with diamonds", saving his signature outfit of "purple satten embroidered ... with ritch orients pearls" for more formal occasions. Although there was in the end no time to ship over such an enormous entourage, the order occupied high-end clothiers for months. On his return to London from Paris, Buckingham and his French guests repeated this exhibition of conspicuous consumption, to the fascinated horror of many English observers. The sight of "our Court ... in its full beauty" dazzled John Wolley, who knew enough about fashion to predict that the English "shall goe nigh to imitate" the "very apish and indeed uncomely" French style. The resulting Anglo-French fashion war was "the greatest that ever I sawe".[6] Such extravagance, while expected of a major court ceremony, could become a serious political liability when asking the Parliament-men for money.

Figure 52: Willem Jacobsz Delff's 1626 engraved copy of Michael van Miereveld's stunning portrait (plate 5) of Buckingham (National Portrait Gallery).

But the real fiscal problem was the daunting cost of war. In early 1625, James had begun paying his brother-in-law Christian IV £30,000 monthly to keep the Danish army in the field. But the Exchequer could not make the monthly payments. For Parliament-men raised on tales of Elizabethan seadogs looting Spanish shipping, such continental commitments seemed only a drain of resources from the blue-water policy that attracted most domestic support. With Charles's accession came an array of strategic proposals, almost all of which called for operations in the Atlantic and the Caribbean, where prizes and plunder, it was assumed, would defray the costs of war. Although these maritime plans interested Buckingham, his ambition was broader, and his continued pursuit of expensive land projects never found parliamentary favour.[7]

If mounting costs and baffling priorities weakened popular support for the war, military failure nearly killed it. The calamitous fate of Count Mansfelt's expedition early in 1625 had stunned observers. Ralph Hopton, a talented young officer, was shocked to see the swift disintegration of Mansfelt's army: "I confesse the miseries we suffred in the last jorney . . . makes me afraid to have charge of men where I have any doubt of the meanes to support them." He retired rather than accept a new commission. Sir John Ogle, a veteran colonel, worked on preparations for Buckingham's great expedition to Spain, which, the duke boasted, would be "such as never went out of England" supplied with "victualls as will last a whole yeare". But Ogle found only all kind of "knotty and cumbersome buysnes"—daily riots, too few junior officers, too many troops who were "very unfit . . . by reason of age, impotencye, sicknes and other infir- mities". Most men were poorly clad, and the pressed men from Hampshire were nearly naked. More importantly, the vaunted victuals were rotten. By June, Ogle was convinced that victory would only come by infecting the enemy with the diseases then rampant among the Englishmen.[8] He too decided to retire.

These starving, sickly men, billeted across Devon and Cornwall, also frustrated Ogle's replacement, Sir Edward Cecil, soon to be made Viscount Wimbledon. And in October 1625, when Wimbledon eventually disembarked his troops outside Cadiz, the invasion quickly degenerated into a drunken revel after the troops discovered a cellar full of wine. On the return voyage, the expe- dition was battered by severe winter storms and by near-open rebellion among the senior officers. The survivors eventually staggered ashore in Ireland and the West Country, and because no supplies awaited them, they began to sicken and die. In Plymouth, Sir John Eliot reported that the bodies were "in greate nombers continually throwen over board", and in Galway, the bedraggled survivors so alarmed the mayor that he closed the town gates against them.[9]

The expedition's fiercest engagement was fought on its return. After Lord Delaware lamented the army's "disorder and ill government", the humiliated commander, Wimbledon, responded by denouncing his own officers as incom- petents, swindlers and malingerers. Inevitably critics began to focus on Buckingham, and they began whispering that "it might have been better had not you guided the King".[10] Cadiz marked a terrible conclusion to a terrible year in which the duke had apparently squandered thousands of lives and about half a million pounds, and all for naught. The Spaniards could barely restrain their contempt. "Throw but a Butt of Sack in the way of the English", one Spanish jest maintained, "and with their own help killing one another being drunk, [it] will do more hurt in an English Army, then a thousand Spaniards can do in Arms".[11]

But the Cadiz fiasco was only one of Buckingham's problems. Fast Flemish warships based in Dunkirk had begun ravaging English and Dutch shipping, repaying the Dutch for instituting the practice of "foot-watering"—drowning prisoners—by tossing captured seamen overboard. Panic quickly spread along the English North Sea coast with the "fearfull and troublesome" news that the Dunkirkers "are now become Masters of the narrow seas". In Aldborough the bailiffs begged the Privy Council for help since the town was "verie open to invasion" from "donkerk (the daylie Enemy to these coasts)".[12] In King's Lynn the Corporation searched frantically for twelve cannons, offering to pay almost any price. The panic was most evident in Great Yarmouth whose Corporation flooded Whitehall with letters stressing "the grand danger that this Towne is in". The town instituted weekly militia drills, sacked a lazy Muster Master, appointed a drummer to give an instant alarm, and ordered all householders to keep a musket in readiness. In March 1626 the townspeople toyed with sending a large delegation of mariners to "make their complaints unto the kings Majesty, the Parliament, the Lords of his Maisties Counsell or the Lord Admirall".[13]

Amid these debacles, a far greater disaster loomed as English relations with France began to deteriorate. The Anglo-Spanish war and the Anglo-French marriage should have brought the two countries closer together, but Louis XIII's refusal to join a military league with England had prompted Charles to bow to parliamentary pressure and enforce the penal laws. In response, Louis dispatched the abrasive envoy, M. de Blainville, to London. Meanwhile important issues festered. After the English began seizing French vessels for allegedly carrying Spanish goods, the subsequent ownership disputes proved almost impossible to untangle.[14] The English arrest, release and then re-arrest of the *St. Pierre de Havre* prompted an aggrieved French merchant to protest to the Parlement of Rouen, which late in 1625 ordered the retaliatory seizure of English vessels in Norman ports. These reprisals in turn became entangled in a dispute about eight English ships loaned by James I to Louis XIII. In January 1625 news of the revolt of the Huguenot Duc de Soubise had infuriated James, for a new Huguenot rising might well spark another religious war and sabotage a non-confessional anti-Spanish coalition. After many Huguenot leaders denounced Soubise, James offered Louis eight ships, but this gesture became a grave liability once the entire Huguenot community belatedly swung behind the rebels. The French then pestered Charles to fulfil his father's promise, and after extended foot-dragging he finally ordered the transfer when it seemed that Louis and Soubise had come to terms. But the projected peace collapsed, and the English vessels played a prominent role in the ensuing naval campaign. Soubise eventually fled to Cornwall, bringing with him a captured French warship—and a French squadron sent to reclaim it. Back in France, Louis besieged the Huguenot stronghold of La Rochelle. These developments were potentially disastrous for the Duke of Buckingham, and in December 1625 he ordered the preparation of a naval squadron to secure the return of the loan ships, by force if necessary. While this strike was in preparation, English envoys brokered a tentative peace between Louis and the Huguenots, but neither side had formally agreed to the settlement by the time the Parliament-men entered Westminster in February 1626, leaving the English uncertain whether they were allies of the French king or his Huguenot foes.[15]

Ruinous expense, military defeat, alienated allies and triumphant enemies: Buckingham's war had brought nothing but disaster. Without consulting Parliament, the duke had sent a country ill-prepared for war headlong into battle against the most powerful state in Europe. The 1625 Parliament had registered its misgivings about Buckingham's strategy, somewhat softly during the London session in June and then much louder in the August Oxford session. "In the government there has wanted good advice", Sir Robert Phelips argued, for "counsels and power have been monopolized". Sir Edward Coke indicted the "want of providence" and cited "vanity and excess in costly buildings, diet and apparel"; he also explicitly called for important offices like the Admiralty to be taken from "young and unskillful persons" and given instead to "men of sufficiency".[16] Sir Nathaniel Rich simply asked that "when his Majesty does make a war it may be debated and advised by his grave council". Sir Francis Seymour identified the realm's chief problem: "the Duke of Buckingham is trusted".[17] Heavy pressure from the regime in August 1625 failed to convince the Commons to fund Buckingham's ambitious plans.

Their refusal placed the administration in an awkward position. Charles could have cancelled Wimbledon's expedition, then gathering at Plymouth, and focused instead on coastal defence and the militia. After all, as Bishop Williams noted, "a King must make himself sure in the Love of his own People at home, before he bid War abroad to such a rich and mighty Nation". Such a retreat would have embarrassed Buckingham, but to proceed without full parliamentary support courted further disasters. Nevertheless Buckingham pressed ahead. The Oxford session, he explained to Christian IV, did not worry him, since the problem was limited to a few dissidents, and Charles would "soon be able to address his subjects from horseback, as they say, like a king and not like a beggar on his knees". To ease the Exchequer's immediate cash-flow problem, Buckingham persuaded Charles to launch a Privy Seal loan campaign and to send some royal jewels to be pawned in the Netherlands. On this flimsy financial basis—neither the Privy Seal nor the pawned jewels produced much money—Buckingham launched the assault on Cadiz. "To show the Greatness of his Power", Hacket later lamented, "he made haste to destroy himself".[18]

Looking at the Duke with More than a Curious Eye

"Theare are twoe many boathe in the Courte and kingdom", Sir Henry Mildmay noted in October 1625, "whoe looke upon my lord Duke his proceedinge with more than a curious eye." In August 1625, Buckingham had urged his parliamentary critics to trust him, confidently insisting "You may judge by the event". Six months later, after the debacle at Cadiz, the Dunkirkers' depredations, and the use of English ships against French Protestants, many contemporaries had reached a verdict: Buckingham was to blame. In Canterbury, Thomas Scott was convinced that England had earned "the anger of the Lord . . . in the setting foorth and managing of our Sea and land forces that wee doe such foolish things, until, if speedily it be not prevented, the Lord by thus taking away our right witts, cast us out of his presence." Thanks to Buckingham's advice, Charles had made "warre before he made himself and his Subiects readie for warre, by reforming Church and Commonwealth and by preparing meete men and meanes for such an enterprise."[19] A growing number of Parliament-men came to the same conclusion—the only way to make the realm "readie for warre" was to remove Buckingham.

The Flemish agents understood the magnitude of Buckingham's Cadiz wager. "The successe of this fleete", X noted, "shall encourage all good subiects to strippe themselves unto their shirtes for the maintenance of so glorious an enterprise". But the costs of failure were equally high. Buckingham "hath a woolfe by the eares, for if the fleete shall not aunswer the expectation here, his greatenes wilbe in no small danger". Indeed, he would then be "a loste man, for many in courte . . . begin to be weary of his tirany". The Infanta Isabella's foreign secretary predicted that if the expedition failed, "the rage of the people will be so great against him, as he will hardly save him selfe att the next parlament". By January 1626 the Parliament-man Sir John Eliot began preparing for the coming storm by retaining an unnamed agent to "inquire for intelligence from all partes" and to make "a dayly note or remembrance of all ordinary passages".[20]

Buckingham's failures caused a fundamental realignment at court. In 1624, Prince Charles and the duke had pieced together a broad "patriot" coalition—in the Lords, the Earls of Pembroke and Montgomery, Viscount Saye and Sele, the Earls of Southampton, Essex and Oxford; and in the Commons, Coke, Phelips, Sir Dudley Digges and Sir Edwin Sandys—all dedicated to easing King James into war. But by 1625 this coalition had disintegrated; Sandys alone remained loyal to the duke and increasingly powerless in the Commons. Why the others distanced themselves from Buckingham so quickly is not entirely clear. Some were upset with their failure to secure royal appointments, but many had lost faith in the duke's ability to lead, and this disenchantment was especially pronounced among the militant godly peers. The Earl of Warwick spent the winter with the Essex militia guarding Harwich from the Dunkirkers, the Earl of Lincoln witnessed first-hand the misfortunes of the Mansfelt expedition, and the Earl of Essex, having survived the Cadiz expedition, refused another military command.[21]

In their frustration these "patriots" opened quiet conversations with erstwhile opponents like Bishop Williams, the Earl of Arundel, and the disgraced diplomat the Earl of Bristol, who all favoured peace with Spain. Signs of this unusual alliance of pro- and anti-Spanish forces, united only by their resentment of Buckingham, first emerged during the 1625 Parliament. The duke was appalled to discover that Montgomery wanted to take Bristol's old servant, Walsingham Gresley, with him to the marriage celebrations in Paris. Meanwhile, Flemish agents reported an "open defiance" between Buckingham and Lord Keeper Williams and a "more private" antagonism between the duke and the Earl of Pembroke. Furthermore, "the Duke hath discerned a combination between them and Arundell". Reports in Paris predicted that Pembroke and Arundel "would ioyne hands and heads together to accomplish" Buckingham's ruin.[22] Following the 1625 dissolution of Parliament, and to Charles's great dismay, Pembroke and Montgomery visited the Earl of Bristol who was under house arrest in Dorset. Divided over long-term goals, this alliance of pro- and anti-Spanish courtiers was to work together in the short term to diminish, if not destroy, Buckingham's power.[23] As his opponents mobilized, the duke took countermeasures. First, he rounded on Williams, Bristol and the Parliament-man Robert Phelips, forcing them to deny any dealings with one another. Then in September 1625 he persuaded Charles to remove Williams as Lord Keeper, and in November he had the king name Coke, Phelips and four other awkward Parliament-men as sheriffs, thus making them ineligible for re-election. From his East Anglian exile, Williams quipped, "What then? Am I made high-Sheriff of Huntingdon-shire?" Initially, these measures worked. Early in the 1626 Parliament, Owen Wynn noted that the "manie great and active spyritts" who resented Buckingham's power lacked "a good directer, suche as Edward Cooke is, or Sir Robert Phillips".[24] Soon enough, however, a "good director" emerged.

Sir John Eliot and the duke had long been allies, and Buckingham had appointed Eliot as Vice Admiral of Cornwall. In 1624, Sir John still stood high in the duke's favour, and early in 1625, Eliot reiterated "the great desire I have unto your Grace's service", adding "nothing has more unhappied me than the wante of opportunitie" to do so. During the 1625 Oxford session of Parliament, Buckingham summoned Eliot to private meetings in his bedchamber, and in December the son of Secretary Conway, the duke's loyal client, spent the holidays at Sir John's house in Cornwall. But by early 1626, Eliot had had enough. He was upset when Charles named Sir John Coke as Secretary of State, a post he coveted. But Eliot had other compelling reasons for disaffection. Business regularly took him to Plymouth where he witnessed the calamitous preparations for Cadiz.[25] As a Cornish magistrate, Eliot helped billet troops, and he was appalled by the condition of the men who had returned from Spain. "[T]he miseries before us", he wrote at Plymouth, "are greate". He witnessed the standoff between Soubise at Fowey and the French squadron in Falmouth, which both sides spent "threatening one to another" over the captured French warship. The precarious situation prompted the residents of Fowey to warn Sir John of imminent violence.[26] Eliot had also seen the damage that the Dunkirkers had inflicted on coastal shipping. In the Oxford session, even though he loyally supported the Crown, Eliot had admitted that Mansfelt's expedition had brought "no fruit but shame and dishonor over all the world". Early in 1626 a hostile observer reported to Buckingham that Eliot was dithering "in a distraction how to divide himself, between your Grace and the Earl of Pemboke".[27] By the time Parliament opened a few weeks later, Eliot had made his decision. He launched an all-out attack on his old friend.

Common Fame

The 1626 session of Parliament opened on 6 February, and since the first week was devoted to routine procedural matters, the business on 10 February was suitably mundane until Eliot rose to speak. In previous parliamentary sessions the Commons had put the king's concerns ahead of his people's grievances, but now, Eliot insisted, "the King should . . . begin with us as we have with him" and explain how the regime had spent the money voted in 1624 and 1625. After denouncing "misgovernment, misemployment of revenue, miscounsel, misadvising of the King," he turned to Wimbledon's voyage, lamenting how "the incomparable hopes of our sovereign" had been "checked in his first designs". For now, few others shared Eliot zeal for the fight. His motion, reported Joseph Mead, "was not applauded nor seemingly liked by the house".[28] But Eliot had shown his hand, and his boldness steadily attracted supporters.

If he were to challenge Buckingham who enjoyed the monarch's complete confidence, Eliot had to assemble an ironclad case with credible witnesses. He had been pondering the problem of how to destroy the duke for some weeks. Before the session began, Eliot, or men close to him, had drawn up a planning document assessing the "Perticular misdemeanours of the Duke" and the evidence to prove them. The parliamentary attacks on Lord Chancellor Bacon in 1621 and Lord Treasurer Middlesex in 1624 had established the basic procedure for an impeachment: the Commons presented the indictment and the evidence to the Lords who alone determined guilt or innocence. Only a compelling case could guarantee conviction. The magnitude of the task can be seen in the planning document, which outlined possible witnesses and lines of attack. The document highlighted Buckingham's involvement in the sale of titles ("Brybes and monyes unlawfully taken") and his "Iuglyinge in Matters of Religion"—allegations that were to loom large in the impeachment debates. But other charges in the planning document highlighted the fundamental problem of finding reliable evidence and witnesses. The document cited, for instance, Buckingham's "horrible oppression of the late Lord Keeper", but the Commons could not take up that issue without Williams's cooperation, and he declined to help. An even more embarrassing charge concerning the duke's predatory sexual exploits with various court ladies would have required the cooperation of the women in question. And the document's allegations about Buckingham threatening the new French Queen of England would have required the testimony of Henrietta Maria herself.[29]

These possible charges also included one about the duke's "fowle and unchristian like carriage about the kinge towarde his ende". The information was sketchy, essentially summarizing the rumours that had circulated late in March 1625, but plainly the sickroom quarrels had not been forgotten. The document described the duke "bringinge" the king, who "after many fytts of an

Ague" was "almost recovered", the "unfortunate Possett and Plaister after the usinge whereof he never looked cheerfull but sayd he was kylled". It cited the opposition of "Dr. Moore and other Doctors" and noted Buckingham's "violence in quarellinge with Mr. Gibb and for committing Dr Cragge for sayinge the kinge was worse after the receavinge therof". This sequence of events, while not constituting outright murder, was nonetheless "a desperate President about dyinge Princes".[30] The document gave few hints of how to prove this charge, and Eliot must have realized that his assault on Buckingham would fall apart if he led with allegations about James's mysterious death. For the time being, the charge lay dormant.

The planning document began with a simple statement: Buckingham was "Vicious ergo not fitt to be soe neare a kinge". This belief drove the impeachment process as it gathered steam in March and April. By late April, twelve charges were in development, impeaching Buckingham for such offences as selling honours, extorting money from the East India Company, lending English vessels for use against the Huguenots, impoverishing the Crown, engrossing offices, and failing to guard the Channel. Yet none of these grave charges rested on incontrovertible evidence.

Earlier impeachments had depended on numerous witnesses. In 1621 four men, two of whom were Parliament-men, testified in Sir Giles Mompesson's impeachment. The case against Lord Chancellor Bacon that same year rested on evidence from a lady, twelve knights, a London Alderman and a further thirty-six people. During the impeachment of Lord Treasurer Middlesex in 1624, platoons of witnesses testified for nearly three weeks.[31] By contrast, the initial charges against Buckingham were long on rhetoric and short on substance. One of the better-documented allegations—the sale of offices—relied on Sir William Monson's report of the Countess of Nottingham's story that Buckingham had given her husband a pension. But even that third-hand allegation was hard to prove, since by 1626 the earl was dead and the countess was remarried to Monson, a man who had once hoped to supplant Buckingham in James's affections. This charge also relied on four other witnesses, most of them Nottingham's dependents saying the deceased earl "told him as much". Other charges had similarly shaky foundations. The charge about the loan ships depended heavily on M. de la Touche, who said, "the duke is a wicked man (*un mescant homme*)". Officials of the East India Company confirmed Buckingham had extorted £10,000, and Lord Robartes recounted paying Buckingham for his peerage, but none of these men appeared in person.[32]

The difficulty finding witnesses had a simple explanation. James I had invariably, if reluctantly, allowed judicial proceedings against his officials to proceed unmolested. When Bacon stood accused of corruption in 1621, James told the Commons that he was "very sorry, a Person so much advanced by him, and sitting in so high a Place, should be suspected". Nevertheless, "if the Accusation shall be proved", he consented to "punish it to the full". In 1624, James announced that if Middlesex had committed "Falsehood and Treachery, and Deceit under Trust, My Love is gone", for "I will never maintain any Man in a bad Cause". Charles I, however, steadfastly supported Buckingham. In early March 1626, Owen Wynn noted that "the kinge favours him and whoe is he that will question him".[33] On 15 March, Charles himself marvelled at the continuing attacks on Buckingham, since "certain it is, that I did command him to do what he has done". On 20 March he warned the Commons against "reflecting backwards" and casting "an ill order upon our present government or upon the government of our late, blessed father". A week later, the king objected that Parliament's attack on the duke had "strained and blemished" not only "the honor of his father" James but also "his own no less". After endorsing Buckingham, whom Charles insisted he "does know better than any man living", the king issued his "express and final command that you . . . cease this unparliamentary inquisition". He had, John Hacket recalled, "wrapt up the Lord Duke, as it were, in his own Royal Robe, to preserve him".[34]

Charles's unwavering support for Buckingham placed Eliot and his allies in a quandary. Since potential witnesses feared the king's displeasure, the anti-Buckingham faction never marshalled the quantity of testimony used in the great impeachment cases of 1621 and 1624. But having initiated the assault, they had nowhere to retreat. Instead they advanced on different fronts. They pressured the king by holding the subsidy bill hostage, and they escalated their attacks in hopes of separating, if only slightly, the king from his favourite. More controversially, they obviated the need for individual witnesses by anchoring their charges on "common fame". On 10 March, Charles had demanded the Commons end their investigations and pass the subsidy bill. The following day, Pembroke's client Samuel Turner began the formal indictment by posing six queries presenting them as "certain accusations of common fame". He denounced Buckingham as the *causa generalissima* of all grievances, "the mother of the rest". In support, he cited his failure to guard the Narrow Seas and to lead the Cadiz expedition in person, his pursuit of "exorbitant gifts" for himself, his creation of a secret Catholic faction, and his sale of honours. But in response, Sir Robert Pye, a senior Exchequer official, immediately requested that Turner "may bring his proofs to those particulars".[35] Three days later, Charles protested that Turner has spoken "without any ground of knowledge in himself, or any offer of particular proof". In late March, Charles complained that the Commons was "running upon generals whereof you have made fame and report the groundwork". Secretary Conway mocked this "unlegall and unparliamentarie waie" of proceeding "in generallitie and upon report and common fame", and Buckingham defended himself, arguing that although "there may be some errors . . . yet they are no such gross defects as the world would make them appear". Above all, "he had been pressed too far upon common fame". These telling responses forced Eliot and his allies to secure a vote on 22 April permitting the impeachment charges to proceed on hearsay. The vote was crucial; without it the impeachment would founder on the paucity of witnesses and evidence.[36]

Throughout this process, Eliot continued to seek reputable witnesses. His hopes initially centred on former Lord Keeper Williams and the disgraced Lord Treasurer Middlesex. Williams was not interested. After the 1625 Oxford session of Parliament, when Buckingham accused him of secretly helping "the Active part in the House of Commons", Williams retorted, "I had been a Madman to have appeared in any of these." In 1626 he likely felt the same way; he wanted not retribution but rehabilitation.[37] Middlesex, however, was another matter. Impeached in 1624, disgraced and fined £50,000, Middlesex blamed Buckingham for his downfall. Yet the duke was also his best hope for restitution. Middlesex tried various strategies. He sent his wife, Buckingham's cousin, to plead with her Villiers relations for mercy. He retained Buckingham's doctor, John More, as an intermediary, and late in 1624, he managed to persuade James to lower his fine to £20,000. Finally, he negotiated with the duke's mother who demanded, and eventually received, Middlesex's prized London residence, Chelsea House. When Parliament opened in 1626, Middlesex remained in retirement. But in March 1626, in a move widely seen as a diversionary tactic on Buckingham's part, Sir Thomas Monson filed a petition in the Lords claiming £2,000 from Middlesex. After Middlesex's allies defended him, the House promptly dropped the matter.[38] But the incident revealed that Middlesex had acquired new friends. The earl's brother-in-law Arthur Brett reported that many Parliament-men "are soe farre from thinkinge you any preiudice that shoulde there a storme arise against you, you would finde soe many frends among them that they would soon disperse it". At the same time, Brett began dealing with Eliot and passing on news "as Sir John Eliott toulde mee". Eliot needed Middlesex to help him get Buckingham, and in return he was ready to assist the disgraced Lord Treasurer. Unlike Williams, Middlesex had no desire for political rehabilitation: "I am resolved to goe no more to sea," he wrote in late April, adding "I am very well contented with my present state." But his new friends in Parliament could reverse his conviction and perhaps even refund his fines. Cannily realizing that Eliot's overtures might make Buckingham reconsider his own position, Middlesex began quietly talking to both sides. In early April, Buckingham's supporters suggested bringing Middlesex to London "to counsel the Duke". Alarmed, "Eliote and all his frends" paid a visit to Henry Brett, another Middlesex brother-in-law. The delegation "stands well affected towards your Lordshippe, and they hope you will give them no other cause, especiallie in this mans behalf", Brett reported. But if Middlesex were to assist Buckingham, then "they sweare to vex all the vaynes of your hart".[39]

In early May, when Buckingham again tried to divert his enemies into attacking Middlesex, Eliot once more defended his new friend. The select committee on impeachment was then trying to document Buckingham's plundering of the Exchequer. Sir Robert Pye volunteered that Middlesex "had gotten from the king in a shorte tyme £120,000" and suggested "that he might likewise bee examined". Eliot was in the chair and:

> answered that it might bee true for ought hee knewe to the Contrarie, but then it was true that [Middlesex] had merited well of the king and had done him that Service that but fewe had ever done, but they could finde no such matter in the duke.

Nicholas Herman, who reported this scene to Middlesex, begged his master to help Eliot so that "your lordship shall doe your selfe right" and, more important, "make him the more firmely yours".[40] Thus parliamentary observers carefully watched Eliot and Buckingham, who were in turn watching Middlesex, wondering what he—and anyone else who might have hard evidence—was going to do.

Bishop Williams thought the 1626 pursuit of Buckingham misguided. Discussing the impeachment, Williams advanced "this subtle Similitude": "if a Beast were got into a Field of Wheat, if the Neighbours ran in, and hunted it about with their Dogs they would tread down more Corn than five beasts could devour, if they were let alone". Parliamentary whale-hunting left no time for domestic legislation and financing the Spanish war. Furthermore, the impeachment effort might well be pointless, for Charles regarded Buckingham as "in a manner his whole Court". By mid-April 1626 events seemed to have proved the sceptics right. Weeks of trampling parliamentary corn had failed to produce a compelling case against Buckingham. Notwithstanding their public defiance, some of the duke's sharpest critics were becoming desperate. A group of Parliament-men privately visited the Bishop de Mende, the queen's almoner and Richelieu's nephew, to float ideas for additional impeachment articles. Perhaps they could indict the duke for asking James to baptize a pig after a long night of drinking, or for farting in the presence of the King of Spain. But it was not quite time for such desperate measures. On 24 April, Philip Mainwaring sent the Earl of Arundel, who was imprisoned in the Tower, important news. The Commons "hath some thing now on foote . . . which at the least makes a noyse".[41] Eliot had decided that the time had come to examine a charge that Charles could not dismiss out of hand, a charge that also had some obvious witnesses. It was time to discuss Buckingham's "fowle and unchristian like carriage" during James I's final illness.

CHAPTER NINE

A CRYING CRIME

THE PARLIAMENT-MEN INVESTIGATE THE DEATH OF

JAMES I

O N 29 APRIL 1626 the Earl of Middlesex had a change of heart, and sent an urgent letter to his London agent Nicholas Herman so sensitive that he instructed him to return it once it had been read. Middlesex's wife had just returned from Whitehall to report that the Countess of Buckingham, suspecting Middlesex's cooperation in her son's impeachment, was busy "misinforming" the duke "to marke . . . mee and those towarde mee". On his master's instructions, Herman had been exploring an arrangement between the earl and the duke's parliamentary enemies. But now the earl reversed course, telling Herman to ignore "the reasons I gave you at your being last with me". Although still angry at the duke's mother, Middlesex explained that he could not "but be sorry for the duke of Buckingham (notwithstanding his Inhumayne dealing with me)". Such sympathy must have shocked Herman. For two years Middlesex had watched helplessly as Buckingham and his mother had ruthlessly plundered his estate. But on 29 April, after weeks of vacillation, Middlesex had suddenly decided to ally himself with Buckingham. His reason was clear. Buckingham's foes had now gone much further than the former Lord Treasurer could stomach. They were charging him with James I's death. "The examininge such a Cryinge Cryme against him by both the howses of Parliament", Middlesex told Herman, "wilbe a Blemishe to him to all posterity howsoever it speede."[1]

The Forerunner and the Parliament-men

The planning document written before Parliament opened had noted Buckingham's "fowle and unchristian like carriage about the kinge towards his ende", but until late April 1626 no one had publicly mentioned the charge. The decision to open an investigation apparently came at the last minute. On Friday, 21 April the Commons established a select committee "to consider of the state of the great business now in hand", and to use the evidence collected to frame formal impeachment charges. That afternoon the new select committee scheduled a debate on "the question of common fame", and on Saturday the House eventually resolved that "common fame" was "a good ground of proceeding". The select committee then asked for a "full report" from "all the committees concerning this business". They also sent messengers to inform Buckingham of "those things with which he is charged", and inviting him to respond on Monday. By the evening of Saturday, 22 April, then, nothing indicated that a new charge would be added to the impeachment bill. Yet when the House reassembled on Monday, the select committee asked permission to consider a "new matter", something "not heretofore propounded in the House or at the grand committee". After "much debate", the House voted 228 to 168 to allow the select committee to proceed. Only after the vote did Mr Gifford deliver Buckingham's response to Saturday's message, reporting that while he wanted to defend himself, the Lords refused to let him do so.[2]

Sometime between Saturday evening and Monday morning, the select committee had decided to revisit James's death. There were good political reasons for their decision. Unlike many other impeachment charges, this one had an obvious roster of witnesses. A thorough investigation might help the committee develop at least one charge that did not depend on "common fame" and that could not be excused as the duke's obedience to royal orders. It was also a charge so shocking that, by implicating Buckingham in treason against the late king, the Parliament-men might finally force Charles to repudiate the duke and to let the impeachment process move forward unchecked. But it is also possible that someone on the committee had read George Eglisham's pamphlet and knew where an investigation of Buckingham's "fowle and unchristian like carriage" might lead.

We cannot be certain when news or copies of Eglisham's tract first arrived in England. Rubens purchased Meerbeeck's Latin edition on 18 April, five days before the Commons' decision to revisit James's death. While we do not know when the tracts were printed or whether Meerbeeck's Latin edition appeared before his English one, two well-informed commentators later placed the publication near the 1626 parliamentary opening. Late in 1626, Sir Henry Wotton, the Provost of Eton College, told Princess Elizabeth that Eglisham's "abominable pamphlet" had been "published and printed towards the time of the last Parliament, in divers languages". Twenty-two years later, Sir Edward Hyde maintained that Eglisham had "sent over a small Pamphlet" from Brussels "about the beginning of that Parliament". These references would place the publication of at least one of Eglisham's tracts to February or March 1626. Another contemporary, writing much closer to the events, noted that Eglisham's pamphlet had come over "in the verie nicke", suggesting it appeared in England just before, or just as, Parliament began investigating James's death.[3]

The select committee's questioning of the royal physicians began on 24 April and ended two days later. By 1 May, Eglisham's pamphlet—in both

English and Latin versions—was the talk of London. On 2 May, Herman informed Middlesex that there "are bookes sent over from Bruxells to some of the lords from one Doctor Ecclestone a Phisition to king James but a Papist, by which hee chargeth that the Duke ... did poison the king, the duke of Richmond, the Marques Hamilton, Southampton, and Dorsett, and speaks of other lords that were to have been poisoned". The book, he noted, "makes a lowd Crye". London was full of "many speeches", a newsletter reported the same day, "which are not fit to be committed to paper". On 4 May a Parliament-man alluded to the book, while the Dutch ambassador reported the sensation caused by "Geerthuus Eglisemius" and his pamphlet. On 5 May the Venetian ambassador and other intelligencers commented on the tract. Some of these accounts suggest a coordinated effort to put copies in front of important men. Herman implied copies were sent to "some of the Lords"; while the Venetian ambassador noted that the copies had "come from Flanders" and "had been consigned to the king and the Lords of the Council".[4]

Hyde later claimed that copies had been "industriously scattered up and down in the Streets of the City of London", and Wotton maintained that Eglisham "had *scattered* in print" his "malicious defamatory pamphlet". Such broadcasting of illicit texts in public spaces was a common form of underground publication, and was used to publicize other attacks on Buckingham during and after the 1626 parliamentary sessions. Within hours of this alleged scattering, the Earl of Bristol used the same method to spread his charges against the duke. If *The Forerunner* had been scattered, it was clearly part of an attempt by Flemish agents or their English allies to jump-start discussion of the book. Copies would most likely have been left along the busiest thoroughfares and in the large public places where contemporaries gathered to talk news— Paul's Walk, the Exchange and Westminster Hall—and in sites of everyday urban sociability—alehouses, ordinaries, churches, theatres and shops. If a targeted scattering did occur, it is even possible that consignments of *The Forerunner* had been warehoused in London until someone decided to paper the City with the book. Once distributed in the City's "public sphere", copies could then have quickly moved through well-established news networks from the capital to the provinces.[5]

Eglisham's tract may have reached London before 23 April and encouraged some on the select committee to investigate James's death: at least one version was in print in Antwerp by 18 April, which gave it enough time to reach London by the 23rd. And although we will probably never know the exact sequence of events, one salient fact remains clear. Within a few days of the doctors' testimony to the Commons, Eglisham's tract was widely available in London. The parliamentary investigations into James I's death took place in the shadow of Eglisham's secret history; indeed the two became inseparably connected.

The Doctors and the Committee Men

On 24 April the select committee opened its inquiry into what a parliamentary diarist described as "som violent attempt upon his late Maiestie". A typical parliamentary committee consisted of courtiers and officials sitting alongside country gentlemen and burgesses.[6] But the twelve-man select committee contained no court representative. For the preceding two months Sir John Eliot had led the charge against Buckingham, and the attitudes of his eleven colleagues were almost as clear-cut. Sir Dudley Digges, a leading Parliament-man, had witnessed Buckingham's ham-handed intervention in the 1626 Kent election, an experience that made him vow "to see my Lord Duke and his servants know honest men that are no fooles from theire Contraries". Buckingham had forced John Glanville to join the Cadiz expedition, and the experience—he was seasick for most of it—only hardened his opposition. Edward Herbert was a relative of the Earl of Pembroke, who had procured his seat, and Sir Thomas Lake still blamed Buckingham for engineering his dismissal as Secretary of State in 1619. John Selden, Edward Whitby and Christopher Wandesford were closely linked to the men Charles had selected as sheriffs to exclude them from the 1626 parliamentary session. Selden had been offered seats in Parliament by Sir Robert Phelips, one of the new sheriffs, and by the Earl of Hertford, the brother of another. Whitby was a close friend of Sir Edward Coke, and regularly objected to the Crown's growing power. Wandesford, who had emerged as an anti-Villiers stalwart, was the protégé of Thomas Wentworth, another 1626 sheriff. Christopher Sherland, John Pym and Sir Thomas Hoby had all spoken about their concerns for the Church and for coastal defence. Of the twelve, the person most sympathetic to the regime was Sir Walter Erle, and by April even he was distancing himself from Buckingham.[7]

These men would do Buckingham no favours, and they confirmed his worst fears when they asked to hold secret hearings into "great matters of weight". On 24 April there was "much dispute" in the Commons over the propriety of "keeping their examinations private without admitting some other members thereof" and "whether this ... committee shall examine any new matter concerning the Duke". Sir Clement Throckmorton "showed the dislike of the proceeding privately" and thought "estranging the members unparallel[ed]". Sir John Lowther was concerned that since "a select committee [may] take what they will, refuse what they will", the House would be "guided by a few who, prepared, may blind our reason, we strangers". The question could only be resolved by one of the House's rare divisions. In the end, curious Parliament-men were allowed to attend the examinations, but only "without interposition", that is, as long as they remained silent.[8]

On the afternoon of 24 April, as the committee began its work in the Court of Wards, several Parliament-men crowded in to observe and take notes.

Bulstrode Whitelocke, the young burgess for Stafford, attended on the second and third day of the hearings; Sir John Lowther, a country gentleman from Westmoreland, and Peter Peake, the town clerk for Sandwich, attended the first two.[9] Because all three brought their notebooks, we are able to follow the committee's proceedings in considerable, if frustratingly telegraphic, detail.

The doctors who testified were mostly distinguished men, highly educated and richly honoured "princes of the art", as the physician Sir Theodore de Mayerne had described them. Henry Atkins, who had co-written Mayerne's 1624 memorandum on James's health, was in his seventies, while the rest were middle-aged. David Beton, James Chambers, John Craig and Alexander Ramsey were Scotsmen, and the others English. All held prestigious continental degrees. Atkins had graduated from Nantes, Ramsey and Matthew Lister from Basel, and Craig, Beton and William Harvey from Padua, arguably the finest medical school in Europe. All were Fellows of the College of Physicians, and Atkins had served as its president on seven occasions. They were well known at court. Lister had attended Queen Anne and Mary, Countess of Pembroke, while Atkins and Lister had tended to Lord Treasurer Salisbury (Fig. 53). Craig had followed Prince Charles to Madrid in 1623.[10] Their patients sometimes employed them as chaperons. In 1604, James had sent Atkins to Scotland to escort the young Prince Charles south, and in 1610, Lister accompanied Salisbury's son to Italy.[11] The doctors also had unusual access to Whitehall and its powerbrokers. A young Scotsman visiting Westminster was delighted to find that, thanks to John Craig, "I haif gottin accesse and acquaintance with the best about Courte". When Atkins's royal lease on a house was unexpectedly terminated, he protested directly to the Lord Treasurer. With this privileged access came titles, rewards and gifts. James once sent a freshly killed deer to William Harvey as a token of "his Maiesties good opinion".[12] But the doctors also enjoyed far more valuable benefits. James retained six physicians-in-ordinary, four of whom received salaries of £100 a year, and the others £50.[13] The other doctors were extraordinary physicians—William Harvey, for instance, secured that title in 1618, a full twenty years before he became physician-in-ordinary (Fig. 54). Equally lucrative were one-time grants. Queen Anne let Atkins buy Crown land at a discount, while James named Chambers a co-receiver of recusant fines, with a guarantee of an eighth of receipts, as well as granting him £250 as a free gift. The finest reward was a lifetime pension; James granted Atkins one worth £100.[14]

One of the eight physicians who testified did not fit this general profile. John More was not a sworn royal doctor. His brother was a secular priest; his great-grandfather was reputedly the martyred Thomas More; and he himself was suspected of being in holy orders. In 1620, More was also suspected of involvement in a Catholic campaign to raise money to oppose Frederick V of the Palatinate; he was released after Buckingham intervened, but given More's

Figure 53: A 1646 engraved portrait of Dr Matthew Lister, one of James's physicians who testified to the parliamentary committee investigating the king's death (Huntington Library).

sympathies and friends—the Spanish ambassador Gondomar was his patient—the charge seemed plausible.[15] John Gee's 1624 list of "Popish Physicians in and about the City of London" began with More, "a man much imployed, and insinuating with great persons in our State" who lodged with a Catholic apothecary. And in March 1626 the College of Physicians denounced him to Parliament as a Catholic. More's open Catholicism put him at odds with the medical establishment. In July 1618, when the president of the College proposed that, out of deference to "important men", they should ignore More's unlicensed practice, a majority of Fellows had rejected the idea. The following year, after a substantial cash gift encouraged the Fellows to reconsider, they allowed More *de facto* freedom to exercise his art.[16] More's medical career had long relied on "important men" and "great persons". By the early 1620s he was a Villiers family doctor. In 1622, Buckingham gave him £50; in 1623, More attended the Duchess of Buckingham through a dangerous illness; and in 1624, Buckingham consulted More during his own long sickness. By early 1626 the Earl of Clare grumbled that More was so "muche and dayly employed" by the favourite that he had no time for other clients.[17] Buckingham clearly trusted More, employing him in such delicate matters as selling a peerage and negotiating over Middlesex's fine.[18]

The most eagerly anticipated medical witness was John Craig, the Scotsman at the centre of the March 1625 stories about Buckingham's medical interventions. Craig was well connected to the Scottish elite. His father was an eminent

Figure 54: A 1739 engraved portrait of Dr William Harvey by Jacobus Houbraken celebrating Harvey's discoveries about the circulation of the blood (Huntington Library). Harvey was among the royal physicians who testified before Sir John Eliot's parliamentary committee.

lawyer, and he was related by marriage to Robert Burnet, later a Scottish judge, and to Lord Dury, a Scottish Privy Councillor under James VI.[19] But Craig owed much more to his uncle (also John), a former professor at Frankfurt University who had become principal physician to King James. By the time of his uncle's death in 1620, Craig was established at court, becoming a physician to Prince Charles in 1613 and to James himself in 1621.[20] According to the March 1625 newsletters, Craig had challenged Buckingham after his medical intervention, and he was clearly the unnamed doctor in *The Forerunner* "committed prisoner to his own chamber" after crying out "the King was poisoned". Craig had paid a price for this outburst. During James's funeral he did not march with the royal physicians but among the prince's servants. When Charles rewarded the royal doctors—Alexander Ramsey, for example, received £100 "for his paines and attendance about the person of his Maiesties late deare father"—he apparently passed over Craig. The Scottish Privy Council also investigated the validity of James's grant of a valuable annual pension to Craig, who found himself listed with others "whose names, persoinis nor deservingis ar nowayes knowne to his

Majestie" and had to appear "persounalie" before the Scottish Council or face immediate suspension of payments. It is unclear whether Craig managed to retain his pension, but it is striking that the other Scottish physicians—Beton, Chambers and Ramsey—did not have to undergo this procedure. Craig had to wait until 1635 for Charles I finally to reappoint him as his physician.[21]

The king's surgeons, Archibald Hay and Gilbert Primrose, also testified. But there were noticeable absences from the witness list. Sir William Paddy, the veteran royal doctor, had been summoned to Theobalds "butt two daies before the death of my soveraigne Lord", and he appears to have done little for James beyond "telling him that ther was nothing left for me to doe . . . butt to pray for his soule".[22] Paddy had been involved, however, in discussions about the duke's interventions after James's death, but for whatever reason the committee did not summon him. The committee also failed to call Henry Gibb of the bedchamber, who had reportedly been sent from court for reprimanding Buckingham, and summoned neither Israel Wolfe, a royal apothecary, nor John Baker, the duke's barber. Nor did they call the Essex doctor John Remington named as the source of James's plaster and potion. But the witnesses did include two men not directly involved in the king's medical care: John Levinstone, a groom of the bedchamber, and a man called Robert Ramsey who would give the strangest testimony of all.

The Doctors' Testimony, 24–26 April 1626

Since the physicians had every incentive to keep their testimony as anodyne as possible, cynics must have expected a perfunctory hearing. Eglisham had warned his readers that many royal doctors were the duke's creatures and that others, including Craig, had been "threatened if they kept not good tongues in there heades". Moreover, the regime soon revealed its impatience with any doctor who spoke out of turn. The performance of Alexander Ramsey, the first witness on 24 April, infuriated Charles. The Venetian ambassador reported that Charles had ordered that Ramsey "remain a prisoner in his house" for his "unfavourable deposition about the late king's death", and a newsletter-writer observed that Ramsey "spake some thing, which extreamely distasted his Majestie for which cause he is discourted".[23] It is not clear which part of Ramsey's evidence attracted Charles's ire, but Ramsey had the misfortune of going first, and he delivered testimony highly critical of the duke. Uncooperative witnesses had stymied previous Commons investigations; in March members of the Council of War had replied to parliamentary questions by stating "we conceive that we are not bound by the act to make any answer". Even Sir Robert Mansell, one of the duke's sharpest critics, had declined to say more without Charles's express permission. Perhaps Charles assumed that Ramsey, too, would not cooperate. In any event, his arrest had a chilling effect on subsequent witnesses, who, as Eliot later noted, "did not speak so fully as they that were examined first".[24] Nevertheless the doctors did talk, and even their cautious testimony presented an unsettling story.

Reading between the lines of the surviving testimony, we can reconstruct the questions the committee wanted answered. The Parliament-men immediately focused on the plaster and potion Buckingham had given James. They wanted to know what was in the ingredients, who had prepared them and where, and who had given them to the king. They wanted to know James's reactions—what he had said, what symptoms he had displayed—and whether Buckingham's actions had contravened the physicians' plans for the king's treatment. This line of questioning produced a fairly coherent account of what had happened at Theobalds in March 1625. What these events meant would be much harder to pin down.

The doctors testified that they had followed Mayerne's advice and agreed on protocols for the king's treatment. They had diagnosed James's illness as a tertian ague with an intermitting cycle of fevers and chills, and "it was agreed betweene them", Ramsey explained, "that no physicke should be applied but under theire hands". Furthermore, given the vital importance of applying the right medicines at the right time, "they had set downe a rule", Atkins recalled, "that nothinge should be given him 3 howres before his fit Came nor till the Couldnesse was of[f] from him". Every day, Lister testified, the doctors would agree on, and then record, "what thinges should be prescribed for that day". Hence, "there was neither eating, drinking, etc" except by recorded "consultation". When prescribing any medicine, "they always directed theire bills to the kings sworne Apothecary and no other" to manufacture and mix the drugs. Outside interference was expressly forbidden. The physicians, Atkins recalled, had specifically asked the king "not to take anie thing and had prohibited all the Chamber to give him nothing".[25] These rules, however, had been violated. Atkins acknowledged that "there weare som things given to the kinge which he was not acquainted with and without theire direction". Beton was more direct: "there was physick prescribed to the late kinge by the kings owne relation without advice of his owne phisitions."[26]

The first outside interference came on 12–13 March 1625, "about the 5 fit of his disease", when the doctors discovered a plaster "laid to the King's side". This, Chambers testified, "they thought strange beinge without theire advise", and Ramsey added that since "none of the phisitions knew of the application" they ordered it removed.[27] The physicians agreed that the intervention was highly irregular, and since they were about to "purge" the king, they had had to disrupt their planned treatment. Their testimony gave relatively few details about this initial intervention, and the diarists did not record any consensus on the plaster's effects. Chambers insisted that "After it was taken of[f] the kinge had som more ease then he had before", though it is unclear whether the ease came from the plaster or its removal. William Harvey testified that "At the first application [of the plaster] that fit was rather worse then better," while Ramsey thought that once the plaster was removed, the king "a mended". It quickly became apparent that the mysterious plaster had come from Buckingham. Chambers testified that "He knows not who made the plaister", but heard it "reported that it had donne the Duke good and others."[28]

The select committee focused, however, on the events of Monday, 21 March 1625. By 19 March, James appeared to be getting better. Chambers claimed that the king was "well the Saturday . . . and on Monday ready to go abroad". Atkins noted "he was better", while Craig confirmed that the king's "fits were lesser" and that the physicians thought "the disease to be declined". Ramsey testified "He had beene by our iugments well recovered."[29] But on Monday night James took a dramatic turn for the worse. The physicians described the events in some detail. Once again, Buckingham had interrupted the physicians' "regular and methodical cure" by applying another plaster. Harvey testified that the plaster was applied "in the afternoone about the beginning of his fit". Ramsey was more precise; at four o'clock a plaster was applied to the king's wrists and at eight o'clock to his stomach.[30] On 12 March, when Buckingham had first applied a plaster, no doctors were in the room, but this time most of them were aware of his action but either unable or unwilling to intervene. James himself initiated the procedure. According to Harvey, the king had "asked him whether that was redy which the Duke had prescribed him", and Archibald Hay insisted that the whole application was "by King's command". This intervention made Beton apprehensive—"he would not have advised to that plaister at that time the kings state of body considered"—but no one tried to prevent the application. Harvey claimed to have been initially unconcerned: since "he conceaved it a facile thing he gave way to it", thinking there could not come "any great hurt of it, being externally to be applied and to work while they stood by". Besides, since "he saw the kinges desire he did not denie it". Atkins was thoroughly versed in court politics, and he testified that though the doctors "disliked" the plaster "offered in the prohibited time", they "would say nothing les[t] [they] might offend the Duke and the King". Harvey also emphasized that James was particularly difficult to manage since he "undervalued physicians" and "took divers things" without their approval.[31]

In contrast, Hay insisted that "no physician disliked" the plaster when it was laid on that afternoon. The duke's servant John Baker had brought him the box containing the plaster, and Baker had also "tasted" the medicine. Hay explained that he had applied the plaster to a strip of leather and laid it on the king's body while several physicians looked on. Some doctors made the best of the awkward situation. Harvey, Beton and Lister all testified that the plaster was "hot", and Lister even suggested it might have been medically useful during the cold phase of the king's fit. When the hot fit began, Harvey testified, "they took it off".[32]

Others described a far more chaotic scene. Ramsey said that he had begun to worry about the plaster half an hour "after it was laid one" and voiced his concern to the bedchamber men. But the plaster stayed on "till midnight" and was removed only when James's "extremity of soundinge" increased. Atkins agreed; "The plaister was taken of because the kinge complained of the heat of it."[33] The testimony also revealed that Buckingham had recommended the plaster to James, had procured it, and, along with his mother, had helped prepare it. "The King desired it," Harvey recalled, since the plaster had been "commended by [the] Duke as good for him, and the Earl of Warwick". Chambers added Lord Carey to the list of those lauding the treatment. Buckingham had touted the cure, Beton recalled, noting that "sundry times before he heard the Duke tell the King that he had used such a plaster which had done him much good". According to Harvey, the treatment "was a secret of one in Essex that had beene used with good successe", adding that "he thinkes it was recommended by the Duke". Lister also attributed it to "a phisition in Essex which the Duke had used".[34] The "Duke's folks brought it in", Hay testified; and Ramsey insisted the plaster "was made in the Duke [sic] Chamber". Atkins heard it was "laid one [sic] by the directions of the Countesse and with the Dukes consent".[35]

That evening Buckingham had also offered the king something to drink. Hay saw the julep "made in [the] Duke's chamber" with "Many about it". Hay "helped to mix it with gillyflower", and testified that the medicinal "Syrup" had been sent to court with the box containing the plaster. Others sampled the medicine. Hay reported there was "not one in the chamber but did taste of it" and confessed that he himself had tried some, though "a great deal after". Chambers acknowledged drinking the posset, and Lister testified that he "tasted" it, or at least "that which he conceaved was of the posset drinke the kinge dranke of". Again James had initiated the treatment. "The King called for it", Harvey said, and "the Duke prepared" it. While Lister was coy about the duke's role, insisting that "he knows not" "who gave it", others were clearer.[36] "As his fit came", Ramsey observed, "the Duke brought the king som thinge to drinke", and Atkins added that the duke "gave the kinge it once with his owne handes". Over the next ninety minutes James "tooke it once and the second time", but "the kinge pute it away with his hand the 3rd time but shewed no reason". Harvey recalled that Atkins and Lister had "opposed the posset". Atkins thought "the drink was given him in the prohibited time" immediately before a fit. Although Lister "thought it could do no harm", he testified that "he wished [the king] forbear" from taking it because of the timing. Since the doctors had "presumed nothinge would be given", Atkins said, they understandably "did shew amongst themselves theire dislike"—but not "to the king because they would not greave him".[37]

Following these interventions, James grew much worse. Initially, neither the plaster nor the potion produced any ill effects. Harvey testified that "the kinge commended" the potion and "liked [the plaster] as appeared and experimented it", while Lister remembered that James "was loath to have [the] plaster off".[38] But as the hours passed, the king's fever fits grew markedly worse. Chambers, who had been away that evening, returned to learn that "the kinge had beene very ill and sicke".[39] By midnight he was in serious trouble. Beton observed that "After the receipt of his potion and plaister he found the kinge much worse and his fever much increased and in drinking his breath like to be stopped." No one in the room could ignore the king's "extremity of soundinge", and Ramsey's description of the "symptoms that followed" was chilling: "panting, raving, swooning, uncertain beating of the pulse". Eventually, James "swooned", and after "he declared his dislike" to Mr Gibb, Ramsey removed the plaster. Atkins seconded this account: "The plaister was taken of because the kinge complained of the heat of it. He grew worse and worse after it and the fever was never of from him."[40] James had also complained of the posset; after taking two doses without complaint, he then pushed it away. As the alarming symptoms multiplied, recriminations began. Ramsey became seriously concerned, confessing his worries to several royal servants including Sir Thomas Lushington, the Earl of Kellie and Henry Gibb. Yet John Craig had caused the most furor by angrily insisting "that which was given to the King by the Duke was as bad as poison".[41]

The physicians' account of James's reactions riveted the committee's attention. When Chambers returned on Tuesday, 22 March, he was told that "the plaister had binne laid one againe and that the king had beene very ill and sicke that night", and that James reportedly had said "that if he had another such fit he could not endure it". The news stunned Chambers who had left court assuming the king was getting better, and he could only marvel that the plaster had been used again after the physicians "had ordered before [that] it should be taken away". On Tuesday evening Chambers and Ramsey sat up with the ailing king and found him "very ill and much deiected". "The violence" of his continued fever left James feeling "far worse", and he told Chambers that "he abhorred that drink, yea a taste in it", complaining that "They gave me warm drink that makes me burn and roast so, and would have given more." Chambers also recalled hearing James ask, in agony, "will you murder me and slay me?" Ramsey gave a similar account. James had asked the two doctors "what had made him so evil last night". Aware of their delicate position, the doctors "excused it", referring to "the haight of the Disease". Yet the king had refused to be mollifed, telling them "No, it was that I had of the Duke of Buckingham." When the committee asked what James was referring to, Ramsey admitted he could not tell "whether he ment the inward potion or outward" plaster. The doctors' recollections may have been inaccurate, and intonation, or sarcasm, could have altered James's meaning. But his health undoubtedly deteriorated rapidly following the dramatic night of 21–22 March. From then on, nothing the doctors tried helped. In Lowther's laconic account, More testified that "after bleeding, fit less, but no declination of Disease. And ever after [James] had a fever".[42] By midday on 27 March the king was dead.

The select committee was understandably eager to know the exact composition of the plaster and potion. The doctors had judged the plaster by its smell. Ramsey recalled "a stronge smell and of penetrating nature". Chambers thought it was made of mithridate, and Lister agreed: it "was of L[ondon] mithridate .... he smelled it and it seemed so". Beton thought it had "a hott smell as it weare made of a terreacalle composition". Atkins, who claimed to have neither seen nor smelled the plaster, said he had heard it was made of "treacle".[43] Hay, who had applied the plaster, testified that, "Treacle or mithridate predominate". According to More, after the second application, "A letter was written to the maker" in Essex, who replied that the plaster was compounded of "London treacle and juice of citrons". As for the drink, More said that Hay had told him "it was plain posset drink with hartshorn in it". Hay and several other medical men testified that the drink also contained syrup of gillyflowers.[44]

But as the doctors revealed, Craig's outburst—"that which was given the king was as bad as poison"—and the continued "muttering in the Court of the givinge of those thinges" had unnerved Buckingham.[45] "Because Craig and Gibb had spoke it did hurt", More testified, the duke attempted to quell the talk. A day or two after the king's death—recollections varied—at Sir William Paddy's insistence and with the approval of "the Duke and Countesse", More circulated a note listing the ingredients of the plaster and potion, and asked the doctors to sign a statement asserting that neither medicine had done any harm. As Beton put it, they wanted written confirmation "to know whether the plaster or julep did hurt".[46] While the doctors agreed that the listed ingredients were "safe and good" in themselves, several lodged highly problematic caveats. Orthodox medical doctrine held that medicines were not inherently good or bad; everything depended how, when, why and for whom they were used. Thus, some doctors would only endorse the ingredients if it were specified that they were to be applied according to the rules of their "art", which required physicians to take into account the place, the time and the patient's complexion. The second caveat was equally damaging: the ingredients More listed might have been harmless, but the doctors could not be certain that the plaster and potion had contained those ingredients. After all, Ramsey explained, they did not "know which apothecary made it". Atkins agreed: "The bill of the ingredients was shown ... and justified in due time and place to be successful", but whether the plaster and potion had in fact been "made of those particulars he knows not". "It was intended", Ramsey noted, "that they should have subscribed that the ingredients in that bill weare the same given the kinge but they refused it". As for the note itself, Beton thought the royal apothecary Israel Wolfe had it.[47] It has never come to light.

The testimony suggested only in very general terms how these medicines might have harmed the king. Perhaps they had been administered at the wrong times in the fit cycles, or had failed to observe the rules of cure by contraries and had heated the king when he should have been cooled, or vice versa. The alleged ingredients were not inherently problematic. London or Venice treacle and mithridate were part of a family of medicines widely used to treat various illnesses. Compounded, often at significant cost, from multiple ingredients, they had been famed since antiquity as poison antidotes.[48] Most medical writers considered treacle a "hot" medicine to be used against distempers related to the cold humours and against the plague.[49] Yet its application to fevers was limited. Walter Baley, treacle's most enthusiastic champion, thought mithridate helped cure "the shaking fits" and "feavers which depend of naughty and malignant causes". But both mithridate and Venice treacle were therapeutically best suited to treating quartan and quotidian fevers, not "pure" tertians, and their use in tertians was usually confined to cases complicated by obstructions or malign mutations.[50] Unlike treacle, the juice of citrons, another alleged ingredient in the plaster, did have a recognized use in treating tertians. The herbalists thought syrup of citron "prevails against all diseases proceeding from choller". The use of plasters on the wrist or torso to deliver ague remedies was also common; indeed, the royal physicians told the committee that at certain points in James's illness, they had used plasters made by the royal apothecary.[51]

The alleged ingredients of James's posset seemed anodyne. Hartshorn and gillyflowers had well-known medicinal uses: according to the herbalists, hartshorn "bindeth, cooleth, and drieth" and when used in plasters could "take away fits of the Ague", while "yellow Stocke-Gillo-floures" possessed "a clensing faculty" and "taketh away the shaking fits". The official pharmacopeia recommended syrup of the "Infusion of Clove-Gilliflowers" as "a good cordial in feavers". The post-mortem report produced by James's doctors recorded the use of hartshorn, marigolds and syrup of citrus juice in various compound remedies deployed during their regular and methodical cure.[52]

Alexander Ramsey, the witness who most insistently claimed that the plaster had caused problems, was also the only doctor to explain what might have gone wrong. Something in the plaster was of a "penetrating nature", and he believed this unknown substance had "repelled the disease inward", driving it back into the body where it corrupted the major organs.

Strange Faculties

Only a highly compressed account of the committee's final session survives, but Bulstrode Whitelocke's telegraphic notes cannot conceal the drama. First, Christopher Wandesford presented his examination of the royal surgeon Gilbert Primrose, who had repeated that "the King was much worse after the plaster had been applied to him". Like Chambers and Ramsey, Primrose had quoted James himself, who "told him that he was worse for that plaster". He also added a lurid detail: shortly before the king's death, "there came from him a great deal of black matter, very noisome, which was without purging". Primrose's terse, isolated account may have added to the impression that something strange had been at work in the king's body.[53]

The most eagerly expected medical witness on the final day was Dr Craig, who had supposedly directly accused Buckingham of poisoning. Yet his testimony proved anticlimactic. He smoothly explained away his confrontation with the duke. He had been dismissed, he confessed, because "he said he was sorry the Duke should administer anything to the King". In response, Buckingham had accused him of saying that "and worse". Craig flatly "denied the worse", insisting his words were those "spoken by one friend to another". He conceded that "in the Lord Duke's chamber . . . there was a rumor that he should say that which was given to the King by the Duke was as bad as poison." But he again denied saying it, maintaining "he spake nothing of these applications one way or other". Craig did, however, add an important detail. In the previous testimony, the doctors were passive figures unable to prevent James and Buckingham from circumventing their protocols. But Craig testified that the doctors "sent him" and another physician "to this King [i.e. Charles] to desire him that he would advise the Lord [Buckingham] to remit all the care to the physicians". They warned the prince that "finding that fit was higher than his other, they might ascribe it to those applications". In the newsletters, in Eglisham's secret history and in earlier testimony, Charles had been invisible, but Craig had now suggested that Charles knew the doctors' concerns and had apparently done nothing to stop the duke's medical interference. Craig was also sent to Buckingham, presumably with the same message, but Dr More, who accompanied him, left Craig outside and "undertook the business" himself.[54]

The physicians' testimony, while unsettling, had not unambiguously supported the allegation that Buckingham had deliberately poisoned James. It had, however, confirmed many circumstantial details in Eglisham's secret history, and some on the committee clearly suspected a poisoning had occurred. On 25 April, for instance, Lowther's fleeting notes recorded a curious interruption in Archibald Hay's testimony. While Hay was answering questions about the composition of the plaster and potion, someone apparently asked whether it might have contained an extract of toad's flesh. According to Lowther, Hay replied that "He neither said nor thought that [frog's flesh] was in it." At that point Sir Edward Peyton, one of the Parliament-men in attendance, violated the committee's rules banning auditors from participating and shouted "Of toad's flesh"—not frog's.[55] Peyton's outburst offers the only hint that anyone had asked the medical attendants about a specific poisonous substance; but they may well have done so in other, now lost, exchanges.

Unlike the other witnesses, Robert Ramsey was neither doctor nor bedchamber-man. He may have been a relative of John Ramsey, Earl of

Holderness, or perhaps the royal trumpeter and brother of Edward Ramsey, a royal servant.[56] Furthermore, nothing suggests Robert Ramsey was anywhere near Theobalds in late March 1625. But when he appeared before the committee on 26 April, he had come to talk not about plasters and potions, but about magical amulets and the distillation of toads. Over the previous six weeks Ramsey had had several odd exchanges with an Irishman called Piers Butler. In early March, Butler had opined that "so long as the King did entertain the Duke of Buckingham he would lose a great many of better friends". Then he had added an unsettling detail: "The King and the parliament could do nothing to the Duke so long as he keeps one thing." When Ramsey replied that "if I were as he I would make much of that one thing", Butler retorted that "he knew who he might thank for it". Later Butler told Ramsay that he possessed "some strange faculties", implying that he had supplied Buckingham with a magical charm to preserve him from political ruin. For the last fortnight Ramsey had studiously avoided Butler after hearing someone called Redman report that Butler had set "one Rennish" to work "to distill the spirit of toads". Ramsey had immediately passed this disturbing news to George Kirk, a groom of James's bedchamber. Perhaps Kirk had brought the story, and Robert Ramsey, to the select committee's attention.[57]

The committee does not appear to have acted on Ramsey's allusive testimony. But he had ominously linked Buckingham to a man with "strange faculties" who experimented with the flesh of a poisonous creature. And while the committee's inquiries appear to have stopped there, others' did not. Bishop de Mende reported that Ramsey had identified "an Irish gentleman . . . accused of sortilege and magic" and that immediately afterwards Butler "had taken flight". The testimony stung the regime into action. The day after Ramsey's appearance, Buckingham sent bulletins to Kent ordering Butler's arrest, and within forty-eight hours the Privy Council had dispatched couriers to Bristol and Chester, ordering the seizure of Butler before he escaped to Ireland.[58]

Butler's appearance in the hearings was remarkable, for he was as close as Parliament would come to identifying the poisoner-mountebank described in *The Forerunner*. Butler was an enigmatic figure who dabbled in chemistry and physic, operating in the grey zone between natural and magical medicine. Variously classified as a learned physician, a charlatan and a witch, the "strong and well sett" Butler cultivated an aura of mystery. And many felt he practised illicit, and politically dangerous, magic. He claimed to have travelled in France and Spain, and alleged a kinship with the Butler earls of Ormonde. Late in 1623 he alarmed fellow drinkers in a cellar near Somerset House when he pulled a bullet from his pocket and announced that "with this Bullet he should have killed the Duke of Buckingham". A 1626 Venetian intelligence report, written after Ramsey's testimony, characterized Butler as "a poor man of no account" who was "generally believed to be a magician". In the spring of 1626, London rumour held that Butler had boasted Buckingham need "never fear Parliament or doubt the king's favour" as long as he wore "what he had on himself", apparently some kind of protective magical amulet.[59]

A later account of Butler's activities depicted him not as a witch but as an alchemical-mystical physician. Jean-Baptiste Van Helmont, the celebrated proponent of Paracelsian medicine, met Butler sometime in the later 1620s, during the Irishman's imprisonment in the Spanish Netherlands. Butler told Van Helmont that he had been "sometime great with James King of England", but his skills fascinated more than his credentials. Butler claimed to have produced a small stone that could cure "every Disease", and although Butler was "presently suspected" of "some hidden Sorcery and Diabolical compact", Van Helmont dismissed these allegations, arguing that Butler's methods were entirely natural. He also recounted preparing with Butler a remedy—which Butler had used to cure numerous London plague victims—made by hanging a toad by its legs, collecting the "excrementious filths" cast out as it was dying, and combining them with the toad's powdered carcass to form a powerful drug.[60] Although Butler impressed Van Helmont, any man who experimented with toads was bound to arouse suspicions. Indeed, by 1626 Butler had also acquired a reputation as a poisoner. Late that year, when Butler travelled towards Sweden "under the pretext of making a pilgrimage", the Scotsman Sir James Spens warned the Swedish chief minister that Butler was a dangerous man, highly skilled "*in artibus veneficis*"—the arts of poison.[61]

Spens also reported that Butler was Buckingham's protégé, someone who, according to Venetian reports, received a "handsome salary"—perhaps as much as £1,000 a year—for "secret service". Butler may thus have been the man Buckingham called "my divill" in a 1624–25 letter to James, who received £400 to conduct alchemical experiments "to have the Felosifers stone". This "divill" also concocted a preservative drug for James out of a "towrd", possibly a mangled spelling of "toad", which Buckingham playfully noted was appropriate for a toad-like king.[62]

Robert Ramsey's brief testimony had dragged Piers Butler into the spotlight; consciously or not, he had startlingly confirmed elements of Eglisham's portrait of the duke as the patron of witches and poisoners.

The Unauthorized Versions

The doctors' testimony shifted the political landscape. Before the hearings, it was easy to dismiss the unauthorized versions of James's death as malicious slander, but it was much harder to do so once the doctors had collectively proven that something untoward had happened at Theobalds. None of them unambiguously supported Eglisham's contention that Buckingham had deliberately poisoned James, although the committee's decision to question Robert

Ramsey suggests that some members wondered whether Piers Butler had not slipped toad venom into the medicines brought from Essex. But most of the testimony militated against this thesis: too many people had witnessed the preparation and application of the plaster and the potion, and since John Baker and several doctors had sampled the medicines with no ill effects, it was hard to imagine that a toad-poison was present. Nevertheless, troubling questions remained. It seemed strange that Buckingham's second intervention had come when James was apparently on the mend. It was equally clear that the duke's conscience was uneasy: why else had he so quickly assumed that Craig had accused him of poisoning? Likewise, why had Buckingham tried so hard to get the physicians' retroactive endorsement of his treatments? The doctors' testimony had also confirmed some of Eglisham's basic allegations. Plainly the duke had gone behind their backs and treated James, and he had pressed the physicians to sign a note approving his treatments. And while their testimony had not proved that James had been poisoned, neither had it definitively disproved that possibility. Finally, the testimony had also highlighted the role of Buckingham's mother, which Eglisham and others had also emphasized. Mende, for instance, reported that "it has been proved that the Countess of Buckingham, against the doctors' advice, put a plaster on the king's stomach composed of strange medicines (*droques extraordinaires*)".[63]

The testimony had revealed other troubling matters. Why had the Villiers family's Catholic physician been in constant attendance at James's bedside? More himself acknowledged that he was "No sworn physician", and the other doctors were quick to distance themselves. Atkins, for one, claimed that More was "no sworn physician to his knowledge". Beton said he did not know "who appointed him to join with them", but added that James had urged them to "consult with Doctor Moore".[64] More could be plausibly seen as Buckingham's man in the sickroom, managing events for his illustrious patron. It was More who had convinced Craig not to speak with the duke about his medical intervention, and More who had played a central role in the attempt to get the doctors to verify the ingredients of the controversial medicines. The prominent role of a Catholic Villiers client during the king's final days understandably gave some contemporaries pause.

If the committee had not found conclusive evidence of a poison plot, it had uncovered abundant evidence of death by misadventure. Buckingham had twice violated strict rules devised to ensure that only the royal physicians prescribed and administered drugs, and that only the royal apothecary could compound them. He clearly did not understand the cycles of the illness or the "prohibited hours" where no medication was safe. Buckingham had given the king a hot plaster and a cold drink at times in the fit when the doctors would have preferred the king receive nothing at all. The duke might well have intervened without any malicious intent; those who knew the king and his favourite understood that experiencing sickness and sharing physic was at the heart of their intimate relationship.[65] But after the doctors' testimony, it was clear that Buckingham might have inadvertently hastened James's death: even if his medicines had contained only the ingredients the Essex doctor had prescribed, the medicines had been given at the wrong time.

That said, parts of the testimony could be cited to excuse the duke's conduct. The doctors made clear that James played a major role in Buckingham's meddling; at the very least, he had consented to his medical interventions, and may even have encouraged them. By emphasizing that James's condition was improving before Buckingham's second intervention, many of the doctors had left the duke highly exposed. But Harvey had insisted that James's illness was "*not* in declination" on the Monday morning; on Saturday the physicians had "thought not the King was mending", Harvey claimed, and on Sunday, James had "heaviness at his heart". By Monday morning, "He" (whether James or Harvey is unclear) "did feare" that day "that the next fitt would be greater then the fit before".[66]

On 27 April, John Glanville delivered the select committee's report on its investigation, and over the next two weeks the Parliament-men would construct their own interpretations of James's death, framing the story in various provocative ways that sometimes developed and sometimes ignored Eglisham's account. These variant narratives, however, were all intertwined. Thanks to the Parliament-men, no one could dismiss Eglisham out of hand; and thanks to Eglisham, the Parliament-men had acquired a dangerous weapon with which to destroy Buckingham. Mulling over the doctors' testimony, the Tuscan agent Salvetti observed that "there is a whisper of poison", but conceded that "in a matter of such importance" one could not ascertain "the exact truth". The Parliament-men "restrict themselves to blaming the act", he thought, in hopes the Lords "will be able to form a judgment regarding it".[67] Sir John Eliot and his allies would end up pursuing a story about misadventure, not murder. But with Eglisham's version of James's death ever more widely available, Buckingham's enemies would also suggest that darker secrets remained to be revealed.

CHAPTER TEN

THE DUKE'S PALLOR

THE FORERUNNER AND THE ASSAULT ON

BUCKINGHAM

A N INTERVIEW WITH Buckingham in mid-May 1626 left the Venetian ambassador seriously alarmed. The duke confessed his "mind was tossed by a thousand agitations" and he was convinced that Charles must "insist upon his authority in order to counteract the activities of the parliamentarians". The favourite's appearance made his anxiety plain, for "the pallor of his face betrays his deep uneasiness at the embarrassments in which he finds himself". The duke found his situation so hopeless that he had even begun talking about moving to the Dutch Republic.[1]

Buckingham's dismay was thoroughly understandable. Initially, he had reacted calmly to the mounting criticism. In a speech on 30 March he had insisted that "it has been my study to keep a good correspondency between the King and his people", and he confessed that "I am amazed" to find "there are other things laid on me" and "so many and on such a sudden". But these attacks, he vowed, would "not alien my heart from that intention" of uniting king and people. Eager "to vindicate" himself, he welcomed criticism and added that if "my errors may be showed me I shall take him for my best friend that will manifest them in particular". Yet he was certain that whatever errors he might have made were "not such gross defects as the world would make them appear", and so he asked that "what is already passed, I wish that it might be forgotten". Delivered before the Easter recess of Parliament, the duke's intervention appeared to have a positive impact. Secretary Conway thought "the greatest part, and most indifferent men, went awaie well satisfied", and one newsletter-writer reported positive responses from "those who were indifferent or not much his [Buckingham's] Enimies". Conway assumed that after cooling down during the recess, the Parliament-men "will hasten to a great conclusion".[2] He was badly mistaken.

After reassembling on 17 April, the Commons gave Sir John Eliot's select committee its wide-ranging powers to hear new testimony a mere five days later. On 24 April the committee began deposing the doctors, and by the time they finished after a further two days, the duke was in serious trouble. Over the subsequent fortnight, as copies of Eglisham's *Forerunner* washed across the capital, Buckingham's self-confidence evaporated. In late April the Earl of Clare met with the duke, who "discoursed much with me of his parlament business". After promising "a full and satisfactory answear" to his charges, Buckingham fell "upon the envy of his fortune" and lamented that "other men's actions were made his, and put upon his score".[3]

Framing the Charge

Buckingham's impeachment required time, and in late April time was running out. On 27 April the select committee told the House that the duke's behaviour in James's sickroom represented an act of "transcendent presumption of dangerous consequence". The Parliament-man John Glanville explained that the king's "sworn physicians" had ordered that "nothing should be applied but by general consent", that all medicines should be prepared "by the King's sworn apothecary", and that the patient should take "no drink for 2 hours before his fit nor till his cold fit over". Nevertheless, two doctors had testified, "the rest not contrary", that two plasters had been applied to the king "by direction of the duke"; afterwards, James "grew worse", with "symptoms of foundering, raving, and extreme heat". Uncertain of the plaster's composition, the doctors had refused to sign a note endorsing it, since they "could not tell of what it was made". The plaster had a "strong smell", and the doctors suspected "that some-what was in it which was invertive". No less than three times, Buckingham had given James a drink that also had "a strong smell" and was "not made by the King's apothecary, nor by the counsel of the physicians". Glanville concluded with James's statement about why he had become so sick: "it was that which I had from the Duke that did it".[4]

The Commons then pondered this controversial report, and the results of a voice vote being "doubtful", they took the unusual step of dividing, a cumbersome process that required those who voted "aye" to walk into the lobby and then be counted as they came back into the chamber. Those voting "nay" remained seated. The House had used the procedure only six times during the current session, most notably on 24 April when 228 members left 168 colleagues in their seats in order to empower the select committee to hear the physicians. Now the House decided, 191 to 150, to accept the select committee's report. With Christopher Wandesford presiding, the Parliament-men then mulled over the new details. Predictably Henry Sherfield, a godly lawyer, was shocked to learn that John More, "no sworn physician", had attended the king, insisting "a physician that is a recusant convict ought not to practice". Edward Littleton, another lawyer, opined that "if a mad man kill the King it is High Treason", suggesting that the duke's offence might be significantly more serious than "transcendent presumption". This implication was too much for Sir Humphrey May, the Chancellor of the Duchy of Lancaster, but after his angry response prompted Wandesford to call him "to the point", May walked out.[5]

The following day, the duke's clients mounted a spirited defence of their master. Lawrence Whitaker, a clerk of the Privy Council, questioned the committee's overreliance on Dr Ramsey, citing the Roman legal adage that a thing proved by one witness alone is of no importance. Besides "I know him so well", Whitaker added, that Ramsey's "testimony is with me of little force". Sir Richard Weston, the Chancellor of the Exchequer, begged his colleagues to appreciate the extraordinary nature of James and Buckingham's relationship, for "these seem presumptuous to us which [to] kings and their near ones are but liberty". May insisted that since "the King desired this plaster and often called for it and the Duke denied it him and prayed him to have the advice of his physicians", then "this business will but add to the bulk of the charge, but not to the weight of it". Sir Dudley Carleton seconded May's sentiment, maintaining that the charge was "not fit to be added". Finally, Sir Thomas Jermyn, an aspiring courtier, warned against rushing to judgement; "this was a great indiscretion and rashness of the Duke of Buckingham", but "if wisemen were always wise, fools would beg their bread".[6]

Buckingham's foes remained implacable. Confident of the outcome, Eliot simply applauded the "variety of opinions", for only "by debate and reasoning pro and con truth comes to light". Meanwhile Sir Francis Stewart, the king's cousin but a sharp critic of the duke, challenged May's contention that James had asked for Buckingham's nostrums. After pointing out that James "could not endure hot drinks as Chambers said", he asked his colleagues "how [the] King could desire it". Edward Kirton defended Ramsey by noting that the witness whom Whitaker had derided had been "imprisoned for the words which he spoke".[7]

These speeches were essentially rhetorical displays from committed true believers designed to persuade their wavering colleagues. Whitaker, Weston, May and Carleton were royal servants, and Jermyn wanted to be one; Eliot, Kirton and Stewart saw the duke's ruin as something akin to a holy crusade. Far more interesting was the reaction of the undecided. In 1625 and again in 1626, Sir Robert Mansell, a former Vice Admiral, had criticized Buckingham, and Charles would soon dismiss Mansell from the Council of War and his local offices. Yet Mansell was noticeably reluctant to add James's death to Buckingham's impeachment articles. "Why rested so great [a charge] a while", he asked, pointing out that there had been "a parliament before" (i.e. in 1625). And after noting that if there were "no evil intent", there had been "no danger", Mansell eventually announced that he "desires this charge not to be added". But others found the doctors' testimony determinative. Humphrey Newbery was the under-steward of Windsor, a constituency with royal connections, but on

28 April he argued against the exculpatory notion that the duke had no "evil intent", observing that "good intentions will not excuse in an act done against the King". The Knight of the Shire for Caernarvonshire, John Griffith, had been trying to "currie favour with the duke", but on 28 April he told the House that although "the witnesses differed" about whether James was recovering at the time of the intervention, yet "upon the testimony of Dr. Ramsey and Dr. Atkins he would if he had been of the Duke's jury . . . have condemned him to death".[8] Since many others shared these doubts, it did not require another division to add Buckingham's involvement in James's death as the thirteenth impeachment charge.

On 2 May the duke's supporters mounted a last effort to forestall a formal impeachment hearing, urging the Commons to present its charges directly to the king. Sir William Beecher reiterated Charles's earlier promise that "he will reform those things we shall complain of". This effort failed. So too did an attempt to block a request for Buckingham's confinement during his impeachment. The duke's supporters then tried to prune the list of charges, and they eventually convinced the House to delete the accusation that Buckingham was responsible for the increase of popery. Yet amid this activity the duke's supporters made no effort to explain or dismiss the accusation of his "transcendent presumption" in James's death. Sir Robert Harley, Secretary Conway's godly son-in-law, predicted that "2 charges will not take" in the Lords, "[St] Peter and that of the King's physic".[9] But he did not elaborate, and no one seconded his opinion.

Later on 2 May, Sir Dudley Digges reviewed the case on "the King's physic". By this point, the details were so well known that Digges simply noted:

> Where physicians to be sworn, kings' person so sacred as none to minister otherwise. His physicians upon consultation [resolved] nothing to be done but by general advice, and commanded a restraint before [each] fit. Duke contrary [to] his duty and these [rules], caused certain plasters to be prepared and drink to be ministered. Notwithstanding it had evil effects and that physicians refused until removed, he, when the King in declination, made them be applied and given, whereupon great distempers and evil symptoms appeared, and physicians did after advise the Duke to do so no more.

On 3 May the House appointed eight Parliament-men with sixteen assistants to present the charges to the Lords. The charge concerning James's death eventually fell to Christopher Wandesford, a protégé of Sir Thomas Wentworth, who had emerged in 1626 as a major figure in his own right. A member of the select committee, Wandesford had attended the doctors' depositions and presented the committee's report to the whole House on 28 April.[10] Aside from Eliot, no one knew the case better.

On 8 May, barely a fortnight after the physicians' testimony, the Commons delegation, headed by Digges and Eliot, went to meet the Lords. By that time their allegations about James's death had been strengthened by a stunning development in the Upper House.

The Ambassador to Madrid

"If I be brought to the Parliament", the Earl of Bristol had said in 1624, "the Duke is madd" (Fig. 55). It had taken Buckingham some time to appreciate this fact. Following his 1624 triumphs, the duke had imagined he could ruin the earl with another parliamentary impeachment, but by early 1625 he had chosen instead to exclude Bristol from Parliament. In 1626, Bristol decided to push back.[11]

The former allies had fallen out during the 1623 trip to Madrid, and Buckingham's 1624 relation to Parliament had identified Bristol as Gondomar's English co-conspirator, a traitor undermining the English Church and state.[12] Although the Parliament-men cheered the address, Bristol knew it was but a partial truth, and he fashioned a counter-narrative stressing the favourite's willingness to trade religious concessions for the Infanta. In this alternative

Figure 55: Renold Elstracke's engraving of John Digby, Earl of Bristol, the former English ambassador to Spain, c. 1620–25 (British Museum). In 1624, Buckingham made him the scapegoat for the Spanish match; in 1626, Bristol charged the duke with treason.

version, the Spanish marriage, which would have brought peace to Europe and wealth to England, had collapsed not because of Spanish duplicity but because of Spanish horror at Buckingham's behaviour.

Bristol had a mass of evidence supporting his account. "The defence of my doeings in Spayne", he told a kinsman, "is supported by no worse legges then the letters of the King Prince and others tha[t] cannot disavowe theire owne warrants." Placed under house arrest on his return to London and periodically questioned but never brought to trial, the earl protested his fate as "an Example hardly to be paralleled in Christendome". By July 1624 he had begun threatening that if "I shall be forced unto it for myne owne Just defense . . . I shall have recourse unto Gods holy protection and myne owne integritie and labour to maintaine myne honor and fidelity against any opponent whatsoever and by all the meanes I can." Welcoming an investigation, he had prepared a slate of witnesses. Since any hearing involving such a well-armed adversary would likely backfire, Buckingham kept Bristol under house arrest, first in London and then in Dorset. Nevertheless, Bristol made contact with the duke's widening circle of critics, and his influence helped disrupt the Oxford session of the 1625 Parliament. By February 1626 those who wanted to check Buckingham were as determined to see Bristol in Westminster as Charles and Buckingham were to exclude him.[13]

The simplest tactic for the regime was to forget to send Bristol a summons, but this ploy would only work if the earl cooperated. On 22 March, however, Bristol asked the Lords to correct the Crown's oversight, arguing that he had never been charged with, much less convicted of, anything. On 30 March, Buckingham announced that Bristol would shortly receive a summons; he neglected to mention that it would be accompanied by a letter relaying Charles's desire that "your Lordship's personal attendance is to be forborne". In mid-April, Bristol forced the issue. On the 19th his former secretary, Walsingham Gresley, told the Commons that if Bristol "might be heard he doubted not but to make it appear that the ill success in the negotiations for the Palatinate may be attributed to my lord of Buckingham".[14] Meanwhile Bristol complained to the Lords that he was being excluded, "lest he should discover many crimes concerning the said Duke" who had "abused their Majesties, the state and both the Houses of parliament". The pressure worked. Charles ordered Bristol, who was "so void of duty and respect", to present himself for trial before the Lords. On 29 April the peers considered whether Bristol should be "of the House" or stand before it as an accused man. The Privy Councillors—Marlborough, Conway, Bridgewater and Buckingham—insisted that Bristol was a delinquent. They carried the day, but only after determined resistance from Saye and Sele, Warwick, Essex, Montgomery and Pembroke, godly Hispanophobes who were now eager for the Hispanophile Bristol's voice and vote.[15]

On 1 May, Bristol finally stood before the peers on charges of high treason. But as Attorney General Sir Robert Heath began reading out the indictment, the earl interrupted with his own accusation. Buckingham had recently called Bristol "one of the dangerousest traitors that hath byn in this kingdome in many years", but Bristol now turned the tables. "I accuse that man the Duke of Buckingham of high treason", he began, "and will prove it." For good measure, he also indicted Conway. Even more provocatively, he argued that because his preliminary petition had been filed on 19 April, his case against Buckingham and Conway took precedence over Charles's case against him. According to Bristol, Buckingham had plotted with Gondomar and the pope to lure Charles to Spain, where Buckingham had laboured to "have perverted the Prince and subverted the true religion established in England". The plot might have worked if the duke had restrained himself. But not only did he routinely adore the Blessed Sacrament and shun Protestant services, he also horrified his Spanish co-conspirators by offering gifts and favours "for the recompense and hire of his lust". More importantly, Buckingham had "been in great part the cause of the ruin and misfortune" of "the Prince Palatine and his estates". He had also harmed King James. Neatly tying his case both to the thirteenth impeachment article and to *The Forerunner*, Bristol recalled how, early in 1625, James had promised to review the case against him. "I pray God", Bristol declared, "that Promise did him no hurt, for he died shortly after."[16]

Confusion ensued as procedural questions multiplied. Magnanimously, Buckingham initially announced that he would not "interrupt Bristol when he was speaking" because "he has been his friend". But his politesse soon crumbled as Bristol's allusion to Eglisham's allegations sank in: "the accusation of Bristol against him is of treason, etc and *a touch upon the late King's death*." Soon, Buckingham asked that "if [Bristol] prove it not, then he may have *lex talionis*". Meanwhile Conway maintained that his case should "be heard presently". Attorney General Heath was uncertain "whether the E. of Bristol shall be heard first or no". The Lord President thought the king's case against Bristol had priority, while Bishop Harsnett plumped for Bristol. Eventually, the House followed Buckingham's advice and agreed to consider both cases together, and, with some misgivings, placed Bristol under house arrest pending a verdict. This decision caused Bristol to "burst out into angry passion that seeing he had accused the Duke of High Treason, that the Duke might be also used in the same manner". Five days later, Bristol again protested that "I ... do find myself a restrained man and the Duke at liberty sitting as one of my judges". "There are complaints of partiality", Salvetti noted, "and a universal feeling of regret for the position of the Earl of Bristol." Yet in a significant concession, the Lords allowed him "free liberty to confer and advise with such friends and others as he shall think fitting", thus giving Buckingham's enemies ready access. Meanwhile Bristol tried to rally support for his cause. As the old envoy spoke in the Lords, his son, George Digby, and his stepson, Sir Lewis Dyve, handed copies of his address out to the Parliament-men, and then littered others around the city.[17]

Bristol's offensive, which dominated the Upper House for the next six weeks, proved hugely damaging. In effect, he had rewritten Buckingham's own rewriting of the 1623 trip, eroding what remained of the duke's once-glittering reputation as a valiant Protestant hero. His accusations also revitalized older images of the court favourite as sexual predator and religious chameleon, while casting new doubt on the young king. During the 1624 relation, the prince had stood beside Buckingham, periodically confirming details. As an official report on Charles's response to Bristol's allegations acknowledged, the earl's claims concerning the 1624 declaration reflected "as far upon himself as upon the Duke, for that his Majesty went as far in that declaration as the Duke". Bristol's speech also revived the case for the much-discredited Spanish match. He insisted it could have worked: Charles would have found "a worthy Lady whom he loved", the Exchequer would have received a dowry "much greater than was ever given in Money in Christendome", Philip IV would have "engaged himself for the restitution of the Palatinate; for which a daughter of Spain and two millions had been no ill pawn", and James would have given "Peace, Plenty and Increase to his subjects".[18] With England's recent military humiliations fresh in the memory, the earl's talk of opportunities lost contrasted starkly with the depressing realities of Buckingham's war.

Bristol's allusion on 1 May to James's death spoke both to the duke's impeachment charge and to Eglisham's tract, and on 6 May the earl again alluded to the secret history. He asked Pembroke to confirm that in the spring of 1624, Buckingham had berated Hamilton, Lennox and Pembroke for successfully arguing against imprisoning Bristol in the Tower, and had insisted that if Gondomar "did come to the King, he would put new hopes into his Majesty, whereby the breach of the treaties with Spain touching the marriage and the Palatinate would be hindered". Bristol left unstated what Eglisham's readers knew—not long after that alleged confrontation, Lennox, Hamilton and King James had all died. Bristol's allusion to Gondomar's possible return also supported Eglisham's story that Buckingham was terrified the Spaniard "wold secund the Lord of Brestowes accusations against him".[19]

Did Bristol and his allies coordinate these mutually supporting statements? After all, only a few days separated the Commons' decision to investigate James's death, the increasing publicity for Eglisham's book, and Bristol's accusations against Buckingham. The evidence is suggestive but ultimately inconclusive. It is unlikely that Eliot and his colleagues would have cooperated with those disseminating Eglisham's book, but Bristol is another matter. He was highly sympathetic to Spain and good friends with Gondomar. In June 1625, when Gondomar arrived in Paris on his way to Brussels, "the young Lord Digby, the Earl of Bristoll's sonne" was in his entourage. In late April 1626 this same young man appeared before the Commons with Walsingham Gresley to argue on Bristol's behalf. If, as seems likely, Gondomar was one of the men behind *The Forerunner*'s printing,

Bristol's network would have been very useful in coordinating the pamphlet's release with a parliamentary investigation.[20]

In any case, by the time Digges, Wandesford and Eliot were ready to deliver the Commons' charges to the Lords, the launching of *The Forerunner* and Bristol's attack on the duke had encouraged much wider interest in James I's death. The impeachment clause still alleged a "transcendent presumption", not a murder, but Eglisham explicitly, and Bristol implicitly, had raised the issue of deliberate poisoning—and they had suggested a clear motive for Buckingham's actions. None of the three Commons representatives took up the poison charge directly, but their addresses to the Lords each alluded to Eglisham's accusations. This was delicate work. One false step, one hint too far, and Charles might dissolve the parliamentary session and Buckingham would be free. But done carefully, the Parliament-men might persuade Charles to surrender the duke.

In the Painted Chamber

On 8 May a delegation of Parliament-men made their way to the Painted Chamber to present the impeachment charges to the Lords' representatives. Digges delivered the preamble, and Eliot the epilogue; while Wandesford presented the accusation concerning James's death. The presentations broke off around 6 p.m., and resumed and concluded on 10 May. Eight peers then spent two days writing up their reports and comparing notes with materials from the Commons, and they formally presented the charges to the Lords on 13 and 15 May. By then, however, the impeachment had already veered badly off track. On 11 May, incensed by the speeches in the Painted Chamber, Charles had sent Digges and Eliot to the Tower.[21]

Since the arrests halted proceedings in the Commons, triggering a standoff over parliamentary liberties, it is crucial to understand what had angered Charles.[22] Both Digges and Eliot had mixed broad-stroke depictions of Buckingham's corruption with details of his specific crimes, but it was their discussions of James I's death that had enraged the king. Eliot had made incendiary historical comparisons between Buckingham and the notoriously corrupt imperial Roman favourite Sejanus, while Digges had implied that the whole truth of James's death was yet to be revealed. The ease with which Digges's words, in particular, were misunderstood reveals the extraordinary volatility of the charge concerning James's death. Wandesford escaped royal retribution, but he too had ventured beyond the strict letter of the impeachment charge. Since the precise meaning of an "act of transcendent presumption and of dangerous consequence" was unclear, the charge could be glossed in various ways. While it was possible to present Buckingham's behaviour as an error of judgement, it was also possible to insinuate that Buckingham had a murderous *intent* to harm the king. The charge's imprecision thus allowed the Parliament-men to mould it in ways that would pressure the king to end his hitherto adamant defence of the duke before more damaging accusations came forth. But this game had to be played with care.

Digges, Wandesford and Eliot's potent rhetorical performances captured the breadth of Buckingham's corruption and misrule. Salvetti thought the presentations portrayed Buckingham "in vivid colours without the slightest respect for his person", and Bishop de Mende thought the speeches used "words more venomous than a viper" (*plus empoisonée que la vipère*).[23] The three speeches also clearly revealed how easily images of the favourite-as-poisoner could be connected to deeper anxieties about royal power, court politics and national decay.

The Comet

Digges's prologue presented a sad portrait of national decline, of power and honour decayed; "the cause of all" this senseless ruin was "one great man". To illustrate his point, Digges compared the "beautiful composition and fair structure of this monarchy and commonwealth" to the divine creation itself. The earth corresponded to the common people who worked the soil and traded upon the waters. The four higher realms—air, fire, the planets and the stars—represented different rungs in the kingdom's hierarchy, magistrates, clergy, "great officers" of state and peers. All was "lighted and heated" by the "one great glorious sun"—the king. This hierarchy was rigid and natural, but bound together by mutual care. Buckingham's rise, however, had violated this immutable order. For Digges, Buckingham was a "meteor" disrupting the cosmic hierarchy and threatening disaster. "If this glorious sun", the king:

> by his powerful beams of grace and favor, shall draw from the bowels of this earth an exhalation that shall take fire and burn and shine out like a star, it cannot be marveled at if the poor commons gaze and wonder at the comet and[,] if they feel the effects[,] impute them to the corruptible matter of it.[24]

Drawn by royal favour from "the bowels of this earth", Buckingham had transcended his appropriate station, and now his "corruptible matter" afflicted the commons below. But he was not a typical comet. Digges compared him to the strange new star that had appeared in Cassiopeia for sixteen months in the early 1570s. As Holinshed's *Chronicles* had noted, the "best and most expert mathematicians" had established that the new star was "in place celestiall far above the moone, otherwise than ever anie comet hath beene seene, or naturallie can appeere". The new star thus challenged the Aristotelian distinction between a mutable earthly sphere and an unchanging celestial one.[25] For Digges, Buckingham's ascent was as abnormal as the "new star" of 1572:

if such an apparition, like that in the last age in the Chair of Cassiopeia, happen amongst the fixed stars themselves, where Aristotle of the old philosophers conceived there was no place for such corruptions, then, as the learned mathematicians were troubled to observe the irregular motions, the prodigious magnitude, the ominous prognostics of that meteor, so the commons, when they see such a blazing star in course, so exorbitant in the affairs of the commonwealth, cannot but look upon it and, for want of perspectives, commend the nearer examination to your Lordships that may behold it at a better distance.

More worrying still, this abnormal ascent carried "ominous prognostics" of divine anger: as one Parliament-man hurriedly noted, Digges had compared the "Duke to a prodigious comet ... which prognosticates the ruin of common-wealth". When listing Buckingham's "exorbitant will, this transcendent power, this placing and displacing officers, this irregular running into all the courses of the planets, this sole and singular managing of the great affairs of state", Digges did not linger over the question of responsibility. Yet his analogy clearly noted that royal favour had drawn the comet's matter from the bowels of the earth.[26]

Digges then previewed the charges against the duke, but when he reached the thirteenth count, he refused to elaborate: "The last of the charges", he noted, "will be an injury offered to the person of the late King of blessed memory that is with God, of which as your Lordships may have heard heretofore, so you shall anon have further information." What Digges said next became the subject of great dispute. He apparently emphasized that the Commons had instructed him not to say anything reflecting upon the honour of either James or Charles. This loyal disclaimer saved the criticism of the duke from being interpreted as de facto criticism of the king, and it prevented Buckingham from attributing his actions to royal orders. Indeed, Digges chastised the duke for "unworthily" casting "some ill odor of his own ways" on James. Despite his cosmological analogy about the royal sun creating the disastrous comet, Digges wanted to insulate James and Charles from the criticism directed at their favourite. The worst of the duke's crimes had occurred under Charles, but Digges interpreted the young king's favour as the outgrowth of his "piety unto his father", which made him "a pious nourisher even of his affections to my Lord Duke in whom, out of that consideration, he has wrought a kind of wonder, making favor hereditary". Since the favour itself was a manifestation of royal virtue, the "abuse of it", Digges concluded, "must be my Lord Duke's own". Nevertheless, Digges was walking a fine line between criticizing the favourite and criticizing his masters. We cannot know Digges's exact words, but he had begun his defence of royal honour immediately after concluding his discussion of James's death: "upon this occasion", he said, "I am commanded by the Commons to take care of the honour of the King our sovereign that lives." For some listeners, "this occasion" seemed to refer to James I's death and the words that followed to imply that Digges could not say any more without impugning the honour of "the King . . . that lives". Sir Richard Grosvenor noted that "in speaking of the plaster and potion [Digges] said he could speak more but he would not for sparing the king's honor; hence, an inference that something was done which might not be related for questioning the King's honor."[27]

Et tu Brute!

Two days after Digges's preamble, Christopher Wandesford presented the impeachment article on James's death, "an offense and misdemeanor of so high a nature as may justly be called, and is by the said Commons deemed to be, an act of transcendent presumption and of dangerous consequence".[28] We do not know how the select committee came to this phrasing—without evidence of "malice aforethought", they could not claim that Buckingham had poisoned James—but it left many in the Commons dissatisfied. When the select committee first used the phrase on 28 April, it immediately stirred controversy. The councillor Sir Richard Weston challenged the definition; since "presumption" might have *led* to a crime, but was not a crime in itself, the allegation could be "no cause for a charge". In response, the lawyer Edward Littleton argued that Weston had misunderstood what "presumption" meant.[29] Others felt the charge did not go far enough and should be redefined. On 27 and 28 April several Parliament-men argued that Buckingham's lack of malicious intent did not diminish the gravity of his offence. Indeed, Wandesford himself had insisted that the standard of proof changed when the victim was a king. "If a madman kill a common person, it is not felony", but if a madman "kill the King it shall be treason as if it had been done by a man of reason". Humphrey Newbery offered two conflicting precedents. The Earl of Southampton, despite his lack of "evil intention", was convicted of treason for joining the Essex revolt of 1601: "good intentions will not excuse in an act done against the King". But his second example—Sir Walter Tirrel's accidental killing in 1100 of William Rufus—muddied the case, because Tirrel's action was deemed "no treason" as he had "no evil intention" to hurt the king.[30] A treason case might be hard to sustain, but Wandesford clearly thought Buckingham's charge could be upgraded. As he told the Lords, to refer to the duke's crime as "transcendent presumption" was to "speak modestly" of his offence. He thus encouraged the peers to seek out new evidence, arguments or precedents to make the duke's action "appear in its own colors", and he suggested where they might look.[31]

First, Wandesford argued that Buckingham had violated the statutes regulating medical practitioners. The impeachment charge alluded to the "special care and order . . . taken by the laws of this realm to restrain and prevent the unskillful administration of physic", and Wandesford cited the sixteenth-century legislation that made it "penal for unskillful empirics and all others to exercise and practice physic upon common persons" without a licence.[32] Wandesford was on shaky ground here, for a 1543 statute permitted ordinary people to apply plasters to external sores and "drinkes for . . . agues", without fear of punishment. Furthermore, Buckingham was not an unlicensed or irregular "empiric" practising medicine as a trade; and even if he had been, Theobalds was outside the jurisdiction of the College of Physicians, who could have only imposed a £5 fine in any case.[33] But to aggravate the crime further, Wandesford stressed the particular horror of "such experiments" practised "upon the sacred person of a king", repeating his earlier (tendentious) claim that even a madman's assault upon a king was treason. After emphasizing the physicians' strict protocols for James's treatment, Wandesford recalled how Henry VI's doctors had "thought it not safe for them to administer anything to the King's person without the assent of the Privy Council and express licence under the Great Seal of England".[34]

Wandesford also tried to redefine Buckingham's actions as felonious homicide. The duke had usurped "the duty and vocation of a sworn and experienced physician"—an unlawful act; and the law "judges a deed done in the execution of an unlawful act" to constitute "manslaughter", while the same deed done in the performance of a lawful act was "but chance medley".[35] Wandesford's terminology was imprecise, in part because the law's distinction between murder and other homicides was in flux. But his legal reasoning reflected contemporary thinking on accidental homicides, and if Buckingham had caused James's death while unlawfully practising physic, he arguably had, at the very least, committed "manslaughter".[36]

Wandesford then offered another aggressive reinterpretation of Buckingham's offence. He noted that although the Elizabethan jurist Sir William Staunford held that a licensed physician whose patient died could not be charged with felony "because he did it not feloniously", "Mr. Bracton", the thirteenth-century legal oracle, maintained that "if one that is no physician or surgeon undertakes a cure and the party die in his hands, this is felony".[37] At least two Parliament-men had made similar claims a day earlier when debating Buckingham's possible commitment to the Tower. Sir John Strangways, a Bristol protégé, maintained that "The Duke . . . administered physic to the king, he died, which is felony". Mr Long agreed: "It is a felony in the law for a common person to give physic and the person die upon it . . . The Duke is no physician; he has applied potions to the King." If this act constituted felony when the "victim" was a "private person", Long asked, "then what is this" when the victim is a king?[38] Again, this was a contested legal point. Bracton in fact had not commented on the issue; but early Stuart lawyers did cite Bracton's late thirteenth-century follower "Britton", who (as Edward Coke later put it) "saith, that if one that is not of the mysterie of a Physitian or Chirurgion, take upon him the cure of a man and he dieth of the Potion or Medicins, this is . . . covert felony." Other lawyers endorsed this interpretation of Britton. John Wilkinson, for example, wrote that "if a man take upon him to bee a Phisition or a Surgeon, and not allowed to use and practise such faculty, if hee take upon him a cure which dyeth under his hands by his ignorance, it is held to be felony."[39]

Wandesford also tried to use the law governing medical malpractice. Although usually protected from culpability, licensed physicians could be held accountable for a patient's death, "if it appear they have transgressed the rules of their own art". There was as yet no systematic English jurisprudence on the issue, however the late thirteenth-century *Mirror of Justices* had contended that physicians who behaved "stupidly or negligently" were to be considered "homicides or mayhemers" if their patients died, and the courts had recently heard felony cases involving medical negligence and malpractice.[40] Unfortunately for Wandesford's argument, Buckingham, as an unlicensed practitioner, could not have transgressed the rules of his profession. Yet once again Wandesford had suggested that Buckingham's actions resembled other felonious offences; once more, he had nudged the Lords to reclassify transcendent presumption as a capital crime.

Complementing these attempts to reclassify Buckingham's offence, Wandesford also fashioned a powerful narrative of political misrule and disorder. Buckingham had acted at Theobalds with his customary ill-counselled arrogance. Although the king's person was "sacred" and "not to be thought upon without reverence, not to be approached unto without distance", Buckingham had recklessly violated the decorum that hedged the royal body. "The boldness of this Lord admits no warrant, no command, no counsel," Wandesford declared. "Transported by the passions of his own will", the duke had "ventured upon the doubtful sickness of a king with a kind of high, sole, and single counseling. The effects whereof, as in all other things, so especially in such as this, have ever been decried as leading to ruin and destruction." Buckingham had ignored the rules of physic—mistakenly assuming the same medicine would "be so catholicly good at all times in all degrees of age for all bodies". Why, Wandesford then asked, would the duke have repeatedly applied medicines that had already "appeared so unsuccessful?" Rather than answer that question directly, he asked the Lords to consider "whether it were a fatal error in judgment only" or whether "something else", something "in his affection", was to blame. The king's precipitous decline was indeed a "strange effect" to attribute to the "applying of a treacle plaster", but the doctors had testified "that this plaster had a strong smell and an invective [invertive] quality, striking the malignity of the disease inward which nature otherwise might have expelled outward". Rather than directly accusing Buckingham of poisoning James, Wandesford trod carefully, relying on hints and queries. But the implications of his historical analogies were unmistakable. The doctors agreed that James had blamed Buckingham's potion for his worsening symptoms, and surely, Wandesford added, this was "A great discomfort" to the king "to think that he should receive anything that might hurt him from one that he so loved and affected." This personal betrayal reminded Wandesford of Caesar's words when his friend Brutus stabbed him: "Et tu Brute! Et tu fili!"[41] The parallel was provocative, for if James was Caesar and Buckingham Brutus, then James's death was not the unfortunate result of a transcendent presumption. It was an assassination.

Veneries and Venefices

According to his Victorian biographer, Sir John Eliot's concluding remarks on 10 May constituted a "philippic of the bitterest order". In addition to summarizing the case against the duke, Eliot also hoped to give the Lords an "idea of the man, what in himself he is, what in his affections". Like Digges and Wandesford, Eliot had to proceed carefully and try to condemn the favourite without faulting his royal masters. When an unnamed peer interjected that Buckingham had only acted by royal command, Eliot replied that the Parliament-men, far from criticizing Charles or James, strove to "vindicate their fames from such as would eclipse them". After pondering how a man "so notorious in ill" could maintain his standing, Eliot attributed this "wonder . . . in policy" not to royal favour but to the duke's creation of a "party" to "help and underprop" his power. Nevertheless, Eliot was playing a dangerous game, and he played it far more recklessly than either Digges or Wandesford had. Once again, James's death would prove the explosive issue. As a careful student of rhetoric, Eliot was undoubtedly aware of what his words could imply. Like Wandesford, he tried to stretch the charge concerning James's death to encompass actions more sinister than an "act of transcendent presumption". Unlike Wandesford, he looked not to the law but to classical history for his precedents, and in particular to immensely controversial Roman critiques of imperial tyranny.[42]

Eliot grouped the charges into clusters, each linked to a master vice. All the duke's crimes derived from his original sin, ambition, exemplified by Buckingham's "procuring the great offices of power and strength in the kingdom and, in effect, the government of the whole into his own hands". These crimes also derived from the "patterns of his mind", which were "full of collusion and deceit, crimes . . . so odious and uncertain as the ancients knew not by what name to term them and therefore they expressed them in a metaphor, calling them *stellionatus* from a discolored beast so doubtful in appearance as they knew not what to make of it". Other crimes revealed Buckingham's tyranny, his "high oppression" of men, laws and the state itself, all "made inferior to his will". "No right, nor interest may withstand him", Eliot claimed, "but through the power of state and justice he dares strike at his own ends." He then turned to Buckingham's "extortion", "corruption" and "sordid bribery in sale of honors, in sale of offices" in which "the ancient crown of virtue" had become "merchantable, and justice itself a prey to the great man". The duke's predations had left the body politic shattered, its "fountain of supply" exhausted, its "nerves and sinews" broken, "the blood and spirit of the kingdom" emptied from its veins, and "the whole body of the land" cast into a "deep consumption". While the king pleaded poverty, Buckingham lived in splendour. "His profuse expenses, his superfluous feasts, his magnificent buildings, his riots, his excesses" were "but a chronicle of his immense exhausts out of the crown revenues."[43]

At this juncture, Eliot turned to the duke's "act of transcendent presumption", which he linked to his broader indictment of the favourite's reckless ambition. Yet in an act of studied reticence, Eliot refused to name Buckingham's crime. His rhetorical intentions are unclear. He later denied that he had been playing games, but since his words were ambiguous, he likely knew what he was doing. Without ever explaining why Buckingham's actions had been classified only as "transcendent presumption", Eliot magnified the horror of the crime, while leaving the impression that there was more to the case than the Commons had felt able to say. In other words, with Eglisham's charges circulating in the City around him, Eliot could hint Buckingham had murdered the king without saying so outright. "Having thus prevailed in wealth and honors he rests not there", Eliot began:

> Ambition had no bounds, but like a violent flame breaks further, catches at all, assumes new boldness, gives itself more scope; not satisfied with the injuring of justice, the wrong of honor, the prejudice of religion, the abuse of state, or that of the revenues. But his attempts go higher to the person of his sovereign, making in that his practice in such a manner and with such effects as I fear to speak it, nay, I doubt to think it, in which respect I'll leave. Cicero did the like, *Ne [aut] gravioribus utar verbis quam natura fert aut levioribus quam causae postulat.* The examination with your Lordships will show you what it is. I need not name it.

The allusion to Cicero was very deliberate. Ostensibly the phrase—"lest I should use either language severer than man's nature is inclined to bear, or else more gentle than the cause requires"—merely explained Eliot's inability to find words appropriate to Buckingham's culminating crime. But the allusion also raised suspicions that something remained "that could not be said"—presumably, more serious crimes than hitherto alleged.[44]

Roman precedents shaped Eliot's second allusion to James's death. Having delineated Buckingham's crimes and character, Eliot observed that no man "so near resembles" Buckingham "as does Sejanus", the great favourite of the Roman emperor Tiberius. Here Eliot deferred to the Roman historian Tacitus, whose account of Sejanus's career formed a central episode in his caustic history of Rome under the Julio-Claudian emperors. Tacitus's discussion of imperial tyranny and corrupt favouritism spoke powerfully to Eliot's contemporaries anxious about the courtly politics and monarchical ambitions of their own age. Eliot began by citing Tacitus's introductory sketch of Sejanus, noting that the imperial favourite "was *[animus] audax, sui obtegens in alios criminator iuxta adulator et superbia*"—"of mind bolde; in his owne actions secret; an informer against others; as proud as flattering". For Eliot, Buckingham's "boldness" and his secrecy "in his purposes" were evident not only from the charges against him, but also from his arrogant behaviour in the current Parliament. As for Buckingham's "pride and flattery", Eliot added, "what man can judge the greater?" He then noted another "parallel". Sejanus supported his own interests by promoting his allies to office and honours. "Does not" Buckingham "do the like?"[45] Eliot concluded first with "a note upon Sejanus's pride, his high ambition": Sejanus "would mix his business with the prince's, seeming to confound their actions, and was after styled *laborum imperatores socios*, his fellow, his companion in his travails"; Buckingham did the same. Eliot then employed the rhetorical figure of *paralipsis* to air accusations while claiming he would not air them. He would not, he said, mention many other offences associated with Sejanus—"his salaciousness, his neglect of counsels, his veneries [sexual transgressions], his venefices [poisonings]".[46]

Although Eliot would later deny he was comparing Sejanus's other crimes with Buckingham's, several of his listeners clearly believed he was hinting at further parallels, and it is almost certain that Eliot wanted them to do so. Sejanus was a notorious poisoner. Tacitus described in salacious detail the favourite's murder of the emperor's son, Drusus: Sejanus had seduced Drusus's wife, Livia, in order to make her his accomplice, and suborned a servant, a eunuch, into administering the slow-working poison obtained from Livia's physician. Tacitus also reported the rumour that Sejanus had suborned the eunuch by sodomizing him.[47] For Tacitus, Sejanus's "veneries and venefices" were thus deeply interlinked: poisoning was achieved through the sexual seduction of those with intimate access to the victim. The implicit parallel with Buckingham hinted that behind the charge of "transcendent presumption" were suspicions that the duke had committed premeditated murder.

The allusion to the favourite's "veneries" also went beyond the Commons' brief. By comparing Buckingham to Sejanus, Eliot could paint the favourite as a polymorphous sexual predator, an adulterer and a sodomite. These allegations about "veneries" resonated with long-standing libellous discourse about the favourite's sexual appetites, but they also allowed Eliot to allude publicly to charges mooted in the impeachment planning document concerning Buckingham's "Adulteryes and the Like", which alleged he had fathered children with the wife of Sir Charles Howard, seduced Lady Roos in order to get her to testify against her mother, Lady Lake, and tried to seduce his own sister-in-law, Lady Purbeck. More shocking, perhaps, were allegations that "to the scandall of our nation and Religion", Buckingham had exposed himself to Spanish nuns and that, back home in his great house at New Hall, the duke had watched as Feliciano, a Spaniard, had sex "with 3 women one after another". One of the women involved in the escapade had been taken to Buckingham's wife, "who wept for the same". Eliot's allusion to Buckingham's "veneries" may also have helped amplify Bristol's vague allegations about the "scandal given" by Buckingham's behaviour in Spain and about the bestowal of "favors and offices" on "base and unworthy persons for the recompense and hire of his lust".[48]

Eliot closed by insisting that since "all our evils" came from Buckingham, only his punishment would bring our "remedies". He offered a medieval precedent for parliamentary censure of an overweening favourite, and like Eglisham he demanded that Buckingham be tried and surrendered to "law and justice". The Commons, Eliot noted, reserved the right to add additional charges and proofs and to reply to Buckingham's defence.[49]

The following day, Eliot was in the Tower.

CHAPTER ELEVEN

A TRUE CLEARING?

BUCKINGHAM'S DEFENCE

T HE VILLAGE OF Santon Downham in northwestern Suffolk was far from Westminster, but the Reverend John Rous had little trouble getting news. Talk of London events was everywhere, allowing Rous to fill his commonplace books with reports that let him engage with the kingdom's affairs. His surviving notes on the 1626 Parliament reflected the general uneasiness in the country. The pricking of Edward Coke as sheriff dominated East Anglian talk at the beginning of the session. Since it was a plan "as was thought" for "the utter bringing under of parliament power", Rous noted that it caused "much griefe in the country". But another issue soon loomed over the session. In early June 1626, Rous wrote, "This Parliament hath as yet . . . bent almost wholly against the duke of Buckingham." The bitter prosecution of the king's favourite had caused "greate wonder", little surprise, thought Rous, "considering the strange, usuall, and bould reportes that be made of him; which, if true, 'tis pity he liveth; if otherwise, God graunte him a true cleering." Next to this comment Rous copied, in his small, neat hand, a version of the Earl of Bristol's accusations against the duke. Rous and his contemporaries across the country now watched intently to see whether Buckingham could find "a true cleering". In the meantime they pored over news from Westminster.[1]

"Want of oyle"

In early May 1626, Secretary Conway wrote to Sir Thomas Roe, the ambassador in Constantinople, informing him (in a remarkable understatement) that "affaires here are somewhat embroiled" and then adding the operative words: "these being times of want". Earlier in the year, the Exchequer had had very little ready money; by May it had none. Military and naval actions soon ground to a halt, for there was "noe whele to be moved for want of oyle": "the treasury [was] empty".[2]

No one had been paid. In London the naval commissioners fended off shipowners whose vessels had sailed in the Cadiz fleet and now demanded compensation, and they rued "the continuall clamour of poore men and the wante of meanes to give them satisfaction". In May the throngs of unpaid sailors roaming the South Bank caused the Privy Council to close the Globe Theatre, lest it be used as a rendezvous for "riotous action"; it only reopened once the magistrates had sufficient "strength . . . for the suppressing of anie insolences or mutinous intentions".[3] But by far the Crown's most insistent creditor was Charles's Danish uncle, Christian IV. Having taken up arms on behalf of Charles's sister Elizabeth in confident expectation of an English subsidy, Christian had little time for Charles's excuses. In order "to refresh [his] memory", Christian sent two envoys and no fewer than thirteen letters to his nephew. Rumours flew that the Danish king would pay a surprise visit; a Habsburg agent relished the thought, for "the duke of Bukingham is in feare of it".[4]

Equally agitated were the billeted troops and their local hosts. In Southampton the mayor demanded that unless the Exchequer immediately cover the town's billeting expenses, "I must flye the Towne for I cannot indure the Continuall vexation they put me to". In Barnstaple, the billeted troops looted the area for several days, and elsewhere frustrated troops were responsible for "diverse robberies committed in market ways".[5] In south Devon, where an outbreak of the plague greatly complicated the situation, the parishes with billeted men pleaded for their removal, while the parishes without them argued against their redeployment. Meanwhile the commissioners responsible for the men begged the Council for cash "so as officer, soldier, billiter, clothier and our owne credit may speedily be provided for".[6] In Ireland the survivors of the Cadiz voyage were dependent on local charity, which by the spring of 1626 had run out. The Corporation of Cork and the President of Munster explained that "the Inhabitants both of Townes and Countrie protest that they can noe longer subsist". The hungry troops were "almost naked", and their officers were "soe poore that they dare not shew their faces".[7] The situation was highly dangerous and made worse by constant rumours of an imminent Spanish invasion. Since many English soldiers had muskets, but no powder, the Irish authorities offered only bleak assessments of the likely attack. The realm's defencelessness was so obvious that a Habsburg agent began taunting his superiors in Brussels that they were "feble and cowards" if they did not take full advantage of this opportunity to "make invasion on us".[8]

Contemporaries blamed Buckingham. A verse libel from early 1626 told the Spaniards that they need not trouble with invading "since heer at home do staye, worse enemyes unto us".[9] In May, Sir Henry Palmer, a naval captain, learned of "a fellowe in Sandwich" who "beinge lately come from London hath divulged a libel of my lord [Buckingham]". An Admiralty employee, it turned out, could identify the libeller, but "he would not because he would not betray his friend".[10] The criticism now also touched the king. In May, William Wraxthall, gaoled in the King's Bench prison, declared that "the King had need . . . to sitt in Justice to looke to things having many upstarts about him", and insisted that "god doth not blesse the King or Kingdome". He then sketched out an early version of the Stuart dynasty's Black Legend: after noting that Charles's "grandfather was hanged on a pare tree" and "his grandmother was beheaded", Wraxthall argued that although James I had "dyed a naturall death", his son, Prince Henry, "twas thought he was poisoned", and James's daughter, Elizabeth, "is driven out of her Countrey". Surely then "there is a curse layed upon" Charles.[11]

The impeachment charges severely damaged Buckingham's already bruised reputation. Across the country, men like John Rous were transcribing and debating the accusations. William Davenport of Bramhall, Cheshire, who copied out parliamentary speeches and impeachment articles, captioned a 6 May newsletter account of the Earl of Bristol's attack on Buckingham, "B: the beginninge of his ffalle". In Amsterdam, Sir Sackville Crowe had hoped to pawn some royal jewels "till now the reportes of my Lords trubles and the discontents of his Majestie with his lower house of parliament come over in such full streames that it caried away with itt all hope or possibilitie of doinge any farther good here".[12]

The final presentation of the impeachment charges, while embarrassing, gave the duke an opportunity to respond, and thus, possibly, to convince the Commons to pass the all-important subsidy bill. Buckingham's clients rallied around their patron. Captain Palmer forwarded testimony from the chief gunner on board one of the loan ships, who "vowed . . . upon his salvation" that it had been French, not English, warships that had most damaged the Huguenots. When the Earl of Totnes, the Master of the Ordnance, was presented Buckingham's warrant for a large cash payment, he advised the duke to get the entire Privy Council to sign it, for "you cannot be too Cautious".[13] Others sent encouragement. An officer in Southampton fervently prayed "our good god to grante unto his Grace the advantage over his Enimyes". In Bristol another official was delighted to learn that "his grace will give a full answer to the obiections of the Lower house" and hoped the duke's friends would soon hear that he and Parliament "weare fairely reconciled".[14]

For a "true cleering", Buckingham had to make an "honorable satisfactory answer" to the impeachment bill. The first twelve charges, while serious, were relatively easy to handle, but the thirteenth was decidedly more awkward. The duke undoubtedly held Eglisham's accusations beneath contempt, but while the Commons had avoided any direct mention of the scandalous tract, Wandesford and Eliot had both hinted that Buckingham might have poisoned James. Any response to the thirteenth charge would draw further attention to James's death and, inevitably, to *The Forerunner*. Yet because the regime desperately needed money, Buckingham had to answer the charges if the Crown were to have any hope of coaxing the parliamentary financial system back to life. But there was another reason why Buckingham had to answer. Eglisham had not discussed Charles's presence at Theobalds in March 1625, but the doctors' testimony had revealed that the angry physicians had begged the prince to restrain Buckingham. This testimony raised a disconcerting question: was Charles involved in his father's death? Most contemporaries found this almost impossible to discuss explicitly, but once the accusations against Buckingham had leaked into public consciousness, the political ground rules changed. If Charles dissolved Parliament now, he risked accusations of a cover-up. On 29 April, Bishop de Mende explained to Richelieu that as a result of the doctors' testimony, "the king will look like an accomplice if he dismisses the Parliament before the charge is disproved". Three weeks later, the Venetian diplomat Zuane Pesaro drew the same conclusion. A parliamentary dissolution had become bound up with "considerations of [Charles's] own honour, because a rupture would go to show that he himself wished to prevent an enquiry into the causes of the late king's death".[15]

Insolent Speeches

Notwithstanding his reams of documentary evidence, Bristol's accusations against Buckingham and Secretary Conway could be dismissed as another example of what Bishop Williams termed the "Blob-tales" used to smear court rivals. And since Charles vigorously rejected Bristol's charges, his attack was unlikely to bring Buckingham down.[16] The Commons' allegations about James's death were far more problematic. Before Buckingham made any answer, Charles tried to bring the discussion back under his control. On 10 March, when Clement Coke, Sir Edward's son, announced that "it is better to suffer by a foreign hand than at home", his words caused "a general susurrus" in the House, but no one reproved Coke. When on 11 March, Dr Turner posed the six queries that began the impeachment proceedings, Buckingham was so enraged that Conway had to calm him down. "With that wretch Turnors speech to the Committee", Conway noted, "I lost all patience," and he agreed that something had to be done about both Coke and Turner, who "if they should bee suffered unpunished would leave noe maide her modesty, noe man his humor, noe seate of Justice integrity nor noe king the glory of his sacred rule and dignity." Nevertheless, Conway urged his patron to "expect the Justice of the lower howse, the sence of the upper howse and in the extremity have recourse to his Maiesties soveraigne remedy".[17] On 14 March, after the Commons refused to punish Coke and Turner, Charles protested against "such insolency", demanding "justice . . . against these 2 delinquents" lest he "use his regal authority to right himself". The next day he repeated his complaint, and two weeks later he protested that his request had "found nothing but protraction and delay". In the end, although the Lower House agreed that Coke had spoken words "which did displease the House and might receive a sinister construction", they never responded to the king.[18]

The House's disregard encouraged Charles to take a different approach after the presentations of Digges and Eliot on 8 and 10 May respectively. While several aspects of their speeches annoyed him, Charles was particularly angered by their discussions of James's death. Furious at what he heard reported from "not one or 2" but "4 or 5" witnesses, the king demanded confirmation from those peers who had been taking notes, "calling for 4 or 5 table books" in which he found further evidence of the Parliament-men's offensive words. Then he took action. Since the formal opening, Charles had made two visits to Parliament, but on 11 May word of his visit arrived so late that the peers had to keep him waiting while they robed themselves. They need not have bothered, because Charles came in his "wearing" or ordinary clothes. He announced that he had "thought fit to take order for punishing some insolent speeches spoken to you". Alluding to his earlier complaint against Coke and Turner, he confessed that he had been "too remiss heretofore in punishing those insolent speeches that concerned myself" lest he appear to be intervening on Buckingham's behalf. Then, without explaining which "insolent speeches" he had in mind, Charles left to spend the afternoon playing tennis. Shortly after, Sir Nathaniel Rich arrived to deliver the Commons' unanimous recommendation that until the Lords resolved the accusations against Buckingham, they should "commit the person of the said Duke to safe custody". By the time Rich returned, his colleagues had realized that "Sir John Eliot and Sir Dudley Digges were gone". A little earlier the Sergeant at Arms had told the two men that they were wanted in the lobby, where two royal messengers arrested them and took them to the Tower. On hearing of this, their colleagues "brake off all business" and, amid cries of "rise, rise", departed. Later that evening some Parliament-men gathered together, "sadly communicating their mindes one to another".[19] This time, rather than lodge another protest, Charles had decided to act, and by so doing, he revealed the depth of his outrage at the two men's insinuations about his father's death.

Whatever Digges and Eliot had actually said—and that remained contested—Charles had made a bold move. The Parliament-men jealously defended their rights of free speech and freedom from arrest, and while monarchs had occasionally managed to remove offensive members, they had far more often been forced to back down. Unsurprisingly, the latest arrests began a constitutional conflict that halted all progress on the subsidy bill. Since March, Charles had kept the Earl of Arundel imprisoned in the Tower, much to the annoyance of the Lords. The arrests of Digges and Eliot only compounded the problem, triggering an equally dramatic backlash. With these arrests, Mende observed, "Buckingham's affairs go from bad to worse".[20]

The Parliament-men who had stormed out on 11 May were not in a better mood the following day. After a period of complete silence, Sir Dudley Carleton rose amid cries of "sit down" and "no" to explain the king's action. The veteran diplomat had just returned to Whitehall, and Henry Wynn described him as "a favorit of the duke". He now detailed the offences of Digges and Eliot. Both men had gone "beyond the matter" and exceeded the Commons' instructions, and

Eliot had talked of Buckingham as if he were already condemned, using the "contemptible" terms "the man" and "this man". But above all, Charles had taken "high offense" at "certain scandals and words" used in Digges's speech relating to "the end of the last King which was inferred as hastened by a drink and plaster". In particular, Digges had said when discussing the plaster that "he would therein spare the honor, of the King, that is now living". The king's anger, Carleton continued, is hardly surprising since many at court, including foreign envoys, thought that the speech hinted at Charles's complicity in his father's death. Eliot's speech meanwhile had been an "invective" more suited to a courtroom indict-ment than to a Parliament, and it went beyond the sense of the charge. Eliot's presentation on James's death, argued Carleton, implied that "something were in that head which was not discovered"; yet the House "thought there was no ill intention" in Buckingham's actions, however tragic their consequences. Carleton then set out what was at stake. By exceeding their mandates, Digges and Eliot had dragged Charles into the fray, for, as the king explained to Carleton, "if he were not tender of this point of the death of his father, he was not worthy to wear the crown". In the process, the two Parliament-men had put the House itself in danger; they had to be "cut off" lest the session founder. The king would not patiently endure such "tumultuary endeavors", Carleton warned. If they persisted, then Charles would abandon Parliament and embrace "new counsels" that would doom England to the fate of foreign monarchies where representative institu-tions had withered away.[21]

The Commons responded by denouncing their colleagues who had misin-formed the king and by insisting that Digges had said nothing inflammatory. On 13 May they began signing a protestation declaring they had never given "consent that Sir Dudley Digges should speak the words mentioned". Furthermore, they "did never hear, or believe, or ever affirmed that he spoke those or any other words to that effect". While some delayed signing, only Thomas Jermyn flatly refused to do so. In the Lords, however, Digges's case prompted far more controversial scenes.

15 May

As Charles and Buckingham had watched Eliot establish his grip on the Lower House, they could take consolation that the Upper House was still under their control. Since many peers depended on the monarch for offices and pensions, they were reluctant to challenge the king. If they ever did, Charles could create a majority by making new peers or by promoting old ones, thus naming, as Sir Benjamin Rudyerd put it, "so many Cardinalls to carrye the Consistorye if theare be occasion". At his coronation in February 1626, Charles had rewarded several reliable servants with new titles. Lord Treasurer James Ley became Earl of Marlborough; Lord President Henry Montagu became Earl of Manchester; Robert, Lord Carey, a Gentleman of the Bedchamber, became Earl of Monmouth;

and Thomas Howard, Viscount Andover, became Earl of Berkshire. Charles also honoured four old warhorses. George, Lord Carew, Master of the Ordnance, became Earl of Totnes; Sir Henry Danvers became Earl of Danby; Thomas, Lord Wentworth, became Earl of Cleveland; and Edmund, Lord Sheffield, became Earl of Mulgrave. Furthermore, Buckingham controlled no fewer than thirteen proxy votes in the Lords and could rely on almost all the twenty-six bishops and archbishops, who, in the opinion of the Tuscan diplomat Amerigo Salvetti, were "dependent on the Court and will therefore always take his side". Late in April, Charles had told the bishops to follow their "conscience" in the impeachment case, but he warned them to be "led by proofs, not by reports".[22]

In April, Buckingham had assured Mende that he was in no danger from Parliament. If indicted in the Lower House, "he had enough allies in the Lords to preserve him, the house being made up of those who were either his kinsmen or clients". But Mende was dubious: "he will find a surprise there". He was right to be sceptical. On 25 February, although the duke and his allies were all opposed, Buckingham overwhelmingly lost a voice vote limiting each peer to only two proxy votes. Signs of restiveness among the Lords became unmistakable. In March they pressed for the Earl of Arundel's release, ignoring Charles's statement that he had punished "a misdeameanor which was personal to his Majesty . . . and had no relation to matters of Parliament". By early April the Lords were dividing over the Arundel case by 34 to 31 and 37 to 29. Anxious for more reliable votes, Charles used writs of acceleration to summon several trusted young men to the Lords, including the sons of the Lord Treasurer, the Lord President of Wales, and the Earl of Northumberland.[23] These precautions, however, were insufficient.

Buckingham often made pithy interventions during the Lords' debates, but after the impeachment charges, he began speaking at greater length. On 11 May, immediately after Charles's impromptu address, Buckingham, working from a script prepared by Bishop Laud, publicly confessed his uncertainty about how to proceed: "if I should hold my tongue it would argue guilt; if I should speak it may argue boldness, being so foully accused". He admitted he was no "angel amongst men", and he refused to "speak anything else to cast dirt at those who have taken pains to make me foul". Instead, he assured his colleagues that "for such crimes as truly deserve public punishment from the state, I hope I shall ever prove myself free, either in intention or act." Edward, Lord Montagu, thought it "a fine speech".[24] Two days later, Buckingham was back on his feet after the reports on the first half of the impeachment articles. On 8 May, when the Parliament-men had presented this material, the House had denied the duke's request to make a response, but on 13 May, although his colleagues were weary, Buckingham insisted on replying. After complaining that "some things were reported short of that was delivered, and some other things more largely reported than they were delivered", he bombarded the peers with detailed rebuttals. He declared that "he did nothing but by the King's command", denied ever telling the 1625 Oxford session of Parliament to "Judge by the event", maintained that the loan ships were "an engagement of the late King", claimed that the Dutch, not the English, vessels had done most of the damage to the Huguenots, rejected any allegation that he had extorted the East India Company, and swore that "he never treated with any man for offices". His speech did not have the same impact as his earlier intervention; indeed, Montagu found this "intempestive" performance somewhat embarrassing.[25]

Worse followed on 15 May after the final report on the impeachment charges. When the report ended, Buckingham protested that "some words were spoken . . . by Sir Dudley Digges which so far did trench on the King's honor that they are interpreted treasonable". He insisted that when he first heard Digges's address on 8 May, "he would . . . have reprehended him for the same" if he had "not been restrained by the order of the House". In particular, Buckingham had been offended by Digges's comments about "the physic and plaster given the King". The mere mention of "the death of the late King—so good to me that I never heard him spoken of, though in the best terms"—inevitably "brings affliction to me", but to hear his death "spoken of in this manner, much distempers me". Buckingham then began to justify his behaviour in the king's sickroom, responding not only to the Parliament-men but, in effect, to Eglisham too. "The late king", Buckingham maintained, "commanded me to send for that physic which I had used in my sickness" in the spring of 1624, but he had delayed until "trial might be made thereof". The doctors had testified that John Baker, the duke's barber, sampled the plaster, but now Buckingham identified others, including "2 children and 1 man of my own", as well as James Palmer, a Gentleman of the Bedchamber. This last was a name to conjure with, for Palmer owed his seat to the Earl of Montgomery. Since Palmer was then in the Commons, the duke was essentially asking a Herbert man to undercut his patrons' political interests. Having sketched out the elaborate vetting process for the physic, Buckingham then delivered another surprise: directly refuting several royal doctors, he insisted that he had not personally administered any medicine. Rather, "in my absence", James "took it himself before I came". Finally, Buckingham recalled that when he had begun "questioning one of the Bedchamber for suspecting me", James had intervened, saying "none but devils would speak of any such thing". The doctors Alexander Ramsey and James Chambers had electrified the hearings with their accounts of James's own testimony about Buckingham's harmful medicines. Now the duke used the late king's words in his defence. In his diary Montagu noted that Buckingham had answered the charges, but especially "of that which concerned the physic and plaster given to the King"; and he did it "with some tears in his eyes".[26]

Buckingham's speech initiated a long debate. His ally Edward Sackville, Earl of Dorset, had earlier accused the Lords' reporters of omitting two items, most notably "forgetting" Eliot's reference to "the veneries and venefices of Sejanus", and at the end of his speech Buckingham also complained that "somewhat [had been] omitted". William Fiennes, Viscount Saye and Sele, the duke's ally-turned-critic, who had reported on Wandesford's speech about James's death, promptly demanded proof of any omissions. John Egerton, Earl of Bridgewater, a loyal client and another reporter, offered "his notes" for inspection and then volunteered "the notes also of all the rest of the Lords who took" them. After Dorset reiterated Digges's controversial line—"I am commanded by the House of Commons to take care that nothing might reflect upon the honor of the deceased King nor the King now living"—Buckingham spoke. Since "divers constructions have been made of these words" and "diversely reported", he moved that "every one of the said eight reporters would be pleased to produce their notes taken at the said conference". When Saye demanded to "know upon what ground", the duke smoothly replied, "I thought you had imposed upon me to show what was omitted." Buckingham's clients—Manchester, Bridgewater and Dorset—promptly read out their notes, confirming Buckingham's version of Digges's statement. But Mulgrave, one of the newly promoted peers, objected to the entire process. William Cavendish, Earl of Devonshire, confessed that his "notes are so short that you can make no judgment out of them", while Edward, Lord Denny, and the Earl of Clare admitted that theirs were "short taken", simply "a word here and another there" that "may conduce to the memory". Buckingham repeated Digges's ominous final clause: "not to reflect upon the dead nor living King: viz on the dead king touching point of government, upon this King touching the physic". For Devonshire and Dudley, Lord North, however, the actual words did not matter because Digges had "not meant so", and North moved "every man to deliver his sense". Since Buckingham insisted that Digges had used provocative language, the Lords ordered that anyone "make his protestation whether he heard Sir Dudley Digges speak anything that might be interpreted treason".[27]

Given the extreme political polarization in 1626, some responses to the proposed protestation were predictable. Saye maintained that Digges had neither said nor implied anything treasonable and "if he had, he would have presently reprehended him". Saye was seconded by other disillusioned veterans of the 1624 Patriot coalition—the Earls of Essex, Lincoln, Montgomery and Warwick—and by men like the Earls of Bolingbroke, Clare and Devonshire who were aligned with this group. Equally predictable were those with grudges. Two decades earlier, James I had annulled the Earl of Hertford's marriage to Arabella Stuart, leaving Hertford estranged from Whitehall. Equally distant was the Earl of Berkshire, who had served Prince Charles as Master of the Horse but lost that title to Buckingham when Charles became king. Charles had tried to soothe Berkshire with gifts and a new title, but the earl was widely seen as "the Dukes professed opposite" and would soon stand against him in the election for Chancellor of Cambridge University. Lord Vaux, a fervent Hispanophile, had raised a regiment for the Spanish Army of Flanders, and late in 1625 had been embroiled in a fracas when the Northamptonshire magistrates searched his house for weapons and cited him for swearing. He was in no mood to placate Buckingham.[28]

Where Buckingham could have expected support, he found none. Instead he had to watch as a troop of normally quiet "backwoodsmen"—Lords Grey of Warke, Russell, Dudley, Morley, Noel and Percy; Viscount Rochford; and the Earls of Kent, Nottingham and Oxford—joined Saye. A few sat the battle out. The Earl of Exeter, Lord Treasurer Marlborough, Archbishop Abbot and Viscount Wimbledon excused themselves because they were "not present" on 8 May. Although George Montaigne, Bishop of London, refused to comment on Digges's words because "he heard them not", many bishops, including Davenant of Salisbury, Bridgeman of Chester, Morton of Lichfield, and Harsnett of Norwich, backed Saye. Bishop Buckeridge of Rochester "hoped" Digges "had no ill meaning", and Bishop Field of Llandaff "cannot conceive his meaning". Given Buckingham's commitment to the Spanish war, he must have expected the swordsmen's support, but Lord Cromwell, a member of the Council of War, followed Saye, as did the newly created Earl of Cleveland, another military veteran. Even Lord Montagu, who generally followed his brother the Lord President, thought Digges blameless. With the tide running so strongly against Buckingham, some office-holders refused to comment. Villiers loyalists like the Earls of Salisbury and Carlisle and Bishop Laud declined to say anything "without commandment" (presumably from the king). Carlisle's silence, Mende noted, was "a bad omen" for the duke.[29]

The pain of these defections was nothing compared to the damage done by some of the duke's closest clients. Bridgewater had found considerable favour from Buckingham, but he too wavered. He would not "trust my memory nor my pen" and refused to "enter into the thoughts of him that spoke them". Nevertheless he backed Saye. Bishop Neile of Durham, a leader of the emerging Arminian faction, eventually conceded that Digges "had no will to reflect anything on his Majesty". While his words "may be ill taken . . . I think in his heart he meant well." Equally disappointing was the Earl of Northampton, Lord President of Wales and Buckingham's step-uncle. He "heard not the direct words", he said, but "heard nothing that might touch the honor of the King." The Earl of Denbigh owed everything to his brother-in-law, but now endorsed Saye. The young Marquis of Hamilton, making his maiden speech, announced that while he "heard little", he had heard "nothing that can touch the King's honor".[30]

The Digges vote was an unprecedented humiliation for the king and the duke. Charles, understandably angry at Digges's insinuation, had staked a great deal on punishing the slanderer—and had found only trifling support. Thirty-six peers took the protestation defending Digges. Pesaro reported that

Buckingham "only obtained three votes", and that only "after much intriguing", while Montagu set the duke's minority at somewhere between six and eight.[31] Another six to ten peers formally abstained, either because they had not heard Digges's speech or because they refused to act without Charles's direct order, and some twenty peers simply left the chamber. In the final roll call, three particularly close allies were also conspicuously absent—the Earl of Monmouth, a fellow bedchamber-man; the Earl of Rutland, Buckingham's father-in-law; and, most strikingly, Buckingham's own brother, the Earl of Anglesey. The magnitude of the 15 May defeat was plain to see. Mende rightly observed that "if Buckingham survives, it will be a miracle".[32] But despite losing this gambit, neither the king nor the duke was ready to give up.

He Must Intend Himself Tiberius

In order to regain control of the Lords, Charles created three new peers, who would, it was hoped, "waygh downe . . . the balance on the Dukes side"; among them was Dudley Carleton who, happy to escape the mounting turmoil in the Commons, would now become Lord Carleton. Meanwhile, the king halted his pursuit of Dudley Digges. On 15 May the Council summoned Digges from the Tower, and Charles "gave him his hand to kisse and used him most graciously". Digges was back in the Commons the next morning, asking his colleagues that "nothing concerning him may divert the business of the commonwealth".[33]

Digges's release highlighted Eliot's continued confinement. The Chancellor of the Exchequer, Sir Richard Weston, explained that Charles "charges him with some things extrajudicial to this House", and so if he chose to "detain him somewhat longer he hopes you will not take this as a breach of . . . privilege". The majority of the Commons, however, remained obstinate, and Sir John Strangways demanded an explanation of the word "extrajudicial". Since the Commons refused to conduct any other business, Charles again had to back down—but first he wanted Chief Justice Crewe and Attorney General Heath to interrogate Eliot. Their questions reveal the nature of the regime's anxiety. They asked Eliot "when and with whom he had conferences how farr any kings had bene heretofore compelled to give way to the will of the people" and what he knew about "the disposing of kings or any president touching deposition of any kings either of this realme or of any other kingdome" and, in particular, about the deposition of Richard II. Eliot remained calm. His scant knowledge of these precedents had come from his general "readinge of history", he claimed, disingenuously adding that "whenever he hath lighted upon any such thing in reading he hath detested it, as being contrary to the lawes both humane and divine". After denying contact with disaffected lawyers in Grey's Inn, foreign ambassadors and Huguenot representatives, Eliot was released and returned to the Commons on 20 May.[34]

Heath's questions suggest why Eliot's impeachment presentation had so offended Charles. While the king's speech had emphasized Eliot's "insolence" in impugning his honour, observers speculated about the real nature of the perceived offence. In London a report so troubled the lawyer Simonds D'Ewes that he asked his correspondent to keep it "private" by tearing off the "half-sheet" from the letter and "burning it, or concealing it, though there be nothing in it unlawful, or unfit to be said". D'Ewes had learned that Charles had "complained of Sir John Eliot" to the Lords "for comparing the duke to Sejanus, in which, he said, implicitly he [Eliot] must intend himself [Charles] Tiberius".[35] D'Ewes's comment exposed Eliot's dangerous game. The use of historical precedent and parallel was crucial to contemporary political discourse, but the implications could be difficult to control. To compare Buckingham to Sejanus inevitably invited a comparison between Charles I and Tiberius, and Tacitus's portrayal of Tiberius was one of the ancient world's most compelling analyses of tyranny. Eliot had confined his allusions to the opening of Book 4 of the *Annals*, but in this book Tacitus had begun to expose the full panoply of Tiberius's cruelty and perversity. Even an implicit comparison of Charles with Tiberius might suggest England's king was a tyrant and thus pose dangerous questions about the depositions of wicked rulers. Furthermore, the parallel could also hint at royal complicity in his favourite's "venefices", for Tacitus had repeated contemporary stories alleging Tiberius's participation in Sejanus's poisoning of Drusus.

No single interpretation of Tacitus's politics held sway in this period. Some contemporaries read the historian as a political realist, like Machiavelli, offering valuable insights into how monarchies actually functioned in a de-moralized political world. But for others, Eliot's use of Roman history suggested a more general critique of early Stuart monarchy, from which some might derive more radical, quasi-republican messages. In this reading of Tacitus, vicious political actors were the result not simply of individual moral failings, but of a corrupted polity degenerating into tyranny. Placed in this republican Tacitean frame, Buckingham's veneries and venefices were evidence of the broader systemic decay of the English monarchy. Those close to the regime readily understood the danger of this kind of thinking. A year later Charles I would suppress Isaac Dorislaus's Cambridge lectures on Tacitus after being warned that they would contain material "applicable to the exasperations of these villainous times".[36]

Forced to release Eliot, the regime tried to discredit him. On 20 May, the same morning Eliot returned to the Commons, Carleton enumerated Eliot's errors and offered him the chance "to discharge himself of whatsoever might be objected against him". Eliot's speech had offended both in manner and matter. In manner "it was too tart and harsh to the person of the Duke", and used "too much vigor, strength, and vehemency". In matter, Carleton noted several offending phrases and passages, most notably Eliot's comparison of Buckingham's mind to a strange beast called "stellionatus" which could not be found "within the compass of his charge". But Carleton concentrated on two larger problems. The first was Eliot's use of "historical comparisons", including the parallel between Buckingham and Sejanus. The comparison had arguably exceeded the terms of the Commons' charge—Eliot had quoted Tacitus's description of Sejanus as an "*audax superbus adulator* (bold, proud flatterer)", but the Commons had not charged the duke with these offences. "Speaking of Sejanus", Eliot had also "said he would not touch his venefices and veneries. Wherein he was conceived to aim at the Duke", and "it was taken as meant that the Lords should look into it". More important, the Sejanus comparison touched the king, portraying him as Tiberius: "This historical part was applied further to those who were in the top of our government." But the "point of the greatest sharpness" was Eliot's presentation of the thirteenth charge; "He said he could not speak and did doubt to think it, speaking of the last charge, the particular of the plaster, and concluded with words of Cicero, as if Cicero, an excellent orator, had not words to explain so much. He spoke as if that somewhat was yet covered which might be uncovered."[37]

Eliot responded to each criticism in turn. His use of "stellionatus" had good classical precedents as "a metaphorical word . . . used for faults of collusion". He confessed that his quest for rhetorical elegance had led him to avoid repetition by using the umbrella category of "stellionatus" to cover three sections of the charge that dealt with "fraud or collusion". He admitted that, to save time, he had sometimes referred to the duke by what Carleton had called the "contemptible" contraction "that man", but again, Eliot had classical precedent on his side—*ipse ille* was often used in Latin. And he also made clear that the duke did not deserve constant reverence: "I do yet believe him no god." Carleton, he suggested, had over-interpreted his historical analogies. Eliot denied he had applied Sejanus's "veneries and venefices" to Buckingham; he had simply mentioned them out of fidelity to the historical record. Anyone who read Tacitus, Eliot noted, would see that next to the material on Sejanus's "preferring his friends", as Buckingham had, "comes in his lechery with Livia and his poisoning". Yet "these I spoke exclusively and had no relation to this man." Slyly, he insisted that no parallels could be drawn on these issues, "except [the duke] so apply them". Eliot then unabashedly defended the political utility of the Tacitean world view to this fraught moment, noting that the stationers had sold more copies of the *Annals* "since this charge than in a year before".[38]

Before Eliot could turn to the thirteenth charge, Wandesford interrupted, urging him to respond to Carleton's insinuation that the Tacitean parallels had touched King Charles. "I gave no words", Eliot responded, "that could admit an interpretation that any person greater than the Duke [was implied]. If they mean my Sovereign, I make this protestation: that I carry a heart as loyal and as faithful to his service as any man that is about him and had not manner of such intention as to touch him in those comparisons." About his alleged allusion to secrets yet undiscovered, Eliot explained little. Since his words had been misunderstood or misinterpreted, he repeated what he thought he had said: "I feared to say I would leave it as Cicero did the like, hoping their Lordships would discover the rest, and ergo to them I left it." As for his manner, Eliot confessed to having a vigorous, perhaps even "violent" expression, but he insisted that "what I spoke then I spoke not in passion, but to do this House service", working "to give life to that I was commanded".[39]

The House quickly and unanimously resolved that neither Digges nor Eliot had exceeded his instructions. But the duke's supporters remained unhappy about Eliot's implication that Buckingham could be linked to "venefices". Sir Robert Pye had been told that Eliot's speech "was very bitter", and nothing he had learned since had convinced him otherwise. He reiterated that the House had not charged Buckingham with intentionally harming the king, but only with an "act of transcendent presumption". Consequently, Pye continued, "by that application of Sejanus" Eliot had "expressed that which was against the sense of the House", because the committee had been "satisfied that there was no ill intention" in Buckingham's medical interventions. Sir Robert Harley observed that all such trouble would be avoided in future if "never any should be allowed to aggravate any matter without first delivering in the heads of what they would speak to the House".[40]

Charles's display of righteous anger had succeeded only in vaulting Digges and Eliot to greater prominence. Sir Bevil Greville had closely followed the case of his fellow Cornishman, Eliot, and writing to his pregnant wife with news of Eliot's release from the Tower, Greville mused that "if god send us a boye, I have a good minde to have him called John".[41] From these events, there was one clear conclusion: if Charles had any hope of reasserting control over the parliamentary session, Buckingham had to respond to the impeachment articles, and he had to take special care answering the thirteenth charge.

"L'oraison funèbre du Duc"

Buckingham's position steadily deteriorated. By mid-May several commentators reported that he was pressing for an immediate dissolution of Parliament, but more cautious councillors persuaded the king to keep working with it. Stories circulated that the worsening situation in Westminster would force Buckingham to leave the country, either to take a fleet out or to move to The Hague or even Turin on an extended diplomatic trip. Meanwhile the Parliament-men continued to be difficult. They usually supported efforts to root out crypto-Catholics, but on 23 May with sentiment running strongly in favour of the imprisoned Earl of Arundel, the Commons unanimously overturned a Surrey report naming him a recusant. The following day in the Commons, the Chancellor of the Exchequer reportedly "in two houres could not gett leave to speak", and on 25 May, "when

the Duke stood up to have spoken" in the Lords, "they would not heare him".[42]
When Buckingham's clients engineered his narrow election as Chancellor of
Cambridge University in early June, his parliamentary opponents were outraged.
In mid-May Mende reported that "I have learned from secret and reliable
sources" that Buckingham "will be condemned to death or banished for life on
pain of death if he ever sets foot in England again". Indeed, some were saying
that the duke would be "degraded from his nobility and all his posterity made
infamous", a fitting fate for "someone accused of the death of a king".[43]

On 8 June, Buckingham finally responded to the charges against him.
Charles had eventually released Arundel, who sat next to Buckingham in the
Lords that day, but all eyes were on the duke. His lengthy statement was very
much a collaborative effort. While others were probably involved, both Laud
and Edward Nicholas, the duke's secretary, provided detailed feedback on a
draft, and the text's careful language betrayed the influence of Buckingham's
legal advisers. Opinions about the effectiveness of the response reflected the
fractious political environment. Mende forwarded to Paris the charges and
Buckingham's response, which in his opinion collectively formed "the duke's
funeral sermon (*l'oraison funèbre du Duc*)". In Dorchester, William Whiteway
thought the duke's response was only "very sleightly framed", and Sir Ferdinando
Fairfax, a Parliament-man, privately deemed it "a modest answer ... some
things he seemes to excuse and for the rest he pleads the 2 generall pardons". In
contrast, Sir Thomas Meautys, Clerk of the Privy Council, thought Buckingham
had made "an ingenuous and clear answer, and very satisfactory ... to all indifferent ears", while Lord Grandison hoped that his "faire and full answeres ...
will geeve good satisfaction to the world". Perhaps the best assessment came
from a London newsletter-writer who reported that the duke's answer was "very
modest and voyd of all bitternes and in some ways satisfactory—his sectaries
say, in all".[44]

Buckingham asked his fellow peers for their understanding, reminding
them that "what is my cause now may be yours and your posterity". He remained
undaunted: "although the House of Commons have not willingly wronged me,
yet I am confident it will be at length found that common fame has abused it
and me." Having been "born and bred" in the service of the state, he was inca-
pable of damaging it willingly; indeed, he added, "If my posterity should not
inherit the same fidelity, I should desire an inversion in the course of nature
and be glad to see them earthen before me." The specifics of his case the duke
left to his lawyer, but Buckingham's answer repeatedly emphasized his obedience to royal commands. His numerous offices and titles came from James,
who "was more willing to multiply his graces and favors upon him than the
Duke was forward to ask them". The cash payment from the East India Company
"was not moved by the Duke, but his late Majesty himself". The loan ships
"were lent to the French King at first without the Duke's privity". And it was

James, who "having honored the Duke himself with many titles and dignities of his bounty, did also think fit to honor those who were in equal degree of blood". Nor had the Commons truly understood James's numerous grants of land: most were so encumbered with debts that they were "small or no present value to him", and the rest were so modest that "by this grant the revenue of the crown is little diminished". Furthermore, the bulk of the money Buckingham had received had gone to fund various operations of the state. While he admitted to "many weaknesses and imperfections", the duke was confident that he had not committed "heinous and high misdemeanors and crimes". But if he had, they would be covered by the two generous royal pardons issued at the end of the 1624 Parliament and at Charles's 1626 coronation.[45]

Amid the lawyerly language, Buckingham spoke at length about the events at Theobalds. The duke insisted that "he did neither apply nor procure the plaster or posset drink", and objected to the Commons' use of the term "potion". He denied being "present when the same was first taken or applied". Countering the narratives of both Eglisham and the Commons, he insisted that "The truth is this". He began with a familiar scene of two friends helping each other through illness. "Being sick of an ague", James "took notice of the Duke's recovery of an ague not long before and asked him how he recovered and what he found did him most good." The Earl of Warwick lived a few miles from Buckingham's Essex country house, and in the spring of 1624, when the duke fell dangerously ill, the two men had been political allies. Warwick had offered help, and "one who was the earl of Warwick's physician had ministered a plaster and posset drink" to Buckingham, though "the chief thing that did him good was a vomit, which he wished the King had taken in the beginning of sickness". The story had a useful political edge. Warwick and Buckingham were now rivals, so if these medicines had been poison, then they had been prescribed by the favourite doctor of one of the duke's most vocal opponents.

After hearing Buckingham's recommendation, James "was very desirous to have that plaster and drink sent for". But the duke was uneasy; while "he wished the King had taken" the medicines "in the beginning of his sickness", he was apprehensive about administering them to an elderly man who had been labouring with his illness for a fortnight. Therefore "the Duke delayed", and the king "impatiently asked whether it was sent for or not". Eventually James over-rode Buckingham and "sent for John Baker, the Duke's servant, and with his own mouth commanded him to go for it". But Buckingham intervened, and far from urging James to take this physic, he "besought his Majesty not to make use of it but by the advice of his own physicians". It certainly should not be taken "until it should be first tried by James Palmer, of his Bedchamber, who was then sick of an ague, and upon two children in the town." James agreed to the trial.

Safe in that understanding, Buckingham rode to London for a quick visit, but when he returned, he learned that "in his absence, the plaster and posset drink was brought and applied by his Majesty's own command". (Buckingham's use of the passive voice masked the names of those who had applied the physic.) As the duke entered the sickroom, he found "his Majesty . . . taking the posset drink"; James "then commanded the Duke to give it to him", and Buckingham obeyed. At this critical point the duke employed language suggested by Nicholas, claiming that he had given James the medicine "in the presence of some of the King's physicians, they then no ways seeming to dislike it". The medicines could not have been problematic, Buckingham argued, again following Nicholas, because "the same drink" was "first taken by some of them and divers of the Kings Bedchamber". Nevertheless, "the King grew somewhat worse then before"—a very mild way of re-describing what others termed a dramatic decline—and rumours flew "as if this physic had done the King hurt, and that the Duke had ministered that physic unto him without advice". Buckingham "acquainted the King therewith", and James, "with much discontent, answered thus, 'They are worse than devils that say it'". Buckingham ended with a line supplied by Laud: he asked his fellow peers "to commiserate [with him for] the sad thoughts which this article has revived in him".[46]

While a few peers probably did commiserate, others might have compared his testimony with that of the doctors and Eglisham. Buckingham's narrative was cleverly wrought, making Warwick and Palmer leading figures in his story. In place of Eglisham's terrifying "poysonmunger mountibanck", the actual physician who prepared the plaster and the posset was Warwick's doctor, and the sinister posset had been tested in part by a protégé of the Herbert brothers. While Buckingham's narrative thrust Warwick, Montgomery and Pembroke forward, it also hid his mother from view. The countess had loomed large in Eglisham's secret history and in the doctors' testimony. Female, disorderly and Catholic, the countess made a culturally plausible accomplice to a poisoning. Obscuring her role, however, protected her reputation and weakened the plausibility of the poison talk. Buckingham's narrative also cleverly challenged Wandesford's unsettling depiction of him as a reckless, uncounselled upstart; in the duke's own version, he was a cautious and careful bystander, reluctant to act without the prior authorization of the royal doctors, conscious of the rules of physic, and devoted to his master's health. Ever a loyal servant, he had simply obeyed royal commands; indeed if anyone had been impetuous, it was James, not Buckingham.

Buckingham's formal answer did invaluable political work. Eliot had reserved the Commons' right to respond to Buckingham's defence, but the duke need not fear a rigorous cross-examination. On 9 June the Lower House requested a copy of the answer, "whereunto we may make our reply if there be cause", and the Lords duly obliged. But time was running out. That same day Charles sent the Commons an ultimatum: either pass the subsidy bill "by the end of next week at furtherest" or he would "take other resolutions". The final crisis came three days later, when the king's spokesmen again pleaded for passage of the subsidy bill. Secretary Coke stressed the need for funds to repel "a great and imminent invasion", while Weston reminded them of their commitment to "make the King safe at home and feared abroad". And Richard Spencer argued that their worst fears had proven unfounded, since "all the Duke said was justified for true both by the King dead and this King". But the majority refused to abandon the whale hunt. William Coryton maintained that without "justice in the Duke of Buckingham's case, I think it not reasonable to pass the bill of subsidy". Wandesford thought "the Duke's growing greater and greater in power is nothing but setting himself against the commonwealth". And Long wondered in "what state will the kingdom stand if this great improvident man may be still in that great office?"[47]

Instead of passing the subsidy bill, the members prepared a Remonstrance listing their grievances. The document reiterated their discontent at the 1625 dissolution and the pricking of parliamentary leaders as sheriffs, recounted the impeachment articles, and expressed their displeasure at Buckingham's acquisition of yet another office, this time in Cambridge. The Remonstrance echoed Eglisham's powerful account of the duke's corrupt hold over the kingdom, which allowed him, "so much as in him lay", to make "his own ends and advantage the measure of the good or ill of your Majesty's kingdoms". Echoing Eglisham's call for justice, the Parliament-men insisted that the nation's ills were susceptible of only one solution. We "beseech you", they addressed the king, "that you will be pleased graciously to remove this person from access to your sacred person."[48]

Anxious to forestall the presentation of the Remonstrance, and to silence Bristol, who had been constantly pressing his case, Charles made a decision. On 14 June, when the Lower House sent a delegation requesting a formal audience, Charles assured them that they would "have answer" to their message "tomorrow morning". When it came, the answer was Parliament's dissolution. Very few in Westminster took the news lightly. The young Parliament-man Bulstrode Whitelocke concluded his diary with an ominous Latin tag: "*sic abeant omnes et cessat gloris regni*"—let everyone leave, and let the glory of the kingdom cease.[49]

Nothing Being Done

The forces that wrecked the 1626 Parliament were varied and complex, but one crucial factor was the Commons' decision to investigate James I's death. Before then, some thought it still possible Buckingham might ride out the parliamentary attacks; indeed on 6 April, Sir Benjamin Rudyerd had observed that "the stormes of this Parliament have bin veary highe but I hope they are nowe well overblowen".[50] But the allegations about James's death—in Eglisham's pamphlet, in the doctors' testimony, in Bristol's charges, in the impeachment article, and in the speeches of Eliot, Digges and Wandesford—created unmanageable political turbulence. Stories of what had happened at Theobalds in March 1625 inflamed and polarized opinion. When Charles struck back at those who had dared hint at where these stories might lead, he triggered a constitutional standoff that effectively ended any prospect of collaboration on the vital subsidy bill. By dissolving the parliamentary session in anger, he left key matters unresolved, not least the question of how, or if, the king could still wage war, pay his debts and salvage his bruised honour. By foreclosing the impeachment process, Charles also left the mystery of James's death open. As accounts of the impeachment articles joined copies of Eglisham's secret history in ever-broader circulation, the claim that James I had been murdered began to take deep root in popular political consciousness. Most talk continued to focus on Buckingham, but by sacrificing a subsidy bill to save the man who had been accused of involvement in his father's death, Charles had left himself open to suspicion. Some wondered what he had to hide.

Back in Santon Downham, John Rous tried to make sense of the dissolution. "About June 11", he wrote, "the Parliament was dissolved, nothing being done," adding that "the cause was that the nether house delayed the grante of subsidies untill the duke had beene tried, which the King was against." News quickly circulated in Suffolk that Buckingham had made "answere for himselfe" against the Commons' charges. Rous heard that the "answere is in writing", circulating in manuscript, but he had not yet found a copy. The duke did not deny "many articles, but intreating favourable construction, as namely, his offensive incontinency, that it might be imputed to his youth; and the miscarriage of maine busines to error of judgment, which the happiest counsellor of all is subjecte to, &c." The cautious Rous did not comment on Buckingham's response to the thirteenth charge, yet he had heard nothing that would constitute "a true cleering" of Buckingham's involvement in King James's death.[51]

CHAPTER TWELVE

SINGING LESSONS

DISSOLUTION AND RETRIBUTION

SLIPPING PAST THE numerous warships patrolling the North Sea, Thomas Morgan, an Englishman, entered the Spanish Netherlands via the neutral French port of Calais. Yet his most unsettling experience occurred not in transit but in a Brussels bookshop. Because of his obligation to "the House of Rutland", and because Buckingham "hath matched" with the Earl of Rutland's daughter, Morgan felt compelled to write to the duke in mid-July 1626 about "a filthye pamphlet" he had seen in Brussels, a publication containing "matter not fit to bee mentioned, nor indeed to be thought upon". He did not repeat the tract's allegations, which "I presume your Excellency hath heard, if not seen it". The tract in question was *Prodromus Vindictae*, and Morgan sensed an opportunity. He asked Buckingham "whether it were not fitt to have this fellow brought to England to see what songe he will singe when hee shall come ther".[1] This could be arranged, Morgan thought, provided Buckingham covered Morgan's expenses and supplied the necessary passports.

We do not know whether the duke responded or whether Morgan ever attempted the operation. But it would not have been the first time the Stuart regime resorted to extra-judicial actions against its foreign critics. In 1614, English agents had tracked down the Catholic polemicist Kaspar Schoppe in Madrid, planning to cut off his ears and nose in revenge for his "vile . . . abuse" of the king; in the event they only slashed his face. And during the manhunt for those responsible for *Corona Regia*, James's agents attempted several kidnappings.[2] Morgan's proposal was one of several plans—some fanciful, some implemented—to manage the fallout from the 1626 Parliament. The regime struggled to stabilize the situation, finding alternative, though controversial, means to finance Buckingham's war and responding, albeit hesitantly, to parliamentary allegations about James's death. In the process a number of prominent men would be forced to take unwelcome singing lessons. Despite Thomas Morgan's offer, George Eglisham was not among them.

Nothing but Thunder

Edmund Moundsford thought the dissolution of Parliament had left London "melancoly and empty". The king and his people could not agree on mundane legislation, much less on the all-important issue of taxation, and amid reports of an imminent Spanish invasion, a dark pall settled over the country. In Cambridge, Joseph Mead lamented "What will become of us now, God knows." "Amazed", Archbishop Ussher prayed that, "the Lord prepare us for the day of our visitation."[3] The dissolution left Sir John Scudamore in despair. It was, he wrote:

> good for no party. It looseth the King 500,000 besides his reputation abroade and at home. It sharpened hatred against the Duke, who being twice Parliament-blasted will be hardly acceptable to the third. It is ill for the people for they have gotten the Kings displeasure and may feare the effects.

In July 1626, Edward Misselden, who represented the Merchant Adventurers in Delft, longed for "good news out of England! Jesu what a world is this, nothing but thunder come thence!"[4]

Many Parliament-men left Westminster, Owen Wynn reported, "with great discontent". The Habsburg agent X echoed the grim assessment; the session had ended "to the very grete discontent of the kinge and kingdome without givinge one peny to the kinge to suppli his wantes or to maintain his warre abroade". In order "to save" Buckingham, the king inexplicably had "hazarded the losse of his owne honor and love of his people at home and off his allies a broade".[5] The Palatine camp was distraught. Charles's sister Elizabeth assured the king and Buckingham of her full support, but in October a letter from Ludwig Camerarius, a senior Palatine administrator, fell into English hands. Camerarius lamented that "the yong king is as it were kept a prisoner by One proude man, so that those that would give good Councell have no accesse, Or if by chance some wholesome advice is put in his head, That man putts it suddenly out againe." Since Buckingham acted like "a sworne Servant to the Spaniards", Camerarius predicted that the Protestant cause was doomed "if God doth not deliver the king of Great Brittain from present slavery" and "reconcile him againe with his people". Given Charles's intransigent support for Buckingham, some began to talk about assassination: "all the talk is of throwing him in the river", Bishop de Mende noted, "so that his death can give the state life."[6]

Meanwhile, protests swept the country. In July the crew of Sir Henry Palmer's Channel squadron "denied to woorke unlesse they might be fedd". At Chatham the dockworkers protested that "being verie poore Men much in debte and having a great charge of Children" they would have "to leave his Maiesties worke and labor els where" unless they were paid.[7] At Portsmouth, when the officers presented the men with only a month's wages, five hundred "presently cryed away away" and set out for London, shouting "one and all, one and all". When the sheriff of Hampshire spotted the "rowte passinge towards London", his efforts to calm the unpaid men only made them "very importunate", and he warned the Privy Council that trouble was heading their way. And in Devon, where some 3,000 hungry, ragged men were billeted, the local magistrates reported that "in all likelihoode wee are to expect as much danger from them as from our enimyes".[8]

Charles's impotence was most starkly apparent on the Continent. In his desperation to soothe Christian IV, Sir Robert Anstruther, Charles's ambassador, flatly denied reports of the dissolution, insisting that Charles had merely adjourned Parliament. Once the truth became known, Christian began delivering diatribes, which, as Anstruther delicately put it, "I deare or must not commit to paper and incke". The polite version of the complaint was that Christian "doeth venter his lyfe, his Crowne, his posteritie and more his reputation . . . at the intreatie of our gracious kinge and maister". In Paris, Louis XIII's ministers had long doubted English military power. In March 1626 they said that "the English have neither power nor money".[9] By early June, Mende assured Richelieu that "there is nothing to fear from England, the king lacks the wherewithal to fit ten boats in two months". In subsequent weeks he steadily revised that modest estimate downwards. The authorities in Brussels remained concerned about a possible English strike against Flemish ports, but William Sterrell, a Habsburg agent, reassured them: "I can not conceave what you neede to feare about Duinkirk or Mardike."[10]

At Whitehall conversations focused on Parliament and its future. Some encouraged the exploration of "new counsels" and prerogative funding. Henry Clifford, a Yorkshire gentleman, acknowledged that "parliaments have been the waie allwayes by which our former kinges have supplied their publique occasions", but those days were over, for "to hope any longer for Remedy from Parliaments is to expect a Phisition after Death". Yet parliamentary taxation remained the easiest and quickest way to avert looming bankruptcy, especially since the Crown had anticipated its future income to the tune of £440,458, well above its ordinary annual receipts. Secretary Coke noted that cooler heads in Whitehall were careful not "to rayse any ielousies betwixt the kinge and his People, or to make invective against the late Parliaments".[11] In early August, Mende told the Venetian ambassador about ominous conversations in which Charles "had spoken to him of the means used by the kings of France to rid themselves of Parliament". But Charles's alternatives were unattractive: he would either "have to cut down his private pleasures and abandon all foreign affairs, with loss of reputation to himself and the state, or have recourse to Parliament." While some courtiers, notably Buckingham, supported the former option, the Council's remaining moderates urged the latter, and intelligence reports suggested that Charles had "a purpose to make further use of parlament", with a possible meeting planned for the autumn.[12]

Until then, the regime struggled to raise money. "There are at this instant", Owen Wynn told his father, "straunge proiectes afoote in this kingdome such as cannot be paralld in anie former tyme synce the Conquest." The Council, Secretary Coke reported in July, "labor day and night to put in order such things as concerne the publique defence . . . [and] for settling the revenue".[13] In short order the king stopped paying all pensions and established a high-level commission to retrench Household expenses. Whitehall once again became a projectors' paradise. The regime toyed with debasing the coinage, and it implemented William Anys's audacious monopoly on the production and sale of Virginia tobacco.[14] To protect against invasion, Charles upgraded the militia-men, all 118,400 of them, and he ordered London and the coastal towns to pay for thirty-seven vessels for three months, commanding neighbouring inland counties to share the cost. The regime's energies, however, were focused on raising revenue through Benevolences and Privy Seal loans.[15] But the rhetoric supporting these projects was so anaemic that Mende likened it to asking Englishmen "to give to the poor box (*tronc*)".[16]

Buckingham also helped stabilize the situation. After parliamentary criticism of his imperious rule, the duke "is carefull to act nothing but by advise of the councell", Simonds D'Ewes noted with some surprise. Buckingham also reportedly considered resigning some of his many offices.[17] Meanwhile he pulled off a masterpiece of factional realignment that promised to insulate him from aristocratic intrigue if Parliament met again. After the dissolution, agent X had confidently reported that Buckingham would "supresse Pembroke, Arondell and the temperate councellors of state" and advance "Holland, Carlile, Conway, Coke and the rest of his begerly creatures". Instead, the duke performed a stunning *coup de théâtre*. In July, Charles appointed Pembroke as Lord Steward and named the earl's younger brother, Montgomery, to succeed him as Lord Chamberlain. These appointments were part of a package deal in which Montgomery's seven-year-old son, who was also Pembroke's heir, was contracted to marry Buckingham's even younger daughter, Mary, who came with a dowry of £20,000. Lest the Herbert brothers become restive, Buckingham also dangled the prospect of making Pembroke a marquis or even a duke.[18] In one stroke the favourite had removed the courtly keystone of the broad coalition that had badgered him in Parliament, thus separating men like Sir John Eliot from their aristocratic backers. Well might the Earl of Clare wish it had happened "sooner, ear a Parlament, ear the whole Kingdome had been a party". While agent X thought "the peace made betweene him and Pembroke" only made "the duke odious and the king contemptible", others scented an opportunity. "This greate Alliance betwixt theise two families", one prospective courtier observed, "cannot but cause some notable alteration in our most important affayres on [sic] way or other".[19] The bold move had its costs. It poisoned Buckingham's relationship with his old ally the Earl of Carlisle, who wanted to be Lord Steward, and left him, Mende noted, in "extreme jealousy". Such collateral damage, however, was acceptable. "This will not only put an end to the mortal enmity between the two houses", the Venetian envoy concluded, "but will firmly establish the duke's greatness". As one diarist gloomily noted, "This the Duke did to make himself strong".[20]

Buckingham's court power was strengthened in other ways. During their first year together the young king's relationship with his teenage French bride had failed to thrive. The abrasive French ambassador Jean de Varigniez, Sieur de Blainville, worsened things by haranguing Charles for abrogating the marriage treaty and by delving into court and, more controversially, parliamentary politics. Secretary Conway blamed the "little republique" around Henrietta Maria, effectively blocking her "from soe frequent conversation with this nation as she ought". The truth was, Sir Benjamin Rudyerd noted, that "theare was soe much disorder and equallitye in hir Maiesties Corte as she would never have bin Queen of England so longe as the French had stayed". One English report denounced "their obscenities and baudye talke at table and in Cabinett" and "their contempt derision and scorne" for English courtiers, even "them in higest degree".[21] By late July, Charles had had enough, and dismissed Henrietta Maria's servants from court. This brash move initially won the king "much honor and good affection among his people", but with her French attendants shipped away the queen was now left in the hands of the Villiers women, as Buckingham's wife, mother, sister and niece Mary, Marchioness of Hamilton, became her daily attendants. With the "argus eyes" of the favourite's relations trained upon her, Henrietta was under near-constant surveillance, and the Venetians concluded that the duke had planned the purge "to win that influence over the queen . . . in the same manner as that which he enjoys with the king".[22]

Cursed be the Inventers

Sir Richard Beaumont told his cousin Buckingham of his delight "that this black Tempest and Confluence of Confounding Malice cast upon you by the passions of some people is past", and he added a pious wish: "cursed be the inventers". Beaumont's enthusiasm for retribution was widely shared at Whitehall. The dissolution of Parliament, the Venetian agent observed, had prompted the duke's adherents to "call for punishment against those who have spoken loudly against Buckingham".[23] With a new Parliament potentially looming, Charles and the duke were constrained from expressing their full displeasure, but some opponents were too tempting to ignore.

The day before the dissolution Charles ordered the rearrest of the Earl of Arundel, eventually allowing him to retire to any of his residences, as long as he stayed away from court. Arundel remained in political limbo for the next eighteen months.[24] The Earl of Bristol was not so fortunate. He was "tower[e]d" immediately after the dissolution, and charges against him were drawn up in Star Chamber. The king instructed Attorney General Heath to examine Bristol's actions "in the time of the late dissolved Parliament" during which the earl, his son and his "instruments" had informed "the Houses of Parliament of divers things tending much to our dishonor and to the stirring up of divers of the members of both Houses for the furtherance of their private ends". This "seditious" and intolerable behaviour required "exemplary punishment". Charles ordered Heath to question Bristol and his son Lord Digby, as well as his stepson, Sir Lewis Dyve, his secretary, Walsingham Gresley, and his allies, Sir John Strangways, Edward Kirton and Simon Digby.[25] By late July, Heath had completed his case: in addition to his errors during the Spanish match, Bristol had refused to listen when Charles "forbadd his accesse to your person or the Parliament", instead using "all the meanes he could both by himselfe and his friends to possesse the members of both the houses of Parliament that he was much iniured by the restrainte". Once in the Lords, he had "endeavoured all the meanes he could seditiously and wickedly to stirre up the ill affections of the members of both the houses of Parliament". Worse still, "he gave your Maiesty the lye", challenging the veracity of Buckingham's 1624 relation even though "every part thereof . . . was confirmed by your Maiestyes owne expresse testi-monye". In effect, Bristol had "cunningly and seditiously" corrupted the parliamentary session, blocking the passage of the subsidy bill, a crime "of such high and dangerous consequence and of such an ill example for any subiect to dare to attempt against his Soveraigne".[26]

Bristol's initially vigorous defense soon collapsed. By October 1627 he had surrendered, making "a personall and publicke submission unto his Maiestie", and announcing that "I should esteeme it as an Act of his Grace and goodnesse that this suite might be noe further prosecuted". After that the only remaining issue was the precise form of his submission. Preoccupied with more pressing business, the king's lawyers delayed final judgement. When Parliament returned in March 1628, Bristol's gentle statement that "I should be loath to have anything that hath relation to me to be touched upon there" was all it took to persuade Heath to drop the case, vowing "neither now or heerafter the[r]e may be either further proceedings or memory of what is past".[27]

The Parliament-men were much harder to discipline, at least as long as the regime hoped for harmony in future sessions. While precedents existed for briefly detaining and interrogating members, harsher penalties would almost certainly produce a hostile response from the next Parliament. But while Charles could not imprison the offending Parliament-men, he saw no reason to reward them. Local offices were vital for any aspiring gentleman, and traditionally the central government was too busy to scrutinize the hundreds of such men who served as Justices of the Peace. But late in 1625, Lord Keeper Coventry had sacked dozens of magistrates, mostly on grounds of inefficiency or religion. Another purge followed on 8 July 1626, this one aimed at "that ungratefull villain Elliott" and his allies. Both Eliot and Sir Dudley Digges lost their seats on county benches, as did Sir John Strangways, Sir Robert Mansell, Christopher Wandesford, Edward Kirton and William Coryton. Coventry also ejected four of the six men whom Charles had pricked as sheriffs in 1626: Sir Robert Phelips, Sir Guy Palmes, Sir Francis Seymour and Sir Thomas Wentworth. And the purge included even minor figures like William Walter, Edward Alford, Walter Long, Sir Thomas Hoby and Sir Walter Erle. Eliot also lost his post as Vice Admiral of Cornwall and Coryton as Vice Warden of the Stannaries. Sir George More's protests could not save the seventy-year-old's lucrative post as Chancellor of the Order of the Garter. Nothing on this scale had ever befallen awkward Parliament-men before.[28]

In the Star Chamber

Shortly after the dissolution of Parliament, John Rous had heard of "an offer made" to the Parliament "to permitte the duke to a triall by his peeres at the King's Bench barre". The offer had reportedly been "refused", and sceptics mocked the idea that any regular court with a jury full of the duke's "speciall frends if not creatures" would rigorously pursue charges against Buckingham. Nevertheless the idea of putting the duke on trial outside Parliament was appealing, especially since an acquittal would protect Buckingham from any future parliamentary prosecutions. Star Chamber, where Buckingham would be judged by his fellow Privy Councillors, was the ideal venue. Amerigo Salvetti thought "a favourable sentence" would be obtained by pressure, but only "in a manner repugnant to the general feeling of the nation". The Venetian agent, however, believed a trial would legally "secure him against further trouble".[29]

On 17 June, two days after the dissolution, Heath ordered the members of the former select committee to attend him on the following Monday. The Attorney General asked them to name the witnesses for each charge against the duke, to specify any additional proofs the House had in hand, and to state whether they of their "owne knowledge knowe any thinge which may be usefull unto mee . . . in provinge any parte of those Charges". Initially, the Parliament-men stalled. Eliot explained that since they had indicted the duke in Parliament, they could not participate in a Star Chamber prosecution.[30] He stood his ground, but others eventually offered token cooperation. Both John Selden and Digges claimed "weak memory", but Digges offered up "Dr. Rawson" (i.e. Ramsey), "Dr. Atkins and divers others of the King's physicians and surgeons whose names I remember not". Wandesford and John Glanville offered partial lists of the doctors, surgeons and bedchamber staff in James's sickroom. John Pym, still a royal office-holder, suggested Atkins, Ramsey, Lister, Craig, Hay, Primrose "and some other Phisitions". But all rebuffed Heath's request for additional proofs, and none suggested new witnesses.[31]

This reluctant cooperation did not halt proceedings, and in late June one of Mead's correspondents reported that Buckingham had been ordered to appear in Star Chamber. Heath continued collecting depositions, including a lengthy one on the loan ships from Edward Nicholas, the duke's naval secretary. By July, Heath had an "exhibit" ready for the Star Chamber suit—essentially a word-for-word copy of the Commons' articles of impeachment, minus the original preamble and postscript. The thirteenth charge was identical to the Commons' version, classifying the offence as "an acte of Transcendent presumption and of dangerous consequence". Heath's new postscript categorized Buckingham's offences as crimes of "highe nature" that caused the weakening of the king's private estate and the general impoverishment of his realm. Heath noted, too, that "all or most" of the offences had occurred "since anye generall pardon" (thus negating one of the duke's defences), and he requested the king to summon Buckingham before Star Chamber "to Answer the premises, and to stand to & abyde such further order, sentence & direccon" from the court. A bill of indictment was duly filed, Buckingham submitted a formal answer, and "Divers Witnesses were examined".[32]

There the case ended, and while the precise reasons for its abandonment are unclear, it was undoubtedly related to an abrupt change in the Crown's political calculations. Immediately after the dissolution of Parliament, Secretary Coke had explained that Charles was determined "to take no violent or extraordinarie way to levie monies"; instead, he would "rely uppon a common case and affection that al men must have that wil not wilfully bee guiltie of abandoning there religion Prince and contrie to the enimies power". But although the king asked the ratepayers to pay "freelie and voluntarily", the overwhelming majority remained uncooperative.[33] In Worcestershire the subsidymen responded that since "they had beene used to supplye by Subsidyes or fifteens, graunted in Parliament . . . they were unwilling to geve in an other waye". In Suffolk the request was "answered with lowde cries" from coastal residents whose "Shippes were taken and fired in their havens before their faces".[34] And in Westminster they simply chanted "a Parliament, a Parliament". The actual sums raised were notional: Kent, one of the wealthiest shires, offered a mere £90.[35]

Events in Lower Saxony transformed the situation. It had been an inauspicious campaign season for the Danes. In April, Christian IV's army was rebuffed at Dessau Bridge, and in July he fell from a wall, leaving him unconscious for two days. Finally, in early August, he advanced into Lower Saxony against Tilly's Catholic League army, only to pull back after Catholic reinforcements arrived. At Lutter the Danish king turned to confront his pursuers. Confident that a stream would slow any imperial advance, Christian went back to get his wagons moving and left no one in charge. When Tilly's men turned both flanks of the Danish position, Christian lost a third of his army. With imperial soldiers now driving into Jutland, Anstruther sketched out the implications:

> if this kinge be not speedlie souplied with sommes of monnie . . . hee is lost, his crowne and posteritie in hazard, the publiq cause concerninge the common good of Christendome will receave a mighte blowe and those princes of these pairts, made tennants at will.

As Christian reiterated, these disasters came of "trustinge to much" to Charles's "promises". The situation was so uncomfortable that Anstruther broke off personal contact, communicating with the Danish court only by "letters and messages".[36]

The news of Christian's defeat at Lutter put Charles in a quandary: either he could immediately summon a new Parliament, or turn to a new form of prerogative finance. The answer seemed so obvious that in Somerset some "popular" men began to "looke after places" in the new session, while in Cornwall, Eliot and his allies "labored for places allreadie". Charles, however, chose the other path. Royal officials stopped asking politely for financial assistance; instead, they demanded it. As Conway explained, the king would "persuade" the subsidymen "to lend such a portion as may by a just calculation rayse the summe" of £400,000, roughly the four subsidies and three-fifteenths that Parliament had declined to authorize. Those who refused the Forced Loan were imprisoned without being charged, much less tried. The Crown's hard-line stance was legally provocative, and although the judges declined to intervene to block the Loan, some former Parliament-men and lawyers argued that the regime had violated Magna Carta and other statutes. Whatever the legal situation, the Forced Loan made clear that Charles was in no mood to recall Parliament. Without the prospect of a new session, Buckingham now had nothing to gain by answering the impeachment in Star Chamber. Charles did not forget the case, however. On 16 June 1628, amid renewed parliamentary attacks on the duke, Charles ordered the Star Chamber to remove the bill of information, the duke's reply, "and all other proceedings thereupon off the File, that no memory thereof remain of Record against him, which may tend to his disgrace". Charles insisted that he was "fully satisfied of the innocency of that Duke in all those things mentioned in the said information, as well by his own certain knowledge, as by the proofs in the cause".[37] While Charles was "fully satisfied", many others still awaited a "true cleering".

Mastering Fame and Report

"A book has come from Flanders printed in English", Zuane Pesaro reported on 5 May. It was "the work of the physician who attended the Marquis of Hamilton in his last moments", and "The king is incensed against the author." Charles's fury was understandable, but it was unclear how, and whether, he should respond to George Eglisham. His ministers knew the author's identity and his potentially embarrassing career in England, and, despite the fake imprints, they knew where the book had been produced. William Trumbull, the former English agent in Brussels and now a Privy Council clerk, had reported Eglisham's arrival in Flanders in 1625 and his boasts about Hamilton's conversion. Trumbull knew, too, about Eglisham's compromising long-term connections to Jean Baptiste Van Male, the Flemish agent in London, and about the *modus operandi* of the Flemish disinformation machine. It would thus have been relatively easy to unmask Eglisham as a Catholic agent in Habsburg service and to discredit his allegations about James's death as a tissue of Spanish Catholic lies.

Already there was hostile chatter in London about the "popish" agenda of *The Forerunner of Revenge*. As early as 5 May the London cleric James Meddus reported talk of Eglisham's "pestilent pamphlet":

> A Papist he is, and papistically he sayth, that whereas we taxe Jesuites and Roman Catholiques with poison and other kind of murthers and cruelties, is it not (saithe he) a foule shame *Proditorem illum Buckingamium* [that the traitor Buckingham] who hath bene author by way of poison of the deathes of the D. of Richmond, the Marquis Hamilton . . . and lastly of K. James, should be nestled in the bosome of King Charles?

"In breife", Meddus concluded, "the whole book is nothing but a bitter accusation of the Duke." The regime clearly knew how to exploit the situation. On 4 May, Sir Dudley Carleton made the only reference in Parliament to the book—"a libel written by a Scottishman"—in a speech defending Buckingham against allegations of crypto-popery. Carleton claimed that since the French and Spanish Catholics and the Dutch Arminians all hated the duke for his staunch Protestantism, this Catholic libel "from Brussels" only confirmed that the duke was no papist.[38]

The regime had also collected other damaging evidence against Eglisham. On 19 May, four days after Buckingham's rout in the Lords and the day Eliot was released from (Fig. 56) the Tower, the Privy Council instructed Sir Henry Wotton, the Provost of Eton, to undertake "a business which his Majestie hath committed to your trust". Charles wanted him to find Anne Lyon. She was the eldest daughter of Sir Thomas Lyon of Auldbar, a central figure in the turbulent world of Jacobean Scotland, and someone James purportedly considered "the boldest and hardiest man of his dominions". After serving the young James VI, Lyon had fled Scotland and then returned in 1585, with Elizabeth I's help, to oust the Earl of Arran from power. Until his death in 1608, Lyon served as Lord

High Treasurer and a Lord of the Session. By his first wife, he had two daughters, the eldest of whom was Anne. Thanks to Scotland's interlocking family networks, she was related to many prominent aristocrats, including the Marquis of Hamilton. In 1626 the Privy Councillors thought she could be found "as we heare at Windsor", but such was their eagerness to talk to her that they authorized Wotton to search, if necessary, "where els you shall finde her". In the event, on 23 May, Wotton only had to cross the Thames from Eton College to find her living quietly in Windsor with her sister and another woman. He took with him Michael Branthwaite, a protégé who had long served as his secretary. Since Anne was understandably apprehensive at the arrival of two distinguished visitors armed with a Council warrant, Wotton "laboured to take from her all manner of shadow touching herself". But after confessing that he was there to discuss a matter "somewhat harsh and umbrageous", he presented the startled women with a copy of *The Forerunner of Revenge* and informed her that George Eglisham had named her as "a witness of this foul defamation".[39]

Eglisham had drawn attention to "a paper ... founde in kingstreete" in Westminster, about the time of the Duke of Lennox's death in February 1624. The doctor reported rumours that Lennox, Southampton and indeed "all the noblemen that were not of Buckingham's faction should be poisoned", rumours that gained new substance when "the daughter of Lord Oldbarre" found a "scroll of noblemen's names who were to be killed". Although the scroll included the peculiar notation, "The Marquis of Hamilton and Doctor Eglisham to embaume him", Eglisham wrote that the discovery initially caused "no terrour to me". But after he saw "the Marquis poisoned" and realized that he was the only person on the scroll still alive, Eglisham became alarmed. "Lord Oldbarre's daughter" was thus one of the few witnesses who could confirm Eglisham's allegations.[40] After Wotton had read out the relevant passages, Anne Lyon proved eager to talk. The provost settled in by the window where the light was good and began transcribing her detailed response.

She remembered the incident clearly. A "carman" (carter) working for a Westminster woodmonger had found the paper and given it to Lady Auldbar's footman, Thomas Allet, who brought it to his mistress. The scroll consisted of:

> half a sheet of paper laid double by the length, and in it was written in a scribbled hand, the names of a number (above a dozen) of the Privy Council; some words had been written more, which were scraped out. The names were not writ in order as they were of quality. In it, next to the Marquess of Hamilton, was writ, "Dr. Eglisham to embalm him". No mention of poisoning, or any such thing, but very names.

Not knowing what to make of the list, Anne sent it to Lennox, whose secretary, Alexander Heatley, soon returned it, suggesting the note came from "a cause to

Figure 56: An engraved portrait of Sir Henry Wotton published in 1657 (British Museum). A Jacobean ambassador to Venice who became Provost of Eton College, Wotton investigated some of Eglisham's allegations in 1626.

be heard before the Privy Council, or in the Star Chamber", and that the author had compiled the names "to help his own memory, to reckon who could be with him or against him". It was unnecessary, Heatley told her, "to trouble his Lord withal". Still curious, Anne sent the paper to David Strachen, one of Hamilton's servants, who reported that "his lord had read it" and then "put it in his pocket".[41]

In the letter to Buckingham that accompanied his report, Wotton offered his "critical . . . judgement" on Eglisham's claims. "I have seen many defamatory and libelous things of this nature" both in England and abroad, he told the duke, and although most were "always without truth", many were "contrived with some credibility". Eglisham's tract, however, was "utterly void" of both. The only men who paid attention to the suspicious scroll—"found . . . not" in a courtier's "cabinet" but "in a dirty street"—were a carman and a footman, who were hardly "authentical instruments that should give it credit". In contrast, their superiors had ignored the paper. Heatley, "a gentleman indeed . . . of sound abilities", thought the scroll not worth troubling his master "with a sight of it". As for Hamilton, Wotton noted, "What doth he with it? It sleeps in his pocket". Eglisham's sinister interpretation clearly had no validity, and Wotton noted how Eglisham had "concealed" the fact that the paper had been first taken to Lennox's secretary, a "gentleman of sober judgement", who thought it "too frivolous to be so much as showed to his master, howsoever named therein". This note was the kind of thing that might intrigue a credulous carter or footman, but men of rank and discernment had paid it little mind. The paper, Wotton later told Princess Elizabeth, was "a bare note of a few council-lors' names, found at first in the very kennel of King-street by a carman, servant to a woodmonger: secondly, by him brought to a footman; by which honour-able degrees it came to the gentlewoman all dirty".[42]

Wotton did not explain why Anne Lyon, a gentlewoman, was puzzled enough by the paper to send it—not once, but twice—to the nobles it named. Yet Wotton praised "this noble gentlewoman" for her "very frank and ingen-ious spirit" and noted that she made a "clear, a free, and a noble report of all that had passed". Her word was reliable. Before he left, Anne asked to borrow Eglisham's pamphlet, and the next day Wotton requested her "full judgement of it". She "freely" responded "that Eglisham had gone upon very slight grounds in so great a matter". Wotton appeared completely unconcerned that someone appearing before Star Chamber had written "Doctor Eglisham to embalm him" after Hamilton's name, an odd detail that both Eglisham and Anne Lyon had highlighted. Instead, Wotton dismissed the whole tract out of hand. "I am doubtful what passion it will most stir in your Majesty", he wrote to Elizabeth, "whether mere laughter at such a ridiculous slander, or a noble indignation at so desperate impudency". The pamphlet itself was "abominable", a "cobweb" intent on "painting, in effect, a nature far beyond that of Richard the Third, when he was Duke of Gloucester". Wotton could only lament that it was the fate of "the greatest men" to be stained by "the foulest and falsest reports", of which Eglisham's book was a "monstrous example".[43]

By the end of May 1626 the regime's file on *The Forerunner* was thickening nicely. In addition to material on the tract's Flemish Catholic origins, which Carleton had used in the Commons, they now had Wotton's plausible demoli-tion of one of the tract's few pieces of verifiable evidence. Men close to Buckingham had also begun making semi-public attacks on Eglisham. On 28 May, Edmund Bolton, a scholar-poet and a distant kinsman of Buckingham, sent the duke a blueprint for navigating the new world of political publicity. After reminding him that "no sort of people under heaven is finallie maister over fame, and report, but the able writer only", he warned that Buckingham's enemies could marshal "fresh orators ... smart poets ... wise historians ... [and] deep discoursers" against him. If he was to master "fame, and report", then the duke needed his own "able penmen". Bolton gave him a taste of what could be done. He told the duke that he had written some "verses against the villain Eglisham", designed for transmission in the very same underground manuscript networks that circulated the libellous poems that had long plagued the favourite. To heighten the verses' effect, Bolton had masked their origins; the poem, he told the duke, was "spred in anothers name, who is a Catholick, and ambitious of the service, and the envie on your beehalf".[44]

Unfortunately, no copies of Bolton's verses have survived, though his choice of a Catholic front suggests he may have been playing some subtle confessional politics. We do, however, possess a fragment, probably in Bolton's hand, of possibly another early attempt to counter Eglisham. Only the opening chapter survives of "The End of King JAMES his reign & the beginning of King CHARLES", but it contained a compelling version of the authorized version of James's death. "Irregular diet and want of corporal exercise" had weakened the king, and from the first, James knew how gravely ill he was. He complained that "hee could not last" and muttered repeatedly "I am durt". James had bitterly dismissed "the vulgar proverbial rime, 'An ague in the Spring is Physick for a King'", the very rhyme Eglisham had cited to demonstrate how little danger the king had faced. According to Bolton, a dream haunted James in which his old tutor George Buchanan predicted that death would come "when his CARBUNCLE should boil with burning fire". Bolton took this prognostication seriously. Carbuncle Street once ran where the walls of Theobalds Palace now stood, so the prophecy "may not only seem to have insinuated the name of the place of his decease, but also the efficient cause thereof, a burning fever, of which hee did undoubtedly die". The narrative also mythologized Buckingham, idealizing him as the creation of James's virtuous favour. In his final days, Bolton wrote, the king found comfort in:

> the only two persons in whom hee had stored up all the chief tresures of his naturall, or elective love; the one his derest sonn (and the same also the very best of sonns) Prince CHARLES ... the other, the principal work of his equitie, power, and favour, his dearest friend, and nearest servant, GEORG, the Duke of BUCKINGHAM.[45]

By June 1626 the regime had enough ammunition, and several possible vehicles, for a devastating attack on Eglisham's book. Commissioning scribal poetry from "able penmen"—the method Bolton had suggested—was one option, and extensive Elizabethan and Jacobean precedents existed for officially sponsored print campaigns, whether through proclamations or pamphlets, to counter dangerous libels.[46] Wotton's investigations had also produced useful material for a systematic denunciation of Eglisham, and Bolton's history of James's death showed how to deploy the authorized version of James's death to undercut rumours of poisoning. Those who paid attention to events across the Channel would have noticed how Cardinal Richelieu responded to the barrage of Habsburg-sponsored attacks on his administration by setting talented writers to work on sophisticated counter-propaganda.[47] Yet printed attacks on the credibility of *The Forerunner* did not appear in England for more than two decades.

The regime's inaction needs explaining. The chief argument for holding fire was strategic: any official response would draw further attention to Eglisham's tract and increase the already considerable demand for *The Forerunner*. Worse still, a response might elicit further editions or even a reply from Eglisham, thus creating more problems than it would solve. Writing in the 1630s, Wotton maintained that Buckingham himself would "not suffer any answer to be made on his behalfe", instead resolving to "trust his owne good intentions which God knew" since "hee sawe no fruite of Apologies but the multiplying of discourse".[48] In practice, Buckingham was not at all averse to strategic publicity; he used everything from parliamentary speeches to printed newsbooks, from engraved portraits to popular stage plays, to manage his popularity.[49] Charles's attitude to public opinion, however, was far more ambivalent. Part of him found the very idea of having to explain his policies to his people repugnant to his elevated sense of royal dignity. But he did not always hide behind the *arcana imperii*. Indeed, in the wake of the 1626 dissolution of Parliament, he quickly issued two printed explanations of the session's failure. A 16 June proclamation "prohibiting the publishing, dispersing and reading" of the Commons' Remonstrance reiterated Charles's belief that attacks on Buckingham struck "through the sides of a Peere of this Realme" to "wound the honour of their Soveraignes".[50] In early July the royal printer issued *A Declaration of the True Causes* of the calling and failure of the last two Parliaments. Designed to stop "the mouth of malice", it inveighed against the "violent and ill advised passions" of a small knot of Parliament-men who had pursued Buckingham instead of funding the "iust and honourable" war with Spain. True Religion and "the publike defence of the Realm" meant nothing to Buckingham's enemies, whose disorderly pursuit of "private and personall ends" only served the interests of the popish "band of Ioab" who were behind "these diversions and distractions".[51] The claim that the Parliament-men had been the unwitting stooges of the "Common Incendiaries of Christendome" might have worked well in a printed rebuttal of *The Forerunner*. But despite his willingness to use print to manage the immediate fallout of the dissolution, Charles was acutely aware of the risks of a public debate with Eglisham.

A series of political miscalculations may account for the final decision to hold fire. The dissolution had stopped the impeachment and obviated the immediate need to discredit Eglisham. Charles and Buckingham may also have assumed that by neutralizing Pembroke and by targeting the "seditious" incendiaries they held responsible for parliamentary unrest, they had dealt with the main sources of potential trouble at Westminster. In any case the setback at Lutter and the decision to launch the Forced Loan made the prospect of a new Parliament increasingly dim, and with no pressing need to defend the duke,

Charles and Buckingham may have thought the best idea was to let the controversy wither away. Perhaps it was here that the duke told Wotton that "hee sawe no fruite of Apologies but the multiplying of discourse"; perhaps Wotton's disdain for the "monstrous", implausible libel convinced Buckingham that few readers would ever take Eglisham seriously. If they made these assumptions, the king and his favourite were gravely mistaken: they had misunderstood the nature of the political disillusion of 1626, and had not grasped the centrality of Buckingham's scandalous image to the anxieties of the age. They had also misunderstood the rules of the new media politics that were competing to shape contemporary perceptions, and were in danger of ceding the mastery of "fame" to "smart poets" and libellous historians. Although Charles issued a forceful, if general, printed defence of his favourite, and although copies of Buckingham's response to the impeachment charges circulated in manuscript, Eglisham's secret history had more staying power. *The Forerunner* spoke to contemporary anxieties in powerful ways, and was about to begin a long, damaging journey through English political culture.

A Tavern Outside Brussels

George Eglisham probably never felt truly safe in Flanders. As long as England and Spain were at war, he need not worry about English complaints to Brussels about his presence, but Thomas Morgan's kidnapping offer shows there were other ways of dealing with awkward controversialists. In the summer of 1626 the militant Protestant pamphleteer Thomas Scott, who had ridiculed James I's foreign policy, was assassinated in Utrecht. The murderer was a mentally unbalanced English soldier who reportedly confessed under torture that "he was hired for money to do it". Joseph Mead heard that Scott was killed "for preventing the coming forth of a book he was writing of our last Cadiz action", but a diarist thought that "his murthering" was designed to forestall a new tract on the "proceedings of the last parliament". Neither commentator mentioned Buckingham's name, but it was obvious who had the most to lose if Scott turned his pen to the Cadiz fiasco or the 1626 impeachment.[52]

In late November or early December 1626, John Brickdale was drinking in the company of some Scottish and Irish emigrés in a tavern outside Brussels. Among them, Brickdale was astonished to find George Eglisham. Having read his book "against the Ducke of Buckingham", Brickdale was shocked to hear the doctor, whose tract had acknowledged "many favours" from King James, now speak "such woords of that famous king and of his Queene, as should seeme intolerable to anie human man". While the "rest of the Company" enjoyed the doctor's stories, Brickdale was so upset that he rebuked the group for their "unhumanitie". After accusing them of being "treacherously adicted towards our Prince", he upbraided Eglisham for his ingratitude and his "strang . . . Doctrine that offered to speake one thin[g]e and write an other". As he recounted the incident to Secretary Coke, Brickdale made clear that, had he not been in a "strange Contry, farr from any sanctuary beinge in a Taverne withoute the Citty", he would have made Eglisham's "hart feele" the insult of the "woords spoken".[53]

We cannot tell whether Brickdale seriously intended to harm Eglisham or whether his report that Eglisham "would willingly be" his friend again was a hint to Coke that Brickdale could still get to the doctor. But the incident revealed that if Charles and Buckingham ever wanted to hurt George Eglisham, either polemically or physically, they knew where to find him. And Eglisham surely realized that, even in Catholic Brussels, he needed to watch his back.

PART IV

THE POISONOUS FAVOURITE
1626–28

PROLOGUE

THE HUNTING OF BUCK, KING OF GAME

Connoisseurs of the chase agreed that the buck was "king of game". But this particular "King . . . Of Brittish Beasts" whose "Game and fame through Europe ringe", was no ordinary stag. He was undeniably magnificent, "faire in sight", his "horne exalted" keeping the "lesser flocks" in fear. But he was also ungovernable, a beast whose "Will's a Lawe". This untamed buck scarred the landscape, "The tender thicketts nere can thrive,/Hee doth soe barke and pill the trees". Contemporaries quickly recognized who this buck was. For our "Charlemaine", King Charles, "takes much delight/In this great beast" and "With his whole heart affects the same,/And loves too well Buck-King of Game." Thus the poet turned the royal favourite, the Duke of Buck-king-game, into the huntsman's quarry: "When hee is chac'd, then 'gins the sport". As the Parliament-men had learned, this beast was hard to bring down:

> The huntsmen have pursu'd this Deare,
> And follow'd him with full careere,
> But such his craft, and such their lott,
> They hunt him oft, but take him not.

But they would not give up, for when they caught their prey, all would be well again, "the Hunter's gladd/The hounds are flesh'd, and few are sadd." This vision of Buckingham ripped open and fed to the dogs ended with the poet assuring the duke, "This bee thy destinie."[1]

Buckingham had survived the huntsmen in 1626; and he quickly tried to outmanoeuvre them. Reconciled with the Earls of Pembroke and Montgomery, his main court rivals, Buckingham tried to isolate and harry his more implacable foes. He had the Earl of Bristol confined to the Tower, and saw many of the rash tribunes of the Commons stripped of local office. The Commons' attempt to compel Charles to surrender the duke by withholding the subsidy bill had failed. The Forced Loan generated great anger but brought in significant funds to revive the faltering war effort. Most importantly, the Parliament-men's assault had only strengthened Buckingham's relationship with Charles. For all the abuse at Westminster, the duke could rest assured that the king did indeed love him.[2]

Buckingham knew that the huntsmen and their dogs were still on his trail. Admittedly, he might yet throw them off. A stunning triumph in the new war against France would have won him great acclaim, and he continued to woo the crowds, commandeering a flourishing newsbook to publicize his first major military command in the summer of 1627 (Fig. 57).[3] But the parliamentary assault of 1626 had left him badly damaged. He had lost the support of the broad coalition he had mobilized in 1624, and the number of his supporters dwindled further as he urged aggressive countermeasures against those who refused to pay the Loan. His hard line alienated zealous Protestants, many of whom found themselves among the list of prominent refusers imprisoned by the regime. Desperate for support, Buckingham turned to Arminian clerics and openly Catholic courtiers, thus fulfilling the godly's worst fears about his religious commitments. Most damaging of all, the duke's bid for military glory ended in humiliation. His 1627 expedition to relieve the siege of La Rochelle floundered on the Île de Ré; forced to evacuate the island in early November, the duke left behind him 5,000 English dead, and scores of banners that would soon fly in the aisles of Notre Dame de Paris. Charles forgave him, but many contemporaries, especially among the surviving officers, did not. By the end of 1627 there were mounting calls for his assassination; these calls became louder still after the Parliament-men of 1628 again failed to check Buckingham's power. When John Felton finally killed the "great beast" at Portsmouth in August 1628, he was acting out many Englishmen's fantasies. The hounds were fleshed and, indeed, few were "sadd".[4]

Those who dreamed of hunting the buck had many grievances. They blamed the duke for the kingdom's ills, for arbitrary government in the state, "popish" innovation in the Church, and military humiliation overseas. And for the rest of his days the duke was dogged by George Eglisham's secret history and by the unfinished business of the 1626 Parliament. The Parliament-men recalled to Westminster in 1628 decided not to revisit James's death—focusing instead on the fight for the people's much-abused liberties—but the claim that Buckingham had murdered James, Hamilton, Lennox and the others refused to disappear, and Buckingham the poisoner would haunt the popular political imagination. Printed and manuscript copies of Eglisham's secret history passed from hand to hand, while contemporaries, frustrated at Parliament's inability to restrain, much less to punish the duke, increasingly gave voice to bitter, seditious words. Over the last two years of Buckingham's life, the poisoning charges would be constantly reinvented and reworked in different forms and contexts, their meanings mutating in the shifting political currents. The secret history's continued relevance was both symptom and cause of the profound political

1 Daniel Mytens, *King James I of England and VI of Scotland* (1621). The aging king in his garter robes during the period of his attempt to settle the Palatinate crisis through a marriage alliance with Spain. James's motto "Beati Pacifici" (Blessed are the Peacemakers) adorns the tapestry behind him, while the odd angle of his right foot suggests the congenital weakness in his legs.

2 William Larkin, *George Villiers* (c.1616). The earliest major portrait of the court favourite, commissioned from the early Jacobean court's most skilled painter of material splendour, depicts Villiers in garter robes and thus commemorates his elevation to the Order, one of the first of a long series of honours and titles granted him by the crown.

3 Daniel Mytens, *Prince Charles* (1623). Charles as Prince of Wales, painted around the time of his trip with Buckingham to Madrid in 1623.

4 Daniel Mytens, *James Hamilton, 2nd Marquis Hamilton* (1624). Painted the year before his controversial death, the portrait depicts Hamilton in his court office as Lord Steward.

5 Michael Jansz van Miereveld, *George Villiers, Duke of Buckingham* (1625–26). A stunning example of the royal favourite as a work of art. Painted during Buckingham's diplomatic trip to The Hague in 1625, Miereveld's portrait captures the duke's calculated use of sartorial splendour – ornate ruff, ropes of pearls, fashionable lovelock – to project his authority.

Figure 57: William Marshall's engraved portrait of George Villiers, Duke of Buckingham, in armour, c. 1627–28 (British Museum).

crisis that engulfed England in the later 1620s. This was a crisis of proto-revolutionary proportions: political opinions polarized; religious beliefs clashed; the power of the state buckled; and large numbers of Englishmen read and expressed dangerous political ideas. With the angry words came the threat of political violence, even of popular resistance to the Crown, while calls for divine deliverance mingled with fears of divine retribution. Anger focused on the duke—the buck—but Charlemaine was not protected from his subjects' discontent. His uncompromising "delight" in Buckingham meant that the king could not distance himself from his favourite's alleged crimes, and many contemporaries were forced into uncomfortable thoughts about Charles's motives for saving the duke in 1626. Some of these thoughts could not safely be put on paper; but at least one contemporary was willing to analyze at length the vexed question of the young king's guilt in his father's murder. The author of "Of Brittish Beasts the Buck is King" also could not avoid touching the king. Unpacking his compound pun, the poet found himself on the cusp of treason, imagining the death of kings:

A Buck's a beast; a King is but a Man,
A Game's a pleasure shorter then a span:
A beast shall perish; but a Man shall dye.

CHAPTER THIRTEEN

THE STAPLE OF NEWS

THE FORERUNNER AND THE LITERARY UNDERGROUND

"WHAT NEWS OF Gondomar?" Earlier in the decade many members of the audience might have asked or heard that question, but now they were supposed to be laughing at the man asking it onstage. His name was Lickfinger, a London cook about to cater a large dinner party and desperate for "a parcel of news/To strew out the long meal withal". And so he had come to the "Staple of News", an office that collected, and sold, "all the News . . . o' the time". The Staple's agents who gathered the "commodity" from every place where news was "made", "or vented forth", took their richest pickings from the "four cardinal quarters": the royal court, St Paul's Cathedral, the Exchange and Westminster Hall. Meanwhile, back at the central office, the clerks sorted and classified the news, transcribing it onto scrolls and filing it away alphabetically where it could be easily retrieved, copied, and "made up and sealed" into packets. To season his dinner party, Lickfinger wanted news of the court, the latest "proc-lamations/Or edicts", as well as news of the theatre. But he was especially keen for reports on the Conde de Gondomar, the former Spanish envoy to London, and here he was in luck. For the Staple had a sensational new report: Gondomar had suffered "A second fistula", the clerk informed Lickfinger:

> Or an excoriation, at the least,
> For putting the poor English play was writ of him
> To such a sordid use, as is said he did,
> Of cleansing his posteriors.

The news delighted Lickfinger. Londoners had cruelly mocked Gondomar's anal fistula for years, and his new physical affliction seemed a just punishment for using copies of *A Game at Chess*, Thomas Middleton's 1624 anti-Spanish play, as toilet paper. But the Staple also had less reassuring news of the old envoy. Gondomar remained in Brussels, "condemned" to the special chair designed to ease his fistula pain: "And there sits filing certain politic hinges,/To hang the states on he has heaved off the hooks."[1]

Ben Jonson's *The Staple of News*, a comedy about the misuse of money, opened in February 1626. Its central characters were the old standards of early Stuart city drama—a young prodigal, his miserly uncle, a philosophical rogue, and a gallery of cynical urban cheats. But Jonson also satirized the contemporary appetite for political information and the new commercial enterprises designed to feed it. The fictional creation the Staple of News indiscriminately peddled false information and self-evident nonsense to the "curious and the negligent,/The scrupulous and careless", the "wild and staid,/The idle and laborious". The "news here vented", Jonson later explained, was not the kind of news a rational man would entertain, but "news made like the time's news (a weekly cheat to draw money)" which:

> could not be fitter reprehended than in raising this ridiculous Office of the Staple, wherein the age may see her own folly, or hunger and thirst after published pamphlets of news, set out every Saturday but made all at home, and no syllable of truth in them; than which there cannot be a greater disease in nature, or a fouler scorn put upon the times.[2]

Echoing Charles I's own distrust of popular political engagement, Jonson stereotyped news-mongering as dishonourable and disorderly, plebeian and puritanical.[3] But while the Staple was Jonson's invention, it was a response to real phenomena, and provides us with a revealingly distorted image of an important fact of political life in early Stuart London—the emergence of a thriving, socially heterogeneous and increasingly commercialized culture of news-gathering and exchange. Dealing in printed, manuscript and oral reports of political affairs, this news culture catered to a diverse audience, circulating the latest texts and information from London's "four cardinal corners" throughout the city and into the English provinces. Feeding a rapidly growing demand for information, this news culture helped sustain a precocious and expanding public sphere where all types of political issues were fodder for discussion and debate.[4] Jonson's satire touched on well-known players in the emergent London news business, including the newsbook publisher Nathaniel Butter, and parodied important practices of filing, sorting and copying news that contemporaries were developing to cope with information overload.[5]

In early May 1626, when Nicholas Herman told his master, the Earl of Middlesex, about the tract "sent over from Brussels to some of the Lords from one Doctor Eglisham", he promised to send copies of "the books, as soon as they may be gotten".[6] As we have seen, there is good reason to believe that the first copies of Eglisham's pamphlet reached London shortly before the Parliament-men opened their investigation into James's death. We have also seen evidence of a strategic book launch—copies "scattered industriously" in the streets and sent directly to court and to the Lords—timed to capitalize on the parliamentary assault on Buckingham. Any such scattering would no doubt have targeted the city's "cardinal quarters" for the collection and dissemination of news. But given the lack of any centralized news mart, and given that anyone who possessed or circulated such a self-evidently seditious libel faced the possibility of punishment, the question remains: after this initial publication, how did copies of *The Forerunner of Revenge* circulate?[7]

This text could not be handled and traded openly. However poor his reputation, Butter could freely (at least for now) sell his weekly newsbooks, as long as he stuck to foreign affairs and avoided controversy. By contrast, the secret history had to move in the shadows, through the less visible zones of the emergent public sphere. To explore how the secret history became public, then, we need to follow Eglisham's work through the early Stuart English literary underground, where dangerous texts could circulate beyond the regime's reach.[8] *The Forerunner* may have originated in a print shop in the Putterye in Brussels; it may have been yet another of Gondomar's plots—his "politic hinges"— designed to heave a state off its hooks. But it was the robust and socially diverse English news culture, and the literary underground that operated within it, that ensured Eglisham's work would reach its most avid readers. This literary underground had links to the Continent, but its dynamism was homegrown, and it involved a cast of characters far broader than Jonson's collection of conmen, silly women and prodigal fops. Although some of its activities were thoroughly commercialized, the literary underground was far more reliant on older forms of exchange, in which sociability and ideological commitment, rather than commodification and profit, facilitated the circulation of dangerous books. These underground systems of exchange disseminated *The Forerunner* and many variations upon it, thus prolonging Eglisham's political impact far beyond the 1626 Parliament, and allowing his allegations to acquire a settled place in contemporary political consciousness where they could ferment and mutate in a rapidly changing world.

The Flanders–London Book Trade

Some readers probably secured copies of Eglisham's pamphlet from the tried and trusted networks that had long peddled seditious foreign books in England. The trade in Catholic books from Flanders was well established; if Eglisham's backers in Brussels had needed help distributing his book, they could have employed a range of experienced actors and well-honed strategies.[9] Agents in Flanders and London arranged shipments and distribution. Books were put on boats in Dunkirk and Gravelines in the Spanish Netherlands, or Rouen and Calais in northern France.[10] Sometimes captains and crew were unaware of their dangerous freight, but other skippers were committed to the cause and carried not only popish books but also priests and "Churchstuffe". If they were anxious about the watchers at the customs houses, captains could offload cargoes "at secrett places", at small anchorages between major ports, or onto small boats, before continuing on to port.[11] Once ashore, books were deposited at secure metropolitan locations, sometimes at diplomatic embassies and the great houses of the recusant elite, sometimes at less conspicuous residences: in the mid-1590s a man who may have been unaware of what he was carrying delivered "divers packettes of sedycious bookes" from "partes beyond the seas" to the house of a Fleet Street tailor.[12]

In London a Catholic book-distribution system—a network of ideologically committed receivers, brokers, dealers and retailers—was already in place.[13] John Gee alleged that a Jesuit lodging near the Savoy in the early 1620s had "two or three large roomes filled up with heapes" of pamphlets, a "greater store of books", Gee wrote, "then I ever beheld in any Stationers Ware-house".[14] From Catholic warehouses a book could follow a variety of distribution routes. In the 1590s the Jesuit Robert Parsons relied on priests to circulate his publications, and the Catholic clergy continued to play a crucial role in distribution in the 1620s. Parsons also employed "young men of birth" to scatter texts around London and Westminster, disseminating Catholic literature "into the dwellings of heretics" while diverting attention away from the more vulnerable recusant consumers.[15]

Experienced book dealers were also crucial to the Catholic distribution system. In the early 1620s, Gee identified more than twenty of them, many working in the book-selling neighbourhoods around Holborn, Fetter Lane, St Paul's and Little Britain.[16] Most were active members of the legitimate book trade—printers, stationers, booksellers and binders—and a significant number were women. While many maintained robust licit businesses, others primarily dealt in prohibited wares. Some were devout Catholics, but others were motivated by the steep profits to be made by selling rare and dangerous writings.[17] The business was inherently risky, requiring dealers to dodge informants and the regime's pursuivants, and many on Gee's list had served time in London's prisons. The substantial risks no doubt helped account for these books' typically inflated prices.

Despite the harassment, the system worked, circulating a significant volume of Flemish-produced Catholic material in late Elizabethan and early Stuart England. Some print runs were quite large. An Antwerp printer produced 4,000 copies of Robert Parsons' *Newes from Spayne and Holland* in 1593, and an informer in 1608 warned that 2,500 new Catholic books were on their way.[18] Seized shipments also indicate the scale of these operations. The informer William Udall, no doubt exaggerating, claimed to have helped intercept 10,000 "seditious bookes" between 1604 and 1608. The authorities seized 700 copies of a "most vile book" in 1608 and another 700 of a Flemish libel in 1609.[19]

The trade flourished for many reasons. Policing was inconsistent, with intense periods of enforcement often followed by long stretches of neglect. The

Hispanophile moment of the early 1620s also undoubtedly eased the pressure on Catholic distributors. Furthermore, the punishment for distributors, if they were ever caught, proved ineffective deterrents. The standard precautions—avoiding heavily policed ports, using aliases and disguises, warehousing stock in embassies—helped shield illicit activity. So too did official corruption. William Udall warned his handlers that some pursuivants sent to search Catholic houses were frequently paid to turn a blind eye to books and that others would sell back confiscated books to their owners.[20] Customs officials were also corruptible: in return for a fee, they would allow illicit material to pass through the ports. In some cases, customs officers were reported to have seized books in order to resell them.[21]

The circulation history of that "terrible booke" *Prurit-Anus* neatly reveals how a printed libel from a Flemish press made its way to English readers through these networks. François Bellet in St Omer printed the book; John Wilson of St Omer College orchestrated its shipment; while John and Joan Dabscot of St Bartholomew's parish, London, coordinated its distribution. The books travelled, probably from Calais, in a boat skippered by Henry Parish, a fisherman based in Barking who moonlighted as a book- and priest-runner. Parish dropped off six bales of books near Lord Mounteagle's house outside London, although it is unclear whether Mounteagle, a Catholic sympathizer, or any of his household was involved. Four of these bales were collected by the Dabscots, who warehoused them at the Venetian embassy under the supervision of the ambassador's new Anglo-Flemish chaplain, a priest with strong Douai connections. The priest stored 700 copies in the porter's lodge, and stockpiled twenty-four additional titles in the embassy cellars. Although the priest may have disseminated a handful of books, the Dabscots controlled the retailing, with copies "taken out one by one" from the embassy warehouse "by the agent of a certain person, as they were required for sale and circulation among Catholics". The scandal caused by *Prurit-Anus* stung the authorities into action. They arrested the Dabscots, who in turn fingered the priest at the Venetian embassy and Henry Parish. Although hundreds of copies were ceremoniously burned outside St Paul's in August 1609, some remained in circulation for years, and a second major shipment may have arrived in London in 1610.[22]

Perhaps the men who produced and sponsored *The Forerunner* used these pre-existing Anglo-Flemish Catholic distribution networks. Eglisham himself must have known how the business worked. According to Protestant sources, Father Wood, the priest Eglisham allegedly brought to the Marquis of Hamilton's deathbed, regularly met other priests at the Fetter Lane house of a London goldsmith who distributed "thousands & thousands" of Catholic books.[23] But given *The Forerunner*'s sensational content—and its effort to conceal its Brussels origins and Eglisham's religion—book dealers outside the usual Catholic circles may also have taken an interest in the pamphlet. Copies might have been offered wholesale to stationers without Catholic connections. In the later 1620s, for instance, a London chandler whose brother-in-law in Amsterdam had sent him two packets of a printed poetic libel, *The Spy*, attempted to offload the goods to a stationer for sixpence a copy. When that deal fell through, the chandler passed the books onto another man to dispose of—anyone would do, just as long as they paid.[24] Some London stationers specialized in banned books, and savvy consumers knew where dangerous material was sold under the counter. Ferdinand Ely, whose personal religious inclinations are unknown, sold all kinds of illegal material from his shop in Little Britain. A report in 1609 alleged that Ely "buyeth and selleth all prohibited bokes, and stoln bokes. He dealeth with them who have warrant from the Highe Commission, and what bokes most of them take in search they sell to this stationer". Gee listed Ely as a purveyor of popish books in 1624, and he continued to trade in illicit material of all kinds during the 1620s.[25] Men and women like him were prepared to run a certain amount of risk to deal in printed books with unusually large profit margins.

A Friend Passing Lately this Way

The full history of *The Forerunner*'s English circulation in print will probably remain hidden, but we do have a revealing account of one reader's lengthy quest for a copy. Joseph Mead, fellow of Christ's College, Cambridge, and an insatiable news consumer, first learned of Eglisham's book early in May 1626, when his London correspondent, James Meddus, reported the tract's arrival in the capital. It is not clear whether Meddus had actually seen the Latin text he described, and he did not offer to send Mead the "pestilent pamphlet".[26] Four months would pass before Mead saw Eglisham's book for himself. On 16 September, Mead wrote to Sir Martin Stuteville in Suffolk that "A friend passing lately this way" had showed him "a printed copy of Dr Egglesheim's" book. Mead had then borrowed it in order to make his own copy. To that end he cut the pamphlet into "pieces", which he "distributed to three of my pupils to transcribe". Presumably this division of labour hastened the copying process, although Mead possibly wanted to spare his students full exposure to the illicit text. Now he was sending this three-handed manuscript copy to Stuteville "to read and return me again sooner or later, as you please".[27]

How Mead's unnamed friend obtained his printed copy of Eglisham's tract, and whether his version was in Latin or English, we cannot tell. But Mead's letter provides a precious glimpse of the way underground texts like *The Forerunner* circulated. The transactions Mead recorded were sociable, not commercial. The text was shown, borrowed, copied and lent out again, not as a commodity but as a gift. Equally significant, Mead's letter also documents the transformation of Eglisham's text from a printed book into a "scribally published" manuscript. The illicit political literature of the 1620s resists quantification—textual survival is too erratic for numbers to mean much—but it is nonetheless interesting that while modern bibliographers have tracked down only five copies of the printed 1626 "Frankfurt" English edition of *The Forerunner*, we know of at least two dozen surviving contemporary or near-contemporary scribal copies of the English tract.[28] Some of these copies can be traced to specific individuals or families: the Percy Earls of Northumberland; Sir George More of Loseley, Surrey, a royal official and victim of the political purge of 1626; the descendants of the Elizabethan courtier Sir Nicholas Bacon; William Ingilby of Ripley Castle in Yorkshire, a gentleman at odds with the Caroline regime during the 1630s; and Sir Jerome Alexander, a justice of the Irish Court of Common Pleas.[29] Some copies can be traced back only as far as their second or third owners, the collectors who bought and compiled early Stuart texts later in the seventeenth century, like the antiquary Peter Le Neve or the natural philosopher Hans Sloane.[30]

These scribal copies took various material and textual forms. Some were transcribed in folio, some in quartos that aped the feel of a printed pamphlet, some as smaller octavos.[31] Some survive as separate manuscripts, loosely stitched together or with pages unbound.[32] Some were compiled, either at the time or later, into bigger collections of political news items.[33] Many scribal *Forerunners* carefully imitated the visual features of a printed book, with title pages, imprints, section breaks, catchwords and regular margins (Fig. 58). One featured an exuberant version of Eglisham's signature at the end of the petition to the king; another used a stylish, distinctive hand to emphasize key words on its title page. One version elegantly inscribed the title page, complete with the Frankfurt imprint, into the blank area of a pre-printed engraved decorative frontispiece, bought from the publishers Sudbury and Humble. Eglisham's title thus appeared inside an incongruous border of flowers, birds and insects, with a squirrel, its feet perched upon a cornucopia, prominently occupying the bottom edge of the frame (Fig. 59).[34]

Like the copy Mead sent to Stuteville, many of these manuscript editions were produced sociably, transcribed by individuals for their own or their friends' collections. Because this form of scribal reproduction was labour- and time-intensive and required sufficient funds for paper and ink, it tended to thrive (though never exclusively so) in socially elite circles.[35] Some collectors had pupils or servants to do the dull work of transcription, but others had the skills and leisure to transcribe the texts themselves. This "user publication" was both relatively safe and surprisingly efficient, for the whole process occurred in places and along networks that the Crown could not police. When Mead had his students transcribe a pamphlet he had borrowed from one friend, and then sent the copy on to another, it was unlikely that anyone involved would betray

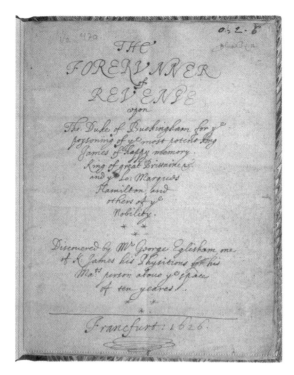

Figure 58: Title page of a scribal copy of *The forerunner of revenge upon the Duke of Buckingham* associated with Ralph Starkey's scriptorium (Folger MS V.a.470).

the operation to the authorities. Over time, sociable copying and exchange could disperse a text quite widely, albeit within predominantly elite circles. Because copying and transmission were enmeshed in social networks, the denser the network—the more links it had to other networks, the more people involved and interconnected—the greater the number of points at which a borrowed copy might be transcribed anew, or might jump from one network to another. Collectors who belonged to multiple overlapping or intersecting networks—familial, professional, local or religious—could act as intermediary nodes, spreading scribal material into new circuits, enlarging the geographical and social scope of its circulation.[36]

Things of Worth and Rare

Sociable scribal publication could move texts far and wide; the only profit was the invaluable social capital that came with gift exchange. But copies of *The Forerunner* were scarce, and demand was robust; for those willing to take risks, there was good money to be made in the underground market. An important proportion of the extant scribal *Forerunners* was commercially produced.

Figure 59: An elaborately transcribed scribal title page for *The fore-runner of Revenge* inserted into a pre-printed decorative border (British Library Add. MS 22591, fo. 31r).

Commercial scribal reproduction of illicit texts was risky, since the more exchange was monetized and depersonalized, and the more it operated without the trust and friendship that shielded sociable scribal publication, the easier it was for the authorities to detect. But because the state's policing powers were weak, the illicit transcription business had flourished in London for years. Among the dangerous wares found in Ferdinand Ely's Little Britain shop in 1609, for instance, was "that vile book" *Pruri-Anus,* "coppied out".[37] When demand for Thomas Scott's sensational 1620 *Vox Populi* far exceeded the supply of printed copies, contemporaries turned to manuscript versions. Some were produced non-commercially—the Suffolk vicar, John Rous, transcribed his version into his commonplace book—but others were commissioned and sold by booksellers. Several London stationers hired young men to make multiple copies for sale under the counter, and the competition among pens-for-hire could be fierce. One informant reported that a young scrivener had agreed with a stationer to supply a dozen copies of *Vox Populi* but had completed only one when the stationer took back his master copy and hired another supplier at a cheaper rate.[38]

Fortunately, we have two tantalizing glimpses into the illicit commercial trade in scribal copies of *The Forerunner*. In early 1627 the authorities found Alexander Bushy in possession of "foure paper coppys" of underground books, two of which were "coppys of D Egleshams publication concerning the duke of Buckingham". Bushy confessed that the copies had been "written" with his "owne hand" and that he had obtained the original from "one Freke a schoolmaster dwelling neer leadenhall". He also admitted to selling an earlier copy for the substantial sum of "a marke" (13*s* 4*d*)—he claimed not to know the buyer— as well as to receiving "thirty shillings" for the four copies—two of *The Forerunner* and two of another work—now in the authorities' possession. Bushy insisted he had no political agenda, that "he writt thes only to relieve his wants, & had noe other ende therin". It is unclear whether Bushy was a professional copyist or merely an opportunist who saw the chance to make money. His ultimate fate is unknown, and while there are hints that the schoolmaster Freke was also arrested, nothing indicates that the authorities ever tracked down Bushy's customers or any other contemporary copyist.[39]

Commercial scribal copies of *The Forerunner* also moved through the hands of the London merchant Ralph Starkey, a well-connected collector, copyist and trader specializing in historical state papers, guides to royal offices, legal precedents, court documents and contemporary news.[40] Starkey's sophisticated business moved awkwardly between two modes of scribal publication, the traditional exchange among friends and the nakedly commercial trade for paying customers.[41] Although he copied some material himself, Starkey employed several scribes to transcribe a wide variety of often scarce political materials—"thinges of worth and Rare", as he put it—that could be sold, lent or traded to public-minded and politically ambitious friends and clients.[42] Early in 1626 he wrote to one client, Sir John Scudamore, offering a range of materials for sale, including copies of official documents and records, sometimes illicitly obtained, which Starkey claimed were useful as either "presidente" or history. For £10 he offered Scudamore a volume of materials outlining the responsibilities and jurisdictions of the High Constable, the Steward of the King's Household and the Earl Marshal; for another £10, Scudamore could have "a coppie of the blacke booke of the order of the Garter". For £7, Starkey could supply a transcription "of the blacke booke of the kinges howsehould", kept at court, which listed the rules of the royal household and the allocations made to each officer, and for £6 he offered "a perfecte Jurnall of all the preceeding in the upore howse of parleamt" during the reign of James I. But Starkey also traded in news, including manuscript separates, and the summaries of recent talk and events he incorporated into his correspondence. In the letter to Scudamore, Starkey apologized that he could send only "litle newse at present", but included a "true coppie" listing the fifty-eight new Knights of the Bath created at the king's coronation. He promised that next week's letter would include transcripts of the formal speeches at the opening of Parliament.[43]

Amidst this heavy traffic in the useful, illicit and rare, copies of Eglisham's *Forerunner* also moved. On 1 October 1626, Starkey sent Scudamore a copy of "doctor Egleshames petycon". Starkey insisted that the copy had cost the significant sum of 30s, and he sent along with it a document on the "canvase in Cambridge", which cost 10s. Perhaps to justify their expense, Starkey warned Scudamore that these were works "that passe with much privacie and danger, wherefore I desire you to be cautious of them". "I am informed", Starkey added later, "that doctor Eglesham hath written an other booke as a second parte of his first worke[;] if it com to my handes you shall have knowledg thereof."[44] This "other booke" is a mystery. It is possible, though unlikely, that Starkey had sold Scudamore only Eglisham's petition to the king and that the "other booke" was the petition to the House of Commons. More likely, Starkey had heard talk of a sequel, perhaps sparked by Eglisham's claim that he had more to report about Buckingham's other murder victims. In any case, Starkey kept a copy of *The Forerunner* in his permanent collection where it was catalogued among the items found in his study at his death late in 1628. How many copies he sold is impossible to say, though at least one, identifiably written in Starkey's own hand, still survives (see Fig. 58 above).[45]

If Bushy and Starkey's prices were anything like the going rate, only the more affluent among the news-hungry public could afford a commercially produced scribal copy of *The Forerunner*. A Bushy Eglisham cost the equivalent of fourteen days' wages for a London craftsman in the building trade; the Starkey version cost twice as much.[46] We have no evidence of prices for printed copies in England. Rubens bought his two copies of a Latin edition for 7 stivers (slightly more than a shilling) apiece, but the English retail cost was probably higher.[47] Despite the steep price of commercial transcription, however, the paid and unpaid labours of men like Ralph Starkey and his scribes, Joseph Mead and his pupils, and Alexander Bushy and Freke the schoolmaster, helped disperse manuscript copies of *The Forerunner* across the country. If the authorities' failure to discredit Eglisham was ultimately a failure of will—a sign of deep ambivalence about how far to engage its critics publicly—the failure to suppress the pamphlet's circulation was ultimately a failure of means. The regime lacked the police power necessary to suppress texts like *The Forerunner*, allowing Eglisham's allegations to be broadly disseminated and appropriated in the later 1620s. Having entered the nation's political bloodstream in 1626, his accusations would remain there for decades.

Scribal Appropriations

Scribal publication played a crucial role in disseminating the secret history of James I's murder. But the process could also rework the text in interesting ways, shaping the impact that Eglisham's pamphlet had on individual readers.

Manuscript copying sometimes introduced textual variants, while the collation of copies into larger compilations of news material allowed readers to reassess the secret history in the light of other texts. Commercial retailers also shaped reader-response by exposing customers to other texts to read alongside Eglisham. Because Starkey and his competitors stocked numerous items from the 1626 Parliament, their customers had the opportunity to read Eglisham alongside reports of the impeachment process. Sir John Scudamore's copy of *The Forerunner* came bundled with the "canvase in Cambridge", a critical account of Buckingham's controversial June 1626 election as chancellor of Cambridge University, which many considered a perfect illustration of the duke's insatiable ambition—a theme central to *The Forerunner*.[48]

Nearly every surviving manuscript *Forerunner* contains a complete transcription of Eglisham's text, and some even aped the feel and look of the printed copy. But scribal reproduction also produced significant variants. Some surviving copies are incomplete, and some make relatively minor cuts, with Eglisham's poetic effusions often falling to the editor's pen.[49] But some scribal copies made much larger changes that, in effect, reinterpreted the original's meanings.

One contemporary manuscript copy, for instance, severely abridged *The Forerunner*, effectively creating a new version that shifted the original's emphases (Fig. 60).[50] Perhaps the most obvious difference between the complete and abridged versions was the amount of space devoted to Eglisham's self-presentation. Eglisham spent much of *The Forerunner*'s opening pages discussing the "humane obligation" that prompted him to take up his pen. The abridgement, however, cut virtually all of Eglisham's extensive account of his personal ties to Hamilton and James, condensing three pages of print into a brief summary.[51] Many of the book's remaining allusions to these connections were either compressed or eliminated.[52] These cuts continued throughout the abridgement, with the editor even attenuating Eglisham's prominent role as eyewitness to Hamilton's sickness and death.[53] The cumulative diminution of Eglisham's autobiographical presence effaced the eyewitness testimony that animated the original, downplayed the rhetoric of honourable revenge, and reduced the implied contrast between Eglisham, the good servant, and Buckingham, his monstrous antithesis. The political effects of these cuts are difficult to pin down. While Eglisham's careful self-presentation had helped deflect suspicions of his ulterior political motives, the abridgement removed this defence. For a reader aware of Eglisham's religious affiliations and Hispanophile sympathies, these omissions might undercut his credibility. On the other hand, by partially depersonalizing Eglisham's story, the abridgement made the secret history of James's death less dependent on one man's potentially problematic perspective.

Other cuts weakened the original's Hispanophilia. The abridgement retained Eglisham's bruising language about the betrayal of Charles's "kind usage in Spain", but cut Eglisham's assertions that James had vowed to revive

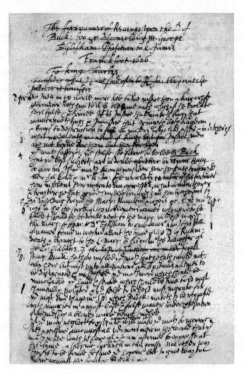

Figure 60: The first complete page of a heavily abridged scribal version of *The Forerunner of Revenge* (Bodleian MS Ashm. 749 III fo. 16v).

the Spanish match and that Gondomar's imminent return had spurred Buckingham to murder the king.[54] While these cuts rendered the text less "popish", one mistranscription had the opposite effect. Where Eglisham scoffed at the "Atheists, Lucianists, or Machiavellists" who thought their crimes immune from providential judgement, the abridgement replaced "Lucianist" (one who mocks religion) with "Lutheranist", turning Eglisham's Christian assault on the irreligious and atheistic into an apparently Catholic conflation of a major Protestant confession with godless Machiavellianism.[55]

The abridgement removed other important parts. Gone was Eglisham's attack on Buckingham's relationship with the "ringleader of witches" John Lambe, removing *The Forerunner*'s most explicit allegation of the duke's demonic witchcraft.[56] Gone too were Eglisham's references to Buckingham's "meane" family, weakening the original's powerful contrast between the aristocratic Hamilton and the upstart Villiers. Initially, the abridgement compressed much of *The Forerunner*'s discussion of justice, but the editor changed his mind and added some extracts back into the text, restoring most of Eglisham's radical language, including his assertion that kings had a contractual obligation to exercise justice, and his threat that unjust monarchs would "die like asses in ditches". The summation of the case for Hamilton's murder and the explicit comparison with the evidence from the Overbury proceedings were both eliminated, while Eglisham's heightened rhetoric about the heinousness of murder in general and poisoning in particular, complete with James's claim that he would not pardon his own son if he were found guilty of such a crime, also disappeared.[57]

The abridgement did retain certain key elements. Buckingham's arrogance, cruelty and dissimulation remained strong recurring themes, while the medical evidence for his crimes was left almost completely intact. Significantly, *The Forerunner*'s lurid description of the external and internal state of Hamilton's corpse appeared in full—indeed, it was one of the longest unedited sections in the whole abridgement. But even here, the abridgement tended to simplification. By cutting Eglisham's account of the physicians' initial bafflement at Hamilton's symptoms, the abridgement made the autopsy evidence less mysterious, but removed Eglisham's explanation of the symptoms and his claims about the foreign "art and artist" capable of pulling off such a "subtle art of poisoning". The mysterious poisoner-mountebank remained, but much of the original's rich poison lore had disappeared.[58]

The cuts became less aggressive when the abridgement arrived at Eglisham's account of James's murder, which may suggest the editor (perhaps naturally) considered the king's death more significant than Hamilton's. The abridgement reproduced Eglisham's account of James's sickness almost in full, retaining the two medical interventions by Buckingham and his mother, the king's verbal and physical reactions to the powder and plaster, and the angry conflicts in the sickroom. Arriving at the tract's final page, however, the abridgement compressed the last third of Eglisham's text, retaining his claim that Buckingham had dissimulated concern for James's illness and death but cutting his description of the duke's use of threats to silence the physicians. The abridgement then proceeded to Eglisham's description of the king's postmortem condition— "The kinges bodie & head swelled above measure his haire with the skin of his head stuck to the pillow, his nayles became loose upon his fingers & toes"—and abruptly ended there. Eglisham's allusion to the way "understanding men" would interpret these symptoms and his final call for justice against "the traitor" and his "accessories" failed to make the cut.[59]

If this particular appropriation attenuated Eglisham's presence, another scribal version of the pamphlet exaggerated it. Among the manuscripts collected by the Mores of Loseley in Surrey is a loosely stitched, quarto-sized pamphlet scribal separate of *The Forerunner*.[60] This neatly copied manuscript completely transcribed the original "Franckford" edition, though Eglisham's motto and poetic declaration of revenge were placed before the beginning of the text and then keyed to their position in the original using symbols.[61] But the end of the petition to Charles included a major variant—an interpolated poem of twelve four-line stanzas. Transcribed in the same hand as the rest of the tract, nothing indicates that the poem was not part of the original. How, when and by whom the poem was interpolated is impossible to say, but its presence added new dimensions to Eglisham's self-presentation. The poem was almost certainly not by Eglisham himself. Drenched in Biblical allusion, the verses offered a spiritual meditation on loss and suffering, sin and contrition, forgiveness and redemption, taking the narrator from despair in the lion's cage to eternal life in God's heavenly palace. The verses begin with the narrator poor, imprisoned and exiled, but end in a quest for Christ's mercy, a yearning for forgiveness and salvation: "Larkelike I flie unto the liveinge springe/desiringe pardon of my heavenlie Kinge . . . Make mee a sparrow in thy howse o Kinge . . . O let mee in thy temple keep a doore/that I may prayse thy name for evermore."[62] The poem appears in at least two other seventeenth-century copies, both of which are transcribed among other religious texts.[63] The poem made sense in these contexts, but is far more mysterious in the middle of *The Forerunner*'s two peti- tions. In some ways it made very little sense there at all—the poem's tone and themes were very different from the surrounding prose. But if we read the "I" of the poem as an extension of the "I" of Eglisham's petition to Charles, we can see the verses refashion "Eglisham", highlighting his introspective piety, perhaps even Protestantizing him, while further legitimating his pursuit of justice. Perhaps more significantly, the poem's images of suffering and exile might have supplemented Eglisham's own presentation of his flight abroad. In the petition to Charles, Eglisham's flight from "these dominions where" Buckingham "raigneth and rageth", his refuge "amongst Buckingham his enemies", his knowledge of the duke's "bloodthristie desire of my blood to silence me with death", all signalled the doctor's escape to a place where he could speak freely. Read alongside the poem, in which the narrator is cast "Mongst Lion fell in Daniells den" and "in lowest prison" with Jeremiah, in which he is "banish'd with David from my native land/cast up with Jonas in the Ninivites land", Eglisham's political narrative of exile acquired a newly spiritualized colouring. The land of Eglisham's exile was now a place of suffering, not a refuge.[64]

The Forerunner of Vengeance

Among the many surviving manuscript versions of *The Forerunner*, only one is not based on the English "Frankfurt" edition. It is possible that *Prodromus Vindictae* preceded *The Forerunner* across the Channel, but once English- language copies arrived, demand for the Latin version probably plummeted. At least one contemporary, however, found himself without an English translation and so attempted his own (Fig. 61).[65] The work is unfinished—it omits the final section on James's death—but survives in a polished draft that looks as if it was originally intended for a broader audience. All translations are acts of appropriation, and by following this translator at work, we can see how at least one educated contemporary appropriated Eglisham's Latin text.

The translation is attributed to "W.W. Master of arts", probably of Oxford. It was presumably begun in 1626, but W.W. or another reader revisited some of the trickier translation problems even after a fair copy had been made. Moreover, at least one person revisited the translation at a slightly later date, adding a marginal note recording the June 1628 murder of Dr. Lambe, the man Eglisham identified as Buckingham's servant and one of the "ringleaders of the witches".[66] W.W. proudly displayed his linguistic and poetic facility, keeping the Latin text of Eglisham's poems alongside his own translations, presumably to highlight his virtuosity.[67] But some of the Latin puzzled him, and W.W. occasionally resorted to highly Latinate English equivalents to render Eglisham's more obscure vocabulary. "Clanculariam caedem", given as "secret murder" in the official translation, appeared here as "clanculary murther". Sometimes a marginal note, perhaps again the work of a second hand, provided the reader with the original Latin for a problematic or puzzling word in the translation. When W.W. translated Eglisham's critique of Buckingham's ungrateful breach with Spain, for instance, he puzzled over the phrase "gratissima in Hispaniis

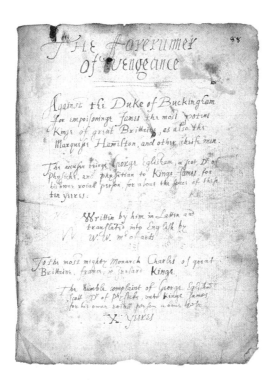

Figure 61: Title page of W.W.'s English translation of *Prodromus Vindictae*, "The Forerunner of Vengeance" (Bodleian MS Wood D. 18, fo. 88r).

promythia". What the official translation rendered as "your most kind usage in Spain", W.W. offered as "a most acceptable promythy in Spaine"; the marginal note added the comment, "promythia, a fable".[68]

In a handful of places W.W.'s translations differed from the official English version in more politically significant ways, suggesting, at the very least, that readers who encountered Eglisham in Latin may have picked up resonances that were occluded in the English *Forerunner*. In one case W.W. faced a choice about how to translate the Latin word "veneficus", which could mean both "witch" and "poisoner", a confusion that neatly captured the ancient cultural associations between the two. In his translation of a passage where Eglisham talked of the risks he faced, W.W. wrote "What hopes then is left for your so humble suppliant, that his complaint should be heard, or if heard to be vindicated? to despaier of obtaininge iustice, to provoke the duke to send away a *Witch* or a cut throat in killinge him." In the official translation, Eglisham worried that he would "provoke the Duke to send forth a *poysoner* or other murtherer". Either translation works with the Latin; W.W.'s choice, however, underlined the charges made elsewhere in *The Forerunner* that Buckingham was allied with the servants of Satan.[69] In another case, W.W.'s translation made greater sense—or, at least, a different sense—than the official version. Eglisham claimed to have good reason to suspect his own life was in danger, because his name had appeared on a mysterious list of Buckingham's intended victims. According to the official translation, Eglisham's name was "set downe next to the Marquis of Hamilton in these wordes, (*The Marquis of Hamilton and Doctor Eglisham to embawme him*)", a phrase that at first glance seems not to threaten Eglisham but to imply that, as Hamilton's doctor, he would embalm the marquis's corpse. W.W.'s translation, however, made the note a direct threat: the doctor was "placed in the calender of those nobles to be killed next unto the Marquesse Hamilton, in such words . . . 'Marq Ham & Dr Eglisham to be embalmed'".[70]

Perhaps the most interesting variant came with W.W.'s rendering of "amasius" to describe Buckingham's relationship to the king. The official English translation rendered "amasius" as "favorite", but classical usage typically had "amasius" denote a lover, and W.W. followed the ancient sources. When Eglisham argued that Buckingham had implanted suspicions of Hamilton in James's mind, the English version of his text noted that "if any other had done it, he [James] would have acquainted his favorite therewith". W.W. rendered this as "if any else had done it the King would have communicated it unto his Paramour". A little later, W.W. reminded the reader that Hamilton had aided Buckingham's political career by advising the king "not to give free accesse to new Paramours", a phrase rendered in the official translation as "keeping the King from giving way to introduce any other favorite".[71] W.W.'s translation suggests that Latin readers had access to a sharper, more sexualized characterization of the king–favourite relationship than appeared in the printed English translation.

Our survey of the ways in which scribal reproduction could introduce significant variants into the text reveals just how malleable Eglisham's tract could be. Our next chapters explore appropriations of Eglisham's secret history on a much broader scale, analyzing how the poisoning charges against Buckingham were reproduced and exploited during the sustained political crisis that lasted from the end of the 1626 Parliament until the duke's assassination in August 1628. Throughout this crisis, Eglisham's allegations continued to circulate in the English literary underground. They were also reworked in other underground texts—pamphlets printed on the Continent and verse libels written at home—and they were articulated in a broad range of popular political discourses—libellous speech, seditious words and panicked rumour. During this period the favourite and his crimes remained the primary focus of critique, with the image of "Buckingham the poisoner" neatly connected to the duke's other alleged transgressions. But at the same time we can also glimpse uneasily repressed anxieties about the possible part that Charles I had played in his father's death.

CHAPTER FOURTEEN

REAPING THE WHIRLWIND

RADICAL TALK AND THE PROBLEM OF JUSTICE

IN THE LETTER accompanying the copy of *The Forerunner* he sold to Sir John Scudamore, Ralph Starkey mentioned another rare and possibly dangerous piece of writing. "Since my last", Starkey wrote:

> there is come to my hands The Apparance of the goast of Edward the second kinge of England, It is com to warne the tymes of his misfortunes havinge ben misled by Gavaston and others: it is written in verse verie ellegant full of stade [state?] and storie of that tyme, not common stuffe, but much observacon of Record . . . I will presume to saye you never Readd a better pennd thinge and fuller of observacion, and that which is not common.

The poem would not be cheap—its 581 seven-line stanzas would consume "a quire & halfe of paper", some three dozen pages.[1]

Sir Francis Hubert, a former royal official long since retired to his country seat, had first drafted the poem in Elizabeth's reign, and then expanded it during James's. In the mid-1620s the poem leaked into the literary underground, becoming a high-end scribal separate traded by men like Starkey. In 1628 a stationer used these manuscript copies to print two issues of the poem, forcing Hubert to produce an authorized revised version in 1629.[2] It is clear why Starkey thought the poem worth Scudamore's investment, for it narrated the rebellions against a notoriously weak English monarch dominated by his favourites, and meditated on the role that divine providence, fortune and political skill played in the fall of kings.[3] Although the poet explicitly denied comparing Edward II or his favourites to their contemporary analogues, Hubert's readers could hardly help doing so. Aware of the risks involved in drawing too close a parallel, Hubert insisted that, for all Edward's horrific failings, the rebels who overthrew him had acted illegitimately; a good subject's only legitimate response to royal misrule was patience.

Released into public circulation in 1626, Hubert's bootlegged poem reinforced many elements of the secret history's portrayal of Buckingham, while at the same time drawing attention to questions *The Forerunner* awkwardly repressed.[4] Whereas Eglisham refrained from direct criticism of King James and King Charles, Hubert made Edward II's responsibility for his favourites' corruption fully explicit. The poem emphasized Edward's inability to control his passions, a failure that "makes a slave even of an Emperor/If once they growe to get the upper hand".[5] Seduced by Piers Gaveston's outward charms, Edward became his favourite's slave, leaving him "at the Helme" to steer "the Sterne at pleasure", while Edward received an education in tyranny and sexual dissolution.[6] Hubert's Gaveston matched Eglisham's Buckingham in several ways. Like Eglisham, Hubert thought that too rapid a social and political ascent was intrinsically dangerous. Kings could raise "such as they please", but they should do so cautiously, always weighing the favourite's ascent against the aspirations of other ambitious men and the rights of established families. And any recipient of royal favour had to be worthy. "Gaveston unworthily was grac'd", Hubert asserted, "And made too great a monster, huge and vaste,/Who in his growth being unproportionall,/Became offensive to himselfe and all." Instead of heeding the plain-speaking counsel of his peers, instead of distributing reward among the many rather than the few, Edward became subject to the "oyled Tongue" of the flattering favourite. The results were disastrous. With the king "suncke in sinne and drown'd in lust", the favourite "almost wrackt the Realme". The noble revolt that resulted in Gaveston's death failed to solve the problem, for Edward remained a slave to his "affections", following "no Law but will", and he was soon in thrall to a new pair of overweening favourites—the Spencers, father and son, men of "ambition" and "swelling spirit".[7]

Hubert's parallels could expose how much Buckingham's corrupt rule owed to the moral failings of James and Charles. And like Eglisham, Hubert insisted that a prince's security depended above all on the execution of justice. None:

> shall invent a better way,
> By which a Prince may with assurance raigne,
> Then to be truly iust.

A good king must punish his subordinates' misdeeds, lest "you make their wickednesse, your owne,/By suffering them to sinne, without controule".[8] But what if royal justice shirked its God-given responsibilities? This question worried both Eglisham and Hubert, and after the 1626 Parliament the Edwardian dilemma of justice denied spoke very clearly to Caroline readers. Yet whatever the ruler's misdeeds, Hubert would not justify taking up arms to remedy wrongs. God eventually overthrew Gaveston, the Spencers and the king, but the human agents of this revolt, the rebellious barons, were guilty of "foule treason":

Ev'n wicked Kings must be endur'd by us.
What ere the cause be, Treason is a sinne:
. . .
The Sword is not the Subiects: his defence,
In all extremes, is prayer and patience.[9]

The Parliament-men of 1626 had turned to the medieval past for guidance in dealing with Buckingham. Hubert's poem about a weak ruler dominated by his favourites and deposed by rebels, offered particularly disturbing precedents for the dangerous political questions that the thwarted assault on Buckingham had already raised. Yet Hubert declined to embrace the most radical solutions, diagnosing profound political corruption but refusing to endorse resistance. Throughout 1626 many of his contemporaries wrestled with troubling questions about a murderous favourite and a misled king, about justice denied and providential anger, and about the practice and ethics of resistance and extra-judicial execution. These debates surfaced in musings on prodigious weather, in scabrous verse libels, seditious speech and popular street unrest, in disturbing news reports and in yet more Flemish mischief-making. Although the regime worked hard to close down critics and criticism, it could neither curtail the circulation of Eglisham's pamphlet nor shut down the widespread debate it aroused. The 1626 dissolution of Parliament was the key turning point of Charles's young reign. Frustrated in their desire for justice and convinced of Buckingham's role in James's murder, many of Charles's subjects engaged in disillusioned and seditious talk. Much of this talk has passed historians by; but by eavesdropping on this chatter, we can trace in often startling detail the capacity of elite and plebeian English men and women to engage in radical political thought.

Tempest

At about three in the afternoon of Monday, 12 June 1626, "a fearful storm of hail, rain, lightning, and thunder" descended on London.[10] The deluge was startling. Water ran through the city streets "like channels of rivers", cellars flooded, and so much hail fell that the great "heapes" of it took more than two days to melt. The storm, thought one witness, was "the greateste shower of rayne and hayle, that ever any livinge man sawe". For about an hour it fell with such "violence" that many thought the city had been struck by "an Earthquake". "The like hath seldome bene seene", another contemporary noted, "and much hurt done thereby". The storm brought down parts of several churchyard walls, and at St Andrew's in Holborn and St Botolph's near Bishopsgate "the force of the storme" tore coffins loose from their graves. Under the pressure of the flood water, some coffins "burste . . . in peeces", tumbling the "dead corpes" out into view, and reports spoke of dead bodies swimming "up and downe" the streets and washing into ditches. Edmund Howes assured his readers that the unearthed dead were "with all speed . . . taken up, and new buried", but John Rushworth described how curiosity got the better of "the ruder sort", who "would ordinarily lift up the lids of the Coffins to see the posture of the dead Corps lying therein, who had been buried of the Plague but the year before".[11]

But the flooding, hail and washed-out graves that "terrible monday" paled in comparison to the "strange spectacle" that appeared on the Thames near Whitehall. Among the astonished spectators were "many very great courtiers, who beheld it out of their windows" and numerous Parliament-men who watched "out of the windows of the House".[12] So startling was the sight that witnesses grasped for words to describe it: a "tempest whirling", "a cartaract or bursting of a cloud (which seamen call a spout)", "a whirlpoole" that caused "the water to seethe and boyle", a "whirlwind of water", a "whirlwater", a "water-pillar".[13] It began with a troubling of the water at Lambeth that sent a sculler's boat spinning out of control. As the water continued to churn, it appeared to become "very much rarified like a mist" and then "began to rise into the form of a circle", forming what appeared to be a "whirlwind of water". Some estimated it at 10 feet high and 30 yards in circumference, while others compared it to "a stacke of haye . . . mounted alofte as high as a steeple" or thought it "as big as a colly [coal] barge". The whirlwind looked hollow at the core, and the water that comprised its exterior was "much condensed, and very black". Enveloped in mist, the whirlwind of water began to move, initially heading eastwards along the south bank of the Thames before "very impetuously" shooting across the river "like an arrow shot", glancing against the stairs at Whitehall Palace before crashing against the walls, gate and stairs of Buckingham's residence at York House. The collision at the York House watergate "broke" open the whirlwind of water, which appeared then to dissolve into a "thick", "great and gross" smoke that spun around like the fumes belched from a brewer's chimney, "ascending as high as a man could discern".[14] One reporter described the astonishing violence of the collision: "itt strocke upon the garden walles with a great force, and mounted it self as highe as an house and soe went over the walles and broake some cherrie trees, and from thence ascended upp into the ayre in a twyninge manner and soe vanished away lyke smoake".[15]

The "strange spectacle" shocked contemporaries, who struggled to explain it. Some thought it a freakish natural phenomenon, but others detected supernatural forces at work. And as they argued about what had happened, they found themselves talking parliamentary politics. The tempest's timing seemed significant—it happened the Monday following the king's final ultimatum to the refractory Commons and three days before the dissolution—and the whirlwind's location on the Thames alongside Whitehall and Westminster seemed equally pregnant with significance. But it was the storm's apparent focus on Buckingham's grand London mansion that fascinated observers. The whirlwind of water had launched a spectacular assault on the York House gardens, gate and stairs, all of them projections of the favourite's wealth and authority. For many this suggested that the storm was a sign—a supernatural political message—targeting Buckingham.

Fascinated by prodigies and portents, Joseph Mead collected accounts of the Thames whirlwind from two London friends who struggled for the correct terminology to describe what they believed was a natural, if freakish, event: one settled on "whirlwind of water", while the other reported that "it is not yet certain" whether this "meteor" was a "turbo, cataract, thunderstorm, or mass of crusty matter", although the great smoke that appeared at York House inclined him to the latter option. Both correspondents realized that this debate over classification and interpretation had political stakes. One confessed that "those that will be wise" call it "the whirlwind of water", "for you must not say it is prodigious"; the other concluded that "I leave you to judge what it was in nature, *ne quid dicam prodigii*".[16]

Others were unafraid to classify the tempest a prodigy, a warning from God putting Englishmen on notice that unless the nation's sins were rectified, further divine chastisements were guaranteed. Some discerned a pattern, linking the tempest to sightings of the Devil and "balls of fire" in Ireland, or to the prodigious discovery of two sixteenth-century religious works inside a fish sold at a Cambridge market, or to recent accounts of a "great noyse" heard at a well in Oundle known "to roare ag[ainst] great events". Preaching to Parliament in April 1628, Jeremiah Dyke argued that God always warned of His "wrath, and iudgements comming" through "prodigious signes, and strange wonders", and that England had to take heed: "God gave us warning in that wonder of the doubled tydes in the river of Thames. God gave us warning in that Earth-quake March 27. 1626. God gave us faire warning in that prodigious storme in the Citie, that fetcht the dead bodies out of their graves: together with that stupendious sight uppon the water."[17]

It was possible to interpret the tempest as a prodigy without being certain what was being foretold or what sins had angered God. "What all this will prognosticate", wrote one man, "god himselfe knoweth and not man." But prodigies usually signalled divine displeasure with something in the polity or the Church. Others read the crashing of the water-pillar into York House not as a warning of providential punishments to come but as a more direct divine rebuke, a providential judgement clearly directed at Buckingham. "There was a tempest whirling", a diarist noted, and it "did light upon" York House. "Everybody", he added, "took it as a judgment against the D." The diarist linked the judgement to the decision, reportedly made by king and favourite "that very day in the afternoone", to break up the Parliament.[18] But it was clearly possible to read the tempest's assault on York House as a more general divine rebuke for the duke's offences catalogued by Eglisham and the Parliament-men. Eglisham had called on God to help him uncover Buckingham's crimes and to urge Charles to carry out justice; God, speaking through a whirlwind of water, had warned of the consequences of leaving justice undone.

Instead of seeing God's hand in the tempest, others had more unnerving supernatural explanations. In Oxford, Thomas Crosfield noted "Newes of a strange tempest & apparitions from London", and reports of strange "apparitions" circulated alongside the more naturalistic descriptions of the storm. Henry Wicliffe reported the "extreme thunder lightning and raine" that had torn coffins and corpses from the graveyards, adding that "it was saide that there was a spirit at the same time seene upon the waters, which did sore affright all the beholders."[19] Some reporters gave these apparitions and spirits a demonological gloss—they were the works of demonic forces, harnessed by witchcraft. In these narratives the duke was less the target of divine wrath than the ally of satanic agents wreaking havoc on the Thames. The same diarist who thought that everyone read the whirlwind as a judgement upon the duke later added news of rumours "that a gentleman should be pillor[ie]d for saying one of the D[uke's] divills did arise at the tempill upon the thunder on the tempestuous Monday". John Rushworth later recalled that the whirlwind "occasioned the more discourse among the Vulgar, in that Doctor Lamb appeared then upon Thames, to whose Art of Conjuring they attributed that which had happened".[20] Eglisham had shocked readers with his claims about Buckingham's relationships with Lambe, the ringleader of the witches, and with the skilled mountebank who made poisons capable of killing at preset times. The demonic interpretation of the York House tempest suggests that some contemporaries took the duke's demonization very literally. Indeed, after the dissolution of Parliament, Buckingham's connection to Lambe appeared increasingly in discourse about the duke. On 11 November 1626, Mead reported "a scurvy book come forth, called *The Devil and the Duke*", whose appearance caused "much inquisition"—whether by the authorities or by interested customers—at the bookshops around St Paul's. No copies survive, but its title suggests that the book linked the favourite with his witches. Some months earlier the Venetian ambassador, Alvise Contarini, despairing of Charles's ability to perceive the "confusion" at large in his realm, had reported that "the credulous vulgar maintain" that Buckingham had "bewitched" the king.[21]

The supernatural readings of the tempest thus provided three equally uncomfortable lessons. They confirmed the royal favourite's close alliance with the servants of Satan, they made God's displeasure with the duke strikingly evident, and they made startlingly clear the high price of forestalling justice's righteous vengeance upon the murderous favourite.

To Unduke the Wanton Duke

"The King and his wyfe the Parliament/are parted both in discontent", mused one angry contemporary. He had a bawdily caustic explanation for what had happened. Initially, the poet blamed Buckingham and "his faction". Drawing on the rich vein of sexual libel that had dogged the duke since the early 1620s, the poet imagined the favourite as "Englands wanton Duke", a sexual predator who had attempted to "rape" the king's wife, the Parliament, by trying to "robbe her of her antient right". This attempted rape exposed not only the favourite's wilfulness but also ripped apart the militant Protestant image that Buckingham had so carefully cultivated since 1624. The only precedent for the duke's actions, the poet mused, was Guy Fawkes's plot to blow up Parliament in 1605. If Fawkes had succeeded in setting off "his vessell/of Sulphure" in Parliament's "sepul-chrall walks", he "Could not have soe disperst our state,/Nor opened Spayne soe wyde a gate,/as hath his gracelesse grace". Buckingham was thus Spain's engine, a regicidal papist, and "till time comes which is at hand,/that all speake Spanish in our land,/We are bound to curse his face". But his sexual debauchery offered some hope of deliverance, for Buckingham had syphilis—"the Pox", "A hungry Mounsieur that will eate,/his joyntes". This disease exemplified the duke's personal and political corruption—his body was rotting with pox just as the kingdom was rotting under his misrule—and tarred him with the charge of popish foreignness: an engine of Spain, the duke was undone by the French, who had sent "her Countryman the Pox" to afflict him.

But the problem was not just the duke. Charles had been separated from Parliament by Buckingham's faction, "those that with the Duke combinde"—the Earls of Holland, Carlisle and Dorset, Viscount Wimbledon, and Lords Carleton and Conway. As individuals they were worthless: Holland was an "effeminate . . . vile worm", Carlisle a spendthrift, Dorset a man of "nimble tongue". But their collective ascent revealed how Buckingham controlled the kingdom by elevating his faction to positions of power. Holland will "all Englands Lords surmount", and Conway, Wimbledon and Dorset "May look without a bribe,/To have in Court the cheifest graces,/and in the state the highest places/next the Villerian tribe". This new court elite, like the Villerian tribe, were made of "base mettle" and would, in a redolent image stolen from Walter Ralegh, "shine like rotten wood".

The poet's language replicated Eglisham and the Parliament-men's indictments of Buckingham's misrule, and like the other critics, the poet had to confront the thorny issue of royal culpability. Initially, he appeared to excuse the king, but by the poem's midway point, Charles's steadfast defence of his favourite had raised increasingly uncomfortable questions. "Say what you will", the poet wrote, but Buckingham's "foote is fast", for "the kinge will nere rebuke him/but love him dearely". The only way for Charles to separate himself from Buckingham's stain was to surrender the duke to justice: To "withdraw from him his grace,/he knowes he must unduke him./Which he may not unlesse he make/him lower by the head." But since Charles would not act, the libeller engaged in ever more dangerous speculations. Dreaming daringly, if obliquely, of a new king, the poet mused that Charles could leave his throne to his brother-in-law, the Elector Palatine, but for now the king seemed intent on giving his kingdoms "to his minion". As for "Turner, Eliot, and Digges", the patriots who spoke out against Buckingham, they shall "scourged be like whirlegigges". The libel ended by praying for the king's reconciliation with Parliament, a reconciliation only possible on the Parliament-men's terms. The Commons "may helpe" the king "to monye", but only if "he will heare her most just groanes/and chase from him those busy droanes/That eate up all the hony."[22] The duke must die, and the Villerian tribe must be destroyed.

Desperate Speeches on Drury Lane

Similarly dissident sentiments surfaced in popular political discourse. In July 1626, John Brown, a Suffolk churchwarden, exclaimed that "it woulde never be good worlde till he that is so gratious with the kinge the Duke of Buckenham be cutt off which he did hoope woulde not be longe". The following month an informant in Ipswich alerted Buckingham's secretary to a local minister who had:

> used some passedge or phrase of speeche that the kingdom hade need to pray and that all things ded not prosper soe well as formerly hathe done and that thay might see bie the breaking up of the parlament that thear some thinge was done bie a great person to be the means for the desolving of it which if it wear or shood prove a dishonor to god he wisht and desired that God woold cutt him off in tyme.

A local preacher who had had his own run-ins with the Privy Council tried to protect his colleague, insisting that the words were too general and the speaker too insignificant to take seriously, but acknowledged that Ipswich was plagued with "vulgar rumors" about the duke, as well as "some muttering & privy whispering".[23]

It is not clear how seriously the Council or the duke took these reports, but in early November 1626 they paid careful attention to a case brought to them by Henry and Dorothy Manners, a married couple from Cheswick in Durham. Two or three weeks earlier the couple had dined in Drury Lane with John Brangston, the tailor with whom they were lodging in London. Joining them at the table was a "countryman" of Dorothy Manners, one Thomas Brediman (also spelled Bridiman or Brodeman), a soldier "borne at Barwick". Over supper, Brediman began to make what the Privy Council would later classify as "desperate and seditious speeches". Both Henry and Dorothy Manners testifed that Brediman had warned that they would all soon see an armed insurrection, "a shew of souldiers" in London against Buckingham and "against the king alsoe". According to Dorothy, he had complained that "the king was so much ruled by the Duke"; according to Henry, Brediman had stated that "it was a shame that one unworthy man should have all the cheife offices in the Commonwealth." In response, Henry had asserted that God would thwart any "unlawful courses" and deliver the duke if he were "innocent", and he reminded Brediman of the Earl of Essex's revolt in 1601, for which he was "overthrowne and perished". Brediman replied that Essex's revolt had not angered God but that the earl "was a foole" for allowing the City to bar the gates on him. Brediman then added that "the auncient men's councells are refused, and Justice had not lawfull proceeding, and that papists encreased and grew bold, unto whom it is held the duke of Buckingham is a greate patron". Brediman grew increasingly reckless. He asserted "that if the State stood as it doth it would not continue long", and when asked what would become of the kingdom, speculated that maybe "it shall bee a free State", adding "perhaps the Palatine and the Lady Elizabeth shall have it". When Brangston's wife warned Brediman that such talk would "cost him his eares", he replied that "if it cost him his eares" there "would be a great manie lost besides". Warned by his companions "to forbeare speaking", Brediman answered that he "tooke God to witnes that hee spake not out of mallice to the duke or any body, but out of his Love that hee wished the State, the land and the people".[24]

Working from the Manners's testimony, Secretary Coke compiled questions for Brediman, demanding information not only about the supper on Drury Lane but also about the alleged "conspiracie or sedition". It is highly unlikely that Brediman knew of any real plans to assault the duke. Far from any actual plot, his words document a fantasy generated by Buckingham's recent escape from justice. But these speeches also reveal the real pressure that the duke's continued favour placed upon ingrained habits of obedience, and how much the king's protection of Buckingham had alienated Charles's subjects. Brediman's talk of a "free state" under the Elector Palatine, for instance, reveals a quite ordinary man thinking outside the norms of English monarchical government—just as, Brediman suggested, "a great manie" others were doing. Furthermore, the conversation exposed how polarized contemporary perceptions of the political landscape had become. Brediman had asked his host whether, in the event of an uprising, "hee would bee for the king or the Country". Although Brangston admitted "a while after" that he would be for the king, his initial response was an intriguing one: "hee had", he confessed, "bin asked that question before".[25]

According to the witnesses, Brediman had begun talking insurrection after Mrs Brangston described some militia men marching down Drury Lane. Brediman may have had in mind other recent, and far less comforting, sightings of soldiers in London. Through the summer and autumn of 1626, bands of soldiers and sailors had marauded in the capital demanding unpaid wages and threatening violence against those they held responsible for their mistreatment.

In mid-August a group of twenty sailors had stopped Buckingham's coach in the street, forcing him to give them "fair words" and empty promises. In October, 150 veterans of the Cadiz expedition reportedly "attacked the duke's coach with bludgeons, while he was sitting in Council, smashing and destroying it utterly"; other reports spoke of a "tumultuous demanding of their pay" and great "insolence, attacking . . . the carriage and servants of the Duke of Buckingham". "The duke", one newsletter reported, "was so hotly encountered by the sailors . . . that he was since fain to get a guard about his house." The king and Council reacted by distributing small sums of money to the crowd, by mobilizing the London-trained bands to mount "guard at the Court" and "safe-guard the gates of the duke's palaces", and by issuing a proclamation forbidding soldiers and mariners, under pain of death, from "disorderly resorting to the city of London in companies". Yet a sense of menace remained. One Londoner described an uneasy encounter with a group of men walking noisily in the street who claimed "they had been with the duke, for money, and they should have it, they said, when the devil was blind on both eyes"—in other words, never.[26]

In late November, defying the proclamation, the protesting soldiers returned. A group of six captains were reported to have "entered forcibly into the duke's chamber at Whitehall as he sat at dinner, and told him they so long served the king without any pay, and were cast [off] without any pay at all, that it was not wont to be the use of his majesty's predecessors, nor of any prince in the world besides". When the duke reminded them of the proclamation, they replied that "if they were hanged, there were more others to be hanged with them for company, and from this proceeded to such uncouth language, as his excellency was fain to yield, and to promise them upon his honour they should very speedily be satisfied." The city bands were once more mobilized, and "companies of veteran soldiers" set "to watch" the protestors "and to repress any tumult which may take place". The proclamation was reissued, arrests were made, and once again, some money was found to disperse the protestors.[27]

Like many contemporary crowd actions, these protests were, in effect, violent negotiations. Property or symbolic objects were assaulted, individuals were confronted, demands were made, and threats of further violence were levelled. The authorities responded with small, targeted concessions, accompanied by a show of force and an attempt to reimpose order. It was a precarious dance that constantly risked escalation into something more serious. During the autumn of 1626 the regime contained the protests, but it could not end them. And, as some contemporaries noted, the small financial concessions merely encouraged the protesters to return.[28] When the protests resumed in February 1627, significantly greater numbers were involved, and the violence, both real and threatened, acquired additional menace. Guards again patrolled Whitehall and watched outside Buckingham's houses, but the attacks escalated, with mobs of soldiers and sailors now "insulting" the coaches of anyone they believed "to be dependent on the favourite", forcing the passengers to pay off their attackers on the spot. The attacks on coaches escalated to the smashing of windows, and some warned of riots planned for the traditional Shrovetide festival of misrule. The protests continued to work within an idiom of loyalty to the Crown, focusing their hostility on Buckingham, not the king. On 1 February some sailors massed outside Whitehall, but dispersed once the king promised them redress if they would reassemble near the Tower. Charles's intervention produced symbolic gestures of loyalty—hats flung in the air and cries of "God Save King Charles"—but not complete satisfaction. The sailors proceeded to Tower Hill, where they performed some theatre of their own. A boy perched on the Tower scaffold issued a mock proclamation announcing that the king had "promised them their pay in that place on the morrow". But "if they had it not then, they made known that the duke should lose his head there" the day after.[29]

Thomas Brediman's fantasy of armed insurrection to execute justice upon the duke, and perhaps also on the king, may have been one contemporary's response to the underlying logic of the protests that brought angry soldiers and sailors into London's streets. Indeed, according to Dorothy Manners, Brediman had mentioned during his anti-Buckingham tirade that already "the marriners came about his Coach". The protests almost certainly encouraged the authorities to take the Brediman case seriously. The Privy Council ordered Secretary Coke to interrogate him, and the Lord Chief Justice and Attorney General to frame a prosecution. The reactions to Brediman's arrest and prosecution reveal a widespread mood of anxiety. "The bold speakers", one letter reported early in November, were now being rounded up. "Captain Brodeman", it continued, was sent to the Gatehouse prison "for speaking more than his part; and, if he be not saved by twelve men, he may have liberty, perhaps, to speak his mind in his last confession. I must not repeat his words, but himself is taught better manners, to put a greater difference hereafter betwixt a duke and a king." By the end of the month it was "generally spoken" in London that Brediman had been taken from the Gatehouse to the Tower, where he had died under torture. Joseph Mead was sceptical: "Captain Brodeman hath been racked", he told Martin Stuteville, "but I cannot hear it confirmed by any other that he died upon the rack, and therefore I think it untrue, and my author deceived."[30] In February 1627, Brediman, still alive but suffering in both spirit and body after "100 days in a Dungon", petitioned Secretary Conway for his release, insisting he had spoken "in Drinke" or in "a Dreame" and thus "Deprived of sences". Only in September was he let go.[31]

"The king", Thomas Brediman had claimed, was "ruled by the duke". "Your majestie," George Eglisham had fretted, "suffereth your selfe so farre to be led" by Buckingham "that your best subiects ar in doubt, whether he is your King or you his". This fundamental fear—that the king's creature had become his master—remained at the heart of anti-Buckingham discourse.[32] Mead's letters repeatedly returned to the problem. Late in 1626 he reported that Charles's lavish entertainment at York House had caused some to "prate that his majesty is in very great favour with the duke's grace". Early in February 1627 he wrote anxiously to Stuteville, "Will you believe that the duke should be carried in his box by six men to St. James's to tennis, and the king walk by him on foot? It is true. I doubt not", he added, "but you have heard of the play in Christmas, which was begun again at the duke's entering, the king having heard one full act". These tales of inversion—of symbolic gestures that made the duke into the king's superior—were so unnerving that the man who had sent them to Mead had written his account in invisible ink; Mead had to hold the bottom of the letter near the fire "till it grew brown" before he could decipher the news. Unsurprisingly, he warned Stuteville that he "thought not fit" to make this news "so common as the rest".[33]

The Marquis of Hamilton's Discontents

There was also troubling news from Scotland. In 1626 the twenty-year-old Marquis of Hamilton stood near the apex of power; a leading noble in both England and Scotland, a cousin of King Charles and the nephew by marriage of the Duke of Buckingham, he was one of the kingdoms' most important men. But he was crippled by his debts, and neither the king nor the favourite could spare the funds to ease his woes. As Hamilton grumbled to the Earl of Morton, though he knew that "tymes are so harde with all our nasion", he was tired of being "put of with delayes".[34] By late 1626 the pressure from his creditors was too much and Hamilton fled from England to Scotland, leaving his thirteen-year-old bride behind. The Earl of Carlisle chided him for abandoning "your noble lady" who "languisheth for your returne"; and like others at court, Carlisle was awkwardly aware that Hamilton's marriage remained unconsummated. He no doubt also sensed that the absence from court of the king's cousin was a potential embarrassment to the Crown. Hamilton's estrangement from the English court was further complicated by the 1625 Act of Resumption, by which Charles had ordered Scottish aristocrats to surrender royal or church land grants made since 1566 for review and possible re-grant. Charles expected Hamilton to "give good example unto others" and "be one of the first there who shall signe the submission", and he promised him compensation. But the marquis had no inclination to be "one of those that should come first on the stage".[35]

Buckingham alternately chided and cajoled his nephew to return, but money remained a sticking point. Buckingham was "greved that att this present there is not so much monie to be had as will be fitting to satisfie your creditors", but promised ample rewards if Hamilton returned to court, while Charles insisted that "the more freelie you give way to what which may import our good wee will deale with you".[36] Hamilton remained obdurate, neglecting routine royal business, and when, early in 1628, his father-in-law, the Earl of Denbigh, rode north to coax him back to Whitehall, he decided to stay north of the Tweed.[37] Hamilton's brother, the Earl of Arran, made clear the family's financial predicament, explaining to Buckingham "how the burthings that now ly so heavie upon me wer first contracted by my father (comeing to court at your desire) and since his death augmented by my stay". And Hamilton himself refused to ride south unless either the king "performe some of those promis long sins maid to me" or Buckingham "take so fatherly caire to see me spedely relieved of the heavie burthengs which without your help will make me to sink".[38]

Those close to events knew the real reasons for Hamilton's absence, but those outside the court, with George Eglisham to guide them, placed a far more sinister construction on the young man's flight north. After all, according to *The Forerunner*, Buckingham had poisoned Hamilton's father in a dispute over the young marquis's marriage to the duke's niece. One London newsletter reported that Hamilton had left court "discontented and with a purpose to return no more, because his pension is taken from him, for that he would never conde-scend to lie with his wife"; a later account alleged that the pension had been suspended "to make him the more willing to be persuaded to bed his wife . . . which he refused to do, though the duke, they say, brought her to him to that end". One ambassador reported "The vulgar say that he is disgusted with his wife, that he will have nothing more to do with her, and will not return to court."[39]

The widespread sympathy for a husband who refused to perform his patri-archal duties was strange enough, but rumour also connected the incident to the broader crisis in the new king's relationship with his Scottish elite. The Venetian ambassador Alvise Contarini heard that Hamilton's chief grievance was "the annexation . . . of Church property to the crown", and reported that "people in general blame the king for allowing so great a personage to depart while affairs are in their present state and discontent at its zenith." Some even predicted armed Scottish resistance, perhaps with Hamilton at its head. A diarist noted that the marquis had "speeded into Scotland" out of "distast between [him] & the Duke" and had written a letter defying the favourite. "A rumer was", the diarist continued, that the "Scottish lords had bought up all the horse in the north parts of England, as if they would make some hurliburleyes." In Dorchester, William Whiteway noted that Hamilton, "being discontent with the Duke of Buckingham, rode post into Scotland, and standeth upon his guard."[40]

Some suggested that these angry Scottish nobles would also demand an inquiry into the deaths of Hamilton's father, the Duke of Lennox and King James. These rumours began in the summer of 1626, as talk spread that the Scottish Privy Council was pressing Charles to call a Parliament. The Venetians thought the intended Parliament would be "certain to institute an enquiry about the deaths of the late king, the Dukes of Richmond and Lennox, and the Marquis of Hamilton, all with the object of attacking Buckingham." Mead reported in

July that "They of Scotland cry out amain of the Duke of Buckingham, saying they will know how King James, the Duke of Lennox, the Marquis of Hamilton, came to their end." And in late October the Venetian ambassador thought that young Hamilton had demanded "an inquest upon his father's death, which is generally attributed to poison". Two months later, he heard that several delegations of leading Scotsmen were riding to London to seek an audience with the king, allegedly "requesting inquests about the deaths of the late king, the Dukes of Lennox and Richmond, and the Marquis of Hamilton, which are generally supposed to have been caused by poison". The ambassador regarded this as a very serious charge, already "in print, being published at Cologne by one Eglinton, a Scotch physician". The allegations, "fiercely maintained" in the last Parliament's assault on Buckingham, left Charles little room for manoeuvre, lest he be accused of lacking "filial affection" for James and "paternal love" for his subjects.[41]

Nothing suggests that any of the Scots who came to court in December 1626 and January 1627 demanded an inquest into Eglisham's charges. It is possible that Charles's concessions on the Act of Resumption mollified the Scots elite, who no longer needed the poisoning allegations as leverage against the king. It is also possible that the rumours reflected English anxieties, not Scottish agendas. After Buckingham's 1628 assassination, Hamilton would return at last to Whitehall, where he was granted the duke's office of Master of the Horse and a significantly enhanced pension. These rewards came at a price. "To satisfy his majesty's pleasure", Jean Beaulieu reported, the marquis was "forced from the first night, though much against his will, to take his bed with his young wife." The king, Mead heard, had lent Hamilton a "shirt, waistcoat, and nightcap", sent his own barber to freshen up his road-weary kinsman, and "would not be satisfied till he had seen them both in bed together".[42]

Hamilton's re-absorption into Charles's inner circle did not end Scottish talk of the murders of King James and other Scottish nobles. Eglisham had claimed a particular Scottish interest in seeing justice done on Buckingham, informing Charles that *The Forerunner*'s case would "serve for . . . a whitstone to me and many other Scotsmen". The possible revival of Eglisham's charges among the Scots in 1626–27 suggests that those charges did have a particular purchase north of the border, especially during what its leading historian has termed the "disruptive and difficult opening phase" of Charles's Scottish kingship.[43] As we shall see, a distinctively Scottish appropriation of Eglisham's secret history would remain one of the defining features of the allegations' many afterlives.

"Le Favorit d'Angleterre"

North and south of the border, Charles I's failure to see justice done on his favourite provoked discontent. Some hoped that God would follow through on the prodigious warning He had hurled at York House on "terrible Monday". Some Scots may have hoped for judicial hearings to pick up where Parliament had left off. Others, like Thomas Brediman, fantasized about armed revolt, deposition and a free state. But the Habsburg propaganda machine, which had helped put the secret history into print, was also quick to capitalize on the damage Eglisham and the Parliament-men had inflicted on the duke. The *Mercure François* reported that, in the wake of Bristol's charges against Buckingham, copies of the earl's "Articles" were printed and published in diverse languages on the Continent, and that this publication was seconded by "some who carried from Flanders into England a pamphlet entitled, '*Le Favorit d'Angleterre, dedié au Duc de Bucquingham*'"—"The English Favourite, dedicated to the Duke of Buckingham".[44] No English copies or translations of this pamphlet appear to have survived, and it is possible the attack was directed primarily at French readers, whether in France or among the francophone elites in Flanders, Holland and London. But, as the Flemish sequel to *The Forerunner*, the pamphlet demands consideration. Like Hubert's poem, it allowed contemporaries to use the rise and fall of Edward II and his favourites to interpret Buckingham's career. But to a greater extent than Hubert, this tract defended the possibility of radical political action to bring a corrupt favourite and his tyrannical king to justice.

As the *Mercure* recognized, *Le Favorit d'Angleterre*, a twenty-page quarto with a fake Paris imprint, was a reworked version of a notorious 1588 pamphlet issued shortly after the radical Catholic League seized control of Paris from Henri III.[45] This *Histoire Tragique et Memorable, de Pierre de Gaverston Gentilhomme gascon iadis le mignon d'Edouard 2. Roy d'Angleterre* was "dedicated" to Henri's much-hated favourite, the Duc d'Épernon. The original version, written by the Parisian Ligueur Jean Boucher, had included a prefatory epistle spelling out the parallels between Épernon's "nationality, family, character, counsels, tricks and artifices, fortunes and actions" and those of Piers Gaveston—and warning that Épernon, like Gaveston, and all those who abused royal favour and oppressed the people, would meet a disgraceful end.[46] The epistle was cut from the 1626 reworking, but the mock dedication "to Monseigneur the duke of Buckingham", like the 1588 dedication to Épernon, invited the reader to identify parallels between the two favourites and between the monarchs they served. Although most of Boucher's ultra-Catholic polemic was cut, his critique of corrupt favouritism still had significant purchase.[47] But the new target, and the new context, also generated resonances and critiques specific to the 1620s.

Much of the pamphlet's portrait of Gaveston conformed to Eglisham's depiction of Buckingham as an upstart whose arrogance and ambition led him to disdain the traditional aristocracies of blood, sword and virtue. Governed solely by his appetites, "*l'ennemy public*" corrupted justice, consumed the kingdom's wealth, betrayed the nation, violated the law, sowed division, and tarnished the king's reputation abroad. But the pamphlet went further than most contemporary critiques by offering an unsettling portrait of failed king-ship. Like Hubert, *Le Favorit* diagnosed corrupt favouritism as both cause and consequence of royal weakness. Because he loved Gaveston, the besotted king rejected all good counsel and surrendered his person, his wealth and his power to his "*mignon*", doing everything he could to protect his favourite from those who tried to destroy him. Forced by his nobles and Parliaments to make concessions, Edward II reneged on his promises at the first opportunity, plot-ting his exiled favourite's return, and then welcoming him "with as much joy as if he was an angel come down from heaven".[48]

Early modern histories of Edward II and his favourites agreed on Gaveston's crimes and the king's flaws, only to diverge on the question of resistance. Hubert could not justify the rebellions that destroyed Gaveston and the king, but *Le Favorit*, shaped by the radical politics of the Catholic League, was far less cautious. Ideally, the king should listen to his barons' and his Parliaments' counsel to redeem himself and his kingdom from the favourite's thrall. This line of reasoning would have appealed to those who clung to hopes that Charles would eventually listen to Parliament and punish Buckingham. But the history of Edward's reign posed the more troubling question: when the king refused to reform, when he violated his concessions and reneged on his promises, what could be done? *Le Favorit* argued that the barons (though perhaps not the Parliament) had legitimate grounds to take matters into their own hands. With no hint of condemnation, the pamphlet described how the barons raised an army, hunted down Gaveston and then summarily executed him. The book legitimated the extra-judicial killing of a "man who despised and violated the laws" and "a traitor who had betrayed the realm".[49] In this account the revenge that Eglisham insisted be executed on Buckingham could lawfully be imposed outside the institutions of royal justice. More controversially, *Le Favorit* also justified direct resistance to the bad king. According to the pamphlet, Gaveston's execution initially brought political unity to England. The queen gave birth to an heir, and as Edward's love for his son grew, Gaveston's memory faded. But before long the "weak and changeable" Edward became infatuated with another favourite, Hugh Spencer, who reignited baronial resistance. Oppressing his people "to please his minions", Edward eroded the trust essential to political life, abandoning virtuous rule for the amoral political dictates of the "damned Machiavelli". For these crimes, *Le Favorit* contended, Edward II brought a just war and subsequent deposition upon himself.[50]

Even denuded of its ultra-Catholic trappings, *Le Favorit* introduced into English debates the League's justification for anti-monarchical resistance. It also tapped into anxieties about the unnatural intimacy between king and favourite. Gaveston so "effeminated and infatuated the king's heart", the pamphlet alleged, that he convinced the king to break his promises to his barons and his Parliament.

This charge of effeminacy did not necessarily imply sodomy. Indeed, *Le Favorit* downplayed accusations of sodomy, editing out sensational material from the 1588 original. The 1626 version retained the original's account of the death of Edward's last minion, Hugh Spencer, who was castrated "in detestation of his sodomy", but it silently omitted the passage in Boucher's version that depicted Edward's own horrific punishment for passive (and thus effeminate) anal sex. It was a death, Boucher wrote, "as shameful as his life": deposed and degraded from his royal dignity, Edward was killed with *"une broche rouge de feu,"*—a red-hot spit—with which the barons stabbed him *"par le fondement"*.[51] The Flemish editors who repurposed Boucher's pamphlet as their sequel to *The Forerunner* clearly calculated that there were some fears about Charles I's relationship with Buckingham which were much too dangerous to articulate.

In the aftermath of the parliamentary dissolution, most English discourse on the problem of justice denied was anxious rather than regicidal. Nonetheless, it played with dangerous ideas about armed resistance as it continued to demonize Buckingham as the root cause of the kingdom's suffering. At least one contemporary reader of Eglisham came to believe that the secret history of James I's murder had implicated Charles as well as Buckingham, but for the time being most contemporaries remained preoccupied with the duke, and the image of Buckingham the poisoner became a prominent part of the monstrous portraits fashioned by libellers and rumour-mongers during the turbulent final months of the favourite's life.

CHAPTER FIFTEEN

LONDON ON FIRE

BUCKINGHAM THE POPISH POISONER

IT WAS, NATHANIEL Butter insisted to Secretary Coke, his only mistake in a long career. Butter's record spoke for itself. "He never published" scandalous books, he claimed, only books that "stoode for the honor of his Maiestie, his kindred and allies, the good of this state, and the true religion therein maintayned"—at least, not until the "twoe" that had now landed him in prison. To be entirely accurate, Butter had produced three and a half handwritten copies: two had been sold, a third lent out, and a fourth was half finished when he was arrested. Their market value was temptingly high. Ralph Starkey was charging 30s a copy and assuring customers that "40s cannot buye it in printe". When informed that the work in question was "a scandalous railing booke", Butter feigned ignorance; he regarded it "as wast paper" and given his well-known "want of understanding in the Latin tongue", he could make neither head nor tail of its complex Latin prose. Unconvinced, Coke had him imprisoned.[1]

Butter's mistake was to copy the *Altera secretissima instructio Gallo-Britanno-Batava*, a clever Latin treatise printed on the Continent late in 1626 and circulating in England, mostly in manuscript, by early 1627. The book was the third in a series of "Secret Instructions", the first of which, published in 1620, had been much reprinted. These sophisticated works of political disinformation were closely related to the 1626 Flemish print campaigns that had produced Eglisham's *Prodromus Vindictae*; indeed, Eglisham's publisher, Meerbeeck, also printed a volume of the "Secret Instructions" series. The *Altera secretissima instructio* sported a fake Hague imprint—the Elector Frederick was in exile in Holland—and may have originated in Vienna, though some copies might have been produced in the Spanish Netherlands. It was probably written in August 1626, and its author knew about both the 1626 dissolution of Parliament and *The Forerunner of Revenge*.[2] As Nathaniel Butter was now all too well aware, the offences in the *Altera secretissima instructio* were legion, and among them was its author's assumption that the secret history was a self-evident truth.

The *Instructio* was only one of many reworkings of Eglisham's allegations that flowed through the turbid stream of critique and scandal that engulfed Buckingham in his last two years of life. Elements of the secret history appeared in many forms—seditious talk and rumour, verse libel and underground print, political disinformation and Tacitean history. Each retelling deployed the poisoning stories for different ends, adding layers of new meanings to Eglisham's narratives. Some reproduced his emphases, others made explicit those questions left implicit in the 1626 parliamentary debates. In the course of these redeployments, the secret history's political meanings shifted markedly, especially when anti-Catholic Englishmen embraced allegations that Eglisham had originally intended to advance the international Catholic cause. By tracking the widespread circulation and appropriation of the poisoning charges, we can not only document this shift in meanings, but also explore how the secret history of James I's murder dovetailed with other anxieties about Buckingham and Charles in the later 1620s. The poisoner-duke had become a resonant symbol of what ailed the kingdom.

"Nayles in the Scabbe"

The "scandalous railing booke" discovered in Butter's shop made several uses of Eglisham's accusations. The *Altera secretissima instructio* aimed to exploit tensions within the anti-Habsburg alliance, while playing upon the increasingly problematic relationship between Frederick and Elizabeth on the one hand, and Charles and Buckingham on the other.[3] In 1625, Charles had gone to war to restore the Palatinate, but had thus far achieved nothing. Persistent failure was complicated by other suspicions and resentments. Until Henrietta Maria produced an heir, Charles's sister Elizabeth stood next in line to the English throne; and many godly Englishmen daydreamed of a reliably Calvinist Queen Elizabeth II. Her popularity had made James and now Charles apprehensive, and this mistrust was easy to exploit. The two camps were also divided on military strategy. Frederick wanted English troops marching up the Rhine to Heidelberg. A land war on this scale would require significant parliamentary subsidies, and for all their private assurances of devotion to the duke, Frederick and Elizabeth may well have thought Buckingham's head a small price to pay for parliamentary support and the liberation of the Palatinate.[4]

The *Instructio* began by tallying Frederick's reasons for despair. "Your hope depends on other mens ayde", it warned, but the Elector's ostensible allies had neither the "Will" nor the "Power" to help. Since there was "No hope . . . from the armes of your frends", the tract urged Frederick to be cunning and to gain power through the deception—and even the subversion—of his ostensible allies. "When the Lions skin is worne out", the tract counselled, it was time to put on the "Foxes case".[5]

James's murder played different roles in the *Instructio*. In the opening section, the secret history appeared in subtle allusions, drawing from pre-existing critiques of Buckingham's ambition and insinuating that Frederick and the favourite had plotted a regicidal course to the English throne. Frederick could expect no help from Charles, the tract advised, for the king "hates you out of iealousie". In the early 1620s, Englishmen had raised more than £100,000 for the relief of the Palatinate, and Charles bitterly "remembers that the nobility denied to him the contribution which in his fathers time they gave unto you". Charles was also "suspicious of the Puritans' love for you", fearing they "ayme at you for their Kinge". He thus kept news of England's domestic troubles from Frederick, "least you . . . have your nayles in the scabbe". But Charles could do little to help Frederick in any case. His treasury was "empty", "Trade fayles", and the Parliament-men were exasperated. "He that feares at home", the *Instructio* concluded, "playes no gambols abroad. When London is on fire; will he carry water to Heydelbergh?"[6]

Charles's continued friendship with Buckingham only deepened his unpopularity. "He defends the Scottish king's favourite", the pamphlet alleged, "as if he were Jove's Ganymede", plainly hinting at the unnatural lusts that had secured Buckingham's influence over the throne. England's allies were frustrated with the duke's continuing dominance: the Danish ambassador had warned Charles that "his love to one man hindred him of mony" and thus sabotaged Anglo-Danish efforts to recover the Palatinate. The tract warned Frederick about his own friendship with Buckingham. The nobles and Puritans who had fantasized about King Frederick of England had now "altered their mindes" because "they thinke you frend to Buckingham". Many in England suspected Buckingham of planning a "royall match for his daughter" Mary, presumably to one of the Elector's sons. Frederick had "a wolfe by the eares": an alliance with Buckingham would "offend the nobility" and scuttle another Parliament—but if Frederick broke with the duke, he would "exasperate the kinge", who would take his revenge "by giving you nothinge".[7]

There was another reason why Charles would not help his brother-in-law. He was worried that Frederick would poison him: "Charles is afraid of the White powder out of your Box". According to Eglisham, Buckingham had murdered James to prevent the revival of Anglo-Spanish negotiations. The *Instructio* implied that Buckingham had conspired in the crime with Frederick and Elizabeth, who had had much to gain from the death of *Rex Pacificus*. Charles was their next target, and he knows "that you love nothinge in him so much as sickenesse, nor hope for any thinge more then his death". The French king was also worried. Louis XIII was "persuaded that you are a client of Buckinghams" and thus hostile to Henrietta Maria, the French king's sister. Louis would not commit France to the Palatine cause because he feared that Frederick was plotting a "divorce"—or perhaps something worse. Louis knew that Frederick was "acquainted with poisoned powders. That Villers does noth-inge without your privity. That by your devises the Queene suffers contumely and the Papists persecution".[8]

The treatise then offered Frederick several Machiavellian alternatives to military action. Instead of waiting for a divided England to come to his aid, Frederick should exploit those divisions and seize the throne. He could easily "drive out the young King . . . as one that is hated by the nobility", and could use as a pretext Charles's failure to surrender Buckingham to the 1626 Parliament. "You the sonne in law do but revenge the death of your father in law which his sonne neglecteth. Nothinge can be more acceptable to the kingdome, to which nothinge is more odious than Buckingham". By acting as the avenger, Frederick would rally his natural allies—the discontented "Puritans", the "dry and covetous" Scots nobility, and the "needie" and "ambitious" English elite. He had only to remember that "They are yet alive, and flourish that make the White Powder, and gave it to Hamilton, and your Father in law. Undertake the cause, the kingdome will take you into her bosome."[9]

Eglisham's *Forerunner* had been part of a Habsburg disinformation campaign to discredit Buckingham, and the *Instructio* was a cunning follow-up, a work of "unusual sophistication and complexity" that exploited the secret history to weaken the Protestant cause.[10] It did not have to convince Protestant readers, only unsettle them. Disinformation created doubt, and doubt would damage a wounded, but still dangerous enemy.

"Thy Swolne Ambition Made His Carkasse Swell"

Resonant images of Buckingham-the-poisoner reappeared in the numerous verse libels circulated in the last two years of his life. Poisoning was never the sole, nor often the main, charge the poets hurled at the duke; indeed, it was nearly always part of more complex, multi-faceted portraits. But poison was good to think with, and had an uncanny capacity to crystallize contemporary anxieties about the perversions of social, political, religious and sexual order that Buckingham personified. By 1627 the libellers did not have to belabour the poisoning allegations, but could rely on an audience familiar enough with Eglisham's charges to catch even a passing allusion. When roving fiddlers sang in the spring of 1627 of King James rising from his grave to "commend" the "trueth of [Buckingham's] service", the "cleane contrary way", it was easy for contemporaries to hear the reference to the false "service" the duke had done the king at Theobalds.[11]

One libeller, astonished at Buckingham's decision to command the disas-trous 1627 expedition to the Île de Ré, facetiously asked "Hast not a Foe/To poison heere at home?" The poem nestled its allusion to Buckingham-as-poisoner within a catalogue of other crimes, including his pursuit of "Whores in Court" and his scavenging of rewards for his predatory kin. Eglisham attributed Hamilton's murder to his opposition to the duke's attempt to foist his niece on Hamilton's son, and the libeller alluded to the duke's marital ambitions when he asked Buckingham, "Hast thou no Neece to marry? Cannot an Inne/ Or bawdyhouse afford thee any kinne/To cuckold Lords withall?" But the real horror was that Buckingham dominated the king so completely that the poet had to ask:

wilt thou goe, great Duke, and leave us heere
Lamenting thee and eke thy Pupill deare
Great Charles? Alas! who shall his Scepter sway,
And Kingdome rule now thou art gone away?[12]

Fragments of Eglisham's secret history also appeared in one of the most widely circulated libels of the decade. Composed after Buckingham's defeat at Ré and sometimes given the punning title "In ducem reducem" ("On the Duke's Return"), the libel offered an angry reckoning of the treacherous duke's many sins. The poet introduced the poisoning charge through a simile, redeploying Eglisham's trope of true nobility suffering at the hands of upstart ambition. As Buckingham fretted about the need to return home, his thoughts "with a restlesse motion" vexed his "bespotted soule", just as "that black Potion/Tortur'd the noble Scott, whose Manes tell/Thy swolne Ambition made his carkasse swell." The libeller noted the swelling of Hamilton's corpse, so central to Eglisham's secret history, but used the distorted body not simply as proof of Hamilton's murder but as illustration of the perverted motivation that lay behind it. Other parts of Eglisham's narrative recurred throughout the poem. Buckingham was allegedly vexed by the "feare" that "The King (thou absent) durst wrong'd Bristoll heare". And the poem evoked the duke's homicidal collaborators—his mother, the Countess of Buckingham; and his conjurer, John Lambe: "Lambe's/ Protection" failed to shield Buckingham from the "French Ramms", and neither his "Mothers Masses, nor her Crosses,/Nor Sorceries" could "prevent these fatall losses". The taint of the unholy trinity of poison, witchcraft and, now, popery clung to the favourite's tattered reputation.[13]

Buckingham's soaring ambition loomed large in other poems. *The Spy*, attributed to "I.R" and written in the early summer of 1628, was printed in Amsterdam and smuggled into England. It described how brazen ambition had led the duke into irreligion, sorcery, murder, and the subversion of justice and rank:

So boundless is ambition, that no lets
Right, virtue, friendship, or religion sets
Before 't, can stay its course. But wrong or right,

> In spite of justice, with a restless flight,
> She seeks her ruin. Poniards, poisons, swords,
> With plasters, potions, witchcraft, coining Lords,
> Corrupting, selling justice: wasting treasure
> In oyster-voyages, and feasts of pleasure.[14]

The allusion to "plasters" and "potions" was unmistakable, but the poet's key point was that poisons, plasters and potions were promiscuously jumbled together with the duke's other crimes, including "witchcraft", all of which were symptoms of the master sin of ambition.

Perhaps the most complex appropriation of the secret history appeared in a poem written towards the end of the 1628 Parliament and known as Buckingham's "most excellent Rotomontados" ("brags"). The poem purported to be the duke's message to the Commons, its sneering tone an indictment of Buckingham's upstart nature. Boasting of his invulnerability, the duke reeled off charges that would never be proved against him, and thus, in effect, confessed his crimes:

> Nor shall you ever prove I had a hand
> Ith poisoning of the Monarch of this land,
> Or the like hand by poison to intox
> Southampton, Oxford, Hamilton, Lenox;
> Nor shall you ever prove, by Magick charmes
> I wrought the Kings Affection, or his harmes,
> Or that I need Lambes Philters to incite
> Chast Ladies to give my fowle lust delight;
> Nor feare I if ten Vitrii were heere,
> Since I have thrice ten Ravillacks as neere.
> My power shalbee unbounded in each thing,
> If once I use these words: I, and the King.
> Seeme wise, and cease then to perturb the Realme,
> Or strive with him that sitts and guides the helme.

The passage began with the poisoning allegations, rehearsing Eglisham's list of Buckingham's victims and adding the Earl of Oxford who died early in 1625 at Breda. Poison was linked to "Magick charmes" to seduce and hurt the king, while sorcery bled logically into sexual debauchery, with Buckingham using Lambe's love potions (philters) to violate chaste ladies with "fowle lust". The libel then had Buckingham the poisoner-sorcerer-seducer unmask himself as a papist and, in a telling allusion to recent French history, as the kind of papist whose religion spawned regicidal violence. Buckingham claimed he had no fear, even in the face of "ten Vitrii", for he had "thrice ten" Ravaillacs beside him.

The number of variant spellings of "Vitrii" in copies of the poem suggests that contemporaries were unsure who or what was intended, but the poet was alluding to Louis d'Hôpital de Vitry, captain of the royal guards under Henri IV and Louis XIII. In 1610, Vitry was unable to prevent François Ravaillac from murdering Henri IV. More pertinently, in 1617, Vitry had, on Louis XIII's orders, orchestrated the assassination of the Queen Mother's much-loathed Italian favourite, Concino Concini. Against Vitry, the protector of kings and killer of corrupt favourites, Buckingham has thirty "Ravillacks", eager to emulate the Jesuit-inspired assassin.[15] Thus, Buckingham the king-killer was paralleled with the Jesuit-inspired Ravaillac and James's murder with Henri IV's. The passage concluded with a dramatic claim about Buckingham's "unbounded" power, which permitted him to justify any enormity with the words "I, and the King", as if he were the king's equal or even his superior. Buckingham warned the Parliament-men to stop competing "with him that sitts and guides the helme". Ideally, the man at the helm was the king; but in 1628 the helmsman was not a Stuart but a Villiers.

"Veneries and Venefices" Revisited

Recent French history also shaped a more overtly Tacitean reassessment of Buckingham's crimes. In 1626, Sir John Eliot had sensationally compared the duke to Sejanus, the Tiberian favourite notorious for his "veneries and vene-fices". In response, Charles I had had Eliot imprisoned. Two years later, two versions appeared of a translated French book that would allow English readers another chance to reflect on Eliot's parallels. Neither version had a publisher's name, and both carried fake Parisian imprints. Both were titled *The Powerfull Favorite, or, The life of Ælius Seianus* and attributed to "P. M."; both were trans-lations (one full, one abridged) of the *Histoire d'Aelius Sejanus*, first published in 1617 by the French royal historiographer Pierre Matthieu.[16]

Matthieu's much reprinted and translated book had retold the Sejanus story to comment on the rise and fall of the favourite Concini.[17] But Matthieu's apho-ristic approach made his book easily applicable to other monarchies, and the 1628 English translations implicitly but unmistakably presented Matthieu's version of Sejanus's story as a mirror of Buckingham's. Whether the two books appeared before or after Buckingham's death in August 1628 is not known, but they contained a provocative, classical republican analysis of court favourites and political poisoning.

Matthieu thought royal favourites posed a delicate political problem: monarchs had the freedom to choose their friends and councillors, even to elevate obscure men to great power, but because those choices affected the state's well-being, they were inescapably matters of public interest. A balance had to be struck. "Seeing that Princes dispose soveraignely of their hearts"—with only

God as their judge—"and that they forme in them love and hatred, to whom and how they please", Matthieu argued, "Wee had need therefore to desire that their affections to particular men might be iust and well regulated. For if they bee disordered they draw with them publike ruine: they render Princes hatefull, and their Favourites miserable."[18] The careers of Sejanus, Concini and Buckingham were all examples of the "indiscreet" distribution of royal favour.

Matthieu's English readers would have noticed many parallels between the Tiberian and Caroline favourites. Both were monsters of prodigality who shamelessly promoted their kindred and allies, while barring others from advancement. Both acquired a virtual monopoly of appointments to office, and aspired to marry into the royal family. And both were so laden with honours and authority that they appeared more powerful than the monarch. It "cannot goe well", Matthieu warned, "when the people perceive that favour transferreth soveraigne honours of superiours upon an inferiour, and that the Prince suffereth a companion in the kingdome to assist him to governe." Above all, Sejanus, like Buckingham, was a monster of ambition: his "minde was franticke with this ambition", which in turn led him into murder; and poison—which "amongst violent deaths . . . was held to be the greatest execration"—was his weapon of choice.[19]

Matthieu's account of Sejanus's poisonings of Germanicus and Drusus spoke to English readers of the secret history, and, as a good Tacitist, Matthieu read these crimes as symptoms of broader political malaise. Germanicus was murdered because he embodied a tyrannized people's only hope for the restoration of "liberty", and poison "entred and mingled it selfe more easily in vessells of gold then of earth", leaving public-spirited men peculiarly vulnerable. Germanicus's poisoning also involved the twinned spectres of disorderly women and maleficent magic. Sejanus co-opted into the plot an ally's wife, Plancina, "a fury disguised in shape of a woman" who deployed "charmes and poysons" with the help of "Sorcerers fetcht out of hell", among them "Martina that famous sorceress and empoysonnesse".[20] Drusus's murder was equally lurid. Sejanus seduced Drusus's wife, Livia, before plotting with her to poison Drusus under the guise of treating his illness—the same opportunity used by Buckingham and his mother against James. But the poisoning was subtle, carried out "so slowly, that his death should be imputed unto nature and chance, not unto violence and treachery". Sex was the glue that held this plot together. Livia was seduced by the doctor who compounded the poisonous drug, while Sejanus "most vildly abused [the] body" of the eunuch slave Ligidus, who administered the poison to Drusus. "These infamous persons combine upon an execrable attempt", Matthieu wrote; "Seianus the assasin conceives it, Livia the adultresse gives her consent, the ruffian Eudemus compounds the drugge, Ligdus the Ganimed presents the same".[21]

These narratives replicated many contemporary images of Buckingham. In Eglisham's secret history he had murdered the virtuous Hamilton who tried to block the favourite's ambition, just as Sejanus had murdered the virtuous Germanicus. Buckingham had also turned to disorderly women—in this case his mother—to assist him, and he had used sorcerers to craft his poisons. Sejanus's "veneries"—the seduction of Livia and the sodomizing of Ligidus— paralleled long-standing libellous images of Buckingham as sexual predator and royal "Ganymede". Furthermore, since Sejanus's "venefices" were symptoms of a tyrannical state where virtuous men suffered for the cause of liberty, English readers might have seen Buckingham's dominance as a token of something similarly rotten in the state of England. Equally unsettling was Tiberius's role in assisting and covering up Sejanus's crimes. According to Matthieu, both men had plotted Germanicus's death and manipulated the legal system to stymie justice. If nothing else, Matthieu's book made clear why Charles had reacted so violently when Eliot insinuated that the king was a new Tiberius, and it forced contemporaries to wrestle with troubling questions: if Charles I was Tiberius, what were his subjects to do about it?

Mr Melvin's "Strange Speeches"

Poisoning was linked to the tyrannical courts of imperial Rome; but in the English Protestant imagination it also remained a quintessentially Catholic crime, indelibly connected to papal politics, Jesuit intrigue and Mediterranean climes. By 1628 contemporaries were drawing increasingly stark portraits of Buckingham not only as a papist, but also as an agent of international popish plots to subvert the Protestant state. The secret history that Eglisham had written to help the Catholic cause was fully integrated into this anti-popish discourse that fuelled much of the criticism of Charles I's court and favourite in the late 1620s.

Robert Melvin (or Melville) spent much of Saturday, 3 May in a drunken haze, slumped in Waterton Payne's tobacco house "neere the Savoy" in London, where he would be overheard by two witnesses speaking many "fowle and undutifull" things "against the Kings honor, the gouverment of the State" and Buckingham "in particular". The authorities quickly hauled Melvin in for questioning. Presented with evidence of nine incriminating statements, Melvin denied all but one. He admitted saying there were only "fower honest Bishopps", the rest being Arminians "and other strange sexes [sects]", but as for the other eight articles, "hee never spake any such words, had never any such thought, nor did ever heare any such thing to his remembrance". He had to concede, however, that he had been "drinking overmuch" at Payne's "and therefore trusts not too much to his memory". With Melvin jailed in the Gatehouse, the authorities set his case aside for nearly a month, until Secretary Conway reminded Buckingham that Melvin's "denyall is nothing against twoe witnesses", adding that "Such scandalous things as theis are should bee silenced with contempt, or punished exemplarily".[22]

By 21 June the authorities had decided on exemplary punishment and charged Melvin with treason. This risky decision was probably prompted by the recent escalation of public attacks on Buckingham. The House of Commons had prepared another scathing Remonstrance against him; a gang of youths had pulled down the scaffold on Tower Hill and announced that Buckingham deserved a new one; and a crowd of London apprentices had brutally assaulted and lynched John Lambe, the man Eglisham had identified as Buckingham's sorcerer.[23] Virtually everyone recognized that the attack on Lambe was an expression of Londoners' violent hatred for Buckingham, but, with no suspects in custody, the authorities saw Melvin's prosecution as a chance to assert some kind of control over a rapidly deteriorating situation.

The prosecution was a disaster. Melvin's alleged "articles" quickly leaked into public circulation, generating a much bigger audience for his allegations.[24] The newsmonger John Pory acquired a copy of "Certain speaches wherof one Mr Melvin a Scottishman is accused", dated Friday, 27 June, and sent a transcript to Joseph Mead, who then sent it on to Martin Stuteville. Other copies began circulating through similar news channels, and Melvin's sensational claims surely stimulated the demand.[25] Melvin's source was an "uncle or neare kinsman", a Catholic cardinal, who had revealed a remarkable series of crimes, committed or plotted by the duke. Melvin alleged that Buckingham met every night with a secret council of "Jesuits and Scottishmen" or "Jesuitish Scotchmen", which was "a stronger Counsell then the king".[26] He claimed that whenever Charles "had a purpose to doe anything of what consequence soever, the Duke could alter it". But the duke's greatest "plott" was "that the parlament should be dissolved" and that with Charles beside him he would lead "a great army of horse & foot"— already 17,000 strong and with Scottish reinforcements promised—against the English commons.[27] "Whilest war was amongst ourselves", Melvin claimed, "the enemy"—presumably Spain or France—"should come". Resistance was futile, "for the kingdome is already sold to the enemy by the Duke". Buckingham's treachery had sabotaged the Ré expedition in 1627, and his Catholic leanings surely explained why Arminians "& other sectes" dominated the bishops' bench.[28]

Inserted into Melvin's account of this popish plot was a variation on Eglisham's secret history. "King James his bloud, and Marques Hamiltons, *cum aliis*, cryed out for vengeance to heaven," Melvin stated, adding, "that he could not but expect ruine upon this kingdom." Like Eglisham, Melvin called for justice and appealed to the concept of blood guilt. Scripture taught that the blood of the murdered called to Heaven for justice, and that God always heard the call. It was up to God's deputed authorities on earth to bring murderers to book, but if they failed to administer the scripturally ordained punishment— the shedding of blood to punish the shedding of blood—then the land remained polluted by blood guilt and God Himself would take vengeance, bringing "ruine upon this kingdom".[29]

Melvin's articles identified James's murder as a "popish" act, part of Buckingham's ongoing "plott" to undermine the Protestant state, and his eighth article implicitly tied the deaths of James and Hamilton to earlier Catholic poison plots. Melvin claimed that Prince Henry "was poysoned by Sir Tho: Overbury who for the same was served with the same sauce, and that the Earle of Somersett could say much to this". This was a variation on rumours that had circulated widely late in 1615 during the prosecution of Overbury's alleged killers. These rumours claimed that, having poisoned Henry, the Earl and Countess of Somerset had planned to poison James, Queen Anne, Prince Charles, the leading Protestant nobility, and ultimately Elector Frederick and Elizabeth too. With the royal family dead, a Catholic insurrection, followed by a Spanish invasion, would install Somerset as puppet king.[30]

It is uncertain whether Melvin intended to allude to the most elaborate versions of these old rumours. Writing in the 1630s, Simonds D'Ewes noted a "constant report" among the Scots that Overbury, fearing Henry would "be a means to ruin" Somerset, had advised the favourite to murder the prince, "and was himself afterwards in part an instrument for the effecting of it". According to D'Ewes, the Scots saw Overbury's poisoning not as a new stage in an evolving Catholic poison plot but as "the just judgment of God, afterwards as a punishment upon him, that he himself died by poison". But whatever Melvin's intentions, his articles implicitly linked the murders of Hamilton and James to the poisoning of Henry and Overbury and situated all four deaths in the context of a continuing popish plot. These allegations played with still-active political memories. In 1623 one of Somerset's former servants had accused the earl as a "contriver of Prince Henryes death", briefly stimulating "much talke of a discovery of the poisoning of Prince Henry", and in the spring of 1626 a prisoner in King's Bench had opined that the Stuart dynasty was cursed and that Henry "twas thought he was poysoned".[31] Eglisham had alluded to the Overbury case as a precedent for the prosecution of murderous favourites, but Melvin had now connected James's murder to the earlier scandal as manifestations of the same, ongoing Catholic plot.

Although Melvin's prosecution helped publicize his version of Buckingham's popish plot, his conviction would have allowed the authorities to neutralize, or at least confront, the rumours about James's murder. But the Crown's plans went disastrously awry. Twice in late June the prosecution postponed proceedings, perhaps because of doubts about their case.[32] Any such concerns were fully vindicated when Melvin eventually appeared in court on 1 July. The grand jury found the treason indictment wanting and issued a verdict of "ignoramus"; without an indictment, the prosecution collapsed.[33] Any hope of using Melvin's trial to regain the initiative vanished, and amid the rampant popular hatred of Buckingham it seemed impossible to counter the monstrous legends that now dominated English perceptions of the duke.

Some observers of the Melvin case detected signs of splits within the regime. One noted that George Hay, Chancellor of Scotland, had walked alongside Melvin "to the bar and back again to the prison, that he might . . . countenance his friend against the implacable malice of, &c"—that ominous "et cetera" referring, no doubt, to the favourite. Technically "freed by the jury" and on bail, Melvin remained imprisoned. On 15 July he wrote to Buckingham begging forgiveness, explaining he had been induced by "an Insolent man" to "inadvisedlie" repeat "the reporte of the common people", the "vulgar error of the tyme". It was an interesting defence, one that suggests just how widespread popular talk of Buckingham's crimes had become.[34]

Even as Melvin sought pardon, his "strange speeches" continued to cause damage. A "paper" containing Melvin's articles came into the hands of Susanna Prince, who was particularly struck by the article about James's poisoning, deducing from it her own troubling conclusions. During a July dinner with Robert Bankworth, Susanna insisted that "a Scotchman coming to London affirmed that the last king was poysoned by the Duke *with the consent of our Soverine* . . . For otherwise they sayde he [Buckingham] shoulde not have bene soe highly favoured". In other words, only Charles's complicity in his father's murder could explain why he had not brought Buckingham to justice. Susanna told Bankworth that these words "against the kings majestye concerning his deceased Father . . . were in writing at her Fathers howse" and offered to show him the evidence. Although he initially dismissed her remarks as worthless gossip "sufficient for a womans tongue", Bankworth eventually denounced Susanna to the authorities lest he be guilty of concealing treason. Under questioning, Susanna admitted owning a copy of Melvin's speeches, although she adamantly denied Bankworth's allegations. Both her mother and brother affirmed that neither of them had heard "any word of the death of King James nor concerninge the duke of Buckingham at that time".[35] The case appears to have been dropped.

A Rod for our own Tails

Buckingham and his supporters made at least one attempt to disrupt these insistent allegations of the duke's complicity in popish plots. Towards the beginning of the 1628 Parliament, Sir John Maynard forged a letter masquerading as secret correspondence taken during a recent raid on a Jesuit conclave in Clerkenwell. The letter read like the confirmation of Robert Melvin's deepest fears, mapping a massive popish plot to subvert the English Church and enslave the nation. But Maynard's goal was disinformation, using the forged letter to distance Buckingham from his supposed popish allies, while undercutting the 1628 Parliament's ongoing attempts to bring the favourite to heel. The "Jesuit" letter thus portrayed Buckingham as the Order's "furyous enemy", and described how popish agents had manipulated Parliament into attacking the duke. The letter also claimed that the Jesuits had stoked popular hysteria against Buckingham by leaking stories "in Paules and the Exchaunge" that left "our irreconcyleable enemy . . . as odyous as a toade; for the people are apt to believe any thinge against him".[36]

As its most astute historian has noted, different readers understood Maynard's "Jesuit" letter in different ways, some taking it at face value, some believing it a Puritan forgery, and some assuming it was a work of ducal disinformation designed to shield Buckingham's real crimes from view.[37] The letter had a political impact that neither Maynard nor Buckingham could control, and the forgery quickly inspired other writers to produce sequels that (at least on the surface) were far more critical of the duke. A letter supposedly written by the emperor's confessor praised Buckingham as "a man fitted to our . . . harts desires", and revealed that the kings of Spain and France had promised to "assist" the duke "to the crowne" for services rendered to the Catholic cause.[38] But it was a letter written in the voice of the Jesuit Rector in Brussels, the supposed addressee of the forged original, that finally introduced James I's murder into the discussion. The "Rector", weary of endless Jesuit political intriguing, cast a sceptical eye over his younger correspondent's report. "Your proiects multiplie as thick as circles after a stone cast into the Water, growing bigger and bigger the farther thay spreade", he wrote; "but as soone as thay touch upon the Banke of solide wisdome, thay vanish". Jesuit plotting was real enough, then; but their plots were in vain. Parliament could not be manipulated, nor would England succumb to internal subversion or external invasion. Much in the English state was sound—Parliament had defended English liberties in the recent Petition of Right; English Protestantism was strong enough to withstand Arminian interlopers; and Charles was a "good" king, "immovablie religious, and wyse above his years". Buckingham, however, was a problem. Charles's virtues would remain compromised, the "Rector" thought, as long as he was "be-witched with that Magitian", and indeed the duke had tried to sabotage the king's accord with Parliament over the Petition of Right. This meddling would backfire on the duke unless "he prevent" it "with some of his precious . . . whyt pocket pouder . . . his *Ultimum refugium* [last refuge] to escape the stumbling block of the tour [Tower]".[39]

This passing allusion was followed by a second more overt reference to the secret history as the "Rector" took stock of his correspondent's report on the Jesuit smear campaign against Buckingham:

> You fly upon the Duke, becaus (belyke) you cannot mould him badd anugh to your bent: If he hade bein an instrument of favour for yow formerly, now then yow ar unthankfull; If he oppose yow now, it will prove indiscretion for yow, *scribere in eum qui potest proscribere* [to write against him who he has the power to proscribe].

And here, with Macrobius's adage in mind, the "Rector" offered a fascinating "Catholic" assessment of the 1626 Flemish campaign against the duke:

> Your policie failed yow when yow instigated your Catholick Scottish phisitian to informe the parliament of the murther of K: James and M: Hammiltoun; were that a treuth, yet was it a rod for our owne tayles.[40]

Untangling political intent from this knotty fiction is not easy. The "Rector" appeared to second-guess the use of Eglisham to make the case against Buckingham; but the problem was not so much that the "Catholick . . . phisitian" was telling lies—the charge was a "treuth"—but that his compromised name and Buckingham's power allowed the duke's supporters to smear the smear, and thus turn the allegation into "a rod" against the popish cause. The "Rector" thus unmasked Eglisham's religious identity without refuting his case against Buckingham, perhaps allowing the reader to dissociate the secret history from its popish origins.

The "Rector" also made a case for killing the duke. It was a mistake for the Jesuits to presume Buckingham was unafraid of the "tour-stumble-blocke"—the executioner—just "becaus he so easelie leaps over Parliaments". It was possible he might suffer at an assassin's hands—"a transcendant Guisean blowe"—but however much the duke now stood in the Jesuits' way, "neither your blessings nor yowr curssings, your inchantings, nor witcheries can remove him till God will". The "Rector" had followed his comments on Eglisham by noting that "the innocent blood of [Thomas] Scott" called out for revenge on the man who procured it, adding that "Blood must be appeased with blood only". If the "Rector" assumed Scott's assassin was on Buckingham's payroll, then he (like Eglisham) was making the case that the murderous duke must die for his crimes.[41]

"Slaine by the Cruell Hands"

Anxious talk of Buckingham the popish poisoner could be found far from the hothouse of the capital. Early on Sunday, 13 July 1628, Edward Cosowarth, a Cornish Justice of the Peace, wrote urgently to Secretary Conway. The previous Thursday two Cornish sailors, Nicholas Browne and Thomas Emmet, travelling from Swansea had arrived near Cosowarth's house close to Newquay and reported "the death of our gratious kinge Charles", who, they claimed, had been "slaine by the cruell hands of the Right Honorable Prince George duke of Buckingham". Anxious lest the report trigger dangerous "distractions", Cosowarth confined the two sailors in a "privatt house" to prevent them from spreading the story and sent his son posthaste to Whitehall with the news.[42] The Crown typically thought such "Irreverent undutifull speeches and false scandalous reports" were "fit" only "to bee sevearrely punished". But such rumours were, in fact, a revealing form of "improvised news", sensitive indices of a population's fears at moments of political crisis. For a few summer days in south Wales and northern Cornwall deeply held popular anxieties about Buckingham the popish poisoner found their voice.[43]

Cosoowarth's report alarmed Whitehall, which hoped to suppress this "false lewde and scandalous" rumour of "dangerous Consequence". Attorney General Heath fumed at "the insufferable licentiousness of spreading false Rumours". His usual inclination when confronted by "that itching & malitious humor" was to punish the offenders, but this particular rumour was "soe transcendent" and its circulation "in the remoter parts" of the kingdom "so daungerous" that Heath thought some kind of "verball inhibition" was required. The Privy Council ordered that the two sailors be strictly examined and punished, while Heath began drafting a proclamation to counter the false report. The Council also instructed Cosowarth that "if this Rumour hath bene divulged and made any apprehentions in the mindes of the people, you are to make knowne that the same is false and the Reporters punishable."[44]

The proclamation was never published. Perhaps once the councillors grasped the full nature and extent of the rumour, they decided that a proclamation would only broadcast yet another tale about Buckingham the poisoner of kings. Questioned on 28 July, the sailor Browne testified that he had first heard the rumour in Swansea on 8 July, when Patrick Jones—Swansea's "portreeve", or mayor—had "publiquelye divulged" the news "in the markett place", with the gentleman Henry Vaughan by his side. The two reputable (and thus reliable) local worthies had announced "the death of king Charles who was there said to be poisoned by George duke of Buckingham". The news, Browne said, had triggered "a generall lamentation of the whole people", who panicked, fearing "that the papists would rise up in Armes & kill them in theire beds". The women from whom Browne bought provisions that afternoon were full of the story, and Browne's colleague Emmet testified that all over Swansea people were "complayning of the danger they stand in being as it were in the face of theire enemies and environed with Papists at home". Browne added that, on his return to Cornwall, he had heard another sailor report that the day after Browne and Emett left Swansea, "diverse of the Counteye souldiers" came to the town "to strengthen it against any enemye that should invade".[45]

Investigations in south Wales uncovered the full story of the rumour's genesis and circulation. It had begun after a robbery near Llanymddyfri (Llandovery) in Carmarthenshire, when the criminals, hoping to divert "the hott persuite cominge after them", had "cryed, and reported that the kings Majestie was dead". It is unclear whether the criminals had blamed Buckingham or warned of a Catholic uprising, but as the rumour spread it was elaborated, with each addition revealing how deeply stories about Buckingham the popish poisoner were rooted in the popular imagination. The rumour moved southwards through

Carmarthenshire to Llanelli, one of the main county towns, and then headed eastwards along the coast. Around noon on 8 July the sound of a hue and cry was heard on the banks of the River Loughor, as about one hundred people from Llanelli headed towards the ford, where they could cross at low tide to warn those on the Glamorgan side of the river. By this point the rumour had acquired damning details about Buckingham, popery and poison. William ap Evan, keeper of the Loughor ferry, was told "the kinge was dead, & poysoned by the duke", while Richard Morgan, a petty constable in Loughor, Glamorgan, soon learned the news that "the kinge was dead, and the Reporte was, that hee was poisoned" by Buckingham.[46] A Loughor alderman testified that the hue and cry had awoken him from a midday nap and that, leaving his house, he had run into a woman who "cryed & said that the Spaniards hadd landed there". The Llanelli crowd was joined by a "great number of people of the towne or borough of Loughor" who marched into Swansea in the mid-afternoon, "Reportinge & cryinge, that the kings majestie was dead & poysoned by the duke". The Swansea trained bands were mobilized, while the portreeve of Loughor—informed of the news in Neath—ordered the watch set up. The region remained on nervous alert until definitive news arrived that the king was alive.[47]

The rumour that Buckingham had poisoned Charles spread rapidly among a population primed to believe it, and to connect the news to a Catholic uprising and invasion. A large and panicked crowd spread the story among three towns—Llanelli, Loughor and Swansea—crying the news along the roads and river crossings. Inside the towns the rumour spread rapidly through the markets and streets, and the boats leaving Swansea soon carried it into Cornwall. The local authorities' initial endorsement of the reports gave them credibility, but ultimately the rumour fed on a widespread predisposition to believe that the royal favourite might poison the king, a predisposition that Eglisham's secret history (and the libellous variations played upon it) had helped nurture over the previous two years.

What John Felton Read

By the time the authorities had interviewed all the rumour witnesses in Loughor and Swansea, Buckingham was dead, murdered in Portsmouth on 23 August 1628 by John Felton, a former lieutenant (Fig. 62). Felton's motivations were complicated. Wounded during the retreat from Ré in 1627, he carried deep emotional as well as physical scars. "Indigent and low in mony", Felton, like many veterans, had petitioned for back pay in vain, and the duke had twice dashed his hopes for a captain's commission. Holed up in London, Felton began to realize that his personal grievances had a broader context. As he walked to the Holborn scrivener who prepared his various petitions, Felton moved through streets and drank in alehouses awash in rumour and libel.

Indeed, his scrivener's office was busy producing illicit underground materials, and Felton might have heard there the ominous rhyme composed after Lambe's lynching and later found scrawled among the scrivener's papers:

Lett Charles & George doe what they can
yet george shall dye like Doctor Lambe.[48]

Felton certainly saw the scrivener's illegal manuscript copy of the June 1628 Remonstrance in the House of Commons against Buckingham. It said nothing about James's death, but the Remonstrance fit the anxious, angry mood that spawned Melvin's nine articles and the anti-popish poison panic in south Wales. It spelled out "the miserable condition" of a kingdom "of late so weakened, impoverished, and dejected". With a "secret working"—a plot—afoot to subvert English Protestantism, the people's hearts remained "full of fear of innovation and change of government", while military defeats had "extremely wasted that stock of honour that was left unto this kingdom". These "evils and dangers" had one cause: "the excessive power of the Duke of Buckingham, and the abuse of

Figure 62: "The lively Portraiture of Iohn Felton" depicting Buckingham's assassin, hat in hand, poised to strike (Ashmolean Museum).

that power". The Commons asked the king "whether, in respect the said Duke has so abused his power, it be safe for your Majesty and your kingdom to continue him either in his great offices of trust or in his place of nearness and counsel about your sacred person." Captured shortly after stabbing the duke, Felton spent the next three months answering questions about his motives and co-conspirators. He consistently claimed that he had acted alone, but freely confessed that, although "the want of his Pay had something moved him", it had been "the Remonstrance that confirmd him", and he "twice or thrice repeated . . . 'Upon my Soule Nothing but the Remonstrance, Nothing but the Remonstrance'". The document had convinced Felton that his woes were England's woes and that by killing Buckingham he would become a patriot hero.[49]

But what else did Felton read? The authorities who searched his belongings found some daring propositions on the safety of the commonwealth, but Felton denied they had inspired him, claiming he had copied them "long ago, out of a Book calld the Golden Epistles". Elizabeth Josselyn, the wife of a London stationer, who had lodged in the same house, described Felton as a "melancholy man, & much given to reading of books", many of which he borrowed from her. Amongst them was one "stiled the history of the Queen of Scotts", perhaps George Buchanan's infamous meditations on the right to resist an evil monarch.[50] Felton roomed in the heart of the city where the apprentices had murdered John Lambe. No doubt he heard reports about Melvin's strange speeches. But did he read George Eglisham? One source suggests he might have.

Henry Wotton was puzzled by Felton's motives. "What may have been the immediate or greatest motive of that felonious conception", Wotton wrote in his short biography of Buckingham from the 1630s, "is even yet in the clouds." Wotton could credit neither of the two rumoured "private" motivations—that Felton was "stung with a denial of his Captains place" or that he resented Buckingham for favouring a man with whom Felton had "ancient quarrels". Wotton assumed Felton knew that military custom did not guarantee him the captain's place, and he considered it improbable that Felton would "make the Duke no more than an oblique sacrifice, to the flames of his private revenge upon a third person". But he also doubted Felton's claims to have acted on public grievances. In a conversation between Felton and Sir Richard Gresham a mere three hours before the assassin's execution, a conversation for which Wotton is now the only source, Felton had confessed "two only inducements". One, unsurprisingly, was the Commons' Remonstrance. But:

> The first, as he made it in order, was a certain libelous book written by one Eggleston a Scottish Physitian, which made the Duke one of the foulest monsters upon the earth, and indeed unworthy not only of life in a Christian Court, and under so vertuous a King; but of any room within the bounds of all humanity, if his prodigious predictions had the least semblance of truth.

Wotton was unconvinced; he suspected that Felton had "studied" these motivations to cover up his real ones, "either to honest a deed after it was done, or to slumber his conscience in the doing". But he was interested enough in Gresham's story to note that Felton had described the Remonstrance as his "second" motivation, "which perchance he thought was the fairest cover, so he put in the second place", a comment that suggests Wotton thought Parliament's indictment looked better as a motivation than Eglisham's pamphlet. But what really motivated Felton, Wotton concluded, "none can determin, but the Prince of darknesse".[51]

"Noe Murder but an Execution"

Felton did become a patriot hero. The poisoning allegations may not have directly inspired him, but they were central to the critiques of Buckingham that surrounded Felton in London and to the torrent of verse libels that would celebrate his actions. Fragments of the secret history appeared in two types of these assassination poems—in the mock-elegiac catalogues of Buckingham's crimes; and in the quasi-legalistic defences of his murder.

One mock elegy connected Buckingham's use of poison to his reckless ambition: the favourite's "excessive power" had abused "The yealding nature of a pious King", and "by abortive means before not us'd,/That hee might mount"—that Buckingham might ascend in power—"Favorites honey tasted,/Whilst others vitall powers by poison wasted." Another elegy had the hell-bound duke proclaim:

> The Flood of my Ambition swelld soe high,
> It overflow'd the bankes of Modestie,
> And with the torrent of unbridled will
> Swept all away, It spared not to spill
> The lives and blood of myne own country men,
> And if I loved One, I hated Tenn.

As the kingdom gazed at Buckingham's ascent, a third poet wrote, its subjects did not dream that his "advauncement" was "groundwork and imition [introduction]/to Murders, Treasons, Incest and ambition".[52]

Other libellers drew different connections. A mock epitaph hailed Buckingham as:

> The Coward at the Ile of Ree
> The bane of noble Chivalrie,
> The night-worke of a painted dame,
> Confederate with Doctor Lambe.

"Bane" could mean "curse", but it could also mean "poison"; the un-chivalric, ignoble Buckingham was thus set in opposition to his virtuous, aristocratic murder victims. A similar allusion appeared when another libeller described the duke as "The courtiers bane, the countries hate/An agent for the Spanish state,/The Romists Frend, the Gospells Foe", with poison this time suggestively linked to Catholicism and treachery.[53] The duke's poisonings may also lie behind another recollection: "Did not thy smiles or frowns make Princes kneele?/Did not thyne Enemies thy Vengeance feele?" While a verse set in hell imagined Lambe welcoming his master and wondering whether the countess would join them:

> Will she be still her grandsir Devills debter?
> Hath she not yet perform'd the task he set her?
> Or are there in the world against her will,
> More honest Nobles to be poyson'd still?[54]

Another verse, also set in hell, asserted that Buckingham would now suffer the murderer's reward: "Caynns deare blessinge, light uppon thy harte".[55]

The conceit of "Thou that on topp of Fortunes wheeles did mount" was that Buckingham, now dead, would have to answer to God, "a righteous Judge". On earth, the favourite had bought the judges, but God was a judge "none . . . of thine owne makeing":

> There thou must show an execrable thing
> how thou so savage a wicked wretch could bee
> to kill thy sacred soveraigne lord and king,
> that had so honored & exalted thee
> Bee sure there thou questioned must bee
> for Richmond Oxford Marquesse Hambleton
> for thy false dealing at the Ile of Ree
> for brave Southampton & his noble sonne.

James's murder was thus the act of a "wicked wretch" who had betrayed the master who raised him from the dust. Buckingham would also have to answer for murdering great nobles, who embodied the ideals of bravery, nobility and True Religion (Fig. 63). Their murderer was their opposite: a cowardly poisoner who had sabotaged the Protestant cause at Ré.[56]

A similar set of connections appeared in a poetic dialogue between the ghosts of Buckingham and Lambe. Upset that his "white Soule" had been "spotted" "By Murther, Pride, Lust, & fowle Treacherye", Buckingham confessed his "black Deeds". He had thwarted Robert Mansell's voyage against the Barbary pirates, allowing the "Turks" to make "Havocke of our men,/And Shipps". He had stymied efforts to support the Elector Palatine; thus, "By me … the Pallatinate was lost". And he had poisoned Oxford and Southampton:

> At last I sent
> Brave Oxford over, unto whose Life I lent
> Some few Dayes, & then did take it from him,
> With Southampton's.

"What with Poyson, Treason & base Treacherie", Buckingham concluded, "My Deedes, like Night, would darke the very skie".[57]

Other poems used the poison charge to explicitly justify the assassination. One epitaph offered two arguments. Since there was no "question made/With" Buckingham "of Murther: 'twas his trade", the duke could not complain about his own murder: "And will his Ghost bee angrie trowe/If any other should doe soe?" The poet's other rationalization was more legalistic. Initially, he introduced Felton as Buckingham's pupil, merely following the duke's murderous example, but then he switched tack, arguing a case for self-defence:

Figure 63: A double engraved portrait of the Earls of Oxford and Southampton as Protestant patriot warriors, published by Thomas Jenner in 1623–24 (British Museum). Verse libels alleged that Buckingham had poisoned both men.

> But he that killd this killer thus,
> Did it to save himself and us:
> Thus farr then with him wee'l dispence,
> Hee did it in his owne defence,
> Besides, his Act redeem'd agen
> Great multitudes of honest Men.
> Then all the Fault, and all the Wrong
> Was, that hee let him live soe long.[58]

Another libel justified the assassination by using Herodotus's story of Queen Tomyris, who plunged King Cyrus's severed head into a bloody sack in revenge for her son's murder. The poem addressed the duke:

> What once was said by valiant Tomyris
> to mightie Cirus haveing lost his head
> applied to thee will not bee thought amisse
> for thou more worthie blood then hee hast shedd.

The poem again alluded to the poison allegations, scoffing that "The witch thy mother that old rotten drabb" could not protect her son from the assassin's knife "with hir inchantments & her conjuring tricks". The libeller thanked God:

> for thou art well dispatcht
> I trust that shee thy ghost shall shortly follow
> more plotts by damme and sonne weere never hatcht
> pretending faire but haveing hart most hollow.[59]

The most powerful legalistic appropriation of the poison allegation, however, occurred in a noticeably terse contribution to the debate:

> The heavens approve brave Feltons resolution
> that breath'd noe murther but an Execution
> in stabbinge him that stab'd a world of wightes
> with poyson not with poyniards; which were lightes
> to th'Cloudy state of our eclipsed nation
> late tortured by an upstart generation
> of snakeish vypers with their spawny broode
> which had no sence of Ill noe touch of good.
> Thus hath the will of justice murthered thee
> that murthred right, religion, pyetye:
> The lawes in force agayne for hees in hell
> that broake those spyders webs composde soe well

Oh that our prince those lawes would foster more
then should we flourish as we did before.

The libel transmuted Felton's action from a murder into the judicial "execution" of a murderer. With divine approval, the assassin had enacted the true
justice hitherto perverted by Buckingham's power and, as the last lines
hinted, by the king's own neglect. Unlike "brave" Felton, who wielded a
poniard, Buckingham killed underhandedly with poison. Unlike his aristocratic victims, Buckingham came from the "upstart generation" of lowborn
"snakeish vypers". Buckingham was more than a poisoner; he was the murderer
of the moral forces that should sustain the nation. "The will of justice murthered
thee" who "murthered right, religion, pyetye".[60]

"Live ever, Felton", another poet intoned. "Thou hast turn'd to dust,/Treason,
Ambition, Murther, Pride and Lust."[61] In 1626, George Eglisham had forcefully
reminded Charles I of the king's duty to execute justice on the murderous duke;
in 1628, as the king still refused to act, Felton had stepped into the breach. By
the late 1620s, Charles had not only ceded charismatic authority to the melancholic assassin. He had also been seriously compromised by his close attachment to a favourite routinely branded a poisoner. This allegation had implicated
both duke and king in a range of other crimes, and portrayed the royal court as
a seat of popery, social and sexual disorder, witchcraft and tyranny. This crisis
in moral authority was bad enough; but some of Charles's subjects were using
the secret history as a springboard for far more radical thoughts.

CHAPTER SIXTEEN

REVOLT AGAINST JEHORAM

THOMAS SCOTT READS GEORGE EGLISHAM

R ARELY CONTENT AT the best of times, Thomas Scott felt particularly anxious in February 1626, convinced, as he was, that "a Padd"—a toad, a threat—was lurking "in the strawe".[1] As was his wont, Scott confided his anxieties and suspicions to his notebooks, filling dozens of folios with his convoluted political meditations. As he wrestled with his bitter disillusion over the ensuing months, Scott found himself drawn repeatedly to George Eglisham's secret history. And as he pondered the murder of James I, Scott argued himself into a series of conclusions so radical they can only be termed revolutionary.

In 1624, Canterbury's voters had returned Scott as one of their two Parliament-men, an honour that cost him "100 li and gayned . . . much ill will, and little thanks", but as the 1625 election neared, the sixty-year-old Scott reluctantly told his friends he was willing to serve "if I were now desired agayne". Unfortunately, Scott had quarrelled with the "Kinges of Canterburie", a group of leading citizens including "the Maior, the Sheriffe, Towne Clarke" along with a "faction of Brewers, Alehouse keepers and Alehouse hunters, Papists, Atheists, Nonresident Priests and dumbdoggs, such as rob the poore of theire right and oppresse the Commons". Against the "Kinges" stood the "honest Commoners", led by a popular minister, a hatter, a mason, a retired captain and Scott himself. In 1625 the "Kinges" prevented Scott's return to Westminster, holding a snap election before his supporters arrived. And when Scott stood again in 1626, the "Kinges" engineered a similar result. This time the "Kinges" wanted to humour the Lord Lieutenant of Kent, the Earl of Montgomery, by backing James Palmer, the bedchamber-man who had tested Buckingham's plaster and potion on his own ague, despite the fact that his non-residency made him ineligible to run. While Scott mobilized the city, his opponents recruited the one man who would determine the election, the city's sheriff Mr Pepper. Although four men stood for the two seats, Pepper announced that the result was a foregone conclusion; rather than winnow out ineligible voters, he decided to "iudge by the sight and without Polling" and quickly returned Scott's rivals. Because the sheriff had illegally allowed non-residents to elect non-residents, Scott thought the result revealed that anyone, "a Welchman, Irishman or Scott", and in fact "a Frenchman, Fleming, Spaniard, Italian, or Turke is as eligible in Canterburie as a Londoner".[2]

Scott poured his considerable anger into a long tract, *Canterburie Cittizens for the Parliament*, which portrayed the Canterbury election as a local symptom of the corruption pervading the kingdom. The failure to enforce electoral regulations had generated nothing but "confusion, disorder, tyranny and Anarchy", leaving "Hells yron Gate sett open". Canterbury had become "a wretched Captive in the Iron hands and bands of a tyrannous Maior, Al[d]ermen and Sheriffs . . . a ruined heape . . . the dead and stincking carkasse of a free Corporation now miserably slaved". The House of Commons, so essential "when Kings incline too much . . . unto Tyranny", was also seemingly beyond redemption, "a den . . . of Court or other forren usurpers or robbers", full of "boyes, serving men, dependants, shallow fellowes, such as seeke theire owne ends, Adiaphorists in religion, or worse . . . forreners".[3] Since the king and his ministers failed to follow Biblical principles, the realm was beset with "Poperie and innumerable disorders in the Church, oppression and a world of grevances and confusions", systemic problems that explained the recent failure at Cadiz, which "hath brought our Royall Navie to this shame and makes us now even afraid of them to whome wee were terrible". While Scott longed for the godly to "bind their (Anti-Christian) Kings in chaines and their (ignoble) nobles in fetters of yron", he prepared for the worst, warning England to "looke to thy owne liberty and freehould: which already grones, as did our Saviour . . . under a most heavie crosse and is nowe verie neere nayling unto it."[4]

Scott took three months to finish this protracted jeremiad. It was far too forthright to present to the Commons, as he had initially planned, but as he finished his work in April 1626, he had already found a new focus for his restless pen. At the end of the manuscript, Scott made cryptic references to "King James" and to "poyson".[5] What he had in mind is now obscure, but in short order he would refocus his energies and spend the next ninth months brooding over the murder of James I.

Thomas Scott of Canterbury has long been overshadowed by the famous pamphleteer of the same name. But his protracted analysis of Eglisham's tract reveals a political thinker far more radical than his famous namesake. Indeed, Scott's manuscripts allow us to trace in unparalleled detail how one contemporary read and understood *The Forerunner of Revenge*, and they reveal the potentially radical consequences of belief in James I's murder. Much of what Scott had to say about Buckingham the poisoner recalls other contemporary assessments of the favourite circulating in popular rumour and libel, underground pamphlets and seditious speech. But Scott's worries, and his analysis, cut much deeper. Drawing on English and Biblical history, his analysis of the 1626 Parliament's failure to bring Buckingham to justice led him to an inescapable conclusion:

Charles I must have been complicit in his favourite's crimes, after, if not before, the fact. Dudley Digges and John Eliot had come close to implicit criticism of the king, and after the dissolution of the 1626 Parliament, the widespread mutterings about justice-denied reflected discomfort with Charles's defence of his favourite. Scott was far more explicit in his criticism, and he used Eglisham's indictment of Buckingham to develop a radical case for active political resistance against Charles Stuart.

A Peaceable and Quiet Spirit

Thomas Scott thought of himself as one of the "Religious, grave, learned, wise and honest men, true to the Realme and the Church"; he declared that "No man is more conformable or more commended for his peaceable and quiet Spirit." But he was a difficult and deeply disaffected man with a caustic tongue. Part of his disaffection stemmed from profound insecurity about his social status. He could boast a descent from great medieval families, yet he clung precariously to the outer edge of the lower gentry. Economic necessity kept him in Canterbury, a city of some five thousand souls, and he found life there "altogeather intollerable", surrounded by "confusion and disorder" and beset with "presumptions, insolencies, disdayne, indignities, disgrace, violence and innumerable wrongs". He resented the extraordinary Jacobean "inflation of honours" that had unmoored the traditional social order. Since upstarts were everywhere, knighthoods were "not desired of any but vaine and fond men", Scott lamented. He longed for a return to better order, when "a Clowne could not . . . from the rise of his mony bagg, leape over the heades of antient and honorable Gentlemen", and when civic offices were filled by "Knights, Gentlemen and men of honest Trades", not by "Maior Thatch-my-Barne", Aldermen "hold-my-Stirrip", Common Councillor "Fill-my-Barrell", and Constable "Mend-my-breech".[6]

Many shared Scott's disaffection, but few shared his compulsion to write. He knew the dangers of committing unfettered political comment to paper, and that "the prudent" should "keep silence" in an "evill tyme". But he could not restrain himself. His writings sometimes unnerved him, and he constantly feared being hauled before the Privy Council. But Scott felt the compulsion to write as a moral duty. His writings were often convoluted, so drenched in Biblical and historical allusion that their meaning was, as he once confessed, "wrapt . . . up in" so "many allego[r]ies and obscure phrases" that only "the intelligent" could decipher the jumble of tenses that blurred the lines between past and present, historical analogues and contemporary events. But sometimes Scott could "speake playnely my minde and the truth"; sometimes, he knew, "I must speake unto all; even the dullest Reader". He often wrote in pulpit rhythms, using repetition and rhetorical elaboration to drive a point home.[7] In full swing, these rhythms could become mesmerizing. And to this preacherly style Scott added a distinctive wit. He bestowed mocking sobriquets on his enemies: the sheriff of Canterbury was "Beaten" Pepper; Philip Herbert, Earl of Montgomery, was "Philip the Conqueror"; the militant last Tudor was "King Elizabeth" and her successor, "Queen James"; the Duke of Buckingham's clients and followers were "ducklings". And he could run doggedly with a pun.[8] Who Scott wrote for is unclear, but he imagined various kinds of readers, even though much of what he wrote was far too dangerous for public consumption.

Religion was central to Scott's world view. His notebooks mapped his place on the contemporary religious spectrum, distancing him not only from the "Idolators" and "holy water pissers", the Catholics and ceremonialist Arminians "of the new cutt", but also from the Erastian conformists, the "king Harrie or Court Protestants", and even from the "lesser Puritans" who sought to remain within the national Church while sympathizing with the godly.[9] Scott placed himself among the true godly, readily embracing the once-derogatory label of "Puritan". The true Puritan did not feel bound to the Church of England, and Scott, though he would donate a balcony in St Alphege's, Canterbury and a lecturer's stipend to his parish, wrote glowingly of the exiled congregationalist separatist Henry Ainsworth.[10] Scott disdained bishops and ceremonies, the twin centrepieces of the Elizabethan settlement of the Church. He found it impossible to believe either that "Christ or his Apostles did ever ordayne or left unto us, Crossings, Copes or Surplices" or that anyone would "have brought the sacraments of Christ to be used now as a Stage play". The Jacobean bishops were, for the most part, "the most seculer and carnall Beastes in the world, ever false to Christ and all Christian States and Princes". "Some few"—"our better or lesse bad Bishopps"—remained uncorrupted, but only "so long as the good moode was uppon them".[11] Under James, the Church had fallen away, and "Truth hath ever almost beene called Treason at Court and banished the Chapel". Scott admired religious "seers", and thought that "Prophets and visions wee may have in as greate eminence as ever if wee will". His own rhetoric had a prophetic colouring. After one particularly exuberant passage of denunciation, Scott praised God for filling him "with indignation".[12] This inspired indignation filled page after page of his notebooks.

Scott's religion shaped his politics and fuelled a profound scepticism about the divine right of kings. He ridiculed James I's "tract entituled falsly the True law of free Monarchies", which "doth talke and teach fooles" that "Kings are more then Gods and Subiects no better then Slaves". He argued that "it cannot be for the good either of the king or kingdome that any king should be thus free from and above all lawe". Not only did "nature, reason, and love of libertie and every noble courage" argue against such a government, but "God abhours it". Since prerogative rule was "an uncivill, ungodly, unhumane, unreasonable and voide lawe", monarchs "must be authorized, lymitted and bound". A well-governed state had a place for a king to whom "wee must yeelde . . . his due" and "right". But the subject had to "take heede how we give" the king "or suffer him to arrogate more", for "if they yeelded him an inch he would take an ell". The king was simply "an officer to doe his dutie and not of absolute power to doe what he lusteth without checke or controle".[13] James I's contention that free men had willingly surrendered their sovereignty to kings made no sense. "O good Lord", Scott exclaimed, "was ever any free people, such as the Jewes were, of whome this is spoken, so madd, as to sue for such a yoake?" Against what "Tyrants and theire Jades and doggs call the true lawe of free Monarchies" Scott maintained "the lawe of truth", "the true lawes of the kinges limitted authoritie and the peoples freedome and dutie to God".[14]

Suspicious of kings, Scott was also sceptical of Parliament's ability to restrain them. He praised the Parliament-men of 1626 who "could neither be tickled with [Buckingham's] promises, nor terrified by (his scarre crow) threatning, from resolute standing to those fundamentall points and reasons of State, which most concerne the honor of their King (and Realme) and the securitie of his person." The crippling problem was the Upper House, the home of "ambitious and vayne Prelats" and "degenerate Peeres". The Bishops docilely followed the king, and the secular peers, who should have been "fathers of the people and fortresses of the Commonwealth", instead "prostitute and sett as it were to sale (unto any Ludovic [Sforza], or George [Villiers], or Pope) the dignitie of their King and the honor libertie and wealth and safety of the kingdome". To compound the corruption, Buckingham had packed the House with his kindred and allies, "his debauched, his beggarly, his servile and vile crew". The people could expect nothing but abject cowering from nobles "hewed out of Buckingham's Blocke", while the king was powerless to intervene in the corruption of his peerage, for he was surrounded by "Flatterers" and "toothlessse Traytors . . . dyed deepe in hypocrisie, policie and Courtcraft".[15] Scott was equally dismissive of Buckingham's calculated pursuit of "fine politique marriages" at court, and noted with interest the continuing strains in the "profoundly politique" Feilding–Hamilton match, reporting that "they shall not cleave one to another . . . ever as yron cannot be mixed with clay". Scott was aware of factional infighting at court, but had no illusions about the ability of the Herbert brothers, the Earls of Pembroke and Montgomery, to lead the fight against Buckingham. He did detect some weaknesses in Buckingham's grip on power. The duke's Machiavellian manoeuvrings with Europe's great powers, for instance, were doomed to fail: "Thou shalt be forced . . . to breake with Popish France as thou hast with Spayne to thy sorrow and shame", for "the Lord hath reiected thy confidences, first in Spayne and now in France, and in otherlike Gaddings about to change thy way, from one silly shifte to another." Because he had separated foreign policy from God's Word, Buckingham would be undone by his erstwhile allies: "the strength of Lewis [will] be your shame and the trust in the shadow of the French alliance your confusion."[16] But for Scott, the future for both commonwealth and Church looked dark:

we shall ere long have such lawes and Statutes enacted and such taxes and Impositions established and such faction and division grow ... and such transcendencie and treason of favourites and such Poperie, Arminianisme and detestable and most pernitious Nonresidencie, Simonie, lazinesse and lewdnesse among the Prelates and theire underlings, creep in or rather rush in upon us as wee shall not be able to endure.

This was all thanks to "Buckingham and his more then bloudie house"—bloody "because he slew King James".[17] The strange tragedy of James I's murder fit all too neatly into the pessimistic world view of this angry, "true" Puritan.

Streona

Most of Scott's writings survive as undated fragments, and his meditations on James's murder are spread across 120 folio pages. Scattered throughout these sheets are a number of clues to the meditations' date. Near the beginning, Scott noted that it was the last day of Lent, which in 1626 would have been either Maundy Thursday, 9 April, or Easter Eve, 11 April. Near the end, he makes a cryptic reference to the eighth day, fifth month and second year, which could be either 8 May or, if he was referring to regnal years, 4 September 1626. At the end comes a clearer reference to 22 March 1627. Scott only mentioned Eglisham directly once, but the influence of *The Forerunner* is unmistakable. From the beginning, Scott was obsessed with uncovering not the ill-advised medical interventions investigated by Parliament, but "that villaine who murthered our laste Martyr". By folio 6, Scott had linked the old king's death to those of "the duke of Lenox, the Marquis of Hamilton, the Earle Southampton and other worthies".[18] Clearly, then, Eglisham was setting the agenda, and it seems likely that, if Scott began his writing in April, he had seen the tract some weeks before it became the talk of London, perhaps even a week before Rubens bought his copy in Antwerp. His skill in Latin would have allowed Scott to read *Prodromus Vindictae* if that was indeed in wider circulation before the English translation. Alternatively, word of Eglisham's tract may have reached Kent, which had excellent trade connections with the Netherlands, before actual copies arrived there. Either way, Eglisham's allegations had a profound effect on Scott, who processed them through his favourite mode of analysis—historical and Biblical analogy.

Scott initially struggled to find the appropriate historical analogue for Buckingham. From the Old Testament, he pondered Hushai, Levi, Simeon, Achan, Agag, Amaziah and Saul, before giving more serious consideration to Achitophel, who betrayed David; to Joab, David's nephew, who murdered Abner, Amasa and Uriah; to Jehoram of Judah, who killed his brothers; to Nimrod of Shinar, tyrannical master of the Tower of Babel; and to Adonibezek, who cut off his rivals' thumbs and toes. But Scott was not limited to Biblical parallels. Herodotus inspired him to consider the Pharaoh Sesostris, and modern history suggested Ludovic Sforza, Piers Gaveston and Sir Walter Ralegh. Early in his meditations on Eglisham, however, Scott urged those of his imagined readers who "can read Latine" to find a copy of Henry of Huntington's *Historia Anglorum*; the less learned he referred to Ranulf Higden's *Polychronicon*. Then he began citing the Croyland Chronicle, John Foxe's *Book of Martyrs* and William of Malmesbury's *Gesta regum Anglorum*.[19] In the deep English past, Scott had at last found the perfect parallel for England's tortured present.

Scott found his analogue in a blood-soaked corner of late Anglo-Saxon England. In 959, Alfred the Great's great-grandson, Edgar the Peaceable, reconquered the Danelaw and reunited the realm. His triumph proved fleeting, for Edgar had become besotted with the beautiful Æflthryth and, after arranging her husband's murder, had married her. Æflthryth soon bore Edgar a son, Æthelred, but it was Edward, Edgar's son from a previous marriage, who would succeed him as king in 975. Within three years, Edward was dead; his stepmother Æflthryth had poisoned him to put her son Æthelred on the throne. Æthelred II's reign proved tumultuous. The Danes returned, and in 991 compelled Æthelred to begin annual Danegeld payments. The Danish invasions provided opportunities for other men to rise, most importantly a man of obscure birth known as Eadric *streona*, "the Grasper". Eadric became Æthelred's favourite; the king repeatedly rewarded him, making him ealdorman of Mercia and giving him his daughter in marriage. Streona's most useful virtue was his talent for murder. When the earldorman of Northumbria quarrelled with Æthelred, Streona killed him and blinded his sons. Streona was also was involved in the St Brice's Day Massacre of Danish settlers in 1002. But when Sweyn Forkbeard and his son, Canute, invaded, Streona became their agent, using his authority to sabotage English counter-measures and betray the fleet. In 1015, after Æthelred's death, his son, Edmund Ironside, battled the Danes to a stalemate, forcing Canute to divide the kingdom with him. Streona now openly cast his lot in with the Danes, and his sons arranged Edmund's assassination by rigging a crossbow to fire when the king sat down to the privy. Although Canute initially reappointed Streona earldorman of Mercia, he eventually had him strangled for boasting of Edmund's death and set the head of this arch-traitor on London Bridge, much to the satisfaction of his new English subjects.[20]

In the murderous Streona and the feckless Æthelred, who inherited the throne after the poisoning of the legitimate king, Scott had found the perfect parallels for Buckingham and Charles. Streona had betrayed his country to the Danes who, Scott wrote, were "as dangerous then unto England" as were "the Spaniards or French Arminian faction" now. "Hath not England of late, loste and Spaine gayned more by this", Scott asked, "because they have theire Streonas among us?" Streona's betrayal of the English fleet echoed fears about the Lord Admiral, Buckingham, who might defect with the royal navy, for "howe else shall he escape the Justice of England, but by letting in Spinola and his forces?" After all, "our Papists now and Arminians were by his art tollerated and trusted that they might be in a readinesse for such a day." Thus, "you see how it comes to passe that our greate preparations and high intentions comes to nothing."[21] Streona's betrayal had destroyed Anglo-Saxon England: "all England (through the damnable Treason of this Slave) slaved for ever, first to the Danes, then to the Normans, and since unto other forrenners and Cruell Lords, more then once or twice." History, Scott feared, would soon repeat itself. "Such a day is not farre", he worried, when invaders might strike his neighbours and take "all their wealth, all their little ones and their wives".[22]

Some in Canterbury doubted that Buckingham was a Spanish agent, but Scott knew better: "the breach of the two Treaties [for the Spanish match and the recovery of the Palatinate] and all which hath beene done, ever since, was never meant by him, I am perswaded and it many wayes appeares too plainly." Contemporaries had to see through Buckingham's public mask and to under-stand that in 1623 the duke was:

> displeased belike with the peace, or for some other such causes as fell out in
> Spaine, when our Streona was there. So can these traitors turne everie way.
> They will be Pentioners unto and factors for Spayne; and suddenly the
> greatest enemies that Spaine hath; at the least in seeming and as suddenly
> they will be all Spanish againe.[23]

Scott then linked Streona's appalling murders to Buckingham's catalogue of crimes, drawing uncomfortable parallels, as he did so, between Charles and Æthelred. Streona assassinated "the noble duke ... Aldhelmus ... (like that villaine, who murthered our laste Martyr, by the like practize, it is suspected)". This crime "increased the descontentments and devisions that were in the Realme and made this unreadie Ethelred, more and more hatefull, untill he had brought himselfe and the Realme to distruction". Similarly, "the hatred of the Subiects against the King (for suffering himself and his Subiects to be thus abused by his Buckingham) did rise and doe great harme in this Realme". Ever scrupulous, Scott admitted that "Buckingham ... hath not made himselfe so odious" as Streona, but the duke had (as Eglisham made clear) slaughtered many men, and the list of murdered courtiers and patriots since 1612 was enough to give anyone pause:

> when Princes (as Prince Henrie) and dukes (as Lennox) and Marquesses (as
> Hamilton) and Earles (as Southampton) and other gracious men of meaner
> condition (as our laste Martyr, Sir T. Overbury and others) gow to the Pott
> (whether by the shambles or by Poison) it is tyme for kings (as king Charles)
> to looke about them and take heede of these Edricks and their Butchers,

Souldiers (such was the last kilde our loved and renowned [Thomas] Scott) Poysoners, their white powders and theire playsters, theire spitt rapiers.

Scott's only consolation was that the murderers would eventually receive their deserved rewards. Buckingham could do nothing, aside from trying to:

drowne, or poyson, or stabb himself (if God doe not gyve him more grace and remorse for which I will pray) to escape the sworde of Justice and severe examination and torture; such as you have heard Achan and shall heare Streona did suffer, and as it is meete such detestable and execrable Parricides should suffer, and that all other kingkillers and ungrateful Monsters may feare.

Not all the duke's victims were innocents. The Duke of Lennox, another meddler in Canterbury's elections, would certainly have continued his nefarious ways, and so "the revengefill God did, in so terrible a manner cut him off from doing any further mischiefe", allowing "one Traitor to poyson another".[24]

Streona's outrages culminated in "the Catastrophe" of King Edmund Ironside's murder, "the prologue of our subsequent and not yet ended Tragedie", a murder that Scott directly paralleled with James's. Scott sketched the inexorable pattern of crime and calamity. "Never was this land in more securitie and safetie" until the murders that paved the way for Æthelred's rule—his mother's first husband and his half-brother King Edward. These killings angered God and caused the Danish invasion. Scott likened the Anglo-Danish partition of England to "a Spanish peace", a subtle scheme "to lay honest English men and theire English king in a sleepe whilest the perfidious Tyrant and his trayterous faction made readie theire gunpowder plot". English hopes of redemption had resided with Edmund Ironside, who vowed "they would never yeeld to the Danish yoak so long as they could have a Captayne under whome to fight in the defense of their liberties and right". Streona, however, had other ideas: as Edmund "sate on the privie, to discharge natures burthen, he was thrust into the bottome of his bellie, so as he dyed of it, after such greevous torments as our late poysoned king [James] did endure, before he could dye of the poison". This much Scott drew straight from the chronicles, but to tighten the connection with Buckingham, he developed a role for Streona's mother, "the Witch", who prepared Edmund for his fateful last call of nature "with theire white powder and Playster". What made these murders so heinous was the fact that the perpetrator was "a sworne Servant, and most ingrate Creature whom he had raised . . . out of the dust of povertie and lifted upp from the dunghill of beggarie, to sett him among Princes".[25]

An independent England died with Edmund Ironside, and the Danes seized the country. "After them", Scott continued, came "others as badd, or but a little better, sometimes worse." This story of national annihilation presented "a notable mirrour for us who yet live; to behould our owne faces in". As he looked into that mirror, Scott turned from Streona's crimes to those of King Æthelred who had taken the throne after his halfbrother's murder. Scott thought this history showed:

> what it is for a State or king to suffer the innocent bloud of theire Soveraigne and Predecessor, especially yf he be theire naturall brother, or father much more, to goe unrevenged, yf it be possible to find out and lay hould of the murtherers and Traytors, be they men or women, favourites, Parents, Children or wives.

"Behould", Scott warned, "what murther, unpunished, will bring upon a Nation, and their guiltie kings and Successors, if but in this, that they let the Murtherers escape."[26] King Æthelred, and thus England, was doomed because he failed to avenge his murdered stepbrother.

Scott remained committed to the rule of law, and wanted Buckingham put on trial. But he knew that God would also impose justice for these and other crimes: "the Lord will send upon thee, cursing, vexation and rebuke in all that thou settest thy hand unto . . . untill thou be destroyed." Buckingham could not escape this fate, "neither the dissolving of the Parliament, nor . . . swearing that there shall be no more Parliaments . . . nor the loane, nor the excise, not the plotted peace with Antichrist nor all that the devill and the duke can devise, nor anything" would save him.[27] By 1626 many shared Scott's harsh opinion of Buckingham. More startling was his assessment of Charles I, the Æthelred who had succeeded a murdered king yet never punished his killer.

Jehoram

"Alas, alas", Scott asked, "cannot king Charles hang Buckingham, as easilie as king Ahasuerus hanged Haman?" He thought there were at least two explanations for Charles's failure to act. The first, and the one Scott wanted to believe, was that neither Charles nor his father could think objectively about Buckingham because "they were bewitched by him". In this interpretation the duke had poisoned James on his own initiative, because he knew that he "and a few other knaves would have bene hanged if king James had not beene poysoned". It was, Scott told Charles, "not with thie consent, wee hope", that "thy Buckingham Poysoned thy father, that he might hasten thy Succession and his owne greatnesse". But Charles's decision to end Buckingham's impeachment by dissolving Parliament rendered this interpretation deeply problematic, for it made the young king appear as an accomplice after the fact. Æthelred had been "a Parricide most inhumane in that he did not doe iustice on the Parricides", Scott argued, so "what then is he that calls not his owne fathers and Soveraignes death in question; of which there is such talke and opinion, I believe certayntie?" "Oh God", Scott prayed, "lett not this be king Charles his sinne."[28]

An even more frightening explanation was possible, an appalling explanation that Scott claimed he would "not yet so much as suspect, or would dare, if I could avoide it". But he had to admit that "the secret of secrets", "which others so much speake of" but which "I so much abhorne to heare, or once imagine in my loyall minde", might be true: Charles might have been complicit in Buckingham's conspiracy. The possibility so alarmed Scott that at one point he set down his pen: "I say no more now", he wrote, and "shall not willingly hereafter." But "if I must", he conceded, "I shall a great deale." "Marke this well", he told his readers, "and be affraide and Repent. He hath kild his own father and King, and hath ascended the throne by murther and treason," for "Who doth not, if it be possible, revenge his father and Predecessors death?"[29] Again Scott searched for historical and Biblical parallels to think through the problems of his own times, and while he continued to draw on Anglo-Saxon history, he repeatedly returned to the Old Testament to help him work out the implications of Charles's possible involvement in James's murder.

Since heinous crimes could incur collective punishment, Scott feared that many innocents might pay the price for James's death. Unless Charles punished Buckingham, Scott warned, God "shall slay some of thy seede (or royall line)" and England shall "be transferred unto a strang nation (the danes then, the Austrians or whom else God will, now)". Even more catastrophic divine judgements were possible. Addressing Charles/Æthelred, Scott wrote:

> Thus saith the Lord (yf thou repent not, and cause thy Buckingham to answer to the lawe without all favour and partialitie) the sinne of thy ignominious Mother [AEflthryth], or Buckingham … and the rest of that accursed conspiracie shall not be blotted out without great bloudshead of the miserable Subiects, and then shall come upon the Nation of England … such evills, as never were since, wee were England.

Charles bore as much guilt for this national suffering as Buckingham did, and Charles "must ruine himself and us by his too much favour and trust in this Traitor, notwithstanding he did see enough if he would have seene the wood for the trees". Scott could only lament, "so are kings, even wise and valient kings … bewitched, that must make themselves and theire Subiects wretched, through theire owne fatall follie."[30]

Scott also drew ominous parallels with the stories of King Saul and King David. As David lay dying, his nephew, the warrior Joab, had tried to be king-maker. But while Joab plotted, the old king met with Solomon, and after rehearsing Joab's involvement in the deaths of Absalom, Uriah, Amasa and Abner, convinced Solomon to execute him. Scott asked "cannot, dares not, king

Charles call the murther of his Abner, nay of his father and Sovereigne into Question? Is Buckingham an other Ioab?" Scott tried to force the comparisons into an argument that might excuse Charles. He suggested the king might be "as unguiltie of his fathers, as Ethelred was of his Brothers murther", and imagined Charles saying to himself: "I am this day weake (though newlie Anointed King) and these Buckinghamists are too hard for mee; I dare not meddle with him." Perhaps the king did not act straightaway because he could not "with his own safetie . . . call Buckingham unto his answere; and without all difficultie gyve him the reward he is worthie of." But this hypothetical defence of Charles's inaction could not excuse others who failed to act. Drawing on further Biblical parallels, this time the story of Saul, Agag and Samuel, Scott argued that "if the king will not" execute justice, then "the state may, nay they must . . . Execute Agag, of whom it is said not that king Saul did it, but rather that when he neglected his dutie, Samuel did it." Scott drew the parallels closely. He had Agag/Buckingham ask "King Saul hath pardoned mee and who now shall condemne mee?" Samuel responded "the State, if the King will not, must say, unto Buckingham" that "as thy sword hath made women Childlesse (as thy Potion and Playster hath made England an Orphan or widdow) so shall thy mother be childlesse among women." Samuel then "hewed Agag in peaces".[31]

But who was the English Samuel? In optimistic moments, Scott cast the Parliament-men in the role. If Charles refused to punish Buckingham, then "it is a verie difficult thing or impossible if ever the Parliament that had him in chase, meete agayne, [for Charles] to forbid the doing of it". But Scott knew the powerful forces undercutting the independence of the House of Commons. He wondered whether the judges of King's Bench might collectively assume Samuel's duties. But the more he recalled the limitations of the judges, the more Scott looked to other solutions. In the process he was drawn to ever more radical propositions. After Saul refused to execute Agag as God had commanded, Samuel "had no hart to visit him [Saul] that had no better hart to doe God and the State right and such a minde to save from death such a damned enemie of God and his Countrie." Samuel's attitude only stood to reason, since "Good mens courage cooles when kings zeale to God and the State decayes." Naturally enough, Samuel prayed "for mercie and grace to so gracelesse and ungratefull a king", but unfortunately for Saul/Charles, "God too much provoked by unthank-full and rebellious kings will not be intreated, no not by Samuel." Then Scott imagined God's response to Samuel's prayers:

> See here the duty ever of good Subiects; more to respect God then theire King; and not too much to preferre mercie before iudgement and that which they owe unto one member, though the head, before that which they owe unto the whole body; forgetting that It is better that one perish, be it O Samuel thy owne Saul, then the unitie of all.

Here Scott underlined the importance of letting one person, even a king, die so that "the whole nation perish not". England shall perish, Scott argued, "if Saul [Charles] and his house contynew; yf God provide not for himself and us, a david." God should send a deliverer "not for us onely, but that allso he may gather together in one, the children of God that are scattered abroade."[32] The greater Protestant cause depended on it.

Charles's refusal to execute his father's killer, then, had led Scott to argue, by way of complex Biblical analogies, that the godly cause would be better off without the Stuarts. He was well aware of the radical implications of what he was suggesting. When God commanded Samuel to select a new king from among the sons of Jesse, Samuel responded "I shall be a traitor by his lawe of free Monarchies." And after Samuel made his choice, Saul tried to kill David. But God's omnipotence was the key, as Scott insisted in rhyme:

As yf God might not send when, whome he thinketh best;
And as to him seemes good, releeve a State distrest,
    As yf God might not sett
    On Shepheards head the Crowne
    When they themselves forget
    That must be tumbled downe.

While English law made it treason for a contemporary Samuel to select an alternative monarch, Scott pointed out that Samuel "was an ordinarie Magistrate, or keeper or executor of the lawe, though subordinate". It followed that "if Kings will not doe iustice, other Justices and iudges may and ought, yea though the king forbid them". After all, "God the State and theire lawe have authorized kings and subordinate Magistrates to execute, not to hinder iustice, to punish not to patronize and protect Traitors against God and the State and the lawe."[33] Scott's evocation of the power of "subordinate magistrates" over wicked kings drew directly on the controversial 1579 French Calvinist resistance tract, *Vindiciae contra Tyrannos*, which Scott described as a "learned and honest Booke . . . barked at by the devills doggs and Currs of the Court". Certainly, "Kings are iustly called Gods", but that was "no more then all other Magistrates; for all and not kings onely, are Gods . . . . everie Justice of peace, Mayor or Cunstable, is as much a God, as a king."[34] By empowering the lesser magistrates, *Vindiciae* provided a blueprint for the kind of godly revolution that Scott was now busy imagining.

Such a revolution was unavoidable while Charles continued to intervene to thwart Buckingham's prosecution. In Canterbury, Scott noted, "everie man is silent and still, wee gaze and gape on one another, but whoe (as the Prophet speaketh) puts himself into the breach?" To encourage action, Scott ridiculed the reasoning that demanded political passivity, asking "When did the State

Parliament or people of England", these "free and noble men, such as God created us, create our selves Slaves; and our Ministers omnipotent and solipotent Soveraignes?" Instead of dreading the regime's wrath, Scott's nervous contemporaries should recall Moses's challenge to the Israelites: "who is for Iehovah? who is zealous and couragious to execute Gods vengeance?" The cowering English should emulate the sons of Levi, who slaughtered the enemies of Israel. In any event, there was no viable alternative, because until James's murder was avenged, "the whole people or State was guiltie" of his blood and lay under God's judgement. Charles might try to avert that judgement by calling for a day of repentance, but these efforts, like his efforts to raise the money for his wars, were doomed: only after the old king was avenged would "your Armies and Navies and other honest endeavours . . . prosper", but until then they "will never be; no, not for all your hypocriticall and MockGod fasting and prayer; and all these other your dayntie devises of five Subsidies and such like fetcxhes [sic] to work wonders." Scott exhorted his contemporaries to "hate the evill (the Murther of your king) and love the good (iustice agaynst the Traytors) and establish iudgment in the gate (bring foorth Buckingham to his arraynment and execution)". Finally, Scott alluded to Jonathan's exhortation to his armour-bearer: "Come, and let us go over unto the garrison of these uncircumcised" to slaughter them. After we punish "them that have poysoned our king and Nobles, It may be . . . these uncircumcised Spaniards, Antichristians, Arminians, should not thus laugh at us, as they doe."[35]

Scott's application of these Biblical stories was provocative enough, but even more unsettling was the parallel he drew between Charles I and King Jehoram of Judah. Notwithstanding his military strength, Jehoram's "loathsome Idolatrie, tyrannie and bloudguiltinesse had made him . . . odious unto God who hath the harts of the people at his disposal and doth inspire them with sacred furie and courage when he pleaseth." The people thus soon learned "not to feare him and his dreadfull dukes and ducklings". God sent Philistines, Arabians and Ethiopians against Jehoram and, more important, encouraged the town of Libna to revolt. "The rebellious Libnites", Scott facetiously argued, mouthing conventional pieties against the right of resistance, "should have knowne and acknowledged, that their king Jehoram Gave the Lawe, tooke none and was above the lawe"; they "ought to have knowne, that all they could lawfully doe, against this detestable Tyrant was to pray and to whine; or like the Sheepe, silently and without struggling, to suffer this Butcher to cut theire throates." But instead they defied their king, and for their boldness "God did marveylously blesse Libna".[36] Here Scott feigned sympathy for "poore, poore Jehoram", for "if one Cittie and Countie for Gods cause revolt and rebell, arme not the rest, to thy owne unrest and ruine; looke to it, if by seeking to recover one, thou loose not all." Jehoram—and, by extension, Charles—was a "despicable and base Tyrant", "childlesse" too, "a man that shall not prosper in his daies". Jehoram was doomed: "such a stinke have thie abominable murthers, treasons, tyrannie and Idolatries raysed in the nostrills of God and godly men; and all that have any goodnesse humanitie or courage in them, to avenge the blouds of our Father the King and fathers, the Peeres."[37]

"Such Levits, Libnites, Kentishmen, Canterburie men as will not revolt as when wee must", Scott pointed out, had no viable alternative. The Israelites under Jehoram "were guiltie of Idolatrie, as now England is, of the Idolatrie which is permitted in the Queenes Chapells and other infinite places; at least wincked at and (not without our fault) thus they provoked the Lord to anger." Then he linked the very limited Catholic toleration, which by then was effectively confined to Queen Henrietta Maria's rooms, to the plague that had decimated the English population in 1625–26, and to the lessons of Eglisham's secret history. There was "scarcely ever such a plague in England as that which came in with the Queenes Masse and after king James his murther," Scott wrote. To those reluctant to defy Saul/Jehoram/Charles, Scott asked, "o Jerusalem, wilt thou not be made cleane?"[38] He urged the waverers to take Libna as a model for godly revolt—ignore "the sayings of Tyrants, Court Currs and the divels divines" and seek the truth from the "messenger of [God's] lawe". They should recall that the Libnites acted "in the iust defence of this and other thie duties and their rights and agaynst Idolatrie and tyrannie". Thus God would surely bless "his sacred Ministrie and his no lesse acceptable Rebellion against prophane Jehoram". In this "sacred revolt and rebellion, for God and your owne libertie", Scott advised his fellow citizens to chant a revolutionary creed: "I respect him not. He is not my father. He is not my King but an usurping Tyrant and Traytor." The Libnites "knew well to difference a Tyrant from a king, slaverie from loyaltie, wicked rebellion and treason, from iust defence and revenge in their owne and Gods right." Anxious Englishmen need only observe that God was:

> pleased with this Rebellion . . . and hath beene in all ages, namely since the revolting from Anti-Christ and Anti-Christian Jehorams, in so many Nations, and will be, with all them, that in good advice and holy resolution, rend themselves from their obedience and subiection, whome to obey and serve, is to disobey and rebell against God, the Church and Commonwealth.[39]

The English should cling to Scripture and defend "the true lawes of the kings limitted authoritie, the peoples freedome and dutie to God", acting only "in the iust defense of . . . their rights and against Idolatrie and tyrannie".[40]

The militant Calvinist Thomas Scott had made the secret history of the Catholic George Eglisham his own. Scott had accepted Eglisham's lengthy bill of indictment against Buckingham, and he had followed to its logical conclusion Eglisham's call for justice. Scott agreed with Eglisham that God demanded justice from kings, and he had asked himself the question Eglisham had also asked: what if a king refused to execute justice? Eglisham had evoked the spectre of unjust kings dying like asses in ditches. Scott had watched Charles dissolve Parliament to prevent justice being done on the murderous duke. In Anglo-Saxon history, Scott had found parallels for Buckingham and his crimes in the career of Eadric Streona, and parallels for unjust monarchy in the fate of Æthelred II. In the Hebrew Scriptures he had found even more disturbing parallels for Charles I: either he was a Saul, who had forfeited his throne for injustice, or Jehoram, an idolatrous tyrant. Working through these parallels, Scott arrived at a revolutionary conclusion: the lesser magistrate's right to become Samuel and replace a wicked king, and the people of God's right to "Revolt from Jehoram and take Arms".[41] He had made explicit the anxieties about justice and resistance that the Thames whirlwind had provoked, and that the French history of Edward II and Gaveston had posed anew. The secret history of the murder of James I had led Thomas Brediman and Susanna Prince onto radical terrain, to dreams of a free state or fears of a blood-guilty king; it led Thomas Scott to imagine a godly revolution of the saints. When that revolution came two decades later, Scott was long dead. But the murder of James I, the complicity of King Charles, and George Eglisham's secret history would all live on to play equally telling roles in the revolutionary crisis of the 1640s.

PART V

STRANGE APPARITIONS
1629–49

PROLOGUE

"KING CHARLES HADD A HAND IN ITT"

B Y 16 JULY 1642 the portents of violent conflict were easy to spot. The previous day, when Royalist horsemen clashed with Manchester townsmen, Richard Perceval became one of the first English casualties of what William Waller would call this "war without an enemy", a war that would soon take thousands more lives.[1] Earlier that week the House of Commons had voted to raise an army, appointed the Earl of Essex as its general, and declared they would "live and die" for "this Cause, for the Safety of the King's Person, the Defence of both Houses of Parliament . . . and for the Preservation of the true Religion, of the Laws, Liberties, and Peace of the Kingdom". They petitioned the king "to prevent a civil war", but amidst all the bellicose rhetoric, the gesture seemed futile. Simonds D'Ewes, one of the more cautious Parliamentarians, saw only a terrifying future in which "the lives of innocent men" would be exposed "to mutual slaughter and destruction", while the realm drowned in "an ocean of blood" with no guarantee of the "very thing for which we strive".[2]

On 16 July, Richard Robertson (alias Whitman) paid a visit to Richard Mumford in Winchester.[3] Robertson knew a thing or two about war and the experience of defeat, for two decades earlier he had volunteered to defend the Palatinate from Habsburg invasion. He was not a Winchester local, and though he usually lodged with "a shoemaker att the signe of the Last in Grubb street London", we do not know whether he shared his landlord's profession. Like Mumford and Thomas Ridley, the third man present that Saturday night, Robertson was, at best, only partially literate; he signed his name with a mark. Yet he was deeply engaged in the unfolding political crisis and in its strange prehistory. That evening he told Mumford and Ridley a story of early Stuart poison politics: "Prince henrye was poysoned," Robertson insisted, "the duke of Leanox was poysoned and . . . King James was poysoned." Like Robert Melvin in 1628, Robertson had connected James's poisoning with Henry's death. Yet what Robertson said next about James's murder was more startling: "King Charles hadd a hand in itt." The following day Mumford denounced

Robertson to the civic authorities, and Ridley confirmed Mumford's testimony, adding that Robertson had claimed that "hee could bring a hundred more beesides himselfe that should iustifie" his account of James's death.

Robertson's words were ominous. As supporters of the king and Parliament prepared for battle, this old soldier had voiced a new and highly infectious mutation of Eglisham's secret history, a mutation that was, Robertson insisted, already widespread. Gone was Buckingham, the central actor in *The Forerunner*, and in his place Robertson had directly and unambiguously named a new moral monster: "King Charles hadd a hand in itt." During the 1620s suspicions of Charles I's complicity in his father's murder went largely unspoken. Eglisham had implied that the king was in Buckingham's thrall, and he had warned that Charles would suffer if he failed to see justice done on the poisoner. Yet Eglisham had levelled no direct charges against the new king. During the 1626 Parliament, Sir John Eliot and especially Sir Dudley Digges had come danger-ously close to hinting at Charles's involvement in the murder, even though both men vehemently denied doing so. Charles's dissolution of the 1626 Parliament, apparently to protect his favourite, had raised doubts about the young king, but for the most part Buckingham remained the primary focus of national anger. Thanks to the survival of Thomas Scott's musings on Eglisham, we have seen how easy it was to move from *The Forerunner* to the chilling conclusion that Charles I must have been involved in the murder. There is no evidence that Scott ever voiced these thoughts, though it is hard to imagine that he could have restrained himself among his friends. By 1642, however, what had been effectively unmentionable in 1626–28 was now being spoken aloud. Having haunted Buckingham for the final months of his life, Eglisham's secret history had shifted its form and its quarry—it would now follow King Charles to the grave and beyond.

The following chapters explore the course and the consequences of this radical mutation. We begin in the 1630s when the secret history, muted but not forgotten, festered beneath the superficial calm of the Caroline Personal Rule. We then turn to the dramatic re-emergence and reinvention of the story during the English Revolution. Early in the civil war, hard-line elements in the Parliamentarian coalition co-opted Eglisham's accusations to bolster their case for armed struggle against Charles I. During the war years, hard-liners would continue to mobilize elements of the secret history to shore up militant resolve. But the most dramatic reappearance of Eglisham's secret history would come in 1648 when radicals in the Army and Parliament revived allegations about James's murder to justify ending negotiations with his son. This revival provoked a powerful Royalist response that offered its own account of James's last days, but by early 1649 stories of James's murder would be used to reinforce the regicides' case for Charles I's tyranny and blood guilt. Having helped justify the king's trial and execution, allegations of Charles's involvement in his father's death quickly hardened into revolutionary dogma. The ironies here are rich. A work written by a committed Catholic under the protection of prominent figures in the Spanish Netherlands was now used by militantly godly Protestants to justify the execution of a king they had repeatedly accused of complicity in a "popish" plot.

This story of dangerous political mutation is also a story of media revolution.[4] During the late 1620s and 1630s *The Forerunner* had circulated within an underground media system of illicit print and manuscript texts; from 1642 the secret history was fully absorbed into a new and truly revolutionary media politics driven by a largely unregulated printing press. Political actors across the expanding ideological spectrum began using print to advance short- and long-term agendas, and to inflame, persuade, deceive and mobilize a variety of local, national and international publics. This revolutionary print culture was remarkably inventive and flexible. Printers, publishers and polemicists experimented with new forms that blurred traditional genres, combined words with images, verse with prose, and personal letters with "impartial" reports. Eglisham's *Forerunner*, which had quickly passed from print into scribal communication during the 1620s, continuously shifted its shape as it was reprinted, refashioned, repurposed and reappropriated inside this new media world. The early Stuart past became a central focus of partisan print debate in the 1640s, and the many afterlives of George Eglisham's little book provide us with remarkable new insights into some of the key dynamics of the English Revolution.

CHAPTER SEVENTEEN

NERO IN WARWICKSHIRE

THE SECRET HISTORY AFTER BUCKINGHAM, 1629–40

GEORGE EGLISHAM REMAINED an exile for the rest of his days. He was still in Brussels at the beginning of the 1630s, perhaps practising as a physician; he signed a letter, dated January 1630, as "M. George Eglisham Doctor of Physicke". His wife, Elizabeth, had died, probably quite recently, leaving one surviving child, a daughter. Early in the 1630s, Eglisham was preoccupied with "providing" for his daughter's future, "setling . . . with all the possible care that I can yeeld", and because questions had arisen about the legitimacy of his marriage, he had to write to a Benedictine monk in England for credible testimony confirming his clandestine 1617 wedding in the Clink. Whether Eglisham's letter ever reached the "right Reverend father" is unclear. It eventually fell into the hands of the English Secretary of State, Dudley Carleton, Lord Dorchester, who filed it away. Whitehall had not forgotten the author of *The Forerunner of Revenge.*[1]

Eventually, Eglisham left Brussels for Liège, some fifty miles to the southeast, the chief city of an independent territory ruled by a long-time Habsburg ally. While living in Liège, sometime during the 1630s, Eglisham attempted to come in from the cold. The only source for this episode is Sir Balthazar Gerbier, Buckingham's art procurer, who served as Charles I's envoy to Brussels from 1631 to 1641 (Fig. 64). In two separate (and slightly variant) accounts—a manuscript relation penned in June 1648, and a book published in French at The Hague in 1653—Gerbier described Eglisham's efforts to secure a pardon. The intermediary was Sir William Chaloner, an English baronet then resident in Liège, whom Eglisham may have known in London. Sir William's father, Sir Thomas Chaloner—tutor to Prince Henry and eventually chamberlain of his household—was an advocate of chemical physic, precisely the kind of man Eglisham might have sought out in his early years in London. The Chaloners also appear to have had property interests in the London neighbourhoods near Bacon House, and they had patronage and business connections with the Scottish courtier Sir David Foulis, who probably owned a house just across the

Figure 64: Paulus Pontius's engraved 1634 portrait of Sir Balthazar Gerbier, Buckingham's art procurer and Charles I's agent in Brussels, who allegedly received Eglisham's offer to recant his allegations (National Portrait Gallery).

road from Eglisham's Noble Street address. Eglisham trusted William Chaloner with the delicate task of delivering a letter and a message to Gerbier in Brussels. "His propositions were", Gerbier recalled:

> that iff the king would pardon and receave him into favour and protection againe, with some compitent subsistence he would recant all that he had said, or written to the disadvantage of any in the Court of England, confessing that he had been urged thereunto by some combustious Spirits, that for theire malitious desseings had sett him on worke.[2]

Gerbier's later French account included more details about the identities and motives of these "combustious Spirits". Eglisham had confessed that several English and Scottish enemies of the Stuart dynasty had encouraged him to write his "libel", and that Buckingham's rivals had paid him to suggest that the plaster given to the king had hastened James's death.[3]

In both accounts Gerbier claimed that, on receiving Eglisham's offer, he immediately sent an express courier with letters to Whitehall but got no response. In his 1648 "Relation", Gerbier speculated that the authorities thought it hardly worth their effort to secure a public retraction, since "the World had long since receaved satisfaction thereon; Egleshem being generally known for a foulle ditractor". Gerbier's 1653 account, however, offered a more sinister explanation: the duke's enemies had suppressed the report to keep the truth of their guilt hidden.[4]

There is much we cannot know about these overtures. In 1648, Gerbier insisted that his "Journall" contained a "copie of the dispatch wherein I have account of this bussinesse", but no trace of the correspondence remains in either Gerbier's letter-book or the State Papers Flanders. It is unlikely that Gerbier invented the incident, but he certainly told his story in ways designed to catch the shifting political winds and further his own ambitions.[5] Even if Gerbier was telling some version of the truth, crucial questions remain unanswered. Eglisham's motives, for instance, are opaque. Gerbier said Eglisham was motived by remorse ("*touché d'un remors de conscience*"), but since we cannot date the overture precisely, we can only speculate about what might have provoked his change of heart.[6] Perhaps Charles I's peace with Spain made Eglisham feel vulnerable to possible reprisals, or perhaps with Buckingham dead, Hispanophilia and Catholicism resurgent at court, London seemed an increasingly attractive alternative to the war-torn Netherlands. Perhaps the outbreak of resistance to Caroline ecclesiastical policy in Scotland in 1637-38 revived Eglisham's anti-Presbyterian Stuart loyalism. Or perhaps he simply longed for some "compitent subsistence" to ease the financial strain of impending old age.

If Whitehall did rebuff his approach, Eglisham may not have heard the news. Not long after bringing Eglisham's request to Gerbier, Chaloner reported a new development: "the unfortunate Egleston had died in the street as he was leaving his lodgings". Gerbier's French here is slippery. The verb he used, "*crever*" (literally, "to burst"), could mean to die violently, or simply to die. It is unlikely Gerbier meant to report that Eglisham had died from a violent assault—indeed, he insisted that his account of Eglisham's death disproved claims circulating in the early 1650s that Eglisham had been assassinated on royal orders. Gerbier could well have meant simply that Eglisham had been struck down by a sudden apoplexy. But Gerbier clearly thought the manner of Eglisham's demise shameful, a "fatall end", perhaps even a providential punishment of this "foulle ditractor".[7]

Eglisham's most infamous work, however, continued to percolate through English and Scottish political culture during the 1630s. Discussion of James's murder had not ended with Buckingham's assassination in 1628. Contemporaries continued to circulate and read copies of *The Forerunner*, and other documents on the secret history, as they tried to understand what had gone so disastrously wrong under Buckingham's rule. In one particularly sensational case, elements of the secret history found their way into a play about the Emperor Nero, his favourite, and the problem of tyranny, a drama written, and perhaps even performed, in the English provinces during the 1630s. Despite the surface calm of the Personal Rule, the political culture remained frayed and, on some questions, deeply polarized; and memories of the 1620s remained dangerously contested.

Copying and Compiling Eglisham

For William King, a professional scrivener with customers in the Middle Temple, business was good in 1634. The scribes around the Inns of Court earned a steady income reproducing legal documents, but could make significant extra money by copying controversial political manuscripts, and King boasted that "there was few manuscripts [but] that he had them or could procure them". Along with an eye for quick profit, these scriveners also needed a good instinct for self-preservation as they dabbled in the murkier reaches of the literary underground. Within a few minutes of meeting Christopher Clough, William King sensed trouble. Clough, a visitor from Cheshire, might have been mistaken for an ill-informed provincial news collector shopping for a recent scribal publication, Sir Henry Wotton's parallel lives of Buckingham and the Elizabethan Earl of Essex. But Clough had come to trade rather than to buy, and offered King a book that he claimed was worth at least £40. At first glance, it seemed innocuous enough—a chronicle of the kings and queens from the Norman Conquest to Charles I. But in addition to the various royal "lives, conditions, [and] qualities", the book also purported to record the "vices and vertues" of these monarchs. What happened next is unclear. Clough insisted that King "intreated me to help him to a copie" of this history, an allegation the scrivener stoutly denied, and since King denounced Clough to the Privy Council, which in turn forced Clough to post a £500 bond, it is likely that the scrivener was telling the truth. King maintained that when Clough offered him this chronicle of royal vice, he wanted no part of it: "this discourse ... he conceived to be so dangerous that he replied he had no desire to see, not to looke [at it] thorough a two inch boord".[8]

William King had ample reason for caution. After the disastrous 1629 Parliament, Charles I had withdrawn from the continental wars and embarked on a "personal rule" without Parliaments, hoping to restore the Crown's credibility and finances. During this period, the Privy Council tolerated little dissent, and hoped to reduce the volume and intensity of popular political discourse. An increasingly broad segment of the population had developed a taste for the controversial manuscript tracts and poems circulating in the literary underground, and the regime hoped to avoid the kinds of inflammatory issues that excited libellous scribblers and their audience. The policy largely worked; in the 1630s the volume of new underground material began to ebb. But as Clough's exchanges with William King suggest, interest had not disappeared. Furthermore, despite the decreasing amount of fresh material, older writings continued to circulate, and many devotees of the once-burgeoning news culture took advantage of the lull to organize and to rear-range their collections as a way to search for patterns in England's recent history.[9] During the 1630s several contemporaries reassessed *The Forerunner* in this fashion. By tracking how these readers incorporated this pamphlet into larger collections of underground political materials, we can glimpse contem-poraries wrestling with the secret history's significance in the new political world after Buckingham's assassination. These compilations from the 1630s placed the secret history next to other materials, old and new, some of which supported Eglisham's claims, some of which undercut them, but all of which refracted the secret history in important ways.

Sometimes compilers placed *The Forerunner* alongside new materials from the 1630s. One collection, for instance, included a copy of Eglisham's tract alongside the work that Clough had sought out—Wotton's parallel lives of Buckingham and Essex, a book that disdained *The Forerunner* and offered a mostly positive assessment of the duke. The same compilation also contained reports of the 1631 rape and sodomy trial of the Earl of Castlehaven, a prosecu-tion widely seen as an exemplary act of royal justice against a monstrous aristo-crat. Juxtaposed with *The Forerunner*, however, the history of the king's righteous pursuit of Castlehaven looked far more ambiguous. Charles's rigorous punish-ment of the sodomite earl, who was executed in May 1631, perhaps made his refusal to execute justice upon the poisoner duke all the more puzzling.[10]

Other compilations in the 1630s similarly complicated *The Forerunner*'s meanings. One scribal *Forerunner*, a small octavo 1640 transcript of the 1626 Frankfurt edition, was bound with other items, all in the larger quarto format, to create a coherent collection of texts. The collection included the 1584 *Leicester's Commonwealth*, another infamous Catholic attack on a poisonous English court favourite, and thus situated Buckingham in a genealogy of poisoner-favourites stretching back to the Elizabethan age. Another copy of Eglisham appeared at the end of a volume of speeches and documents from the 1628 Parliament, immedi-ately after a transcript of the 14 June "Remonstrance" against Buckingham. The juxtaposition suggested interesting continuities and tensions in the anti-Buckingham politics of 1626 and 1628. Attentive readers may have wondered, for instance, why the "Remonstrance", which replicated some of the 1626 impeachment charges, made no mention of James I's suspicious death.[11]

Perhaps the most interesting of these 1630s compilations was the one most sceptical of Eglisham's tract. The copy of *The Forerunner* included here was elegantly produced: it replicated the "Frankfort, 1626" title-page imprint and provided catchwords at the foot of each page. It also incorporated a strikingly decorative version of Eglisham's signature at the end of his petition to Charles. Yet the compilation's owner condemned Eglisham's book at the top of the first page as "A damnable Libell" (Fig. 65). Its owner clearly thought the secret history worthy of preservation, if only to illustrate the recent past, but he did not believe its charges. Other materials in the compilation reframed Eglisham's charges in different ways. The compilation contained, for instance, three poems celebrating Buckingham's assassination. Two praised his murderer John Felton, while the third catalogued the duke's offences, alluding to elements central to *The Forerunner*'s narrative. The libel had Buckingham describe his rapid conquest of Hades's court and his new place as "heire-apparant to th'infernall State". Reunited with his witch Dr Lambe, Buckingham now plotted to advance his kindred in Hell, just as he had on earth, telling his mother that she would make a good wife for "Don Pluto". Buckingham's witchcraft also featured in another of the Felton poems, which celebrated the assassin's brave resolve "In spight of charme/Of Witch or Wizard", to free "our land/From Magique thralldome."[12]

While these verse libels echoed Eglisham's allegations, other documents re-categorized such libellous charges as forms of dangerous political speech. The collection included two separates from the 1626 Parliament, but instead of the

Figure 65: Scribal copy of "The Fore-runner of Revenge", c. 1640, adjudged "A damnable Libell" by the copyist (BL Egerton MS 2026, fo. 51v).

much-copied Bristol accusations or impeachment charges, it contained only a procedural ruling in the Bristol case and King Charles's 11 May speech rebuking the Parliament-men who sought to destroy his favourite and offering to "cleare him in every particular". Two other documents from the early 1620s also offered an implicit critique of Eglisham's tract. One was a highly critical commentary on Sir Henry Yelverton's 1621 parliamentary speech comparing Buckingham to Edward II's favourite, Hugh Spencer. The account rejected Yelverton's claim that the comparison with Spencer implied no comparison between James I and the deposed (and sodomitical) Edward II, and denounced Yelverton's "spitefull" speech as "full of poison against his Majesties most sacred person" and "right Puritan-like". This gloss on Yelverton provided the compilation-reader with a frame for interpreting other criticism of Buckingham, whether in *The Forerunner* or in the verse libels, as similarly unruly, popular and Puritanical.[13] The second document was a 1622 examination of Edward Hawley, in which the Crown's lawyers sought information about the Parliament-men imprisoned after the 1621 dissolution and about possibly treasonous behaviour by the Earl of Oxford, another Buckingham critic. Hawley's testimony made clear the real threat that scandalous speech posed to royal "governement or honour". Hawley denied ever hearing Oxford say "That the King was but a Vice-Roye to the Kinge of Spaine". Nor had Hawley seen "anie verses, that did touch the Kinge, the State, the Government, the Lo: Marques Buckingham, or anie other Lord or person of the State", nor the specific poem entitled "the Teares of the People". He knew nothing about "anie plott, or practice against his Majestie" by Oxford and his friends.[14] Read according to the presuppositions of the Crown lawyers in the Hawley manuscript, Eglisham's pamphlet looked like another seditious, "popular" attempt to attack not just the favourite but the Crown as well. Placed in that context, the anti-Buckingham material in this compilation could be taken as evidence of the popular, Puritan, seditious tendencies that the Personal Rule had set out to contain and destroy.

D'Ewes and Wotton Look Back

Late in the 1630s the godly antiquarian Simonds D'Ewes began a memoir, weaving his life story into a history of the strife-torn age. The result was a powerful narrative of the public events of the 1620s, events overshadowed by the "losses and desolations" afflicted on the European Protestant Cause. D'Ewes's memoir also emphasized the lingering effects of the "sad and fatal" breakdown of Charles I's three Parliaments and recorded the role that poison politics played in their demise. He certainly knew *The Forerunner* and he accepted the plausi-bility of its accusations about the murders of Lennox and Hamilton. Lennox's sudden death in February 1624 was "generally reported to be natural", D'Ewes wrote, "though many suspected it to be violent by poison". These suspicions grew after Hamilton's demise a year later, "the manner of whose death, and the view of the dissected body upon his decease, much confirming men's suspicions that he perished by a violent intoxication." D'Ewes found ample cause for suspicion; Hamilton's death was "so sudden as many feared it was violent, by poison; but whether the Duke of Buckingham were the author of it, as Doctor Eglisham, a Scotchman, hath published in print, I cannot say". Unlike Eglisham, D'Ewes ruminated on the murder in the distinctive language of the godly patriot, judging the marquis's loss a great blow to "all good men and true Protestants".[15]

D'Ewes's account of James's death did not allude to Eglisham's claims of deliberate poisoning. But he rejected the authorized version of the king's final illness, endorsing instead the narrative produced by Sir John Eliot's 1626 Select Committee. After James's ague turned into a burning fever, D'Ewes wrote, "it was at first reported that he fell into that extremity by his own wilfulness, neglecting the advice and remonstrances of his physicians." Yet in 1626, "Doctor Ramsey . . . and other learned practitioners in that faculty" testified that James "was reasonable well recovered, and in their judgments past all danger, till, in their absence, George Duke of Buckingham ministered to him a potion, and gave him plasters, after which he soon fell into a great burning and distemper, which increased more and more till his decease." D'Ewes believed that these accusations, and Charles's stubborn defence of the favourite, played the central role in the "abortive dissolution". When that "great assembly" questioned Buckingham "for his life", Charles had abruptly ended the session "to prevent his further danger". The political costs were steep. "Infinite almost was the sadness of each man's heart . . . that truly loved the Church or Commonwealth at the sudden and abortive breach" of the session. After the Commons found Buckingham "guilty of many great and enormous crimes, and *especially because he had given a potion and ministered plasters to King James, in his last sickness, of which it was doubted he died*", and after the Lords resolved "to question the said Duke for his life", then:

> all those proceedings received a sudden check and stop by this heavy and fatal dissolution; which happened not only most unseasonably in respect of the many blessings we missed at home by it, but also because the King had at this time many great and noble designs abroad for the restoring of God's oppressed Church and Gospel in foreign parts.

D'Ewes was not certain that Buckingham had murdered Hamilton, and he rejected Eglisham's claim that Buckingham had murdered James. Nevertheless, he agreed with the Parliament-men that Buckingham's medical interference had damaged any hope of James's recovery. For D'Ewes, Buckingham's "fatal end" in 1628 was a providential judgement on his "extreme lust, ambition, pride, gluttony, and other sins".[16]

Sir Henry Wotton also turned to "Historicall Imployments" during the 1630s, but he came to markedly different conclusions. Before his death in 1639, Wotton wrote two perceptive accounts of Buckingham's career, both eventually printed early in the 1640s. *A Short View of the Life and Death of George Villers* puzzled over the hatred Buckingham had inspired, arguing that envy and obloquy were the inevitable results of the "naturall Incompatibility" between popular and "Soveraigne favour". Since popular opinion cared only for "good success", and thus changed rapidly, like the "Contrary motions of popular waves", Buckingham's popularity in 1624 had been "a meere Bubble", doomed to burst. For Wotton, the "sudden and marvellous conversion" of the duke's reputation from "the most exalted . . . to the most depressed", while unprecedented, was explicable. Parliaments might be capable of "shrewd" criticism, but England in the 1620s had provided "Ranke soile" for "free Witts" addicted to carping critique. The 1626 session was a case in point. Whatever the ostensible reasons given in the impeachment articles, Wotton insisted that the assault on the duke was, in fact, the result of a secret, envy-driven aristocratic conspiracy that had deployed agents in the House of Commons to mobilize discontent. Wotton did not discuss the impeachment articles that this plot produced, but he insisted that Buckingham's answers were "diligently and civilly couched". Furthermore, Charles's protection of Buckingham was entirely justified; the young king had been "engaged in honour, and in the sense of his own naturall goodnesse, to support" his favourite.[17]

Wotton may have had *The Forerunner* in mind when he castigated the "wild Pamphlet" that "would scant allow" Buckingham "to be a Gentleman", but he insisted that Buckingham had behaved honourably in Spain and that James's affection for him had never ebbed. As we have seen, Wotton did refer explicitly to Eglisham in his analysis of Felton's motivations for murdering Buckingham, but he did not bother to rebut *The Forerunner*'s claims; he simply excoriated its falseness. This "libellous book made the Duke one of the foulest Monsters upon the earth", unworthy not only of power "but of any room within the bounds of all humanity"—or it would have, if the libeller's "prodigious predictions" had possessed even "the least semblance of truth".[18]

Wotton's other book drew parallels between Buckingham and the late Elizabethan favourite, the Earl of Essex. Again, Wotton brooded over the intensity of parliamentary attacks on Buckingham, and blamed their virulence this time on the election of a generation of young, ambitious and impetuous men. He also used the Eglisham case to analyze how the two favourites managed "fame". Unlike Essex, who liked to issue apologies "which hee Wrot and dispersed with his owne hands at large", Buckingham "saw no fruite of Apologies but the multiplying of discourse". Wotton then told the story of his interrogation of Lady Auldbar "about a certayne filthy accusation grounded upon nothing but a few single names taken up by a Foote man in a Kennell, and streight baptized: A list of such as the Duke had appoynted to be empoysoned". Wotton recalled how he:

> found it to bee the most malicious and Franticke surmize, and the most contrary to [Buckingham's] nature that I thinke had ever beene brewed from the beginning of the World, howsoever countenanced by a Libellous Pamphelet of a fugitive Physition even in Print; and yet of this would the Duke [not] suffer any answer to be made on his behalfe, so constant hee was to his owne Principles.[19]

Vehement Presumptions

These English reckonings with the 1620s reveal ideologically polarized perspectives on the recent past. Eglisham's secret history also continued to resonate in Scotland. In 1625, David Calderwood, an outspoken Presbyterian critic of James VI's ecclesiastical reforms, returned from exile and began writing a history of the Kirk. By the early 1630s he had completed a "second digest" of this work, more than two thousand pages in length. So significant was Eglisham's secret history to this enterprise that, as Calderwood revised his history, he added in more and more details from *The Forerunner*. According to Calderwood, reports of Hamilton's death had caused "small regrate" in Scotland, but they were accompanied by a "brute . . . that he was poysoned". The accusation was then "avowed . . . in print" by "Doctor Eglesheim" who "fledd to West Flanders". Calderwood extracted several key elements from *The Forerunner*: the mysterious scroll of names, the rumours that Buckingham would poison his enemies, the mountebank who "offred to sell poyson" that could kill at a certain time, and Hamilton's post-mortem blistering and swelling. Calderwood also endorsed Eglisham's account of the motive: Hamilton "wold not accomplishe the matche betuixt his sone and the duke's neice, whereupoin the duke thus revenged himself upon him."[20]

Calderwood's account of James's death was more caustic. The day before the news reached Edinburgh, a terrible storm hit the Scottish coast—a portent, argued Calderwood, "of some great alteration". He thought it fortunate that the king had died two weeks too early to enforce Easter Communion in conformity with the controversial "Act of Perth": "honest men"—the Presbyterian hardliners who defied James's "terrours and threatnings"—had no reason to mourn his death. Calderwood's hostile account of James's last days expressly contradicted the picture of pious resignation painted by John Williams, Dr Paddy and the court newswriters. James "lay all the time of his sickness almost silent", and "what he spake was to litle purpose: 'Sone Charles, Sone Charles!' and the like". Furthermore, the king's last words before he became "speechlesse" were no testimonies of piety. When his courtiers urged him "to take courage, for he wold be well again", James swore "By God's wounds! . . . I will dye if ye had all said it!" As for the famous last communion, Calderwood was contemptuous: this ritual was but a taking of "his viaticum after the English fashioun".

Calderwood added two further damning details to this portrait. While James was ill:

> Buckinghame caused baptise a gryse [pig] in the chamber where [James] lay sicke, with the ceremonies requisite, godfathers and the rest; and efter it was baptized it was chassed up and doun the chamber. The pretense of this horrible profanation or mockerie of the Sacrament was to make the king to laughe.

For Calderwood, such "mockerie" was further evidence of James's impiety and a sure sign that the king had, in fact, died badly. Indeed, some thought this travestied sacrament represented something altogether more sinister—"plaine magicke". Calderwood turned to Eglisham for his second damning detail: there were "vehement presumptions that [James] was poysouned" by the Countess of Buckingham's plasters and a "white powder sprinkled in his drinke".[21]

Calderwood quickly summarized Charles's proclamation in Scotland, noting that the time-serving Edinburgh preachers who "commendit King James for the most religious and peaceable prince that ever was" had failed to "move the people" to any real grief. He then described James's funeral, again rejecting the authorized version: the rituals were "performed with great magnificence for mater, but without forme and order", and the "funerall night" in London witnessed another portentous storm that "passed the rememberance of man". Finally, Calderwood returned to Eglisham. He quoted *The Forerunner's* demand that Charles exact justice, and Eglisham's claim that his work would be a "tuichestone to . . . manie other Scotish men". Calderwood then transcribed Eglisham's account of James's poisoning "word by word".[22] Nowhere did Calderwood refer to Eglisham's 1619 defence of James's Kirk reforms or to his attacks on George Buchanan and Andrew Melville, nor did Calderwood pursue the implications of Eglisham's flight to "West Flanders". Shorn of his popery and his Stuart loyalism, George Eglisham served the militant Presbyterian's political purposes all too well.

It is unclear when Calderwood condensed this second digest into the shorter history that eventually appeared in print in 1678, but he probably was still working on the project in the mid- and late 1640s. The final version dramatically pruned the accounts of Hamilton and James's deaths, repeating that Hamilton had been poisoned and that "Doctor Eglisheime . . . avouched it in print, and spared not to impute it to Buckinghame", but cutting all the supporting details. Although the printed version retained accounts of the portentous storms that accompanied James's death and funeral, it excised the account of the king's spiritually mediocre death, the porcine baptism, and Eglisham's poisoning allegations.[23] If Calderwood made these cuts during the 1640s—and we can only speculate about this—the explanation for this radical surgery may lie in the increasingly revolutionary, and ultimately anti-Presbyterian and anti-Scottish, uses to which the secret history was put during the course of the English Revolution.

A Greater Man than Nero

Throughout the 1630s, in commonplace books and manuscripts, memoirs and histories, contemporaries brooded over Eglisham's tract. But perhaps the most astonishing appropriation of the secret history appeared in a play, written early in the decade and possibly performed in a Warwickshire gentry parlour. John Newdigate, a Parliament-man and theatre devotee, is the most likely author of *The Emperor's Favourite*, a play set at the court of the tyrant Nero: the sole copy is in his hand and survives in his family's papers.[24] Like other early Stuart writers, Newdigate used the Roman past to illuminate the English present. The parallels between Crispinus, Nero's favourite in the play, and Buckingham were unmistakable. Like Buckingham, Crispinus hailed from an obscure social background, and his sudden rise upset social norms. Like the duke, Crispinus promoted his relatives, securing them lucrative offices and advantageous marriages. Like Buckingham, the upstart Crispinus became arrogant, lording it over "the best men" while riding through the city in a lavish litter; he perverted the common good by trading in monopolies and patents; and his sexual appetite was as rapacious as his thirst for power. More troubling still, Crispinus, like Buckingham, had recourse to witches.[25]

The play also drew parallels with several scandalous incidents in Buckingham's career. The coerced marriage of Crispinus's doltish brother Hillarius to the virtuous Aurelia, and the favourite's subsequent prosecution of Aurelia for adultery, closely mirrored the notorious match between Buckingham's brother, Viscount Purbeck, and the daughter of Sir Edward Coke.[26] The play also alluded to Buckingham's military misadventures: Crispinus deliberately undermined the Roman war effort, taking bribes from Rome's enemies, and boasting that "there's not a forraine state/with whom Rome hath a difference but keeps/Me in continuall pay".[27] Newdigate also highlighted the favourite's close relationships with his mother, Locusta, the "mistress of my councell & the contriver of all my designes", and with their client witch, Promus, who had "skill ith' black art" and with love philters. Like the Countess of Buckingham, Locusta embodied contemporary gender anxieties: she was an ageing but still sexual woman who consorted with witches and wielded perverse political power within a supposedly patriarchal system.[28] Although the favourite's power stemmed from his control over the emperor—Crispinus boasted, "I/have Nero now in a string"—Crispinus was dominated by his mother: "Nero commands

Rome, my son Nero[,] I him," Locusta proclaimed. Finally, Crispinus, like Buckingham, hungered for more than royal favour; he wanted popularity, "pleasing words/ . . . from the vulgar mouthes", and he delighted when the "mechanicks . . . doe acknowledge me/A greater man then Nero".[29]

These parallels encouraged Newdigate's audience to see Nero as Charles. A secondary character, both pathetic and tyrannical, Nero articulated a philosophy of arbitrary rule. He imagined political obedience as analogous to slavery: since "the meanest man in Rome commands his slave/And gives no reason why", Nero reasoned that "our priviledge/Sure goes as farr as his". He unabashedly claimed to be above the law, and since he would only advance those who abased themselves to his will, the country's "brave spirites" either left Rome voluntarily or were forced out. Nero's court was also a sink of sexual corruption, although nothing hints that Nero was attracted to his favourite's fine leg and "dayntie shape".[30] While some characters blamed Rome's disastrous condition on the favourite rather than the monarch—"Cesar is good", one honest Roman declared, "I would the men about him/were as good servants as he is a maister"—the play itself refuted this line of exculpation. Nero alone had ordained Crispinus's rise to power, and the emperor repeatedly rejected sound counsel about how to use his favourite. He did not want a wise advisor, or even a lightning rod to deflect criticism; he wanted a companion "in our sportes/ Such as our leisure shall give licence to".[31]

This deeply disillusioned portrait of the recent past made muted, but unmistakable, references to James's murder. Both Tacitus and Suetonius had presented Nero as an orchestrator and a beneficiary of poisoning. To ease his way to the throne, his mother, Agrippina, engineered the murder of her husband, the emperor Claudius, and Nero himself had Claudius's son Britannicus poisoned. The poison artist employed in both murders was Locusta, a woman with "a vast reputation for crime". Newdigate's play did not claim that Crispinus's mother, and the notorious historical poisoner of the same name, were the same woman. But the echo, and the ensuing parallel with the Countess of Buckingham, was surely intentional. And with her close ties to Pronus/Lambe, the play's Locusta reinforced the poisoner-woman-witch triad so central to contemporary images of the crime. At one point, Locusta's daughter urged her to invite "those that envy you" to a banquet of "Italian figs", a commonplace shorthand for poison. These allusions set up the play's one direct reference—brief but clear—to the old king's poisoning. The playwright Datus read Nero a script that cut close to a dangerous truth: "The day was fatall/wherein the conscious successor prepar'd/A draught to hasten his adopters death". Here was licence to conclude that Nero/Charles was complicit in the murder of Claudius/James. Nero, unsurprisingly, ordered the author of these lines hanged.[32]

The Emperor's Favorite also revisited the vexed question of justice denied. In a scene harking back to the Parliaments of 1626 and 1628, Crispinus's enemies presented Nero with evidence of his treason, only for the emperor to stymie any investigation. This denial of justice provoked a dissident conspiracy to assassinate Crispinus, an act his enemies justified in neo-republican terms as liberation from "timorous servitude". Newdigate had the virtuous Tigranes stab Crispinus, just as Felton stabbed Buckingham, and represented the assassination in language nearly identical to the rhetoric used to lionize Felton in 1628. Tigranes's bold action had "a brave intention" to "Take the common wealths revenge". Like Felton, Tigranes confessed his deed with pride and submitted to his fate while the populace hailed him as an agent of justice and liberty.[33] Although the plotters expected a new political dawn, the play did not provide one: without even a hint at a royal awakening or an end to tyrannical misrule, this was a troublingly inconclusive end to a dangerously critical play.

Dining in Fish Street, London, 1634

William Hardly had known Christopher Clough for years, certainly long enough to feel comfortable walking the political wild side in his company. Late in 1634, as the two men dined together at a London hostelry in Fish Street, Hardly, a draper's apprentice, recited for his friend several verses from the 1627 libel "In ducem reducem", which indicted the military fiasco at the Île de Ré and included unmistakable allusions to Buckingham's poisonings and witchcrafts. Clough did not recognize the poem, and asked Hardly whether it were new, and whether he could have a copy. In marked contrast to his dealings with William King the scrivener, Clough did not need to barter: Hardly promised him a free transcript.[34]

The continued circulation of verse libels such as "In ducem reducem", with its allusions to the murder of James I—like the continued copying and compilation of *The Forerunner*, the scribal publication of Wotton's parallel lives, the history-writing of D'Ewes and Calderwood, and Newdigate's *The Emperor's Favourite*—all reveal the continuing fascination with Buckingham's England in the years after the favourite's death, and the ideologically divided responses his England still aroused. Although the English literary underground was not as densely thronged as in the 1620s, it was still a flourishing concern. Yet this literary underground, with its bold authors, scriveners and readers busy producing or tracking down the latest libel, was on the cusp of a great change. The revolutionary crisis that returned *The Forerunner* to the thick of political discourse in 1642 would not only reshape the book's meaning; it would also present its charges to a much broader set of audiences. Eglisham did not live to see the day, but his secret history would become a major beneficiary of a media revolution.

CHAPTER EIGHTEEN

EGLISHAM REDIVIVUS

THE SECRET HISTORY AND THE CASE FOR WAR, 1642

O<small>N 8 OCTOBER</small> 1642, Thomas Hill, a husbandman from the north Devon parish of Bishops Nympton, was drinking at the Bear Inn in Exeter when he overheard a city gentleman railing against the House of Commons. Francis Giles announced that "it was exprest or sett foorth in some printed booke or paper that King Charles had poisoned his Father and was consent to the poisoning of the Duke of Lennox," and asked his companions "Be not these roages that sett foorth such things, and is it not pittye that such roages should be suffered?" The following day, Hill recounted this exchange to a local weaver, telling him that "the said Giles had spoken against the Parliament, and had saide that the Parliament as he did think had declared or sett foorth that King Charles had poysoned his Father." Three months earlier, when Richard Robertson, a Londoner visiting Winchester, had announced that "king Charles hadd a hand" in the poisoning of Prince Henry, the Duke of Lennox and King James, all Robertson could say was that "hee could bring a hundred more beesides himself that should iustifie it". Giles, by contrast, could cite "some printed booke".[1] Eglisham's secret history had just gone public for the second time, and on a scale far beyond anything imagined sixteen years earlier.

In 1626, Jan van Meerbeeck had produced perhaps several hundred copies of *The Forerunner of Revenge*, and subsequently scriveners and copyists had done their best to meet the demand for more. But late in 1642 many hundreds, perhaps thousands, of copies of Eglisham's book were flying from London's now essentially unregulated printing presses. While chance largely accounts for the survival rates of individual tracts, the rough totals suggest something about the scale of the new print runs: Meerbeeck's *Forerunner* survives in five copies, but the London 1642 editions in sixty-seven.[2] The scale of republication suggests that the secret history had a real impact on the revolutionary events now convulsing the British Isles.

Over the summer and autumn of 1642, sometimes with fervour, often with reluctance, men mobilized for war as king and Parliament accelerated their search for soldiers, weapons and money. On 22 August, Charles I raised his standard at Nottingham, and on 9 September the Parliament's Lord General, the Earl of Essex, left the City with 300 horse and "his coffin and winding sheet and funeral scutcheons ready drawn". The first major skirmish took place on 23 September at Powick Bridge near Worcester, while moderates continued to search for a settlement. But attitudes were rapidly hardening. On 27 August and again on 6 September, Parliament had turned away royal overtures, and moderates in Westminster fretted that a cabal of "fiery spirits" had met the king's "gracious" messages with an "insolent resolution" reflecting an emergent "spirit of violence grown amongst us". England was already suffering from "rapine and pillage", both from soldiers and the "rude multitude" who plundered "the houses of the nobility, gentry, and others".[3] During these tense early autumn days Eglisham's secret history returned to the centre of English political discourse, as those committed to the Parliamentarian cause of religious and political reformation appropriated the murder of James I to mobilize popular opinion against any easy accommodation with Charles I.

Eglisham's book reappeared in a sequence of works published between early September and early November 1642. The first reappearance occurred just before the Earl of Essex left London with his coffin in tow; the second, more intense cluster of reappearances began late in September, days after the clash at Powicke Bridge, and continued through the battle at Edgehill on 23 October. The last reappearance came early in November, after the strong Royalist showing at Edgehill had made Parliament more willing to talk peace. Changing contexts and divided partisan agendas meant *The Forerunner* carried no stable meaning during the autumn crisis of 1642. Both radical and more mainstream elements of the Parliamentarian coalition appropriated the alleged murder of James I in different ways and for somewhat different ends, but by tracking the reproduction and redeployment of Eglisham's story, we can see how a weapon forged in Brussels against a royal favourite was now refashioned in London for use against the king.

King James His Judgement

One of the earliest 1642 printed allusions to James's death was also one of the most radical, a sign of the profound disgust some Parliamentarians already felt for the monarchy. *King James His Iudgement of a King and of a Tyrant*, printed on 8 September, was an eight-page quarto designed and priced for a mass audience. Although the tract listed no author, printer or publisher, parliamentary investigators later attributed it to Abigail Dexter, wife of the Puritan printer Gregory Dexter. The pamphlet claimed to be the work of a Scotsman and included ostentatiously Scottish vocabulary like "Kirk" for Church, "anent" for "about", "geud" for "good", but at least one contemporary thought the Scottish persona masked an author who was "by most of his language, as by common fame . . . english bred".[4] The pamphlet commented on a speech James I had given to Parliament in March 1610. Since monarchs, by natural law and by their coronation oaths, were explicitly bound to govern according to the laws, James had maintained that the ruler who did not do so was "a Tyrant". Silently excising the king's comment that "no Christian man ought to allow any rebellion of people against their Prince", even a tyrannical one, the pamphleteer now appropriated James's words to justify the popular right to resist tyrants once a king broke his "Covenant . . . with his people". Charles I, the pamphlet argued, had become a tyrant, for he had "left off to rule according to his Laws" and "(which is one infallible marke and property of all Tyrants) doth take up Armes against the faithfullest, honestest and godlyest liege people of his Land; yea aginst the whole body of the Land, when assembled in Parliament sitting for the good of the Kirke and State." Since to obey such a "perjured Man . . . odious to God" was to become "his Slaves", the king's subjects had not only a right but also a duty to resist, lest they assume "the tyranicall yoake of perpetuall slavery".[5]

Citing Calvinist resistance theory, classical republican concepts, and the Caroline past, the tract warned readers to focus not on Charles's recent moderate declarations, but on his actions "from the first entrance of His Reigne". Against Charles's claims to stand for Protestantism, the tract set his 1623 letter to the pope, nothing less than a "precontract made" to introduce popery into England. The tract then listed "Certaine Quaeries of things done since King Charles his Reign began". This catalogue of misdeeds placed the blame squarely on Charles himself, not on his evil counsellors, and it ended by stating that the king was "now intending and indevouring with Might and maine . . . to set up a lawlesse and Tyrannicall Government over His Land." The bill of particulars began with James I's murder: "When our geud King Iames his death was by one of his Phisitians tendered to the King and Parliament to be examined", the tract wondered, why was "the Parliament . . . eft soone dissolved?"[6] The implications of this allusion to Eglisham's charges were clear: Charles had dissolved the 1626 Parliament to prevent the investigation of the poison allegations and was thus implicated in (at least) the cover-up of a murder. Like publicizing Charles's letter to the pope, unearthing the secret history of James's death cast a penetrating new light on the past to reorient political action in the present. The cover-up of James I's poisoning was refigured as one of his son's original sins and became a central part of the Caroline popish plot against English religion and liberty.

King James his Iudgement went far beyond the official Parliamentarian rhetoric that defended the war as a fight "for the king", and so on 10 September the House of Lords ordered the pamphlet burned and instructed the Lord Chief Justice to "examine the printer, publisher and author". The Commons quickly followed suit, directing the Committee for Printing to investigate the tract for advocating "the deposing and killing of tyrants". A month later, two suspects had emerged. Although Gregory Dexter had been on military duty when the book was printed, William White, one of his men, confessed to printing the book on Dexter's premises, as did Abigail, Gregory's wife. White denied knowing the author, and Abigail claimed she had found the copy of *King James His Iudgement* "in her husbands workroome". She admitted that she knew the author but refused to name him. After seven weeks in the King's Bench prison, she continued to deny any seditious intent since the book was "a work of the late King and therefore inoffensive", and she played on expectations of female weakness by begging the Lords to excuse her "imbecility and ignorance". Still imprisoned five weeks later, she lamented that "her husbands trade (hee being still absent in the Army) is almost lost, their estate wasted", and thus pleaded for mercy.[7]

One observer, sceptical of the pamphlet's alleged Scottish origins, thought it the work of a "subtle Machiavillian [*sic*] . . . who, I am well assured is either Brownist, Anabaptist, or Separatist". Royalist authors regularly, and stereotypically, linked political radicalism to religious sectarianism, but in Abigail Dexter's case this linkage to the radical heterodox wing of Parliamentarianism made sense. In the 1630s, Gregory Dexter had participated in underground Puritan print campaigns, and by 1641 he was working with the stationer Richard Oulton on books supporting political and godly reformation. By 1643, Dexter would be the printer of choice for the most radical voices in the capital. Late in 1642, Abigail Dexter was almost certainly working with the same kinds of radical Parliamentarian factions.[8]

On 9 November 1642, George Thomason, a London bookseller and voracious book collector, bought a response to *King James his Iudgement*. Aping the visual appearance of the original, which it damned as a "shameles, unjust and trayterous Impeachment", *King Charles His Defence* insisted that the king was "no Tyrant" and noted that even Parliament had not called him one. Yet even if Charles were a tyrant, the tract reminded readers, only God could punish bad kings. Although the pamphlet deployed several Royalist polemical tropes, it cultivated a scrupulously moderate tone, admitting that Charles's regime had made errors, most notably in Church policy, while blaming his wicked counsellors, not the king himself. The response did not focus directly on the revival of Eglisham's charges, but its attitude towards those charges was clear. Commenting on the "Quaeries" headed by the murder of the king, the author claimed "I doe accompt them altogether so scandalous and divellishly invented that they are not worthy to be answered, but the writer and publisher of them ten times more worthy to dye a cruell death then Shimei that cursed and threw stones at King David." Nevertheless these slanders had to be taken seriously, for they "assaulted his Majestie, attempting thereby to kill him in his honour and royall estate".[9]

Eglisham Redivivus

By the time Thomason purchased *King Charles His Defence*, the full story of James I's death "made by one of his physitians" had already re-emerged in print. "About October 10", John Rous wrote in his diary, "my brother sawe a booke that shewed the grounds of suspition that the old marquesse Hamilton and king James were both poysoned by the duke and his mother." The entry suggests that Rous himself had not seen the book before, but he had long been aware of the impeachment charges that in 1626 were "the greate wonder of the country". The "large and well pend discourse" that Rous's brother had seen in London in October 1642 quickly attracted widespread notice.[10]

Perhaps as many as six different versions of *The Forerunner* appeared late in 1642. Thomason procured his copy on 30 September, while another version carries a handwritten date of "No[vember] 2d 1642" (Figs 66 and 67).[11] The Thomason version appeared in at least three variants. All were two-sheet, sixteen-page quartos, and all had slightly different spelling, typesetting and punctuation. Two of them corrected the title-page typographic slip of "Farle" for "Earle" found in Thomason's copy, and one carried a redesigned title page.[12] A fourth version, with a different title page, different ornamentation and a reset text, retained the sixteen-page quarto format.[13] The version that one owner dated 2 November presented the text in a more spacious three-sheet, twenty-four-page quarto. Its title page dropped some of the ornamental bordering that had appeared on the Thomason copy and its variants, though it retained the Thomason version's odd reference to the "most Honourables Houses of Parliament". This "November" version appeared in at least two different print-ings, one of which introduced even more eccentric pagination.[14]

None of the six versions of the 1642 *Forerunner* named the printer or publisher, and it is probably impossible to establish whether all six were produced on the same press or whether several printers and publishers were at work. Taking as clues the various printers' ornaments—decorative headbands, title-page borders, distinctive ornamental capital letters—one scholar has suggested that the Thomason version of the Eglisham reprinting was part of a series of publications issued by a radical group of printers around George Bishop and Richard White, who were eager to support the "fiery spirits" in Parliament led by John Pym and William Fiennes, Viscount Saye and Sele.[15] Drawing conclusions from shared ornamentation is at best uncertain—many ornaments were mass produced, and were often loaned or traded—but it is clear that the Eglisham editions were republished as part of an effort to advance the militant Parliamentarian case for war in the uneasy autumn of 1642.

All the 1642 versions included a title-page suggestion that among the lessons to "be observed" in Eglisham's book was "the inconveniences befalling a State where the Noble disposition of the Prince is mis-led by a Favourite".

The Fore-Runner

OF

REVENGE,

Being two Petitions:

THE ONE

To the KINGS moſt Excellent Majeſty;

THE OTHER

To the moſt Honourables Houſes of Parliament.

Wherein is expreſſed divers actions of the late Farle of *Buckingham*; eſpecially concerning the death of King *James*, and the Marqueſſe *Hamelton*, ſuppoſed by Poyſon.

Alſo may be obſerved the inconveniences befal- ling a State where the Noble diſpoſition of the Prince is miſ-led by a Favourite.

By *George Eglisham* Doctor of Phyſick, and one of the Phyſi- tians to King *James* of happy memory, for his Majeſties perſon above ten yeares ſpace.

Printed at *London*, in the yeare, 1 6 4 2.

Figure 66: Title page of George Eglisham, *The Fore-Runner of Revenge*, one of several versions of Eglisham's tract published in the autumn of 1642, and purchased by the bookseller George Thomason on 30 September (British Library).

Given Eglisham's claims, "inconveniences" was a clear understatement, but the key lesson concerned the political problem of "the Prince"—even one of "noble disposition"—"mis-led by a Favourite". The lesson now applied to Charles, rather than James, whom Buckingham had misled in the 1620s. In the polemical context of September–October 1642, this title-page alert connected the Eglisham reprints to one of the core Parliamentarian justifications for taking up arms. Official parliamentary declarations in September 1642 avoided direct attacks on the king and depicted Charles not as the "tyrant" imagined by *King James His Iudgement* but as a dangerously misled ruler surrounded by "Delinquents", the agents of "a wicked partie, who have long plotted our ruine and destruction". In some declarations Charles seemed almost a victim; one petition claimed the king's life was in danger from these evil men if he did not "in all things concur with their wicked and traitorous courses". But others blamed Charles for serving as "a shield and defence to those instruments" against parliamentary judgement, and in doing so he was responsible for the "innocent blood which is like to be spilt in this cause". The declarations urged Charles to "withdraw your royal presence and countenance from these wicked

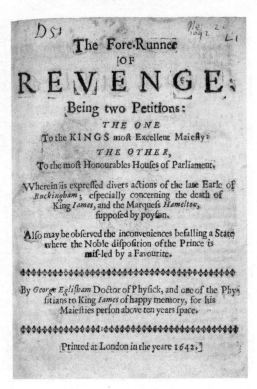

Figure 67: Title page of another 1642 version of George Eglisham's *The Fore-Runner of Revenge*, this one purchased on 2 November (Bodleian Library).

persons", and in fact, Parliament effectively instructed Essex "by battle, or otherwise" to "rescue his majesty's person . . . out of the hands of those desperate persons who were then about". Charles's refusal to follow this script drove some of his opponents into more dangerous polemical territory. The House of Commons ordered the burning of a pamphlet written by "A. H.", who stressed the miserable fate of those bad kings who had refused to "forsake" the "wicked counsell of all Achitophels" and those "wicked sonnes of Beliul that are thy councellors against all right and law of God, of nature and of kingdome".[16]

The reprinted *Forerunner* played into this Parliamentarian discourse on kingship, evil counsel, and the costs of retaining wicked advisors whom Parliament had identified as delinquents. By returning attention to 1626, when Charles had interrupted the parliamentary investigation of his favourite, the reprinting confirmed those Parliamentarian narratives that traced Charles I's misrule back to the very first days of his reign. Moreover, by reviving Eglisham's uncompromising verdict on kings who failed to administer justice, these republications supported more radical meditations on what would happen if Charles continued to neglect Parliament's "Good Councell". Eglisham's startling image of unjust kings dying like asses in ditches echoed the Biblical imagery of the radical A. H., who warned of a new political world exalting "him that is low" and abasing "him that is high".[17]

For the first time in its history, Eglisham's book was widely and publicly available in England, and the sheer volume of copies produced in the autumn of 1642 indicate how useful his secret history could be in this time of early revolutionary flux. As we have seen, in the 1620s, *The Forerunner* had told a complicated mix of political stories that could be framed in several different ways. In 1642 it again spoke in many voices, resonating with different themes in the unfolding polemical warfare. Eglisham's allusions to John Lambe and Buckingham's witchcraft, for instance, surely resonated with other pamphlets issued in November 1642 that warned of the Royalist Prince Rupert's supernatural or demonic powers.[18] But *The Forerunner* spoke more clearly to pressing arguments about royal misrule, evil counsel, and the right to armed resistance. The republication of *The Forerunner* turned the secret history into a highly visible, and flexible, polemical tool, and versions of the story would recur in several different forms and for several different purposes for the remainder of the Civil War.

The Ghost of King James

The flood of reissued *Forerunners* also spawned a highly creative adaptation. John Aston had set up shop as a stationer in Cateaton Street near London's Guildhall late in the 1630s. After a few early publications, his output had slowed, but the breakdown of the Caroline regime gave his work new impetus, and by 1641 he had fully embraced the commercial and political possibilities of revolutionary print culture. That year his printers churned out pamphlets highlighting *causes célèbres* like the trial of the Earl of Strafford, reporting parliamentary debates, and publicizing a broad range of works by the militant John Pym, the leading Presbyterian Denzil Holles and the episcopal champion Sir Thomas Aston.[19] John Aston's coverage did not always please the Commons. In May 1641, upset by his "presumption" in publishing a parliamentary document, the House ordered him to cease production and leave official materials to the Commons' own printer. To feed the demand for news and comment, Aston also published timely historical revivals. During the Strafford trial, for instance, he printed two of the earl's speeches from the 1628 Parliament.[20] His output slowed over the course of 1642, but with the Eglisham reprints, Aston found himself busy again. In late October or early November he may have been the "I. A." responsible for the *Articles Drawn up By the now Iohn Earle of Bristoll and presented to the Parliament, against George late Duke of Buckingham, in the yeare 1626*. By late 1642 many Parliamentarians regarded the Earl of Bristol as one of the notorious malignants around the king, and they eventually demanded his head as the price of any serious peace negotiations. But I. A.'s republication showed another side of Bristol's career and tied him to the burgeoning interest in James's death. The pamphlet's title page summarized the 1626 articles and explained how Bristol's insider knowledge of the Spanish match helped expose the larger popish plot against England's Church and government. But high on the title page, privileged in large type, was Bristol's last charge, which in the wake of Eglisham's republication became the most significant of them all: "Concerning the death of King James, on which Articles", the publisher confidently affirmed, "the Parliament was dissolved &c".[21] This gloss made two controversial claims: that Bristol's last article had to be read as an accusation of murder, even though it only hinted at the possibility of foul play; and that the 1626 Parliament had been dissolved because of Bristol's articles, the murder charge most prominent among them. This last point raised uncomfortable questions about Charles's complicity in his father's death, either as an accessory after the fact, or, more worryingly, as a co-conspirator who, as Richard Robertson put it, "hadd a hand in" the poisoning.

Aston's role in this publication remains at best only a good possibility. But he definitely published the most creative late 1642 appropriation of Eglisham's tract. On 21 October, George Thomason purchased an eight-page quarto pamphlet issued under Aston's imprint (Fig. 68).[22] *Strange Apparitions, or The Ghost of King Iames* recycled *The Forerunner's* lengthy petitions into a fast-paced dialogue in which James, Hamilton and Eglisham accused Buckingham of murder. The narrative followed many of the tropes of early modern crime writing, heightening the drama by staging the case as an interpersonal confrontation in which Buckingham's arrogant denials eventually gave way to abject confession. The large woodcut on the title page heightened the effect, capturing the four interlocutors shrouded in their winding sheets, each holding a lighted brand in his left hand. To the right stood Buckingham, isolated, with a ducal coronet perched on the tied knot of his shroud; on the left were Eglisham, Hamilton and James, in ascending social order, angled in such a way that the king occupied not only the highest but also the most central space in the image. Hamilton carried his coronet and James his crown, and in their right hands all three Scots held the palm of martyrdom and salvation. Buckingham, by contrast, held nothing in the right hand he raised towards the three accusing shades.

By rewriting *The Forerunner*, the tract was also able to introduce new information, including updates on the fates of the original participants and an emotional dramatization of the king's horrified reaction to the news of his own murder. These additions and compressions are as fascinating as the tract's theatricalized form. Many of *The Forerunner's* claims about motivation and proof survived the reworking, although often in a compressed style that reduced the original's eyewitness detail. Where the original gave far more attention to Hamilton's murder than to James's, the balance now was roughly

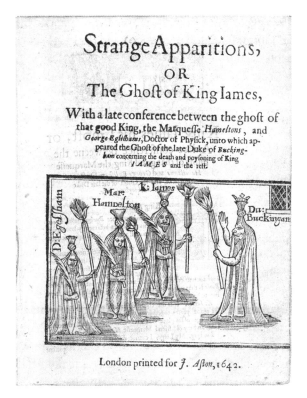

Figure 68: Title page of *Strange Apparitions, or The Ghost of King Iames*, published by John Aston in 1642 (Huntington Library).

even, and this editorial decision marked the beginning of Hamilton's gradual disappearance from the secret history over the course of its reinventions in the 1640s. Eglisham's ghost now moved swiftly through a condensed account of Hamilton's murder: Buckingham's ascent from "meane bloud to honour", the ill-fated marriage alliance, the quarrel, Hamilton's illness and death. The original pamphlet's vivid description of the corpse survived only in the bare line that Hamilton's dead body "swel'd to a strange and monstrous proportion" that revealed to "all the Physitians" that he had been "poysoned". The "brute" with the list of the duke's murder victims—though not the paper containing the list—reappeared, as did the claim that Buckingham had employed a "poyson-monger or mountebank" to supply the murder weapon.[23]

The dialogue form allowed the pamphlet to augment *The Forerunner*'s portrayal of Buckingham as an arrogant upstart by showing him scoffing at his accuser ("this urinall observer") and stoutly denying his "lyes" until Eglisham forced him to admit the truth. Only then was Buckingham humbled, acknowledging the torments of his guilt-wracked conscience and begging in vain for his victims' pardon. The dialogue also heightened the nature of Buckingham's crime against the king. Almost from the outset, James branded him "ungratefull Buckingham", a "most ungratefull murtherer", and the king's shocked and some- times pathetic interjections emphasized the personal betrayal. After Eglisham recounted how "the dead body of King Iames like as Marquesse Hamiltons corps sweld above all measure, their haire came off, and their nailes became loose", James bitterly rebuked Buckingham: "did I not love thee as if thou hadst been my dearest son?" The king's ghost lamented too that if Buckingham had poisoned other men, perhaps envy or "some cruell passion" could explain the crime, "but to kill him that was thy gracious Prince, whose favour had created thee Duke, and gave thee honours farre above desert, it was the highest steppe of base ingratitude." A little later, James concluded that princes should "learn from thee never to trust a Favourite", reiterating the lesson inscribed on the title pages of the republished editions of The Forerunner. In addition, James's admis- sion that Buckingham had been given "honours farre above desert" implicitly undercut the original pamphlet's seemingly untroubled presentation of James as a "good king".[24]

Most importantly, the tract reinvented Eglisham. Some elements of his earlier self-presentation remained: James welcomed Eglisham as his "most faithfull" servant and as Hamilton's "old friend", and like the original, Strange Apparitions privileged Eglisham's medical expertise and political acuity. But the dialogue also revised Eglisham's self-portrait. His shade first appeared as a pale-faced "Scholler" whom Buckingham mistook for some "Ghost of Aristotle", a flattering description that dovetailed with the doctor's own claims to intel- lectual authority. More significantly, the dialogue transformed Eglisham's confessional identity, recasting him as a Protestant. In The Forerunner, Eglisham had said that he fled England before the 1626 Parliament, and, while he admitted taking refuge among the duke's enemies, he did not broadcast the fact that he had gone to Brussels. In Aston's reworking, James's ghost explained that it was only after the 1626 dissolution of Parliament that "to avoid the fury of thy malice" "Eglisham was faine to go over"—not to Catholic Flanders but to Protestant Holland. Later in the reworking, after Buckingham confessed to murdering Hamilton and James, Eglisham accused him of a third murder: "for feare that I . . . should discover you . . . I was sought to be murthered, but I fled into Holland; and there by your appointment I was stabb'd and killed." In this fictional assassination at Buckingham's hands, Eglisham appropriated the fate of the celebrated Puritan pamphleteer Thomas Scott, killed by a deranged English soldier in Utrecht in 1627. The doctor's new Protestant identity also altered Buckingham's motivations for killing James. In the original Hispanophile version, Buckingham killed James to thwart his plans "to bring the Spanish match about againe". In Strange Apparitions, however, Buckingham confessed that he acted to preserve his own power after James's "wonted affection" waned and the king became "jealous of all my actions and sayings", adding that the

"intemperate" old king had become a "burthen to your selfe and to your people",
who were now "sick of an old government & desiring a new change". Buckingham
could never have secured his place as the "Favourite to a succeeding King", the
duke's ghost averred, without first removing James.[25]

Amid the omnipresent anti-Catholic rhetoric of 1642, Eglisham's new
Protestant identity lent his story new credibility. Such credibility was essential
when addressing the highly vexed question of Charles's possible guilt in his
father's murder. *Strange Apparitions* hinted at answers. When first confronted
with the charges, Buckingham asked "if I had beene to wicked, why was not I
when living brought to tryall and sacrificed to Iustice?" James's ghost initially
responded that, although Eglisham's petitions to king and Parliament had
"most lovingly amplified the ingratitutde of thee my Favourite", neither Charles
nor the Commons took "course for the examination of the guiltinesse, by
reason of thy plot which dissolved that plarliament [sic]". The dissolution that
saved the duke was thus reimagined as a result of Buckingham's "plot", not
Charles's will. But the pamphlet later reopened the case against Charles with a
list of Buckingham's motives for killing James, which made Charles into a
direct, even if unwitting, beneficiary of his father's murder. More teasingly,
Buckingham later confessed that "Many more besides my selfe; whom I dare
not reveale as yet", were his accomplices; "time", he asserted, "shall produce
them, and their foule actions".[26] Even though the dialogue concluded with
Buckingham's final confession and plea for God's mercy, his announcement
that only "time shall produce" his accomplices left the vital question of Charles's
guilt dangerously open.

"This Vilinous Pamphlet"

At the end of 1642, as Royalists and Parliamentarians faced off in bookshops
and on battlefields, Eglisham's secret history underwent several major transfor-
mations. Hitherto, notwithstanding the best efforts of scriveners and collectors, the tract itself had remained relatively hard to find, something that
ordinary contemporaries were more likely to have heard about than to have
read. After 1642, however, Eglisham's allegations were openly available for sale
in London's bookshops. Furthermore, his story had been updated, dramatized,
illustrated and Protestantized in John Aston's *Strange Apparitions,* an entertaining précis of the secret history for a large audience. The scale of this revival,
with its multiple editions and copies, was significant. By early October, as the
cases of Francis Giles and Thomas Hill reveal, the Eglisham revival had reached
not only the city of Exeter but even the little Devonshire village of Bishops
Nympton. Later in the decade, Sir Edward Hyde vividly recalled when "this
Pamphlet written so long since by Eglisham was printed, and publickly sold in
Shops, and about the Street".[27]

As Francis Giles's angry fulminations in The Bear make clear, the Eglisham revival outraged the king's supporters. No evidence suggests a coordinated Royalist response to Eglisham redivivus, but in the flood of printed texts produced in 1641–42, some older, critical images of Eglisham were introduced into broader public circulation. In 1641, Sir Henry Wotton's *Parallell betweene Robert late Earle of Essex, and George late Duke of Buckingham* finally appeared in an anonymously printed edition, complete with Wotton's dismissal of the "filthy accusation" and "most malicious and Franticke surmize" contained in that "Libellous Pamphelet of a fugitive Physitian" (Fig. 69).[28] Wotton's *Short View of the Life and Death of George Villers, Duke of Buckingham* (Fig. 70) appeared in October 1642 from the stationer William Sheares, who clearly hoped to capitalize on the renewed interest in Eglisham and Buckingham, and sold enough copies to justify a second edition. Thomason purchased his copy on 22 October, the day after buying Aston's *Strange Apparitions*. The Sheares

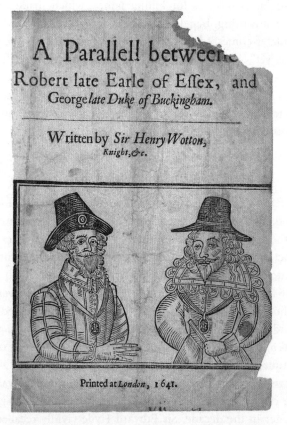

Figure 69: Title page of Sir Henry Wotton, *A Parallell betweene Robert late Earle of Essex, and George late Duke of Buckingham*, written in the 1630s and published posthumously in 1641 (National Portrait Gallery).

edition reproduced a much-admired Dutch engraving of Buckingham (Fig. 71), a courtly image that contrasted markedly not only with Eglisham's pen portrait but also with the crude woodcut rendition in *Strange Apparitions* of the murderous duke in his winding sheet. As we have seen, *A Short View* dealt with Eglisham obliquely, critiquing the 1626 impeachment, praising the duke's self-defence, lauding Charles's honourable decision to rescue his favourite from the aristocratic plot to destroy him, and dismissing Eglisham's tract as a "libellous book" crammed with "prodigious predictions" without "the least semblance of truth".[29] Thanks to Sheares, Wotton's scepticism now offered a potential antidote to the old poisoning charges that were now the talk of a nation.

Viscountess Feilding had no interest in arguing with George Eglisham; she was much too horrified at the sudden reappearance of his book. Elizabeth Bourchier had married Basil, Viscount Feilding, only a few months before the outbreak of civil war. Feilding was Buckingham's nephew, and according to Eglisham, it had been the marriage of Feilding's sister to Hamilton's son that had led to Hamilton's poisoning. Basil's allegiance to Parliament in 1642 had shocked

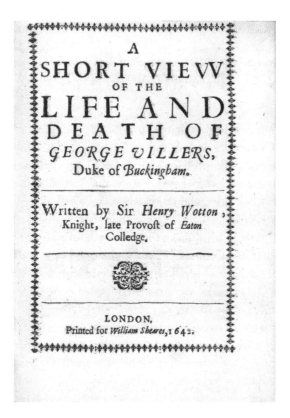

Figure 70: Title page of Sir Henry Wotton, *A Short View of the Life and Death of George Villers, Duke of Buckingham*, 1642, his posthumously published account of the favourite (Huntington Library).

Figure 71: Frontispiece to Sir Henry Wotton, *A Short View of the Life and Death of George Villers, Duke of Buckingham*, 1642, adapting Delff's 1626 engraved portrait of the duke (see Fig. 52) (Huntington Library).

his family; his mother, Buckingham's sister Susan, Countess of Denbigh, sent him a stream of letters urging him to join the king, and his Royalist father, the Earl of Denbigh, died at Edgehill in October 1642 where Basil was commanding a regiment of horse in Essex's army. The young viscountess hoped that her husband would switch sides, and she thought that news of the republication of *The Forerunner*, with its shameless assault on his family, might make him reconsider. "Hear is a booke in print about the duke your unkill", she wrote, and "your good Grandmother [the Countess of Buckingham] is in the booke too." Since "it says both the duke and the king [Charles] poysoned King James", the viscountess pronounced it a "Libelous Booke" and "a damnable booke" that "troubles mee and I belev it will doe the like to you". Her initial shock gave way to hopes of retribution: "Oh without doubte God will [let] Just Judgments fall one them that publish it, for itt rongs the dead and the innocent. The parliament is sayd to defend it, and though they deny the putting of itt forth yett they defend it." But whoever was behind the reprinting, as the viscountess acknowledged, republishing *The Forerunner* represented a dramatic end to the deference customarily shown to the king. "The king may have faults", she concluded, "but none like the publishing this vilinous pamphlet."[30]

Lady Feilding understood the crux of the matter. Like Francis Giles, she was convinced that Parliament itself had orchestrated the Eglisham revival, and that the tract, no matter its actual content, accused Charles of killing his father. Although their identities remain hidden, those who spearheaded the republication had indeed wanted to broadcast Charles I's faults, not Buckingham's; in doing so, whether intentionally or not, they encouraged more contemporaries to ponder the conclusions that Thomas Scott had reached in 1626 and Richard Robertson in July 1642: the king's reign had begun with regicide, and Charles I "hadd a hand in itt".

CHAPTER NINETEEN

ROME'S MASTERPIECE

CIVIL WAR POLEMIC AND THE MURDER OF JAMES I,

1643–45

O N 1 APRIL 1645, George Thomason obtained nine handwritten stanzas of a vitriolic anti-Royalist ballad. While it is unclear whether the song ever appeared in print, it obviously referred to the Earl of Essex's humiliating surrender near Lostwithiel, Cornwall, in September 1644, a defeat that negated the advantages Parliament had won at Marston Moor two months earlier. Although the author lamented the internal divisions among the Parliamentarians and noted how "merrie" the Royalists had been since Essex dishonourably slipped away "in a wherrie", the military humiliation had not diminished the writer's anger at the king and the Royalist cause. The ballad's tone was robustly indecorous—even Elizabeth I was hailed in overly familiar style as "Queene Bettie". The poet reserved his venom, however, for James and Charles, depicting them as weak, effeminate rulers, subservient to their Catholic wives and the Catholic cause. James, the ballad scoffed:

> was both cunning and fearefull wee find
> And loose in his Sockets [Pockets?] before and behind
> He kept on with Pattents to make the state Poore
> And still kept a Minion in stead of a whoore.[1]

The poet daringly juxtaposed James's preference for a minion to the looseness of his pocket or socket—slang for vagina—"behind", insinuating a royal taste for sodomy. The ballad was even more contemptuous of Charles. The king's attack on the "honest" Scots, his complicity with the Irish rebels, and his attempts to turn the army on Parliament in 1641, all proved Charles a man whose "word's a Toy". But Charles was not simply untrustworthy: he was also an agent of a popish plot:

> Let no man believe him what ever he sweares
> Hee's so many Jesuits hangs at his Eares

Besids an Indulgence procured from Rome
To pardon his sinnes both past and to come
   Which is more then the whore
     Er'e would have granted
   But to see Poperie
     Here againe Planted.

The balladeer made James I's murder the starting point for his son's pursuit of popery and arbitrary government. Charles's misrule began immediately after "George had rewarded King James with a Figge". "Figge" was well-known shorthand for poison and was usually described as "Spanish" or "Italian". The word thus connected Buckingham's poisoning of James to the Catholic Mediterranean and to the popish plot delineated elsewhere in the ballad. Although Buckingham, not Charles, had committed the crime, James's murder had begun Charles's attempt "to see Poperie/Here againe Planted".

The 1642 republication of *The Forerunner of Revenge* had made Eglisham's secret history well known and widely discussed, and his narratives helped stiffen militant resolve during the tense opening months of civil war. In October 1642, John Aston's *Strange Apparitions* translated Eglisham's pamphlet into dynamic dialogue and transformed Eglisham into a Protestant martyr. The doctor's confessional transmutation in 1642 proved decisive, enabling the widespread assimilation of his secret history into the most powerful strain of Parliamentarian political discourse: the fear of a long-standing, many-stranded popish plot working to destroy English religion and liberty. In the 1641 Grand Remonstrance, John Pym and his allies in Parliament had set out an authoritative account of this popish plot stretching back to 1625, and in the months and years that followed a steady stream of pamphlets poured from London's presses, adding new plots to the central narrative. The process of making James's murder "popish" had begun in the anti-Buckingham discourse of the later 1620s; by the early 1640s the transformation was complete, and the secret history was easily absorbed into the omnipresent rhetoric of "innumerable plots", "treacherous and hellish", "wonderfull, bloudy and dangerous", that fascinated, terrified and mobilized Parliament's supporters.[2]

Poison made perfect cultural sense as a Catholic crime, and well-worn images of papists as regicidal poisoners were propaganda staples. In 1643 one pamphlet recalled the time of Elizabeth and James, when "that Jesuiticall faction, were active in treason by poyson, stabbing and blowing up Parliament, destroying posterities of Kings Nobles and massacring whole kingdomes", while another explained how experienced princes guarded against the pope and "his powder, poysons and poynards".[3] In 1644, *A New Invention* noted that Catholics who "were wont to make nothing of stabbing and poysoning Princes, now become so pious and zealous that none are forwarder to take their Kings part". Others warned of ongoing popish poison plots against heroic Parliament-men, who "goe in feare of poyson and of knives". In October 1641 a pamphlet had breathlessly narrated Pym's providential escape from contamination by a "Contagious Plaster of a Plague-Sore" sent to him by a Catholic poison plotter "Wrapt up in a Letter".[4] George Eglisham—Louvain student and Habsburg agent—was an unlikely collaborator in the rhetorical elaboration of a popish plot, but his secret history fit seamlessly into these narratives of ongoing popish malice.

During the First Civil War (1642–46), contemporaries regularly deployed Eglisham's secret history, but most of them carefully avoided directly implicating Charles I in his father's murder, which (as Abigail Dexter had discovered) would have breached the acceptable limits of Parliamentarian discourse. But Eglisham's primary allegation—that Buckingham had poisoned James— flourished in the early 1640s as a telling example of the evil actions of those counsellors from whom Charles I needed protection and of the grim Catholic determination to overthrow Protestantism. In 1645 as in 1642, Eglisham's secret history remained especially valuable to Parliamentarian militants who refused to contemplate peace with the king. In these hard-line Parliamentarian texts Charles and the Royalist cause remained deeply implicated in a pattern of evil counsel and popish plotting whose most notable victim had been King James himself.

The Indian Nut

William Prynne, the legal scholar and Puritan polemicist, made a formidable opponent (Fig. 72). Twice pilloried and mutilated in the 1630s for seditious libel, Prynne had returned to London at the beginning of the Long Parliament as a living martyr. The "S.L." branded on his cheek became to him a badge of honour denoting not "Seditious Libeller" but "Stigmata Laudis", the marks inflicted by William Laud, Archbishop of Canterbury. When Parliament began formal legal proceedings against the archbishop, Prynne volunteered his formidable learning and immense appetite for work to the prosecution. In August 1643 the Commons' Committee on Printing made public some of Prynne's detailed research into the archbishop's papers. By working through mounds of secret correspondence, much of it in cipher, the Presbyterian martyr had found not only evidence of an ongoing popish poison plot and of official attempts to cover it up, but also material linking this plot to the events at Theobalds in March 1625.[5]

Romes Master-peece reached its first readers during a dark phase of the military struggle against the king when Royalist power was expanding in the west and south-west, and Parliament was riven with bitter infighting. Prynne's revelations made clear how important it was to resist any calls for a quick and easy

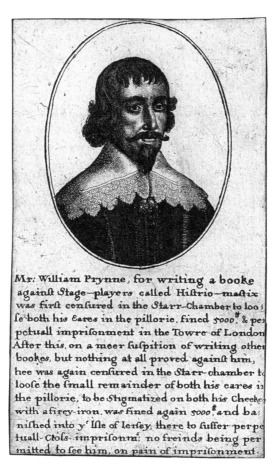

Mr. William Prynne, for writing a booke
againſt Stage-players called Hiſtrio-maſtix
was firſt conſured in the Starr-Chamber to looſ
ſe both his Eares in the pillorie, fined 5000ˡⁱ & per
petuall impriſonment in the Towre of London
After this, on a meer ſuſpition of writing other
bookes, but nothing at all proved againſt him,
hee was again cenſured in the Starr-chamber to
looſe the ſmall remainder of both his eares in
the pillorie, to be Stigmatized on both his Cheeks
with a firey-iron, was fined again 5000ˡⁱ and ba:
niſhed into yᵉ Iſle of Ierſey, there to ſuffer perpe
tuall-Cloſs impriſonnᵗ; no freinds being per
mitted to ſee him, on pain of impriſonment.

Figure 72: Wenceslaus Hollar's c. 1641 engraved portrait of William Prynne, the lawyer, Laudian martyr, and tireless investigator of popish plots (British Museum).

peace. Directed in part at those who doubted the reality of "The Grand Conspiracy of the Pope and his Iesuited Instruments, to extirpate the Protestant Religion, re-establish Popery, subvert Lawes, Liberties, Peace, [and] Parliaments", the pamphlet published secret documents revealing a nefarious Jesuit poison plot.[6] The documents included letters and memoranda from Charles I, Archbishop Laud, Sir William Boswell, English ambassador to the Dutch Republic, and an unnamed renegade Catholic informant. The most sensational material appeared in a lengthy memorandum written by a former Catholic priest who had worked for George Con, the papal nuncio in London. Horrified by what he was witnessing in London, the priest had abandoned the Church and reported Con's plotting to Andreas Habernfeld, an agent at the Palatine court in The Hague. The memorandum outlined the role of Jesuit agents in England in fomenting the Scottish crisis in order to allow English

Catholics to extort toleration from Charles I in return for financial and military aid against the Scots. James I's murder appeared in article 10 of the memorandum. If Charles refused to cooperate with the Catholic extortion, he was to be "dispatched". "For an Indian Nut", the informant alleged, "stuffed with the most sharp poyson is kept in the Society [the London Jesuit headquarters] (which Cuneus [Con] at that time shewed often to me in a boasting manner) wherein a poyson was prepared for the King; after the example of his Father". In the margin, Prynne noted that the Jesuits were experienced in the art of poisoning princes and that "the Iesuites it seems know very well King James was poysoned, belike by some of their Instruments".[7]

In his conclusion Prynne returned to these allegations, asserting that, after Parliament had thwarted their designs, the popish plotters had triggered the Irish Rebellion and the English Civil War. They still aimed to secure religious toleration in return for their assistance against Parliament, and they would murder Charles if he continued to refuse them:

> they have an Indian poysoned Nut reserved for him amongst this Jesuiticall society, or if it be lost, a poysoned Knife perchance, or some other Instrument, to dispatch him out of the World, and to get the possession and protection of the Prince, whom they will educate in their Antichristian Religion.

Such a plot was utterly plausible given the papists' track record as assassins:

> their poysoning of the Emperour Henry the seventh, in the sacred host; of King John in the Chalice; their stabbing of Henry the third of France with a Knife in the belly; of Henry the fourth his successor, first in the mouth, next in the heart-strings; though all of their owne Religion, because they would not humour the Pope in every unreasonable demand. . . . Together with their pistolling of the Prince of Orange, and poysoning of King James himselfe (as the Legate boasted).

Another marginal note here advised Prynne's readers to "See Doctor Eggleshams Booke, and the Commons charge against the Duke of Buckingham", a pairing that suggested Parliament's charge of "transcendent presumption" should now be understood, like Eglisham's pamphlet, as a murder allegation.[8]

Prynne saw James's murder, like the other royal assassinations in his catalogue, as yet another episode in ongoing Catholic plots against England. Buckingham, whom Prynne mentioned only in passing, was thus refigured as an "instrument" of the Jesuits.[9] Neither the original memorandum nor Prynne's gloss on it suggested that Charles was in any way responsible for his father's death, and neither source discussed Charles's dissolution of the 1626 Parliament. Indeed, in the original memorandum, both Charles and Laud appeared to be innocent victims of Catholic machinations. But Prynne glossed the story to support the Parliamentarian cause. He was amazed that the authorities had allowed Con such freedom at court, and used Laud's writings to highlight the archbishop's popish proclivities and friends. Furthermore, Prynne blamed Charles for allowing the Jesuits free rein in his kingdom, thus ceding them significant power "over the King himselfe". Charles, he wrote:

> either cannot, or dares not (for feare perchance of poysoning, or other assassination) oppose or banish these horrid Conspirators from his Dominions and Court, but hath a long time permitted them to prosecute this plot without any publike opposition.

In the circumstances Prynne could only wonder:

> what will become of the poor sheep, when the Shepherd himselfe, not onely neglects to chase and keep out these Romish wolves, but permits them free accesse into, and harbour in the sheepfold, to assault, if not devour, not onely his flock, but Person too?[10]

Since Laud and Charles had ignored credible intelligence of Catholic threats as early as 1640, Prynne maintained that they deserved some of the blame for the plot's subsequent metastasis. And although Prynne never posed the question, attentive readers clearly had licence to wonder why, if Charles had evidence in October 1640 that Jesuit "instruments" had poisoned his father, he had chosen to ignore it. These stories from 1643 about James's murder thus neatly illustrated the ongoing threat from a popish plot in which Charles was both victim and collaborator. For Prynne the message was clear. There was no room for compromise or peace; to preserve king, Parliament and religion, Parliamentarians had to unite and emulate the Jesuits' own steely resolve.[11]

Prynne returned to *Rome's Master-peece* in subsequent publications, repeatedly warning that a royal victory would establish popery in England—"or else" the Jesuits would "poyson" Charles with an Indian "poysoned Nut after the example of his Father".[12] "They have a poysoned Fig reserved for him", he noted later in 1643, "in case he should refuse it." In 1645, Prynne again insisted that the Jesuits refused "to ayde" Charles's cause "except he would grant them a free toleration of their Religion, yea resolving to poyson him with an Italian figge, in case he condescended not to their demands."[13] In his 1646 report of Laud's trial, Prynne again cited the plot to give Charles "a poysoned figge (as his Father was poysoned)" and accused the archbishop of being:

> so far from crossing this ... Jesuiticall designe, that he confederated and joined with the Jesuits and popish party in fomenting, maintaining the war

against the Scots, and revived it when it was ceased, by perswading the King
to break the first pacification, and denounce a second war against them.[14]

Although the suppression of the plot's 1640 discovery was one of the charges at
Laud's trial, it is not clear whether the trial proceedings included any mention
of the poisoning threat; Laud's defence against the charge that he had "concealed
these papers" did not mention it, though his notes on *Romes Master-peece*
included some marginalia around the allusions to James's death, suggesting
that Laud had given Prynne's allegations serious thought.[15]

Eglisham's tract had become in Prynne's hands a means of saving Charles I
from the Catholics and from himself. James I's erstwhile physician and polemicist
was still a royal champion, but now an unambiguously Protestant one. Prynne's
portrait of Charles, like Eglisham's, was profoundly ambiguous. In both readings
Charles was dangerously passive, in one instance manipulated by his favourite
and in the other by Jesuits and his archbishop. Charles was not a murderer, but
his inaction rendered him deeply complicit in the woes afflicting his nation.

A number of other 1643 publications found contemporary political significance in James's death. John Vicars, a Presbyterian poet and Prynne's "most
affectionate kind Friend", alluded to James's murder in his *Prodigies &
Apparitions or Englands Warning Pieces*. Like Prynne, Vicars told a story about
the long-term origins of the Civil War, cataloguing the "mercifull premoni-
tions" sent by God as a "visible demonstration of his just wrath and displeasure"
to persuade the English to adopt "true repentance and hearty reformation". But
the sin-loving English had neglected these warnings, and disasters inevitably
followed as Protestants were massacred in Germany, France and Ireland, and as
civil war engulfed England. But providential judgements had also claimed the
lives of the great and the good: "the death of Queene Anne, and of King Iames
also himselfe, not long after; yea and many most eminent Peeres and Nobles of
this Land, suddenly taken away, but by what stroke is not yet fully discovered,
though greatly suspected; as the Marquesse of Hamilton, the Duke of
Richmond, and the Lord Belfast, &c. all eminent Common wealths men." Here,
Vicars deployed elements of Eglisham's narrative to illustrate the wages of
collective sin. Vicars was unclear whether James's death was among those
whose cause was "not yet fully discovered, though greatly suspected", although
in the context of the Eglisham revival many readers must have assumed it was.
But Vicars was not interested in assigning criminal responsibility for specific
murders; for him, these deaths merely illustrated the workings of God's providence against a sinful nation.[16]

The continued republication of materials from the 1620s also stimulated and
reshaped politicized memories of James's death. In December 1643, Joseph Doe
printed Sir Dudley Digges's 1626 speech presenting the impeachment charges
against Buckingham to the House of Lords. The title page billed it as a disquisi-

tion on "the evil Consequences, that doe attend this State, by committing Places of trust, into the hands of Court-Favourites", by which "it doth plainly appear, to be the Originall of all the publick grievances, and combustions of this Kingdom". Like the title-page editorializing on the republished *Forerunner*, the reissued speech focused on Buckingham; but whereas the title page of the reprinted Eglisham claimed that the duke had misled Charles's "noble disposition", the title page of the Digges speech blamed those who gave favourites "places of trust", making Charles an agent of his own undoing. The speech itself appeared without editorial comment, leaving the reader to apply its lessons to the present crisis. The original speech's passing comment on the "injurie offered to the person of the late King of blessed memory" remained in the printed version. But Digges's insistence that "upon this occasion I am commanded by the Commons to take care of the honor of the King our sovereign that lives", a phrase that Charles had thought implicated him in his father's death, was effectively neutralized by the pamphlet's compositor whose typesetting made it harder to link Digges's caveat back to his comment on James's death.[17]

These old materials also tantalized readers in the United Provinces eager for news about the dramatic events on the other side of the North Sea. In February 1644 a translation of Eglisham's *Forerunner* appeared for the first time in Holland; it too focused on the problem of the wicked favourite (Fig. 73). The Dutch prefatory address suggested that the "following discourse" taught at least three lessons. The first recapitulated one of Eglisham's own central themes, captured in a Dutch proverb meaning "he who rises too fast, easily becomes arrogant". The second was that Buckingham's assassination at the height of his power provided "evidence of the just judgment of God, who can destroy such proud and ambitious people when they least expect it". While the final lesson warned kings "not to make such favourites too prominent". The publisher hoped his readers would take pleasure as well as instruction from the text and, like English contemporaries determined to expose the *arcana imperii* to public scrutiny, he declared "it would be a shame if such an example remained covered and concealed in the darkness".[18]

The reworked variations on the secret history in 1643 and early 1644 met with little direct Royalist response. But in his 1643 *Chronicle of the Kings of England*, Sir Richard Baker anticipated key components of what would become the standard Royalist critique. Baker acknowledged the "scandalous rumours" about James's death and, with Eglisham in mind, noted that "some were so impudent, as to write that he was poysoned". Such audacity was beneath contempt, but Baker used medical evidence, which had loomed large in Eglisham's allegations, to refute them. James's autopsy had found "no signe at all of poyson", wrote Baker, and no suspicious marks, save for the spleen problems that had caused his ague. James was an old man and had traversed "The Ordinary high way . . . to a naturall death".[19]

Figure 73: Title page of George Eglisham, *Een moordadich, schrickelijck, ende heel wonderbaer Secreet, in Engelandt ontdeckt*, a 1644 Dutch translation of *The Fore-Runner of Revenge* (British Library).

The True Britanicus

By the beginning of 1644, George Bishop had become a major figure in the most popular and lucrative of the new political media, the weekly newsbook. In January he and his co-publisher, Robert White, were running a formidable operation, bringing out no fewer than four periodicals—*Certaine Informations*, *The Parliament Scout*, *The Kingdomes Weekly Intelligencer* and *Mercurius Britanicus*. By the end of February, however, Bishop's business was in ruins. *Certaine Informations* had ceased operations altogether, while the colophon on the other three titles now recorded only White's name. It is hard to tell what happened, but the most likely explanation is political. White was aligned with the Earl of Essex, a moderate willing to negotiate with the king, while Bishop, a known supporter of "fiery spirits" and a protégé of the more militant Lord Saye, Sir Henry Vane and Oliver St John, wanted to see the war through to the end. Since these newsbooks were too important for Essex and his supporters to leave alone, an editorial coup had likely driven Bishop out.[20]

He did not go quietly. In late February he took over another newsbook, the *Military Scribe*, but could not revive its fortunes. Then, for three weeks in March, loyal readers of *Mercurius Britanicus*, the partners' marquee publication, were confronted with two versions of the popular newsbook, one published by White, the other by Bishop. White reacted angrily, insisting that he was the authentic voice of the celebrated periodical: "I tell you", White boasted, "who are honest, who are faithfull, who are Parliamentarian, who are new Pyms and Penningtons," and he plastered the city with notices denouncing "Bishops Britanicus". For his part, Bishop warned that his former partner "had best be more wary" lest Bishop "spoil his revenues by Pamphlet-plotting" and "unmaske these hypocrites to the full". But above all else, Bishop assured his readers, "you shall finde mee to be the true Britanicus". For all Bishop's bluster, his parallel operation lasted only three weeks.[21] In April he tried again, launching *Mercurius Aulico-Mastix* to attack the leading Royalist newsbook, *Mercurius Aulicus*, but his new venture also quickly folded. In late April, Bishop issued *A True and Perfect Journall of the Warres*; but it soon closed. Bishop was understandably frustrated. In the long term he would return to what he knew best, publishing a reasonably successful newsbook, the *London Post*, at the end of the year. But in the short term he took another approach, blending his personal frustrations with the mounting chorus of alarm from other parliamentary militants.

The first half of 1644 was an anxious period for the Parliament. John Pym had died in December 1643 after completing Parliament's military alliance with the Scottish Covenanters. Meanwhile King Charles secured thousands of Irish troops after negotiating a ceasefire with the Catholic Confederacy. The gap between the war and peace parties in the House of Commons steadily widened, and serious disagreements about the future religious settlement erupted with the January 1644 publication of the Independents' manifesto, the *Apologeticall Narration*. One of Bishop's ill-fated newsbooks, *A True and Faithfull Journall*, sounded the tocsin in April, urging Parliamentarian militancy: "now is the time for England to recover its almost lost Religion and Liberty, and since God and the Parliament have called us out, let every mans heart and hand and purse concurre". The newsbook exhorted its readers:

> to bring Delinquents to condigne punishment according to the Covenent, and to expell the Irish and all other forraign Enemies, that are lately crept in amongste us, to suck our blouds, seize upon our goods and estates, and to enthrall our soules and bodies in a perpetuall captivity of Popery and slavery.[22]

In the summer of 1644, Bishop adopted an alternative polemical strategy for stiffening Parliamentarian resolve and for proving that he, not White, was "the true Britanicus". Between June and October he printed seven satirical tracts playing a sequence of variations on central elements of Eglisham's secret history. It is possible Bishop had been involved in the 1642 republication of *The Forerunner*, but in any case he knew the text and its uses well. His campaign rolled out over several turbulent months. On 2 July 1644 parliamentary and Scottish troops defeated the Royalists' northern army at Marston Moor, but they were unable to exploit the victory. The Earl of Essex was trapped in Cornwall, while the Earl of Manchester refused decisive actions against the king lest a total defeat make an honourable peace impossible. By late October, Charles was able to threaten London again before being turned back at Newbury.

On 5 June 1644, less than two months after abandoning the newsbook trade, Bishop printed *The Second Part of the Spectacles*. The pamphlet adopted the persona of a loyal Royalist pondering various awkward facts about the king. The author began by noting that "when hee was but Prince, he [Charles] was by the Physitian (shall I call him) or Poysoner in ordinary, Buckingham, even made to take the Aire in Spaine, as a sure remedy to preserve our Religion." Here was another possible starting point of the popish plot: "some would make me believe, that at this voyage about the marriage, the Plot for propagations of Popery in England was first layd in Spaine," and although "the match with Spaine was broken off, yet the generall Plot of bringing in Popery held on." The next step in the popish conspiracy was "the necessary Translation of King James", which Buckingham "first plotted" in Madrid. The narrator admitted that, although he was a loyal Royalist, he had to "confesse" that the business "concerning King James and Marquesse Hamilton, doth somewhat stalle me", for "the Plot might be more currant . . . if they were both removed out of the way". Like Eglisham, the author claimed that corrupt courtiers had suppressed the truth about the murders: "it is said some Phisitians were dealt with under-hand, and either submitted their mercenary tongues to flattery for gold or their mindes to base timiditie". These details made the "Royalist" narrator waver, for "if I knew the certainty, all my doubting were at an end". Further reflection, however, had removed his doubts, and the author switched his allegiance to Parliament.[23] Connecting widespread contemporary fears of popish plotting to Eglisham's account of James's murder, the satirist produced an image of the Stuart court so thoroughly corrupted by poison and popery that it would make a Royalist desert his cause.

A little over a month later, on 13 July 1644, Bishop returned to Eglisham's secret history by printing *A Prognosticall Prediction of Admirable Events*, which this time focused on Buckingham's links to Charles's later evil advisers. "The Duke of Buckingham was a brave man and had the love of two Kings," the pamphlet said, but "rumor ran about the Country and told strange tales of him", the strangest being that "he was thought to be guilty of taking away [James's] last breath". Once the duke proved "above the reach of a Parliament", God used John

Felton to cut him down. Nevertheless "the English had been slow in executing Justice", and the nation still "smarts for it". It was obvious that "our king (that hath now given over his government, and fights for a new one) rul'd the Kingdom then, but the Duke rul'd him, the Jesuites rul'd the Duke, the Pope the Jesuites, and who (d'ye think) rul'd the Pope?" Furthermore, Buckingham left behind a fearful legacy, for both Laud and the Earl of Strafford were his protégés. With an appropriately courtly image, the author concluded that Charles:

> that lov'd musicke so well, was now furnished with admirable instruments, the Bishop was his great Organ-pipe, the Duke Base-Violl, Strafford his Irish Harpe, and Cottington, Finch and Windebanke, were the Meanes to make up a cursed Consort.[24]

This tract's ability to link Buckingham to the misdeeds of the 1630s played into themes circulating in earlier Parliamentarian texts. A 1643 *Satyre* on the Cavaliers, for instance, had dubbed Strafford and other Royalists "the forlorne Imps of great Buckingham", left behind after the favourite was "stopt by Felton". The *Protestant Informer* observed that though the duke "ruled, and swayed, the course of things in the Kingdome", it was obvious that "the Jesuites swayed him". Strafford had simply implemented Buckingham's plan to use Irish Catholics to subvert the Protestant Parliament. Fortunately for England, the "Lictors axe tooke off this actor [Strafford], as Felton's knife the other".[25]

On 19 July 1644, six days after *A Prognosticall Prediction*, Bishop published the latest instalment of the feud between the Parliamentarian astrologer John Booker and the Royalist John Taylor, the Water Poet. These celebrity pamphlet wars utilized dense, playful texts that mixed inventive personal insult with scathing ideological assault.[26] Booker's *No Mercurius Aquaticus* smeared Taylor as an "Antichristian Prick louse", one of the debauched "Liars" who "pumpe and Pimpe . . . in the behalf of Popery, Murder and Rebellion against the State". His attack concluded with a satirical recipe for a "Medicine which will cure thee and all thy Malignant Companions, of their railing and malignant fits" and of their unquenchable "thirst after Popery and Slavery". The recipe's ingredients—Royalist crimes and deceits, including doses of Prince "Rupert's Religion", "His Majesties Protestations", the queen's "good Intentions to the Kingdome", and a "Case of Conscience . . . in the behalfe of Tyranie"—were all to be boiled together for "the length of a Masque at White-Hall" in a basin plugged with clerical vestments and sweetened with "a Bucket or two of Irish Protestant Blood". This much was par for the polemical course, but the first ingredient in this medicinal brew came straight out of *The Forerunner*: "One dram of King Iames his Cordiall, that was made by Buckingham." Clearly, Booker assumed that his readers would understand an allusion that effectively equated James's poisoning with other Royalist crimes. By implicitly comparing the murdered king with martyred Irish Protestants, Booker's pamphlet, like so many other Civil War variations on the secret history, also framed James's murder as a "popish" act. In response, Taylor (or his surrogate) branded Booker "a Rebell, that revil'd his King" and countered with a medical recipe of his own. But he steered clear of any comment on Buckingham's "cordiall" and James's death.[27]

Eight days after publishing Booker's pamphlet, Bishop issued the satirical *Dog's Elegy*, commemorating the death of Prince Rupert's notorious poodle, "Boy", at Marston Moor (Fig. 74). The poem depicted the Royalist general and his dog as the witch-spawned agents of a demonic plot against the kingdom that had begun with the 1588 Armada and now reached into the civil wars in which Rupert:

> Duke of Plunderland,
> This Dogs great Master, hath receiv'd command
> To kill, burne, steale, Ravish, nay, any thing,
> And in the end to make himself a King.

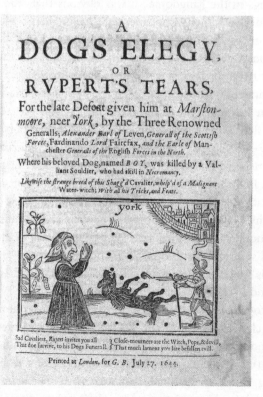

Figure 74: Title page of *A Dog's Elegy*, one of the variations on the secret history published in 1644 by the hardline Parliamentarian George Bishop (Beinecke Library).

Playing with stereotypical links among poisoning, witchcraft and popery, the poem recounted the dog's endeavours to advance the Catholic cause. When the discovery of the Gunpowder Plot of 1605 thwarted his aims, the "Dog turns Courtier", serving "the Fav'rite Buckingham" and trying through him to "bring this land to Popery". The Spanish match, the fall of La Rochelle, and Laud's promotion were all part of the devil-dog's machinations. So too were several poisonings. Quoting from the 1627 libel "In ducem reducem", the *Dog's Elegy* began its catalogue of victims with "that noble Scot" (identified in the margin not as Hamilton, but as Lennox) whose dead body revealed "Twas they [*sic*] Ambition made his carcase swell". Then, with little concern for chronology, the poet turned to the death of Prince Henry in 1612, before returning to James. In this reworking of Eglisham's pamphlet, the devil-dog, frustrated by the collapse of Anglo-Spanish rapprochement:

> must finde out a way
> By Poyson still, how that (O monstrous!) Hee
> More home may strike at Sacred Majestie,
> Great Brittains KING, and Europs chiefest glory,
> Scarce parallel'd in any English Story,
> Must with White Powder given him in his drinke,
> Cry out on him that made his Carcasse sinke.

Since Buckingham was the murderer, his assassination was divine retribution for "all this blood" he had shed. But the favourite was part of a larger, and still active, popish conspiracy, embodied in the ongoing crimes of the demonic dog and the Royalist cause.[28]

During July 1644, Bishop had printed three variations on Eglisham's work, but he was not yet done with *The Forerunner*. Published on 24 August, *Parliaments Kalender of Black Saints* imagined the drumhead trial of such Royalist villains as Laud, Strafford, Cottington, the Earl of Bristol's son, and Bishop Williams, "one of Buckingham's Chaplains". At their head was Buckingham himself. The judges charged the duke with "High Treason against God, the King and Country" because he had "Confederacy with Jesuites, and other notorious Papists" for "planting Popery in the Kingdomes and to that end did further all their Popish designes by an uncontroled Power". The sole particular against him, however, was that:

> by the help of Dr. Lamb thy learned Physician, thou didst remove some great Personages out of the way, as the Duke of Lenox and Richmond, King James of blessed Memory, and some others who were likely to crosse thee in this thy wicked purpose.

After the duke confessed his crimes, the judges summoned the assassin Felton to "Take him". A month later, Bishop issued a sequel. *A Nest of Perfidious Vipers* now put the Scottish Royalist Duke of Lennox on trial. "His Father was truly Noble and lov'd Parliaments", the pamphlet noted, and for that reason, in 1624, he had been "unfortunately stung to death by those poysonous Vipers". Lennox's son, however, "loved the murderers better, and hates the Parliament he should love". He was merely another of the "malignants, Jesuites, Arminians, and cabinet-counsellors" who had plotted against "the Parliament, our religion, laws, and lives".[29]

Hell's Hurlie-burlie, Bishop's final Eglisham variation of 1644, arrived on 5 October. The prose prologue reported that Satan, outraged at the pope's pretensions, had blocked Catholics from entering Hell. Yet a flood of Cavalier "malignants" made this restriction awkward, and as Satan vacillated, one of the Cavaliers sought to break the impasse by asking to speak to Buckingham, for "I am certaine he is here". The tract then printed two verse libels that had originally circulated at the time of the favourite's assassination. In the first, Buckingham—England's "Ad-mar-all"—was about to enter Hell, and the poet expressed pity for those already there: "Alas poor friends I grieve at your disgraces/You must lose all your Offices and places." Even Lucifer should worry that Buckingham would force him to "resigne thy Crowne/For thou shalt meet a Duke will put thee down." The second poem, also set in Hell, imagined Buckingham encountering his sorcerer, Dr Lambe. After initial pleasantries, Lambe asked why the duke's mother was not there with them:

Hath she not yet performed the task he [Satan] set her?
Or are there in the world against her will
More honest Nobles to be poyson't still?[30]

Bishop's months-long fascination with Eglisham is highly revealing. Aside from various newsbooks, a few short news reports and a reprinted theological text, Bishop printed fifteen short tracts in 1644, and seven of them referred to *The Forerunner*.[31] Crucially, his polemic was directed as much at internal Parliamentarian enemies as at his Royalist foes. Ejected from his newsbook operation by more moderate men, and angry at the squandering of military advantage over the king, Bishop was eager to rearticulate the Parliamentarian hard line. By linking *The Forerunner*'s revelations to ongoing fears about the king and his party, Bishop set the current crisis of popery and evil counsel in a long historical context and underscored the risks inherent in negotiating with a dangerous and deluded monarch.

None of these tracts directly linked Charles to his father's alleged murder, and nothing suggests that Bishop wanted to depose, much less execute, the king. In fact, *Mercurius Aulico-Mastix*, his short-lived 1644 newsbook, predicted that "we can presage his Maiesties return to his Parliament" no later than 1645.[32] Yet readers were certainly free to apply Eglisham's accusations in more radical ways, and the Bishop tracts intersected with other more radical readings of the secret history. The tracts repeatedly linked James's poisoning to the presence of demonic witchcraft at court. *Parliaments Kalender* and *Hell's Hurlie-burlie* both recalled Buckingham's patronage of Dr Lambe, and the *Kalender* identified Lambe as the mountebank who had concocted Buckingham's poisons. A *Dog's Elegy* drew on various polemical attempts to represent Prince Rupert as a witch and his pet dog, "Boy", as his demonic familiar, rewriting the popish plot as a literally devil-hatched plan in which the poisonings of Henry, Lennox and James were all associated with witchcraft. These connections between Royalism and witchcraft were picked up elsewhere in 1644. In his comparison of the "Two Incomparable Generalissimos of the World", Jesus Christ and Satan, George Wither depicted the devil's entourage led by "his nimble Mercuries/Intelligencers, Scouts and Aulick lyes", with Dr Lambe bringing up the rear.[33] This demonization of the Royalist cause could implicate Charles. In early August 1644, *A Survey of Monarchie* presented a comprehensive catalogue of rulers so misled by councillors that they became "but Emperors and Kings in name". Much of the pamphlet conformed to standard Parliamentarian rhetoric on evil advisors, but its conclusion moved in more radical directions. Naples and Catalonia, like England, Scotland and Ireland, were then in revolt, and the Dutch had long struggled against their rulers. These widespread uprisings clearly suggested that "The alteration which we see happen in our age in so many Countryes might serve for a notable Table to behold the Judgements of Gods, cleane abolishing whole Empires for cause of our sinnes." Some of these sins were unsettling: God had "cast the people out of the land of Palestina, for the Sorcerers which they used", and He had poured out his wrath not only upon those who employed sorcerers but also upon "those likewise that suffereth them to live". Readers were then referred to Jeremiah 15:4—"he will scatter them in all kingdomes of the earth because of Manassas for that which hee did in Jerusalem." Readers seeking to puzzle out the reference could turn to 2 Chronicles 33, where Manassas had done "that which was evil in the sight of the LORD, like unto the abominations of the heathen". In part, Manassas's crime had been to restore the old pagan temples, altars and idols, an obvious reference to Charles's toleration of the Catholic revival at court and Laudian ceremonialism in the English Church. But Manassas had even more disturbing vices, for "he observed times, and used enchantments, and used witchcraft, and dealt with a familiar spirit, and with wizards". In His anger, God sent invading armies who took Manassas, "bound . . . with fetters", to Babylon.[34]

Searching "to the quick"

Parliament's failure to capitalize on the victory at Marston Moor led to bitter recriminations at Westminster in late 1644 and early 1645 and to renewed power struggles pitting the peace party against the war party and Presbyterians against Independents. By January 1645 the king was in a much stronger position than he had been back in July 1644. While hardliners and Independents pushed through a remodelling of the army in hopes of preventing what Oliver Cromwell termed "a dishonorable peace", the peace party allied itself with the Scots commissioners and crafted a set of proposals for direct negotiations with Charles at Uxbridge. In late January 1645 the Presbyterian Christopher Love, chaplain to the parliamentary garrison at Windsor, twice took to the pulpit to warn his listeners against hastily embracing a peace deal with the king. As negotiators gathered, Love insisted to audiences in Windsor and Uxbridge that a "just War" was far preferable to a "wicked Peace" and that the army's duty was to fight "the Lords battels" and "avenge the blood of Saints which hath been spilt". Love promised that God would heal a kingdom sickened by the "poyson-full food" of arbitrary government and idolatry, but that no cure was possible unless the patient submitted to the physician (in this case, to Parliament and its army). A peace that failed to secure a genuine religious reformation and to purge all malignancy from the body politic was no peace at all. In fact, Love argued, no "safe" or "just" peace could exist until "all the guilt of the blood be expiated and avenged, either by the Sword of the Law, or law of the Sword". Some of England's current woes stemmed from the patient's neglect of the physician's assistance. In particular, the patient had refused to let the physician examine some of the less visible wounds that had weakened the body politic. If these wounds were not "searcht to the quick", they would "rot, rancle, and fester, and never be perfectly healed". Love's list of public wounds in need of thorough investigation included the ill-fated Parliaments of the 1620s, the fall of La Rochelle and the Irish Rebellion. But Love also wanted to discover "whether King James and Prince Henry his son, came unto a timely death, yea or no". Only after a proper examination could there be a proper "healing of this poor Nation".[35] What truth Love expected such an investigation to uncover is clear, at least in outline, for James's death did not stand alone; it was part of a longer catalogue of "popish" crimes and plots, with Henry's death in 1612, the betrayal of the Huguenot cause in 1627–28, and the Irish rebellion in 1641. It seems unlikely that Love, who would stridently oppose the trial and execution of Charles I in January 1649, intended to implicate the king in his father's murder, but by placing a call for the truth about James's death alongside references to the sudden dissolution of "some Parliaments" that had dared talk of an "enquiry", he might have encouraged more sinister constructions of the secret history. Coming amid warnings that the nation would find no peace until the blood of the innocent was avenged, Love's comments shortly became more explosive than he himself dreamed.

Three years after Love's sermon, when, despite Parliament's military triumph, a permanent settlement still seemed far out of reach, radicals in Westminster and the parliamentary Army would declare that they were finished dealing with the king. When they sought to justify breaking off all further talks, they would turn once again to Eglisham's allegations and the events of the 1626 Parliament. And this time, the question of Charles I's responsibility would occupy centre stage. Printers and polemicists had mobilized variations on the secret history throughout the first Civil War, using representations of the early Stuart past to legitimize a range of (mostly) hard-line Parliamentarian positions at key moments of crisis and debate. In 1648 the secret history of James I's murder would help pave the way for regicide.

CHAPTER TWENTY

THE HELLISH WESTMINSTERIAN LIE

THE SECRET HISTORY AND THE CRISIS OF THE

ENGLISH REVOLUTION, 1648

W HAT IF IT "could be ... demonstratively proved" that Charles I was a murderer? It was a startling question for a Royalist to ask, even in the desperate days of February 1648. His answer, however, was entirely orthodox: even if such a horrific charge could be proved, the king's subjects would still lack lawful grounds for resisting and deposing their monarch. The only permissible response would be to "set our selves to the duties of Fasting, and Prayers, and Teares, for the lamentation and expiation of so horrid an iniquity from his Majestie and the Kingdome". Nothing the king could do would "discharge ... the bond of our allegiance", as Scripture made perfectly clear. King David committed adultery and procured a man's death, but this justified neither the rebellions against him nor Shimei's "foul-mouthed railing". The Emperor Nero was a "Devill incarnate", yet during his reign St Paul had preached the doctrine of absolute subjection "unto the higher powers". Charles I's "Right unto his Crowne and Government" thus remained "entire", no matter his crimes.[1]

These questions were no longer academic. On 11 February 1648, only a few days before this tract appeared, Parliament had approved a sensational *Declaration of the Commons of England* (Fig. 75). All the newsbooks covered the event. *The Weekly Intelligencer* named it the item "which this week is most remarkable", *Mercurius Bellicus* said it scourged the king "with Scorpions", and *Mercurius Aulicus* declared that, after the Parliament-men approved the document, Satan sat "grinning ... to see his pretty Impes with what brazen Browes and Diabolical Imprudence they have out-fac'd the Publique".[2] One author later dubbed the *Declaration* "the Master-peece of treachery", while another called on the heavens to "Blush ... at the divelish, Imprudency" of the "viperous genera-tion of cruel and inhumaine Canniballs" who had forged this "Hellish Westministerian lye". The *Declaration* deserved such dramatic reactions. The document attempted to justify Parliament's refusal to continue negotiations with the king, signalling a significant hardening of attitudes among the Parliament-men that raised the stark possibility of a final political settlement without Charles on

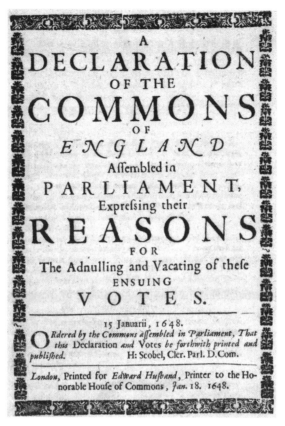

A

DECLARATION

OF THE

COMMONS

OF

E N G L A N D

Aſſembled in

PARLIAMENT,

Exprefsing their

REASONS

FOR

The Adnulling and Vacating of theſe

ENSUING

V O T E S.

15 Januarii, 1648.

ORdered by the Commons aſſembled in Parliament, That this Declaration and Votes be forthwith printed and publiſhed.   H: Scobel, Cler. Parl. D.Com.

London, Printed for Edward Huſband, Printer to the Honorable Houſe of Commons, Jan. 18. 1648.

Figure 75: Title page of *A Declaration of the Commons of England*, 1648, the official justification of the Vote of No Addresses breaking off negotiations with the king, which reintroduced the murder of James I to the centre of political debate (Huntington Library).

the throne. Equally startling were Parliament's stated justifications, and one claim, in particular, struck many with horror. "O implacable monsters", intoned *Mercurius Bellicus*, the Parliament-men "will sure proceed next, to question the Almighty Iehovah about the death of his Son, as they now dare to doe his Viceregent, our gracious King Charles, for the death of his Father."[3]

As the English Revolution approached its crisis, the secret history re-emerged to dominate political discourse and debate to a degree it had never done before. In 1626, George Eglisham had urged Charles I to execute justice on his father's murderer; early in 1648, Charles's failure to do so would become the polemical centrepiece of a campaign to discredit and perhaps destroy the king. This revolutionary appropriation of *The Forerunner* would in turn provoke a powerful Royalist counter-offensive that portrayed their opponents as cynical regicides and tried to pick apart Eglisham's credibility. As the nation careered into a revolutionary future, the past was close behind.

To Make a Bonfire of Monarchy

By January 1648 it was sometimes hard to believe that Parliament had won the Civil War. The winning coalition was hopelessly divided over the nation's future. Parliament's attempts to demobilize the Army in 1647 without paying arrears or guaranteeing indemnity had incensed and then radicalized the officers and soldiers. The Scottish Covenanters, having assisted in Parliament's victory, were increasingly apprehensive about the religious and political intentions of their ostensible allies. Meanwhile the king played the various factions off against each other as popular sympathy for his plight began to grow. Increasingly nostalgic for the tranquillity of the 1630s, many contemporaries were apprehensive about further religious and political chaos. Householders struggled under an unprecedented tax load, most notably from the hated excise, and many were forced to give soldiers free quarter in their homes. Unflattering comparisons with the illegal exactions of the 1630s became commonplace: one poet asked "was Ship Money more heavie then Excise" and added that "Free quarter eates up all Monopolies".[4] Parliament's godly war on Christmas provoked pro-Royalist riots in Kent over the winter of 1647–48, and with the Parliament-men too badly divided to respond effectively, stinging Royalist critiques of the Westminster regime poured from the presses, forcing frustrated radicals into increasingly drastic solutions to the crisis. In February 1648, as the crisis worsened, the Royalist *Mercurius Pragmaticus* warned of a "Paper-plot . . . to make a Bon-fire of Monarchy"; among the most combustible materials was Eglisham's secret history.[5]

After the first Civil War ended in 1646, rumours had surfaced periodically of plans to re-investigate James I's death. In June 1646, French diplomats reported that "the Independents are on the verge of pronouncing Charles guilty of his father's death (*coulpable de la mort de son père*)". Nine months later, Royalist agents heard that Parliament, unable to "fixe any other calumnies on his Majesty", would try him "for his Father's death". In March 1647, Nicholas Oudart, former secretary to Charles I's Secretary of State, Sir Edward Nicholas, wrote of "3 queres come or coming from Scotland", one of which asked "Whither the death of K. James shall not be inquired after". Oudart added that a "Dr. Henderson offers his oath to prove the latter, so as that it will appeare the King now had a hand in it." Later in June of that year, Presbyterians in the House of Commons were reportedly anxious that "the Army and the Independents will accuse the king of Poysoning his Father and soe endeavour to take away his leif".[6] These rumours suggest that James's death had begun to interest the more radical Independents, who were increasingly sceptical of any settlement with the king. Yet in 1647, with the leadership of both Parliament and Army committed to negotiation, Eglisham's stories remained only as background noise to other discussions.

By early 1648 the situation had changed. Parliament had sent a delegation to Carisbrooke Castle on the Isle of Wight to negotiate with the imprisoned king, but Charles was evasive, and, while ostensibly talking to Parliament, had secretly concluded an "Engagement" with Scottish agents that would lead to a Scottish invasion on his behalf. Apprehensive of a Royalist–Covenanter alliance and angry at the king's intransigence, a majority in Parliament opted for drastic action. The Army had already pressed to break off the negotiations, and on 3 January 1648, "after many houres debate", the Commons agreed. Although "cried downe by some that were in their wits", the radical Henry Marten led "a whole regiment of New-lights"—among whom Colonel Herbert Morley was characterized as one of the "principall Fire-men"—in favour of the vote. John Maynard called for the House "to lay the King aside", while Sir Thomas Wroth prayed, "From divells and Kings Good Lord deliver me . . . I desire any government rather than that of Kings". As the discussion dragged on, some slipped away and "left the remnant to that opportunity which they fought for". By a vote of 141 to 92, the House decided that it would make no further addresses to the king, and, as one newsbook put it, "THAT THE HOUSE WILL NOT ADMIT OF ANY" overtures from him. Furthermore, anyone who conducted unauthorized negotiations would be guilty of treason. Having "set this Kingdom all on Flame", as *Mercurius Dogmaticus* lamented, the House appointed nine men to draw up a declaration justifying its actions.[7]

The committee's composition virtually guaranteed a provocative result. It included mostly younger men. Thomas Chaloner, the oldest, was fifty-three, and Lord Grey, the youngest, was twenty-six; the rest were in their thirties or forties. All were radicals. In 1643 the Commons had found Henry Marten's outspoken animosity to Charles so appalling that they had suspended him for three years. Grey, a veteran officer, had openly supported the radical Levellers in 1647, and Chaloner shared not only Marten's politics but also his antagonism towards organized religion. In December 1648, when over two hundred conservative Parliament-men were purged from the Commons, all but one of the nine committee-men kept their seats; indeed, Grey helped conduct the purge. In January 1649, when thirty-eight members signed the king's death warrant, four of the nine-man committee—Chaloner, Grey, Marten and John Lisle—were among them; another three—Herbert Morley, Edmund Prideaux and Richard Salwey—were appointed to the trial commission but did not sign the warrant. Nathaniel Fiennes and William Pierrepont were more moderate. Fiennes was the sole committee member purged in December 1648, and Pierrepont, though not formally secluded, soon withdrew in protest. In January 1648, however, the committee members were all frustrated with the king. Fiennes, in fact, probably took the lead in drafting the *Declaration*, though some Royalists thought the Independent lawyer John Sadler helped him.[8]

The committee worked amid relentless Royalist criticism. After denouncing these "Earth-quakes in the State", *Mercurius Pragmaticus* reasoned that "if there must be no further Addresses, it is evident there can be no Accommodation, and if no Accommodation, then they must have some other Government". Clearly, Charles's life was in danger; the Parliament's "heav'nly Cause . . . which first baptized the Round-head in noble Strafford's blood . . . now/Must on the King's be founded".[9] Emotions ran high. The Army's General Council quickly resolved to "stand by the Parliament in those things . . . concerning the King", but the House of Lords, fearful of counter-revolutionary unrest in the unsettled capital, took nearly two weeks to support the Commons.[10] The drafting committee also faced direct abuse. One newsbook scoffed at "their wild Sophistria" and another sneered at their "pritty side-wasted Declaration (that the people of the Land may fall in love, and comitt fornications with) for the justification of all their Divelish devices and odious conspiracies". Amid the clamour, the committee focused on its dangerous assignment of "setling and securing of the Parliament and Kingdom . . . without the King, and against Him".[11]

The committee worked slowly. On 3 January 1648 the Parliament-men had assumed the task would take four days, but by 15 January they had still only seen a general preamble. On 24 January the House called for the draft document, but it did not appear until 2 February. Over the next nine days, the Commons debated it almost daily. The text predictably indicted Charles I's misrule and his refusal to negotiate in good faith. More startling was the inclusion of what a Venetian report characterized as "old and almost forgotten charges" that "his Majesty hastened the death of his father by poison or that Buckingham attempted it with his consent".[12] We do not know who revived these charges, but the few surviving glimpses of the Commons' deliberations reveal that the members repeatedly returned to the language used on James's death. On 3 February the members considered the draft declaration word by word. On 5 February the Commons recommitted the "Clause . . . concerning the Death of King James", authorizing the committee "to proceed to the thorough Examination of this Business; and to send for Parties, Witnesses, Papers, and Records".[13] The following day it expanded the committee, adding the future regicide Thomas Scot, as well as Thomas Reynolds, Thomas Stockdale and John Moyle, all of whom would eventually serve in the post-revolutionary Rump Parliament. The larger committee had the power to "add marginal Notes" to the document "for directing to the Proofs and Evidences", but ultimately decided not to clutter the margins with citations.[14] On 10 February the House reviewed the final text, and of nine small emendations, four related to James's death. One newsbook noted that "the particulars about the death of King James took up a great part of this dayes consultation", and another reported that there was "most dispute . . . about the death of King Iames; because every particuler is made very cleare, before it passe".[15]

We know little of these debates, save for two references from Royalist sources. Sir Henry Mildmay, James and Charles's Master of the Jewel House, had supported Parliament in the Civil War, and when sceptics cited the lack of hard evidence about James I's murder, he allegedly offered "to be deposed that his Majestie was guilty of his Fathers death". Other veterans thought otherwise. John Selden, the celebrated antiquarian, then in his sixties, was one of the few survivors from the 1626 Parliament. He reportedly regarded the draft language on James's death as an accusation of parricide and recalled the examination of "the business of poisoning King James in the Duke of Buckingham's time, but could find nothing at all reflecting upon this King [Charles]". He thus urged the House to delete the article. According to Royalist reports, when Oliver Cromwell called for Selden's expulsion, another parliamentary veteran rose to his feet. Like Selden, Simonds D'Ewes "troubled himselfe much in relickes and records", and he took Cromwell's suggestion "much in snuff". D'Ewes added that he had "a premeditated speech upon that particular but finding (his comrade) Mr Selden like to speed so ill for discharging his minde he desired that he might have liberty to sitt downe and say nothing", which was, the anonymous reporter added, "his wisest course".[16]

On 11 February the Commons finally approved the text. In a thinly attended House, eighty members voted for it, but, an observer reported, "there were 50 . . . out of their tendernesse to the King that dissented". The House ordered the committee to see the text "true and well printed" and the members to "send Copies thereof to be published and dispersed" in their constituencies. By 17 February the Commons' printer had produced 5,600 copies, 3,500 of which were "to bee sent into the Countrie".[17]

The *Declaration* catalogued Charles's continuous "Breach of Trust" in rejecting offers for a settlement. Then, broadcasting "what hath long been suffered in too much silence", it made two bold claims: Charles clung to the "most Destructive Maxime or Principle" that he owed no one but God an account of his actions—"a fit foundation for all Tyranny"; and he had a long-standing "Correspondence . . . with Rome" threatening the "Peace, Safety, Laws, Religion here established". The text then surveyed Charles's many crimes: his betrayal of La Rochelle, his attempts "to enslave us" using foreign mercenaries and "grinde us" with illegal taxes, his plan to lead his people "captive into Superstition and Idolatry" and to deny them a Parliament, the only "hope for liberty". But the crime given the most space in the text concerned the "Proceedings and Passages of the Parliament held in the second year of this Kings reign, concerning the Death of His Royal Father".[18]

Here the *Declaration* followed the 1626 parliamentary record. Using a slightly larger font and a mix of italic and roman letters to highlight the more significant passages, the pamphlet reprinted the thirteenth impeachment charge accusing Buckingham of "An act of transcendent presumption". Charles's constant "Messages and interruptions" had wilfully sabotaged the Commons' attempt to prosecute his favourite for this crime, and he had imprisoned Digges and Eliot, the men who had "specially managed" the charge concerning James's death. Finally, as the Commons prepared a "judgement against the said Duke", Charles had "a suddain purpose to dissolve the Parliament" before "Justice could be done". Since there was no subsequent "legal inquiry" into "the death of the said King", the *Declaration* concluded ominously, "We leave the world now to judge where the guilt of this remains." In spite of confident reports that the document would accuse Charles of "the death of his father", the text let readers decide whether Charles had become an accessory after the fact by thwarting the course of justice or whether he had connived in James's poisoning. This evasiveness surprised one Royalist observer, who noted that the *Declaration* was "short of what was expected".[19] The ambiguity was likely deliberate. While radicals like Grey, Marten and Chaloner wanted to end negotiations, moderates like Fiennes and Pierrepont probably hoped to frighten the king back into serious talks. The text was framed to allow for both outcomes.

Nevertheless the *Declaration* represented a dangerous development. Years later, Edward Hyde would argue that the vote and the *Declaration* marked a major watershed, because for the first time a majority in the Commons had focused their "invective" directly on the king, casting aside the "duty and respect" hitherto used when talking of "the King's person". Gone was the rhetoric of wicked counsel that had diverted parliamentary attacks onto Charles's ministers; instead, the *Declaration* cast its "particular reproaches" directly "upon the person of the King". Further, Hyde wrote, the clause about James's death could be read as a "direct insinuation as if he had conspired with the Duke of Buckingham against the life of his father". Other Royalists agreed. "They accuse him of his Fathers Murther", wrote one pamphleteer, and another opined that "these desperate and bloody usurpers" have used the "grand manifesto" of the Commons to accuse Charles "of parricide". The news that this charge was under consideration had reportedly made Charles "very melancholy, and good reason hee hath, for now to render him absolutely odious a declaration is frameing, and horrid crimes pretended against him". If the charges stuck, warned the newsletter, Charles's "life will not stand in their way".[20]

Some radicals hoped the revived accusation would lead to a formal inquiry into James's death. On 24 February 1648 the Commons read a letter from Thomas Heselrige, brother of the radical Parliament-man Sir Arthur, reporting that Francis Smalley, a former Star Chamber functionary, had "notes . . . of the Principal passages" of the abortive Star Chamber hearings into Buckingham's role in James's death. The House ordered Smalley to Westminster, and when he finally appeared, he brought the 1628 royal warrant instructing Attorney General Heath to take the case documents off the file. Although, as a

Presbyterian writer later recalled, Smalley brought "no notes", the House ordered the committee that had drafted the *Declaration* to examine him and indeed any other "Parties, Witnesses, Papers, [and] Records". The investigation produced nothing; definitive evidence was as difficult to come by in 1648 as it had been in 1626.[21]

More importantly, the *Declaration* triggered widespread public discussion of James's death, a discussion that dominated debate for months in ways and to a degree that scholars have almost completely ignored. Brief summaries of the document appeared in Parliamentarian newsbooks, further publicizing the charges, and the tract itself would have been hard to avoid, with over five thousand copies in circulation. A later Royalist pamphlet insisted that the *Declaration* had also been "carefully read in our parish churches, according to order, and vehemently pressed by the ministers that you have placed amongst us". The text was also translated into both Dutch and French.[22]

Yet this was not enough for some radicals. On 10 February 1648 a Royalist agent reported that the Commons was finishing its declaration "to make his Majesty . . . more odious to the people", but "in the mean time as a forerunner . . . an other scandalous and base booke is sett out by Henry Martin with the good leave of our Patriots". That "scandalous and base" book was almost certainly the pamphlet published by the London stationer George Horton that George Thomason purchased on 14 February (Fig. 76). The tract bears no evidence of Marten's involvement, but the radical Parliament-man and the publisher were fellow travellers. In 1647, Horton had produced several tracts articulating Army grievances, and in February 1648 he printed the hard-line exhortation *Englands Remonstrance to Their King*. Horton's latest "base book" was another remodelled version of Eglisham's secret history. Retitled to highlight its connection to Parliament's *Declaration*, *The Forerunner* was now *A Declaration to the Kingdome of England, Concerning the poysoning of King James*. The text was heavily edited to fit into the cheapest single-sheet, eight-page quarto format. Hamilton's murder, which had dominated Eglisham's original, was now relegated to a half-page coda. More significant, Horton's title page reframed the edited text to make an implicit but unmistakable accusation. After summarizing the case against Buckingham and his mother, Horton urged the reader, in a slightly bigger font, to take note of "King James His Protestation concerning our Soveraign Lord the King that now is". This protestation appeared, italicized, as the preamble to the account of James's death, and noted that James had:

> often publikly protested even in the presence of his apparent Heire, *That if His owne sonne should commit Murther, or any such execrable act of injury, he would not spare him, but would have him dye for it, and would have him more severely punished then any other.*

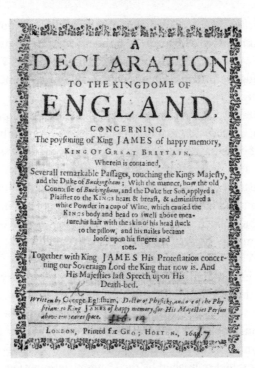

Figure 76: George Eglisham, *A Declaration to the Kingdome of England*, an abridged edition of *The Forerunner of Revenge* published by the radical printer George Horton in 1648 to coincide with Parliament's *Declaration* on the Vote of No Addresses (British Library).

In the 1626 *Forerunner* this statement appeared at the beginning of Eglisham's petition to Parliament as part of his paean to justice, but in the Horton edition it was ripped from context to insinuate that Charles was his father's murderer and deserved no mercy.[23] Whether orchestrated by Marten or not, Horton's tract reinforced the most radical gloss on the *Declaration*'s enigmatic presentation of James's death.

The Horton *Forerunner* reproduced Eglisham's narrative of James's murder and restored the references to the Earl of Bristol, the Conde de Gondomar and the Spanish match that John Aston had omitted in his Protestantized 1642 version. The 1648 edition also emphasized the medical evidence from the autopsies. The title page, as well as the text, highlighted Eglisham's claim that the poisons "caused the Kings body and head to swell above measure, his hair with the skin of his head stuck to the pillow, and his nailes became loose upon his fingers and toes". And all that remained of Eglisham's lengthy account of Hamilton's murder was his vivid description of the marquis's grotesquely swollen corpse.[24]

The *Declaration*'s insinuations about Charles's involvement in his father's death, insinuations that Horton's edition turned into virtual indictments, fit neatly into the broader contemporary debate at this crisis point of the English Revolution. Regicidal speculation was rife, and a full discussion of radical resistance theory soon followed the *Declaration* into print. In late February 1648, Matthew Simmons, a printer with ties to the parliamentary Army and the Independents, produced the first English edition of the *Vindiciae Contra Tyrannos*, the famous 1579 Huguenot justification for the deposition of wicked monarchs. Touted in newsbooks, the tract sold well, and Simmons soon issued a second edition.[25] Some radicals were clearly hoping that the revival of the secret history and the translation of the *Vindiciae* would together help fuel a "bonfire for monarchy". In this bold radical endeavour much depended on the provincial reaction, and initial responses from the activists were encouraging. In mid-February petitioners in Taunton in Somerset announced that "we are fully satisfied in our Iudgements and Consciences, of the Necessity and Iustice" of the Vote; and in early March, Buckinghamshire presented a petition to the Commons endorsing the position "in your late Votes and Declaration concerning the King (after his rejecting so many Applications) having so fully cleared your selves, as may stop the mouth of Envy and Malice it self for ever".[26] But the polemical battle had just begun.

"This Off Scumme of Hellish Plotts"

Mercurius Aulicus immediately pounced on Horton's *Forerunner*, sneering that this "old patch'd piece with a new facing to it" was a "yelping Iacall before the roaring Lyon hunting for his prey". The Royalist editor, who understood the implications of Horton's revisions, doubted whether James would ever have made the protestation attributed to him. Since a "learned prince" surely knew that "to slay the King, or the Kings eldest Sonne, is the highest Act of Treason", this ridiculous claim was twisting the words of a supposedly murdered king "to take away [the] life" of his son. The newsbook also challenged the medical evidence. James had died of transparently natural causes, for " 'tis well known" that "being an excessive drinker, his body was very Hydropicall, and his disease being a Quartan-Feaver, nature was too weake to resist the violence of it". Eglisham's description of James's distorted corpse was a "report as false as hell", *Aulicus* insisted, as "false and scandalous as the jugling knave that writ it".[27]

The radicals had hoped to use the *Declaration* and the relaunched *Forerunner* to mobilize the public against settlement with the king. Their strenuous efforts provoked a furious Royalist response. Confronted with the unpleasant realities of confiscatory taxation, oppressive military power and heterodox religious fanaticism, many longed for stability, and the king's supporters orchestrated petitions from Essex, Kent, Sussex and even London to denounce the Vote. When the Surrey freeholders presented their petition, a riot broke out before the Parliament-house amid cheers of "for King Charles, for King Charles", and the Army eventually shot several protesters. The freeholders of Hampshire denounced these developments as "a president so full of horror, injustice and more than Turkish tyranny" and registered their firm opposition to "those that had a designe by taking away Monarchicall Government, of making themselves high and mighty States, and engrossing all Dominion".[28]

As they sought to undermine the *Declaration*, the Royalists paid particular attention to Eglisham's sensational charges, recognizing that they were the most dangerous part of the document. "The maine wheele or spring of your Engine", wrote one Royalist, "which if any thing must doe your feat of dis-uniting the hearts of the Kingdome from his Majesty, and justifying your protested rejection of him, is that which concerneth the death of the late king." Another author urged the public to "Looke upon" the *Declaration* "as the bane and poyson of Aspes, spit abroad to envenome your soules, resolving never to believe more therein, then themselves dare speake or utter (I meane concerning the death of the King his father)." That was too much for *Aulicus*, who begged its readers to avoid the tract and "shut your eyes" and "stop your eares" against it.[29]

Two decades earlier, Buckingham and Charles had refused to answer Eglisham in public, but now the Royalists carried the polemical fight to the king's critics. Parliament was acutely aware of the threat still posed by Royalist penmen and printers. On 19 February it instructed messengers "to repair to any house, shop, or other place" where the newsbooks "Pragmaticus, Melancholicus, Elencticus, or any other unlicensed pamphlets" were "printed or sold and seize on them" as well as their "printers, sellers, and authors".[30] Although *Mercurius Elencticus* mocked Parliament's spies who "Listen and Evesdrop the City", the dragnet soon caught the printer of *Pragmaticus* and the author of *Melancholicus*.[31] Nevertheless, enough of the network survived to launch a punishing Royalist counterattack. As Sir Edward Hyde later recalled, "many private persons" decided on their own initiative "to publish answers to that odious Declaration".[32] The Royalist leadership in exile—Hyde in Jersey and Sir Edward Nicholas in Normandy—also monitored, coordinated and contributed to the campaign (Fig. 77). On 20 March, scarcely a month after the *Declaration*'s publication, Nicholas fretted to Sir Richard Browne, the Royalist agent in Paris, that "I did hope to have received before this a sollid Aunscweare to the villainous Declaration published against the king, but it seems it was not soe soone finished as I was advised it would be". He hoped to receive the response within the week, vowing to forward it to Browne "if I shall find it aunsweare my expection". He thought it "a shame that (there being soe many good pens of the kings party) none did use more diligence to vindicat his honor from such false, unworthy and traiterous aspersions". And at the heart of Nicholas's anxiety were the *Declaration*'s allegations concerning James I, which he felt would prove particularly damaging among continental readers. "Nothinge in that libel", he noted to Browne, "did leave a worse impression among strangers then the

Figure 77: A mid- to late seventeenth-century engraved portrait by A. Hertochs of Sir Edward Nicholas, Buckingham's former secretary who became Charles I's Secretary of State in the 1640s and attempted to coordinate the Royalist response to the 1648 *Declaration* (National Portrait Gallery).

particular malicious and false aspersion concerning the death of K. James," and Nicholas was painfully aware that several people in France already believed that Charles had been aware of "such a villainy".[33] But even without Nicholas's direct prompting, his allies had already begun staging a response to the *Declaration*.

The Royalists produced two almost instantaneous ripostes. *An Antidote Against An Infectious Aire*, which Thomason purchased on 17 February, offered "A briefe Reply". While conceding that the section on James's death was crucial, the tract wondered why it was so ambiguous: "You are loth to expresse your selves therein, yet it is not hard to discerne what thoughts you would thereby commend unto." The *Declaration* relied on "insinuations" and "assertions" to convince readers "to thinke more than it selfe dares speake or utter", and it did so because the House of Commons had no solid evidence. "If you can clearly make good what you intend," asked the *Antidote*, "why did you not speake it plainly? if you cannot, why doe you goe about by malicious art to insinuate that which you are not able to make good?" The pamphlet mocked the inherent implausibility of using "quodlibeticall and uncertaine conjectures" to under-mine the virtuous king. And since everyone knew that Charles had held his father in "deare affection", they would understand that the charge had been "forged by some against him" for their own wicked ends. *The Antidote* attracted attention, and when copies became "very hard to be got", the Royalists printed an abridged version.[34]

Four days after the *Declaration* appeared, *Treasons Anatomie* exposed the inherent flaws in that "Poysonous (and till now) unheard of peece of treason" and offered to vindicate "His Gracious Soveraigne, against those horrid Aspersions . . . conserning His Fathers Death". Incredulous at "this off scumme of Hellish plotts", the author claimed to "quiver and tremble in the carriage of my quill through the bloody and villeinous Scandall". Parliament's "Infernal Strategems" made him ask God why "thy dearest servant, and our dread sove-raigne be thus intolerably slandered?" The answer was simple: "how many Parliament men, so many monstrous Kings, so many Monsters, so many Tyrants". Having glossed the charge (in the common counter-revolutionary style) as a symptom of Parliament's tyranny, the tract offered more specific objections to the *Declaration's* case on James's death. "Let any man that hath but common sence Judge how their other Arguments do hang together". Far from being murdered, James "dyed in a good old age, having finished his course", and Parliament in 1626 had discovered that much from "divers Chiurgions . . . who were at the embalming" and found James's "corps to be as free from any the least imperfection, or change of colour". Buckingham had been a victim of the malice of "rebellious villaines" in 1626, and clearly had no motive to kill a king who had so handsomely rewarded him. The 1626 dissolu-tion of Parliament, so central to the *Declaration's* insinuations, had a simple explanation: after the poisoning charge "was answered on the Dukes behalfe" and Charles "cleered [Buckingham] of that envious aspersion", the king had dissolved Parliament "least they should murther that English Hero".[35]

The Royalist newsbooks were equally energetic. Parliament, *Mercurius Bellicus* argued, had "done a better service to their King in publishing . . . their Declaration, then his best friends could possible have invented", for any "judi-cious" reader could see both the "uncertainties" on which the "allegations are founded" and Parliament's "implacable hatred to their gracious Soveraigne; their Trayterous intends, to aspire to his throne, and their cursed machavillian pollicies, to inslave a free people". "Let the Committee enterline, dash in and dash out what they will", railed *Mercurius Elencticus*: the people would not be "charmed" and would stand "a gast" at the "deformed, shaplesse, and saplesse" document. *Mercurius Aulicus* called the charges "poyson-poynted arrows, to murder Majesty withall", and likened the *Declaration* to "a Basilisk" whose "very breath is able to infect the Universe".[36] In 1626, *Mercurius Pragmaticus* noted, Charles had cleverly perceived that Parliament struck "principally at himselfe", and in 1648 the king again understood that "their present Insinuation" aimed at "the dishonor of his Majesty". The *Declaration*, reasoned *Pragmaticus*, attempted to "render his Majesty odious in the eyes of his people" by charging

him with "Treason . . . . against his Father King Iames, as if hee had been accessary to his Death". For *Mercurius Bellicus*, Buckingham's great affection for
James proved his innocence—"the duke was the King's darling", and the two
men "were reciprocally affectionate even a second Pilades and Orestes".[37]

The newsbooks also responded with ridicule. *Pragmaticus* used parliamentary diagnoses of James's illness to mock the religious derangement at
Westminster. "Our State-mountebanks":

> never knew what belonges to Ague-fits, unlesse it were in Religion, and
> those they are taken with oftner than the Spring and Fall: And because they
> are able to quit their Consciences of the malady . . . they are bold to imagine
> it could not bee mortall.

Mercurius Melancholicus offered its readers rude verses fit to "break thy very
sides":

> Men where are your hearts become,
> Lood (*sic*) you what here is, look ye what here is
> A DECLARATION, kisse my bumme,
> Now the Fools jeare us, now the Fooles jeare us.

Aulicus libelled the *Declaration*'s authors, and while it singled out Chaloner,
"that cursed Cannibal" who produced "This Declaration out of his base block-
head", it focused its scorn on the sexual adventurer Henry Marten:

> We wonder not at the cursed fruit of such an accursed Stock as thou art,
> who loves a Whore better then God, prefers liberty before Loyalty, and had
> rather commit fornication with Sea-cole ashes, then pay the tribute of
> Allegiance which by nature and grace too (if thou hadst any) thou doest
> own unto thy Lord and Soveraigne.[38]

Other tracts also exploited Marten's scandalous reputation: the "Accusation"
concerning James's death was so ridiculous that even "H. Martin himselfe, the
most professed enemy unto the King, thought so meanly" of it "that he onely
made sport of it". When others brought it up, Marten claimed that "if it were
true", the murder "was the only good action" Charles "had ever done in his life".[39]

Since the confined space and restricted news cycle prevented more systematic critiques, the newsbooks harried their opponents while others readied more
substantial responses. Three weeks after the publication of the *Declaration*, *The
Kingdomes Briefe Answer* arrived in London. Parliament, the new tract insisted,
had used the *Declaration* as a "warrant for introducing a new government over
us". The author offered the beginnings of a detailed alternative version of James's

death and the events of the 1626 Parliament. "The present King had no hand in the applying" of medicine to James, and the charge "against the Duke, who did all this" was not for murder but merely for "a transcendent Act of presumption". Yet somehow "it must now be insinuated as murder, and patricide in King Charls". The *Declaration* had also omitted inconvenient evidence; why else "did you not print the Examinations you have on this businesse, of the sworne Physitians you speak of, and of the Apothecary that made and tempered this Playster and Drink?" Parliament had similarly suppressed "the story how the same Playster and Drink had cured a great man a little before, and King James, impatient of pain, resolved to make trial of it". There was no poisoning—the "Physitians and Apothecaries knew all the Ingredients"—although it was possible that the medicines, while "good in themselves", might have been "improper for his age". Yet James's body, when "opened", was "found fair and clear". Finally, the 1626 dissolution of Parliament had a clear explanation. Charles had not acted to save Buckingham from a murder charge; rather, after "finding it only an Act of policy to remove his Favorite, He exprest an Act of power in preserving him from his adversaries".[40]

The Royalist counter-offensive continued in April, again resorting to a variety of tones and strategies. The satire *White-hall Fayre* imagined Colonel John Barkstead as a street vendor trying to sell "Orders, Questions, Proclamations/Covenants, Contracts, Compacts, Protestations", all designed "to kill the King, and all his Progenie". When his customers proved uninterested, Barkstead offered them "the Master-piece of treachery", that:

> thing
> Some call a Declaration, 'gainst the King;
> Taxing him for his Life.

Parliament's "vipers" would "sell sinne, at any rate", attempting to "perswade the world, the kings command/Did send his Father, to the Stygian strand".[41]

But in Normandy, Secretary Nicholas still anxiously awaited a more persuasive answer to "the House of Commons Declaration".[42] It finally came in the 5 April issue of *Mercurius Elencticus*.[43] The newsbook opened with a prophecy that the rebels' "reigne is at an ende", and insisted that the *Declaration*, "that damnable Alcharon", was the "forerunner" of the rebellion's fall—its allegations were so incredible that they had been "exploded, and hiss'd at by every Schoole-boy". But to destroy the *Declaration*'s "most pernicious Ingredient", the charges that "accuse his sacred Majesty to have had some hand" in his father's death, the newsbook now printed an "answer . . . which will give the world . . . full satisfaction . . . and . . . stop the mouths of all Divelish Detractors". What followed was the most systematic response to Eglisham's accusation since Buckingham had addressed the 1626 Parliament.

This "answer" was powerfully framed, focusing on the details of James's last illness and supplying the names and addresses of many surviving witnesses. It replicated much of Buckingham's 1626 defence, emphasizing James's active participation in his treatment and the harmlessness of the medicines involved. But thanks to the testimony of John Baker, Buckingham's barber, the narrative offered vivid new details. On James's orders, Baker had ridden to Dunmow to consult Dr "Kimington" (Remington), "famous in those parts for curing of agues", who had recently treated both Buckingham and the Earl of Warwick. Finding the physician ill in bed, Baker had prevailed on him to write a prescription that a local apothecary then prepared. Baker returned with "a potion and a Plaister", pieces of leather on which the plaster could be spread, and instructions "how and where to apply them". The narrative stressed the precautions taken before the medicines were given to the king. An aguish Sir James Palmer, groom of the bedchamber, asked to "make a tryall" of the medicines, and after drinking the posset "boyled with Harts-horne" and putting the plasters on his "Breast and Wrists", he "not only mist his fit, but afterwards lost his Ague". When the medicines arrived "about the time the King's next fitte was to come", Baker tested them in front of the royal physicians, drinking a full dose of the potion that the Countess of Buckingham's maid, Mary Fowler, had prepared and eating a walnut-sized portion of the plaster. The royal apothecary, Israel Wolfe, then applied the plasters. Unfortunately, "it pleased God, the good effect succeeded not". Yet the medicine remained potent. Patrick Mawle, another aguish bedchamber-man, "tooke of the residue of the Medicine that was left and drank the like Potion, and applyed the like plaisters . . . and thereby was cured". The narrative concluded by noting that Wolfe the apothecary, then residing in Twickenham, could testify that the potion consisted of "Sirrop of Gilly-Flowers" and the plaster of "Treakle and Mithridate". Likewise, Mary Fowler and John Baker had married and were living near New Hall in Essex; they could swear that the potion was "ordinary possit, boyled only with Harts Horne".

More powerful still was the narrative's depiction of James's good death. Horton's edition of *The Forerunner* had described James turning away from Buckingham with the words "Poysoned me!" on his lips.[44] In this Royalist counter-narrative, however, the king proclaimed only love for his favourite. After taking the sacrament on the Thursday before his death, the king told Buckingham "Steny, I am willing to die, but am sory I must leave the World, before I have done that for thee my love intended." These, the narrative added, were "almost the last words the King spake, with an articulate voice". The intimacy implied by James's use of the nickname was underlined by Buckingham's response to his master's death. When James died in Palmer's arms, "grasping the Dukes hand", Palmer asked Buckingham to "close the eyes of the best Master in the World", but overcome by "Teares", Buckingham could not do it. Palmer then "tooke the Dukes hand in his, and with his Fingers ends closed up the Kings eyes". Although the document did not list his whereabouts, Palmer, like Baker, was still alive, living outside Windsor.[45] The radicals had launched an abortive inquiry into the facts of James's death, but only this narrative offered witnesses who could set the record straight.

The Royalist exiled leadership was highly impressed. Secretary Nicholas confirmed the narrative's accuracy, noting to Browne that "I was present att the back staires att Theobalds and saw John Baker eate a pillet of the plaister". And the Royalists quickly deployed the material to counter the damaging impression the *Declaration* had left on European opinion. Nicholas in France handed out copies to foreign agents "hereabouts", while Sir William Boswell arranged a Dutch translation that was in print by early May 1648. Yet Nicholas wanted to put the narrative before a much broader public audience. In mid-April he instructed Browne to commission a French version and to have it published in the official Paris *Gazette*. A week later, he was beside himself over delays in getting it out, and on 1 May he urged Browne to hurry the publication because "diverse . . . have said that they believe the king was not unknowing of such a villainy because no full Aunsweare is given to that particular". He only relaxed when the account appeared in the *Gazette*'s 10 May issue.[46]

This resonant narrative was soon reinforced by two lengthier Royalist tracts that systematically dismantled both Eglisham's pamphlet and the *Declaration*, and together with the *Elencticus* narrative, these tracts finalized what would become the set Royalist rebuttal of the secret history. On 19 April, Thomason bought *The Regall Apology*, in which "their whole charge . . . is cleared, and for the most part retorted". It was almost certainly the work of George Bate, Charles's former physician. Bate revisited Buckingham's 1626 defence, discussing the duke's successful use of Remington's plaster and potion and James's own "urgent desire" for the remedy. He conceded that Buckingham's intervention had upset the king's physicians, but James himself, "impatient both of his disease, and of his Physicians prescripts", had begged for a second round of treatment. Bate found Remington's ingredients—London treacle in the plaster, hartshorn and marigold in the posset—unobjectionable, but he noted that a royal apothecary and the duke's mother had made the second plaster with Venice Treacle. Although the posset and the new plaster were clearly efficacious, Bate conceded that these were not the right medicines for the king at that particular juncture. Moreover, Venice Treacle was "hotter" than London and thus had aggravated the king's hot fit, prompting James's outburst that "these had done him hurt". Bate blamed Buckingham's ignorance "of the distinction between Agues" and his "Imprudence, to meddle in an Art, he was not Master of", but insisted the medicines were "no cause of the Kings death". They were given "out of a good affection" and at the king's entreaty, and all the doctors reckoned them "innocent". Bate then offered his own explanation of James's death. Whatever the Parliament-men had claimed, James's illness was

not "in the declination" when Buckingham intervened. The fever's long duration had worn the king down, and the fever itself was unusually dangerous, for
James had fallen ill shortly before a plague visitation, a time when "diseases
have much Malignancy" and defeat even "the best Physicians". Furthermore,
James was an "aged man", "kept an ill Diet", and was "full of humors, corpulent,
and of an evill constitution". What ultimately killed him was a mixed quotidian
and tertian ague "call'd a Hemitritea", a disease "known to be mortall in its
owne nature", especially in a patient with James's constitutional weaknesses.[47]

Bate also attacked the medical "experts" supporting the case for James's
murder. "The chief Witnesses against the Duke" were the king's Scottish doctor,
Alexander Ramsey, and Eglisham, men with "so bad a Reputation, that their
testimony was not to be taken against a private man". Ramsey "will lie, swear,
flatter, do any villany", Bate claimed, and had been "expell'd, or enforced to
relinquish the Colledge of London for his ill-behavior", while Eglisham had
been "expell'd from his University". Bate also undid John Aston's posthumous
Protestantization of the secret historian: Eglisham, he wrote, was "a Papist, or
rather of no Religion, and of as little honesty or learning, a man of a crackt
Braine too". Bate argued that Sir John Eliot had brought the two men's lies and
half-truths before Parliament solely to settle a private grievance with
Buckingham and to force Charles either to abandon Buckingham or to "beare
the reflection of that Dirt, which they would bestow upon the Duke". Charles
had indeed rescued the duke, someone who had "done King James no hurt" and
who was being "prosecuted . . . upon another Score".[48] By patiently analyzing
James's medical history, highlighting Eliot's ulterior motives and unmasking
Eglisham's true confessional colours, Bate had undercut both The Forerunner
and the Declaration.

A few days later, a second lengthy Royalist work offered a complementary
analysis. Here Nicholas may have been participating in, rather than simply
orchestrating, the Royalist response. Draft material from the Royall Apologie
survives among his papers, and it is possible this pamphlet was the "sollid
Aunsweare to the villainous false Declaration" that Nicholas had been
attempting to "hasten" into print in late March. It quickly reviewed the medical
evidence and argued that James's death had been natural. James was "hard to be
ruled and governed by his Physitians", and his intermitting tertian "turned into
a continual Fever, whereof he died". "Certaine plaisters and posset-drinks were
applied"—the tract does not say by whom—but these were "such as are ordinarily given by women in the country". Like other Royalist commentators, the
pamphlet stressed that "the King was embowel'd and embaumed publiquely,
and no Symptomes appeared, but that he dyed naturally of His Sicknesse".[49]

The heart of the pamphlet's refutation focused on the Parliament-house.
The 1626 evidence, so central to the Declaration's insinuations, was also the
radicals' Achilles heel. The Parliament-men had said nothing about James's

death in the 1625 session, and only took up the question a year later when, "being highly incensed" with Buckingham, they lent "a ready ear ... to all complaints". Such was the passion against the duke that "it was with great vehemency pressed, that there might have been an accusation of Treason drawn up against him". The duke's opponents surely would have done so:

> if there had been any the least ground, or evidence of any wicked intention, in the Duke to destroy the King, or any Symptoms that the Kings death had been caused or hastned by those things that were given; or that the said drinkes and plaisters had beene of any noxious or hurtfull quality.

But with "the evidence falling short" of this, "it was carried in the House for an impeachment only of *Misdemeanor, and a transcendent Presumption, and not of Treason*". Hence the Parliament-men did not, indeed could not "lay to his charge the death of King James". Furthermore, the *Declaration* had not reprinted Buckingham's extensive reply to the charge, readily available in the Lords' Journals. If the duke's response had been weak, the tract reasoned, the Parliament-men would surely have publicized the fact. But Buckingham's defence had actually been so strong that the members had let the charge "lie asleep almost this 20 years, untill their malice, and desire to blast their King, hath awakened it". In short, Parliament, not Charles, had dropped the prosecution. The pamphlet emphasized the *Declaration* was simply attempting "to make the King odious, as judging that nothing could more incense the world against Him". The charge was a cynical "artifice" deployed by desperate men to transform the people's natural "compassion" for Charles's ongoing maltreatment into a "prejudice" against him.[50]

Key elements of this case also appeared in the undated but probably relatively early *Declaration Declared*, a tightly argued attack on Westminster's "masqued monsters" and their "wormeaten stories". Drawing on considerable, perhaps even eyewitness, knowledge of the 1626 session, the tract reiterated that the House of Commons had not charged Buckingham with murder, and it claimed that the duke's defence in 1626 had been so compelling that his opponents did not pursue the allegations in 1628. The pamphlet also rebutted the *Declaration*'s insinuations about Charles's arrests of Eliot and Sir Dudley Digges. Whatever Parliament now claimed, neither had been "the principall men" handling the charge on James's death; that task had fallen to Christopher Wandesford, whom Charles had not imprisoned. The tract also noted that Digges had been arrested on a "misinformation" and had loudly protested that he had not implicated the king in his father's death. The Commons' ostentatious insistence that Digges had made no such insinuation was also evidence that the House, already "satisfied of the Dukes innocency", had thought the king entirely blameless. The dissolution of Parliament itself stemmed not from the king but from "some unquiet spirits" who "tooke occasion to necessitate a breach". The Parliament-men of 1626 had thus unanimously denied the suggestion that Charles bore any responsibility for his father's death. The Parliament-men of 1648, on the other hand, were driven by "malice, insolence, and impiety" to distort the truth; how could "any man thinke theise men are any way tender of the death of King Iames that soe maliciously seeke the bloode of his sonne?"[51]

By the late spring of 1648 the pace of the Royalist response slowed as a spasmodic set of uprisings in Kent and Essex began what would soon become the Second Civil War. But the king's supporters had not forgotten about the *Declaration*. In May a broadside, *Troy-Novant Must Not Be Burnt*, urged London's citizens to beware "the compilers of the scandalous Declaration". The aim of *A Satyrical Catechisme* was more precise. When a "Newter" asked whether the king did ever "conspire against his owne Father King James", the Roundhead assured him "Believe it and credit it, for it is as sure as I am a saint." The author then interjected, "Tis as false as God is true thou son of Belial."[52]

Early May also witnessed a more sober Royalist reply from Sir Edward Hyde, Charles's advisor now exiled in Jersey, who entered the fight over the secret history with a slight piece refusing to clear the king "of such Slaunders, for which there are no Proofs alledged; for, Malice being once detected, is best Answered, with Neglect and Silence". He flatly dismissed Eglisham's charge, asking "was there ever greater, or more apparent, Malice, then to offer to put the horrid Slander of Paricide upon Him, who was eminently known to be as obedient and loving a Son to his blessed Father?"[53] But Hyde was already working on a more systematic response (Fig. 78). *A Full Answer to an Infamous and Trayterous Pamphlet* finally appeared in late July, offering what Hyde later described as a "very large and full answer" to the *Declaration*. The pamphlet set out to prove "his majesty's innocence in all . . . particulars" and added "such pathetical applications and insinuations as were most like to work upon the affections of the people". Hyde sent the manuscript to Nicholas in Normandy, who in turn sent it to "a trusty hand in London, who caused it to be well printed" by the Royalist Richard Royston. *A Full Answer* was clearly designed as the authoritative reply to the *Declaration*. Bristling with obscure legal references, emblazoned with the royal coat of arms, and translated into Latin for continental audiences, it weighed in at an impressive 188 pages.[54]

Hyde believed the centrepiece of the *Declaration's* "infamous and scandalous" attack was "the odious and groundlesse discourse of the death of King James", and so he focused on "this most impossible Calumny and Scandall", identifying the long-festering plot to destroy royal authority that Eglisham had begun. James had died "after many terrible fits of an Ague which turned to a quotidian Fever, a disease usually mortall to persons of that age and corpulency of body". Buckingham's remedies were "such as unlearned people upon observation and

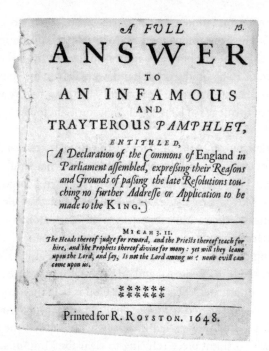

A FULL 13.

ANSWER

TO

AN INFAMOUS

AND

TRAYTEROUS *PAMPHLET,*

ENTITULED,

[*A Declaration of the Commons of* England *in Parliament assembled, expressing their Reasons and Grounds of passing the late Resolutions touching no further Addresse or Application to be made to the* KING.]

MICAH 3. 11.

The Heads thereof judge for reward, and the Priests thereof teach for hire, and the Prophets thereof divine for mony : yet will they leane upon the Lord, and say, Is not the Lord among us ? none evill can come upon us.

✻ ✻ ✻ ✻ ✻
✻ ✻ ✻ ✻ ✻

Printed for R. ROYSTON. 1648.

Figure 78: Title page of Sir Edward Hyde's anonymously published 1648 work, *A Full Answer to An Infamous and Trayterous Pamphlet*, a detailed Royalist rebuttal of the secret history (Huntington Library).

experience . . . believe to do much good, and the learned acknowledge can doe no hurt". Because "there was never the least whisper or imagination of the King's death, to be otherwise then naturall", even Buckingham's enemies did not mention the matter in the 1625 Parliament. The publication of *The Forerunner*, however, had changed everything. Eglisham was "an infamous Scotch-man, and a Papist" motivated by "an ambition to be taken notice of as an Enemy to the Duke". After fleeing to Flanders, Eglisham had "sent over a small Pamphlet", "industriously scattered up and down the streets in the City of London", that set in motion the drafting of the thirteenth impeachment article. In other words, the *Declaration*'s central charge could be traced back to the machinations of an "infamous . . . Papist". Further, Hyde insisted that Buckingham had presented an able response, which the *Declaration* should have printed so that "the people would have understood that there was nothing *administered to the King, without the privity of the Physitians, and His own Importunate desire and Command*". Charles's behaviour had been scrupulously correct. After Buckingham offered his defence, the king waited "above a Week" and yet "no one person appeared in that time to offer the least evidence concerning that Clause". As for Eglisham, "the miserable wretch, who raised the Scandal" later confessed his "Villany" with "great penitence" and "died with the horrour of his guilt".[55]

Hyde, like Nicholas, noted that the 1628 Parliament did not revive the charge, and although Eliot and Digges were still "nothing reconciled to the Duke", there was then "not the least word of that aspersion". For Hyde, this proved that the charge was utterly "groundlesse". Hyde attributed the Eglisham revival in 1648 to a long-festering plot orchestrated by the Machiavellian "chief Agents" responsible for all the "confusion" of the civil wars. Early in 1642 these men had whispered that soon "they would examine the matter of the Death of King James", and to that end "this Pamphlet written . . . by Eglisham was printed, and publickly sold in Shops, and about the Streets". Hyde thought this initial republication had been plotted by "a very powerfull person of that Faction" to damage Secretary Nicholas, or even Charles himself. This schemer had told Nicholas of an informant who knew "a Papist" who "could prove, that King James was poysoned". Assuming that Nicholas would do nothing, the plotter hoped to expose him for concealing a crime. But Nicholas informed the king, who ordered a thorough investigation. By calling the plotters' bluff in 1642, the king had, however, only postponed the day of reckoning. The malcontents agreed "amongst themselves, 'that the time was not yet come, that they might make use of that matter' ".[56] By February 1648 things had changed.

The moral of this dark, convoluted tale was clear: the secret history was a cynical lie, originally manufactured by an "infamous . . . Papist", seized on by Buckingham's enemies in 1626, and then exploited in the 1640s by traitors who used the new "licence of Talking and Preaching seditiously" to precipitate the Civil War. Hyde's polemical agility was impressive. He took a story from 1626 that had later been recycled to fit the Parliamentarian master narratives of popish plot and evil counsel and then reworked it to present a Royalist counter-narrative that exposed the real roots of the Great Rebellion in the Machiavellian manoeuvres of seditious and factional malcontents. The only response that "sober honest understanding" men could make to the revived allegation, Hyde thought, was "horrour against the Contrivers of it", men "drunk with the bloud they have spilt, and confounded with the sense of their own wickednesse", whose "wits are as near an end as their Allegiance". These men "have no other stock left, but of despaire and madnesse, to carry them through their impious undertakings".[57]

"To Un-king his Majesty, to Murther Him"

The Royalists mounted a dynamic, multi-directional assault on the *Declaration*. But they also countered stories of an old poisoning plot with tales of a new one. In June 1648 details emerged of a conspiracy to poison Charles in Carisbrooke Castle.[58] A former royal attendant claimed that Robert Hammond, the governor of Carisbrooke, "had received severall Letters from the Army, intimating they desired the King might . . . be removed out of the way, either by poyson or otherwise".[59] The ensuing scandal quickly erupted into fierce printed debate, spawning a parliamentary investigation and eventually judicial proceedings.[60] The resulting polemical exchanges divided not only Parliamentarians from Royalists, but also radical from moderate Parliamentarians.

Royalist polemicists implicated Hammond and leading radicals—Lords Wharton and Saye and Sele, Edmund Rolfe, Major-General Skippon and Cromwell—either in the "hellish plot" or in the subsequent cover-up.[61] The Royalists detected an increasingly confident regicidal spirit at work in the Army and the Commons. According to one account, the Vote and *Declaration* had encouraged the men around Hammond to brand the king "the cheif Murderer" who "ought therefore to die by the same meanes". After the Vote, a broadside claimed, Charles had lost the "reverence . . . due to his Royall Person" and was now "exposed to private *Murder* and *Poyson*".[62] What, another tract asked, was "That base and scandalous Libell or Declaration of lyes . . . but an antedated sentence before his Majestie was heard one word?" More important, "what could it presage, but an assault upon his Person, after the murther of his honour?" Utterly "undone", the king was "scorned and reviled, and more Ballads made of him, and abuse put upon him, then ever King David had", and he was "in danger every hour to be murthered or poysoned". Another pamphlet claimed that the radicals planned to "pistol" or "poyson" the king since the Vote had prepared the way to "un-King His Majesty, to murther Him", and the *Declaration*, written by the "unclean spirits of the Houses", had charged him "with murthering His naturall and deare Father, and other shamfull and wicked slanders and obloquiues to make His people hate him".[63]

While the *Declaration* implied Charles's guilt in his father's death, the Royalist exploitation of the Hammond plot transformed the king from perpetrator to victim of poisoning and allowed his supporters to smear the radicals as the real king-killers. Royalist writers thus deployed the supposed plot to mobilize popular support for their threatened king, and worked feverishly to enhance the royal image, fitting the suffering monarch for the charismatic role of martyr. The king, concluded the most detailed Royalist analysis of the plots against him, "is a rare example of Wisdome, Patience Fortitude and other Vertues", and while Army officers panicked that they would be poisoned, Charles readily ate his food, "though it were Cooked by the hands of a mortall enemy, and passed through the hands of many more". The king's "Devotions", his "Temperance" and "Clemencie" all showed him to be a true godly ruler whom "ought to bee pittied above all men, and deserves to be rescued from this danger by His Subjects".[64]

The Vote and *Declaration* marked a dramatic turning point in the crisis of the 1640s, and at the polemical centre of this extraordinary political watershed was a bitter and extensive debate about events that had happened nearly a quarter century before. As the English Revolution approached its climax, a confused and unsettled public was thus confronted not simply by the horrors of renewed civil war and the spectre of regicide, but also by a barrage of sophisticated, emotive polemic offering rival accounts of old parliamentary history and clashing expert opinion on agues and poisons, plasters, potions and autopsies. To a remarkable degree, revolutionary and counter-revolutionary politics took shape around the contested secret history of James I's murder. Late in August 1648, Parliament won the Second Civil War after Cromwell crushed the Scots at Preston, capturing, among others, the Duke of Hamilton, whose youthful marriage to Buckingham's niece had played such a large role in *The Forerunner*. But victory divided the victors. Charles's utter defeat made some Parliament-men nervous, and, shying away from radical options, the Commons reversed the Vote of No Further Addresses and reopened negotiations with the king. At the same time, the renewed Civil War had hardened the resolve of others to bring Charles Stuart, "that man of blood", to account for his crimes. In February 1648 radicals had used the secret history to justify cutting off negotiations with the king, and for many of the "saints" it became an article of faith that Charles was guilty of his father's death. But the prominence that the *Declaration* had given to the charge had also exposed it to withering Royalist critique, and by highlighting the regicidal implications of the Vote and the *Declaration* the Royalists were able to frighten moderates back to the negotiating table.

Plainly, the Royalists had inflicted damage; they had exposed Eglisham's Catholicism, questioned his medical evidence, and revealed the malicious, "private" political interests of the Parliament-men who peddled stories of James I's murder in 1626 and 1648. Their propaganda success arguably encouraged counter-revolutionary sentiment in 1648 while burnishing Charles's severely damaged image. As they defended Charles from the horrific charge of parricide, Royalist pamphleteers had made the slandered king a stoic hero. Held a close prisoner, separated from wife and children, maligned as a murderer and prey to assassins, Charles became more sympathetic than he had ever been before. In his own (spurious) pamphlet response to the Vote, Charles had spoken in an unusually intimate tone, presenting himself as a pitiable figure, deprived of liberty and family but resolved to bear his afflictions with patience, and the text cleverly aligned the king and his people as fellow victims of Parliament's tyranny.[65] Several tracts celebrated his filial piety, and Bate's *Regall Apology* maintained that Charles could not have had a hand in killing James because instead of displaying the mental torment that afflicted murderers, he remained serenely calm. Months before the regicide, then, Royalist authors were already rehearsing Charles's future role as martyr, and the men who would help him produce the great testimony of his martyrdom, *Eikon Basilike*, would conclude that powerful narrative with a chapter of "Meditations upon Death, After the Votes of Nonaddresses and His Majesty's Closer Imprisonment in Carisbrooke Castle".[66] As we shall see, the ghost of James I would accompany his son to the scaffold. But the ghost's return in 1648 had not only inspired the regicides, it had also helped Charles craft the image of patient Christian suffering that would ensure the survival of monarchy's sacral power after the king's death.

An Ill-shap'd V

When John Felton assassinated Buckingham at Portsmouth in 1628, the duke's oldest son, George, was less than a year old and his youngest, Francis, was still in his mother's womb. The boys therefore had no memory of their father, but grew up in Charles's household among those who had loved him. Neither son played an active military role in the first Civil War, but they were young men of honour, and when the *Declaration* resurrected their father's alleged crimes in 1648 they took up arms to avenge his name. The Royalist James Fenn heard that the Commons' "late remonstrance ... concerning his father" had "infinitely troubled" the young duke, and that the "violent partye" among the Royalists had urged him to join their insurrection. On 4 July, George and Francis left London with their father's old friend the Earl of Holland and assembled several hundred men in Kingston-on-Thames. Two days later, they declared their determination to fight "for the King and Parliament, Religion and the known Laws, and peace of all His Majesties Kingdomes". Calling for new negotiations with the king, Buckingham and Holland denounced the "confused and level-ling undertaking to overthrow Monarchy". The following day parliamentary troops caught up with them. After what one soldier thought was "as sharp a charge ... as ever I saw", the small Royalist force fled the field. By 10 July, Holland was in custody, Buckingham had fled into exile, and nineteen-year-old Francis Villiers was dead. After losing his horse in the melée, Francis fought "most valiantly" on foot until he was struck down from behind. Royalist eleg-ists, including Andrew Marvell, mourned his heroic death, while the news-books decried the savagery of his killing. His body was eventually interred beneath the great monument to his father in Westminster Abbey. A far more prosaic memorial marked the place where he had fallen in the quest to avenge his father's honour. There, "in memory of him", an unknown hand cut into the bark of an elm tree "an ill-shap'd V for Villiers".[67]

CHAPTER TWENTY-ONE

UNDER THE POWER OF THE SWORD

BLOOD GUILT AND THE REGICIDE, 1648–49

AT WESTMINSTER HALL, the morning of 6 December 1648 began with unsettling signs. Normally, a guard from the London militia stood by to keep order, but as the London detachment marched towards the Parliament-house, they found their way blocked by a thousand soldiers who "told them that for the good will they bare towards them, and in regard of their long under-going that toil, they would for ever hereafter ease them of it". Amid warnings to go home, some "to their shops, others their wives", the militiamen turned around. After a cavalry force arrived at the Parliament-house, the soldiers established "a strong guard" around the "doors, in the lobby, stairs and at every passage leading towards the house". Their purpose soon became clear. As the Parliament-men tried to enter the house, Colonel Thomas Pride politely greeted them with "a courteous salutation, and with his hat in his hand". Senior officers checked names against a list, and sympathetic Parliament-men helped identify their colleagues. Some were let through, some were turned away, and forty-one were arrested. Two burgesses, mistakenly let pass, had to be "violently pulled out of the House". After waiting in a room without chairs or heat, the purged members were escorted away between lines of troops who rained "opprobrious Speeches" upon them.[1]

The detained Parliament-men wanted explanations. When William Prynne demanded to know "by what Authority or Commission and for what cause they did thus violently seize on, and pull him from the house", Colonel Pride pointed to the "armed Souldiers standing round about him" and announced that "there was their Commission". Prynne characteristically decried the arrests as "nothing else but the designs and projects of Iesuites, Popish Priests, and Recusant[s]". Among those initially arrested, Nathaniel Fiennes was one of the odd men out; although he now backed a negotiated settlement with the king, he had helped draft the *Declaration* justifying the Vote of No Addresses, and he was soon released. Fiennes naturally asked "by what power he was committed", and was told "By the power of the sword". The phrase was soon on everyone's lips. Indeed, as one anonymous author observed, the whole Parliament now found itself "under the Power of the Sword". Charles I was in the same perilous situation. In late December a pamphlet in his name protested against "his present restraint under the Power of the Sword". A month later, he was to kneel outside his father's Banqueting House under the executioner's axe.[2]

Pride's Purge and Charles I's subsequent trial and execution are justifiably famous events, and have recently become the topic of fierce scholarly debate about the intentions of those who put the king on trial. But scholars have scarcely noticed the prominent role that the secret history played in these revolutionary actions. In spite of the sophisticated Royalist campaign to discredit the February *Declaration*, variations on the secret history remained a central part of revolutionary political discourse, shadowing the prolonged discussions about Pride's Purge and Charles's trial and execution. The secret history thus helped legitimate and even precipitate actions that others thought unjustifiable exercises of illegitimate force. Evoking the February 1648 *Declaration* as their warrant, the radicals presented the Army's actions on 6 December as an attempt to bring Parliament back to its senses. By tarring Charles with responsibility for his father's death, or with a cover-up, the radicals helped define the king as an unnatural tyrant and a man of blood whose death was required to appease God's wrath. The supposed murder of James I thus allowed the radicals to invoke God's law as their warrant against Charles—a power far greater than that of swords.

Mr King, Mrs Parliament and Captain Army

Resounding victory in the Second Civil War set Parliament and its Army on a collision course. In the late summer and autumn of 1648, attendance in the House of Commons steadily climbed. Only 120 members had decided on the Vote of No Addresses early in the year, but attendance rose to almost 180 in October, and nearly 240 in early December, and the higher numbers diminished the influence of the radicals who had dominated the thinner House at the start of the year. The new, more moderate majority agreed on 24 August to repeal the Vote of No Further Addresses, and they reopened talks with the king on 18 September at Newport in the Isle of Wight.

These developments heartened Royalists and Presbyterian Parliamentarians but infuriated the radicals, and especially the officers and soldiers of the New Model Army. News of the reopened negotiations baffled the troops. "It cannot but lye heavy upon our spirits", Colonel Ingoldsby's men noted in early November, "to apprehend that all our harvest should end in chaffe, And what was won in the field should be given away in a Chamber." In November, as a settlement seemed likely, the *True Informer* wondered "whether, upon this offer of the Parliament to enslave us to the King, the People are not bound in conscience, especially to oppose the Parliament, as the King?" Soldiers asked

whether, if the Army accepted these terms, "they should not contract to themselves the guilt of all the bloud of the Cavaliers which they have shed?"[3]
Individual units began petitioning against any compromise settlement, and
they did so by invoking the February *Declaration*. A radical newsbook, *The
Moderate*, noted that earlier in the year Parliament had charged Charles "with
all the blood that had been shed by this War in the three Kingdoms, the death
of his father King James, etc, and therefore no further addresses to be made to
him", which made it strange that "now his most sacred Majesty [is] to be Treated
with by both Houses of Parliament, as one innocent, and cleer, of any such
Charge". A petition from Leicestershire in late September expressed dismay
over renewed negotiations after Parliament "did Vote, That no farther Addresses
should be made unto him, or received from him, and declared him to be guilty
of the death of King Iames".[4]

Perturbed, the discontented radicals continued to brood over the secret
history. In October 1648, *Mercurius Militaris* mocked the divine aura of a
monarch, the "master of as many fools as would down of their knees to his
sword", and ridiculed the idea that Charles was the Lord's anointed; "when was
it done? after the poysoning of his brother Harry or his Father?" Attacking the
king's tyrannical treatment of parliaments, *Militaris* noted that "Parliament, in
the third year of Charles, could not ask whether King James was poysoned, but
immediately his black Rod scourged them all home". Meanwhile a Royalist
tract used the radicals' faith in the secret history as the central conceit of a
satirical scene in which "Captain Army" interrupted the wedding of "Mr. King"
and "Mrs. Parliament" to forbid the banns. The Captain's reasons were clear;
"we say he is a delinquent, and a Trayter to the Kingdoms trust, guilty of the
murder of his Father". It thus followed that "we pronounce him a capitall
Traytor to the Kingdom (that's the Saints)" and hope "with all speed" to "bring
him to exemplar Justice for all the Treason, blood or mischief, that we shall
judge him to be guilty of, that so he may speedily dye without mercy".[5]

The Royalists thus sought to undermine the radical cause by associating it
with a set of charges that they thought discredited. Although this approach satisfied moderates, it could not hope to persuade the radicalized Army and its civilian
allies, who still insisted and believed the charges had merit. By repealing the Vote,
Parliament effectively had negated the February *Declaration*, but some Royalists
still feared its power, and the continuing radical evocations of the *Declaration*
encouraged the publication in November of a final Royalist critique. *The Returne
of the People of England* presented itself as a Grand Jury verdict on the *Declaration*.
Although "the Common People" were "little vers'd in State-Matters", they were
"sufficiently informed" about the *Declaration*'s charges and found them "uncertain and insufficient". The pamphlet tellingly concentrated its attack on the case
"Concerning the death of King James", and reiterated many elements of earlier
Royalist critiques: The ingredients of Buckingham's potion and plaster were

known and harmless; Dr. Remington, a witness "yet living", had prescribed the medicines to Buckingham and Warwick to "good effect"; and the royal doctors knew of Buckingham's interventions, as the duke's formal answer, "which", the pamphleteer told Speaker Lenthall, "you have by you" in the parliamentary record, made perfectly clear. The pamphlet then cleverly reworked the *Declaration*'s notorious open question about "where the guilt" lay to indict Parliament itself: "We have reason to beleeve that you [i.e., Parliament] did acquiesce in the Dukes answer, as true, and satisfactory", for the Lower House had failed to resume prosecution in 1628. "We appeale to your Journall Books" to know "whether there be any mention of the businesse in either of your Remonstrances of that Parliament". Hence, "(if there be any guilt) we leave the world to judge where the guilt remaines, that this businesse was not farther prosecuted".[6]

Given the increasingly militant mood in the Army, *The Returne* held out little hope for the Newport negotiations. In mid-November a correspondent at Army headquarters reported that the officers could not comprehend how, "after all objections made against no Addresses to the King, and a full Vote passed in the House to governe without Him", a majority had reversed themselves so that "now addresses made, and [Charles] courted as one that hath not had the least finger in all that innocent bloud that hath been shed". The Army's officers thus moved that "all those of both Houses, who voted with those that would have further addresses may bee sequestred the House". Angry over the Second Civil War, the Army and its civilian allies demanded extensive retribution. In September a London petition had asked that everyone, "Kings, Queens, Princes, Dukes, Lords and all persons alike", should be held equally subject to the law, so that "all persons even the Highest might fear and stand in aw".[7] In October the men of Henry Ireton's regiment demanded that "impartial and speedy Justice may be done upon all criminal persons" who have "bin Authors of shedding that innocent blood, which calls to Heaven for Vengeance, that so we may be at peace with God". Yet "instead of Iustice", the garrison at Newcastle lamented, "behold a Treaty with them for Peace, that God speaks no peace to".[8]

The division between the parliamentary majority, eager for a settlement with Charles, and their troops, who wanted nothing more to do with the king, steadily widened. Senior officers, most notably Henry Ireton, were convinced that the king was a "man of blood" who had to be brought to justice. Although Royalist polemicists feared that Charles I, like Edward II and Richard II, would be imprisoned and then quietly murdered, the troops themselves wanted to see him placed on public trial. On 15 November, after lengthy debates over Ireton's preliminary draft, the General Council of the Army approved a text calling for the king to be brought to justice; they presented it to the House of Commons five days later, and quickly produced summary, abridged and full-length printed versions.[9] The Army's *Remonstrance* marked the radical turning point of the revolution, mapping a road towards regicide, "the Capitall punishment" of the "principall

Author" of the kingdom's wars. Although it mobilized a complex set of political and religious arguments to make its case, the document also explicitly drew support from the Vote of No Addresses and from the February *Declaration*, which had resurrected the secret history of James's murder. "All men", Ireton insisted, had understood the Vote "to imply some further intentions of proceeding in Justice against" Charles "and setling the kingdome without him". The Vote "*and your reasons for them*" constituted the "light" by which the God of battles had so clearly signalled his assent in the Second Civil War.[10]

Several printed declarations endorsed the *Remonstrance*. Colonel Valentine Walton's regiment, for one, heartily approved the idea that "the King, that Capital Destroyer of, and Shedder of the Blood, of some hundred thousands of his good people . . . may be brought to publique Justice".[11] And as the Army and its supporters roused themselves to challenge Parliament, elements of the secret history continued to appear in print. On 24 November a *Humble Petition* from the county of Rutland declared that the Newport negotiations had left them aghast; "how durst our Parliament think of Treating with such a man", the petitioners exclaimed. Again, the February *Declaration* was the touchstone; to resume negotiations was:

> a giving them the ly, as though all that they had said of him, as touching the betraying of Rochell, *the death of his father*, the Irish rebellion, bringing in the German horse, the violence done to the Parliament at the beginning of their sitting, with divers other evils of a high nature which they laid to his charge, had no truth in them.[12]

The crisis soon came to a head. On 1 December 1648 the Commons rejected the *Remonstrance* and debated instead the king's latest peace terms. The soldiers of Colonel Pride's regiment protested that the Commons had repealed the Vote of No Addresses and decided "to beg mercie of him [Charles], the very hours that Armie of his was begging mercie of us". They demanded that "justice may be sodainly and equally be dispensed" according to "the Parliaments Declaration concerning the Kings evills". Early in December the Army began taking unilateral action. Without Parliament's approval, it moved Charles to a more secure location on the Isle of Wight, and several regiments marched into London. On 5 December the Commons voted 129 to 83 to accept Charles's latest answer as the basis for a peace settlement.[13] The next morning, Colonel Pride and his men were waiting to welcome Prynne, Fiennes and their colleagues at the Parliament-house.

Cannibals in Council

There was no need for alarm, Hugh Peters preached in mid-December. Parliament was like an elder brother who "keps the key a long time in their pocket, while the door is locked" and "who can blame the Army (though they be the yonger Brother) for breaking open the door to relieve their mother from being utterly destroyed". But behind such appealing domestic analogies was the stark fact that the Army and a minority in the House of Commons had seized control of Parliament by force. Unsurprisingly, the Royalists protested that "the Puppets run all upon wire now in the House of Commons" where "their Votes are but the Ecchoes of the military Junto".[14] Royalist satirists mocked the radicals as "mad Sainted Elves" who had driven "away all Members that are not of the sanctified Faction, and so not fit to tread upon that holy ground". All that remained were "the refined Brethren", the simple "Mechanicks and Politicks", who were now to erect "the blessed Tabernacle of Democracy". *Mercurius Pragmaticus* dubbed the purged House "the grand Conventicle of King Choppers" and its members "Cannibals in Councell".[15]

The first order of business was to reverse the votes recently cast by the more moderate House. On 13 December the purged Commons rejected the latest proposed settlement and repealed the August repeal of the Vote of No Addresses. The House ordered Thomas Chaloner and Thomas Scot, who had helped draft the February *Declaration*, to prepare a new one, but in an extraordinary action the House also adopted Colonel Gurdon's proposal that "every member set his hand to it, in detestation of those former Votes". This procedure, *Mercurius Pragmaticus* observed, served "as the Sibboleth to try who were their Friends", and it initiated a second purge of moderate Parliament-men: the resolution prompted two dozen "dissenters" to abandon the House, dropping attendance from seventy-eight on 7 December to fifty-three a week later. The new *Declaration* not only denounced the king as "a Person uncapable of any further Trust" and "our implacable Enemy" and called for "a Universall Reformation", but it also endorsed the February *Declaration* "as we judg it needles here again to repeat".[16] This blanket endorsement of the text that had resurrected the secret history had thus become part of the shibboleth for the radical cohorts intent on forging a revolution.

The remaining Parliament-men moved swiftly to "Proceeding against the King", and on 28 December they passed what *Mercurius Elencticus* termed "the Rebellious Bloody Ordinance for Murdering" him.[17] Before Charles's trial opened in late January 1649, however, his prosecution had to decide on the charges against him, and a number of tracts speculated on those charges. Some claimed the indictment would be narrowly construed. After "departing from the Parliament" in 1642, Charles had waged war "to uphold and establish himself" with an "absolute, tyranicall power", and he had taken actions "contrary to the Liberties of the Subject, and tending to the destruction of the fundamental Laws and Liberties of the Kingdom".[18] Other pamphlets, however, speculated about the possibility of more expansive charges. Some of this speculation was satirical, some serious, but it reflected actual debates among the radicals that reveal the continuing significance of the allegation that Charles had murdered his father.

One pamphlet, for example, offered readers seven "Articles of Impeachment" proving that Charles "hath been the most capital and grand Author of all the bloud which hath bin spilt in England". Such rhetoric was commonplace, but the articles also charged Charles with complicity in various popish plots. Since the articles were "collected" from the works of William Prynne, the best-known casualty of Pride's Purge, the whole list was likely designed to embarrass the Presbyterian who violently opposed trying the king.[19] In other tracts, the February *Declaration* loomed large. In late December one argued that medieval precedent, and thus the Common Law, justified the parliamentary deposition of wicked kings. Charles's crimes were far worse than those that had cost Edward II and Richard II their thrones. The two medieval kings had been misled by their favourites, but Charles had been "hurryed on by his own inordinate desire of Arbitrary Power". The pamphlet compared Edward II's relationship with Gaveston to Charles I's with Buckingham; and once more, the secret history provided the crucial seed of regicidal justification. Edward had chosen Gaveston because of their long-standing love. But Charles had chosen:

> to be governed by the Duke of Buckingham, whose enemy he was till a few
> moneths before his fathers death; and it is more then doubted by honest and
> discreet men, that they contracted friendship, and agreed to divide the
> Empire upon condition of poysoning the old man.

Pressed by the House of Lords, Edward had banished his favourite. But when Buckingham was "charged in Parliament upon Articles of high Treason, of which one was the murder of King James", Charles had protected the duke "against Law" by dissolving Parliament "lest his fathers death should be inquired into, (fearing that himself might be found too much concerned in it)". The pamphleteer did not speculate about formal charges, but he clearly rested his case for regicide on the *Declaration's* catalogue of Charles's crimes, which began with James's murder.[20]

Royalists exploited public curiosity about the possible charges for their own ends. Contemporaries would naturally have been attracted to *The Charge of the Army, and Counsel of War, against the King*, which George Thomason purchased on 29 December. But its polemical intent emerged clearly in "a brief ANSWER thereunto by some of the Loyall Party". In print so large that a handful of sentences covered two pages, the Royalist tract laid out a nine-point prosecution, following the lead of the February *Declaration*. The only charge that ran for more than a sentence was the very first: the king's "favourite, (the Duke of Buckingham) by his consent, laid a Plaster to King Iames, and gave him a Drinke, when he was sick of an Ague, although the sworne Physitians had forbidden any to presume to give the King any thing without their Direction". The charge then added the telling detail, derived from Eglisham; because of the "Plaister and Drink", James had "dyed not long after, his body presently blistering and swelling up with the poyson thereof". The charge harkened back to the 1626 Parliament, which had accused Buckingham of "an Act of a transcendent presumption", which "cannot be judged by us any other then Murder and Patricide".[21] This hypothetical indictment neatly blended elements from *The Forerunner*, the 1626 impeachment and the 1648 *Declaration*, but it went well beyond all three by explicitly charging Charles with active complicity in his father's murder. Its presence in this Royalist publication suggests that many Royalists feared Charles might well face a parricide charge; after all, the Royalists had been arguing for months that the February *Declaration* had revived the secret history solely to justify regicide, a claim apparently now confirmed by the Army's continued enthusiastic endorsement of the text. And clearly the murder charge fit neatly within the emerging regicidal discourse depicting Charles I as a "man of blood" who had to be put to death lest an angry God punish the kingdom for spilling innocent blood.[22]

Of course, *The Charge of the Army* promulgated the supposed article so that the pamphlet's Royalist author could refute it; he did so using many of the arguments already advanced against the February *Declaration*. The "Martiall Tyrants" of the Army, the pamphleteer argued, sought to blacken Charles I in order to change a "well-regulated Monarchy into a Military Anarchy". The poisoning charge was absurd. First, even if Buckingham had done something wrong, there was no evidence he acted "by consent of the Prince". Second, Charles lacked motive: he was James's sole heir, and with the king ageing "it could not be long before" he succeeded to the throne. Besides, no son was "more dutifull to a parent" than Charles was to his father. These points, however, were ultimately irrelevant, because James had died of natural causes, and the medicines he took were harmless. The actual culprits were lack of exercise and a fondness for drink, which had "occasioned" James's "Feavorish Ague, and a droppicall humor". Impatient with his illness, James had asked for the medicines that had "cured a great Person of the same Disease", and his doctors "knew all the Ingredients to be good". Finally, the evidence from the autopsy clearly refuted Eglisham's claims, for "The kings body being opened was found fair and cleer".[23]

Non-Royalist commentators also speculated about whether the murder of James I would find its way into Charles's indictment. On 4 January *The Manner of the Deposition of Charles Stewart, King of England* reported that after the king's arrival in Windsor on 23 December, the Commons had "nominated a Committee, to consider how to proceed in a way of Justice against the King". This much was well known, as was the fact that the Committee had the authority "to send for Papers and witnesses to examine". More interestingly, however, the

Committee reportedly was to examine "the bunesse [sic] of Ireland, the poys-oning of King James and other particulars". The tract then offered a report on the charge the Committee supposedly adopted, but it included nothing on James's death.[24] The secret history shadowed the debate about the charge and the trial through early January. On 11 January, Thomason acquired *The Armies Vindication*, a refutation of William Sedgwick's attack on the November *Remonstrance*. This comprehensive response argued that Sedgwick "should have cleared the King of the things laid to his charge"; instead he had ignored "what hath beene reported about his Fathers death, and Marquis Hambleton".[25]

Amid the mounting tensions, the Army and its parliamentary allies pressed on with the revolution. On 2 January 1649 the nine peers in attendance at the House of Lords pondered two controversial bills from the Lower House, one making it treason for a monarch to take up arms against Parliament and another establishing a High Court of Justice to try the king. The Lords unani-mously rejected both bills, and adjourned themselves for a week. Undeterred, the Parliament-men on 4 January "passed such Votes as never any House of Commons before them dream'd of", authorizing them to proceed on their own "although the Consent and Concurrence of King, or House of Lords, be not had thereunto". Whatever Charles I's subsequent fate, his state had dissolved.[26]

Speculation about the charges ended on 20 January, when Charles appeared before the High Court of Justice (Fig. 79). The charge focused tightly on the king's actions between 1642 and 1648, which had cost "much innocent blood of the free people of this nation", and left him "guilty of all the treasons, murders, rapines, burnings, spoils, desolations, damages and mischiefs to this nation, acted and committed in the said wars or occasioned thereby".[27] But although the final indictment narrowly focused on the 1640s, there is good evidence to suggest that the commissioners of the High Court had also discussed draft charges concerning Charles's misrule in the 1620s and 1630s. Official news-books described a draft charge circulating on 15 January, for instance, as "very large", incorporating material from the *Declaration* on Charles's crimes in the 1620s. The reports mentioned a possible charge about "the ill mannaging of the Navall businesse at the siege of Rochell in the yeare 1628" but nothing about James's murder. John Cook, the Solicitor General appointed to draft the indict-ment and prosecute the king, later claimed that "some would have had a very voluminous and long Charge" but that he had been "utterly against it", thinking it "not fit and requisite, that any thing should be put in". Contemporary news-books indicated that the majority of his fellow commissioners came to share this pragmatic view that the charge should "be abreviated". On 17 January the commissioners still thought an edited version "too large" and ordered that it "be yet made more brief".[28] A witness later recalled hearing some commis-sioners, intent on "the Contracting of the Impeachment", fret over the "length of that, as it was drawn" and insist on more emendations. Meanwhile Colonel

Figure 79: *The High Court of Justice for the Trial of Charles I*, published in John Nalson, *A true copy of the journal of the High Court of Justice* (1684), with the prosecutor John Cook standing to the right of the king (Huntington Library).

Thomas Harrison reportedly argued for a longer, more inclusive charge since "It will be good for us to blacken him, what we can".[29]

No copies of any of these drafts survive, but it seems possible, at least, that the case against Charles set out in the 1648 *Declaration* was under active consideration as a basis for the king's prosecution just days before his trial began. Whether formally charging Charles in the murder of his father would have helped or hindered the prosecution's case is not easy to gauge.[30] On the one hand, the charge, as critics of the *Declaration* had noted, had blackened the king's reputation, branding him a poisoner and a parricide. The allegation fit perfectly into the regicidal discourse on the king's "blood guilt" in which James's poisoning was merely the first murder undertaken by a "man of blood". The prosecution also might have had little difficulty construing the act as treason according to traditional legal definitions. On the other hand, proving the charge in court would have been difficult. The Royalist responses to the *Declaration* had exposed all kinds of problems with the allegation. And while Parliament would have trouble finding good prosecution witnesses, Royalist writers had already located a number of people who could have confirmed Buckingham's account of the medicines' origin, composition and use. Dredging "the king's reign to the very depths", then, would not necessarily have made for a more effective legal case.

King Charls his Case

Charles refused to acknowledge the court's authority and declined to enter a plea, which prevented John Cook from presenting the complete prosecution case in open court. Within ten days of the king's execution on 30 January 1649, however, the radical stationer Giles Calvert published *King Charls his Case*, allowing Cook to make his arguments to the public (Fig. 80). The book, Cook acknowledged, was a composite. The "most part" consisted of "that which was intended to have been delivered at the Bar" if Charles had entered a plea, but Cook had added what he called "additional Opinion", focusing on "the Death of King James, The loss of Rochel, and, the Blood of Ireland". The book is thus both an invaluable record of what Cook might have said at the trial and an important early printed defence of the regicide. In the ambitious print propaganda campaign aimed at justifying what many felt could not be justified, the secret history of James I's murder had a significant polemical part to play.[31]

It is hard to disentangle the planned speech from the additional material, but Cook apparently had intended to make a passing reference to James's death to illustrate the broad strokes of the official indictment. In particular, Cook sought to amplify the charge's opening remarks about Charles's "wicked design to erect" tyrannical rule, and to do so, Cook turned to the 1620s. The king's "restlesse desire to destroy Parliaments" was first revealed by his "untimely dissolving" of the 1628–29 Parliament and by Sir John Eliot's subsequent commitment as "close prisoner to the Tower, where he lost his life by cruel indurance". But Cook's description effectively implied that Eliot's fate in 1628–29 was linked to his actions in the 1626 "Conference with the House of Peers concerning the Duke of Buckingham, who amongst other things was charged concerning the death of King James". At this point, Cook planned a brief aside on the already well-publicized claims about James's death: "I may not passe over without a special Animadversion: for sure there is no Turk or Heathen but will say that if he [Charles] were any way guilty of his Fathers death, let him die for it."[32] This powerful, albeit glancing, aside, delivered in open court, would have insinuated Charles's guilt in his father's death without having to prove it, while invoking natural law to magnify the horror of the crime.

Cook's pamphlet then interrupted his intended courtroom presentation with an "additional Opinion" on James's murder. "I would not willingly be so injurious to the honest Reader", he politely noted, "as to make him buy that again which he hath formerly met with in the Parliaments *Declaration* or elsewhere." Instead, he

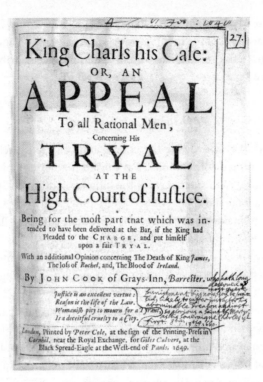

Figure 80: Title page of John Cook's 1649 *King Charls his Case*, which presented the detailed charge against the king that Cook had planned to deliver if Charles had entered a plea at his trial (Huntington Library).

thought, "a marginal reference may be sufficient", offering only "a Students mite which satisfied my self" until a future declaration on the case "for more general satisfaction" appeared. Cook's account was starkly condensed and circumstantial, omitting the medical and political details found in *The Forerunner* and the *Declaration*. "Instantly upon the death of King James", Cook observed, Charles's attitude to Buckingham had changed from open enmity to "special protection, grace and favour", a change of heart so abrupt that it could only suggest the king was in the duke's debt. Cook then turned to the 1626 Parliament: "When the Earl of Bristol had exhibited a Charge against the said Duke, the 13. Article whereof concerned the death of King James, He instantly dissolved that Parliament, that so he might protect the Duke from the justice thereof, and would never suffer any legal inquiry to be made for his Fathers death." The few facts on offer were badly garbled. Cook confused Bristol's accusations and the Commons' impeachment charges and failed to mention that several weeks had elapsed between the presentation of the articles and the dissolution of Parliament. Yet the narrative followed the logic set out in the *Declaration*: Charles had dissolved Parliament "so he might protect the Duke", thus preventing all "legal inquiry" into his father's death. While the *Declaration* had stopped here, Cook spelled out what it had left unsaid. What, Cook asked, could have restrained a son from discovering the truth about his father's death, especially when the son was a monarch who "hath all power in his hands to do justice"? Cook sketched out the conundrum: "there is one accused upon strong presumptions at the least, for poisoning that Kings Father", and yet "the King protects him from justice". The next question was obvious: "do you believe that [Charles] himself had any hand in his Father's death?" After all, "Had the Duke been accused for the death of a begger, he ought not to have protected him from a Judicial Trial". At the very least, Cook argued, Charles helped conceal his father's murder, and "to conceal a Murder, strongly implies a guilt thereof, and makes him a kind of Accessary to the fact".[33]

This additional material about James's murder strengthened Cook's central claim that the king was a capital felon, indelibly marked with blood guilt. Good kings sought justice, but Charles had "no nature to do justice" even "to his own Father". Good kings were paternal rulers, but Charles lacked "natural affection" even "to his own Father". Cook could not understand how Charles could "love a Kingdome" if he made no "Inquisition" into an injury inflicted on his own blood. The full truth of how James died, Cook conceded, might remain "a riddle" until Judgement Day, but at the very least Charles's failure to act made clear not only how unnatural but also how ungodly a ruler he was. An apt precedent was provided by *2 Kings* 12–15. When Amaziah, the new king of Judah, "did justice upon those servants which had killed his father Joash: he did not by any pretended prerogative excuse or protect them". Charles, however, was not Amaziah, and did not make "the Law of God his delight".[34]

Retelling the secret history thus allowed Cook to establish his case for regicide. Charles was a lawless, ungodly and unnatural tyrant, a man of blood who had slaughtered thousands in the quest for arbitrary power, and his victims now called to Heaven for vengeance and to the High Court for justice. Charles Stuart's death, Cook concluded, would stand as a warning that "the Kings of the Earth may hear, and fear" and "do no more so wickedly".[35]

Other justifications of regicide recycled the secret history in very different styles. On 26 January, the day before the judges ordered Charles's execution, Theodore Jennings licensed a pamphlet that gave Charles's trial and execution a prophetic warrant. The mysterious prophecy of the "White King" was nearly a thousand years old, but the pamphlet claimed recent events had unlocked its true meaning: the White King was Charles I. The interpreter insisted that the prophecy predicted the Scottish rebellion, the civil wars, the bringing of the White King "to tryall by the supreame power of the Commons", and the White King's subsequent death. The prophecy had also indicated that the White King would be the successor of the "Lyon of Righteousnesse", the first king to rule both England and Scotland, but would take the throne only after his father was "dead, poysoned, or cut off" and his elder brother "removed out of the way by poyson, death, banishment, or some way or other". Of course, the original prophecy had said nothing about poisoned fathers and brothers, but the interpolation of the secret history into a regicidal reworking of ancient prophecy spoke to the broader sense in these bewildering late January days that Charles's execution could be linked to (and justified by) his role in James's murder.[36]

Some contemporaries were left wondering what, if anything, the king could have said to answer Eglisham or the *Declaration*. One newsbook claimed to know. According to the *Kingdomes Weekly Intelligencer*, on 29 January, the night before his execution, Charles dismissed his dogs, along with anything or anyone else who might distract him from his devotions. But someone got in, and asked the king "to say somewhat how farre hee was guilty of the Death of his Father and the Rebellion in Ireland". Charles's response was terse: "he had done nothing that he needed to aske pardon for".[37] There is no telling whether Dr Eglisham's ghost actually haunted Charles I's final hours on earth, but the urge to invent such a story demonstrates yet again the powerful hold the secret history exercised on the English political imagination at the very climax of the English Revolution.

An Inquisition After Blood

A Perfect Cure for Atheists, Papists, Arminians and all other Rebels and Traytors, published in June 1649, contained enough ingredients to make even a seasoned apothecary gasp. Thrown into the brew were the events and personalities of the previous quarter-century, including "three grains of Salt brought from the Isle of Ree", "two or three years paiment of Shipmoney", "three quarters of a yard of the Kings morning cloak he wore when he broke the last Parliament", and "three bricks of the little Popish Chappell built in [Charles's] Chamber at Whitehall, where he might lie in bed and hear Mass". Ingredients from the civil wars were also well represented: "the Ashes of all those Towns the Cavaliers have burned", "two Kilderkins of Irish Protestants blood", and "Prince Rupert's Religion". Nor did the recipe omit the tragic death of Buckingham's youngest son, calling for "three of my Lord Francis last God-dam-ye when he ran himself headlong into Hell, rather than take quarter of a Roundhead". All of these, along with "fifteen drops of his Maiesties tears", went into the pot, "covered with Straffords night cap", then set on the embers of Colchester, boiled for "the space of a Masque", and strained "with one of Canterburies lawne Sleeves when he stood to see Burton, Pryn and Bastwicks ears cut off". The conceit here was an old one, and similar mock recipes were traded back and forth in civil-war polemics. But the ingredients of this recipe included no fewer than three early Stuart court poisons: "Prince Henries perfumed Gloves, of each two graines", "one ounce of Sir Thomas Overburies Potion", and "one dram of King James his Cordiall made by Buckingham".[38] In contemporary satire, the secret history of early Stuart poison politics clearly still mattered: Charles's death had not killed the discussion of his father's murder.

Indeed, the new Republic was ready to use James's death as part of its official legitimating "script" justifying its rule to the world. In mid-March 1649 the Republic ordered a new declaration to justify their "late Proceedings", and instructed the circuit judges to publish it in the assize towns. This official statement presented Charles as a king who had violated "the Trust of that Office" and chosen to destroy rather than nurture his people. The document dwelled on the "cry of the blood of Ireland and England", which gave more than "sufficient cause to bring the King to Justice". According to the Biblical principle, "wherein is no dispensation for Kings", it followed that "the Land cannot be cleansed of the Blood that is shed therein, but by the Blood of him that shed it". Charles bore the guilt of all the blood shed since the 1641 Army Plot and the brutal slaughters of the Irish rebellion. But the Republic's declaration also surveyed the opening years of Charles's reign, in which he surpassed "his Forefathers in evil". Out came the usual evidence of Charles's tyranny—La Rochelle's abandonment, the forced loan, Ship Money, monopolies and projects, "unlawful imprisonments", and the "long intermission of our Parliaments". But once again, Charles's original sin was the 1626 dissolution of Parliament, which was in turn linked to James's murder, for "afterwards [Charles] shewed an unnatural forgetfulness, to have the violent Death of his Father examined". Charles was not explicitly depicted as a parricide in this official declaration, but James's "violent Death" was taken as an uncontroversial fact and Charles's refusal to prosecute that murder explained his angry dissolution of Parliament and exposed his "unnatural forgetfulness".[39]

Commentary on the king's execution dominated print debate early in 1649, and both supporters and critics of the regicide used arguments about the past—about the 1620s in general as well as about the secret history in particular—to justify their interpretations of the present. Much of the writing was hostile, and some of these critiques directly attacked the secret history. In February, *The Returne of the People of England*, first printed late in 1648, reappeared under a new title, *The Charge Against The King discharged*, and a new date, "The first Yeere of Englands Thraledome". Its dismantling of the *Declaration*'s reworked secret history remained in place, although the pamphlet now implied that Charles had faced the *Declaration*'s full panoply of charges during his trial.[40] In July, James Howell anonymously published *An Inquisition after Blood* that acquitted Charles of all charges against him. Howell had little patience for "This businesse about the playster". It had been "sifted & winnow'd as narrowly as possibly a thing could be in former Parlements", and so it was "strange that these new accusers shold make that a parricide in the King, which was found but a presumption in the Duke". But Howell also cited the legal maxim that "The King can do no wrong", arguing that even if James I "died a violent death, and his Son had been accessary to it, (which is as base a lie as ever the devil belch'd out)", Charles could not be charged with murder because "his accesse to the Crown had purg'd all".[41]

Samuel Butler took aim in manuscript at John Cook's *King Charls His Case*, branding its charges as contemptible "Riddles of Contradiction". Butler was especially angered by Cook's additional material on James's death, the "prodigy of your Injustice, as well as Inhumanity". He questioned Cook's use of circumstantial evidence: if Charles had been as "politick a Tyrant" as Cook claimed, surely he would have silenced Buckingham for killing his father, not advanced him. Likewise, Butler found no evidence that Charles had dissolved Parliament in 1626 to protect the duke, but even if he had done so "in such cases Princes may as well protect their Favourites from Injury as Justice". He noted that Cook had smeared Charles "after his Death, for what you were ashamed to charge him with alive"; so by interpolating these additional charges into his pamphlet, Cook had revealed the real weakness of the main charge against the king. Butler also offered a fascinating alternative genealogy of the secret history. Like other Royalists, he believed that some Parliamentarians had plotted the "alteration of Government" for decades and argued that Buckingham's 1626 impeachment was simply a "politick Course" to further this plot. The allegation about James's death was carefully designed both to appeal to the credulous "People", always eager to see great men fall, and to bend the king to their will by preventing him from "protecting the Duke (though he knew his innocency) lest the envy and fancy of all should fall upon himself". These traitors simply used stories of James's murder to advance "some Design they had in hand". The eleven-year gap in parliaments between 1629 and 1640 revealed not Charles's tyranny, but his concern to protect his people from seditious malcontents.[42]

Other Royalists interpreted the secret history's origins differently. *The Royall Legacies of Charles the First*, published in May 1649, charged that Parliament had "falsly loaded Him with horrible Reproaches, viz. the Death of His Father, and the Blood of His People", and that these false allegations had come "from persons of His own creating and advancing" whom Charles "had fed from their Cradle". Although the anonymous author never mentioned Eglisham, he characterized the charge as a Scottish invention. In part, it fit the national character, for "so seditious and murtherous" were the Scots "towards their Kings" that James reportedly exclaimed, if not for his hope of succeeding Elizabeth, "He would sell all He had in Scotland, and goe live a private Gentleman at Venice, rather then rule such a faithlesse and ungovernable People". The *Royall Legacie* flatly rejected the poison allegation: "(without going to a Witch) every man knowes that King James dyed in the Cold Fit of a Tertian Ague, a Disease most incongruous to the operation of Poyson". The only fortunate aspect of the charge was that it had given Charles early in his reign "a full sence of the ever Traiterous Scots . . . [and] their rancorous Malice towards English men".[43]

The most powerful, albeit indirect, Royalist response had appeared within hours of Charles's execution. *Eikon Basilike*, a collection of the king's musings and prayers, ghostwritten partially, if not entirely, by a royal chaplain, became an unprecedented publishing phenomenon; in 1649 alone, no fewer than forty-six English editions appeared, as well as another ten editions in French, Latin, Dutch and German. *Eikon Basilike*'s description of Charles I as a pious martyr had real purchase, and it posed an existential threat to the fledgling English Republic. The book did not engage directly with the secret history, though it made much of Charles's profound spiritual introspection in the wake of the Vote of No Addresses. But the secret history proved an important weapon for Republican writers tasked with tearing down the revitalized image of the martyr king.

Eikon Alethine, an early response to the king's book that Thomason purchased on 16 August, denounced it as a "counterfeit Piece" written by the "Presumptious Preist" who was exposed behind an opened curtain on the title-page. In its mockery of *Eikon Basilike*, it used the murder of James I as a sharp polemical tool. "Can any beleeve the late King would professe that . . . he never wilfully opposed or denied any thing that was in a faire way, after full and free debates propounded to him by the two Houses", the author asked. Surely readers remembered "the dissolving the Parliament, for questioning the D. of Buckingham for poysoning his Father, when he was bound by all ties of justice and Nature, to have heard them". Confronted with Charles's alleged boast about "a 17 yeares reigne in such a measure of Justice, Peace, Plenty and Religion, as all Nations about either admired, or envied", the author began listing examples of "the base neglect of his subjects blood so perfidiously slain", among which was "the breaking up the Parliament for questioning the poysoners of his Father".[44]

Eikon Alethine prompted its own Royalist rebuttal, *Eikon e Piste*, that derided the "Presumptious coxcombe" who presumed to "Murder the issue of the Kings owne braine". In its point-by point refutation, *Eikon e Piste* denied that Charles had dissolved the 1626 session to stop "questioning the Duke of Buckingham for poysoning his Father", and offered alternative explanations for the dissolution of Parliament, including Charles's fear that the House of Commons would have murdered Buckingham as the 1641 Commons had murdered the innocent Strafford. Since the Parliament-men "would have condemn'd him right or wrong", it was wiser to judge Charles's actions "charitably" than "to revile the gods upon trust". In any case, the suggestion that Charles had been "a conniver at his Fathers murder" was as preposterous as it was wicked.[45]

A few weeks later, John Milton brought out *Eikonoklastes*, the most ambitious assault on the martyr-king's seductive image, and used the secret history to undercut *Eikon Basilike*'s rewriting of Charles's relationship with his parliaments. Against the king's book's insistence that Charles had summoned Parliament in 1640 out of his "own choice and inclination", believing in "the right way of Parliaments", Milton simply catalogued Charles's long-standing hostility to the institution, which he "never call'd . . . but to supply his necessities; and having supply'd those, as suddenly and ignominiously dissolv'd it, without redressing any one greevance of the people". Following the 1648 *Declaration*'s lead, and conflating the parliaments of 1625 and 1626, Milton explained that Charles had dissolved his first Parliament "for no other cause then to protect the Duke of Buckingham against them who had accus'd him, besides other hainous crimes, of no less then poysoning the deceased King his Father".[46]

Cannot a Man Speak of King James's Death?

Early 1645 now seemed a lifetime ago. On 18 January 1649, two days before the king's trial began, a cohort of Presbyterian ministers presented *A Serious and Faithfull Representation* to the Army leadership. Still in shock from Pride's Purge, they rejected the Army's November *Remonstrance* and protested that they had not taken up arms in 1642 "to subvert and overthrow the whole frame and fundamentall constitution of the Government". With Charles's trial imminent, and fearful that "Religion" would be "made to stink by reason of your miscarriages, and like to be a scorn and a reproach in all the Christian World", forty-seven ministers signed their names, among them the prominent London preacher Christopher Love.

In a hard-line sermon in 1645, Love had cautioned against making peace with the king before the nation's hidden wounds had been "search't to the quick". Among these wounds were the alleged murders of Prince Henry and James I. Opponents of the January 1649 Presbyterian *Representation* were quick to remind Christopher Love of his words. In mid-February, John Price's vindication of "the Capitall punishment of the Person of the King" quoted from Love's 1645 sermon. He marvelled that the same ministers who had helped "in setting the people at first against the King and his party, firing mens spirits against him, charging him with the guilt of the blood of England, Scotland and Ireland" now objected to "the staining the Protestant Religion with the blood of a King". In his 1645 sermon, Love had called on the nation "to find out whether King James and Prince Henry his sonne, came to a timely death", and, Price wondered, "what is this but to incense the people to an implacable spirit of revenge against the King?" The Presbyterian petition against Charles's trial revealed them as "false, bold, pertenacious, scandalous, mutinous, seditious, rebellious fellows"; just four years earlier Love had "spoken . . . of the bloode guiltinesse of the King, yea intimated unnaturall and horrible blood-guiltinesse in him, as if he had been guilty of K. James his death, and Prince Henrie's death". A few days after Price's intervention, an anonymous author joined the attack. He doubtless enjoyed reminding the Presbyterian Thomas Gataker of the famous Bibical tagline for militant resistance, "Curse yee Merose", that Gataker had trumpeted in numerous sermons from the early 1640s:

> you cryed, Cursed be he that doth the worke of the Lord negligently; and Cursed be hee that keepeth back his sword from blood. . . . And said, God was making inquisition for blood, mentioning the blood of Rochel, of King James, of Ireland, etc, and all to stirre up the people.

Has "God . . . given over making inquisition", the tract asked the Presbyterians, "when you give over crying?"[47]

In April 1649, Christopher Love's supporters printed his defence, which switched uneasily back and forth from the first to the third person. Insisting that his reference then to the "man of blood" referred, not to Charles, but to "those who were the chief instruments to engage the King in the late bloody War", Love admitted that he "often wisht that the contrivers of the Rebellion in Ireland, the Betrayers of the Protestants in Rochell, the Conspirators of King James and Prince Henrys death (if they did come to an untimely end) might be found out". Yet "I demand of you, is there any clause in that Sermon or any tendency that way to charge the King with the death of King James or Prince Henry"? Slipping into the third person, the defence protested that the claim that "hee spake therein of the blood-guiltinesse of the King is utterly false", adding "I have read over his Sermon from the beginning to the end; and can find no mention of the King . . . but in two places, and there too, without the least reflexion or accusation". Finally, Love's defence lamented, "cannot a man speak of King James or Prince Henries death, but must it be interpreted that he said King Charles had a hand in it?"[48]

By 1649 the answer to that question was obvious. As Love had discovered, what was still possible in 1645 became all but impossible after the February 1648 *Declaration* had so sensationally revived the secret history. The murder of James I had acquired an indelibly regicidal cast—to accept that James had been poisoned was now to assume Charles's guilt in the crime. It is equally obvious that historians cannot fully understand the regicide—its causes, its rationales, its supporters and its critics—without recognizing the key role played by the secret history of James's murder.

Waiting for Denbigh

Early on 9 March 1649, James, Duke of Hamilton, the last surviving protagonist of *The Forerunner of Revenge*, awaited execution at Whitehall, having been convicted a month earlier by the same High Court and prosecutor that had tried Charles I. Hamilton made an unlikely Royalist martyr. Imprisoned by the king during the First Civil War, he had belatedly taken up arms in early 1648 to lead a Scottish force south in an ultimately unsuccessful effort to liberate his royal cousin. As he stood on the scaffold, Hamilton pinned his hopes for a reprieve on his brother-in-law, Basil Feilding, Earl of Denbigh: "he is my Brother", the duke explained, "and has been a very faithfull servant of this State, and he was in great esteem and reputation with them". Those who overheard (or later read) Hamilton's words might have remembered George Eglisham's sensational story of Hamilton's marriage to Denbigh's sister and the murderous quarrel that ensued between Hamilton's father and Denbigh's uncle, the Duke of Buckingham. Later in the 1620s, news collectors had avidly followed stories of the marriage's near disintegration and fretted anxiously over reports of young Hamilton's hurried flight from the Caroline court. But Hamilton had eventually been reconciled with his wife and her family. The couple lived in a house once occupied by the great favourite, and Hamilton later buried his wife alongside her grandmother, the Countess of Buckingham. Over the years, he and his brother-in-law Denbigh became close friends, and this friendship survived the ideological fractures of civil war. In 1642, Denbigh had joined the Parliamentarian cause, and not even the republication of *The Forerunner* that so horrified his wife could shake his resolve. His long record of service meant that Denbigh might have had the influence to secure his brother-in-law's reprieve, and Hamilton begged the sheriff to delay his execution "in regard of the Earl of Denbigh sending to speak with me". But when Denbigh finally arrived, he brought only bad news.[49]

The public execution of a duke drew a large crowd, some of whom would have had only a jumbled knowledge of Eglisham's accusations. Others, however, doubtless knew the secret history well, and would have recalled the lurid details of the sudden death of Hamilton's father and the grotesque discolouration and swelling of his corpse. That March morning they knew they were witnessing yet another of the sons of the secret history's three main characters join Francis Villiers and Charles Stuart in the grave.

PART VI

SPEAKING REPROACHFULLY OF
THE DEAD
1649–63

TRVTH
Brought to light and
discouered by
Time
or
A
discourse
and
Historicall Narration
of the first XIII yeares
of King Iames Reigne

PROLOGUE

AN ENGLISHMAN IN UPPSALA, 1653–54

UPPSALA IN DECEMBER 1653 was bitterly cold and very dark, but the harsh climate was the least of the problems facing England's new ambassador to Sweden. Charles I's execution in January 1649 had made diplomatic service dangerous. Royalists had murdered the new Republic's representatives in Holland and Spain, and Bulstrode Whitelocke would hear of several assassination plots against him during his time in Sweden (Fig. 81). A reluctant rather than an ardent revolutionary, Whitelocke had loyally served the new Republic as its chief legal officer. Angered when Oliver Cromwell dissolved the Rump in April 1653, he had nonetheless kept his office and accepted the Swedish assignment. In mid-December 1653, while Whitelocke was travelling north, Cromwell was installed as Lord Protector following the disintegration of the Nominated Assembly that had replaced the Rump. Whitelocke thus well understood Swedish concerns about his government's stability; privately, he shared them. But the Swedish authorities were at least ready to do business with him. Others remained far less inclined to overlook the regicide. One night during his stay, a gang of Danes and Dutchmen gathered outside Whitelocke's house, taunting the "English dogges" and "King killers" within.[1]

To secure a treaty of amity, Whitelocke had to deal not only with the ageing Chancellor Axel Oxenstierna, but also with the enigmatic Queen Christina, daughter of King Gustavus Adolphus. She made a striking first impression. Dressed in an oddly masculine outfit, "her countenance pale but sprightly, her demeanor full of Majesty & Sweetnes", she toyed with Whitelocke, drawing "close to him" as he spoke and using intimidating "lookes & gestures" to disconcert him. If this was a test, he passed it, and Whitelocke soon began meeting with Christina in private. The queen admired the way he behaved "not as a Marchant butt as a gentleman & man of honor", and she repeatedly questioned him about England. She asked about Cromwell, lay preachers in the Army, and the state of the English Navy, and she confided troubling news that young Charles, the executed king's exiled son, had offered to marry her. The queen

Figure 81: William Faithorne's 1656 engraved portrait of Bulstrode Whitelocke (National Portrait Gallery).

was especially curious about the contentious issue of "liberty of Conscience", and she doubtless dismayed the godly ambassador when speaking strongly "in favor of the Papists". On occasion their meetings ended "in much drollery".[2]

On 30 December their conversation took an awkward turn. Although Whitelocke had brought the latest news from London, Christina was more interested in the English past. "Among other things", Whitelocke wrote, she "fell into discourse with him concerning King James, who she had heard was poisoned, and his son Prince Henry also." Her inquiries caught the ambassador off guard. He probably had much to tell her; after all, as a young Parliament-man in 1626 he had taken notes during the hearings into James's death. But Whitelocke tactfully "declined this discourse", explaining that he did not want "to speak reproachfully of the dead". His reticence soon vanished when Christina then asked about "the extraction and favour" of "the great Duke of Bucks". Since his wife was a cousin of Buckingham's duchess, Whitelocke willingly gave the queen "a particular account" of the favourite. As Christina kept probing, asking questions about various aristocrats and scholars, Whitelocke's admiration grew. "One would have imagined that England had been her native country", he noted, "so well was she furnished with the characters of most persons of consideration there, and with the story of the nation." For her part, the queen thought his refusal to "reproach princes or any other behind their backs" both "honourable and very becoming a gentleman".[3]

Oxenstierna, who had taught Christina her English history, may have long been aware of stories about James's murder, for his London agent in the late 1620s had warned him about the enigmatic Piers Butler who had allegedly supplied magical amulets and (perhaps) poisons to the Duke of Buckingham. Christina may also have heard variations on the secret history from Claude Saumaise (Salmasius), the French scholar she brought to Sweden after his 1649 attack on the regicide. Whether she wanted to unsettle Whitelocke or to satisfy a genuine curiosity, Christina was clearly intrigued by the story of James I's murder. Whitelocke's reticence is equally revealing. Although ambivalent about the regicide—he had left London rather than serve on the committee preparing the king's indictment, and he spent the day of Charles's execution in prayer— Whitelocke had assumed prominent positions in both the Commonwealth and the Protectorate, and many of his colleagues regarded James's murder as a matter of fact.[4] Indeed, stories of James's poisoning had become part of the foundational mythology of the English Republic.

Faced with mortal threats from within and without, the new regimes struggled to establish legitimacy. To justify the regicide, the new Republic and, eventually, the Protectorate, the revolutionaries drew from many sources: they invented new (or repurposed old) rituals and imagery; they pioneered increasingly skilful media campaigns; they borrowed ideas from classical republicanism, Calvinist resistance theory and radical millenarianism; they invoked God's Providence and applied Hobbesian philosophy.[5] But these regimes and their supporters also drew explicitly and repeatedly on politicized histories of the early Stuart age. Like all polities, whether traditional or revolutionary, they constructed origin stories that gave meaning and authority to the present. During the 1650s the secret history of James I's murder became part of the English Revolution's usable past. It was absorbed into short-term polemic and incorporated into larger historical narratives about the fall of the House of Stuart. It was turned into a story of God's providential workings, and invoked as damning evidence of monarchy's inherent sinfulness and corruption. It was glossed, elaborated, annotated, documented and, eventually, vigorously contested. And it would continue to be avidly discussed deep into the eighteenth century. The cautious Whitelocke may have declined to discuss James I's murder, but many of his contemporaries were more than happy to "speak reproachfully of the dead". They did so to validate the revolutionary present.

CHAPTER TWENTY-TWO

TRUTH BROUGHT TO LIGHT

THE SECRET HISTORY AND THE DEFENCE OF THE

ENGLISH REPUBLIC, 1650–53

THE IMAGE IS designed to grab attention (Fig. 82). Truth and Time pull back the curtains to reveal a republican *memento mori*: James I, slumped on his throne, his head propped on his left hand, his outstretched right hand resting on a skull, his crown and sceptre tumbled to his feet—reminders that "crowns, sceptres, and all things" must pass. But the open curtains also invoked a novel republican transparency, a promise to reveal the long-hidden secrets of kings to the critical gaze of the revolutionary reader.

This evocative image appeared on the frontispiece to Michael Sparke's 1651 *Truth Brought to light and discovered by Time*, a book that promised to discover "all the policies, Dissimulations, Treacheries, Witchcraft, Conjurings, Charmes, Adulteries, Poysonings, Murderings, Blasphemies and Heresies" of the Jacobean era.[1] This exercise in revolutionary demystification—which focused primarily on the scandal around the poisoning of Sir Thomas Overbury—belonged to a much bigger assortment of publications in the early 1650s about the first Stuart king. Official newsbooks mined early Stuart scandals to ward off the threat of resurgent Royalism, while other publications opened Whitehall's "closets" and "cabinets" to expose the "mysteries of state and government" to public scrutiny. Histories became a common genre. Some were salaciously anecdotal, others were sober and unusually well documented, but all were deeply partisan retellings of early Stuart history designed to speak to present concerns. And all of them spoke about James I's murder.

Astraea Is Returned

On 20 March 1650, George Thomason bought *Somnium Cantabrigiense*, a short pamphlet of undistinguished verse that restated the case for regicide against the late king's champions, William Prynne the Presbyterian, Salmasius the Huguenot, and the Royalist poet John Quarles who had insisted the martyr-king's "hands ... [were] clear from blood". *Somnium* told the story of a man

Figure 82: John Droeshout's frontispiece to Michael Sparke's 1651 collection of early Stuart histories, *Truth Brought to light and discovered by Time* (Huntington Library).

"Frantick with rage and griefe" at the regicide, who was visited in a dream by England's Genius who explained to him how Justice "thought good" that Charles "who in slaughter liv'd, should dye in blood". Charles's tyrannies had outdone the worst deeds of Rome's most corrupt rulers, the Genius declared, and chief among the king's crimes was murder. His most prominent victim was his own father. Just as the Roman tyrant Tarquin Superbus had seized the throne after ordering his father-in-law murdered, so it was that "poyson'd James" had "made room" for Charles in 1625. Charles had proved his complicity in the murder, as the 1648 *Declaration* had insisted, by dissolving the 1626 Parliament to protect "Endeared Buckingham". Echoing John Cook's questions about the natural duties of sons to fathers, England's Genius wondered, "Who could have thought but justice would be done/The Father murthered, and the Judge the Sonne". But the fact remained that:

> The Sonne whom you judge fit,
> To follow the inditement, hindred it.
> But this was like the rest, an Act of grace,
> And Charles would not be judge in his own case.

Least truth unvail'd, prerogative might marre,
And George call Charles along unto the Barre.

This crime, along with the massacre of English troops at Cadiz in 1625 and the Île de Ré in 1627, should silence all Royalist lamentations: the "light of truth . . . robs Charles of the Crowne of Martyrdome". Charles's death had set England "free", but it had also marked the return of Astraea, goddess of justice and harbinger of the Golden Age. All those:

who did so long
About Astraea's Throne for justice throng:
Now cease complaints; for Charles hath paid that due
By the keen Axe, which he did owe to you.

This dawning Golden Age would encompass a whole continent: the "oppressed" would be liberated and their kingly oppressors destroyed. Europe's "Tyrants though they hate/Englands example, yet feare Englands State", for the High Court's "Thundring sentence" against Charles I "shall awake/The drowsiest slaves, whil'st proudest Tyrants quake".[2]

The secret history, fused here with regicidal discourses of blood guilt, providential deliverance and tyrannicide, and mobilized within a proudly republican vision of Europe-wide revolution, continued to exert a significant purchase on English political imaginations in the early years of the English Free State. But by the time *Somnium Cantabrigiense* appeared, the Republic's defenders not only had to worry about the cult of Charles the martyr; they also had to wrestle with a new threat, one that *Somnium*'s mock dedication to "the famous Dreamer John Quarles" made clear. For John Quarles was not simply an idolater at the shrine of the martyred Charles I; he was also "Ordinarie Poet to Charles the Second".[3]

A Ticklish Time

"Is not this a ticklish time . . . to write Intelligence?" Marchamont Nedham asked the readers of *Mercurius Politicus*'s first issue in June 1650. A year earlier, in the last issue of *Mercurius Pragmaticus* before Parliament closed it down, Nedham had imagined the regicides suffering traitors' deaths, but now he was writing "in defence of the Common-wealth, and for the Information of the People". His new quarry was Charles I's son and the Scots whose "Kirk in time may chance to mount him . . . and send him a hunting into England like his grand-sire Jamy". Initially, Nedham mocked the Stuart threat: the young Charles lived "like a Scotich Emperor" on the £2,000 that the cash-strapped Scottish Parliament had "strained the Sinews" of their "State" to find.[4] But

Nedham's drollery could not conceal the ominous situation north of the Tweed. In May 1650, Charles agreed to the Covenanters' demand for a Presbyterian Church across the three kingdoms. In June he landed in Scotland, where the entire country rallied around him. Alarmed by the prospect of a Stuart prince leading a large army of seasoned Scottish veterans, and by reports of tactical alliances between English Presbyterians and Royalists, the Commonwealth sent Oliver Cromwell north. His soldiers had twice defeated the Royalists, but this Third Civil War was a radically different affair, pitting reformed Protestants against errant former allies and brethren. At the same time, English contemporaries had to rally to the Republic and to reject the Stuart pretender. In response, the regime and its supporters launched a concerted press campaign to stiffen English resistance and to make their former Scots allies think long and hard about their potential new king. To do so, they turned again and again to scandalous stories from the secret history of the House of Stuart.[5]

Charles himself had acknowledged his family's heavy curse. In June 1650, shortly after his arrival in Scotland, he declared that though he honoured "the memory of his Royall Father" and "the person of his Mother", he was "afflicted in spirit before God, because of his Fathers hearkening to, and following evil Counsels, and his opposition to the work of Reformation". Lest God visit "the sins of the Fathers upon the Children", Charles now confessed "the sins of his Fathers house".[6] Marchamont Nedham took his confession as the centrepiece of his propaganda against the prince, repeatedly deploying a counter-history of the cursed dynasty in which the murders of James I and Prince Henry loomed large. The Kirk ministers, Nedham noted in August, "were the Beagles wherewith they hunted his great Grandam [Mary, Queen of Scots], grand-sire [James VI and I], and Daddy [Charles I]"; and none of these three monarchs "dyed a naturall death", while "Jamy's was more unnaturall than any, except Prince Henry". This was no reason for sorrow, for in James's reign "the seeds of our misery" had been "plentifully sown". Subsequent issues of Nedham's newsbook elaborated this polemical history. The following week he praised the Kirk ministers who knew to "threaten him, except he publickly disavow and dis-own His and his Fathers opposition to the Covenant". The next letters, Nedham quipped, would likely report that the new king was "asleep with . . . his Father: For, it is a Solecism in Scotland that a King should be said to die in his Bed". After all, Charles's great grandfather, Lord Darnley, ended up "truss't . . . up upon a Peartree".[7]

By the 12 September issue of *Mercurius Politicus*, Nedham had a better-developed and increasingly providentialized argument. Although Cromwell's decisive victory at Dunbar a few days earlier made Nedham fear that "I and my man Mercury should be out of employment", the situation remained uncertain as the Scots army withdrew behind the River Forth. Nedham now appealed to the Scottish "Brethren" to abandon their quixotic effort "to repair the ruines of a Scottish Fatall Family". Disaster had "followed the whole Family for many Generations". James's father—"if we may say the Lord Darnly was his Father", Nedham snidely added—"was hanged in Scotland, and by the consent (or rather conspiracy) of his own Wife". Mary, Queen of Scots and her grandson Charles I were both beheaded, while "K. James himselfe, and his eldest Son Henry" were "more then suspected to be both poysoned". James's daughter Elizabeth and her husband Elector Frederick "were driven out" of the Palatinate, and James's favourite Buckingham "stabb'd". Plainly no cause could thrive "that admits of a Combination with that wretched Family".[8]

Other defenders of the Republic were equally anxious in the summer of 1650. The veteran Parliamentarian polemicist Henry Parker edited (and may have written) a detailed critique of the young pretender's claim to the throne.[9] *The True Portraiture of the Kings of England*, purchased by George Thomason on 7 August, celebrated the regicide as a providential liberation: since the people had reassumed their sovereign authority, it would be an act of "stupidity, and blindness" to abandon it. "We have conquered the Conqueror, and got the possession of the true English title, by justice, and gallantry", the pamphlet concluded. "Let us not lose it again, by any pretence of a particular, and debauched person." Parker insisted that these conclusions derived not from philosophy but from "visible Politicks" and "Precedents". For centuries, English liberties had been sacrificed on the altar of divine-right monarchy, a process the Stuarts had taken to new heights. Too timid to engage in open tyranny, James I worked to "insensibly and closely undermine the Liberties of England", and Charles I became "the most absolute . . . example of tyranny and injustice that was ever known in England". But before Charles could act, James had to die:

> He now grows old and was judged only fit to lay the Plot, but not to execute it; the design being now ripe, and his person and life the only obstacle and *Remora* [hindrance] to the next Instrument, he is conveyed away suddenly into another world, as his son Henry was, because thought unsuteable to the Plot, it being too long to waite, untill Nature and Distemper had done the deed.

Parker's passive construction masked the identity of James's killer, but there was no doubt the murderer was Charles I. The "young Pretender" now among the Scots was his father's son, "bred up under the wings of Popery and Episcopacy", and doubtless "suckt both brests". Whatever concessions the young prince offered now would be worth nothing once he returned to the throne and could avenge his father's death.[10] The *True Portraiture* was less playful than Nedham's newsbook, but the message was similar: the secret history of Stuart family murder would help the English and the Scots understand what was at stake in

this existential challenge to the revolutionary regime, and thus clarify the legitimacy of both the regicide and the Republic.

Others soon entered the fray. But unlike Parker's pamphleteer, who insisted
he would "not rip up" James I's "personal failings after his death", they were
quick to situate the secret history in a richer, more scandalous catalogue of
royal debauchery.

Kingcraft Exposed

Sir Anthony Weldon's *Court and Character of King James* was easily the most
popular of these histories of royal debauchery, and its appearance in 1650–51,
"Published by Authority", strongly suggests that it was part of a coordinated
campaign to wean contemporaries off Stuart kingship (Fig. 83). Weldon, a
former court official and Parliamentarian activist, probably composed his
history in the mid-1640s. Only after his death in 1648 would enterprising

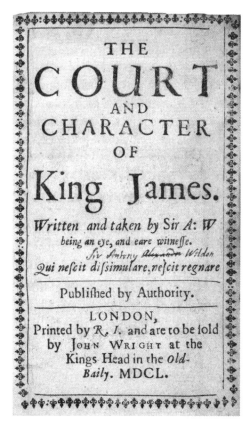

Figure 83: Title page of the Robert Ibbitson and John Wright edition of Sir Anthony Weldon, *The
Court and Character of King James*, 1650 (Huntington Library)

publishers retool his account into revolutionary propaganda. On 1 October 1650, Thomason purchased his copy of Weldon from one of the two, or possibly three, editions that John Wright and Robert Ibbitson published that year. In 1651, Ibbitson and John Collins issued another three editions, expanding the text to include "The Court of King Charles", also attributed to Weldon. Roughly one hundred copies have survived from these editions, testimony to the book's undoubted popularity and to the skill with which Weldon and his publishers turned an insider's revelations about the Jacobean court into a scandalously gripping moralistic secret history.[11]

Ibbitson was a committed radical printer based in Smithfield. He had printed for the Army in 1647, helped produce the 1648 translation of *Vindiciae Contra Tyrannos*, published widely on the regicide in 1649, and was also involved in the official newsbook *Severall Proceedings in Parliament*. Although occasionally in trouble with the censors, Ibbitson remained close to the revolutionary regime, and in 1653 he would be a candidate for the position of official printer to the new Council of State.[12] In 1650 he worked on the first editions of Weldon with the veteran John Wright, who had a shop in the Old Bailey. These Wright–Ibbitson editions clarified Weldon's relevance to the current crisis with a preface encouraging readers to "give glory to God, in acknowledging his Justice, in the ruining of that Family". Their warning to the supporters of the King of Scots was stark: "take heed how they side with this bloody House, lest they be found opposers of Gods purpose, which doubtlesse is, to lay aside that Family" (Fig. 84). The preface identified five "remarkable passages" in the book that exemplified this message. One was "the fearfull imprecation made by King James against himselfe and his Posterity, in the presence of many of his Servants, and the Judges, even upon his knees, if he should spare any that were found guilty in the poysoning businesse of Sir Thomas Overbury". James's failure to fulfill this oath, the preface argued, had incurred God's wrath, which first fell on the king himself. "How the Justice of God hath been, and is upon himselfe and Posterity, his owne death, by poyson, and the sufferings of his Posterity, doe sufficiently manifest".[13]

In 1651, Ibbitson and John Collins produced an expanded edition, and their new preface characterized the book as "an Epitomee of some secret Passages" once too dangerous for publication. An unsigned prefatory poem promised that the book would expose "the foulest secret Crimes" and "Tricks of State", revealing:

> Favourites Rise and Fall,
> Greatnesse debauched, Gentry slighted[,] all
> To please those Favourites, whose highest ends
> Were to exhaust the State, to please their friends.

Figure 84: Frontispiece portrait of James I in the Ibbitson–Wright 1650 edition of *The Court and Character of King James* (Huntington Library). The prophetic gloss beneath the image depicts James as "Vulpes", the Fox, the master of kingcraft, and predicts the end of monarchy in England (Huntington Library).

Quite simply, "Prerogative's sole life" was "the Kingdomes death".[14]

Weldon's history did not disappoint. He presented James as a weak king "easily abused" by his courtiers and addicted to the Machiavellian "art of dissimulation, or, (to give it his own phrase) King-craft": he "was very crafty and cunning in petty things", Weldon wrote, "as the circumventing any great man, the change of a Favourite, &c. insomuch as a very wise man was wont to say, he beleeved him the wisest foole in Christendome, meaning him wise in small things, but a foole in weighty affaires."[15] Weldon's detailed narrative of James's murder offered a parable about the fatal limitations of this royal kingcraft, in which the king was destroyed by a monster of his own creation. A true Machiavel could curb his passions, but James could not restrain his sexual appetites. James's courtiers exploited his taste for "young Faces, and smooth Chins", and after the "King cast a glancing eye" on young George Villiers, a faction of men groomed the young man for royal favour. Villiers's rise had calamitous consequences. The favourite swelled "with pride, breaking out of these modest bounds, (which formerly had impaled him) to the high-way of pride and scorne, turning out, and putting in all he pleased". By promoting the wicked and the incompetent, selling office to the highest bidder, making the "great Officers" of state "his very slaves", and marrying off "numerous beggerly kindred" to prominent men, he was soon beyond James's control. None was "great with Buckingham", Weldon wrote, "but Bawds and Parasites, and such as humoured him in his unchaste pleasures; so that since his first being a pretty, harmlesse, affable Gentleman, he grew insolent, cruell, and a monster not to be endured."[16]

George Eglisham had claimed that James and Buckingham had quarrelled over the Spanish match, but Weldon insisted that they had fallen out much earlier, and for sexual reasons. Soon after Buckingham's marriage, James grew "satiated" and "weary of him, for his now stalenesse". But fearful of Buckingham's "over-awing power", the king dared not cast him aside. Confronted with James's cooling ardour, Buckingham "made Court to the Prince", winning Charles "to bee so deare with him, as to be governed by him all his life time, more then his Father was in the prime of his affection". But the favourite also developed an "extreame hatred" for James. Unable to repudiate Buckingham, James resorted to kingcraft. The king suborned Sir Henry Yelverton to make a speech in the 1621 Parliament against the favourite, but when the ploy backfired he abandoned Yelverton in the Tower. Buckingham then befriended the imprisoned knight, who revealed James's scheming. Henceforth king and favourite were united in mutual hatred. But while James still dared not act openly, Buckingham had "more courage", and "although the King lost his opportunity on Buckingham, yet the black plaister and powder did shew Buckingham lost not his on the King".[17]

Weldon's vivid account of James's final illness elaborated on the 1626 narratives. The king "was seized on by an ordinary and moderate Tertian Ague, which at that season, according to the Proverb, was Physick for a King"; Buckingham's "Empirick" applied medicines "whilst those Physitians appointed to attend him, were at dinner"; and James complained of the "black plaister and powder given" him. For Weldon, the duke's guilt was incontestable:

> Nor could any but Buckingham answer it with lesse then his life at that present, as he had the next Parliament, had it not been dissolved upon the very questioning him for the Kings death, and all those that prosecuted him, utterly disgraced and banished the Court.

Weldon also offered new revelations. He reported that James had often begged the Earl of Montgomery, "whom he trusted above all men, in his sicknesse", to make sure "for Gods sake" that he had "faire play". Embellishing Eglisham's account of the recriminations among the bedchamber staff, Weldon reported that an "honest servant" told Buckingham to his face that he had "undone us". When the angry favourite kicked him, the servant tipped him over. Buckingham rushed to the dying James, crying "Justice, Sir, I am abused by your servant, and wrongfully accused". And then "the poore King (become by that time speechlesse) mournfully fixed his eies on him, as who would have said, not wrongfully".[18]

God Hath Cursed That Kingly Race

Nedham's and Weldon's success encouraged other variations on the secret history. In January 1651, as the stalemate along the Forth continued, Charles II was crowned King of Scotland at Scone (Fig. 85). The English polemicists reacted with a scandalous book about his father entitled, with dripping sarcasm, *The None-such Charles His Character*. Again "Published by Authority", the book was another product of the Ibbitson–Collins partnership which was at that point also rushing hundreds of copies of the updated *Court and Character* to the bookstalls. *The None-Such Charles* occasionally referred to Weldon's best-seller, explicitly supplementing its case against James.[19] But the two books had significant differences. Unlike Weldon's history, *The None-Such*

Figure 85: "Charles the IId. Crownd King of Scotland Janu 1. 1651" (Huntington Library).

was a compilation drawn from "divers Originall Transactions" and the "Notes of severall . . . Councellours of State". The only counsellor it mentioned was Sir Balthazar Gerbier, Buckingham's servant and Charles I's agent in Brussels, whose "Diurnalls", housed in the "Paper-Roome at White-Hall", detailed Charles's betrayals of the Protestant Cause.[20] Whether Gerbier actively contributed to the book is unclear. He had strong ties to Ibbitson and to his newsbook partner Henry Walker, and by 1651 Gerbier was eager for the regime's favour following the closure of his Academy at Bethnal Green. Some Royalists blamed Gerbier for *The None-such*, but he is unlikely to have been more than a partial collaborator, and he might not have been directly involved at all.[21]

Whoever assembled the book, it was clearly attuned to the regime's imperatives. *The None-such* mocked Charles I while praising his conquerors. The execution of a king who was a papist idolater and preferred poetry and paintings to Scripture was a blessing from "the incomparable Mercy Seat of God". Charles's misrule revealed how much better off the English were without kings, while the Republic's legitimacy had been demonstrated by its recent military triumphs, so many "witnesses of Gods consent to that Blow".[22] The unfolding crisis in Scotland haunted *The None-such*, which reiterated Nedham's and Weldon's trope of the providential curse upon the Stuart dynasty. The tract noted, for instance, the lingering effects of God's anger at the crimes of James I and Henri IV, the "two Stemmes of this dismall Race". Generations to come would pay the wages of their sins. Both kings were hypocrites, blasphemers and dissemblers, and both were polluted by sexual excess. The history of "fatall . . . curses on their Posterity" only confirmed the divine sentence against the dynasty. James I and Henri IV were "the chief Ringleaders unto all the ensuing disasters which befell the late King, together with his owne pernicious, horrid depraved courses". These excessive sins had caused Charles I to be "cut off, not in his Coach" like Henri IV, nor in his bed like James I, but, most shamefully of all, on "a Scaffold, before his own Palace".[23]

Initially, *The None-such* argued that James's demise was caused "by the misapplying of Medicaments with a precipitated death", and situated his murder within a providentialist calculus of monarchical sin and divine punishment. But when the tract returned to the king's death some sixty pages later, its tone became more cautious—an inconsistency no doubt explained by the tract's patchwork construction. Having narrated, much as Eglisham had, the growing quarrels over the Spanish match, *The None-such* turned to address the reader:

> The publick may perhaps expect in this place a more ample explanation concerning the Plaister, and the Drinke which the Duke had administred to King Iames, for that known jealousies on both sides, may have been extreame grounds for some action between these two Parties, who were known to be so violently passionate.

But that "more ample explanation" was not forthcoming. Since Parliament had termed the duke's offence only a "high presumption", it would now "savour of a presumption" to claim something more than Parliament had intended. James's death was, in fact, a "riddle", and to spend more time on it might only encourage sceptics to abandon the broader case against James and Charles, which was "not wrapt up in any Riddles at all". Although the "Publick" was invited to acknowledge the "crying Sins which have brought downe so signall a wrath from God upon that Family", *The None-such* had effectively agreed with a key Royalist critique of the secret history: Charles could not be accused of murder if Parliament itself had refused to charge Buckingham with that crime.[24] Fully committed to justifying the regicide, *The None-such* had opted not to use the murder of James I as part of its legitimating script.

The None-such promised that Charles I's "domestic transactions" would be more "fully treated" in a separate volume. It is possible that this separate volume was the material on Charles's reign, over which Buckingham had loomed "like an impetuous storme", that Ibbitson appended to the new editions of Weldon's *Court and Character* in 1651. The Weldon narrative of the 1626 Parliament contained no trace of the hesitations in *The None-such*, instead emphasizing that the 1626 dissolution marked a fatal watershed. The Commons had investigated Buckingham "for the death of his old Master, which had been of a long time before but whispered; but now the Examinations bred such confessions, that it looked with an ugly deformed poysonous countenance". The dissolution, "ill relished by the people", only confirmed the accusations, as did Buckingham's vengeance upon "all those that followed that businesse, in that Parliament, or that seemed inquisitive thereafter". The Weldon narrative also told of an "old Parliament man" whose initial scepticism had ended after hearing the doctors' testimony before the select committee. Ever after "he both hated and scorned the name and memory of Buckingham; and though man would not punish it, God would, which proved an unhappy prediction". Buckingham's assassination was clearly providential justice for James's murder, but to Ibbitson and Collins's readers such language implied that God's revenge, begun at Portsmouth in 1628, was not complete until Charles's execution in January 1649.[25]

In February 1651, a month after the appearance of *The None-such*, George Thomason acquired another Ibbitson work, a large broadside, "Published by Authority", which offered a narrative report, an engraved image and an analysis of *The True Manner of the Crowning of Charles the Second King of Scotland*. The broadside ridiculed the "swarthy" young man as an "Artificiall Meteor", a "Scottish vapour, exhaled by French distillation", and a puppet of "his mothers counsels". Indeed, the writer marvelled that anyone would support the new Scottish king, given "such evident manifestations of the Lords so visibly owning" the anti-Stuart cause. "He that sitteth in the heavens shal laugh", the text predicted, and "the Lord shal have them in derision". The new Scottish king would surely follow his "fatall Progenitors":

> His Father was beheaded, His Grand-Father (as some Phisitians have declared) poysoned, His great Grand-Father, and so on to several assents before, successively cut off, by disastrous deaths.[26]

Similiar arguments came from two of Nedham's friends. John Milton's *Pro Populo Anglicano Defensio*, published in February 1651, was the regime's official (and widely reprinted) Latin refutation of the celebrated attack on the regicide by the French scholar Salmasius. Milton marshalled a formidably learned case, but, as in *Eikonoklastes*, he cleverly used the secret history to sharpen his critique. Milton challenged Salmasius's praise for the late Stuart king. "If you take such great delight in parallels", Milton suggested, "let us compare Charles with Solomon". The Israelite king began by justly punishing his brother, while the Briton's reign began "with his father's funeral". Milton scrupulously claimed he would not "say 'murder' (although all indications of poison were beheld on his father's body". But when Buckingham was suspected, Charles not only absolved "the murderer of the king and of his father" of "all guilt in the presence of the highest council of the realm", but then dissolved Parliament "lest that matter be . . . subjected" to its examination. This sin was one of many that Charles committed in concert with his favourite, and Milton asked how Salmasius could "praise the chastity . . . of one whom, together with the Duke of Buckingham, we know to be covered with every crime?" But James's death stood at the head of Charles's crimes. Dismissing Salmasius's claims that the English Parliament had acted towards Charles "more like Nero than the Roman senate", Milton mocked "this malignant itch of yours for cobbling together the most inept comparisons", for it was the English king who most obviously resembled the Roman tyrant:

> How like Charles was to Nero, I will show. "Nero", you say, "killed his own mother" with a sword. Charles did the same with poison to his father who was also the king. For to pass over other proofs, he who snatched from the clutches of the laws the duke who was charged with the poisoning, cannot but have been guilty himself too.[27]

While Milton addressed a continental audience, John Hall's *Grounds and Reasons of Monarchy Considered in a Review of the Scotch Story*, published first in Edinburgh and then in London, spoke to the Scots, who were "strangely blinde as to Gods Iudgement perpetually powred out upon a Family". Hall revelled in the long Scottish tradition of king-killing and the Stuarts' taste for adultery and murder. James, conceived in his mother's adulterous bed, had inherited her bloodlust. Suspecting his wife, Queen Anne, to be "too much in

League" with the Earl of Gowrie, James had Gowrie murdered before Gowrie could murder him. "From this Deliverance", Hall noted, echoing a charge made in the Ibbitson–Wright preface to Weldon's history, "he blasphemed God with a solemn Thanksgiving" every year for "the remainder of his life". On Elizabeth I's death, James cannily circumvented the statutory prohibition on foreigners inheriting the throne. By playing off the "Cecilians and Essexians" and imprisoning the lawful heir, Lady Arabella Stuart, James illegally seized the English crown. While mocking James's poetry and philosophy, questioning his Protestantism, and deriding his statecraft, Hall also emphasized the secret history and the dynastic curse. Prince Henry had died "of Poyson, and that as is feared by a hand too much allyed", insinuating that James or even Charles had been involved. Then James himself died "a violent death (by poyson) in which his son was more than suspected to have a hand". Charles's guilt, Hall insisted, could be seen in "his own dissolution of the Parliament that took in hand to examine it" and in his alleged "indifferency at Buckingham's death . . . as he was glad to be rid of so dangerous and so considerable a Partner of his guilt".[28]

In May 1651, as Cromwell prepared to cross the Forth, Marchamont Nedham returned to the theme of the "fatall Family". The 15 May issue of *Mercurius Politicus* insisted that since the Scots had first declared "the late King a man of Blood", the English "did no more but execute the sentence which they had long past [put] upon him"; but now the Scots were inexplicably in love with kings again. Nedham's next issue proclaimed that the English had good "cause to cast off that Tyrannick Family". Hitherto, discussion of the Stuart black legend had centred on Mary, Queen of Scots, James and Charles, but with rumours spreading of a French invasion of Ireland, Nedham extended the discussion to Mary's mother, Marie de Guise, for "it must not be forgotten how much was spilt by the Lady of the hous of Lorraine that was K. James his grandmother". Naturally enough, Marie's daughter Mary "massacred her husband . . . for the love of a Fidler, and another of her Adulterers by name Bothwell". And since Mary followed up these sins with still worse ones—she "persecuted all the reformed Religion with Sword and Fagot, endeavourared to poyson her own son, shed blood likewise by raising Civill Warre at home and conspired with forein Papists for the destruction of Queen Elizabeth"—Nedham thought her a serious contender for the title "Whore of Babylon". As for Mary's son, James "wrote his Beati Pacifici in Blood". His victims included the Gowries, killed after their "pretended conspiracy"; Sir Walter Ralegh, whose death "was no lesse than a downe right Murther"; and Prince Henry, "who also came to an untimely death". Nedham scrupulously conceded that it was "not directly known by what hand [Henry] was taken away", but "there was a strange connivence, and little mourning after it was done". The Scots knew this history well, because they had compelled Charles II "to acknowledge the sins of his Fathers bloody and Idolatrous House".[29]

Nedham returned to this theme on 29 May, reiterating "the blood-guiltinesse of that pernicious House", which descended "from Father to Son, for divers generations". He cited the Royalists' recent murders of republican envoys to Spain and Holland, killings that proved the pretender Charles a true "Heir apparent of that Blood and vengeance". Since Charles was "guilty of Blood, let all the world (but especially the Scots themselves, be Iudges), whether we had not farre more cause to reject him than they have to receive him". Later Nedham took a new tack. He responded to "their designe in endeavouring to force a Brat of their own upon us" by listing the "late line of Succession, which indeed was made up of nothing else but successive usurpations, cruelty and Tyranny".[30]

In mid-July 1651, Cromwell launched an amphibious attack across the Forth, and Charles marched into England. The day after the Scots army crossed the border, the best-selling political astrologer and parliamentary pensioner William Lilly published several old prophecies that spoke to the Scottish crisis, together with "Passages upon the Life and Death of the late King Charles", who was "not the Worst, but the most unfortunate of Kings". Although self-consciously moderate, Lilly fully supported the new regime, mocking the "foolish Citizens" who went "a whoring" after Charles I's image "set up in the old Exchange", and praising "the learned Milton" for demolishing *Eikon Basilike*. Lilly took it as a given, "evidently proved before a Committee" of Parliament, "that King James was really and absolutely poisoned by a Plaster, applied by Buckinghams Mother unto King James his stomack". But he was cautious about the identities of the other alleged murderers; "Whether Buckingham himselfe, or the late King, was guilty either in the knowledge of, or application of the Plaster, I could never learne". Nevertheless, "many feared the King did know of it", because Charles had ended the session to stop Buckingham being "questioned concerning King James death" and had given "Buckingham his hand to kisse" when the impeachment articles were brought up. "Even the most sober of his friends", Lilly noted:

> held him very much overseen to deny a Parlament justice in any matter whatsoever, but in matter of poyson, and the party poysoned being his Father . . . to prohibit a due course or a legall proceeding against the party suspected . . . was to deny Justice with a refractory hand.

"There is no pen, how able soever", Lilly concluded, "can take off the blemish that will ever hang on him, for falling out with his Parliament, because they questioned, how and by what meanes his Father came to his death." Whatever his motivations, the former king would be forever "suspected guilty".[31]

Cromwell's defeat of Charles's Scottish army at Worcester in early September 1651 was accompanied by yet another major polemic against the Stuart dynasty, this one endorsed by Nedham's newsbook and eventually running to three editions. Like Nedham, the author of *The Life and Reigne of King Charls; or the Pseudo-Martyr Discovered* made much of the Stuart family curse. A delayed response to *Eikon Basilike*, written by an anonymous official who had once been the king's "poor Servant", *The Life and Reigne* enumerated England's tyrannical rulers while invoking the Scots' tradition of resisting "perverse and intractable" kings. James I was just another high-handed monarch in the Scottish mode. His abuse of justice was vividly displayed when he harshly punished "the accessaries in Sir Tho. Overburies case" while granting royal mercy to their aristocratic paymasters. He was also "the onely occasion of all the after Wars throughout Germany" and had been the "utter undoing of his Son in Law the Count Palatyne". Charles I had proved "no ill scholler in putting in practice his Fathers precepts for the better invading of the libertyes of the Subjects".[32]

The Life and Reigne offered no firm opinion on whether James had been murdered, although it strongly hinted that Buckingham was responsible. But Charles was clearly guilty of the cover-up. When the Commons charged the duke with James's death, Charles offered to "be a witnesse to clear the Duke in evry particular". Then "in terrour to the lower House", he arrested Sir Dudley Digges and Sir John Eliot, and "notwithstanding the House of Commons having the proofes and examinations in preparation against the Duke, the King to make all sure, and in arrest of further proceedings against his chief privado", dissolved the session. Charles was a "most unhappy Prince, who in affront and despight of the Iustice of a Court of Parliament, would not suffer his own Fathers death to be called to accompt, or any further examination thereof to be taken for clearing the Duke". Yet neither the murderous duke nor the blood-guilty tyrant escaped justice, for God "will in his own good time bring to light, and to Iudgment, that crying sinne of Blood". The stunning evidence of God's providential wrath was manifest: Buckingham had been killed "by the stab of a knife", while Charles had ended "his dayes at his own Gates, by the axe of Gods just judgment". In *The Life and Reigne* the possible murder of James I did not simply legitimize the regicide; the regicide could be read as a providential punishment for James's murder (or its cover-up), an act of God responding to the "crying sinne of Blood".[33]

A final variation on the secret history was written in the late summer of 1651, as Charles II marched from Scotland to Worcester, although it was not printed until the following year. Milton's nephew, John Phillips, was intervening in the still-simmering Salmasius controversy, responding to the attack on the poet's book by John Rowland, the exiled Royalist polemicist. Rowland had justified Charles's protection of Buckingham in 1626, and his logic made Phillips ask:

> Are you really a butcher? Do you suppose the king has sufficient excuse
> because he considered the Duke his familiar, his closest friend—a man who

had been arraigned by the Supreme Council of the kingdom for poisoning the king's own father? What more frightful accusation could you have made against the king?

Phillips was equally dismissive of Rowland's attempt to play down the tensions between James and Buckingham in 1624–25: "Everyone knows that the conduct of Buckingham at length became gravely displeasing to James", and that this alienation caused Buckingham to embark on "two capital actions—to contrive the death of the father, and to bamboozle the son by ingratiating himself with every conceivable effort".[34]

Triggered by the Scots' alliance with Charles I's son, the republican polemics of 1650–51 were remarkably wide-ranging and sophisticated. They repeatedly and luridly described the blood guilt and providential curse afflicting Charles I and his family, and in learned Latin texts, weekly newsbooks, polemical tracts, astrological musings and scandalous histories, they addressed an unusually broad English, Scottish and continental public. The campaign added James to a list of murder victims that included Lord Darnley, David Riccio, the Earl of Gowrie, Prince Henry and Sir Thomas Overbury, and the message was clear: the history of the Stuart dynasty was written in blood, and God had imposed a providential judgement on its crimes. Back in January 1651, as Cromwell wondered how to get an army across the Firth of Forth, an intelligence agent had urged that great student of God's providences to take heart, for "Certainly God hath cursed that kingly race".[35] Retelling the secret history may not have weakened the Covenanters' support for Charles II, but it helped legitimate and strengthen the revolutionary cause in England.

History and Anatomy

Arthur Wilson spent much of his life among aristocrats alienated from the early Stuart court. He had accompanied the Earl of Essex to the Palatinate and Cadiz in the 1620s, and he underwent his religious awakening in the Puritan household of the Earl of Warwick during the 1630s. At Oxford he debated Laudian scholars, advocated "a naturall and just freedom for the subject", and bemoaned churchmen who made "themselves great by advancing the king". Appalled by the "giddy multitude" rioting against Catholic gentry in the Stour Valley in 1642, Wilson nonetheless worked with Warwick to frustrate the Royalists in Essex.[36] At some point in the 1640s he began writing a history. Taking Tacitus as his model, Wilson announced that he would write fearlessly, but "without the passions of Love or Hate", vowing to "shape my Course in the middle betwixt both". His subject was the reign of James I, analyzed "without prejudice to his Person, or Envy to his Dignity". Wilson's historical method paralleled the medical techniques he had studied at Oxford. "Histories are like

Anatomies", Wilson wrote. With a "gentle hand" guided by "Authority and Knowledge", the historian could examine "the waies and passages of the Body ... where Diseases have bred" and apply "fitting Remedies for prevention of such Evils". By anatomizing the early Stuart past, he could diagnose the ailments that had brought a sickly body politic to its knees.[37]

Where Weldon's book was scandalous and anecdotal, Wilson's *History of Great Britain*, published posthumously in 1653, was sober and detailed (Fig. 86). His anatomy identified the origins of various distempers that had sickened the Caroline polity, exploring the cause and effects of the parliamentary quarrels of the 1620s, and Buckingham's support for "popery".[38] He also stressed the damage wrought by James's personal failings. The king's tendency to anger, for instance, led him into "Prophaness" and an amoral cunning that became the "super intendent of all his Actions; which ... often makes those that know well, to do ill". Some compared James to Tiberius "for Dissimulation", and critics soon took every opportunity to libel him, a phenomenon that Wilson regarded as a dangerous symptom of political distemper. The long Jacobean peace had encouraged poetry, which "swelled to that bulk in his

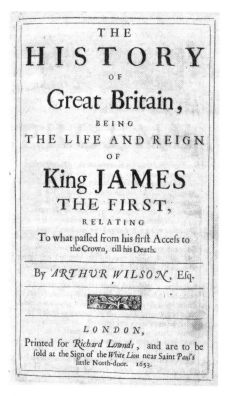

Figure 86: Title page of Arthur Wilson's posthumously published 1653 *The History of Great Britain* (Huntington Library).

time, that it begot strange Monstrous Satyrs, against the King['s] own person, that haunted both Court, and Country".[39]

Wilson knew these "Satyrs", and he clearly knew *The Forerunner of Revenge*, some of which he dismissed. Buckingham had not poisoned the Earl of Southampton and his son: rather "burning feavers", then rampant, had claimed the son, while the father "dyed of a Lethargy" shortly thereafter. And Wilson also appeared to attribute the Duke of Lennox's death to natural causes. But he strongly endorsed Eglisham's account of Hamilton's demise: the marquis was "suspected to be poisoned", and his post-mortem symptoms were "very Presumptious". Wilson adopted Eglisham's description of the quarrel between Hamilton and Buckingham, the marquis's swollen, blistered corpse, and the attempt to "huddle up" the post-mortem inspection, all of which encouraged "tumourous Discourses, which reflected much upon the Duke". But of the king's physicians, "onely Doctor Eglisham a Scotchman" dared speak out, and the scandals "never broke out in this Kings time, being bound up close (as it was thought) more by the Dukes power, than his Innocency".[40]

James's death fascinated Wilson; indeed, he narrated it twice. At first, he offered a terse verdict citing natural causes. Fear, stubbornness, poor diet, the "continual use of sweet wines", and the burdens of rule had all "set the gross Humors awork"; the resulting tertian ague, usually harmless, had turned into "a Feaver ... too violent for him". But when Wilson returned to James's death a second time, he identified an array of suspicious circumstances. He was uncertain whether the king had been given something "that extorted his Aguish Fits into a Feaver" and hastened his end. But clearly Buckingham and his mother, a woman "whose Fame had no great favour", had much to explain. No one disputed that they had administered a plaster and a potion during the doctors' absence. The king had "complained of" the drugs, and indeed they "did rather exasperate his Distemper than allay it". Understandably, "some of the King's Physicians mutter'd against it, others made a great noise, and were forced to fly for it". For Wilson, the contents of the medicines were irrelevant—the very act of applying them without medical approval was "Daring". Unlike most other post-regicidal narratives, Wilson did note Buckingham's dealings with Dr Remington, but he observed that there was nothing to prove that the medicines given to James were the same ones Remington had prescribed. Wilson also offered additional circumstantial evidence against the duke. Buckingham had used "insinuating perswasions" to convince James to accept the unorthodox remedies, and both mother and son were notorious for their dealings with "Montebancks". John Lambe, the convicted witch and rapist, "was much imployed by the Mother, and the Son", who also "much confided" in Piers Butler, another specialist in "Distillations" and strange "extracting practices". While never explicitly claiming that Butler had supplied Buckingham with poison, Wilson nonetheless reported the story that Buckingham had arranged for Butler's murder in a Jesuit "Room of

Death" where "the floar that hung upon great hinges on one side, was let fall by Artificall Engins, and the poor Vermin Butler, dropt into a Precipice". Wilson thought this account of Butler's murder "(if it be true) . . . one great evidence of some secret Machination betwixt the Duke and him". Why else, Wilson implied, would Buckingham have Butler silenced? For all its caution, Wilson's emphasis on the favourite's ties to Lambe and Butler revived Eglisham's powerful linkage between courtly poisoning and demonic witchcraft.[41]

Wilson also entertained a version of Eglisham's account of Buckingham's motives for killing James. He thought the Spanish envoy Hinojosa's accusations against the duke in 1624 not far from the truth; there was "cause to suspect, that the great intimacy, and Dearness, betwixt the Prince and Duke (like the conjunction of two dreadful planets) could not but portend the production of some very dangerous effect to the old King". Again echoing Eglisham, Wilson speculated that Buckingham might finally have killed James because he was afraid that "the King being now weary of his too much greatness, and power, would set up Bristoll his deadly enemy against him". Wilson also stressed the importance of the failed 1626 impeachment. Although the "Dukes power" had silenced the doctors who "muttered" against him, Parliament was harder to cow. Since the Parliament-men would never have acted "upon false Rumor, or bare Suggestions", the charges had to be taken seriously, and thus "it will be a hard task for any man to excuse the King his Successor, for dissolving that Parliament, to preserve one that was accused by them for poisoning his Father".[42]

O Ye Princes of Europe

Charles I's execution in January 1649 unleashed a wave of radical speculation and millenarian exultation in which the secret history also loomed large. Weldon's success encouraged others to rake over the Jacobean past, and by the summer of 1652 an unknown writer, possibly Marchamont Nedham, had reworked elements of Weldon's *Court and Character* into the more brazenly republican *A Cat May look upon a King*.[43] Playing on the radical claim that native English freedoms had been lost under the Norman Yoke, the pamphlet catalogued the "blood, oppression, and injustice" of every king since the Conquest. Not even the greatest monarchs escaped the *Cat*'s rough tongue. Henry V was interested only in "wars, raising of monies and spending the blood of this poor Nation"; and Henry VIII "never spared man in his anger, nor woman in his lust". Equally bad were the "honourable, Noble, and right Worshipfull Families . . . which have been maintained by the blood and treasure of this oppressed Nation". This unabashedly radical history was designed explicitly for "the Common people" who were too busy to wade through the chronicles, and so "this little Book" taught them "for whom and for what they fight, and pay".[44] The *Cat* presented James I as the "fountain of all our late

Afflictions", and "as great a Tyrant as any of the rest". Summarizing Weldon's account of James's murder, the *Cat* described how Buckingham, after realizing that James, "not withstanding his slabbering expressions of affection", had grown tired of him, "made him amends for all his favours" with a "Plaister and a Powder": "King-craft" had "met with his match". The tract was less certain about Charles's complicity: "How far King Charles might be privy to this busines, I determine not; but the private familiarity between them, continued so long after, and protecting him from being questioned for this very particular in Parliament, is no small presumption". Again following Weldon, the tract noted that God, and Buckingham's assassin John Felton, eventually delivered the justice that Charles had denied.[45]

But the regicide was only the latest of God's judgements upon the House of Stuart. Recycling the trope of the cursed Stuart dynasty, *A Cat* listed all the signs of the Stuarts' providential doom, beginning with the murder of James's father and the execution of his mother, and culminating in the regicide and the exile of Charles I's two sons. Again, poison allegations were central: James's "eldest son Pr. Henry, by the jealousie, and consent of his Father, in the flower of his youth and strength of his age, is poysoned". So too was James, "by the act of his Favourite Buckingham" and, *A Cat* concluded, finally abandoning its earlier caution, by "the consent of his son Charles". The book then urged its readers to "lay all these things together, the lives of all our former Kings, and the lamentable condition of this Nation under these two last; and tell me if it were not high time to consider of the honour, welfare and security of this Nation, by reducing it to a Free-State".[46]

A Cat's use of James's murder for radical republican purposes was striking. But an even more baroque reworking of the secret history appeared in April 1652. *The Divine Catastrophe of the Kingly Family of the House of Stuarts, or a Short History of the Rise, Reign and Ruins Thereof* was, its author admitted, more "a Rhapsody, then a continued History". Nevertheless it revealed "the most secret and Chamber-abominations of the two last Kings", and used these crimes to vindicate the regicide and the abolition of monarchy. This republican rhapsody was the work of Sir Edward Peyton, a Cambridgeshire baronet who was nearly seventy when Giles Calvert, who had earlier issued John Cook's *King Charls His Case*, printed the *Divine Catastrophe*. Peyton, a Parliament-man from 1621 to 1626, had little direct contact with Whitehall. Early in 1621 he lost an important local office to a Buckingham protégé, an incident that no doubt prompted him to join the parliamentary attack on monopolies that ensnared both Buckingham and Eglisham. But most of Peyton's time in Westminster was spent pursuing religious reform, backing bills to regulate the Sabbath, repress Catholics and police sexual irregularity. By the mid-1630s, heavily indebted, Peyton had lost his local offices, and with the coming of civil war his more turbulent tendencies found free rein. In 1642 he refused to kneel when receiving communion, insisting that the Second Commandment banned "bowing to Creatures, Sun, moon, Starrs, Men, Beasts, Vegatables, Mineralls, etc", and then quickly set out his case in print. That same year Attorney General Sir Robert Heath deemed Peyton's draft tract on Charles's attempted arrest of the Five Members so outrageous that he was condemned to death *in absentia*. Early in the Civil War, Peyton rallied to Parliament, and in 1642 at the age of fifty-eight led an infantry company at Edgehill.[47]

A man of Peyton's convictions was not a natural courtier, but he had tried at least once to find favour. In 1633, anxious for a patron to fend off his creditors, Peyton presented the young Duke of Lennox with a moralistic treatise on "Court & Courtiers". The shadow of the now-dead Buckingham loomed over his discussion, but Peyton did not criticize the murdered favourite. Instead he suggested that favouritism and virtue were perfectly compatible, for recent "illustrious Starres" like Cardinal Richelieu, the Conde de Olivares and Buckingham had enhanced their "naturall indowmentes" with "a sage discretion, and a discreete wisdome". Of course, courtiers had to guard against "unsatiable devouring, and swallowing of humane things", and avoid "the deepe mine of magicke art . . . Poisons, Philtres, Inchantments the better to marrie with Fortune". But "since the begining of Queen Elizabeths raigne, till this moment", Peyton affirmed, no such "artifices" had been practised in England, and no "such court Cometts . . . appeared in our Horrizon".[48]

Lennox resisted Peyton's overtures, and in the wake of revolution Peyton radically revised his assessment of the early Stuart court's morality. *The Divine Catastrophe* presented what Peyton termed "a little Enchiridion [handbook] of divers remarkable events" that would "prove Gods just revenging hand on the Family of the Kingly Stuarts of Scotland" for their "heavie weight of sin". He admitted his work "will incur the displeasure and hatred of most in this State", but he invoked "a higher power" to show that "the Almighty hand of God hath determined the extirpation of the Royal Stock of the Stuarts, for murthering one of another, for their prophane Government, and wanton Lasciviousness of those Imps ingrafted in that Stock".[49] His narrative jumped wildly across the decades, weaving scandalous narrative threads into a startling portrait of the early Stuart court that proved the Stuarts were tyrants with "unsatiable desires" for power whose outrageous behaviour had brought God's judgement down upon monarchy itself.

Peyton insisted that the Stuarts' appetite for sexual perversity, homicide, popery and poison had cursed the dynasty. Mary, Queen of Scots had been an "apt Scholar" in the French court's "School of Venus" and had returned to Scotland eager for sexual variety, taking and then murdering a succession of lovers. From her lustful womb emerged James VI and I, "a Spiny and thin Creature", unmanned by his mother's sins. Unsurprisingly, this weakling was overmatched by his own lustful queen, whose sexual adventures, little dreamt of by even the wildest early Stuart libellers, cast doubt on the legitimacy of James's children. "Lord Saintcleare, then Ambassadour in Denmark", fathered Prince Henry, while "one Mr. Beely a Dane" confessed that "he was naturall Father to King Charls". Queen Anne had sexually corrupted Henry, initiating him into the "Court of Cupid" by locking him in a room with "a beautiful young Lady now dead", thus behaving "more like a Bawd than a discreet Mother". But Anne suffered a fitting end, killed by the "rotted" skeleton of a child, long-since destroyed by "Physick", that had festered in her womb.[50]

The king's own sexual transgressions had also angered God. "For comple-ment", James continued to visit Anne, but he "never lodged with her a night for many yeers" because, Peyton claimed, he was "more addicted to love males then females". The king's unnatural passions created dangerous intimacies with those who shared his secret; the Spanish ambassador Gondomar, having perceived "how king Iames was addicted", often joked with the king about "back-door" passageways. James's desires also led to the rise of minions who ruled "in the person of the king". Robert Carr, a man so unfit for "wise counsel" that his library contained only "twenty Play-books and wanton Romances", had "defiled his hands" by poisoning Sir Thomas Overbury. But far worse was George Villiers, whom James "would tumble and kiss as a Mistress". Peyton's Buckingham was a Machiavellian plotter with an insatiable appetite for power and flesh. Having prostituted himself to the king, Buckingham used his new influence to procure a steady stream of "gentile and noble virgins". And "to please this favorite", James became his pimp. Buckingham's lusts had catastrophic consequences: his pursuit of Louis XIII's queen, for instance, resulted in the disastrous war with France.[51]

This immorality made "strictness of life" a cause for disgrace, Peyton continued. As the court became "addicted more to pleasure and delights", goodness began to hide and "vice to spread far and neer", with the most "vitious" now "being counted the gallantest men". The debauchery spilled into Charles's reign, and for all his public show of virtue, the new king proved no better than his parents. Charles became famous for "his lubricity with divers Ladies", while his queen Henrietta Maria pursued her own affairs, including one with Buckingham.[52] For Peyton, sexual excess and tyranny went together. James "plotted the ruine of Parliaments" to avenge his mother's execution, and on his deathbed he presented Charles with a last testament advising him "with an inconsiderate fury . . . to settle to himself and his successors an unbridled power of dominion". Charles subsequently enslaved his kingdoms under arbi-trary rule, imposing "ungodly burdens" and "Unlawful Taxes", and plotting to betray England to Rome, for "it is probable King Charles was in his heart a Papist". Fortunately God had delivered the kingdom by raising "Heroes within the doors of the Representative, and without, to awaken the people from a dead sleep". Despite the loss of martyrs like Sir John Eliot, Parliament had eventually defeated and executed the tyrannical and lustful king.[53]

Peyton had seen Eliot at work. In 1626 he had watched Eliot's committee question the royal physicians, and although the Parliament-men were supposed to let the committee's members do the talking, Peyton had intervened; after one witness referred to "frog's flesh", he had reminded him that the flesh in question was a toad's. Peyton had thus long brooded on James's death, and the *Divine Catastrophe* vividly rehearsed Eglisham's accusations. James's murder stemmed from the favourite's unquenchable thirst for power. Once atop the "mount of glory", Buckingham became as bestial as "a ravenous kyte" and quickly "ingrossed all into his hands, to inrich and advance his kindred, and to place and displace whom he listed". In the process he made the king his abject subject. When the gout-ridden James, whom Buckingham dragged from one hunting lodge to the next, tried to reassert his authority, the duke struck back. Like the Catholic Eglisham, the fervently anti-Catholic Peyton argued that the final confrontation came over the Spanish match, when James tried to use the Earl of Bristol to check Buckingham's power. But the duke "perceived the plot" and, using his newly won influence with Charles, he countered James's gambit. Triumphant, Buckingham sat "as a Gyant on the shoulders of king Iames", and his dream of becoming king of Ireland "made the Duke swell like a Toad, to such a monstrous proportion of greatness in vast thoughts, as multiplying to an ocean, from the rivers of pride, power, and ambition". Peyton's image of a bloated toad resonated with his description of the favourite's most horrifying crime: eventually, Buckingham "rewarded the king with poyson, by a poys-oning water, and a plaister made of the Oyle of Toads".[54]

Peyton believed that Buckingham had also poisoned Lennox, Hamilton, and Southampton and his son, and he cited "Doctor Eglestons relation" as proof. Like John Aston in *Strange Apparitions*, Peyton also asserted that Buckingham had arranged for Eglisham to be "killed in forraine parts, for discovering the villany", a fate that further guaranteed his credibility. But Peyton did not rely on Eglisham for his claim that Buckingham, "filled with the venome of greatness", had sent "his Master packing to another world". He depended instead on "the witnes of divers Physitians, especially Doctor Ramsey, in full hearing at a Committee" in 1626. Charles's failure to prosecute Buckingham for these murders raised crippling doubts about the new king:

> King Charles, to save the Duke, dissolved the Parliament, and never after had the truth tryed, to clear himself from confederacy, or the Duke from so hainous a scandal. Now let all the world judge of Charles his carriage, whether he were not guilty of conniving at so foul a sin, though not of the death.

Peyton had little doubt about Charles's guilt, and the king's subsequent misrule had proved him "like Nero the Tyrant", that most poisonous of emperors.[55]

Peyton understood James's murder as part of the divine catastrophe visited on the Stuarts for their egregious violations of God's laws. After all, James had ordered the murder of his own son, Henry, "by some Pill or other", and the evidence of the prince's poisoning was "plainly-shewed", Peyton insisted, when Henry "was cut up to be imbalmed", exposing a "liver-hued and putrefied brain". The condition of the whole corpse was a clear "argument of poison".[56]

Adultery and sodomy, popery and poison, sin and tyranny, a nation stripped of its morals and debauched—this was the Stuarts' legacy and the cause of the "fatal Catastrophe", the revolution that had turned "the spoakes of the Wheel upside down, raising the humble out of the dust, and abasing the proud and high-minded". The Stuarts' crimes both explained and justified the civil wars, the regicide and the Commonwealth. Their sins had released the people from obedience, for "When kings cease to imitate God, they cease to Govern or be Governors". The regicide had executed not a lawful monarch but "a mortal enemy" to the commonwealth who "had his hands in the blood of hundred thousands". Consequently, "the cup of Gods vengeance was filled to the brim, for king Charles his family to drink the dregs". The end of the Stuarts was also the end of the monarchy that had disfigured England from the time of William the Conqueror. The Free State dedicated to the advance of "the Kingdom of Jesus Christ thorow the Universe" would have no more reckless favourites and political poisonings. And England's monarchy was only the first to fall; like other radicals, Peyton hoped to work with God to "bring down the Mountain of Monarchy, which had continued more then five hundred yeers". The recent events in England served as "a Symptome and Harbinger for France, Spaine, Germany, Turkey and Papacy, to change from an unbridled power, to an Aristocratical, or Plebian way of rule". In this new world England would be "the elder brother" to other revolutionary regimes. In a remarkable final passage Peyton directly addressed Europe's remaining monarchs: "O Ye Princes of Europe, that persecute inferiours by Tyranny and oppression, look on the works of God since the creation and you shall see plainly the great Creator will dismount your glory and pride."[57]

No other post-regicidal writing could match the intensity of Peyton's millenarian reflections on the secret histories of the early Stuart age. But the *Divine Catastrophe* was part of a broader shift. By the early 1650s the political meanings of Eglisham's secret history had been utterly transformed. The Catholic physician and Stuart loyalist had told a story that the godly revolutionaries now transformed into a providentialist account of the fall of the Stuart dynasty, an account that equated monarchy with tyranny and debauchery; justified resistance, regicide and republican revolution; and helped sustain the military struggle to save that revolution from its monarchical enemies. George Eglisham had given the English Republic a usable past.

Most Mischievous and Derogatory Defamations

The Scottish crisis of 1650–51 had posed an existential threat to the new Republic, and the many writers who rallied to its defence—Nedham, Parker, Hall, Milton, Phillips, Lilly, Weldon, Wilson and Peyton—all offered variations on Eglisham's allegations. In stark contrast to 1648–49, this extraordinary outpouring met with near total silence from the Royalists. Individual Royalists were dismayed by these republican secret histories. George Thomason was so upset by *The Life and Reigne of King Charls* that he amended the title page with his pen, striking through *Pseudo* to change the subtitle to "*the Martyr Discovered*" and adding that the author was "a Rebellious Rogue". Meanwhile the exiled Secretary of State, Sir Edward Nicholas, may have had Anthony Weldon or Balthazar Gerbier in mind when he lamented that "the most mischievous and derogatory Defamations that were spread of the King's blessed father and his Councils were raised and abetted in his own Household and Court". These defamations passed mostly unchallenged not because the Royalists had nothing to say, but because the republican regime had tightened control over printing. During years when even loyal radicals like Robert Ibbitson fell afoul of the censors, Royalists had fewer opportunities than ever to mount sustained publicity campaigns.[58]

There were a few exceptions to this pattern of silence and repression. In 1651, Joseph Jane replied to Milton's *Eikonoklastes,* and by implication to his more recent attack on Salmasius, by insisting that the poet should consult "the publicke Records of the Kingdome" showing that Parliament never accused Buckingham of "poysoning the deceased King". Rendered "madd" by the "venome of Treason", Milton had wilfully confused "a fact of presumption and of dangerous consequence" with "a poysoning". The same year a Dutch publisher issued *Reliquiae Sacrae Carolinae*, a large collection of the late king's writings, reprinting the shorter of Edward Hyde's two 1648 pamphlets against the *Declaration*.[59]

The burgeoning sales of Weldon's *Court and Character* also provoked an anonymous reply from William Sanderson, writing under the scoffing title of *Aulicus Coquinariae*.[60] *Aulicus* offered readers yet another version of the Royalist response to the 1648 *Declaration*. James had died of natural causes. The king's well-known "Impatience" and "utter Enmity to any Physick" meant that he had been reluctant to follow a regular cure, and he had turned to the "advice" of friends for "Prescriptions as have been helpfull unto others". The plaster used on the king, Sanderson stressed, was made of "harmless" ingredients, and had worked on other patients. Admittedly, it had been applied in the doctors' absence, but they "were assured of the Composition", and at least two of them were still alive "to clear that calumny". In the end, James's ageing body simply could not resist a distemper that might not have proved "Pestilentiall" to "another Constitution". While the 1626 Parliament had investigated the case, they had only accused Buckingham of "a Boldness unpardonable", and in the charge presented to the Lords his actions were "not urg'd as poysonous, but only criminous". Finally, Sanderson dismissed Weldon's vivid story of Buckingham's verbal and physical confrontation with an "honest servant". Why, he asked, had Weldon not named the man in question? And how could Weldon have known what the dying king was thinking as he witnessed the struggle?[61] Sanderson earned a rebuke from the author of *The Life and Reigne of King Charls*, who warned readers "not to value that late impartiall and flattering Author, Aulicus Coquinarie" or anyone else who "palpably and ridiculously" tried to turn James into "the only Platonicall, Peaceable and pious King of his time".[62]

Another Royalist response, published in French and printed at The Hague, appeared in 1653 from the pen of Balthazar Gerbier.[63] Presumably wounded by his alleged role in the *None-such Charles*, Gerbier hoped to confirm his commitment to the king's cause. Five years earlier, following the 1648 *Declaration*, Gerbier had compiled, first in French and then in English, an extended refutation of the charges against the Stuart kings and presented his work in manuscript to the queen, the prince and other Royalist leaders. After rehearsing the usual Royalist arguments against Eglisham, Gerbier, as we have seen, had added a striking new detail: Eglisham's offer to recant the "black Calomnie" he had cast upon the English court.[64] In 1653, Gerbier put that claim into print, and in his defence of James and Charles I he took particular aim at the *"libellistes"* Weldon and Peyton. Gerbier discussed many of the widespread charges about Jacobean and Caroline foreign policy that had appeared in the *None-such Charles*. But he lingered on the supposed *"empoisonnement"* of James and his courtiers and on the *"Libelle diffamatoire"* of the Scotsman Eglisham, a so-called physician (*"soy disant Docteur en Medicine"*), copies of whose work could still be found in Europe's most renowned "Cabinets" and libraries. He fleshed out his story of Eglisham's recantation; the doctor had confessed that Buckingham's enemies had bribed him to say that the plaster given to James had "hastened his end" (*avoit hasté sa fin*). In 1648, Gerbier had suggested that his report to London on Eglisham's offer had been ignored because everyone knew the libeller was a "foulle ditractor"; in 1653 he suggested that the report had been deliberately suppressed. His embellished account of Eglisham's pathetic death in the streets of Liège refuted the manifest falsehood peddled by Peyton and others that Charles had arranged Eglisham's murder. As he had in 1648, Gerbier pointed out that the 1626 Parliament had failed to find any evidence of poisoning and had charged Buckingham only with a presumption in treating the king without medical consent. James's doctors, perhaps uneasy about their own failings, had started the muttering about Buckingham's plaster, but it had been a cabal of English and Scottish courtiers intent on destroying Buckingham and replacing him with a rival favourite who had turned the physicians' annoyance into the stuff of secret history. In 1648, Gerbier had invoked Buckingham's sweet nature as evidence that he would never have poisoned James; this time he argued that Buckingham had every reason to prolong the old king's life since he could not know whether Charles would favour him as James had done.[65]

For the moment, Gerbier's Eglisham revelations were confined to a coterie scribal publication and a French treatise printed in Holland. By the early 1650s the partisans of the secret history, backed by an impressive propaganda and censorship regime, had apparently driven their opponents out of the anglophone public sphere and, in doing so, had established the makings of a usable past that would help legitimate the regicide and the Republic. Intriguing evidence points to at least some official and semi-official coordination in this project. John Milton and Marchamont Nedham were close friends, and both worked for the Republic. John Hall was their protégé, and John Phillips was Milton's nephew.[66] William Lilly received a pension from Parliament, and Gerbier, if he indeed contributed willingly to the None-such Charles, desperately wanted one. Robert Ibbitson, who helped craft the None-such Charles and edited Weldon's manuscript history, had good enough connections with the regime that his newsbook survived strict crackdowns on the genre. In 1653, Giles Calvert, who had published Peyton and John Cook, was a finalist (like Ibbotson) for the position of the Council of State's official printer. The Royalists certainly assumed that these projects had been coordinated. Even Arthur Wilson's sober history, which left out some of the secret history's more inflammatory mutations, was not above their suspicion. Sanderson thought Wilson's book had been compiled by a "parent Presbyter" working from "bare Collections of Old", with "Wilsons Name, set to the Sale" after his death.[67] But whatever the level of coordination, this steady outpouring of prose, all of it broadcasting the providential curse of the Stuarts, saturated the political print culture of the day. Yet this period of polemical dominance was to prove only a brief respite in the war over James I's death. At least one Royalist historian was preparing to bring Gerbier's reports on Eglisham's recantation to a much wider English audience.

CHAPTER TWENTY-THREE

WORSE THAN RAVAILLAC

EXORCIZING EGLISHAM AND THE KING-KILLERS,

1655–63

CONVICTED TRAITORS FACED horrific deaths. Hanged until almost, but not quite, dead and then cut down, the condemned man supposedly remained conscious while he was castrated, eviscerated, and forced to watch his entrails burned before his eyes. The remorseless violence only ended after the executioner beheaded the corpse and quartered the mangled remains, which were then left to rot in prominent locations around the metropolis. While most thought this spectacular punishment fit the crime, James Parry was not convinced, and in 1661 he reminded the Lord Chancellor of the fate of François Ravaillac, who had assassinated Henri IV in 1610. As the French judges pondered an appropriate punishment, some contemporaries proposed to flay him, some to impale him, and yet others thought he should be cut in half and "his bowells . . . clap'd on a hot iron plank, which should preserve the other half of the body, and the noble parts in pangs of agonie a long while". In the end, the French opted for a comparatively swift punishment. First, the hand used to stab the king was pierced by the murder weapon and burned in a fire of sulphur. Next, Ravaillac's legs were thrust into leggings full of hot oil while hot pincers ripped open his calves, thighs and chest, which were then to be filled with "boyling lead, burning rozin and wax melted with sulpher". All the while, cordials kept him conscious. Finally, four horses pulled him apart, and his body was to be "burnt and reduc'd to cinders . . . to make an utter extinction of him in this world". This, thought Parry, was how king-killers should die. Ravaillac's royal victim had died quickly, but the English regicides had tormented their victim with months of captivity before brazenly executing him in public, and then hiring "scurrilous Pamphleteers to bespatter him". Yet although "the English Murthers were far more abominable, yet their punishment was much more easie and short"—a mere quarter-hour of agony. To Parry, this did not seem just, for these men had far "exceeded Ravaillac in a hellish kind of impudence".[1]

When Oliver Cromwell died in September 1658, he governed an exceptionally powerful state, one capable of projecting English military power across the Continent and the Atlantic. Indeed, Cromwell's soldiers had recently taken Dunkirk, that nest of Flemish privateers who had long terrified English coastal towns, and agitated the Parliament-men of 1626. These remarkable military achievements could not, however, hide the underlying political instability of the Protectorate. After Cromwell's death, without the old soldier's charisma to hold them together, the governing coalition of religious radicals, army militants, mistrustful republicans and pragmatic conservatives quickly unravelled. The new Protector, Richard Cromwell, was powerless to save what his father had built. Unruly elements in the Army stationed in and around London first demanded the dissolution of the Protectorate Parliament and then, rather improbably, welcomed back the forty or so survivors of the Rump Parliament that Oliver Cromwell had dismissed in April 1653. Unsurprisingly, the Army and the Rump soon quarrelled, and on 1 January 1660, appalled at the chaos, General George Monck and 8,000 troops stationed in Scotland began marching on London. Initially, Monck's political intentions remained veiled. At first, on Parliament's instructions, he sought to restore order in the City, which had turned against both Parliament and Army. But then Monck abruptly reversed Pride's Purge, using his troops to escort the secluded Parliament-men of December 1648 back into the House of Commons. The returned members, who now represented a majority in the House, quickly called a new parliamentary election, the first since 1640, and began negotiating for the restoration of Charles II, who finally entered London amid riotous festivities on 29 May 1660. It would not be long before the men who had killed Charles I and blackened his name would face their day of reckoning.

By the time Monck headed for London, the secret history's place in the contemporary political imagination had already begun to shift. As the revolution stabilized under Oliver Cromwell, it no longer seemed quite so important to legitimate the regicide and the Republic. Indeed, as the Protectorate incorporated men of a more conservative bent—and as some kind of accommodation with Charles's son seemed possible—repeating stories about the murderous former king may have seemed increasingly counter-productive. In the crisis following Cromwell's death, contentious tracts again poured from the presses, and they again alluded to the secret history, albeit to a lesser degree. By that point, Royalist writers had finally seized back some of the initiative in the battle over James I's death. Within months of Charles II's restoration, some of the men who had engineered the regicide and made James's murder a political shibboleth would be punished for their actions, and the secret history returned to the underground. The regicides' deaths might not have satisfied James Parry, but they did bring the secret history's revolutionary phase to a definitive end, and, after more than three decades, they finally exorcized George Eglisham's ghost.

A Messenger from the Dead

In 1657, Richard Perrinchef, an ejected fellow of Magdalene College, Cambridge, published a solemn dialogue between the ghosts of Henry VIII and Charles I on the horrors of civil war and regicide. Printed in Paris, first in Latin and then in English, as *A Messenger from the Dead*, this exercise in Royalist political piety was quickly hijacked by a satirist who used the "Conference Full of stupendious horrour . . . between the Ghosts of Henry the 8. and Charls the First" to attack the Royalist cause. Perrinchef had bemoaned the indignity of Charles's burial in Henry VIII's tomb at Windsor despite his explicit request to be buried in Westminster Abbey; in the reworked version, Henry objected to the intruder, and when Charles insisted that he too had been a king of England, Henry was incredulous: "What you a King! Did you ever weare a Crown on your head, who have not a head on your shoulders." Where Perrinchef depicted Henry sympathizing with Charles's plight, the satirist had Henry lecturing Charles on his mistakes and "the admirable course and tenour of . . . Divine Justice" on the crimes of kings, which "deserve greater punishment because we commit greater offenses". Henry apologized for his own extensive list of sins, adding "that the measure of my iniquities was compleated in you my successor, and the divine vengeance did mark you out for destruction". Eventually, Charles acknowledged the justice of "the Judgments of God". But there remained the matter of Charles's head, and Henry could not help asking how he had lost it. His reign, Charles confessed, had fallen apart almost immediately, and "a Parliament being called at Oxford I lost the love of my people, for dissolving it at that instant when the Duke of Buckingham was questioned for having a hand in my Fathers Death". In retrospect, Charles should have listened to the Parliament-men, but "I was too constant alwayes to my own Counsailes" and instead of working with the Commons decided "to put unusuall taxes upon my people".[2]

Well into the 1650s, then, the version of the secret history established by the 1648 *Declaration* remained a part of anti-Royalist propaganda. Indeed, in January 1658, as the Commons discussed the revival of a second house of Parliament, the regicide Thomas Scot attempted to turn back the conservative tide by once again invoking the republican Good Old Cause and harkening back to the *Declaration*. Ten years earlier he had helped draft the document, and now he reminded his colleagues of "all the incroachments upon our civil and religious liberties" that they had endured in Charles's reign, noting that "you have them reckoned up, all the incroachments of this kind, in a declaration of that Long Parliament". Further, "I cannot but remember", he continued, "what was charged upon the late king, upon the vote of Non-Addresses, his not suffering his father's blood to come to that question."[3]

Although some revolutionaries still invoked the 1648 *Declaration*, it was the Royalists who had the more sustained engagement with the secret history in the mid- and later 1650s as they sought to discredit the regicidal and republican accounts of James's murder in the works of Anthony Weldon and Arthur Wilson. History was "the great Arbitress of Time and Truth", one Royalist noted, "a Tribunal that summons the Dead to Judgement, a Court of Record to the Living". Thus the verdict of Clio, muse of history, could not be left to an "ignorant, and false erroneous Chronicler" who "wrongs the time passed, the time present and the time to come".[4] Several Royalist writers took up the challenge of rewriting the early Stuart past. Thomas Fuller began work on his *Church-History of Britain* during Charles I's reign, but he finished it only after "Monarchy was turned into a State". In 1650, John Hacket, chaplain to the former Lord Keeper, Bishop John Williams, began the monumental biography of his master in part to correct "Welden, Wilson, [and] Payton". In the same year, Weldon's *Court and Character* so angered Godfrey Goodman, the sequestered Bishop of Gloucester, that he wrote a letter of protest to the publisher; in short order, Goodman was busy penning a more systematic reply.[5]

Goodman objected to Weldon's lack of charity, highlighted his repeated misstatements, "some of them so foolish and malicious, that they were fitter for children", and compared him to Ben Jonson's preposterous "Sir Politic Would-be", who constantly spouted "heathenish, foolish, and political observations". Goodman's account of James' death, which assumed his readers already knew the details of the controversy, began with the Earl of Bristol's charges against Buckingham in the 1626 Parliament, the last of which was "then understood" to imply that "the King had not died naturally". Even though Bristol himself had rejected that interpretation of his words, Goodman admitted that unanswered questions surrounded the king's death. James's final illness, he insisted, was due to natural causes. The king "did feed a little more than moderately upon fruits" in the springtime, and the resulting "great looseness", which in his youth "did tend to preserve his health", "did a little weaken his body" now that he was older. The king's "going to Theobalds, to Newmarket, and stirring abroad when as the coldness of the year was not yet past almost", made it almost inevitable he would "fall into a quartan ague". He died, Goodman argued, because of mismatched treatments, with "the physicians taking one course, and [Buckingham's] plaister another". Yet Goodman remained uneasy. Parliament had examined neither the surgeons who conducted the autopsy nor James's Dutch apothecary, and these well-placed medical professionals had told Goodman things that left him "not well persuaded of the death of the King, nor of the Marquis of Hamilton". Nevertheless Goodman did not suspect Buckingham of murder. He had been in the Lords when Buckingham explained "that a woman had a child sick of a quartan ague in the same town, and that she did use the very same plaster to her child, and she recovered". Goodman had also watched "when Buckingham spake of the King", for "he spake with tears in his eyes, expressing much sorrow that he who had been so infinitely beholden to the King for himself, for his kindred, for all his favours, that he should now be questioned for murdering him". That scene had convinced Goodman to forget the unsettling whispers from the surgeons and the apothecary. "Certainly", Goodman noted, "there never lived a better natured man than Buckingham".[6] Although uncertain about James's death, Goodman removed the keystone of the regicidal variant of the secret history: if Buckingham was not guilty of murder, then Charles could not be guilty for protecting him.

Goodman had witnessed some of the events he described, but Bishop Williams had stood by James's sickbed. For Williams's biographer Hacket, James's death was a crucial moment in the Lord Keeper's career. Hacket's polemical intent was clear: James had died of natural causes, but, most importantly, he had died well, thanks to Williams's interventions. Hacket moved quickly past the medical evidence, though he did note the royal physician William Harvey's entirely natural explanation for the king's deterioration. Hacket's greater concern was what Williams had learned of the king's soul. With Charles's approval, Williams had acquainted the dying king "with his Feeble Estate, and like a faithful Chaplain" reminded "him both of his Mortality, and Immortality". Then, as "the principal Instrument of that Holy and necessary Service", Williams had choreographed the king's good death, becoming as he did so not only the Keeper of the Great Seal but also "the Keeper . . . of his Majesties Soul". Retelling the authorized version of James's death, Hacket reconstructed the spiritual dialogue between king and bishop, noting how James "made Answer" to Williams's "Discoursing", responding "with Patience, and full of Heavenly Seasoning". Hoping to be fortified "against the Terrors of Death, with the lively Remembrance of Christ's Death and Passion in the Holy Communion", James "craved Absolution" for his sins and "rendred the Confession of his Faith before many Witnesses" and "Profess'd he Died in the Bosom of the Church of England". As James received the sacrament, "God did lend [the king] such Strength, to utter himself how well he Relish'd that Sacred Banquet of Christ's Body and Blood, and how comfortably the Joy of the Holy Ghost did flow into his Soul, as if he had been in a way of Recovery." At his words, "his mournful Servants . . . rejoiced greatly, that unto that time Sickness did not compress his Understanding, nor stop his Speech, nor Debilitate his Senses." As James rapidly deteriorated, Williams attended to "every Word the King spake in that extream condition", and "at last shut [the king's] Eyes with his own Hand, when his Soul departed". Hacket's version of the king's good death largely conformed to the details that circulated in newsletters in 1625 and that Williams himself had given at James's funeral. But writing in the 1650s, in a new polity repeatedly legitimized by myths of a providential curse against the Stuart dynasty, Hacket's narrative had a sharp Royalist edge that the authorized version had not needed in 1625. Like *Eikon Basilike*, Hacket's retelling of James I's final hours reaffirmed the tattered myths of sacred kingship for a regicidal age.[7]

Neither Hacket's biography nor Goodman's history were printed in the 1650s. Yet other Royalist histories did find their way into the bookshops in spite of tightened press controls. Fuller's *Church-History of Britain*, published in London in 1655 and 1656, argued the case for James I's natural death, adding new variations on what had become the standard Royalist medical narrative. The tertian ague had struck an ageing, "plethorick Body, full of ill humours". Yet while the "malignity" of the illness demanded cure, James's "aversnes to Physick" complicated his treatment. Yet, "above expectation", the king had "contrary to His custome" submitted to his physicians and become "very orderable". Unfortunately, this cooperativeness was not a good sign, for in "such sudden alterations, some apprehend, a certain prognostick of death, as if when mens mindes acquire new qualities, they begin to inhabit and cloath themselves for a new world". Sticking closely to "the naked truth delivered by oath from the Physicians to a select Committee", Fuller acknowledged two unusual medical interventions. First, "the Countesse of Buckingham contracted much suspition to her selfe, and her son, for applying a playster to the Kings wrists, without the consent of His Physicians". Then Mr Baker, "(the Dukes servant) made the King a Julip, which the Duke brought to the King with his own hand, of which the King drank twice, but refused a third time". Fuller conceded that afterwards James grew "worse and worse" and that Archibald Hay, the royal surgeon, "was called out of his bed to take off the plasters". Fuller also recounted how "Most" doctors had refused to sign the "Bill" presented by their fellow physicians William Paddy and John More, because "they knew not whether the ingredients mentioned in the Bill were the same in the Julip and Plasters". But Fuller also emphasized details from Buckingham's defence, noting that Dr Remington was "honest, able and successful in his practice" and "had cured many Patients", and recording that someone had eaten a piece of the plaster given to the king "without the least hurt or disturbance of nature". Finally, implicitly arguing against the 1648 *Declaration*, Fuller reminded readers that the House of Commons had only termed "the Dukes act a transcendent presumption" and added that "most thought" the duke had acted without "ill intention".[8]

Support for the Royalist case also came from an unexpected quarter. In 1643, William Prynne had broadcast news of the sensational plot in which the Jesuits had threatened to poison Charles just as they had poisoned James. In subsequent years, Prynne had repeatedly returned to the plot, regularly citing Eglisham as proof that James had died an unnatural death. But after the regicide, Prynne used the plot for a new political cause. The Jesuits, he maintained, had eventually murdered Charles I; by bringing him to the scaffold, Cromwell's troops had unwittingly assisted the popish plot. In this final iteration the murder of James I remained an act of popish devilry, but Prynne had now given James's murder an anti-regicidal, and Royalist, twist.[9]

The Story of These Confus'd and Entangled Vertiginous Times

The most systematic Royalist response to the republican histories came from William Sanderson, who had served as the Earl of Holland's secretary in the 1630s (Fig. 87). In 1650 he had written "a Petit Pamphlet" against Weldon's *Court and Character*, but Sanderson had admitted that a thorough refutation required more "mature deliberation".[10] Six years later, the first fruits of that deliberation appeared. His 1656 *Compleat History* of Mary, Queen of Scots and James VI and I was formidable in its scale and learning, comprising six hundred closely printed pages studded with original documents, many printed for the first time. Another *Compleat History*, this time of Charles I, followed in 1658. The Royalist James Howell praised the "exactness and punctuality" with which Sanderson had "confuted a late Paradox, commonly repeated, that it was

Figure 87: William Faithorne's 1658 engraved portrait of the Royalist historian William Sanderson (British Museum).

impossible to compile the Story of these confus'd and entangled vertiginous times". But Sanderson's learned works were also deeply partisan. Some recent Royalist histories—most notably Hamon L'Estrange's 1655 *Reign of King Charles*—simply bypassed the vexed question of James's death. Sanderson tackled it head on. The title page of his first volume announced that it was intent on "Reconciling several Opinions ... and Confuting others, in Vindication of [James I], against two scandalous Authors"—Arthur Wilson and Anthony Weldon. Sanderson thought Wilson mixed truth with falsehood "finely put together", but he found Weldon beneath contempt.[11]

Sanderson flatly rejected the secret history. The rapid rise of Buckingham and his kindred all fell within honourable norms, and his power rested on legitimate royal favour. Sanderson gave short shrift to Wilson's (and Eglisham's) attempts to find portents of James's murder in the court politics of 1624. He dismissed the Spanish envoy Hinojosa's accusations against Buckingham as a "Jesuite trick" and branded as a "horrid infamy" Wilson's imputation that Charles and Buckingham's friendship had threatened James's life. Sanderson then explained the sequence of suspicious deaths at the late Jacobean court. The Marquis of Hamilton was "a man intemperate" who had "hastened his sudden death, by his high feeding very late at Nights, and at all times most disreasonable", and his doctors had warned such behaviour was "impossible for his constitution". A late-night dinner and "too much good fellowship" had proved fatal, for his host's "new French-mode Cook with his Quelque choze and Mushroom Salads" had "surfeited the Marquess to the death". Eglisham's hellish poisoning conspiracy theory was now a cautionary tale against cosmopolitan excess. Furthermore, Hamilton's corpse showed no unusual signs, except those typical of such "distempred Bodies". Sanderson also described how the Earls of Oxford and Southampton, together with Southampton's son, had died outside Breda early in 1625, wryly observing that "certainly had the Duke been but at Breda, all our English Lords had been impoisoned there too, and so might have saved that Authors labour to story their several diseases".[12]

Sanderson's account of James's death followed the standard Royalist narratives, emphasizing the king's "impatience in any pain" and his hatred of physic, which ensured that "nothing was ministred to give him ease in his fits, which at length grew violent". Naturally, "in those Maladies, every one is apt to offer advice", and Buckingham had recalled the Earl of Warwick's recommendation of Remington who "had cured many and him also, of a Quartane Ague". James then "commanded the Duke to send for the Medicine". What came was "a Plaister of Mithridate, made and spead upon Leather, and delivered from [Remington's] hand to One Mr. Baker", who was still alive to tell the tale. The remedy was "shewed to the Doctors, and lay ready prepared upon the Table untill proper time to be applyed to his stomach". Remington also sent "a Possit-drink of milk and Ale, Hartshorn, and Mary-gold Flowers, ingredients harmless and ordinary". Buckingham gave this to James and then left for London. The doctors sat up all night with the king, and then went to lunch as he slumbered. In their absence James fell "into a change of his fit, unto timelyer effect, then usually it had happened before". In response, "the Plaister was offered"—Sanderson does not say by whom—"and put to his Stomach". Unfortunately, "it wrought no Mittigation", and the doctors removed it, being "much offended that any one durst assume this boldness without their consent". But they calmed down on learning the plaster's ingredients and that a "piece thereof" was "eaten down by such as made it". The plaster, moreover, was "many moneths afterwards in being, for further trial of any suspition of Poyson". In support of his account, Sanderson referred readers to witnesses who could still be "examined, with very great satisfaction to cleer that calumny". In passing, Sanderson also sneered at the Earl of Montgomery, who, according to Weldon, James had instructed to see justice done. Sanderson feigned disbelief that the old king would have placed any faith in a peer who betrayed Charles so notoriously in the 1640s. But if James had done so, then Montgomery, "that precious Earl, of successive merit towards the Kings posterity", was surely partly to blame for the abortive investigation into James's death.[13]

Sanderson based his account not only on the parliamentary record but also on the vivid Royalist account of James's illness printed in 1648 by *Mercurius Elencticus*. He also offered his own eyewitness recollections of the 1626 hearings, reporting Buckingham's comment that "my innocency is so cleer, that their malice does the more rivet me into good mens affections". Sanderson added that "the Lords thought the Commons, more busie then needful". And he had little respect for the so-called witnesses against the duke. Dr Ramsey "is a Doctor yet living from that time discontent with the Court; and perhaps to colour his own demerit" would not hesitate to "insinuate . . . his too much resentment of the Kings death". Dr Eglisham meanwhile was "something bitter against the Duke". His book had been written "at Bruxells"—and thus had decidedly Catholic origins—yet had been "reprinted in times of freedom for such like Pasquils, purposely set out to renew the memory of the Dukes crimes, and to taint others with infection". This was the true logic behind the 1642 and 1648 republications: Buckingham's supposed crimes had been cynically revived to "taint" the king. Sanderson thought *The Forerunner* itself unworthy of detailed consideration: as "the surface thereof, at the first sight is frivolous, so be it examined to the full, it will be found malacious, and lastly laid aside as impossible".[14]

Sanderson also knew of Sir Balthazar Gerbier's 1648 and 1653 accounts of Eglisham's effort to come in from the cold. Gerbier was a problematic source; he had switched sides during the 1640s, was suspected of writing *The Nonesuch Charles*, and Sanderson judged his testimony "odious to any man". But

Sanderson confirmed Gerbier's story that "Egglesham dealt with him in Flanders; for a piece of money (not more then four hundred of Guilders to defray the charges) to imprint his recantation", before adding a surprising new detail: Buckingham had agreed to Eglisham's terms and promised "he would pay for printing that also".[15]

By dismantling Weldon's and Wilson's narratives, and by highlighting Eglisham's willingness to recant, Sanderson undercut the 1648 *Declaration's* claim that Charles had dissolved the 1626 Parliament to protect Buckingham from an accusation of "poisoning his Father". Sanderson emphasized that Buckingham "was never accused of any such crime" and argued that the allegation that Charles "should connive (an equal guilt with the Principal) at the impoisoning of the Father" was an act of treason: "what can be more horrid infamy, for a Traytor to surmize to publish, nay to imprint" such accusations?[16]

Sanderson's *Compleat History of the Life and Raigne of King Charles*, published in 1658, declined to re-engage with the secret history. Instead, Sanderson simply excised Buckingham's transcendent presumption from the impeachment charges, leaving the impression that the duke had only faced twelve articles. When discussing the 1648 *Declaration*, Sanderson opted for contempt rather than debate. Quoting directly from Edward Hyde's 1648 response, he insisted that "Malice being once detected, is best answered with neglect and silence", repeating the mantra, "was there ever greater or more apparent Malice, than to offer to put the horrid slander of Parricide upon him, who was eminently known to be as obedient and loving a Son to his blessed father, as any History can make mention of".[17]

Sanderson had produced what would remain the most detailed Royalist response to the secret history. Instead of ignoring Eglisham, he tried to discredit him. He rejected out of hand his account of Hamilton's death and emphasized Eglisham's connection to Catholic Flanders. He cast doubt on the parliamentary account of the sickroom, insisting that the doctors knew about Remington's remedies before they were applied. And he referred to still living, if ageing, witnesses who might set the record straight. Most importantly, he broadcast Gerbier's story of Eglisham's proffered recantation. Still, Sanderson's presentation had its own problems. He had entered Holland's service only in the late 1620s, which rendered questionable his claim that in 1626 Buckingham had spoken to him of his "innocency". His report that Buckingham had offered to pay the printing costs for Eglisham's recantation was consistent with Buckingham's willingness to exploit the press, but Sanderson was supposedly retelling Gerbier's story, and Gerbier had only arrived in Brussels three years after Buckingham's assassination. By the later 1650s, however, plausibility mattered more than accuracy.

Sanderson's work did not pass unscathed, but the critiques, which came from Royalist rather than Cromwellian pens, said nothing about his rebuttal of the secret history.[18] Neither Weldon nor Wilson found new republican defenders—perhaps because the Cromwellians thought the battle had been won, or perhaps because they realized that another Eglisham revival would only further alienate Royalists from the Protectorate. Whatever the reason, the polemical tide was running out on the secret history. Lambert van den Bos's immensely popular 1657 collective biography of the kings of England was uneasy about James's death: "what remains to be spoken of King James is . . . scarce worth recording", he wrote, but he argued, perhaps from Richard Baker's *Chronicle*, that the king had died from "a disease of the Spleen", before hurriedly adding that "there were false reports spread abroad that he was poysoned".[19] Equally sceptical was John Gadbury, an astrologer sharply critical of William Lilly's predictions and politics. Gadbury's 1658 *Nativity of the late King Charls* challenged Lilly's famous horoscope of the king and added "it seems improbable, and most absurd and irrational to me (and I presume to all ingenious Artists) that the report concerning the Duke of Buckingham's endeavouring to poyson the King this Natives Father, was at all known or connived at by him". Gadbury vowed "to make it appear in due time to the world, that King James dyed a natural death". In the meantime he urged his readers to consider that "it is common for the best of Persons to have the basest and most unworthy reports pass on them, though never so innocent".[20]

Not everyone had stopped playing variations on the secret history, however. In 1658, Richard Brathwait, a popular poet then in his seventies, published *An Excellent Piece of Conceipted Poesy*. The volume included "The Critical Ape", an extended reflection on the 1620s that branded Buckingham "an Hispaniolized Favorite" and "a very sensual fleshly Sibarite", and held him responsible for "th'massacre of Reze" (Île de Ré), where English troops were slaughtered as "their Generall . . . slunke away". But Buckingham had met a violent death of his own, thanks in part to "the dismall shot of Eglesham/Whose fate was this Dukes fall, enforc'd to loose/Those Honours by a stabbe".[21] Three decades after the event, Brathwait confidently linked *The Forerunner* to John Felton's fatal blow. Whether Brathwait believed Eglisham is another matter. Although he could be critical of James and Charles, and had no time for Buckingham, Brathwait's political sympathies were fundamentally Royalist. His 1659 "royal romance" *Panthalia*, which offered a lightly fictionalized account of recent English history, decried the regicide and anticipated the return of the exiled prince "Charicles". It also offered a deliberately indeterminate account of the death of "old King Basilius". Brathwait refused to endorse any of the "diverse reports . . . dispersed" of the king's final illness. Some blamed natural causes (intemperate diet, a "declining Constitution", fatal "hydropick humours, with other contingent infirmities"); but others, from "Experienc'd Physitians and Philosophers", insisted Basilius had "died of Poyson". Basilius's favourite, the sybaritic Silures, was "publickly accused and impeached . . . as a principall Instrument of the

Regicide", but proceedings against him were "wholly suppressed by the especiall grace and Favour" of the new king Rosicles. This was highly contested historical terrain. But Brathwait refused a definitive verdict. On the one hand, Rosicles's actions to protect the favourite were "strangely interpreted by many"; on the other, the accusations against Silures were "too full of presumption" to be entirely convincing. Brathwait left the verdict to God: "whether the grounds of his accusations were just or no, we shall not here determin. They are left to an higher scrutiny, whose judiciall eyes cannot be deluded". Brathwait noted that after Basilius's death, in which Silures's "hand was reported to be instrumentall", the favourite's designs "by Land or Sea" all came to naught. Yet Brathwait did not explain these failures (or even Silures's assassination "by a Common Souldier") as God's verdict on the poisoning charge. He attacked Silures as a "Courtly Libertine" and criticized Basilius for "his infinite affection to Favorites", but in *Panthalia*, James I's murder had become a possibility, not a certainty. In any event, it was no warrant for revolt against Rosicles or a sign of God's curse upon the dynasty. Translated into the idioms of romance, the secret history may not have been exorcized, but it was very nearly neutered.[22]

The Dissolution of New Atlantis

After Oliver Cromwell's death in September 1658, the regime gambled that an ostentatious funeral might help secure its longevity. To the disdain of the Royalists and the horror of his more radical comrades, the Lord Protector's funerary rituals closely resembled the lavish spectacle Charles I had devised for his father in 1625. As a political exercise, the funeral signally failed. "It was the joyfullest funeral that ever I saw," the Royalist John Evelyn noted, and "there was none that Cried, but dogs." Early in 1660 a satirist imagined Cromwell slipping out of Hell to visit Westminster. In St James's Park he encountered his old friend, Hugh Peters, who explained that, shortly after the Lord Protector's death, Britain had witnessed another unexpected revolution, which would now see the "restoring of the Line of King James to the Kingly power, the redintegation [sic] of Monarchy and Hierarchy, and the dissolution of our new Atlantis, and Utopian Common-wealth".[23] Incredulous, Cromwell fled back to Hades.

As dissension paralyzed Whitehall in 1659–60, a new polemical struggle erupted in which the secret history would again play its part. A Restoration satire on Cromwell would later claim that "a great number" of copies of "those vile and impious Pieces, called, *The Court and Character of King* James, and *The None such* Charles" had been "bought up" during the regime's death throes. Although Roger L'Estrange argued that events "before 1648 [1649] is beside the present Question", new authors still returned to the early Stuart past. As the prospect of Charles II's restoration became ever more real, some proponents of the Good Old Cause revived the 1648 *Declaration*'s charges against the dynasty. An *Eye-Salve for the English Armie* warned the soldiers that their substantial arrears were the least of their problems, since to the Royalists "you are Traytors for what you have done". The tract reminded the troops of the hallmarks of Charles I's reign, all of which would surely return with his son:

> His inforced Loanes, privie Seales, Coat and Conduct money, and Ship-money, enlarging of Forests, incloasing of Commons, ingrossing of Gun-powder, with innumerable Pattents and Monopolies . . . besides his Cropping of Eares, sliting of Noses, Racks, Stocks, Pillories for Conscience sake.

But at the head of Charles I's litany of offences was the "Covering the poysoning of his Father, and dissolving the Parliament June 15, 1626 to save the Duke of Buckingham and Committing Sir Dudley Diggs and Sir John Eliot close Prisoners in the Tower, for managing the examinations against the said Duke". In March 1660, *Plain English* declaimed "against the return of that Family" and facetiously sought to remind the public "how good a King, and how great a Saint [Charles I] was". The details had become jumbled "because the memories of men being frail, cannot retain all particulars". But the tract asked a series of pointed questions: "Who it was that interposed betwixt the Parliament and the Duke of Buckingham, and would not permit the Proofs to be made against him concerning the death of his own Father?" "Would you hear who it was that . . . destroyed several eminent Patriots for their freedome of speech in the Parliament on behalf of the Publick; and in particular, touching the death of his Father?" Lest anyone needed reminding, the anonymous author reprinted the 1648 *Declaration*, beseeching his readers to "read the following . . . and be satisfied to the full, whether or no the late King and his Father deserved death and extirpation". And he warned General Monck and his officers of the danger of "returning to our old Bondage under that Family which God so wonderfully cast out before us".[24]

This revival of the 1648 *Declaration* inspired a reply, *Treason Arraigned*, that once more recounted the events of 1626. The Commons' journals made clear that "this businesse had been ventilated and examined against the Duke, and no mention made of Poysoning, or Killing King James"; when Sir Arthur Hesilrige had claimed in 1648 that Mr Smalley had proof of James's murder, the Commons had quickly found he had nothing to offer, and the "Chimera vanished". More important, there was not "the least Reflection upon King CHARLES". Any serious search for the worst offenders against parliamentary liberties would lead not to the king but to "Cromwel and the secluding Members, the RUMP", who had used Pride's Purge to establish the hated "Rumparchy".[25]

A few weeks later, the Royalist who had recounted Cromwell's visit from Hell offered another ghostly colloquy. The satire purported to describe the making of the late king's indictment early in 1649. Cromwell's ghost recalled that Hugh Peters had been "most intimately consulted with by my self, my son Ireton, Tom Harrison and Henry Martin, for the abridging and shortning the charge and Impeachment against the King". Isaac Dorislaus and John Cook "had prepared a long draught of almost a hundred sheets of paper for a Charge", and John Bradshaw, the president of the tribunal, "would have made a tedious piece of businesse of it, by drawing into question the death of King James, and the defeat at the Isle of Ree, with other miscarriages in his Government". Fortunately, Cromwell continued, "thy policy concurred with ours to charge him with Generals . . . and so we resolved onely to lay the Cause of the War in England at his doore, and make him the Author and Fomentor thereof". A fuller charge would only have led to "a formal Tryal", allowing Charles to mount a detailed defence. Instead, "we assured our selves, that he would never own our Jurisdiction, and then we should the sooner dispatch him for his Contumacy out of the world". The politic Protector's boastful recollections were cut short in the pamphlet by news of Charles II's proclamation. Peters knew what awaited him and the other surviving regicides: he would be "tortured and torn in pieces with wild horses, as Ravilliac was". Already "There's nothing but Hue and Cries after us", Peters wailed, "and no one will shelter us".[26]

By the end of the 1650s, the secret history was under assault in sober tomes as well as breezy satires. Loyal service in the Army and the Commonwealth had provided John Rushworth with unrivalled access to all kinds of documents, and in 1657 he presented Cromwell and his Council with the draft of a first volume of *Historical Collections*, a documentary history of political events between 1618 and 1629. Ostensibly, Rushworth wanted to show how royal actions had proven "a Seminary of all Evils hurtful to a State". But he adopted a novel, and potentially unsettling, approach; unlike such historians as Peyton, Sanderson, Wilson and Weldon, who were "crook-sided, warped and bowed to the right, or the left", Rushworth wanted to be "unbiased" and "of a Party, and yet not partial". He thus provided only "a bare Narrative" and let the documents speak for themselves. It took Rushworth nearly two years to secure permission to print his collection. Among the many political myths he quietly subverted was Eglisham's account of James's poisoning. Rushworth noted that James had died from "a Tertian Fever" and added a few details about the king's good death and funeral. For additional commentary on James, he offered snippets from Hamon L'Estrange (a Royalist critic of the king), Francis Bacon and Arthur Wilson, and he referred in passing to Weldon's book, which, he blandly observed, "renders a further Character of that King". Then he left "the Reader to his freedom". Rushworth did not even hint at anything irregular in James's death. In his account of Buckingham's impeachment, James's death appeared only in the Commons' indictment; Rushworth did not include the doctors' testimony or the debates over the thirteenth charge. He did record the mysterious water spout on the Thames just before the 1626 dissolution of Parliament, as well as the rumours connecting it to Dr Lambe, and he noted the Scotsman Robert Melvin's accusation in 1628 that "King James his blood, and Marquesse Hamiltons, with others cries out for vengeance to heaven", but did not explain these references. In short, enthusiasts of the secret history would find little support in Rushworth's "unbiased" account. Later readers could use the material for various ends, but the sober *Historical Collections* left Eglisham's charges as potentially insubstantial as the revolutionaries' new Atlantis.[27]

Elijah's Fiery Chariot on Fleet Street

Most contemporaries knew the story of the prophet Elijah, who "smote the waters" of the Jordan and crossed "over on drie ground" before climbing into a chariot of fire that carried him "up by a whirlewind into heaven". The Israelites continued to look for Elijah and his chariot, because they remembered what the Lord had told the prophet Malachi: "Behold, I will send you Elijah the prophet before the coming of the great and dreadful day of the Lord." In mid-October 1660, Elijah and the day of the Lord were very much on John Jones's mind. A soldier, Parliament-man and signatory to the king's death warrant, and Oliver Cromwell's brother-in-law, Jones was scheduled to die on 17 October alongside three other regicides. Condemned traitors were pulled from Newgate Prison to their place of execution on a sledge or "hurdle", their feet in the air and their heads to the ground, inverted and degraded before the eyes of the massing crowds. Jones, however, was certain that he would die a martyr; the humiliating sledge was, he said, "like Elijah's Fiery Chariot", "only it goes through Fleet Street" (Fig. 88).[28]

For months little doubt had attended the fate of those radicals who had made the secret history a warrant for regicide. Late in 1659 a poet insisted that when "Traitors Heads shall swim in blood,/We shall be happy then again."[29] A mock execution of the Rump Parliament, published in March 1660, elaborated satirically on how traitors die, "carried back to the place of Execution upon a Sledge, where thou shalt be hanged up by the heels, with thy Rump upward, fleed and salted, then cut off, and thrown into the fire, thy Members also shall be cut off, and burnt with thy bowels."[30] The manhunt began in June 1660, when a proclamation ordered all those involved with the king's trial and execution to surrender themselves within two weeks. Some did, and others were arrested. John Carew was taken from his house in Cornwall and reviled along the way to London. Many others fled, or tried to; "some that knew him" seized Colonel Jones as he took an evening stroll, and Gregory Clement was arrested after a blind man recognized his "remarkable" voice. Edmund Ludlow

Figure 88: The frontispiece to W.S., *Rebels No Saints* 1660, depicting the execution of the regicides (Huntington Library).

and John Cook lay low in London but were betrayed by friends, although Ludlow eventually slipped overseas. A secure refuge was hard to find. A few regicides found shelter in the Connecticut wilderness and some in the Swiss cantons, but much of Europe remained unsafe: the Royalist dragnet caught John Okey, John Barkstead and Miles Corbet in the Netherlands, and Thomas Scot in Flanders.[31]

Prisoners willing to repudiate their crime and call in powerful friends generally escaped the executioner, and of the eighty-odd who were tried, only eleven were executed in 1660. Some of those men lacked the right connections, but all were determinedly unrepentant. Adrian Scrope maintained that "he did believe" Charles's execution "to be no Murther". Thomas Harrison began his defence by announcing "I would have abhorred to have brought" the king "to an account, if the blood of Englishmen had not bin shed". Thomas Scot found himself confronting a former Parliament-man who testified that, in the Commons, Scot had announced "he desired no greater honour then to have it

Engraved upon his Tomb-stone, Here lies Tho. Scot, one of the Judges of the late King". When invited to contradict this testimony, Scot claimed the Parliament-man's freedom of speech: "you speake of words that I should utter in the Parlament. I doe humbly insist upon it, that they are not to alleagde, nor I to answer to anythinge of that nature, it being a high breach of priviledge." When the judge maintained that no Parliament could exist without the House of Lords, Scot argued "there was no more than a House of Commons in the Saxons' tyme". John Cook was even more defiant; he would promise "to live quietly", but he would not admit any guilt, "For to this day I am not convinced of any, as to the Death of the King." Even on the scaffold, Cook announced his "desire never to repent of any thing therein I have done".[32]

According to most accounts, the eleven men remained resolute throughout their gruesome executions, and shrugged off cruel attempts to intimidate them. Harrison's severed head accompanied Cook on his hurdle, and the Sheriff's men made Peters come closer to watch Cook being butchered. When his guards taunted Harrison, asking "Where is your Good old cause?" he smiled and tapped his chest, saying "Here it is, and I am going to seal it with my blood." The old soldier did not submit meekly; according to one report, as Harrison was being disembowelled, he mustered enough energy to strike the executioner.[33] John Carew urged his grieving friends to "Think not your prayers lost, for your prayers and tears, with our blood, shall come down shortly upon Babylon." Cook was certain that "an Army of Martyrs would willingly come from heaven to suffer in such a cause as this that I come here to suffer for", and Daniel Axtell wore his wedding gloves to his execution, since he was on his way to "marry immortality". All in all, it was a grisly business even for a professional. After carving up Scot, Scrope and Clement on 17 October, the executioner "was so drunk with Blood" that "he grew sick at stomack"; he left it to his boy to dispatch Colonel Jones, who met his death with astonishing cheer.[34]

Crowds thronged the executions. Samuel Pepys counted himself lucky to have seen both Charles I and Harrison die, and the latter, he remarked, "looked as cheerful as any could do in that condition". A few days later, Pepys went to see another party of men leave Newgate Prison on their sledges, but a last-minute postponement thwarted him. These spectacles of restored monarchical power were a form of political catharsis. When Harrison's head and heart were shown to the crowd, Pepys observed "there were great shouts of joy", while *Mercurius Publicus* reported that when Hugh Peters's head was "held up aloft upon the end of a spear, there was such a shout as if the people of England had acquired a Victory". John Evelyn missed the executions of Scot, Scrope and Jones, but later in the day he saw "their quarters mangld and cutt and reaking as they were brought from the Gallows in baskets on the hurdle". His diary records not even a hint of disgust, while Pepys marked Harrison's death by going with friends to a tavern for a dinner of oysters.[35] Amid the celebrations one poet imagined

Londoners building bonfires that make "the pale Phanatick Grin/to see our general Ioy". When the wood ran out, the crowds burned the symbols of the revolutionary past: the "rotten boards" containing the Protectorate's arms and the mounds of paper that had accompanied the revolution—"the Rebellious votes", "th'Infernal Act . . . When they abolish'd Regal Power" and "that Vote which Commonwealth'd us". Next to be cast into the flames, the poet proposed, were men like Arthur Hesilrige, Thomas Scot, Henry Vane and Henry Marten. With the regicides reduced to ash, "all Rebellion may be buri'd/While we dance round".[36]

Onto this metaphorical bonfire went Eglisham and his secret history. Several of the condemned men whose quarters now decorated the city were intimately associated with the revolutionary reframing of Eglisham's allegations. Early in 1649, as committees prepared Charles's indictment, debate had raged over whether the particulars should be limited simply to Charles's actions in the Civil War or should begin with James's death. In that debate, a royalist tract noted, Thomas Harrison had stood out as "one that upon the trial [of] our most innocent Sovereign used this expression, That they should blacken that white person as much as they could, in drawing up their charge against him" by using the lengthy indictment in the 1648 *Declaration*.[37] Thomas Scot had helped draft the *Declaration*, the document that had publicly aired the question of Charles's guilt in his father's death, and ten years later, Scot was still invoking James's supposed murder to stall the revolution's conservative drift. A few days after Charles's execution, John Cook had printed *King Charls His Case*, a version of the more comprehensive "blackening" he would have delivered in open court if Charles had entered a plea. Cook's pamphlet had deployed the secret history for the regicidal purposes of the Good Old Cause, which Harrison, Cook and Scot now hoped to seal with their "martyred" blood.

While Mr Vigures Dozed by the Fire

The Restoration in 1660 was met with widespread and spontaneous joy, but it also excited anti-monarchical outbursts. In May 1660, Margaret Dixon of Newcastle declared that nobody loved the restored king "but drunk whores and whoremongers", and she prophesied that he would "sett on fire the three king-domes as his father before him had done". John Bott, a Yorkshire preacher, urged his congregants to take up swords against the king who would reintro-duce "superstition and Popery". Others looked back on recent events with pride: Richard Abbot thought "Cromwell ruled better than ever the King will", and William Lawson argued "It was justly done that the late King was beheaded".[38] Among the discontented was John Careuth, a gentleman from Tynemouth. Early in March 1660, Robert Allyson, a butcher from neighboring Shields, heard Careuth say that "the King was a son of a whore", adding "The rogue, your master, is comeing over into England, but he hath never a man that followes him that hath a principle of God in him except Sir Ralph Hopton". As for George Monck, the army commander who had cleared the way for the Restoration, he was "a traytor, and worse than Jezabel that was eaten by doggs". Like old Sir Edward Peyton before him, Careuth had branded the king's mother, the French Catholic Henrietta Maria, a whore. And he had worse to say about Charles I: he had "poison'd his father".[39]

The secret history would survive the Restoration and the cathartic bloodletting that helped legitimize Charles I's son. With the Privy Council once again policing the realm, only the most reckless would attempt to print a tract that so much as hinted at James I's murder. As we shall see, during the Exclusion crisis of 1678–81, a neutered version of the story would briefly reemerge, and it would reappear in radical Whig discourse of the 1690s after the revolution against James II. But for long stretches of time the secret history effectively vanished from Restoration print culture. Yet it still lingered in the shadows, resurfacing when drink loosened tongues and political memory and desire took wing.

In December 1663, James Harris, a journeyman fuller from Pelynt in Cornwall, arrived in Liskeard some twelve miles to the north with his master's daughter, Margaret Allen. As Samuel Vigures sat by his own fire, drifting in and out of sleep, Harris told Samuel's son William about his life. He had not always been a fuller; he had "bine a souldier in Cromwells Army", and his military service had taken him to London early in 1649, where "he did see the last kinge Charles beheaded". As Samuel dozed, Harris gave William a history lesson. Charles "was beheaded" for two reasons: "for goeinge from his Parliament [in 1642] and for poysoning his father". William's sister Jane recalled Harris talking about the curse on the Stuarts and claiming that "there were noe kinges dyed but were putt to death, And that this kinges father did poyson his ffather". Margaret Allen remembered similar talk: Harris had claimed "the kings father dyed for poysoning of his father".[40] The mayor of Liskeard sent these reports to the neighbouring magistrate, Jonathan Trelawney. Eager for compensation for his own suffering in the civil wars, Trelawney seized on this incident as a way of reminding Whitehall of his deserts. He soon had Harris in custody, but he could learn nothing further about either this outburst or "any further designe of Mischiefe". Trelawney did glean some evidence of Harris's religious inclinations, recording his master's statement that "hee hath often heard Harris say that the king allowes the Prophanation of the Sabbath".[41] Trelawney asked Whitehall for instructions about what to do with Harris, but no answer has survived.

James Harris can hardly have been the only former soldier who had internalized the version of the secret history advanced by the Army and parliamentary radicals in 1648–49, and historians would not have known of his comments if the local magistrate had not been so eager for royal favour. But for mainstream Restoration political culture, and even for its dissidents, this particular political memory had lost much of its utility. It was tainted by a seemingly indelible association with the king-killers dragged through Fleet Street on their chariots of fire.

SCANDALOUS AND LIBELLOUS DISCOURSES

THE MURDER OF JAMES I FROM PARTISAN HISTORY

TO FORENSIC MEDICINE, 1663–1862

IN EXILE IN 1646, Sir Edward Hyde had busied himself by beginning a history of the Great Rebellion; late in the 1660s, after falling into Charles II's disfavour, he returned to his work. The first volume of his history, which finally appeared in print in 1702, quickly became the indispensable Royalist contribution to the flurry of memoirs and histories of the civil wars published in the late seventeenth and early eighteenth centuries.[1] Hyde opened by looking back to the beginning of Charles I's reign to identify the long-term roots of the political tragedies to come.[2] Buckingham loomed large, and Hyde offered an unusually complex portrait of the great favourite. Hyde thought the duke had many excellent qualities and a real, though mostly unfulfilled, potential. Buckingham was a loyal, generous friend. Courtly and elegant, he danced like a god, but he also understood the business of government, which he had learned from his master James I. Yet Buckingham was also impulsive, too readily led astray, and once crossed, vindictive. What the favourite had needed, Hyde thought, was a close friend to pull him back from "the current, or rather the torrent, of his impetuous passions". His personal anger at the Spanish in 1623 and the French in 1627 had dragged the kingdom into ruinous military confrontations and generated dangerous domestic discontent. Although that discontent had focused temporarily on Buckingham, it had never really dissipated: "The venom of that season" eventually "increased and got vigour until from one licence to another, it proceeded till the nation was corrupted to that monstrous degree that it grew satiated and weary of the government itself". Buckingham, however, was far from the monster his detractors depicted. If he had lived and matured, Hyde thought, he could have done much to ease the tensions his youthful errors had caused.[3]

Hyde's history, like his 1648 pamphlets, gave short shrift to allegations that Buckingham had murdered James. While he admitted that James had grown weary of his favourite in 1623–24, Hyde insisted that their deteriorating relationship had no bearing on James's death. His account of the king's end was tellingly brief. In the spring of 1625, "after a short indisposition by the gout", James "fell into a quartan ague, which, meeting many humours in a fat, unwieldy body of [fifty-eight] years old, in four or five fits carried him out of the world". Hyde's medical details were imprecise, but the point was clear: the king had died of natural causes. As for the poisoning allegations, Hyde offered an oblique but unmistakable refutation. After James's death, "many scandalous and libellous discourses were raised, without the least colour or ground; as appeared upon the strictest, and [most] malicious examination that could be made, long after, in a time of license, when nobody was afraid of offending majesty, and when prosecuting the highest reproaches and contumelies against the royal family was held very meritorious." Hyde acknowledged that Charles's dissolutions of the 1626 and 1628 Parliaments to protect Buckingham had been mistakes, leaving the false impression that the king was complicit in his favourite's offences.[4] What is more, the clash with Parliaments created collateral political problems that would haunt the king in years to come. Hyde never once specified what the "scandalous and libellous discourses" after James's death had been. He likely believed that since his readers would know very well what he was talking about, an allusion was all that was needed. Even in 1702, when the *History* first appeared in print, no editor felt it necessary to remind readers of the murder of James I.

In the 1660s and 1670s many other survivors were also raking over the recent past. Lucy Hutchinson's husband John had narrowly escaped a ride to Tyburn on Elijah's chariot, only to be arrested in 1663 for allegedly conspiring against Charles II. His subsequent death in prison prompted his widow to write a memoir to vindicate his life and the Good Old Cause. Her account of the early Stuart court owed much to the radical assessments of the 1640s and 1650s. At James's court, full of "fools and bawds, mimics and catamites", Buckingham had reached a "pitch of glory . . . by the favour of the king, upon no merit but that of his beauty" and, Lucy added, "his prostitution". James's death was highly suspicious. Under threat from Parliament, Buckingham was uncertain of James's continued support and "it was believed he added some help to an ague that killed that king". Although Charles I brought a "temperate, chaste, and serious" face to Whitehall, the duke remained "high in . . . favour", and the new king would prove "a worse encroacher upon the civil and spiritual liberties than his father". Among the early signs of Charles's misrule was the 1626 dissolution of Parliament. Following the logic of the 1648 *Declaration*, Lucy recapitulated core elements of the regicidal variation on the secret history. Buckingham was "impeached concerning the death of King James, and other misdemeanours". But "to deliver him from it", Charles "broke up the parliament, which gave too just a suspicion that he favoured the practice". There was a case to answer, as "it is true that the duke's mother, without the consent of the physicians, had made an application to the wrists of the king for his ague, after which he died in his next fit".[5]

Although it would never again play a sustained political role, the secret history of James's murder was far from forgotten after the Restoration. Samuel Pepys would reread John Rushworth's account of "the charge and answer of the Duke of Buckingham", and he had his copies of Weldon's and Peyton's scandalous Jacobean histories rebound in early 1665.[6] Although Lucy Hutchinson's book would not be published until the early nineteenth century, the regicidal version of Eglisham's accusations survived in "underground" political discourse, and it would eventually resurface in the 1690s. The attribution of James's murder to a nefarious Catholic conspiracy, partially articulated in the later 1620s and reworked by William Prynne and others in the early 1640s, continued to play a small but conspicuous role in anti-popish rhetoric during the Restoration. And competing narratives of James's death would circulate in all kinds of politically engaged historiography well into the eighteenth century.

The Indian Nut and the Popish Plot, 1678–81

During the Restoration, William Prynne often seemed like a curious relic of a distant past. Charles II rewarded his devotion to the monarchy in the 1650s by appointing him as Keeper of the Records in the Tower, and Samuel Pepys was bemused by a man who insisted on wearing his hat at dinner, who would not drink to the health of anyone, not even to the king, and who in conversation predictably "fell upon what records he hath of the lust and wicked lives of the nuns heretofore in England".[7] Yet in 1678, nearly a decade after Prynne's death, Titus Oates's allegation of a vast Catholic plot to murder Charles II by gun or poison revived the old lawyer's famous 1643 revelation of the Jesuit plot to poison Charles I with an Indian nut "after the example of his father". Prynne's plot story had always been flexible in its application. Initially, he had revealed the plot to blacken the reputation of William Laud and to steel Parliamentarian resolve to rid the king of his Catholic favourites. After Charles's execution, he deployed it to attack the regicides whose actions, Prynne contended, were the latest manifestations of the Jesuit plot against the nation. Late in 1678, Prynne's narrative acquired new currency in the wake of Oates's explosive claims.[8] Contemporaries quickly connected Oates's story to the older plot narratives. Early in November 1678, Henry Hills republished Prynne's account, complete with the story of the Jesuits' murder of James I and details of the poison-filled Indian nut intended for Charles. Hills retitled Prynne's narrative *The Grand Designs of the Papists, In the Reign of our late Sovereign Charles the I* and made clear that these designs were "now" being "carried on against His Present Majesty", Charles II. Another adaptation of Prynne's account—*A True Relation of the Popish-Plot Against King Charles I*—appeared in 1679, while the Whig polemicist Henry Care issued a third, compressed version as the *History of the Damnable Popish Plot* in 1680.[9] By the spring of 1679, Oates himself had also co-opted parts of Prynne's plot narrative, borrowing in particular from the post-1649, anti-regicidal version. Oates's dedicatory epistle to Charles II, printed before his full-length account of the *Horrid Plot and Conspiracy of the Popish Party Against the Life of His Sacred Majestie*, sketched out how the papists had committed "many past Treasons" and detailed the "many tragical instances against Your Majesties own Family and Person". Catholics had murdered both of Charles II's grandfathers: Henri IV of France "was basely and villainously stabbed in the Heart", and "Your Grandfather King James, though he escaped their Powder, is well known not to have escaped their Poyson". The papists' "diabolical art of inflaming Parties and Passions against each other" had caused the Civil War, and these same plotters brought Charles I to his "unspeakable Sufferings".[10] Thus, the murder of James I had been incorporated into an ostensibly loyalist but politically unstable version of the popish plot, where it served to corroborate Oates's revelations about the murder conspiracies against Charles II. Sir Roger L'Estrange, the most energetic Tory critic of the new popish plot allegations, argued that the close structural similarities between Prynne's version and the conspiracies outlined by Oates suggested that Oates had modelled his fiction on the earlier narrative, with "One Forgery Grafted upon Another". Hills's republication of Prynne in 1678, argued L'Estrange, had been designed to make the old "Sham" vouch for the new.[11]

A Letter from Major-General Ludlow

As his fellow regicides were being rounded up in 1660, Edmund Ludlow had escaped to Switzerland. In the aftermath of James II's deposition in 1688–89, someone, either Ludlow or someone posing as him, offered English readers another take on the regicidal version of the secret history. Public discussion of all variants of Eglisham's accusations had been decidedly muted for three decades, but the ouster of what the radical Whigs regarded as another Stuart tyrant provided a precious opportunity for reassessing and repurposing the past. To argue their point, the radicals published several accounts emphasizing the structural continuities between the despotic regimes of Charles I and James II.[12] In 1691 the first of four printed letters attributed to Ludlow compared "the Tyranny of the first four Years of King Charles the Martyr, with the Tyranny of the ... four Years Reign of the Late Abdicated King".[13] The attribution to Ludlow capitalized on his continued standing in radical circles as a symbol of the republican cause, connecting the political struggles of the 1690s to those of the 1650s.[14] The pamphleteer's starting point was the fawning sermons in honour of Charles I delivered on the anniversary of his execution every 30 January. But the tract argued that Charles, far from being a martyr, was as great a tyrant as his son James II, and to praise one while repudiating the other made no sense. The pamphlet offered the standard litany of

Charles's offences: he had promoted popery, betrayed the Huguenots, violated English laws, perverted the courts, and plotted to use foreign mercenaries to quash opposition. Because "No Rank or Order of Men stood clear from the Oppression of this Tyrant", the pamphlet concluded that "I cannot see how I ought to have expressed the Despotick and Arbitrary Pranks I have mentioned, by any other Name than Tyranny; nor to have stiled him, who acted them, other than a Tyrant".[15]

Central to this radical Whig portrait of Caroline tyranny were James I's murder and the 1626 dissolution of Parliament. Alluding to rumours that Charles II had been poisoned in 1685, the pamphlet paralleled the beginning of Charles I's reign with the beginning of James II's: "That King Charles the Second went off by Poisoned Chocolate, to make way for his Brother, when Matters were well prepared to set up the Romish Idolatry, is a thing generally believed: And so it was, that King James the First, was so dispatch'd." The pamphlet directed the reader to materials in Rushworth's *Historical Collections* documenting the Earl of Bristol's charges against Buckingham, Sir Dudley Digges's speech to the House of Lords, and the thirteenth article of the Commons' indictment, "which charged the Duke with a very suspicious Plaister and Potion adminstred to that King". It recounted how Charles tyrannically oppressed "our best Patriots" while "he upheld and sheltred the grand Enemies of the Commonwealth". Charles had cast Digges and Sir John Eliot into the Tower while he attempted to protect Buckingham. "When the Commons impeach'd him", the pamphlet claimed, returning to the language of the 1648 *Declaration*, "and by one of their Articles charg'd him (in effect) with the Murder of King James, The King told the House of Lords, that to approve Buckingham's Innocence, he could be a Witness to clear him in every one of the Articles". When his word would not suffice, the king dissolved Parliament.[16]

The first Ludlow letter prompted bitter responses. The cleric Edmund Elys dismissed it as an unrepentant regicide's attempt to justify his crimes, and he argued that the case for the murder of James I was "a thing so Incredible, that the bare mention of it is sufficient to Enflame any one of common Ingenuity with an Everlasting Indignation".[17] Further "Ludlow" letters targeting Charles I's contemporary apologists were soon in print.[18] *Ludlow no Lyar* listed twelve charges from the original letter that the king's defenders had somehow "overlookt". One was Charles's protection of Buckingham from Parliament's "intent upon the Duke's Prosecution" that had "charged him in effect with the Murder of King James". To the original presentation of the case, the "Ludlow" pamphleteer added an extract from the "Treatise called the Divine Catastrophe", written by Sir Edward Peyton, "a Member of Parliament in that time".[19]

Although Peyton's book would not be reprinted until Sir Walter Scott's early nineteenth-century compilation of Jacobean "secret histories", radical Whig printers published several other post-regicidal reworkings of James's murder in the decade or so after the 1688–89 Revolution.[20] In 1688, Henry Parker's 1650 edition of *The True Portraiture of the Kings of England* reappeared with a new conclusion that took the story through James II's deposition. Richard Baldwin, the leading radical Whig publisher, reissued Weldon's *Court and Character* in 1689, retaining both the providentialist prefaces of the Ibbitson–Wright editions and Weldon's account of James's murder. The 1652 republican tract *A Cat May Look Upon a King* appeared in a revised and updated version published (ostensibly in Amsterdam) in 1714. Sections on the crimes of Charles I, Charles II and James II were added to the original indictment of James I, while the original's advice to the "Free State" was replaced by a radical Whig gloss on the 1688–89 Revolution. Like the "Ludlow" pamphlets, the revised *Cat* castigated those who praised Charles I as "a Saint and Martyr". Retaining the original's account of James I's murder, the new *Cat* introduced Charles I as a man:

> as like his Father as one Egg is like another, only with this odds, his Father had not Courage answerable to his Intentions; but this Man durst attempt any thing, that his perverse and inflexible Temper put him upon. . . . He was shrewdly suspected to have had an Hand in his Father's Death, together with his Favourite Buckingham, whom he protected to the last, against the Justice of the Kingdom.[21]

In the mid-eighteenth century, the radicals also revived John Cook's *King Charls his Case*, adding it to the appendices of documentary materials that were included in the second and third editions of the widely read, radical Whig adaptation of Edmund Ludlow's memoirs. Thus, Cook's regicidal gloss on the murder of James I survived in the back matter of one of the most significant books in the canon of the Hanoverian "country" party.[22]

Secret and Complete Histories

A broad range of histories written and published after the 1688–89 Revolution also used the murder of James I for contemporary political purposes. Many of these histories shamelessly recycled older works, although some did offer novel details and perspectives. Large swathes of Anthony Weldon's prose, including his narrative of James's death, appeared without acknowledgement in the Whiggish *Secret History of K. James I and K. Charles I*, published in 1690.[23] Such "secret histories" were then much in vogue, with most of them serving mainstream Whiggish ends by castigating Stuart misrule and celebrating the new Williamite regime.[24] Roger Coke's 1694 *Detection of the Court and State of England*, for instance, depicted how "the Kings of the Scotish race" had regularly violated "the Constitutions and Laws of the English Monarchy". His account of James I's death followed the case made in the parliamentary

impeachment articles, again cited from Rushworth, and while Coke acknowledged that it was "but a Charge upon the Duke", he nonetheless concluded
that the charge "was next to positive proof". Charles's dissolution of Parliament
to protect Buckingham was thus a clear "Failure of Justice".[25] David Jones's
Tragical History of the Stuarts, published in Part Two of his *Secret History of
White-Hall*, offered a far richer narrative, woven out of Weldon's and Wilson's
accounts of James's murder. Like various 1650s commentators, Jones asserted
that the king's death mirrored the fates of his murdered ancestors—but
unlike the earlier writers, Jones did not give this reading a providentialist
gloss.[26]

Jones's borrowings from Wilson's 1653 *History of Great Britain* were not
unusual. Wilson's work was reprinted in full in the multi-part *Complete history
of England* (1706) whose third volume contained White Kennett's highly influential Whig history of the later Stuarts.[27] Other eighteenth-century "complete
histories" told the story of James's death in different ways. The Huguenot Paul
de Rapin-Thoyras's multi-volume work, the "standard history of England" for
a whole generation of English and European readers, was more circumspect
than the work of many earlier historians.[28] Rapin acknowledged that tertian
agues were "not dangerous in the Spring" and that the king's death, "happening
... suddenly and unexpectedly", aroused suspicions about Buckingham's
medical meddling. But Rapin offered no judgement, noting only that
Buckingham "was afterwards impeached by the Commons, not directly for
poisoning the King, but for daring to apply Remedies without the Advice of his
Physicians". A note by Rapin's translator supplied some possible motives for
murder, but Rapin himself neither defended nor prosecuted the duke.[29] Other
eighteenth-century historians offered variations on the authorized versions of
James's death first circulated in 1625. The Anglican cleric Laurence Echard's
1707 *History of England* borrowed heavily from John Hacket's recently
published narrative of James's last days, replicating his highly sacralized
account of James's "good death". Echard attributed the king's death to natural
causes, dismissing as "scandalous Rumours" the stories of poisoning "occasion'd
by the too bold Officiousness of the Duke of Buckingham". The standard
Royalist gloss on the autopsy evidence provided the definitive rebuttal: "upon
opening his Body there was found no Mark or Sign of Poison, his inward Parts
being all sound; only his Spleen was a little affected, which might be Cause
enough to throw him into an Ague".[30] David Hume's mid-eighteenth-century
account of James's death made no mention at all of the poison rumours
and echoed what he took to be the king's own sense that a tertian ague, though
not dangerous to a young man, posed real dangers to an old one. Hume also
offered a distinctly secularized version of the authorized narrative of the king's
good death, describing how James "with decency and courage ... prepared
himself for his end". Hume's analysis of the 1626 impeachment articles made

clear his scepticism: "All these articles appear, from comparing the accusation and reply, to be either frivolous or false, or both," he wrote. Buckingham's answers were "so clear and satisfactory" that it was "impossible to refuse our assent".[31] Writing a few years later, Oliver Goldsmith agreed, dismissing as a "frivolous accusation" Eliot and Digges's allegation in the 1626 Parliament that Buckingham had "applied a plaister to the late King's side which was supposed to be poisonous".[32]

One earlier work of history, much read in the eighteenth century and beyond, added a new wrinkle to the secret history. Gilbert Burnet's posthumously published *History of My Own Time* (1724) began with an abbreviated account of British history in the six decades before the Restoration. Burnet, a Whig cleric, had scant regard for James I, the "scorn of his age", whose policies in Scotland, leniency to popery in England, and pusillanimity during the Bohemian revolt had helped create long-term difficulties for Stuart rule. Burnet also argued that James's "inglorious" reign had been tarnished by scandal. Hedging his bets on whether Prince Henry's militant anti-popery had cost him his life, Burnet nonetheless reported hearsay that Charles I himself had confessed to being "well assured" that his elder brother "was poisoned by the earl of Somerset's means". Furthermore, "The whole business of Somerset's rise and fall, the matter of the countess of Essex and Overbury, the putting the inferior persons to death for that infamous poisoning and the sparing the principals, both Somerset and his lady, were so odious and inhuman, that it quite sunk the reputation of a reign that on many other accounts was already much exposed to contempt and censure". The Scotsman Somerset also figured in Burnet's teasingly inconclusive account of James's death. Burnet agreed with others that James had grown tired of Buckingham. But Burnet had heard from Somerset's friends that the king had decided early in 1625 to restore "the earl of Somerset again into favour". According to Burnet's sources, the king and his disgraced former favourite had met secretly in the gardens at Theobalds, where James had "embraced him tenderly" and voiced his frustration at Buckingham's overbearing behaviour. But, according to Somerset, word of the secret meeting leaked, and soon after "the king was taken with some fits of an ague, and died of it". Without ever definitively concluding that the king was poisoned, Burnet reported the contemporary suspicions: "My father [the eminent Scottish legal official Robert Burnet] was then in London, and did very much suspect an ill practice in the matter: but perhaps doctor Craig, my mother's uncle, who was one of the king's physicians, possessed him with these apprehensions; for he was disgraced for saying he believed the king was poisoned". Burnet's ambivalent reworking of the secret history, complete with new "inside" sources and familial recollections, offered no definitive conclusions, although it served to further bolster his argument about James I: "certain no king could die less lamented or less esteemed than he was".[33]

Dr Eglisham and the Eighteenth Century

George Eglisham and *The Forerunner of Revenge* were conspicuously absent
from many of these retellings of the secret history. The Popish Plot republications on the intended poisoning of Charles with the Indian nut and on James's
murder omitted Prynne's marginal notes alluding to Eglisham, and the radical
Whig accounts of the murder in the early 1690s relied primarily on the parliamentary documents in Rushworth's *Historical Collections* or on arguments first
formulated in the 1648 *Declaration*. *Ludlow no Lyar* notably used material from
Sir Edward Peyton, rather than Eglisham. Elements of Eglisham's book and
biography appeared in Arthur Wilson's history, but by the time Wilson was
reprinted in 1706, copies of *The Forerunner* itself were scarce. Indeed, it was
apparently not republished for nearly a hundred years after the George Horton
abridgement of early 1648. John Hughes, who edited Wilson's work for the
Kennett *Complete history*, felt it necessary to include a note by "The Learned
Dr. Welwood" glossing the text's allusions to Eglisham. Welwood, who appears
to have read Sanderson's account of Eglisham's flight to Brussels, claimed that a
decade earlier the Spanish ambassador Pedro de Ronquillo had lent him a copy
of *The Forerunner*. But Welwood's memory played tricks on him. He talked at
length about one of the "Remarkable Passages I remember in the book", a
passage in which Eglisham and Dr Lister questioned Dr Remington after
James's death. The two court doctors showed their Essex colleague the plaster
applied to James and received the shocking news that it bore no resemblance to
the mithridate application Remington had sent to Buckingham. The story was
indeed remarkable—but it also does not appear in any extant version of
Eglisham's pamphlet. Perhaps more telling—and more damaging to Eglisham's
long-term reputation—was Welwood's conclusion that "This Book of
Eglisham's is wrote with such an Air of Rancour and Prejudice, that the manner
of his Narrative takes off much from the Credit of what he Writes".[34]

Until the mid-eighteenth century, copies of *The Forerunner* were hard to
find, and even after that the tract was not widely known. In the mid-1760s,
Horace Walpole, who knew of the book from his researches into Sir Balthazar
Gerbier's career as an art broker, finally learned its title from a list of the antiquarian "Mr Baker's MSS at Cambridge". Walpole's Cambridge contact Thomas
Gray told him that Baker had only transcribed the last few pages of the
pamphlet but that Gray himself had read the whole thing in a college library
and thought he might be able to track it down. "Baker's extract", he told Walpole,
"is only a part of it, relating to King James's death, but there is more of it (as I
remember) about the Marquess Hamilton worth transcribing. If the facts are
true, it is curious, and you shall have it soon".[35] Neither Gray nor Walpole was
aware of the fact, but by the time of their exchange two versions of *The
Forerunner* were back in print. A drastically truncated version of Eglisham's

pamphlet appeared in the second collection of what would become known as the *Somers Tracts*. The publisher's subscription brochure had promised a complete version of one of the 1642 editions, but what appeared in print in 1750 was only the opening petition to Charles I.[36] A full reprint of one of the 1642 editions had, in fact, already appeared in *The Harleian Miscellany*, published in 1744, and John Aston's *Strange Apparitions* was republished in a further volume of the miscellany a year later.[37] Both the Harleian and Somers collections trumpeted their "scarce and valuable" tracts as objects of interest and entertainment for a curious public. Both extended the longevity of seventeenth-century printed and scribal political ephemera, and both gave George Eglisham's secret history new readers and a new life.

"Not with Art but Chymicallie"

It was probably some time in the late eighteenth or early nineteenth century that the public saw the first, and perhaps the only, visual representation of James I's murder (Fig. 89). A broadside titled "The Death of King James I" reproduced a "most rare and curious Print" attributed to the seventeenth-century engraver Wenceslaus Hollar.[38] The image depicted a bearded, ageing man, propped up on his pillows in a four-poster bed, turning to receive a flask from the attending physician, who assured the patient of the cure's efficacy. Meanwhile another man, lurking behind one of the bedposts, leaned out saying "Thanks to the chymist". The patient's ultimate fate was clearly indicated by the pall-draped coffin at the side of his bed and the preacher standing behind it, who gravely intoned "Sumus Fumus" ("We are smoke"). A grieving woman sat at the coffin's head, leaning on her hand and muttering "Not with art but Chymicallie". The broadside commentary offered its own gloss on James's murder. Noting that many authors had implicated James in the poisoning of Prince Henry, and that James had pardoned the Earl and Countess of Somerset, presumably because they had concealed his role in Henry's death, the commentary argued that "If he was in any way accessary to the prince's death, he seems to have experienced the law of retaliation in a singular manner". Buckingham and his mother had procured James's death "by a poisoned plaister and a posset", which, the broadside claimed, had left telling traces on the corpse: "the physicians, who opened him, reported his intestines to have been very much discoloured and his body extremely distorted". The man holding the flask in the sickroom, the broadside suggested, was none other than Dr John Lambe, "an empiric, and supposed necromancer, a great favorite of Buckinghams". Later viewers argued that the man lurking behind the bedpost and giving "thanks to the chymist" was Buckingham himself.[39]

The image was indeed a seventeenth-century work, but it almost certainly had no early modern connection to James's murder. It was originally the third

THE DEATH OF
KING JAMES THE FIRST.

From a moſt rare and curious Print by HOLLAR,
in the Collection of WILLIAM BECKFORD, ESQUIRE.

Many writers have aſſerted that Henry Prince of Wales, eldeſt ſon of James the Firſt, was poiſoned; and that the king was privy to the act; certain it is, that at the trial of Carr, Earl of Somerſet, James was ſo fearful of the earl's ſpeaking of that circumſtance, that two perſons were provided, to ſtand behind him with a cloak, and the moment he ſhould utter any thing reflecting on the king, he was to have been muffled therein, and hurried away : and though James moſt ſolemnly vowed to ſhow no favor to any perſon that ſhould be found guilty of Overbury's death; yet on the conviction of the earl and his lady, he was pleaſed to grant them a leaſe of their lives, for ninety-nine years. If he was in any way acceſſary to the prince's death, he ſeems to have experienced the law of retaliation in a ſingular manner; as a violent ſuſpicion fell on the duke of Buckingham, and the counteſs his mother; of procuring his death by a poiſoned plaiſter, and a poſſet of the duke's preparation: the phyſicians, who opened him, reported his inteſtines to have been very much diſcoloured, and his body extremely diſtorted. Buckingham was greatly declining in favor, and would certainly have been called to account, if James had lived; for adviſing the journey of prince Charles into Spain. In the year 1628 Doctor Lamb, * an empiric, and ſuppoſed necromancer, a great favorite of Buckinghams, was killed in the ſtreets of London by the mob, who hated him as much for his own ſake as the duke's.

 * It is certainly Doctor Lamb who is ſtanding by the bed, holding the bottle, as the portrait very much reſembles that of him publiſhed by Mr. Thane.

Figure 89: After Wenceslaus Hollar, *The Death of King James the First*, an early nineteenth-century image of a seventeenth-century satire on chemical medicine (British Museum).

panel of a triptych of scenes satirizing the practice of chemical medicine, and it depicted the inevitably fatal results of the quackish chemical remedy whose complex preparation was illustrated in the first two frames. All three images had been used in a 1672 satirical broadside ballad titled "The Downfall of the Upstart Chymist".[40] How the image first became identified with James's death is unclear—the broadside making the claim is undated and unsigned, and the only clue to the reasoning behind the identification is a note that the figure carrying the flask was "certainly Doctor Lamb ... as the portrait very much resembled that of him published by Mr. Thane", the great print dealer and publisher of late eighteenth- and early nineteenth-century London.⁴¹ Flimsy though the identification was, it persuaded a number of connoisseurs. The first modern catalogue raisonné of Hollar's work, though aware of the complete triptych, categorized the whole as an "Allegory of James I's death" (*Allegorie auf den Tod Jakobs I von England*). A London exhibition of Hollar's work in 1875 listed the third panel as an "Allegory on the Death of James I", arguing that the other two panels were produced years later.⁴² A catalogue of engraved portraits for purchase by collectors eager to "Grangerize" (to illustrate by later insertion of material) their histories of the seventeenth century offered the image of James "on his death-bed", described as an "accurate copy of scarce print by Hollar", for a shilling. At least one collector was persuaded to buy. The Huntington Library's Grangerized version of Wilson's 1653 *History of Great Britain* includes this image, inserted among the pages on James's death.⁴³

The editions of Eglisham in the Harleian and Somers collections made *The Forerunner* available to a diverse range of Regency and Victorian writers and historians.⁴⁴ Some found the case for murder plausible; some did not. Sir Walter Scott's notes to his 1811 "revised, augmented" and rearranged edition of the *Somers Tracts* dismissed Eglisham's "virulent accusation" as a self-absorbed, absurd mockery of a case, which "quotes no particulars, refers to no living witnesses" and fails to "state distinctly what was to rest on his own testimony".⁴⁵ Partisan historians, however, could still find the charge persuasive. George Brodie, a Scottish historian whose 1822 history of England was intended as an "elaborate assault on the Stuarts and their apologists", included an extended footnote setting out Eglisham's case against Buckingham. Brodie vouched for the plausibility of Eglisham's claims and questioned Sanderson's attack on the doctor's motives. In his main text, Brodie deliberately distanced himself from "Modern authors" who dismissed such stories as the ridiculous "offspring of credulity in a benighted age", noting that the impeachment charge against Buckingham was the work of "the legislative assembly of a great country". "It was not without reason", he concluded, that "the enlightened men of that age were discontented at being so unconstitutionally defeated in their attempt to bring it to trial".⁴⁶

Something of this "modern" attitude towards the credulity of less enlightened past ages found its way into Thomas Babington Macaulay's typically elegant reflections on the poisoning rumours surrounding the death of Charles II in February 1685. "At that time", he noted, "the common people ... were in the habit of attributing the deaths of princes ... to the foulest and darkest kind of assassination. Thus James the First had been accused of poisoning Prince Henry. Thus Charles the First had been accused of poisoning James the First." But the fact that these popular misattributions were wrong made them no less worthy of historical analysis: "Such tales ought to be preserved; for they furnish us with a measure of the intelligence and virtue of the generation which eagerly devoured them." As Macaulay's astute reading of the rumours about Charles II made clear, it was possible to analyze the historical credibility of these stories without vouching for their accuracy. But Macaulay's cultural historicism had its limits. His own age, he thought, had progressed beyond those that so readily believed these tales of courtly poisoning:

> That no rumour of the same kind has ever, in the present age, found credit among us, even when lives on which great interests depended have been terminated by unforeseen attacks of disease, is to be attributed partly to the progress of medical and chemical science, but partly also, it may be hoped, to the progress which the nation has made in good sense, justice, and humanity.[47]

Macaulay's Whiggish faith in moral and intellectual progress was partially rooted in the distinctively "modern" achievements of science, including the newly confident discipline of forensic medicine.[48] It is perhaps fitting that the scholarly discussion of George Eglisham's secret history ended with Norman Chevers, the Victorian physician-turned-historian, writing on the banks of the Hooghly river in north-eastern India. As we have seen, what Chevers offered in 1862 was the first "medical review of Eglisham's story" that aimed to seek out and test "any medical evidence in proof" of the poisoning allegations.[49] By the standards of the day, Chevers's medical qualifications were first-rate—early in his career, he had made significant discoveries in the study of heart disease, and he would eventually become a major figure in the colonial medical regime of British India. His mindset was profoundly influenced by Victorian imperial ideologies; his manual on medical jurisprudence "for Bengal and the N. W. Province", for example, includes an account of the "Criminal Characteristics of the People of India" that is almost a parody of Orientalist assumptions about the exotic inferiority of the Hindu and Muslim "Other".[50] His research on James's medical history was exhaustive, including, in addition to Eglisham, Wilson, Weldon, Clarendon, Burnet, Sanderson, Coke, a range of diplomatic and domestic newsletters, parliamentary documents, and even Dr Paddy's notes on James's final hours, written in the prayer book Paddy left to St John's College, Oxford. Chevers could not find a 1626 edition of *The Forerunner of Revenge*, and he was misled by Welwood's garbled notes to the 1706 edition of Wilson's *History* into thinking that the 1626 edition differed markedly from the 1642 version he had consulted in its modern reprints.[51] But Chevers was firm in his conclusions: "there is not a vestige of evidence", he wrote, "which would be accepted in the present day, to show that King James was poisoned".[52] Using a wide range of documents, he argued the case that

James had died of natural causes. Aware of, but unable to locate, Dr Mayerne's notes on the king's health, Chevers nonetheless assembled a portrait of a man whose "habits of life were a strange admixture of inexpressible grossness"—poor diet, excessive drinking and "other vices" of a "filthy and scandalous life", by which Chevers clearly meant James's supposed homosexuality—"with extraordinary application to recondite study". This combination, Chevers argued, was self-evidently "as little as possible conducive to health and longevity". Chevers diagnosed the "tertian ague" as malaria, and, drawing on contemporary accounts of James's chronic ailments and post-mortem examination, he argued "It is very doubtful whether, even in the present day, with quinine at their command, an equal number of our best physicians would succeed in curing such an attack of malarious fever in an old, intemperate, and gouty man, with a weak heart and diseased kidneys". Chevers did concede that Buckingham's medical interference might have made things worse: James had unfortunately "allowed himself to be dosed at the most critical stage of his illness, with domestic remedies of the least appropriate kind". The posset was indeed composed of usually harmless ingredients, but they might have aggravated the condition of "an old man of broken constitution, with renal disease, who had been suffering for a week from a serious form of low intermittent fever".[53]

Chevers's assessment of Eglisham's medical expertise was entirely critical. Eglisham's sensational account of the Marquis of Hamilton's post-mortem symptoms was based on a (possibly deliberate) misunderstanding of the natural process of decomposition. "Every medical man who reads the above description", Chevers declared, "will perceive that it is a most gross exaggeration of the appearances which usually present themselves in the rapidly decomposing corpse of a full-bodied person rapidly cut off, whether by disease, accident, or poison, but which, although they were, popularly, believed then and long afterwards to do so, are never received now as indicating death by poison". Chevers acknowledged that Eglisham's claims about hair and nail loss did fit modern understandings of the symptoms of "chronic arsenical poisoning", but those symptoms were also explicable as elements of the natural decomposition process: "The separation, early after death, of the cuticle, with the hair and nails, is merely a sign of early decomposition," Chevers noted, "which, *caeteris paribus*, is most liable to occur in persons of full habit of body dying suddenly." The pre-mortem symptoms were equally poor evidence for Eglisham's claims. If the posset had been poisoned, Chevers argued, James would never have lingered for a week after being dosed, and Chevers found it implausible that a toxin administered through the skin, via the plaster, could have caused such allegedly "violent symptoms of poisoning" so quickly. "The probability, if not the fact, that Eglisham was a most unprincipled slanderer", he concluded, "has been, as nearly possible, established".[54]

Chevers used "modern" medical science and forensic reasoning to dismantle the case for poisoning, and, as we have noted, S. R. Gardiner's foundational modern historical account of the early Stuart era cited Chevers's conclusion in support of its own verdict on the implausibility of the charges.[55] But for all his scepticism, Chevers remained convinced that the poisoning allegations had been of immense political and historical significance. At the very beginning of his pamphlet, Chevers made a robust claim: the report of James I's poisoning "was the spark igniting that train which exploded in the Great Rebellion and in the death of King Charles the First upon a scaffold at Whitehall". Having debunked the medical evidence, Chevers then returned to this initial assertion, documenting in detail the volatility of the charge in the 1626 Parliament, and arguing that Charles's decision to dissolve Parliament was a "most rash and calamitous step". Chevers was aware too of the violent hostility that hounded Buckingham to his grave: "There can be no doubt", Chevers argued, "that the suspicion that Buckingham had poisoned King James added greatly to the detestation in which he was held by the public at large". He concluded that Eglisham's account of the king's murder was "unworthy of credit", but that the poisoning allegation "rankled desperately" and played a key role in the aggravation of "the contest between King Charles and his Parliaments". To substantiate his case, Chevers not only printed long extracts from the parliamentary record—Eliot's speech on Sejanus, Christopher Wandesford's presentation on the transcendent presumption charge—but also narrated the murder of Dr Lambe and analyzed a small handful of libellous poetry to document popular hostility to Buckingham and joy at his assassination.[56] It would take political historians well over a century to start reading these kinds of sources again, and to begin taking seriously George Eglisham and his strange political world. Chevers's pamphlet marked the end of serious discussion as to the possibility that James I was poisoned. Yet it left vital clues towards a far more interesting possibility: that the story of James I's murder might offer a way to better understand the origins and nature of the English Revolution.

THE SHADOWS FROM THEOBALDS

T HE PALACE WHERE James I died in March 1625 did not survive the English Revolution. After the abolition of the monarchy, the republican regime systematically assessed the Crown's property as prelude to a mass sale. Initially Parliament voted to spare Theobalds, and even the hard-headed surveyors who came to gauge its "value in timber . . . bricks, blue slate, stone, glass, iron, wainscott and lead" readily appreciated its beauty. They marvelled at its Cupid and Venus statue, "easilie . . . discerned by passengers and travellers to there Delight", and at its "towers, turratts, windowes, chimneyes, walkes and balconies" which "for length, pleasantness and Delight is rare to be seene in England". Yet the regime needed money and, though they left a Presbyterian congregation in possession of the chapel, their workmen soon dismantled almost everything else. They spared neither the chambers that carried the names of old courtiers like the Marquis of Hamilton nor the royal bedchamber where James had died. They removed thousands of bricks from the great wall erected to protect James's privacy and they cut down many of the trees in the park that Prince Charles and Buckingham had helped plant. The surveyors even put a cash value on the eighty-five deer antlers that decorated the palace interior. Whether these trophies of the royal hunt brought in the estimated £22 and 10s, we do not know. But in all, the dismantling of James I's beloved retreat brought the Republic nearly £10,000 to fend off the incursions of the old king's grandson.[1]

Theobalds was gone, but the events there in March 1625 continued to cast a very long shadow. Having spent many pages mapping and analyzing the protracted afterlives of James I's death, we want to conclude with some comments on the significance of this history for students of early modern Britain.

* * *

Our book has focused primarily on the making and meaning of stories about James's death, narratives that were retold, reworked and refuted a bewildering number of times over decades of turbulent history. We have avoided arbitrating these contemporary debates, and to a great extent the truth of what happened at Theobalds in March 1625 is irrelevant to the event's historical significance. Yet tantalizing details about James's last illness continue to emerge from the archive. None of the seventeenth-century polemicists and politicians who investigated or debated the king's death had access to the Duke of Buckingham's private accounts, and so none of them noticed the two payments on 1 and 23 March 1625 to John Remington, the Doctor of Dunmow, who prescribed the plaster and potion that Buckingham and his mother gave to the king.[2] Buckingham's account book confirms Remington's involvement in James's treatment. But more startlingly, it shows that Remington did more than supply the remedies; he also went to Theobalds to consult directly on the king's case. The timing of his first visit—1 March—adds another puzzling detail to the story of Buckingham's medical intervention. James had arrived at Theobalds on 28 February, but Buckingham would not get there until 2 March. In the interim, the duke had arranged for his favoured ague specialist to visit the king. If Remington treated James on 1 March, no record of the treatment emerged during the furore over the king's death. If the doctor left a prescription, then we have to wonder how ill James was on 1 March, three days before the diagnosed start of his ague, and whether the plaster first given to James two weeks later had been prescribed on that day. Remington's visit to Theobalds on 23 March is even more intriguing. While it is possible that the doctor might have slipped in unnoticed on 1 March, it is impossible to believe he could have done so in the wake of the drama surrounding Buckingham's second medical intervention. What Remington was doing at Theobalds on 23 March—helping Buckingham, answering questions, or even examining the king—we do not know. But the fact that no one mentioned his presence, either to Parliament or in later polemic, is interesting. There's nothing here, of course, that necessarily suggests a poisoning or its cover-up. But this archival find makes clear how fundamentally mysterious the events at Theobalds remain. What more might yet be discovered, we can only guess.

What we do know is interesting enough. There can be no doubt that on two occasions Buckingham and his mother gave the ailing king medicines not prescribed by the royal doctors, including two plasters and a potion. But if they were trying to poison James, they were remarkably careless. A plaster was far from ideal for delivering a poison because it involved a lengthy application. The first plaster, though secretly applied, was left on the king for hours and was soon detected. On the second occasion, both the potion and the plaster were administered with other doctors and attendants present. Even if many physicians were initially left in the dark, too many people in and around the royal bedchamber knew that the duke and his mother had treated the king with unauthorized remedies. There is also good evidence that the aguish Sir James Palmer, a groom of the bedchamber, and several others in the sickroom tried the potion, and that John Baker, Buckingham's barber, ate some of the plaster. No one reported any ill effects, and both Palmer and Baker were still alive, and ready to testify, a quarter of a century later. Furthermore, though very few, if any, murderers record payments to their accomplices, Buckingham had his keeper of accounts enter the two payments to Remington. If James was murdered, it was done ineptly.

It remains possible—as Norman Chevers suggested—that Buckingham's interventions were medically inappropriate for a man about to experience a malarial paroxysm; perhaps the duke's interventions hastened James's death. It is equally possible that the royal physicians' regimen of purges and bleeding, to which the king only reluctantly and belatedly agreed, had already seriously weakened James. But without a reliable modern diagnosis of James's illness and absent modern forensic analysis of Buckingham's medicines and the remains of his putative victims, there is no way we could ever know for sure. What we do know is that James and Buckingham's relationship had long been marked—and emotionally deepened—by the shared experience of illness. It would have been shocking if Buckingham had *not* helped nurse James in March 1625. Given James's horror at orthodox therapies and his habit of swapping medical advice and cures, it would have been odd if James had *not* asked for, and Buckingham eventually secured, the ague remedies from Essex that had come so highly recommended. Buckingham's interventions angered and troubled the royal physicians; he violated their rules and their understanding of how best to treat the king's distemper, and Buckingham was no doubt uninformed of the finer points of contemporary fever theory. But by his own lights, the duke did nothing wrong: and it would be hard to identify, from his actions, any evidence of malicious intent.

That said, it is equally understandable why the sickroom erupted in recriminations once the king took a serious turn for the worse. At the best of times a royal illness was a time of peculiarly heightened anxiety. The physicians had devised strict protocols for managing their royal patient precisely because of the high stakes involved; and the costs of making mistakes were huge, as the case of Prince Henry in 1612 had shown. But early in 1625, James's court was also a particularly fraught environment as king, prince and favourite struggled to chart England's course into or around the Thirty Years War. The intensifying political, ideological and factional competition left everyone apprehensive, especially in the midst of Charles and Buckingham's assault on the Hispanophile faction at court. In this poisonous atmosphere even the slightest misstep could provide an opening for rivals to smear a reputation or destroy a career. However benign his intent, Buckingham must have been terrified at the sudden deterioration of the king's condition, and he could not be sure that his interventions had not somehow complicated James's disease. And so he brought Remington back to Theobalds on 23 March, and swiftly tried to silence recriminations;

and then, after James's death, the duke tried to secure the doctors' retrospective endorsement of his medicines in a desperate effort to contain the potential damage that "strange tealles" of his actions might inflict. His one consolation—in March 1625 and again in May 1626—was that his friend, the new king, had absolute trust in him.

While there is space for reasonable doubt about Buckingham's actions, there is no evidence at all of Charles's involvement in James's death. The young king's mistake, the action that allowed Thomas Scott of Canterbury in the 1620s and the regicides in 1648–49 to implicate him in James's murder, was his decision to dissolve Parliament in 1626. Undoubtedly, Charles acted in part to protect Buckingham; not only because of his love for the duke, but also because a king so sensitive to attacks on his honour was genuinely convinced that ambitious "popular" politicians were (to use his own image) wounding him through his favourite's side. But Charles had other political concerns. When he dissolved Parliament, a verdict in Buckingham's case was not imminent, the House of Lords being understandably reluctant to expedite such an explosive case. What was imminent was a reckoning on the battlefields of Europe. Having launched the kingdom into war with Spain, Charles saw parliamentary failure to vote generous supply as a supremely irresponsible action that directly threatened England's independence as well as his own authority. From his perspective, he could not have waited for a verdict; letting the subsidy bill lie hostage to a dishonourable assault on a trusted royal friend would have broadcast his impotence across England and the Continent. We might criticize Charles for inflexibility—in the face of parliamentary pressure, James had cast off Lord Chancellor Francis Bacon in 1621 and Lord Treasurer Middlesex in 1624. But given the powerful bond between Charles and Buckingham, and given Charles's keen sense of his own honour and of his obligations to his beleaguered sister Elizabeth, his actions made perfect sense. No crime was being covered up.[3]

Charles and Buckingham's failure to contain the stories of James I's death had remarkable short- and long-term political consequences. We have seen how these stories were made, contested and mutated, acquiring different emphases and ideological colouring with every turn. And we have argued that this tangled history illuminates the multifaceted, interconnected forces that created so much political turbulence during Charles's reign. But it is worth reflecting on the reasons why so many contemporaries were willing to abandon the authorized account of James's death in favour of Eglisham's secret history.

Part of the explanation was *The Forerunner*'s craft and timing. Eglisham skilfully reworked inchoate allegations into a plausible, coherent secret history. His narrative played off long-standing English stereotypes about poison at court as well as on recent memories of the murder scandal surrounding Sir Thomas Overbury; it connected with deep-rooted anxieties about court favouritism; and it re-energized a host of scandalous accusations that had dogged Buckingham since the early 1620s. Eglisham also capitalized on his status as an insider, an eyewitness with expert knowledge, while cleverly, if never completely, masking the circumstances of his exile and the motives of his Habsburg sponsors. *The Forerunner*'s impact also owed much to the timing of its London release, which suggests a degree of careful advanced planning. Had the tract emerged too early, say in February or March 1626, it could not have capitalized on the concerted parliamentary assault on Buckingham that had yet to develop. Likewise had it appeared two weeks later than it did, it would have missed the presentation of the charges by the Commons to the Lords. But by late April there may have been enough copies in circulation that Sir John Eliot saw them as a way out of the impasse in the impeachment fight. The pamphlet's full release in London, which happened quickly and in volume in early May, was carefully timed to coincide with the Earl of Bristol's attack on the duke, and to capitalize on the addition of the thirteenth impeachment charge by the Commons. The pamphlet's launch immediately heightened the stakes of the Parliament-men's upcoming presentations to the Lords. Eglisham said what the Parliament-men could only suggest obliquely, and his direct accusations, which gave their insinuations real polemical and political force, greatly complicated any easy resolution of the impeachment crisis.

The Forerunner also had a significant impact on popular political opinion. As Edmund Bolton had warned Buckingham, the regime was in danger of losing control over what the king's subjects read and thought. Sharp poets and shrewd historians became opinion makers, with their writings and libels now circulating widely in the capital and the provinces. Yet the Crown remained paralyzed by a fundamental ambivalence towards the new media world of the 1620s; it dabbled inconsistently in opinion management while insisting that politics was not an appropriate subject for popular debate. Buckingham was more conscious of the possibilities of public relations. In 1624 and again in 1627 and 1628 he tried to outflank his critics with strategic acts of media publicity. Yet in 1626 neither the duke nor Charles took action to discredit Eglisham publicly. William Trumbull and Henry Wotton had more than enough material to undercut the secret history, and Bolton was willing to orchestrate a sustained campaign. Yet the regime did nothing.

The contrast with the contemporary situation in France is telling. French *dévots* and Habsburg polemicists repeatedly excoriated Cardinal Richelieu for his willingness to support foreign Protestants. In response, Richelieu mobilized numerous writers of different styles and religious inclinations to mount a multifaceted polemical counter-offensive against the libellers in Paris and across the Continent.[4] They did not silence the cardinal's critics, but they certainly answered them, undercutting the public influence of the attacks. When Charles I and his ministers were forced belatedly to embrace this form of political publicity in the 1640s, they proved highly adept at the game. Indeed by the end of the decade, Charles arguably had a better, and certainly more imaginative, stable of writers, editors and publishers than his parliamentary opponents. As Secretary Nicholas noted in 1648, there were then "many good pens of the kings party", and they mounted a strikingly successful assault on the 1648 *Declaration*'s revival of the secret history. Their campaign could not save Charles's life, but it helped nurture Royalism through its darkest days.[5] If Nicholas and Buckingham had organized a response in 1626 along the lines of the Royalist response to the 1648 *Declaration*, the history of the secret history would have undoubtedly been very different. If the regime had tied *The Forerunner* to a Brussels-based Catholic, it is hard to believe that godly Calvinists like Thomas Scott would have so fervently embraced it in the 1620s or that militant Parliamentarians would have republished and exploited it in the 1640s. The Caroline regime's failure to adapt to and exploit the news culture of the 1620s has to be reckoned among the long-term causes of its eventual collapse.

* * *

Our history of the secret history suggests several new avenues for further research. We did not set out to write a book so focused on the entanglement of English and European history. But chasing George Eglisham required us to cross and re-cross national boundaries, and forced us to see the Channel and North Sea not as barriers cutting the Isles off from the Continent, but as networks of interconnected political and cultural histories.[6] While historians of ideas and high culture have long paid attention to the cosmopolitan formations and transnational perspectives of key early modern thinkers and artists, polit-ical historians have only just begun to explore the role of mobility and exile in the making of religious and political polemicists.[7] Historians have also only just begun to think seriously about the transnational circulation of political texts and news, and thus resituate the new media history of early modern England in comparative and entangled European contexts.[8] Eglisham's story makes it clear that we also need to pay attention to moments of heightened interconnectivity, intervention and cross-fertilization, and thus develop suffi-cient numbers of case studies to allow us to conceptualize the architecture of transnational networks and map the recurrent patterns of longer-term proc-esses of entanglement.

The secret history of James I's murder clearly needs to be situated in a longer history of Flemish and Catholic polemical interventions in English politics. As Peter Lake and Michael Questier's recent work has shown, transnational Catholic agents and networks largely using Flemish presses launched a stag-gering array of polemical attacks into England in the Elizabethan and early Stuart eras.[9] Some fell flat, but a few struck with quite devastating effect. *The Treatise of Treasons* (1582) and *Leicester's Commonwealth* (1584) used a string of lurid accusations to focus attention on the baleful influence of Elizabeth I's favourite the Earl of Leicester and on the queen's own morals. Cardinal Allen riveted English readers, already anxious about the future, with *A Conference about the Next Succession* (1594). And as we have seen, in James's reign, Flemish printers infuriated the king with sensational, scandalmongering works like *Prurit-Anus* (1609) and *Corona Regia* (1615). Yet doubtless the Flemish tract that had the most profound, and longest lasting, impact was Eglisham's pamphlet, printed in Jan van Meerbeeck's Brussels shop early in 1626. Readers with a taste for irony can only marvel at the sight of godly English radicals demanding and subsequently justifying the execution of Charles I based in part on allegations made by a Scots Catholic protected by a Spanish cardinal and associated with a Spanish ambassador, working with a printer in Brussels closely tied to the Infanta Isabella's regime. But the irony highlights a vital historiographical lesson, which points the way towards a British political history repositioned within the entangled, transnational and multi-confessional European histories of the early modern era.

We hope also to revitalize work in other areas of the historiography. Historical fashions come and go. Thirty years ago, the debate on the causes and nature of the English Revolution—the battle of "revisionists", "whigs" and Marxists—commanded the attention of scholars in many different fields. The combat pitted giants of the profession against a generation of rapier-sharp young (and not so young) Turks eager to topple paradigms and reputations. The historiographical and ideological issues at stake, late in the Cold War, seemed unusually pressing; and the level of vitriol was sufficient to satisfy even the most avid connoisseur of academic blood sports. The heat and the noise of those debates have now faded away, leaving work on the English Revolution to continue at a quieter (if more sophisticated) pitch beyond the concern or interest of the profession at large.

Our book remains fundamentally indebted to those debates, and to the "post-revisionist" approaches that emerged immediately in their wake. If labels help, then this is undoubtedly a "post-revisionist" book, and one that also tries to broaden the traditional definition of political history according to the insights of the "cultural turn" in contemporary historiography. This book takes ideological friction and religious belief, text and media, image and perception, seriously as engines and expressions of political conflict. It argues that English politics was the business of more than a narrow courtly and parliamentary elite. And it suggests that the English Revolution had deep and long-term causes; that dramatic confrontation was not inevitable, but that it erupted out of a political culture that was long unsettled, a culture whose fault lines dictated the specific shape the revolution would take. This book also insists that these events still matter, though they remain difficult to know and to explain. The dust has settled on the historiographical wars over revisionism, and although the battle lines are no longer clearly drawn, we hope that scholars continue to revisit the early and mid-seventeenth century with new questions, new sources, and a willingness to experiment in form and method, seeking, as Marc Bloch put it nearly a century ago, to craft a political history "in the widest and truest sense of those words".[10]

If it is to thrive anew, the debate on the English Revolution must continue the turn towards new sources and the difficult task of putting them in productive conversation with the old ones. We have tried in this book to trace a particular story across a range of very different archives: state papers and parliamentary diaries, diplomatic reports and gentry newsletters, poems and printed tracts, images and plays, commonplace books and government investigations, medical treatises and autopsy reports, all scattered in libraries across Britain, the United States and Europe. We have insisted that even the most scandalous and scabrous material deserves careful attention, and that it must be integrated into the traditional political narratives patiently reconstructed from the records of Whitehall and Westminster. We have shown how the competition for power and influence at court was enmeshed in complex struggles over and around the king's fragile, ageing body. We have argued that the parliamentary crises of 1626 and 1648, so central to the traditional high political narrative, do not make sense without attention to the sensational and often lurid dreamscape of a popular political culture awash in political media, in which exaggerated fears and anxieties shaped the perceptions of political actors and destroyed the reputations of powerful men. The words and actions of the great heroes of Whiggish parliamentary narratives, Sir Dudley Digges and Sir John Eliot, acquire new meaning once we resituate them in a contemporary context where debates on the people's and the Parliament's liberties were inextricably interconnected with anxieties about toad venoms, lecherous favourites and a "poysonmunger mountibanck".

George Eglisham's secret history caused neither the crisis of the 1620s nor the civil wars and the regicide. Yet it certainly shaped and reflected these events in important ways, and its passage across time exposes to historical scrutiny a remarkably rich and volatile political culture. By taking fictions, even libellous fictions, seriously, by seeking out the political meanings of different experiences and texts, and by looking for political engagement in different locales, we have tried to see early modern politics on a much broader canvas. This expansive view has allowed us to discover new things. We have found ideological contestation and radical thought where scholars once insisted there was none; and we have found ordinary people, whom scholars once assumed were politically uninformed and detached, deeply engaged in the politics of court, Parliament and nation. Christopher Hogg, Susanna Prince and Thomas Brediman belonged to very different social worlds than Thomas Scott, Robert Melvin and the Parliament-men, but they shared an engagement with the secret history of James's murder that forced them to ponder troubling questions about the early Stuart court, and in some cases to think radical thoughts about the limits of obedience and the right of resistance. We have seen too how "scandalous" allegations about poison and witchcraft, allegations that historians have traditionally found at best bizarre, at worst embarrassing, could intersect with broader concerns about religion, social and gender order, and the balance of power between Whitehall and Westminster. We have seen how poison stories inflamed the confessional divisions of an age on the brink of religious war, and how they resonated with classical republican critiques of monarchical tyranny. And they have led us to rethink Britain's place in a broader European political landscape, a world of international cultural entanglement and mobility.

As we followed the secret history into the age of revolution, we saw it reborn and remade inside a sophisticated "public sphere" that transformed the practice of politics. Print accelerated the revolutionary dynamics of the 1640s, and at key points in the decade the secret history emerged as a focal point of radical action and speculation, constantly inflaming and polarizing political opinion. The struggle to define the meaning of James I's death was at the heart of some of the most contested moments of the revolutionary era: the case for war against the king in the early 1640s, the radical rejection of Charles Stuart in 1648, the trial and regicide of January 1649, and the cultural legitimation of new republican regimes. Indeed, it now seems clear that the pivotal crisis of 1648 cannot be understood without restoring the secret history to its central place in the violent debates over the future of monarchy.

Bitter, arrogant and quarrelsome, George Eglisham remains difficult to like. Lucky finds in scattered archives have allowed us to learn much about his life that we never expected to know, and there is undoubtedly more material out there for others to find. But there is much we will never know about him. Eglisham probably had some idea that his little book would cause trouble. Confident enough in his own powers of persuasion and in his reading of contemporary politics, he knew that, if properly framed and timed, his secret history might wound Buckingham and damage the Protestant Cause. His backers were surely delighted to watch Eglisham's allegations wreck a Parliament and leave the English war effort adrift. If Sir Balthazar Gerbier was right that Eglisham's "conscience" grew troubled in the 1630s, the Scot had good reason to feel guilty. He died probably sometime in the 1630s before he could witness radical Protestants reviving his secret history to smear the king as a papist and then to destroy him and the monarchy. But Eglisham had imagined, at least, how such a thing could happen; after all, in 1626 he had insisted that "iniustice . . . bringeth both Kingdomes and Kings to destruction to fall in miserie, to die like asses in ditches".[11]

Norman Chevers, Eglisham's most astute Victorian historian, thought *The Forerunner* was "the spark igniting that train which exploded in the

Great Rebellion and in the death of King Charles the First upon a scaffold at Whitehall".[12] He was right to take George Eglisham and his secret history seriously, even if he overstated the case. *The Forerunner* did not cause the English Revolution, but its strange history helps us better understand the forces that did.

NOTES

Introduction

1. David Stevenson, "Erskine, Thomas, First Earl of Kellie (1566–1639)", *ODNB*; Neil Cuddy, "The Revival of the Entourage: The Bedchamber of James I, 1603–1625", in David Starkey (ed.), *The English Court from the Wars of the Roses to the Civil War* (London, 1987), pp. 186–7.

2. *M&K*, pp. 214, 216–17 (20 November and 15 December 1624; 10 January 1625); Julian Goodare, "Erskine, John, Eighteenth or Second Earl of Mar (c. 1562–1634)", *ODNB*.

3. *M&K*, pp. 223–5 (9, 16 and 22 March 1625).

4. *M&K*, pp. 226–7 (28 March and 7 April 1625).

5. *M&K*, p. 218 (12 January 1625); Lockyer, *Buckingham*, part one, esp. p. 185; Cuddy, "Revival", pp. 218–21, 223–4; Bellany, *Politics*, pp. 66–9.

6. *M&K*, pp. 225–6 (22 March 1625).

7. On Procopian secret history in Stuart England, see Annabel Patterson, "Marvell and Secret History", in Warren Cherniak and Martin Dzelzainis (eds), *Marvell and Liberty* (Basingstoke and New York, 1999); Noah Millstone, "Seeing like a Statesman in Early Stuart England", *P&P* 223 (2014).

8. S. R. Gardiner, *A History of England Under the Duke of Buckingham and Charles I, 1624–1628* (London, 1875), 2 vols, I, pp. 159–62 and p. 161 n.1; *History of England from the Accession of James I to the Outbreak of the Civil War 1603–1642* (London, 1889–94, 1899–1901), 10 vols, V, pp. 312–14.

9. S. R. Gardiner, *The History of the Great Civil War, 1642–1649* (London, 1891), 4 vols, III, pp. 298–9; J. S. A. Adamson, "Eminent Victorians: S. R. Gardiner and the Liberal as Hero", *HJ* 33 (1990).

10. Norman Chevers, *A Manual of Medical Jurisprudence in Bengal and the North-Western Provinces* (Calcutta, 1856), pp. 64–200 and p. 185 n.; *Did James the First of England Die from the Effects of Poison, or from Natural Causes?* (London and Calcutta, 1862), p. 66; Ivan A. D'Cruz and Robert A. Miller, "Norman Chevers: A Description of Congenital Absence of Pulmonary Valves and Supravalvular Aortic Stenosis in the Eighteen-Forties", *British Heart Journal* 26 (1964), pp. 723–5; Gardiner, *History of England*, V, p. 314 n.1.

11. Chevers, *James the First*, pp. 1–2, 4, 29 n., 36, 42, 65–6.

12. The post-revisionist case on political perception was made initially by Richard Cust, "News and Politics in Early Seventeenth-Century England", *P&P* 112 (1986); Richard Cust and Ann Hughes (eds), *Conflict in Early Stuart England: Studies in Religion and Politics* (London, 1989); and Cogswell, *Revolution*, prologue. On post-revisionist cultural histories, see the introductions to Bellany, *Politics*; and Kevin Sharpe, *Remapping Early Modern England: The Culture of Seventeenth-Century Politics* (Cambridge, 2000); *Reading Revolutions: The Politics of Reading in Early Modern England* (New Haven and

London, 2000); and *Selling the Tudor Monarchy: Authority and Image in Sixteenth-Century England* (New Haven and London, 2009).

13. Shorter analyses of the secret history in this vein include David Underdown, *A Freeborn People: Politics and the Nation in Seventeenth-Century England* (Oxford, 1996), chs 2–3; James Holstun, *Ehud's Dagger: Class Struggle and the English Revolution* (New York, 2000), ch. 5; and Curtis Perry, *Literature and Favoritism in Early Modern England* (Cambridge, 2006), ch. 4. Other recent considerations of Eglisham appear in Debora Shuger, *Censorship and Cultural Sensibility: The Regulation of Language in Tudor-Stuart England* (Philadelphia, 2006); and Hugh Trevor-Roper, *Europe's Physician: The Various Life of Sir Theodore de Mayerne* (New Haven and London, 2006).

14. We thus challenge Conrad Russell's seminal interpretation of 1626 in *Parliaments and English Politics, 1621–29* (Oxford, 1979)—see p. 316 for his marginalization of the secret history; and Robert Ashton's assessment of 1648, *The Second Civil War* (New Haven and London, 1994)—see p. 40 for his dismissive attitude to the charge.

15. See Roger Chartier, *The Cultural Origins of the French Revolution*, trans. Lydia Cochrane (Durham N.C., 1991); and Perry, *Literature*, pp. 1, 3–4, 10, 12–13, 283–5.

16. Alastair Bellany, "Railing Rhymes Revisited: Libels, Scandals, and Early Stuart Politics", *History Compass* 5:4 (2007), surveys the historiography of early Stuart media and the public sphere, to which should be added Jason Peacey, *Print and Public Politics in the English Revolution* (Cambridge, 2014); Mark Knights, *Representation and Misrepresentation in Later Stuart England: Partisanship and Culture* (Oxford, 2005); Noah Millstone, *Plot's Commonwealth* (Cambridge: forthcoming); and David Como's ongoing work on radical printing in the English Revolution.

17. On the legitimation crisis, see Lawrence Stone, *The Causes of the English Revolution, 1529–1642* (London, 1972); William Hunt, "Spectral Origins of the English Revolution: Legitimation Crisis in Early Stuart England", in William Hunt and Geoff Eley (eds), *Reviving the English Revolution* (London, 1988); and Sharpe, *Image Wars*. See too Robert Darnton, *The Forbidden Bestsellers of Pre-Revolutionary France* (New York, 1995).

18. For a similar challenge to revisionist works that minimized the degree of ideological conflict and radical thought in early Stuart England, see David Cressy, *Dangerous Talk: Scandalous, Seditious, and Treasonable Speech in Pre-Modern England* (Oxford, 2010).

19. See, e.g., Hugh Kearney, *The British Isles: A History of Four Nations* (Cambridge, 1989); and Conrad Russell, *The Causes of the English Civil War* (Oxford, 1990), and *The Fall of the British Monarchies, 1637–42* (Oxford, 1991), and the great train of studies in their wake. On Atlantic or global approaches to political culture, see, e.g., Carla Pestana, *The English Atlantic in an Age of Revolution, 1640–1661* (Cambridge, MA, 2004); David Armitage, *The Ideological Origins of the British Empire* (Cambridge, 2000); David Armitage and Michael J. Braddick (eds), *The British Atlantic World, 1500–1800* (Basingstoke and New York, 2002); and Philip J. Stern, *The Company State: Corporate Sovereignty and the Early Modern Foundations of the British Empire in India* (Oxford, 2011).

20. Relevant recent comparative projects include J. H. Elliott and L. W. B. Brockliss (eds), *The World of the Favourite* (New Haven and London, 1999), J. H. Elliott, "The General Crisis in Retrospect: A Debate Without End", in *Spain, Europe and the Wider World, 1500–1800* (New Haven and London, 2009), and Geoffrey Parker, *Global Crisis: War, Climate Change and Catastrophe in the Seventeenth Century* (New Haven and London, 2013).

21. See esp. Jonathan Scott, *England's Troubles: Seventeenth-Century English Political Instability in European Context* (Cambridge, 2000).

22. A focus on entanglement and mobility draws, of course, from the conceptual armoury of the new Atlantic and global historians. The study of early modern transnational news networks has made significant strides in this direction, while Malcolm, *Reason*, models a transnational approach to political polemic.

23. Ida Macalpine and Richard Hunter, *George III and the Mad-Business* (London, 1969), pp. 201–9; A. W. Beasley, "The Disability of James VI & I", *Seventeenth Century* 10:2 (1995); Kristine Williams et al., "Written Language Clues to Cognitive Changes of Aging: An Analysis of the Letters of King James VI/I", *Journal of Gerontology: Psychological Sciences*

58B:1 (2003); Timothy Peters et al., "The Nature of King James VI/I's Medical Conditions: New Approaches to the Diagnosis", *History of Psychiatry* 23:3 (2012), p. 282. See too Hilary Mantel, "Royal Bodies", *London Review of Books* (21 February 2013).

24. Chevers, *James the First*, p. 66 (our emphasis).

Prologue

1. *CJ*, I and *LJ*, III, 23–24 February 1624; "An Account of the Report", 24 February 1624, D. M. Loades (ed.), *The Papers of George Wyatt* (London, 1968), pp. 208–9; NA SP 14/160/33 (Carleton the younger to Carleton: 5 March 1624).

2. "His Maiesties Declaration touching his proceedings in the late Assemblie", January 1622, in J. P. Sommerville (ed.), *King James VI and I Political Writings* (Cambridge, 1994), p. 257. For the European and English contexts, see Geoffrey Parker (ed.), *The Thirty Years' War*, 2nd ed. (London, 1997); Peter H. Wilson, *The Thirty Years War: Europe's Tragedy* (Cambridge, MA, 2009); and Cogswell, *Revolution*.

3. BL Add. MS 72275, no. 43 (Castle to Trumbull: 19 September 1619); Lockyer, *Buckingham*, pp. 82, 85.

4. NA SP 84/111/148 (Calvert to Carleton: 27 February 1623); TCD MS 708, I, fo. 186 (Carleton to Roe: 26 May 1623). See also Glyn Redworth, *The Prince and the Infanta* (New Haven and London, 2003).

5. *CSPV 1621–23*, pp. 576, 581–2 (21 February and 1 March 1623); D'Ewes, *Diary*, p. 121; and Akrigg, *Letters*, p. 394 (James to Charles and Buckingham: 11 March 1623).

6. "The Spanish Labarinth [sic] or a True Relation of that Narrative made by the Duke of Buckingham", Huntington Library, HM 807, fos 3r, 4v–6, 8v, 10r, 12r; BL Add. MS 28640, fos 139–42, "The Relation made by the Duke to the Parlament".

7. BL Add. MS 72255, no. 151 (Beaulieu to Trumbull: 5 March 1624); Arthur Wilson, *The History of Great Britain* (London, 1653), p. 264. See also Edmund Howes's "Relation", BL Egerton MS 2533, fo. 66v; *Scrinia*, p. 190; Bod. Add. MS D111, no. 400 (Spottiswoode to Buckingham: 19 March 1624); and Bod. MS Carte 30 fos 183–4 (Falkland to Buckingham: [March 1624]).

8. Bergeron, *Letters*, p. 165 (James to Buckingham: 18 April [1623]); BL Add. MS 72276, no. 76 (Castle to Trumbull: 28 June 1622); *Chamberlain*, II, p. 441 (to Carleton: 22 June 1622); NLS MS 80 (Melros to Buckingham: 9 March [1625]). On Villiers's rise, see Bellany, *Politics*, pp. 65–71; Lockyer, *Buckingham*, part one and genealogical tables pp. 4, 72, 74; J. H. Barcroft, "Carleton and Buckingham: The Quest for Office", in Howard Reinmuth (ed.), *Early Stuart Studies* (Minneapolis, 1970); and R. Hill and R. Lockyer, "Carleton and Buckingham: The Quest for Office Revisited", *History* 88 (2003).

9. Lawrence Stone, *The Crisis of the Aristocracy, 1558–1641* (Oxford, 1965), p. 113; Alastair Bellany, "'Naught But Illusion': Buckingham's Painted Selves", in Kevin Sharpe and Steven Zwicker (eds), *Writing Lives: Biography and Textuality, Identity and Representation in Early Modern England* (Oxford, 2008), pp. 132–40.

10. James I, *Meditation upon the Lords Prayer* (London, 1619), sigs A4v, A5v.

11. NLS Advocates MS 33.1.7, no. 84 (Buckingham to James: [1625]).

12. D'Ewes, *Diary*, pp. 92–3.

13. Michael B. Young, *James VI and I and the History of Homosexuality* (London, 2000), and "James VI and I: Time for a Reconsideration", *JBS* 51:3 (2012), make the case for James's homosexuality. The most sophisticated case for agnosticism is Alan Bray, *The Friend* (Chicago and London, 2003), esp. pp. 96–103, 146–50, 154, 165–72; anticipated in Alan Bray, "Homosexuality and the Signs of Male Friendship in Elizabethan England", *History Workshop* 29 (1990). On James and Somerset, see Bellany, *Politics*, pp. 30–2.

14. *CSPV 1621–23*, p. 411 (Lando's Relation: 21 September 1622); SP 15/42/41 (Digby to [Conway?]: late 1620). On James's hunting, see also *CSPV 1610–13*, p. 41 (6 September 1610); *CSPV 1617–19*, p. 159 ("Anglopotridia": 10 July 1618); NA SP 94/20, fo. 81v (Digby to James: 22 June 1613). See also Roger Manning, *Hunters and Poachers: A Social and Cultural History of Unlawful Hunting in England, 1485–1640* (Oxford, 1993); Edward Berry, *Shakespeare and the Hunt: A Cultural and Social History* (Cambridge,

2001); D. H. Willson, *James VI and I* (Oxford, 1956), pp. 26–7, 179–86; and Alan Stewart, *The Cradle King: A Life of James VI and I* (London, 2003), pp. 176–81.

15. NA SP 94/20, fo. 81v (Digby to James: 22 June 1613); and *CSPV 1617–19*, p. 80 (22 December 1617).

16. *CSPV 1623–25*, pp. 55, 366 (23 June 1623 and 18 June 1624); James VI & I, *Basilikon Doron*, in Sommerville (ed.), *Political Writings*, p. 56; John Oglander, *The Oglander Memoirs*, ed. W. H. Long (London, 1888), pp. 132–4.

17. *HMC Salisbury*, XVII, p. 572 (Aston to Salisbury: [1605]); *CSPV 1617–19*, p. 259, and *CSPV 1619–21*, p. 150 ("Anglopotridia": 1 July 1618; and 30 January 1620). On James's love for his dogs, see *M&K*, II, pp. 147, 223 (19 December 1623 and 9 March 1625); *Chamberlain*, I, p. 469 (to Carleton: 1 August 1613); Stewart, *Cradle King*, p. 179.

18. *CSPV 1610–13*, p. 448 (6 November 1612); *CSPV 1619–21*, pp. 412, 456 (25 September and 17 October 1620); *CSPV 1621–23*, p. 410 (31 August 1622).

19. NLS MS 33.1.7, vol. 4, nos 72, 75, 79, 89 (Buckingham to James: c. 1622–4). On the three men's enthusiasm, see *CSPV 1619–21*, p. 452 (21 September 1621); *CSPV 1621–23*, p. 380 (14 July 1624); *CSPV 1623–25*, p. 89 (1 August 1624); BL Add. MS 72313, no. 70 (Throckmorton to Trumbull: 7 December 1615); BL Add. MS 72331, nos 140 and 147 (Wolley to Trumbull: 20 September and 22 October 1624); and NA SP 84/111, fo. 193v (Calvert to Carleton: 14 March 1623).

20. Bergeron, *Letters*, p. 154 (James to Charles and Buckingham: 11 March [1623]); BL Harl. MS 6987, fos 178r, 184r (James to Buckingham: [May 1620], [mid-1621] and [c. 1624]).

21. Bergeron, *Letters*, pp. 159, 162 (James to Charles and Buckingham: 25 March and 7 April [1623]).

22. NLS Adv. MS 33.1.7, nos 186, 190 (James to Buckingham: [late 1624?]); Bergeron, *Letters*, p. 150 (James to Buckingham: [late 1622]); BL Harl. MS 6987, fo. 225v (Buckingham to James undated).

23. NLS Adv. MS 33.1.7, no. 81 (Buckingham to James: January–February 1625). On the return of the countess to James's favour, see BL Add. MS 72276, no. 127 (Castle to Trumbull: 9 July 1624).

24. Bergeron, *Letters*, p. 187 (Charles and Buckingham to James: [10 March 1623]); and NLS Adv. MS 33.1.7, no. 79 (Buckingham to James: [undated]). See also MS 33.1.7, no. 89, and Bergeron, *Letters*, p. 192.

25. Bergeron, *Letters*, p. 188 (Buckingham to James: 24 March 1624); BL Harl. MS 6987, fo. 219r (Buckingham to James updated) and NLS Adv. MS 33.1.7, no. 90 (Buckingham to James: [January 1625]).

26. Bergeron, *Letters*, pp. 179, 197, 199 (Buckingham to James: 20 August, 1 September 1623 and undated).

27. Bergeron, *Letters*, pp. 152, 188 (James to Charles and Buckingham: 28 February 1623; Buckingham to Charles: 24 March 1624).

28. BL Harl. MS 6987, fos 23–24v (Buckingham to James: 1623); Bray, *The Friend*, p. 170.

29. Bergeron, *Letters*, p. 100 (Buckingham to James: 1 September 1623); BL Harl. MS 6987, fo. 178r (James to Buckingham: late 1621/early 1622).

30. Bod. MS Tanner 72, fo. 14r (James to Buckingham: [late 1624]); NLS Adv. MSS 33.1.7, no. 79 (Buckingham to James: undated). Akrigg, *Letters*, p. 431 n.1, dates this letter to the early 1620s, but Willson's late 1624 dating (*James VI and I*, p. 445) is more logical.

31. Bray, *The Friend*, pp. 96–103. For different interpretations of the same evidence, see Young, *James VI and I*.

32. Bergeron, *Letters*, p. 166 (James to Charles and Buckingham: [May 1623]); NLS Adv. MS 33.1.7, no. 77 (Buckingham to James: [late 1624–early 1625]). For more on their relationship, see BL Add. MS 4155, fo. 81r (ABCD, "A Post Caution, rather a post monition to the Common Speakers in the Lower House" [1626]); D'Ewes, *Diary*, p. 78; Goodman, *Court*, I, pp. 225–6; Bray, *The Friend*, p. 170.

33. Yale Beinecke MS FB 155, unfoliated (Spanish complaints: 1624). For a later transcription, see *Cabala: Sive Scrinia Sacra* (London, 1654), p. 254.

34. D'Ewes, *Diary*, pp. 56–9, 64, 79–80, 84–5, 87, 98, 100; Bray, "Homosexuality and the Signs of Male Friendship".

35. D'Ewes, *Diary*, pp. 55, 112–13. For the archive of early-1620s' libels on Buckingham, see *ESL*, L, M and N; and Thomas Cogswell, "'The Symptomes and Vapors of a Diseased Time': The Earl of Clare and Early Stuart Manuscript Culture", *Review of English Studies* 57 (2006). On contemporary images of royal sodomy, see Bruce M. Smith, *Homosexual Desire in Shakespeare's England: A Cultural Poetics* (Chicago and London, 1991), pp. 202–3; Curtis Perry, "The Politics of Access and Representations of the Sodomite King in Early Modern England", *Renaissance Quarterly* 53:4 (2000); Curtis Perry, *Literature and Favoritism in Early Modern England* (Cambridge, 2006), ch. 5; James Knowles, "'To Scourge the Arse/Jove's Marrow so had Wasted': Scurrility and the Subversion of Sodomy", in Dermot Kavanagh and Tim Kirk (eds), *Subversion and Scurrility: Popular Discourse in Europe from 1500 to the Present* (Aldershot, 2000); Paul Hammond, *Figuring Sex Between Men from Shakespeare to Rochester* (Oxford, 2002), pp. 140ff; Bellany, *Politics*, pp. 254–61.
36. *ESL*, L8. For other discussions, see Bellany, *Politics*, pp. 258–61; Andrew McRae, *Literature, Satire and the Early Stuart State* (Cambridge, 2004), pp. 75–82; and James Knowles, "'Songs of Baser Alloy': Jonson's *Gypsies Metamorphosed* and the Circulation of Manuscript Libels", *HLQ* 69:1 (2006).
37. On contemporary attitudes, see Alan Bray, *Homosexuality in Renaissance England* (London, 1982); and Cynthia Herrup, *A House in Gross Disorder: Sex, Law and the 2nd Earl of Castlehaven* (Oxford, 1999).
38. *ESL*, Nv16, 17.
39. BL Harl. MS 1581, fo. 80r (Mathew to Buckingham: 29 March 1623); Goodman, *Court*, II, p. 300 (Clarke to Buckingham: 1 August 1623).
40. BL Add. MS 72329, no. 133 (Beaulieu to Trumbull: 24 October 1623); and BL Add. MS 72331, no. 108 (Wolley to Trumbull: 7 November 1623).
41. *Cabala*, p. 275 ("The Heads of the Discourse": 7 April 1624); *M&K*, II, pp. 182, 184 (18 October and 29 November 1623). See also Robert Ruigh, *The Parliament of 1624: Politics and Foreign Policy* (Cambridge, MA, 1971), pp. 257–302.
42. *Cabala*, p. 295 ("Heads of the Discourse": 7 April 1624); *CSPV 1621–23*, p. 443 (21 September 1622); *CSPV 1623–25*, pp. 373, 468 (25 June and 15 October 1624). See also Cogswell, *Revolution*, pp. 263–307.
43. Lockyer, *Buckingham*, pp. 55–8; NA SP 14/109/89 (Harwood to Carleton: 12 June 1619); 14/109/112 (Brent to Carleton: 26 June 1619); Bellany, *Politics*, pp. 28–9.
44. BL Add. MS 64881, fos 92r, 98r (Coke to Brooke: 10 and 19 May 1624); and BL Add. MS 72254, no. 119 (20 May 1624). See also Lockyer, *Buckingham*, pp. 196ff.
45. Akrigg, *Letters*, pp. 436–9; and BL Harl. MS 6987, fo. 221r. On court monitoring of Buckingham's illness, see David Coast, *News and Rumour in Jacobean England: Information, Court Politics and Diplomacy, 1618–25* (Manchester, 2014), ch. 6.
46. BL Harl. MS 6987, fo. 221r. (Buckingham to James: [late Spring 1624]).
47. BL Harl. MS 6987, fos 203v–204r, 224r, 227r. (Charles to Buckingham: [1624/1625]; Buckingham to James: [late Spring 1624]; Duchess of Buckingham to James: [late Spring 1624]).
48. BL Harl. MS 6987, fos 218r, 222r–v (Duke and Duchess of Buckingham to James: [late Spring 1624]); BL Add. MS 64881, Part II, fo. 92r (Coke to Brooke: 19 May 1624); BL Add. MS 12528, fo. 14v.
49. BL Add. MS 72254, no. 120 (Castle to Trumbull: 28 May 1624); BL Add. MS 72331, no. 128 (Wolley to Trumbull: 17 June 1624).
50. BL Add. MS 63081, fo. 137v (R. Townshend to Sir R. Townshend: 3 Jan [1625]).
51. Bergeron, *Letters*, pp. 214–15 (Buckingham to James: [December 1624?]).

Part 1 Prologue

1. Lauren Kassell, "Paddy, Sir William (1554–1634)", *ODNB*.
2. William Paddy's MS notes (unpaginated, p. 5), *The Booke of Common Prayer* (London, 1615), St John's College, Oxford, Cpd.b.2.upper shelf.5. Paddy's "Notes" cover five of the blank pages bound at the very end of the volume.

3. Paddy, "Notes", pp. 1, 3–4. For another copy of the sentences, see Bod. MS Tanner 73, fos 525–27r.

4. Paddy, "Notes", p. 5.

5. Eamon Duffy, *The Stripping of the Altars: Traditional Religion in England, 1400–1580* (New Haven and London, 1992), ch. 9; Ralph Houlbrooke, *Death, Religion and the Family in England, 1480–1750* (Oxford, 1998), ch. 6; Carlos Eire, *From Madrid to Purgatory: The Art and Craft of Dying in Sixteenth-Century Spain* (Cambridge, 1995), esp. book 2; John E. B. Mayor (ed.), *The English Works of John Fisher, Bishop of Rochester*, Part 1, Early English Text Society, Extra Series, 27 (London, 1876), pp. 268ff.

6. Akrigg, *Letters*, pp. 369–70 (James to Christian IV: 2 March 1619); *Chamberlain*, II, pp. 219–20 (to Carleton: 6 March 1619).

7. *Rushworth*, I, sig. X2v; NA SP 16/1/31 (nos 24, 27–8); SP 84/126/111 (Conway to Carleton: 31 March 1625); *M&K*, pp. 226–7 (7 April 1625); SP 16/1/2 (Chambermayd to Elizabeth: 27 March 1625).

8. NA SP 84/126/111 (Conway to Carleton: 31 March 1625); *Rushworth*, I, sig. X2v; SP 16/1/31 (no. 25); SP 99/26/78 (Conway to Wake: 31 March 1625); *Roe*, p. 373 (Abbot to Roe: 30 March 1625).

9. *Ellis*, p. 244 (Tilman to Paul D'Ewes: 1 April 1625); *Salvetti*, p. 2 (1 April 1625); *CSPV 1623–1625*, p. 627 (27 March 1625); *Whiteway*, p. 70.

10. *M&K*, pp. 226–7 (7 April 1625); BL Harl. MS 389, fo. 420r (Mead to Stuteville: 9 April 1625); *Salvetti*, p. 2 (1 April 1625); *Whiteway*, p. 70; *Mercure François*, XI, pp. 335–6. See too Alexander B. Grosart (ed.), *An Apology for Socrates and Negotium Posterorum by Sir John Eliot*, 2 vols (private circulation, 1881), vol. I, pp. 50, 57.

11. See Kevin Sharpe, *Selling the Tudor Monarchy: Authority and Image in Sixteenth-Century England* (New Haven and London, 2009); and *Image Wars*.

Chapter 1

1. *Laud*, pp. 157–9; *Scrinia*, I, p. 222; *Ellis*, p. 244 (Tilman to Paul D'Ewes: 1 April 1625); *Whiteway*, p. 70.

2. *Hardwicke, SP*, I, p. 562; *Progresses*, IV, p. 1,028.

3. Christopher Wirtzung, *The General Practise of Physicke. Conteyning All Inward and outward parts of the body, with all the accidents and infirmities that are incident unto them, even from the crowne of the head to the sole of the foote*, 2nd English ed. (London, 1617), p. 622; Iain M. Lonie, "Fever Pathology in the Sixteenth Century: Tradition and Innovation", esp. pp. 30–42; Don G. Bates, "Thomas Willis and the Fevers Literature of the Seventeenth Century"; and Wesley D. Smith, "Implicit Fever Theory in 'Epidemics' 5 and 7", all in *Medical History*, Supplement no. 1 (1981).

4. See e.g. Wirtzung, *General Practise*, p. 624; Francis Anthony, *The Apologie, or a Defence of a Verity Heretofore Published Concerning a Medicine Called Aurum Potabile* (London, 1616), sigs M1v–2r, M3v–4r.

5. Wirtzung, *General Practise*, pp. 623–4, 634–5, 637; Daniel Sennert, *Of Agues and Fevers* (London, 1658), pp. 55–7; Lazarus Riverius (Lazare Rivière), *The Practice of Physick, In Seventeen several Books* (London, 1672) (orig. 1640), p. 580; Thomas Elyot, *The Castle of Health, Corrected, and in some places Augmented by the first Author thereof, Sir Thomas Elyot Knight Now Newlie Perused, amended, and corrected, this present yeare, 1610* (London, 1610), sig. C4v; Robert Burton, *The Anatomy of Melancholy* (New York, 2001), vol. 1, pp. 147–52.

6. On the debates, see Lonie, "Fever Pathology", pp. 29ff; Sennert, *Agues*, p. 55; Rivière, *Practice*, p. 580.

7. Sennert, *Agues*, pp. 53, 56–7; Rivière, *Practice*, p. 580; Wirtzung, *General Practise*, pp. 634–5, 637–9.

8. Hugh Trevor-Roper, *Europe's Physician: The Various Life of Sir Theodore de Mayerne* (New Haven and London, 2006), chs 14–17. The 1623 report is in BL Sloane MS 1679, fols 42r–51v, and printed in Norman Moore, *The History of the Study of Medicine in the British Isles* (Oxford, 1908), appendix III, pp. 162–76 (cited hereafter as Mayerne,

"Note"). Partial translations appear in Moore, *History*, pp. 97–106; and Ida Macalpine and Richard Hunter, *George III and the Mad Business* (London, 1969), pp. 201–9; and a detailed summary in Trevor-Roper, *Europe's Physician*, pp. 269–72. The 1624 memorandum is printed in Theodore Turquet de Mayerne, *Opera Medica* (London, 1703), pp. 288–307, and summarized in Trevor-Roper, *Europe's Physician*, pp. 273–5.

9. NA SP 14/74/52 (Mayerne to Carr: 22 August 1613).

10. Mayerne, *Opera*, pp. 288–9, 306–7; Trevor-Roper, *Europe's Physician*, pp. 273–5.

11. Bod. MS Barlow 54, fos 2r–5r; W. S. Munk, "Marvodia: Being an Account of the Last Illness of James I and of the Post-Mortem Examination of his Body", in Walford D. Selby (ed.), *The Genealogist*, New Series 1 (London, 1884), pp. 230–4.

12. Bod. MS Barlow 54, fos 2r–3r; Munk, "Marvodia", pp. 230–1; Mayerne, "Note", pp. 162–4, 168–70.

13. Bod. MS Barlow 54, fos 2r–3r; Munk, "Marvodia", pp. 230–1; Mayerne, "Note", p. 163; Elyot, *Castle*, sigs C4r ff, G3r–v, I4v.

14. Bod. MS Barlow 54, fo. 3r; Munk, "Marvodia", p. 231; Mayerne, "Note", pp. 164–5; Elyot, *Castle*, sigs N2r–v, N3v; and Kate Frost, "Prescription and Devotion: The Reverend Doctor Donne and the Learned Doctor Mayerne—Two Seventeenth-Century Records of Epidemic Typhus Fever", *Medical History* 22 (1978), pp. 411–12.

15. Mayerne, "Note", pp. 166, 168–70.

16. Mayerne, "Note", pp. 166–8. On 1613 and 1615, see Bellany, *Politics*, pp. 50–6, 71–3.

17. Bod. MS Barlow 54, fos 3r–4v; Munk, "Marvodia", pp. 231–3.

18. Mayerne, "Note", p. 168.

19. Mayerne, "Note", pp. 169–72; Mayerne, *Opera*, p. 290; Trevor-Roper, *Europe's Physician*, p. 274.

20. Wirtzung, *General Practise*, pp. 628–30, 632, 634, 636; Rivière, *Practice*, pp. 580–1; Sennert, *Agues*, pp. 56–7; and Reginald Scot, *The Discoverie of Witchcraft*, ed. Montague Summers (Mineola, 1972), p. 155 (citing Jean Fernel).

21. Wirtzung, *General Practise*, pp. 629–30, 635–7; Sennert, *Agues*, pp. 57–60; Rivière, *Practice*, pp. 581–2; Anthony, *Apologie*, sig. B3v.

22. Bod. MS Barlow 54, fos 3r–4v; Munk, "Marvodia", pp. 231–3; on sweating, see Mayerne, "Note", p. 165; on wine, see Wirtzung, *General Practise*, pp. 636–7.

23. Bod. MS Barlow 54, fos 3r–4v; Munk, "Marvodia", pp. 231–3; NA SP 14/74/52, 54, 55 (Mayerne to Carr: 22 and 23 August 1613; and to James I: 31 August 1613); Trevor-Roper, *Europe's Physician*, p. 275; Mayerne, *Opera*, pp. 306–7.

24. Bod. MS Barlow 54, fos 3r–4v; Munk, "Marvodia", pp. 231–3. On the remedies, see Wirtzung, *General Practise*, pp. 628–32, 636–7; Sennert, *Agues*, pp. 57–60; John Gerard, *The Herball or Generall Historie of Plantes . . . Very much Enlarged and Amended by Thomas Johnson Citizen and Apothecarye of London* (London, 1633), pp. 427–8, 1,607–8; The College of Physicians, *Pharmacopea Londinensis* (London, 1618), p. 161; Lonie, "Fever Pathology", p. 35; Charles Webster, "Alchemical and Paracelsian Medicine", in Webster (ed.), *Health, Medicine and Mortality in the Sixteenth Century* (Cambridge, 1979).

25. Bod. MS Barlow 54, fos 3r–4v; Munk, "Marvodia", pp. 231–3.

26. Bod. MS Barlow 54, fos 4v–5r; Munk, "Marvodia", pp. 233–4.

27. Mayerne, *Opera*, p. 305 (trans. Frost, "Prescription", p. 410); Paul Slack, "Mortality Crises and Epidemic Disease in England, 1485–1610", in Webster (ed.), *Health, Medicine and Mortality*, pp. 25, 27, 33–4, 39 and *passim*; Charles Creighton, *A History of Epidemics in Britain* (Cambridge, 1894), vol. II, pp. 30–4.

28. Bod. MS Barlow 54, fos 2r, 4r–v; Munk, "Marvodia", pp. 230, 232–3.

Chapter 2

1. *Chamberlain*, II, p. 616 (to Carleton: 14 May 1625); W. H. St John Hope, "On the Funeral Effigies of the Kings and Queens of England", *Archaeologia* 2nd Series 60:2 (1907), p. 557, plate LXV; Anthony Harvey and Richard Mortimer (eds), *The Funeral Effigies of Westminster Abbey* (London, 2003), pp. 68, 70.

2. *APC 1625–26*, pp. 4, 7; NA SP 16/1/17–19 and 103–9; Jennifer Woodward, *The Theatre of Death: The Ritual Management of Royal Funerals in Renaissance England, 1570–1625* (Woodbridge: Boydell, 1997), ch. 10; Sharpe, *Image Wars*, pp. 231–2; Clare Gittings, *Death, Burial and the Individual in Early Modern England* (London, 1984), ch. 10; David Howarth, *Images of Rule: Art and Politics in the English Renaissance, 1485–1649* (Basingstoke and London, 1997), pp. 174–7.

3. *APC 1625–26*, pp. 14, 18; NA SP 16/1/66; *Chamberlain*, II, pp. 232, 616 (to Carleton: 25 April 1619 and 14 May 1625); NA LC 2/6, fo. 26v; *PP1625*, pp. 167, 432; *Salvetti*, pp. 4, 9, 14, 17 (1 and 22 April, 6 May 1625); Gittings, *Death*, pp. 180–1, 226; Lawrence Stone, *The Crisis of the Aristocracy, 1558–1641* (Oxford, 1965), pp. 784–5; Peter Sherlock, "The Monuments of Elizabeth Tudor and Mary Stuart: King James and the Manipulation of Memory", *JBS* 46:2 (2007), p. 272.

4. NA LC 2/6, fos 3r–4r, 5r, 6r, 7v–8r, 18v–19v, 21r, 22r–25v, 27r ff; NA SP 16/2/35; *Chamberlain*, II, p. 224 (to Carleton: 27 March 1619); *Salvetti*, p. 9 (22 April 1625); *APC 1625–26*, pp. 33–4. On cloth and funeral expenses see Bod. MS Ashmole 836, pp. 23–32, 36; Stone, *Crisis*, pp. 785–6; Harvey and Mortimer, *Funeral Effigies*, p. 69; Gittings, *Death*, p. 172.

5. "True Order", in *Progresses*, IV, pp. 1,037–9; NA SP 16/1/34; Bod. MS Ashmole 818, fo. 51r; *Rusdorf*, I, p. 536 (30 March 1625); *Chamberlain*, II, p. 609 (to Carleton: 9 April 1625); *C&T Charles*, I, p. 3 (Neve to Hollonde: 5 April 1625); *CSPV 1625–26*, p. 11 (8 April 1625); John Stow (cont. Edmund Howes), *Annales* (London, 1631), p. 1,036; *Salvetti*, pp. 4, 6 (1 and 8 April 1625); James Shirley, *Poems &c* (London, 1646), p. 57; *Whiteway*, p. 70; Woodward, *Theatre*, p. 196.

6. "True Order", pp. 1,038–9; *Salvetti*, pp. 15–16 (James I's funeral); *C&T Charles*, I, p. 3 (Neve to Hollonde: 5 April 1625); Woodward, *Theatre*, pp. 181–2, 186–95; *Mercure François*, vol. XI, p. 339. On English royal funeral effigies, see Gittings, *Death*, pp. 222–4; Nigel Llewellyn, "The Royal Body: Monuments to the Dead, For the Living", in Lucy Gent and Nigel Llewellyn (eds), *Renaissance Bodies: The Human Figure in English Culture, c. 1540–1660* (London, 1990), p. 229.

7. On elite funerals, see Gittings, *Death*, p. 216, and chs 8–10; on royal rituals, see e.g. Sharpe, *Image Wars*; R. Malcolm Smuts, "Public Ceremony and Royal Charisma: The English Royal Entry in London, 1485–1642", in A. L. Beier et al. (eds), *The First Modern Society: Essays in English History in Honour of Lawrence Stone* (Cambridge, 1989); Clifford Geertz, "Centers, Kings and Charisma: Reflections on the Symbolics of Power", in *Local Knowledge: Further Essays in Interpretive Anthropology* (New York, 1983).

8. "True Order", *Progresses*, IV, pp. 1,039ff; College of Arms, London, Nayler MS, "Royal Funerals 1618 to 1738", pp. 25–62; and draft scripts in NA SP 16/1/98–100 and 102, 16/2/28–29 and 31–32; and Bod. MS Dugdale 28, fos 101 ff. See too *Salvetti*, pp. 14, 16–7 (13 May 1625); *Mercure François*, vol. XI, pp. 337–40; *CSPV 1625–26*, p. 55 (14 May 1625); *Chamberlain*, II, p. 616 (to Carleton: 14 May 1625); D'Ewes, *Autobiography*, I, pp. 267–8; Gittings, *Death*, pp. 173, 222–3.

9. "True Order", pp. 1,045–7; *Mercure François*, vol. XI, p. 340; BL Lansdowne MS 885, fo. 121v.

10. *CSPV 1625–26*, p. 55 (14 May 1625); Bulstrode Whitelocke, *Memorials of English Affairs*, 4 vols (Oxford, 1853), I, p. 1; Sherlock, "Monuments", p. 266; *Rushworth*, I, sig. Z2r; *Whiteway*, p. 72; Sharpe, *Image Wars*, p. 231; Woodward, *Theatre*, pp. 180–4.

11. "True Order", p. 1,047; NA SP 16/1/100; *Salvetti*, p. 16 (James I's funeral); *Mercure François*, XI, p. 340.

12. *Salvetti*, p. 16 (James I's funeral); "True Order", pp. 1,041–4; BL Lansdowne 885, fos 117r–19v.

13. *CSPV 1625–26*, p. 30 (22 April 1625); *Salvetti*, pp. 9–10 (22 April 1625); BL Harl. MS 389, fos 422r, 436v (Meddus to Mead: 13 April and 6 May 1625).

14. *Register PSC*, I, p. 650 (Gilbert Primrose to his father: 10 May 1625); *CSPV 1625–26*, pp. 53–6, 64–5 (14 and 30 May 1625). See also NA SP 16/2/51–2; NA LC 2/6, fo. 34r; *Salvetti*, p. 14 (13 May 1625); *Rusdorf*, pp. 575–7 (5 May); *Mercure François*, XI, p. 339; Maurice Lee, Jr., *The Road to Revolution: Scotland Under Charles I, 1625–37* (Urbana, 1985), p. 11.

15. *Chamberlain*, II, p. 616 (to Carleton: 14 May 1625); *CSPV 1625–26*, p. 55 (14 May 1625); Stow and Howes, *Annales*, p. 1,041; BL Add. MS 72255, no. 178 (Beaulieu to Trumbull: 12 May 1625); *Whiteway*, p. 72.

16. *Chamberlain*, II, p. 616 (to Carleton: 14 May 1625); *CSPV 1625–26*, p. 55 (14 May 1625); *Salvetti*, p. 17 (James I's funeral); Stow and Howes, *Annales*, p. 1,041; College of Arms MS "Partition Book the 2nd", fos 346r, 356v–59v; NA SP 16/2/30; BL Cotton MS Vesp. C XIV, fos 223r–25r; BL Harl. MS 389, fos 432v–33r, 437r (London reports: 27 April and 6 May 1625); Gittings, *Death*, pp. 176, 225; Anthony Wagner, *Heralds of England: A History of the Office and College of Arms* (London, 1967), pp. 113–14; *Progresses*, III, pp. 499–500; John Peacock, "Inigo Jones's Catafalque for James I", *Architectural History* 25 (1982); John Harris and Gordon Higgott, *Inigo Jones: Complete Architectural Drawings* (New York, 1989), pp. 160, 186–7; Francis Sandford, *Genealogical History* (London, 1707), p. 561.

17. John Williams, *Great Britains Salomon* (London, 1625), pp. 37–9, 41, 43–5, 47, 50–1, 54, 56, 58–9, 62–3, 65–7; Sharpe, *Image Wars*, part 1 *passim*.

18. Williams, *Salomon*, pp. 67–71.

19. Williams, *Salomon*, pp. 71–3.

20. Williams, *Salomon*, pp. 75–6. For responses, see D'Ewes, *Autobiography*, I, pp. 267–8; Fuller, *Church*, VI, pp.10–12; *Scrinia*, I, p. 223.

21. "True Order", pp. 1,047–8; NA SP 16/2/31–2; D'Ewes, *Autobiography*, I, pp. 267–8; *Salvetti*, p. 17 (13 May 1625); Charles Cornwallis, *The Life and Death of . . . Henry Prince of Wales* (London, 1641), pp. 92–3; Gittings, *Death*, pp. 176–9; Woodward, *Theatre*, pp. 180–1; Arthur Stanley, *Historical Memorials of Westminster Abbey*, 3rd ed. (London, 1869), pp. 678–86; Sherlock, "Monuments", pp. 267, 273. For evidence that James's body was interred earlier, see *Salvetti*, pp. 15–17 (13 May 1625), and *Scrinia*, I, p. 223.

22. Hugh Holland, *A Cypres Garland. For the Sacred Forehead of our late Soveraigne King Iames* (London, 1625), sig. A3r; Cornwallis, *Henry*, p. 93; St. John Hope, "Funeral Effigies", p. 557; Woodward, *Theatre*, p. 202; Sherlock, "Monuments", pp. 271, 273, 286–8; Llewellyn, "Royal Body", pp. 224–8, 240.

23. Llewellyn, "Royal Body", p. 240; Sherlock, "Monuments", p. 289; Roy Strong, *Britannia Triumphans: Inigo Jones, Rubens and Whitehall Palace* (New York, 1981); Stanley, *Memorials*, pp. 651ff.

24. Williams, *Salomon*; BL Harl. MS 389, fo. 444r (Mead to Stuteville: 21 May 1625).

25. Daniel Price, *A Heartie Prayer, In a needfull time of trouble* (London, 1625); Phineas Hodson, *The Last Sermon Preached Before His Maiesties Funerals* (London, 1625); Holland, *Cypres Garland*, sig. A3v; Thomas Heywood, *A Funeral Elegie Upon the Much Lamented Death of the Trespuissant and unmatchable King, King Iames* (London, 1625); John Taylor, *A Living Sadnes, In Duty consecrated to the Immortall memory of our late Deceased albe-loved Soveraigne Lord, The Peerelesse Paragon of Princes, IAMES* (London, 1625).

26. Hodson, *Last Sermon*, pp. 20–2; Holland, *Cypres Garland*, sigs C1r, C2r–v; Taylor, *Living Sadnes*, pp. 2, 3, 6–7, 9–10; Price, *Heartie Prayer*, p. 3; Francis Hamiltoun, *King Iames his Encomium* (Edinburgh, 1626), sigs B3r–v (mispaginated).

27. Hodson, *Last Sermon*, p. 21; Holland, *Cypres Garland*, sigs B4v, C1r–v; Taylor, *Living Sadnes*, pp. 3–4, 6, 9; Heywood, *Funeral Elegie*, sig. B2r.

28. Taylor, *Living Sadnes*, pp. 3, 4–6 and 9–10; Heywood, *Funeral Elegie*, sigs B2v, C4v–D1r.

29. Hodson, *Last Sermon*, pp. 20–1, 26; Price, *Heartie Prayer*, pp. 12, 17–19, 30–1, 35; see too Holland, *Cypres Garland*, sigs B3r–v, C4v; Taylor, *Living Sadnes*, p. 2.

30. Heywood, *Funeral Elegie*, sigs B3v–4r, D2r–3r; Taylor, *Living Sadnes*, pp. 1, 10; Holland, *Cypres Garland*, sig. C4r.

31. Abraham Darcie and Robert Vaughan, *Maiesties Sacred Monument Erected by A.D.V. Darcie in Memorie of K. Iames* (London, 1625).

32. Taylor, *Living Sadnes*, pp. 3–4, 8; Heywood, *Funeral Elegie*, sigs B2r–v, B3v, B4r; Holland, *Cypres Garland*, sig. B2v; Price, *Heartie Prayer*, p. 33.

33. BL Stowe MS 182, fos 74v–75r (punctuation amended); Holland, *Cypres Garland*, sigs A4r, B3r, C3r–4r.

34. Holland, *Cypres Garland*, sigs A4v–B1r; Heywood, *Funeral Elegie*, sig B4r; Taylor, *Living Sadnes*, p. 7; Price, *Heartie Prayer*, p. 31.

Part 2 Prologue

1. NA SP 16/10/33 (Danby's information: 26 November 1625); 16/10/55 (Hogg's examination: 30 November 1625); 16/12/54 and 54: I–III (Rutland to Conway: 26 December 1625); 16/19/15 (Carr to Conway: 21 January 1625); 16/21/61 (Hogg's examination: 25 February 1626); 16/21/73 (Crewe to Conway: 27 February 1626); 16/23/21 (Thomas Trussell's petition); 16/23/22 (Crewe to Conway: 18 March 1626); Francis Blomefield and Charles Parkin, *An Essay Towards a Topographical History of the County of Norfolk* (Lynn and London, 1769), vol. III, pp. 792–3.
2. Adam Fox, *Oral and Literate Culture in England, 1500–1700* (Oxford, 2000), ch. 7.
3. NA SP 16/3/53 (misc. examinations: June 1625); *C&T Charles*, vol. I, pp. 49, 58 (Mead to Stuteville: 10 September and 22 October 1625).
4. NA SP 16/3/53 (Robert Byrback's testimony).

Chapter 3

1. HHStA, Belgien Fasz. 62, fo. 165r (Van Male to [Faille]: 25 March 1625).
2. TCD, MS 708, I, fo. 380r (Carew to Roe: 14 October 1624); *Chamberlain*, II, pp. 531, 579 (to Carleton: 6 December 1623 and 4 September 1624); Theodore de Mayerne, *Opera Medica* (London, 1703), pp. 305–6; Kate Frost, "Prescription and Devotion: The Reverend Doctor Donne and the Learned Doctor Mayerne—Two Seventeenth-Century Records of Epidemic Typhus Fever", *Medical History* 22 (1978).
3. TCD, MS 708, I, fo. 412r (Elizabeth to Roe: 27 December [1624]); *Holles*, II, p. 301 (to G. Holles: 4 March 1625). See too *Chamberlain*, II, pp. 574, 576, 578–9 (to Carleton: 7 and 21 August, 4 September 1624); *HMC Cowper*, I, pp. 172, 174.
4. NRS Lothian MSS GD 40/2/15 (Melros to Kerr: 9 March 1625); NA SP 31/3/61, fo. 60r (D'Effiat to Ville-aux-Clercs: 1 March 1625); NLW, MS 9059E/1220 (Owen to Sir John Wynn: 4 March 1625).
5. *Chamberlain*, II, p. 605 (to Carleton: 12 March 1625); BL Harl. MS 389, fo. 410r (Mead to Stuteville: 5 March 1625); TCD MS 708, I, fo. 477r (Abbot to Roe: 30 March 1625).
6. NA SP 84/126/39 (Carleton to Conway: 9 March 1625); BL Add. MS 72255, no. 177 (Beaulieu to Trumbull: 8 April 1625); NLW, MS 9060E/1283 (Owen to Sir John Wynn: 12 January 1625); BL Add. MS 72329, no. 168 (Wolley to Trumbull: 15 April 1625).
7. NA SP 101/10/11 (Anon. to James: [1624]); SP 16/1/2 (Chambermayd to Elizabeth: 27 March 1625).
8. Yale Beinecke MS FB 155 (Spanish protest); NLS, MS 33.1.7 nos 72, 92 (Buckingham to James [1624]).
9. *Yonge*, p. 74; BL Add. MS 72275, no. 118 (Castle to Trumbull: 14 May 1624); and NA SP 101/10/11 (anonymous newsletter from Paris: 1624).
10. BL Add. MS 72272, fo. 196r (Hamilton to Trumbull: 4 March 1625); BL Add. MS 72254, no. 144 (Castle to Trumbull, 5 March 1624); *Chamberlain*, II, p. 604 (to Carleton: 12 March 1625); BL Harl. MS 389, fos 408v, 414r–v (Meddus to Mead: 4 March 1625; London report: 11 March 1625).
11. NA SP 14/185/95 (Coventry to Conway: 22 March 1625); *Whiteway*, p. 69.
12. *Ellis*, p. 244 (Tilman to Paul D'Ewes: 1 April 1625); *Cornwallis*, pp. 128–9, 133 (Bedford to Lady Cornwallis: 23 March and 12 April 1625); D'Ewes, *Autobiography*, I, p. 262.
13. NA SP 81/32/84 (Nethersole to Woodford: 7 February 1625); SP 14/182/40 (St Leger to Conway: 23 January 1625); SP 81/30/244 ([Buckingham] to [Mansfelt]: 12 January 1625); SP 84/122/75 (Conway to Carleton: 25 January 1625).
14. NA SP 84/122/178 (Cromwell to Conway: 26 February 1625).
15. NA SP 84/122/180 (Cromwell to Conway: [late February 1625]); SP 84/126/1 (Carleton to Conway: 1 March 1625).

16. NA SP 84/126/1 (Carleton to Cromwell: 1 March 1625); SP 84/126/3 (Cromwell to Carleton: 2 March 1625); *Holles*, II, p. 299 (to Somerset: 2 March 1625).

17. NA SP 84/126/15–17 (Conway to Carleton: 4 March 1625).

18. NA SP 84/126/68 (Conway to Carleton: 21 March 1625); SP 99/26/66v (Conway to Wake: 24 March 1625).

19. NLS Adv. MS 33.1.7, vol. 22, no. 84 (Buckingham to James: [1 March 1625]) BL Harl. MS 6987, fos 203–4 (Charles to Buckingham: [early 1625]).

20. Folger MS L.d.294 (Fotherbye to [Townshend]: 8 March 1625). On James and Buckingham's movements, see *Holles*, II, p. 301 (to G. Holles: 4 March 1625); *Laud*, p. 158; NLS MS 33.1.7, no. 71 (Buckingham to James: [late February 1625]); NA SP 14/185/1 (Conway to Buckingham: 1 March 1625).

21. *M&K*, p. 223 (9 March 1625); NA SP 16/1/2 (Chambermayd to Elizabeth: 27 March 1625); NA SP 31/3/61, fo. 77r (D'Effiat to Ville-aux-Clercs: 9 March 1625); *Chamberlain*, II, p. 606 (to Carleton: 12 March 1625).

22. Hardwicke, *SP*, I, p. 562 (Conway to Carlisle: 16 March 1625); BL Harl. MS 389, fo. 417v (London report: 18 March 1625).

23. HHStA Belgien Fasz. 61, unfoliated (X: 11 March 1625); BL Add. MS 72276, no. 145 (Castle to Trumbull: 18 March 1625).

24. *CSPV 1623–25*, p. 618 (15 March 1625); SP 14/185/63 (Mountaigne to Conway: 16 March 1625); *Rusdorf*, p. 499 (Rusdorf to Frederick: 15 March 1625).

25. NA SP 78/74/60 (Carlisle and Holland report: 14 February 1625); SP 78/74/58 (Goring to Buckingham: 23 February 1625); and Hardwicke, *SP*, I, p. 464 (Buckingham to James: [mid-February 1625]).

26. NA SP 78/74/88 (Conway to Carlisle and Holland: 1 March 1625); BL Add. MS 72255, no. 176 (Beaulieu to Trumbull: 18 March 1625).

27. BL Add. MS 72276, no. 145 (Castle to Trumbull: 18 March 1625); Bod. MS Clarendon 96, fo. 193r (Holland to Charles: 12 March 1625); Hardwicke, *SP*, I, pp. 562–3 (Conway to Carlisle: 16 March 1625).

28. NA SP 16/1/2 (Chambermayd to Elizabeth: 27 March 1625); Hardwicke, *SP*, I, p. 562 (Conway to Carlisle: 16 March 1625); SP 14/185/85 (Morton to Conway: 21 March 1625); SP 84/126/66 and 68v (Conway to Carleton: 21 March 1625); NA 31/3/61, fo. 91r (D'Effiat to Ville-aux-clercs: 21 March 1625).

29. NA 31/3/61, fo. 91r (D'Effiat to Ville-aux-Clercs: 21 March 1625); and *Chamberlain*, II, p. 607 (to Carleton: 23 March 1625).

30. NLS MS 31.1.7, no. 87 (Buckingham to James: [1624]); NA SP 94/32/6 (Buckingham to Aston: 16 January 1625).

31. *Holles*, II, p. 301 (to G. Holles: 4 March 1625); *CSPV 1625–26*, p. 610 (4 March 1625).

32. NA 31/3/61, fos 94–5, item B (D'Effiat to Ville-aux-Clercs: 19 March 1625); NLW MS 9060E/1254 (Owen to Sir John Wynn: 4 March 1625).

33. NA SP 84/126/69 (Conway to Carleton: 21 March 1625); *C&T James*, II, p. 503 (anon. report: 4 March 1625).

34. *Scrinia*, I, p. 222; Hardwicke, *SP*, I, p. 564 (Conway to Carlisle and Holland: 24 March 1625).

35. Hardwicke, *SP*, I, pp. 565–7 (Conway to Carlisle: 24 March 1624); NA SP 99/26/67 (Conway to Wake: 24 March 1625).

36. *Holles*, II, p. 302 (Clare to Somerset: 26 March 1625); *Cornwallis*, p. 129 (Bedford to Cornwallis: 23 March 1625); BL Add. MS 64882, fo. 142r (Apsley to Coke: 11 March 1625).

37. *Rusdorf*, p. 532 (Rusdorf to Frederick: 26 [March] 1625); *CSPV 1623–25*, p. 627 (27 March 1625).

38. *CSPV 1623–25*, pp. 623, 627 (25 and 27 March 1625).

39. *M&K*, pp. 225–6 (22 March 1625).

40. HHStA Belgien Fasz. 62, fo. 165r (Van Male to [Faille]: 25 March 1625); Fasz. 61, unfoliated ("XX": 25 March 1625).

41. HHStA Belgien Fasz. 62, fos 167–7v (anon. letter: 25 March 1625).

42. BL Add. MS 12528, fos 9v, 15r–v, 18v–19r, 31r.

43. BL Harl. MS 6987, fos 234v–35r (Buckingham to James); BL Add. MS 12528, fos 14–15r; Francis Anthony, *The Apologie, or a Defence of a Verity Heretofore Published Concerning a Medicine Called Aurum Potabile* (London, 1616), sigs M1v–2r, M3v–4r.

44. "Introduction", in Arthur Searle (ed.), *Barrington Family Letters, 1628–1632*, Camden Society, 4th Series, 28 (London, 1983), p. 20.

45. Lazarus Rivière, *The Practice of Physick* (London, 1672), pp. 584–5; Daniel Sennert, *Of Agues and Fevers* (London, 1658), p. 59.

46. Nicholas Monardes, *Ioyfull Newes out of the newe founde worlde* (London, 1577), book two, fols 46r–56v; Thomas Hariot, *A briefe and true report of the new found land of Virginia* (Frankfurt, 1590), p. 9; John Gerard, *The Herball* (London, 1633), pp. 389–92, 1,524–5; Ben Jonson, *Volpone*, Act 2, scene 2, ll. 112–23. On therapeutic eclecticism, see Michael MacDonald, *Mystical Bedlam: Madness, Anxiety and Healing in Seventeenth-Century England* (Cambridge, 1981).

47. Anthony, *Apologie*, sigs D1v, D2r, E1v–2r, F1v–2r, G1r–v, G4r–v, H1v–2r, L1v–L2r, M1v–M2v, M3v, M4v, N2v.

48. Gerard, *Herball*, pp. 587–8, 688, 807; G. W. and A. T., *A Rich Storehouse, or Treasurie for the Diseased* (London, 1630), pp. 12–25. For examples of MS remedy books with ague cures, see e.g. BL Add. MS 42115; Egerton MS 2608; and BL Harl. MS 907. See too Paul Slack, "Mirrors of Health and Treasures of Poor Men: The Uses of the Vernacular Medical Literature of Tudor England", in Charles Webster (ed.), *Health, Medicine and Mortality in the Sixteenth Century* (Cambridge, 1979).

49. Reginald Scot, *The Discoverie of Witchcraft*, ed. Montague Summers (New York, 1972), book 12, ch. 18, pp. 153–5; BL Add. MS 42115, fos 2r–3r; BL Egerton MS 2608, fos 27v, 28r, 29v, 31v, 40v, 43r, 46r, 53r, 56v, 62v, 82r, 88r; Gerard, *Herball*, pp. 991–2, 1,169, 1,188; BL Harl. MS 907, fos 74v–5r.

50. Alan Macfarlane (ed.), *The Diary of Ralph Josselin, 1616–1683* (Oxford, 1991), pp. 110–13 (6–19 February 1648); Lucinda McCray Beier, *Sufferers and Healers: The Experience of Illness in Seventeenth-Century England* (London and New York, 1987), ch. 7.

51. On Buckingham and different forms of medicine, see *Chamberlain*, II, p. 558 (to Carleton: 13 May 1624); BL Add. MS 12528, fos 15v, 31r; BL Harley MS 6987, fos 218r, 238r; *HMC Cowper*, I, p. 168 (Sir Francis to John Coke: 15 August 1624); Alexandra Walsham, *The Reformation of the Landscape: Religion, Identity, and Memory in Early Modern Britain and Ireland* (Oxford, 2011), p. 415.

52. MacDonald, *Mystical Bedlam*, esp. pp. 21, 49, 92, 152, 192, 199, 256 n.27; BL Harl. MS 6987, fos 56r–v (Countess to Duke of Buckingham: 6 April 1623); Bod. MS Ashmole 1730, fo. 194r (Napier to Purbeck); Bod. MS Ashmole 240, fos 48r, 49r, 792 (Napier's astrological charts for Purbeck and Buckingham).

53. *Laud*, p. 154.

54. Bellany, "Lambe"; BL Harl. MS 6987, fos 219r–v (Buckingham to James: undated).

55. *The Correspondence of Sir Robert Kerr, First Earl of Ancram* (Edinburgh, 1875), p. 522 ("Sonnet," late 1624); NA SP 84/126/111 (Conway to Carleton: 31 March 1625); TCD MS 708, I, fo. 478r (Abbot to Roe: 30 March 1625); Bod. MS Add. D111, fo. 323r (Exeter to Buckingham: 28 March 1625).

56. BL Add. MS 64883, fos 13r–v (Chudleigh to Coke: 2 April 1625); BL Add. MS 72255, no. 177 (Beaulieu to Trumbull: 8 April 1625); *Chamberlain*, II, p. 609 (to Carleton: 9 April 1625); HHStA Belgien Fasz. 61, unfoliated (X: 29 April 1625).

57. BL Add. MS 72331, no. 164 (Wolley to Trumbull: 8 April 1625); BL Add. MS 72255, no. 177 (Beaulieu to Trumbull: 8 April 1625); HHStA Belgien Fasz. 61, unfoliated (X: [31 March 1625]).

58. HHStA Belgien Fasz. 61, unfoliated (X: [31 March 1625]); *M&K*, p. 227 (7 April 1625); *CSPV 1625–26*, p. 3 (30 March 1625); *C&T Charles*, I, p. 4 (Neve to Hollonde: 5 April 1625).

59. *CSPV 1625–26*, p. 13 (8 April 1625); NLS MS 80 (Melrose to Buckingham: 9 March 1625); HHStA Belgien Fasz. 61, unfoliated (X: 8 April 1625). See too *Salvetti*, p. 10 (2 May 1625); *Cornwallis*, pp. 131–2 (Bedford to Cornwallis: 12 April 1625).

60. HHStA Belgien Fasz 61, unfoliated (X: 31 March 1625).

61. *Holles*, II, p. 305 (to G. Holles: 1 May 1625); HHStA Belgien Fasz. 61, unfoliated (X: 8 April 1625); *C&T Charles*, I, p. 21 (Mead to Stuteville: 6 and 14 May 1625). See also *Chamberlain*, II, p. 611 (to Carleton: 23 April 1625); *CSPV 1625–26*, p. 27 (22 April 1625); NA SP 16/1/43 (Charles to closet council: 9 April 1625).

62. NA SP 84/126/173–3v (Conway to Carleton: 12 April 1625); *Holles*, II, p. 303 (to G. Holles: 10 April 1625); *M&K*, p. 183 (4 November 1623). See also *CSPV 1625–26*, p. 4 (30 March 1625).

63. Somerset RO Phelips MSS, DD/Ph 219, fo. 64r (Tomkins to Phelips: [late March 1625]); KHLC Knatchbull-Astley-Wyndham MSS, U951/C261 (anon. report: 31 March 1625).

64. *CSPV 1625–26*, p. 3 (29 March 1625); NA SP 84/126/109 (Conway to Carleton: 31 March 1625).

65. BL Add. MS 72331, no. 160 (Wolley: 1 April 1625); BL Add. MS 72255, no. 177 (Beaulieu to Trumbull: 8 April 1625); Folger MS L.d. 418 (Mason to Townshend: 3 April 1625).

66. KHLC Knatchbull-Astley-Wyndham MSS, U951/C261 (anon. report: 31 March 1625). See also *Chamberlain*, II, p. 609 (to Carleton: 9 April 1625); BL Harl. MS 389, fo. 422r (Letter to Mead: 13 April 1625).

67. NA SP 84/126/109 (Conway to Carleton: 31 March 1625); *CSPV 1625–26*, p. 4 (30 March 1625).

68. KHLC Knatchbull-Astley-Wyndham MSS, U951/C261 (anon. letter: 31 March 1625); BL Add. MS 72255, no. 178 (Beaulieu: 12 May 1625), in response to Trumbull's 6 May letter.

69. *C&T Charles*, I, p. 5 (Mead to Stuteville: 9 April 1625).

70. *CSPV 1623–25*, p. 627, and *1625–26*, p. 13 (27 March and 8 April 1625); HHStA Belgien Fasz. 61, unfoliated (X: 31 March 1625). On Gibb, see Bellany, *Politics*, p. 70.

Chapter 4

1. Thomas Dempster, *Thomae Dempsteri Historia Ecclesiastica Gentis Scotorum: Sive, De Scriptoribus Scotis. Editio Altera* (1627) (Edinburgh, 1829), p. 271. Eglisham was brought up with the second Marquis of Hamilton, born in 1589, but was probably a few years older than his friend.

2. *Forerunner*, p. 5; George Crawfurd, *The Peerage of Scotland: containing an historical and genealogical account of the nobility of that Kingdom* (Edinburgh, 1714), pp. 188–202; Francis Hamilton, *King Iames his Encomium* (Edinburgh, 1626). In 1616 a George Eglisham was "served heir to his father John Eglisham, a burgess of Edinburgh" (David Irving, *Memoirs of the Life and Writings of George Buchanan*, 2nd ed. (Edinburgh, 1817), p. 114 n.), but while a John Eglisham appears in the right kinds of elite circles (see e.g. John Maitland Thomson [ed.], *The Register of the Great Seal of Scotland, AD 1546–1580* [Edinburgh, 1886], pp. 36, 638), Eglisham's account of his presentation to James VI (*Forerunner*, pp. 5–6) may imply his father died before 1603.

3. *Forerunner*, pp. 5–6; Rosalind K. Marshall, "Hamilton, John, First Marquess of Hamilton (1539/40–1604)", *ODNB*.

4. Dempster, *Historia*, p. 271 ("bonas artes et didicit Lovanii in Belgio operose"); BIUM, "Commentaires de la faculté de médecine" 10 (1604–12), fo. 284v; Alexander Du Toit, "Dempster, Thomas (1579–1625)", *ODNB*; A. Schillings (ed.), *Matricule de L'Université de Louvain* (Brussels, 1962), vol. 5, p. ix; Nicolas Vernulaeus, *Academia Lovaniensis Libri III* (Louvain, 1627), pp. 116–21 (trans. William Hamilton, *Discussions on Philosophy and Literature, Education and University Reform*, 2nd ed. [London, 1853], pp. 736–41). David Buchanan claimed (erroneously) that Eglisham studied at St Andrew's: see *Davidis Buchanani de Scriptoribus Scotis Libri Duo, Nunc Primum Editi* (Edinburgh, 1837), p. 20.

5. *Records of the Scots Colleges at Douai, Rome, Madrid, Valladolid and Ratisbon* (Aberdeen, 1906), vol. I, p. 8; Hubert Chadwick, "The Scots College, Douai, 1580–1613", *EHR* 56:224 (1941), p. 582.

6. On the Reresbys, see *The Visitation of the County of Yorke, Begun in Ao Dni MDCLXV and Finished Ao Dni MDCLXVI By William Dugdale*, Surtees Society 36 (1859), pp. 182–3; James J. Cartwright (ed.), *The Memoirs of Sir John Reresby of Thrybergh*

(London, 1875), esp. pp. 4ff; "The Northern Book of Compositions, 1629–32", in "Miscellanea: Recusant Records", *Catholic Record Society* 53 (1960), p. 343.

7. Edward Peacock (ed.), *A List of The Roman Catholics in the County of York in 1604* (London, 1872), p. 6; Cartwright, *Memoirs*, p. 3; A. G. Dickens, "The Extent and Character of Recusancy in Yorkshire, 1604" (1948), and (with John Newton), "Further Light on the Scope of Yorkshire Recusancy, 1604" (1955), reprinted in A. G. Dickens, *Reformation Studies* (London, 1982). Dickens (p. 199 and n.9) hedges his bets on the identity of "Egleseme".

8. Dempster, *Historia*, p. 271; BL Add. MS 22961, fo. 244r (Hommius to Lubbertus: 9 June 1612); *Plaidoye de Me Iaques De Montholon Advocat en la Cour*, 2nd ed. (Paris, 1612), pp. 179–80; Philip Benedict, *Rouen During the Wars of Religion* (Cambridge, 1981), pp. 170–1; Paul Arblaster, *Antwerp & the World: Richard Verstegan & the International Culture of Catholic Reformation* (Leuven, 2004), pp. 23–4; Jean-Pierre Bardet, *Rouen au XVIIe et XVIIIe Siècles: Les Mutations d'un espace social* (Paris, 1983), vol. II, table 17, p. 34; Guy Lemarchand, "Rouen au milieu du XVIIe siècle: une grande ville de France", and Michel Zylberberg, "Les Relations internationales de Rouen dans le premier XVIIe siècle", both in Jean-Pierre Cléro (ed.), *Les Pascal à Rouen, 1640–1648* (Rouen, 2001).

9. Benedict, *Rouen*, pp. 193–6; Antonella Romano, "Enseignement des mathématiques et de la philosophie naturelle au Collège de Rouen (Première Moitié du XVIIe Siècle)", in Cléro, *Les Pascal à Rouen*, pp. 218–20, 226–7.

10. "Livre des Receveurs et Quaesteurs de la Nation d'Allemagne, 1580–1625", cited in W. A. McNeil, "Scottish Entries in the *Acta Rectoria Universitatis Parisiensis* 1519 to c. 1633", *Scottish Historical Review* 43:135 (1964), p. 85; BIUM, "Commentaires", 10, fo. 284v.

11. BIUM, "Commentaires", 10, fos 284v, 302–3; John Durkan, "The French Connection in the Sixteenth and Early Seventeenth Centuries", in T. C. Smout (ed.), *Scotland and Europe, 1200–1850* (Edinburgh, 1986), pp. 27–8; L. W. B. Brockliss, "Medical Teaching at the University of Paris, 1600–1720", *Annals of Science* 35 (1978), esp. pp. 227–8.

12. Gabriel de Castaigne, *L'Or Potable Qui Guarit de Tous Maux* (Paris 1611), p. 65; Francisque Michel, *Les Écossais en France: les Français en Écosse* (London, 1862), vol. II, p. 221 n.6; BL Add. MS 22961, fo. 244r (Hommius to Lubbertus: 9 June 1612).

13. Laurence Brockliss and Colin Jones, *The Medical World of Early Modern France* (Oxford, 1997), pp. 119ff; Hugh Trevor-Roper, *Europe's Physician: The Various Life of Sir Theodore de Mayerne* (New Haven and London, 2006), chs 1–8; Stephen Bamforth, "Paracelsisme et médecine chimique à la cour de Louis XIII", in Heinz Schott and Ilana Zinguer (eds), *Paracelsus und Seine Internationale Rezeption in Der Frühen Neuzeit* (Leiden, 1998).

14. Castaigne, *L'Or Potable*, pp. 11, 63–5; Francis Anthony, *The Apologie* (London, 1616), sigs A1r, A2r–v; Brockliss and Jones, *Medical World*, pp. 123–5 nn. 144 and 146; 232, 330 n.194; Bamforth, "Paracelsisme"; and François Secret, "De quelques traités d'alchimie au temps de Marie de Médicis", *Chrysopoeia* 3 (1989).

15. Secret, "De quelques traités", pp. 329 n. 93, 337 (quoting *L'Or Potable* [1613 ed.], pp. 54–5); Bamforth, "Paracelsisme", pp. 225, 228–9; BIUM, "Commentaires" 10, fos 367r, 375r–76r.

16. Gabriel de Castaigne, *Le Grand Miracle de Nature Metallique* (Paris, 1615), p. 10; Bamforth, "Paracelsisme", pp. 225–6; and Véronique Luzel, "Une pièce liminaire de Béroalde de Verville dans un ouvrage du médecin chimiste Israël Harvet", *Nouvelle Revue du Seizième Siècle* 21:2 (2003), p. 93 n.50.

17. Some scholars (including the *DNB*) claim Eglisham trained at Leiden, but he does not appear in Edward Peacock (ed.), *Index to English-Speaking Students Who have Graduated at Leyden University* (London, 1883); or R. W. Innes Smith, *English-Speaking Students of Medicine at the University of Leyden* (Edinburgh and London, 1932). On Louvain's conservatism, see François-André Sondervorst, *Histoire de la médecine belge* (Séquoia, 1981), pp. 86–7, 110–11; Walter Pagel, *Joan Baptista Van Helmont: Reformer of Science and Medicine* (Cambridge, 1982), pp. 2–6.

18. Dempster, *Historia*, p. 271; cf. Anthony, *Apologie*, sigs A3v–B4v.

19. See Bamforth, "Paracelcisme", pp. 231–3, on Castaigne's self-presentation.

20. Anthony, *Apologie*, sigs B3r, C2r.

21. [George Browne, trans.], *The Argument of Mr. Peter de la Martelière, Advocate in the Court of Parliament of Paris* (London, 1612), p. 26 (a translation of Martelière, *Plaidoyé de Mᵉ Pierre de La Marteliere fait en Parlement* (1612)); *Plaidoye de Mᵉ Iaques De Montholon*, pp. 179–80.

22. The major sources for Eglisham in the United Provinces are J. A. Worp (ed.), "Fragment Eener Autobiographie Van Constantijn Huygens", *Bijdragen en Mededeelingen van het Historisch Genootschap* 18 (The Hague, 1897); J. H. W. Unger (ed.), *Dagboek van Constantyn Huygens. Voor de eerste mall naar het afschrift van diens kleinzoon uitgegeven* (Amsterdam, 1885); and A. G. H. Bachrach, *Sir Constantine Huygens and Britain, 1596–1687: A Pattern of Cultural Exchange* (Leiden and London, 1962), vol. I, pp. 72–83, 213–14.

23. On the Vorstius affair, see Bachrach, *Huygens*, I, pp. 72ff; F. C. Shriver, "Orthodoxy and Diplomacy: James I and the Vorstius Affair", *EHR* 85:336 (1970); and Jonathan Israel, *The Dutch Republic: Its Rise, Greatness, and Fall, 1477–1806* (Oxford, 1998), ch. 18 and pp. 428–9.

24. Israel, *Dutch Republic*, p. 428.

25. Ralph Winwood, *Memorials of Affairs of State* (London, 1725), vol. III, pp. 310–11, 339, 349; NA SP 84/68, fos 234r–35r, 238r–39v, 242r–v (Winwood to Salisbury: 5, 10 and 20 February 1612); BL Stowe MS 172, fo. 191r (Winwood to Edmondes: 26 February 1612); *Declaratio Serenissimi Magnae Britanniae Regis* (London, 1612); *His Maiesties Declaration concerning His Proceedings with the States generall of the United Provinces of the Low Countreys, In the cause of D. Conradus Vorstius* (London, 1612); Shriver, "Orthodoxy", p. 470.

26. Winwood, *Memorials*, III, pp. 311, 318, 323, 330, 339–40 (Winwood to Trumbull: 11 and 31 December 1611, 11 and 25 January, and 18 February 1612); BL Add. MS 72327, fos 94r–95r, 98r–v (Winwood to Trumbull: 11 and 31 December 1611); Willem Nijenhuis (ed.), *Matthew Slade, 1569–1628: Letters to the English Ambassador* (Leiden, 1986), pp. 11–16.

27. Winwood, *Memorials*, III, pp. 339, 348, 357 (Winwood to Trumbull: 18 February, 16 March and 13 April 1612); NA SP 84/68, fos 238v, 259v (Winwood to Salisbury: 10 February and 19 March 1612); Israel, *Dutch Republic*, pp. 433–4.

28. NA SP 84/68 fos 252r–v (Winwood to Salisbury: 18 March 1612); BL Stowe MS 172, fo. 210r (Winwood to Edmondes: 17 March 1612).

29. Huygens, "Autobiographie", p. 94; *Forerunner*, p. 5; Pierre Bayle, *The Dictionary Historical and Critical of Mr Peter Bayle* (London, 1734), vol. V, p. 512; Christoph Lüthy, "The Confessionalization of Physics: Heresies, Facts and the Travails of the Republic of Letters", in John Brooke and Ian Maclean (eds), *Heterodoxy in Early Modern Science and Religion* (Oxford, 2005), pp. 101–4.

30. Huygens, "Autobiographie", p. 94; George Eglisham, *Crisis Vorstiani Responsi. Qua Conradus Vorstius denuo Atheismi, Ethnicismi, Judaismi, Turcismi, Haereseos, Schismatis, et ignorantiae arguitur* (Delft, 1612); George Eglisham, *Hypocrisis Apologeticae Orationis Vorstianae cum Secunda Provocatione ad d. C. Vorstium missa* (Delft, 1612); Bayle, *Dictionary*, V, p. 512.

31. *Crisis Vorstiani*, sigs B1r, B2r ff, C2v–3r, C4v, G3r; Bayle, *Dictionary*, V, p. 512.

32. BL Add. MS 22961, fos 239r, 240r, 243r, 244r (Slade and Hommius to Lubbertus: 24 April, 5 May, 6 and 9 June 1612); BL Add. MS 72341, fo. 89r (Nieuland to Trumbull: 6 June 1612); *Nicolaus Hasius Leydensis D. Georgio Eglisemmio Scoto, Medico & Philosopho* (Leiden, 1612).

33. BL Add. MS 72326, fos 59v, 61r, 63r; BL Add. MS 22961, fo. 243r (Slade to Lubbertus: 6 June 1612).

34. Eglisham, *Hypocrisis*, sigs C2r–E4v; F3r–H4v, I2r–v.

35. BL Add. MS 72342, fo. 25r (Nieuland to Trumbull: 14 August 1612); Bayle, *Dictionary*, V, p. 512.

36. Huygens, "Autobiographie", pp. 94–6; Winwood, *Memorials*, III, p. 302. On the lost Eglisham publications, see Dempster, *Historia*, p. 271, who says that Eglisham published *Declamationes Philosophicas*; and Buchanan, *De Scriptoribus*, p. 20, who attributes to him *Animadversiones in Aristotelis Logicam*. See too Bachrach, *Huygens*, I, ch. 3, pp. 79–81; and Rosalie L. Colie, *'Some Thankfulnesse to Constantine': A Study of English Influence Upon the Early Works of Constantijn Huygens* (The Hague, 1956), ch. 1 and p. 22.

37. Huygens, "Autobiographie", pp. 94–7, 103–4; Unger, "Dagboek", pp. 7–8; cf. the curriculum in Vernulaeus, *Academia Lovaniensis*, pp. 116–21; Colie, 'Some Thankfulnesse', chs 5–8; Svetlana Alpers, *The Art of Describing: Dutch Art in the Seventeenth Century* (Chicago, 1983), ch. 1; Brockliss and Jones, *Medical World*, p. 121.

38. Bachrach, *Huygens*, I, p. 82; Huygens, "Autobiographie", p. 103; Peter Peerlkamp (ed.), *Constantini Hugenii de Vita Propria Sermonum Inter Liberos Libri Duo* (Harlem, 1817), p. 11.

39. J. A. Worp (ed.), *De Briefwisseling van Constantijn Huygens (1608–1687)* (The Hague, 1911), vol. I, p. 24 (12 June 1618); Colie, 'Some Thankfulnesse', ch. 2 and *passim*; Lisa Jardine, "An Irregular Life: Not a Biography of Constantijn Huygens", in Kevin Sharpe and Steven Zwicker (eds), *Writing Lives: Biography and Textuality, Identity and Representation in Early Modern England* (Oxford, 2008), pp. 41ff.

40. Huygens, *Briefwisseling*, I, p. 24: "Il a obtenu un bon benefice du Roy en recompense de son *Ferio Baralipton* contre Vorstius". "Ferio Baralipton" is a logician's joke.

41. Charles Webster, "William Harvey and the Crisis of Medicine in Jacobean England", in *William Harvey and His Age: The Professional and Social Context of the Discovery of the Circulation* (Baltimore and London, 1979), pp. 13–14; and "Alchemical and Paracelsian Medicine", in Webster (ed.), *Health, Medicine and Mortality in the Sixteenth Century* (Cambridge, 1979), pp. 313, 328–9.

42. Webster, "Harvey", pp. 11–12, 17–18; F. V. White, "Anthony, Francis (1550–1623)", *ODNB*; Allen Debus, *The English Paracelsians* (London, 1965), pp. 142–4; Margaret Pelling, *Medical Conflicts in Early Modern London* (Oxford, 2003), pp. 88–9 n.14; Andrew Wear, *Knowledge and Practice in English Medicine, 1550–1680* (Cambridge, 2000), p. 87; John Cotta, *Cotta Contra Antonium* (Oxford, 1623).

43. RCP Annals, III, fos 17v, 33v, 40r (microfiche pp. 60, 112, 132).

44. William Munk, *The Roll of the Royal College of Physicians of London* (London, 1878); J. Harvey Bloom and R. Rutson James, *Medical Practitioners in the Diocese of London, Licensed under the Act of 3 Henry VIII, c.11* (Cambridge, 1935); Pelling, *Medical Conflicts*, p. 136 n.2.

45. Pelling, *Medical Conflicts*, pp. 171–2, 323ff; Anthony, *Apologie*, sigs C4v ff.

46. William Foster (ed.), *Early Travels in India, 1583–1619* (London, 1921), pp. 193–6, 232–3.

47. White, "Anthony, Francis"; Anthony, *Apologie*, sig. D2v; Webster, "Harvey", p. 12.

48. George Eglisham, *Georgii Egljsemmjj Scoti, Doctoris Medici Regii, Accurata Methodus erigendi thematis natalitii, in diebus criticis disquirendis* (Edinburgh, 1616).

49. George Eglisham, *Duellum Poeticum. Contendentibus, Georgio Eglisemmio Medico Regio, & Georgio Buchanano Regio Praeceptore. Pro Dignitate paraphraseos Psalmi centesimi Quarti* (London, 1618); Foster, *Early Travels*, p. 233; NA C3/373/39, item 3 (Borthwick testimony: 8 February 1623); *Guil. Barclayi Amoeniorum Artium & Medicinae Doctoris, Iudicium, De Certamine G. Eglisemii* (London, 1620), sig. 4r; *CD 1621*, VII, p. 527.

50. S. D. Clippingdale's nineteenth-century *Medical Count Roll* (Royal College of Surgeons, MS 51/2/1, fo. 47) suggests Eglisham's appointment was in Scotland, but his name does not appear in the most recent examination of the pertinent records: see G. N. Clark, "Royal Physicians in Scotland, 1568–1853", *Medical History* 11:4 (1967), pp. 402–6.

51. On the medical staff, see Harold J. Cook, *The Decline of the Old Medical Regime in Stuart London* (Ithaca, 1986), Appendix 3. The only surviving documentation of Mayerne's appointment is among his own papers, see BL Sloane MS 2063, fos 203v–4.

52. Cook, *Decline*, ch. 1, esp. p. 55; Lucinda McCray Beier, *Sufferers and Healers: The Experience of Illness in Seventeenth-Century England* (London and New York, 1987), ch. 2.

53. Eglisham, *Duellum Poeticum*. For its contexts, see Johannes A. Gaertner, "Latin Verse Translations of the Psalms: 1500–1620", *Harvard Theological Review* 49:4 (1956), esp. pp. 282–5; and J. W. Binns, "Biblical Latin Poetry in Renaissance England", in Francis Cairns (ed.), *Papers of the Liverpool Latin Seminar* 3 (1981).

54. Eglisham, *Duellum Poeticum*; I. D. McFarlane, *Buchanan* (London, 1981), pp. 500–6; Binns, "Biblical Latin Poetry", pp. 387, 401–2; David Murray, "Catalogue of Printed

Books, Manuscripts, Charters, and other Documents", in *George Buchanan: Glasgow Quatercentenary Studies 1906* (Glasgow, 1907), pp. 407 ff, esp. pp. 426–8; Gaertner, "Latin Verse Translations"; Roger Green, "Dry Bones of Contention? Picking Apart Buchanan's Psalms", and John MacQueen, "'Return, Buchanan!' The Letter of Walter Denniston to George Buchanan & Buchanan's Reply", in Philip Ford and Roger P. H. Green (eds), *George Buchanan: Poet and Dramatist* (Swansea, 2009), pp. 254–5, 272–3.

55. Eglisham, *Duellum Poeticum*, sigs A2v, B1r–C4r; Gaertner, "Latin Verse Translations", pp. 283–5; and Binns, "Biblical Latin Poetry", pp. 406–7.

56. Eglisham, *Duellum Poeticum*, sigs C4v–D1v; Andrew Melville, *Viri Clarissimi A. Melvini Musae* (London, 1620), p. 24 (trans. in Thomas McRie, *Life of Andrew Melville*, 2nd ed. [Edinburgh, 1824], vol. II, p. 157; and Robert Pitcairn [ed.], *The Autobiography and Diary of Mr. James Melvill* [Edinburgh, 1842], vol. II, pp. 682–3); David Calderwood, *The History of the Kirk of Scotland*, ed. Thomas Thomson (Edinburgh, 1845), vol. VI, pp. 597–600; Antoine Le Fèvre De La Boderie, *Ambassades de Monsieur de la Boderie, En Angleterre* (1750), vol. I, p. 458 (Boderie to Puisieux: 8 December 1606); "Carmina D. D. Melvini Scoti in Aram Regiam", BL Add. MS 81607; *Melvini Musae*, pp. 24–7. See too Maurice Lee, Jr., *Government by Pen: Scotland under James VI and I* (Urbana, 1980), pp. 66–7 and ch. 5; Ernest R. Holloway III, *Andrew Melville and Humanism in Renaissance Scotland, 1545–1622* (Leiden, 2011), pp. 255–60; and James Doelman, "The Contexts of George Herbert's *Musae Responsoriae*", *George Herbert Journal* 2 (1992).

57. Eglisham, *Duellum Poeticum*, sigs D4v–E1v; Arthur H. Williamson, "Maxwell, James (c.1581–c.1635)", *ODNB*.

58. Eglisham, *Duellum Poeticum*, preface 1 sig. A4r, preface 2 sig. A4r, and sigs D2v–3r; MacQueen, "'Return, Buchanan!'", p. 272; Doelman, "Contexts", pp. 53–4 n.23. James had a copy of *Duellum Poeticum* in his library, see T. A. Birrell, "Some Rare Scottish Books in the Old Royal Library", in A. A. MacDonald, Michael Lynch and Ian B. Cowan (eds), *The Renaissance in Scotland: Studies in Literature, Religion, History and Culture Offered to John Durkan* (Leiden, 1994), pp. 407–8, 410.

59. Eglisham, *Duellum Poeticum*, sigs A4v, E3v–4v; Sir William Fraser, *Memorials of the Earls of Haddington* (Edinburgh, 1889), vol. I, pp. 17–33; Nicola Royan, "Blackwood, Adam (1539–1613)", and T. F Henderson, rev. Rachel E. Davies, "Blackwood, Henry (d. 1614)", *ODNB*; Bathsua Reginald, *Musa Virginea Graeco-Latino-Gallica, Bathsuae R. (filiae Henrici Reginaldi Gymnasiarchae et Philoglotti apud Londinenses) Anno Aetatis Suae Decimo Sexto edita* (London, 1616); Jean R. Brink, "Bathsua Reginald Makin: 'Most Learned Matron'", *HLQ* 54:4 (1991).

60. Bachrach, *Huygens*, I, pp. 82, 130–1, 214; Arthur Johnston, *Consilium collegii medici Parisiensis de mania G. Eglishemii* (Edinburgh, 1619)—another edition was published in 1619 in Paris, and a third in Edinburgh in 1631; Arthur Johnston, *Onopordus Furens* (Paris, 1620); William Barclay, *Iudicium, de certamine G. Eglisemii cum G. Buchanano, Pro dignitate paraphraseos Psalmi CIIII.* (London, 1620); Nicola Royan, "Johnston, Arthur (c.1579–1641)", *ODNB*; Holloway, *Andrew Melville*, pp. 283ff; Matthew Steggle, "Barclay, William (c.1570–c.1627)", *ODNB*. For positive modern assessments of Eglisham, see Binns, "Biblical Latin Poetry", p. 407, and Gaertner, "Latin Verse Translations".

61. William Duguid Geddes (ed.), *Musa Latina Aberdonensis: Arthur Johnston* (Aberdeen, 1892), vol. I, pp. 14ff; Green, "Dry Bones", p. 263 n.15; Trevor-Roper, *Europe's Physician*, p. 281; *PP1626*, IV, p. 335.

62. Eglisham, *Duellum Poeticum*, sigs D1v–2r.

63. NA SP 14/119/44E, fol. 137 (Sir George More's report: 6 February 1622 [1621]).

64. Ben Coates and Alan Davidson, "Sir Henry Britton", *HOC*, III, pp. 309–10; *CD 1621*, VII, pp. 411, 449, 446–7, 467.

65. *Proclamations, James I*, pp. 422–4 (4 February 1619). On Spencer, see *CD 1621*, III, p. 130, and VI, p. 106.

66. *CD 1621*, V, p. 105.

67. Anon., *A Briefe of Some of the Principall Points of the Kings Maiesties late Charter* (London, 1619). On the formation of the company, see *CD 1621*, V, pp. 105, 362; VI, p. 106; and VII, pp. 371, 526–35.

68. Goldsmiths' Company, Wardens Accounts, P2, p. 18 (18 August 1620).

69. Charles Nicholl, *The Lodger: Shakespeare on Silver Street* (London, 2007), ch. 6.

70. C. L. Kingsford, "On Some London Houses of the Early Tudor Period", *Archaeologia* 71 (1921), pp. 32–7 and fig. 1, 52–4; Francis W. Steer, *A History of the Worshipful Company of Scriveners of London* (London and Chichester, 1973), vol. I, pp. 43–4; John Stow, *The Survey of London* (London, 1633), pp. 320–1.

71. Kingsford, "Some London Houses", pp. 32–4 and fig. 1; Stow, *Survey*, pp. 320–1; David Kathman, "Barker, Christopher (1528/9–1599)", *ODNB*; Linda Levy Peck, *Consuming Splendor: Society and Culture in Seventeenth-Century England* (Cambridge, 2005), p. 95; Alfred B. Beaven (ed.), *The Aldermen of the City of London* (London, 1908–13), vol. I, p. 58, vol. II, p. 52; G. E. Cokayne (comp.), *Some Account of the Lord Mayors and Sheriffs of the City of London During the First Quarter of the Seventeenth Century, 1601 to 1625* (London, 1897), pp. 53–4; Lyn Boothman and Richard Hyde Parker (eds), *Savage Fortune: An Aristocratic Family in the Early Seventeenth Century* (Suffolk Records Society 49, 2006), pp. 185–6.

72. Kingsford, "Some London Houses", p. 36 n.3; Guildhall MS 8723 part 1 (1628), and MS 28942, bundle 2 (1631).

73. Nicholl, *Lodger*, chs 5–6 and pp. 57–8, 60–3, 65; Stow, *Survey*, pp. 320–5.

74. Buchanan, *De Scriptoribus*, p. 20.

Chapter 5

1. *ESL*, L10.

2. *CJ*, I, 6 February 1621; on the 1621 session, see Robert Zaller, *The Parliament of 1621* (Berkeley, 1971); and Conrad Russell, *Parliaments and English Politics, 1621–1629* (Oxford, 1979).

3. NA SP 14/121/124–25; "Book of Orders", *CD 1621*, VI, pp. 451–66; Elizabeth Read Foster, "The Procedure of the House of Commons against Patents and Monopolies", in Allen D. Boyer (ed.), *Law, Liberty and Parliament* (Indianapolis, 2004).

4. *CJ*, I, 18 April 1621. On Britton, see "Book of Orders", *CD 1621*, VI pp. 462, 465–6.

5. *CJ*, I, 10 March 1621; *CD 1621*, IV, p. 232; Lockyer, *Buckingham*, pp. 89–105; M. A. Abrams, "The English Gold- and Silver-thread Monopolies, 1611–1621", *Journal of Economic and Business History* III (1931).

6. *An Abstract of the Grievances of . . . the Cutlers, Paynter-stainers and Booke-binders* ([London, 1621]); [Bookbinders], *To the Most Honourable Assembly of the Commons* ([London, 1621]); *CD 1621*, V, p. 105 n.8.

7. *The Answer of the Gold-beaters, to the Answers Exhibited* ([London, 1621]).

8. *CJ*, I, 18 July 1620; *APC 1619–21*, p. 252; Sir Julius Caesar's notes, BL Add. MS 34324, fo. 117r.

9. *CD 1621*, V, pp. 105–6; VI, pp. 105–7; and VII, p. 531.

10. Edward Nicholas, *The Proceedings and Debates of the House of Commons* (London, 1766), vol. I, pp. 336–41; *CD 1621*, IV, p. 232; V, pp. 105–6; VI, pp. 105–7.

11. *CD 1621*, IV, p. 288, and V, p. 362; *CJ*, 2 May 1621. On the Goldbeaters' dealings with the Goldsmiths, see Goldsmiths' Company, P2, pp. 448, 461, 487–8 (Wardens Accounts and Company Minutes); and A.IV.1 (Reasons, 1620).

12. *APC 1619–21*, p. 405; *Proclamations, James I*, pp. 513–14.

13. *CJ*, I, 2 May 1621.

14. NA Chancery C3/373/39.

15. NA SP 16/64/77 (Herriott to Nicholas: 27 May 1627).

16. NA Privy Council Registers 2/32, fos 219, 447; 2/33, fo. 66; *APC 1623–5*, p. 321; NA SP 14/150/59 (Mayor of Weymouth's letter: 9 August 1623); 14/151/21 (John Coke's letter: 21 August 1623); 14/151/40 (John Poulter to Mayor and Customer of Weymouth: 23 August 1623); 14/151/65 (Mayor of Weymouth's letter: late August 1623).

17. NA SP 16/521/80:I (John Bere memorandum: 14 June 1625); 16/521/79 (John Harris to Conway: 21 June 1625); 16/521/80 (Arthur Harris to Conway: 21 June 1625); 16/4/35 (James Bagg to Nicholas: 10 July 1625); 16/523/32 (Edward Yates to Nicholas: 7 February

1626); 16/37/89 (Yates to Nicholas: 16 October 1626); 16/136/47 (Yates's petition: 1629); 16/205/22 (Yates's petition: 1634); *CSPD 1628–1629*, p. 297.

18. *Articles to be inquired within the dioces of Ely* (1638), ch. 5, art. 7; Peter Heylyn, *France Painted to the Life by a Learned and Impartial Hand* (London, 1656), p. 60; Eric Partridge, *Shakespeare's Bawdy* (New York, 1969), pp. 81, 161; Alan Bray, "Homosexuality and the Signs of Male Friendship in Elizabethan England", *History Workshop* 29 (1990).

19. Thomas Hylles, *The Art of Vulgar Arithmeticke* (London, 1600), table p. 258; Paul L. Hughes and James F. Larkin (eds), *Tudor Royal Proclamations* (New Haven and London, 1969), vol. II, nos 472–3, p. 158; *Proclamations, Charles I*, no. 474, pp. 1,006–7.

20. Ben Jonson, *The Alchemist*, in G. A. Wilkes (ed.), *Ben Jonson: Five Plays* (Oxford, 1988), Act 1, scene 1, ll. 113–14; Act 3, scene 3, ll. 142–5; Malcolm Gaskill, *Crime and Mentalities in Early Modern England* (Cambridge, 2000), part II.

21. Gaskill, *Crime*, pp. 126, 129, 157; David Riggs, *The World of Christopher Marlowe* (New York, 2004), pp. 287–9; 1 Mary st.2 c.6; 1 & 2 Philip & Mary c.11; 14 Elizabeth c.3.

22. Craig Muldrew, "'Hard Food for Midas': Cash and its Social Value in Early Modern England", *P&P* 170 (2001), pp. 89–90; Hughes and Larkin, *Tudor Royal Proclamations*, II, no. 487, pp. 179–81; Charles Howard Carter, *The Secret Diplomacy of the Habsburgs, 1598–1625* (New York and London, 1964), p. 193.

23. It is possible that Yates was also a Catholic: see John J. LaRocca (ed.), *Jacobean Recusant Rolls for Middlesex* (Catholic Record Society 76, 1997), p. 80.

24. *Chamberlain*, II, pp. 520–1 (to Carleton: 8 November 1623); Henry Foley (ed.), *Records of the English Province of the Society of Jesus* (London, 1877), vol. I, pp. 85–6; Alexandra Walsham, "'The Fatall Vesper': Providentialism and Anti-Popery in Late Jacobean London", *P&P* 144 (1994); Michael Questier, "John Gee, Archbishop Abbot, and the Use of Converts from Rome in Jacobean Anti-Catholicism", *Recusant History* 21:3 (1993), pp. 347–8.

25. John Gee, *The Foot out of the Snare: With A Detection of Sundry Late Practices and Impostures of the Priests and Jesuites in England* (London, 1624), sigs A1r, B2r, B3v–4r; Questier, "John Gee", pp. 348–52.

26. Gee, *Foot*, sigs D4r–v, R4r–S4v, T1r–V4v.

27. Gee, *Foot*, sigs A1v–2r, X1r–2v.

28. William Munk, *The Roll of the Royal College of Physicians of London* (London, 1878), vol. 1, s.v., "Giffard, John", "Palmer, Richard", "Prujean, Sir Francis"; RCP Annals, III, fols 65v–66r; Charles Nicholl, *The Lodger: Shakespeare on Silver Street* (London, 2007), pp. 61, 65. Palmer died in 1625.

29. Vivian Salmon, "Webbe, Joseph (d. c.1630)", *ODNB*; Margaret Pelling, *Medical Conflicts in Early Modern London* (Oxford, 2003), pp. 159 n.81, 326; Munk, *Roll*, s.v., "Lodge, Thomas"; Alexandra Halasz, "Lodge, Thomas (1558–1625)", *ODNB*; J. C. Jeaffreson (ed.), *Middlesex County Records* (London, 1886–92), II, p. 216.

30. Cogswell, *Revolution*, p. 288.

31. NA SP 16/158/60 (Eglisham letter: 18 January 1630); RCP Annals, III, fol. 34r (microfiche pp. 114–15); Gee, *Foot*, sigs V4r–v; W. K. L. Webb, "Thomas Preston O.S.B., alias Roger Widdrington (1567–1640)", *Biographical Studies* 2 (1953–4); Alan Dures, "The Distribution of Catholic Recusants in London and Middlesex, c. 1580–1629", *Essex Recusant* 10 (1968), pp. 74–5; Peter Lake (with Michael Questier), *The Antichrist's Lewd Hat* (New Haven and London, 2002), ch. 6.

32. Dures, "Distribution", pp. 75, 77.

33. NA SP 14/119/83 (More's Report); *HOC 1604–29*, III, pp. 309–10.

34. Cogswell, *Revolution*, pp. 37–8; Questier, "John Gee", pp. 348–9; Foley, *Records*, VII, pt. 2 (London, 1883), pp. 1,098–9; Lyn Boothman and Richard Hyde Parker, *Savage Fortune: An Aristocratic Family in the Early Seventeenth Century*, Suffolk Records Society 49 (2006), pp. xxxviii–xli, xliv–v; *Rushworth*, I, p. 393.

35. Gee, *Foot*, sig. X1v; Questier, "John Gee", p. 348; Anon., *The Fisher Catched In His Owne Net* (London, 1623); BL Add. MS 28640, fos 113r–v.

36. Daniel Featley, *An Appendix to the Fishers Net* (London, 1624), pp. 113–49; Anon., *Something Written by occasion of that fatall and memorable accident in the Blacke-Friers* (London, 1623), p. 14.

37. *Silva de varias Poesias en diversas linguas en alabança del Gran Condestable de Castilla Juan Fernandez de Velasco di Bernardo Cremosano* (Milan, 1622/23), pp. 104–5, 117–18; Robert Cross, "To Counterbalance the World: England, Spain, and Peace in the Early Seventeenth Century", unpublished PhD thesis, Princeton University (2012), chs 4–8.
38. Featley, *An Appendix*, p. 118.
39. Foley, *Records*, VII, pt. 2, pp. 1,100–1.
40. *Chamberlain*, II, p. 531 (to Carleton: 6 December 1623).
41. Anon., *Fisher Catched*, sig. A2r.
42. Gee, *Foot*, sigs M4r–N3r; [George Musket], *The Bishop of London His Legacy* (London, 1623); Peter McCullough, "King, John (d. 1621)", *ODNB*.
43. M. C. Questier (ed.), *Stuart Dynastic Policy and Religious Politics, 1621–1625*, Camden Society, 5th Series, 34 (Cambridge, 2009), pp. 356–7 (Thomas Roper to Thomas More: 4 March 1625); *Chamberlain*, II, p. 605 (to Carleton: 12 March 1625).
44. *M&K*, pp. 222–5 (2, 9 and 16 March 1625); *Cornwallis*, p. 133 (Bedford to Lady Cornwallis: 12 April 1625); NA SP 16/1/2 (Chambermayd to Elizabeth: 27 March 1625).
45. *M&K*, p. 222 (2 March 1625).
46. Questier (ed.), *Stuart Dynastic Policy*, p. 357 (Roper to More: 4 March 1625); NA SP 77/18/149–50 (Trumbull to Conway: 2 June 1625) (copy in BL Add. MS 72386, fol. 334r).
47. Featley, *An Appendix*, pp. 128, 134–42; Anon., *Something Written*, p. 14; Gee, *Foot*, sig. V1v; Thomas Scott, *The Second Part of Vox Populi* (London, 1624), sig. G4v; Walsham, "'Fatall Vesper'", p. 73, fig. 5; Thomas M. McCoog (ed.), *English and Welsh Jesuits, 1555–1650, pt. 2*, Catholic Record Society 75 (1995), pp. 336–7.
48. Thomas M. McCoog, "'Pray to the Lord of the Harvest': Jesuit Missions to Scotland in the Sixteenth Century", *The Innes Review* 53:2 (2002), pp. 156, 187; Francis Shearman, "James Wood of Boniton", *The Innes Review* 5 (1954). Questier (ed.), *Stuart Dynastic Policy*, p. 357 n.1,150, discusses both candidates.
49. Foley, *Records*, I, pp. 153–4, VII, pt. 1, p. 28; McCoog, *English and Welsh Jesuits, 1555–1650, pt. 1*, Catholic Record Society 74 (1994), p. 110; McCoog, "Baker, Alexander", *ODNB*; John Gee, *New Shreds of the Old Snare* (London, 1624), pp. 21–2.
50. Mark Stoyle, *From Deliverance to Destruction: Rebellion and Civil War in an English City* (Exeter, 1996), p. 30; Foley, *Records*, I, pp. 153–4, 185–6; *PP1625*, pp. 152–5, 458, 529–30; Gee, *New Shreds*, p. 22. But see Questier, *Stuart Dynastic Policy*, p. 357 n.1,150.
51. *CSPV 1623–1625*, p. 621 (18 March 1625); *CSPV 1625–1626*, pp. 6–7 (30 March 1625).
52. RCP Annals, III, fol. 65v (29 March 1626).
53. Gee, *Foot*, sig. V1v; Scott, *Second Part*, sig. G4v; Walsham, "'Fatall Vesper'", pp. 37, 65–8, 73 fig. 5.
54. On Buckingham's heroic image, see Cogswell, *Revolution*, ch. 8; Thomas Cogswell, "Thomas Middleton and the Court, 1624: *A Game at Chess* in Context", *HLQ* 48 (1984); Alastair Bellany, "'Raylinge Rymes and Vaunting Verse': Libelous Politics in Early Stuart England", in Kevin Sharpe and Peter Lake (eds), *Politics and Culture in Early Stuart England* (Basingstoke, 1994), pp. 300–1; and Alastair Bellany, "Buckingham Engraved: Politics, Print Images and the Royal Favourite in the 1620s", in Michael Hunter (ed.), *Printed Images in Early Modern Britain: Essays in Interpretation* (Farnham, 2010), pp. 217, 222.
55. Scott, *Second Part*, sigs D2r–v.
56. *ESL*, Oi2 (punctuation modified).

Chapter 6

1. "Discourses Held Between the Sieur Rubens and Gerbier since the Year 1625", in W. Noel Sainsbury (ed.), *Original Unpublished Papers Illustrative of the Life of Sir Peter Paul Rubens* (London, 1859), pp. 68–9; *Mercure François*, XI, pp. 365–6; C. V. Wedgwood, *The World of Rubens, 1577–1640* (New York, 1967), pp. 102–6; C. V. Wedgwood, *The Political Career of Peter Paul Rubens* (London, 1975), pp. 33–4; Alastair Bellany, "'Naught but Illusion'? Buckingham's Painted Selves", in Kevin Sharpe and Steven

Zwicker (eds), *Writing Lives: Biography and Textuality, Identity and Representation in Early Modern England* (Oxford, 2008), pp. 132–40; Peter Paul Rubens, *Rubens Drawings* (New York, 1989), p. 3.

2. Ruth Saunders Magurn (trans. & ed.), *The Letters of Peter Paul Rubens* (Evanston, 1991), pp. 123–5, 130–1 (to Valavez: 16 and 31 December 1625; 10 February 1626).

3. Magurn, *Letters of Peter Paul Rubens*, pp. 125, 127, 130 (to Valavez: 20 January, 2 and 10 February 1626).

4. Leon Voet, *The Golden Compasses: The History of the House of Plantin-Moretus* (1969–72), dbnl e-book edition 2008 (dbnl.org/tekst/voet004gold01_01/colofon.htm), vol. I, pp. 211, 263–4, 266.

5. Voet, *Golden Compasses*, I, pp. 212, 317, 323, 330–1; II, pp. 417ff.

6. "Rekeningen der boeken geleverd door Balthasar Moretus aan P. P. Rubens", in *Bulletin-Rubens: Annales de la Commission Officielle Instituée par le Conseil Communal de la ville d'Anvers pour la publication des documents relatifs à la vie et aux oeuvres de Rubens* (Antwerp and Brussels, 1883), vol. II, p. 200; Max Rooses, *Petrus Paulus Rubens en Balthasar Moretus* (Antwerp and Ghent, 1884), p. 123; Prosper Arents, Frans Baudouin et al., *De bibliotheek van Pieter Pauwel Rubens: een reconstructie* (Antwerp, 2001), section E, p. 176; Magurn, *Letters of Peter Paul Rubens*, pp. 130–3 (to Valavez: 10 and 16 February; 23 March 1626); Albert Loomie, *The Spanish Elizabethans: The English Exiles at the Court of Philip II* (New York, 1963), p. 240; Markus A. Denzel, *Handbook of World Exchange Rates, 1590–1914* (Farnham, 2010), pp. 15, 57.

7. HHStA Belgien Fasz. 62, fos 160r, 243r, 247r (Van Male to Isabella; 18 March and 20 May 1625; to Della Faille, 20 May 1625).

8. NA SP 77/18 fos 149–50, 197v (Trumbull to Conway: 25 July and 2 June 1625); BL Add. MS 72386, fo. 334r (Trumbull letter book: 2 June 1625).

9. Archivo de General Simancas, Flandres, Estado 2516, fo. 115r–v (anon. report, Brussels).

10. Bernard de Meester (ed.), *Correspondance du Nonce Giovanni-Francesco Guidi di Bagno (1621–1627)*, Analecta Vaticano-Belgica 2nd Series, Nonciature de Flandre, vols 5–6 (Brussels and Rome, 1938), vol. VI, p. 653; Henri Lonchay et al. (eds), *Correspondance de la Cour d'Espagne sur les affaires des Pays-Bas au XVIIe Siècle* (Brussels, 1927), vol. II, p. 226; Brendan Jennings (ed.), *Wild Geese in Spanish Flanders 1582–1700: Documents, Relating Chiefly to Irish Regiments, From the Archives Générales du Royaum, Brussels; and Other Sources* (Dublin, 1964), pp. 196–8. J. H. Elliott, *The Count-Duke of Olivares: The Statesman in an Age of Decline* (New Haven and London, 1986), pp. 226–43; Jose Alcala-Zamora y Queipo de Llano, *Espana, Flandes y el Mar del Norte (1618–1639)* (Madrid, 1975), pp. 208–42; Rafael Rodenas Vilar, *La Política Europea de España Durante La Guerra de Treinta Anos* (Madrid, 1967), pp. 58–66, 83–90; R. A. Stradling, *The Armada of Flanders* (Cambridge, 1992), pp. 37–57.

11. De Meester, *Guidi di Bagno*, VI, pp. 661–3, 666, 672; Jonathan Israel, *The Dutch Republic* (Oxford, 1995), pp. 478–505; Peter Wilson, *The Thirty Years War* (Cambridge, MA, 2009), pp. 362–84; Geoffrey Parker, *The Army of Flanders and the Spanish Road* (Cambridge, 1972).

12. NA SP 77/18 fos 185r, 195–6 (Trumbull to Conway: 21 and 25 July 1625); Lonchay, *Correspondance*, II, pp. 246, 254.

13. NA SP 16/32/117 (information: July? 1626).

14. Paul Arblaster, *Antwerp & the World: Richard Verstegan and the International Culture of Catholic Reformation* (Louvain, 2004), chs 3–4; P. R. Harris (ed.), "The Reports of William Udall, Informer, 1605–1612", *Recusant History* 8:4–5 (1966), pp. 234, 239, 245–8, 254, 262, 264, 267; Leona Rostenberg, *The Minority Press and the English Crown: A Study in Repression, 1558–1625* (Nieuwkoop, 1971), chs 9–10; Lewis Owen, *The Running Register; Recording A True Relation of the State of the English Colledges, Seminaries and Cloysters in all forraine parts* (London, 1626), p. 14; John Gee, *The Foot Out of the Snare* (London, 1624), sigs R4r–S4v.

15. Anon., *Prurit-Anus, vel nec omne, nec ex omni. Sive Apologia pro Puritanis & Novatoribus Universis* ("Lutetiae Britannorum", 1609); Harris, "Udall Reports", pp. 202–4, 243–4, 255; *CSPV 1607–10*, pp. 328, 336–7, 351 (24 and 31 August, and 14 September 1609);

Owen, *Running Register*, p. 14; Cyndia Susan Clegg, *Press Censorship in Jacobean England* (Cambridge, 2001), pp. 76, 80–1.

16. Anon., *Prurit-Anus*, sigs A4r–B2v; Harris, "Udall Reports", p. 202; *CSPV 1607–10*, p. 322 (Wotton's speech: 13 August, 1609).

17. *CSPV 1607–10*, pp. 288, 314, 322–3 (reports: 8 June and 28 July 1609; Wotton's speech: 13 August 1609); Harris, "Udall Reports", p. 204. For other responses see Owen, *Running Register*, p. 14; *CSPV 1607–10*, pp. 319, 328 (10 and 24 August 1609); Michael C. Questier (ed.), *Newsletters from the Archpresbyterate of George Birkhead*, Camden Society, 5th Series, 12 (Cambridge, 1998), pp. 61–2 (More to Baker: 31 October 1609).

18. NA SP 77/17 fos 176r–77r (Trumbull report [1624?]); Gilbert Tournoy, "Erycius Puteanus, Isaac Casaubon and the Author of the *Corona Regia*", *Humanistica Lovaniensia* 49 (2000), pp. 382 n.19, 383, 386–8; Winfried Schleiner, "Introduction: The Most Intense Early Modern Detective Story Involving a Book: Trumbull's Attempts to Find the Author of *Corona Regia*", in Winfried Schleiner and Tyler Fyotek (eds), *Corona Regia* (Geneva, 2010), pp. 14–15, 17–18.

19. Schleiner and Fyotek, *Corona*, pp. 34–7, 46–57, 62–7, 78–81, 86–9, 94–101.

20. D'Ewes, *Diary*, pp. 92–3; *Wotton*, II, pp. 92–3 (to Winwood: 23 April 1616); Schleiner, "Introduction", pp. 13–14, and Fyotek, "Translator's Note", p. 25, in Schleiner and Fyotek, *Corona*.

21. *CSPV 1621–23*, p. 53 (11 May 1621); D'Ewes, *Diary*, p. 142.

22. [Richard Verstegan], *Londons Looking-Glasse* ([St. Omer], 1621), sigs B2r–3r, C3r–v; [Verstegan], *A Toung-Combat, Lately Happening, Between two English soldiers* ([Mechelen], 1623).

23. [Verstegan], *Toung-Combat*, sigs D1r ff; Malcolm, *Reason*, pp. 31, 33–4, 50–2; Kevin Sharpe, *Reading Revolutions: The Politics of Reading in Early Modern England* (New Haven and London, 2000); Noah Millstone, "Seeing Like a Statesman in Early Stuart England", *P&P* 223 (2014).

24. NA SP 77/17 fos 354v–55r (Trumbull to Conway: 3 October 1624); [John Skinner], *A True Relation of the Late Cruell and Barbarous Tortures and Execution, done upon the English at Amboyna* ([St Omer], 1624); Anthony Milton, "Marketing a Massacre: Amboyna, the East India Company and the Public Sphere in Early Stuart England", in Peter Lake and Steven Pincus (eds), *The Politics of the Public Sphere in Early Modern England* (Manchester, 2007), p. 179; Cogswell, *Revolution*, pp. 274–5; P. A. Neville-Sington, "The Primary Purchas Bibliography", in L. E. Pennington (ed.), *The Purchas Handbook* (Hakluyt Society: London, 1997), II, p. 525 n.3.

25. [Adam Contzen], *Mysteria Politica. Hoc est, Epistolae Arcanae Virorum Illustrium Sibi Mutuo Confidentium* ("Neopoli", 1625); *Mercure François*, XI, pp. 34–48; William F. Church, *Richelieu and Reason of State* (Princeton, 1972), pp. 122–3; Malcolm, *Reason*, p. 32; A. Lloyd Moote, *Louis XIII, The Just* (Berkeley, 1989), p. 178.

26. Museum Plantin-Moretus, Archive MS 744, fo. 347r.

27. Albertus Miraeus, *Codex Donationum Piarum* (Brussels, 1624); Christopher de Bonours, *La Memorable Siege d'Ostende* (Brussels, 1628). Using STCV—the Short Title Catalogus Vlaanderen (vlaamse-erfgoedbibliotheek.be/en/database/stcv)—and the Plantin-Moretus records, we can identify approximately thirty-seven titles from Meerbeeck's press, 1624–34. Of the thirty-seven, seventeen are in Latin, eight each in Dutch and Spanish, three in French and one possibly in Italian.

28. Antonio Carnero, *Historia de las guerras ciuiles que ha auido en los estados de Flandes des del año 1559 hasta el de 1609* (Brussels, 1625); Adriaen van Meerbeeck, *Nederlandtschen Mercvrivs oft Waerachtich verhael vande geschiedenissen van Nederlandt, ende oock van Duytschlandt, Spaengien, Italien, Vrankrijck ende Turckijen. Sedert den iare 1620. tot 1625* (Brussels, 1625).

29. Balthasar Nardus [Baldassarre Nardi], *Trivmphvs invictissimo heroi Ambrosio Spinolæ* (Brussels, 1626); Bonours, *La Memorable Siege*; and Guido Bentivoglio, *Relationi* (Antwerp, 1629).

30. Richard Verstegan, *Nederduytsche Epigrammen Ende Epitaphien* (Brussels, 1624); Miraeus, *Codex Donationum*; and Albertus Miraeus, *Stemmata principum Belgii: ex*

diplomatibus ac tabulis publicis potissimum concinnata (Brussels, 1626); Arblaster, *Antwerp*, p. 146; Paul Arblaster, "Policy and Publishing in the Habsburg Netherlands, 1585–1690", in Brendan Dooley and Sabrina A. Baron (eds), *The Politics of Information in Early Modern Europe* (London, 2001), pp. 184–5; Arblaster, "'Dat de Boecken Vrij Sullen Wesen': Private Profit, Public Utility and Secrets of Sate in the Seventeenth-Century Habsburg Netherlands", in Joop W. Koopmans (ed.), *News and Politics in Early Modern Europe (1500–1800)* (Leuven, 2005), pp. 84–5; and Paul Arblaster, "Abraham Verhoeven and the Brussels Court: Isabel Clara Eugenia's Staple of News", in Cordula Van Whye (ed.), *Isabel Clara Eugenia: Female Sovereignty in the Courts of Madrid and Brussels* (Centro de Estudios Europa Hispanica, 2011), pp. 288–9.

31. Elliott, *Olivares*, p. 67.
32. (1) Ornamental capital "S": *Prodromus* ("Frankfurt"), sig. A2r, and *Forerunner*, sig. A2r (p. 3); Jan Ruysbroeck, *T'Cieraet der Gheestelycker Bruyloft* (Brussels, 1624), pp. 12, 40, 47, 73; Jean de Marnix, *Resolutions Politiques ou Maximes d'Estat* (Brussels, 1629), p. 232. (2) Ornamental capital "Q": *Prodromus* ("Frankfurt"), sig. C1r; Ruysbroeck, *T'Cieraet*, p. 1. (3) Tail-piece ornament: *Forerunner*, sig. C3v (p. 22); Verstegan, *Nederduytsche Epigrammen*, sig. ***2r, p. 67; Marnix, *Resolutions*, pp. 76, 154, 231, 302, 319, 359, 472.
33. Meerbeeck participated in at least one later campaign. In 1633 he printed *Anti-Puteanus*, an attack on Erycius Puteanus's *Belli et pacis statera* (1633). See Judith Pollman, *Religious Choice in the Dutch Republic: The Reformation of Arnoldus Buchelius (1565–1641)* (Manchester, 1999), pp. 189, 254 ns 136–7; Pieter Geyl, *History of the Dutch-Speaking Peoples, 1555–1648* (Reprint: London, 2001), p. 403.
34. Anon., *Veritas Odiosa* (Brussels, 1626), sigs A2v (epitaph), A3r–v (dating), A4r–B2v (news from Rome), B3r (Boccalini), B3v ff (Proditione Gallicana), C3v–D2r (Maurice and Oldenbarnevelt), D2v–D3r (psalms).
35. *Veritas*, sig. D3v; Church, *Richelieu*, pp. 123 ff; W. J. Stakniewicz, *Politics and Religion in Seventeenth-Century France* (Westport, 1976), pp. 98–101; Moote, *Louis XIII*, p. 178.
36. *Veritas*, sigs A2v, C3v–D2r, D3r.
37. *Veritas*, sigs B4v–C1r, C2v–3r.
38. *Veritas*, sig. B3r. The tract turns the anti-Spanish Boccalini, *Pietra del Paragone Politico* (Venice, 1615), sigs G1v–2v, into an anti-French work; compare the Protestant appropriations in William Vaughan (comp.), *The New-found Politicke. Disclosing The Secret Natures and dispositions as well of private persons as of Statesmen and Courtiers* (London, 1626), sigs S1v–S2v; and Thomas Scott, *Newes from Pernassus. The Politicall Touchstone Taken From Mount Pernassus* ("Helicon", 1622), sigs G2r–3r.
39. *Veritas*, sigs A3v, C1r, D2v, D3v.
40. Malcolm, *Reason*, pp. 35–9, 45; Wolfgang E. J. Weber (ed.), *Secretissima Instructio/Allergeheimste Instruction* (Augsburg, 2002), pp. 123–8.
41. John L. Flood, "'Omnium totius oribis emporiorum compendium': The Frankfurt Fair in the Early Modern Period", in Robin Myers, Michael Harris and Giles Mandelbrote (eds), *Fairs, Markets and the Itinerant Book Trade* (Newcastle, DE, and London, 2007), pp. 21–2.
42. *Prodromus Vindictae* (np. 1626), sig. A2r; *Secretissima Instructio, Gallo-Britanno-Batava, Friderico V. Comiti Palatino Electori Data* ("The Hague", 1627), sig. A2r.
43. *Imp. Ludovici IIII Bavariae Ducis, Sententia separationis Inter Margaretam Ducissam Carinthiae, & Iohannem Regis Bohemia* (Heidelberg, 1598), p. 44; M. Freher, *Originum Palatinarum Commentarii Appendix* (Heidelberg, 1599), p. 77; Andrew L. Thomas, *A House Divided: Wittelsbach Confessional Court Cultures in the Holy Roman Empire, c. 1550–1650* (Leiden, 2010), p. 81.
44. Paul Arblaster, "Posts, Newsletters, Newspapers: England in a European System of Communications", *Media History* 11:1/2 (2005), pp. 23–4; and "Antwerp and Brussels as Inter-European Spaces in News Exchange", in Brendan Dooley (ed.), *Dissemination of News and the Emergence of Contemporaneity in Early Modern Europe* (Farnham and Burlington, 2010).
45. [John Hughes (ed.)], *A Complete History of England: with the lives of all the kings and queens thereof . . . In three volumes* (London, 1706), vol. I (preface); vol. II, pp. 790–1; C.

Scott and P. Skwarczynski, "A 17th-Century Spanish Diplomat's View of Poland", *Slavonic and East European Review* 40:95 (1962), p. 497 and n.1.

46. *Prodromus Vindictae, Das ist: Vorlauffer oder Vorbott der billichen Raach, vber den gifft-mörderischen Fürsten von Buckingham, vmb wegen der grewlichen hinrichtung deß Grossmächtigen Monarchen Iacobi Königs in Groß-Britanien* (Augsburg, 1626).

47. Dorothy Alexander and Walter L. Strauss, *The German Single-Leaf Woodcut, 1600–1700: A Pictorial Catalogue* (New York, 1977), vol. I, pp. 25–6; David Paisey (ed.), *Catalogue of Books Printed in the German-Speaking Countries and of German Books Printed in Other Countries from 1601 to 1700 now in the British Library* (London, 1994), W236 and P88; Hans-Jörg Künast, "Dokumentation: Augsburger Buchdrucker und Verleger", in *Augsburger Buchdruck und Verlagswesen: von den Anfängen bis zur Gegenwart*, eds Helmut Gier and Johannes Janota (Wiesbaden, 1997), pp. 1,237–8; Ute Ecker-Offenhäusser, "Volkssprachlich-medizinischer Buchdruck in Augsburg im 17. Jahrhundert", in ibid., p. 953; Walter Pötzl, "Augsburger Mirakelbücher", in ibid., pp. 660–1, 663, 678–9; Sibylle Appuhn-Radtke, "Augsburger Buchillustration im 17. Jahrhundert", in ibid., p. 764; and Allyson F. Creasman, "'Lies as Truth'": Policing Print and Oral Culture in the Early Modern City", in Marjorie Plummer and Robin Barnes (eds), *Ideas and Cultural Margins in Early Modern Germany* (Farnham, 2009), p. 266.

48. John Gee, *The Foot out of the Snare* (London, 1624), sig. V4r.

49. *Vorlauffer*, sig. A2r; Margaret Aston, "Symbols of Conversion: Proprieties of the Page in Reformation England", in Michael Hunter (ed.), *Printed Images in Early Modern Britain: Essays in Interpretation* (Farnham, 2010), esp. pp. 30–4, quotation from Henry Burton (p. 30). The Jesuit monogram appears in a number of Aperger's publications in the 1620s: see e.g. Bernard Heltfelder, *Basilica SS. Udalrici et Afrae Augustae* (1627), sig. A1r; and cf. *Sacratissimae Caesareae, Ac Germaniae, Hungariae, Bohemiae, &c. Regiae Majestatis, Edictalis Cassatio, Iniquae, Praetensae, & ipso jure nullae Electionis GABRIELIS BETLEN, in Regno Hungariae* (1621), sig. A2r.

50. "Pambon Vreimundima", *Hollandisch Apocalypsis, Oder Offenbarung* (Augsburg, nd); *Veritas*, sig. D3v; *Den Hollantschen apocalypsis* ("Nieustadt", 1626); *L'Apocalipse ou Revelation Hollandoise* ("A Ville Neuve", 1626); *STCV*; Paisey, *Catalogue*, S1718; Julius S. Held, "Carolus Scribanius's Observations on Art in Antwerp", *Journal of the Warburg and Courtauld Institutes* 59 (1996), p. 174.

51. *L'Apocalipse*, pp. 28, 31, 34–5, 42–5, 51; *Hollandisch Apocalypsis*, tp, 20ff. For the Dutch context, see Israel, *Dutch Republic*, chs 19–20.

52. *Mercure François*, XI, pp. 475, 500–2, 504; Church, *Richelieu*, pp. 151–4.

Chapter 7

1. *PP1626*, IV, pp. 334–7 (Browne to anon.: 20 May 1626).

2. Bellany, *Politics*; and "Thinking with Poison" (forthcoming); Curtis Perry, *Literature and Favoritism in Early Modern England* (Cambridge, 2006), chs 2 and 4; Franck Collard, *The Crime of Poison in the Middle Ages*, trans. Deborah Nelson-Campbell (Westport, CT, and London, 2008), esp. ch. 4; Silje Normand, "Venomous Words and Political Poisons: Language(s) of Exclusion in Early Modern France", in Melissa Calaresu et al. (eds), *Exploring Cultural History: Essays in Honour of Peter Burke* (Farnham, 2010), pp. 113–32; Catherine E. Thomas, "Toxic Encounters: Poisoning in Early Modern English Literature and Culture", *Literature Compass* 9:1 (2012), pp. 48–55; and Fredson Thayer Bowers, "The Audience and the Poisoners of Elizabethan Tragedy", *Journal of English and Germanic Philology* 36:4 (1937).

3. "Breviat of Evidence", Huntington Library, Ellesmere MS 5979, fo. 1; *ST*, II, pp. 971–2. For an earlier example of forensic debates in a poison case, see [Francis Bacon], *A Letter written out of England to an English Gentleman remaining at Padua* (London, 1599); M. A., *The Discoverie and Confutation of a Tragical Fiction, Devysed and Played by Edward Squyer* (1599); William Clark, *A Replie Unto a certaine Libell, latelie set foorth by Fa: Parsons* (1603); Thomas P. Harrison Jr., "The Literary Background of Renaissance Poisons", *Studies in English* 27:1 (1948), pp. 35–67.

4. *Forerunner*, pp. 3–4.
5. *Forerunner*, pp. 4–6.
6. *Forerunner*, pp. 4–7, 9–11.
7. *Forerunner*, pp. 4–5, 10.
8. *Forerunner*, p. 8.
9. *Forerunner*, pp. 11–12.
10. *Forerunner*, pp. 12–13.
11. *Forerunner*, pp. 13–14.
12. *Forerunner*, pp. 13–14.
13. *Forerunner*, pp. 14–15.
14. *Forerunner*, p. 15.
15. *Forerunner*, pp. 15–16.
16. *Forerunner*, pp. 16–17.
17. *Forerunner*, pp. 17–18.
18. *Forerunner*, pp. 16–17, 19.
19. *Forerunner*, pp. 7, 19.
20. *Forerunner*, pp. 18–19.
21. *Forerunner*, p. 19.
22. *Forerunner*, p. 18.
23. *Forerunner*, p. 20.
24. *Forerunner*, p. 21.
25. *Forerunner*, pp. 21–2.
26. *Forerunner*, p. 8.
27. Bellany, *Politics*, pp. 144–5, 165–76; Dwight C. Peck (ed.), *Leicester's Commonwealth: The Copy of a Letter Written by a Master of Art of Cambridge (1584)* (Athens, OH, 1985), pp. 75, 80, 85, 92–3, 95–6, 99–100, 103–5, 125–32, 135, 174, 193; Collard, *Crime of Poison*, pp. 95, 133, 148–50.
28. *Forerunner*, pp. 4, 10; Bellany, *Politics*, pp. 174–6.
29. *Forerunner*, p. 9.
30. J. H. M. Salmon, "Seneca and Tacitus in Jacobean England", in Linda Levy Peck (ed.), *The Mental World of the Jacobean Court* (Cambridge, 1991); R. Malcolm Smuts, "Court-Centred Politics and the Uses of Roman Historians", and Blair Worden, "Ben Jonson Among the Historians", both in Kevin Sharpe and Peter Lake (eds), *Culture and Politics in Early Stuart England* (Basingstoke, 1994); Perry, *Literature and Favoritism*, ch. 7; Peter Burke, "Tacitism", in T. A. Dorey (ed.), *Tacitus* (New York, 1969); Kevin Sharpe, *Reading Revolutions: The Politics of Reading in Early Modern England* (New Haven and London, 2000); Noah Millstone, "Seeing Like a Statesman in Early Stuart England", *P&P* 223 (2014).
31. Cf. Ian Burney, *Poison, Detection, and the Victorian Imagination* (Manchester, 2006), esp. chs 2–3, 5.
32. Daniel Sennert, *The Sixth Book of Practical Physick. Of Occult or Hidden Diseases* (London, 1662), pp. 32–3; Franck Collard, "Ouvrir pour découvrir. Réflexions sur les expertises de cadavers empoisonnés à l'époque médiévale", in Dominique Guéniot (ed.), *Corps à L'Épreuve: Poisons, remèdes et chirugie: aspects des pratiques médicales dans l'Antiquité et au Moyen-Âge* (Langres, 2002), pp. 181–2; Collard, *Crime of Poison*, pp. 54–60.
33. [Ambroise Paré], *The Workes of that famous Chirurgion Ambrose Parey, Translated out of Latine and compared with the French by Th. Johnson* (London, 1634), Book XXI, "Of Poysons", p. 775; Janet Doe, *A Bibliography, 1545–1940, of the Works of Ambroise Paré, 1510–1590 Premier Chirurgien & Conseiller de Roi* (New York, 1937, and Amsterdam, 1976), pp. 8, 103, 113, 155.
34. Paré, *Workes*, p. 776; cf. Sennert, *Sixth Book*, pp. 28, 30. Humoural explanations were eventually challenged by mechanistic analyses, see e.g. Richard Mead, *A Mechanical Account of Poisons In several Essays* (London, 1702), sig.A2r and *passim*; M.P. Earles, "Early theories of the mode of action of drugs and poisons", *Annals of Science* 17:2 (1961).

35. Paré, *Workes*, pp. 778–9, 782, 793, 795–6; Sennert, *Sixth Book*, pp. 51–2, 69, 75–8. For the persistence of similar reasoning, see William Ramesey, *Lifes Security: or A Phylosophical and Physical Discourse; Shewing the Names, Natures, & Vertues of all Sorts of Venomes and Venemous Things* (London, 1665), pp. 69, 71, 227.

36. Peck, *Leicester's Commonwealth*, pp. 83–4; *Rhetorica Ad Herennium*, 2:5, 2:27 (Loeb translation); Burney, *Poison*, p. 51; Bellany, *Politics*, pp. 144–8; Olivia Weisser, "Boils, Pushes and Wheals: Reading Bumps on the Body in Early Modern England", *Social History of Medicine* 22:2 (2009), pp. 326–7; Quentin Skinner, *Reason and Rhetoric in the Philosophy of Hobbes* (Cambridge, 1996), pp. 23, 32–3; Sarah Currie, "Poisonous Women and Unnatural History in Roman Culture", in Maria Wyke (ed.), *Parchments of Gender: Deciphering the Bodies of Antiquity* (Oxford, 1998), p. 163.

37. Barnabe Barnes, *The Divils Charter* (London, 1607), sigs K3r, M2v–M3r; "The famous Ratketcher" (c. 1616), Robert Latham (ed.), *Catalogue of the Pepys Library: The Pepys Ballads* (Cambridge, 1987), vol. I, pp. 458–9; see too "An excellent new Medley" (c. 1620), in Latham, *Pepys Ballads*, I, p. 456; and "A Copy of Verses of a Baker and a Mealman", in Latham, *Pepys Ballads*, III, p. 72; J. Payne Collier (ed.), *Kynge Johan. A Play in Two Parts. By John Bale*, Camden Society, 1st Series, 2 (London, 1838), p. 82; John Foxe, *Actes and Monuments* (London, 1570), book 4, pp. 328 (illustration), 329; Cheshire RO, MS Z QSF/30, Crownmote and Quarter Sessions File 1576–77, items 7–14, 20; and Lancashire RO, Quarter Sessions, QSB 1/146/35–9 (January 1634/5).

38. Cheshire RO, MS CR 63/2/19, fos 7r, 8v; *ST*, II, pp. 918–19, 922; NA SP 14/82/2, 27; "A discourse of the poysoninge of Sr Thom: Overbury", KHLC, Knatchbull MSS U951/Z4, fo. 4v. For a well-known classical example, see Juvenal, *Satires*, I, lines 69–72.

39. Sennert, *Sixth Book*, p. 33; Paré, *Workes*, p. 809; Louis Guyon in Thomas Milles comp., *Treasurie of Auncient and Moderne Times* (London, 1613), p. 169; Mead, *Mechanical Account*, p. 103 (citing Andrea Bacci's 1580s treatise 'De Venenis'); and Ramesey, *Lifes Security*, p. 35.

40. See esp. David Harley, "Political Post-mortems and Morbid Anatomy in Seventeenth-Century England", *Social History of Medicine* 7:1 (1994); and Katherine Park, *Secrets of Women: Gender, Generation, and the Origins of Human Dissection* (New York, 2006), ch. 3. Early Stuart examples of pathological autopsy include the scholar Isaac Casaubon (1614) and the diplomat/privy councillor Sir Ralph Winwood (1617): Harley, "Political Post-mortems", p. 10; Hugh Trevor-Roper, *Europe's Physician: The Various Life of Sir Theodore de Mayerne* (New Haven and London, 2006), pp. 193, 219; *Chamberlain*, II, p. 108 (to Carleton: 31 October, 1617).

41. *Chamberlain*, II, p. 220 (to Carleton: 6 March 1619); *Yonge*, p. 42. See, too, examples in *Whiteway*, p. 88; Vittorio Gabrieli (ed.), "A New Digby Letter-book: 'In praise of Venetia'", *National Library of Wales Journal* 9:2 (1955), pp. 134–5; and John Aubrey, *'Brief Lives'*, ed. Andrew Clark, 2 vols (Oxford, 1898), vol. I, pp. 224–7, 229–32. On embalming see Lawrence Stone, *The Crisis of the Aristocracy* (Oxford, 1965), pp. 572–9; Clare Gittings, *Death, Burial and the Individual in Early Modern England* (London, 1984), pp. 104, 166–7, 190–1; Harold J. Cook, *Matters of Exchange: Commerce, Medicine, and Science in the Dutch Golden Age* (New Haven and London, 2007), pp. 270–81; and Collard, "Ouvrir pour découvrir", pp. 184–5.

42. See esp. Michael Clark and Catherine Crawford (eds), *Legal Medicine in History* (Cambridge, 1994); Carol Loar, "Medical Knowledge and the Early Modern English Coroner's Inquest", *Social History of Medicine* 23:3 (2010); Vanessa McMahon, "Reading the Body: Dissection and the 'Murder' of Sarah Stout, Hertfordshire, 1699", *Social History of Medicine* 19:1 (2006); Julia Rudolph, "Gender and the Development of Forensic Science: A Case Study", *EHR* 123:502 (2008); Katherine D. Watson, *Forensic Medicine in Western Society: A History* (London, 2011); Ynez Violé O'Neill, "Innocent III and the Evolution of Anatomy", *Medical History* 20 (1976); Joseph Shatzmiller, "The Jurisprudence of the Dead Body: Medical Practition at the Service of Civic and Legal Authorities", *Micrologus* 7 (1999), esp. p. 229; Collard, "Ouvrir pour découvrir"; and Collard, *Crime of Poison*, pp. 192–3.

43. R. F. Hunnisett (ed.), *Sussex Coroners' Inquests, 1558–1603* (PRO Publications: Kew, 1996), pp. xxxvi–xxxvii, pp. 95–6 (Butcher case); Michael MacDonald and

Terence R. Murphy, *Sleepless Souls: Suicide in Early Modern England* (Oxford, 1990), pp. 226–7.

44. See e.g. [L.B.], *The Examination, confession, and condemnation of Henry Robson Fisherman of Rye, who poysoned his wife in the strangest maner that ever hitherto hath bin heard of* (London, 1598), sigs A4v–B1r; Hunnisett, *Sussex Coroners' Inquests, 1558–1603*, pp. 116–17, case no. 472L; Anon,. *Murther, Murther. Or, A bloody Relation how Anne Hamton, dwelling in Westminster nigh London, by poyson murthered her deare husband Sept 1641* (London, 1641), p. 5; Loar, "Medical Knowledge", p. 479; Shatzmiller, "Jurisprudence of the Dead Body", p. 229; Bellany, "Thinking with Poison".

45. For an earlier example see the rumours around the death of Catherine of Aragon: James Gairdner (ed.), *Letters and Papers, Foreign and Domestic, of the Reign of Henry VIII* (London, 1887), vol. X, pp. 20–2, 51; Garrett Mattingly, *Catherine of Aragon* (Boston, 1941), p. 431; Retha M. Warnicke, *The Rise and Fall of Anne Boleyn: Family Politics at the Court of Henry VIII* (Cambridge, 1989), pp. 186–7; Eric Ives, *The Life and Death of Anne Boleyn* (Oxford, 2004), pp. 327, 340, 345; and G. W. Bernard, *Anne Boleyn: Fatal Attractions* (New Haven and London, 2010), pp. 89, 167–8.

46. Copies of the autopsy report appear in Charles Cornwallis, *The Life and Death of Our Late Most Incomparable and Heroique Prince, Henry Prince of Wales*, (London, 1641), pp. 75–9; BL Add. MS 30075, fos 44v ff; Theodore de Mayerne, "Relation veritable de la Maladie, Mort, & Ouverture du Corps de tres Hault & tres illustre Henry Prince de Valles", *Opera Medica* (1703), pp. 103ff; and W. H., *The True Picture and Relation of Prince Henry* (Leyden, 1634), pp. 44–6.

47. BL Harl. MS 1973, fo. 10v, "The maner of the death of prince Henry"; cf. *Chamberlain*, I, pp. 388–9 (to Carleton: 12 November, 1612); *CSPV 1610–13*, p. 464 (English ambassador to Venice: 13 December 1612); Cornwallis, *Life*, pp. 81–2; Bellany, *Politics*, pp. 202–3; Harley, "Political Post-mortems", pp. 7–9; Trevor-Roper, *Europe's Physician*, pp. 171ff.

48. Cornwallis, *Life*, pp. 75–9; Mayerne, *Opera*, p. 111; W.H., *True Picture*, pp. 44–6, 75.

49. *Chamberlain*, I, pp. 388–9 (to Carleton: 12 November, 1612); *CSPV 1610–13*, p. 464.

50. Cf. the early 1630s case in Charles Goodall, *The Royal College of Physicians of London* (London, 1684), pp. 428–37

51. BL Harl. MS 389, fo. 420r (Mead to Stuteville: 9 April 1625); D'Ewes, *Autobiography*, I, p. 263; William Neve in *Progresses*, IV, p. 1037. Cf *Mercure François*, XI, p. 336. On analogical interpretations see Richard P. Sugg, *Murder After Death: Literature and Anatomy in Early Modern England* (Ithaca, 2007), pp. 89–90; "Digby letter-book", p. 134; *Mercure François*, XII, p. 482.

52. On experimentation with poison, see e.g. William Shakespeare, *Cymbeline*, Act 1, scene 5, lines 21–6, 28, 40–51; Paré, *Workes*, p. 809; Guyon in Milles, *Treasurie*, pp. 163–4; Suetonius, *Historie of Twelve Caesars*, trans. Philemon Holland (London, 1606), p. 195; Barnes, *Divils Charter*, sig. K3r; M. P. Earles, "Experiments with Drugs and Poisons in the Seventeenth and Eighteenth Centuries", *Annals of Science* 19:4 (1963); Thomas Birch, comp., *The History of the Royal Society of London* (London, 1756), vol. II, pp. 31, 41–3, 45–6, 48, 50, 54, 55–7, 59; Mead, *Mechanical Account*, pp. 103, 117, 121–3; and Daniel Carey, "The Political Economy of Poison: The Kingdom of Makassar and the Early Royal Society", *Renaissance Studies* 17:3 (2003), pp. 533ff.

53. *Forerunner*, pp. 14, 19 (our emphasis).

54. Paré, *Workes*, p. 777; Sennert, *Sixth Book*, p. 31; Guyon in Milles, *Treasurie*, pp. 170–1; Ramesey, *Lifes Security*, pp. 10–11; Burney, *Poison*, pp. 46–9.

55. Shakespeare, *Cymbeline*, Act 3, scene 4, line 16; John Webster, *The White Devil*, Act 4, scene 2, line 61; Bellany, *Politics*, p. 147. For other theatrical representations of "artistic" poisonings see *Arden of Faversham*, Scene 1, lines 227–34, 280–1, 609–16; John Webster, *The White Devil*, Act 2, scene 1, lines 299–303, 308; Act 2, scene 2, lines 24–31; Act 5, scene 1, lines 69–71; Act 5, scene 3, lines 27, 157–8, 160–5; Thomas Middleton, *The Revengers Tragedy*, Act 3, scene 5, lines 102–5; Barnes, *Divills Charter*, sigs H1v–H2v. See too Cornwallis, *Life*, p. 82; Anon., *The Cruel French Lady* (London, 1673), pp. 5–6; Lynn Wood Mollenauer, *Strange Revelations: Magic, Poison, and Sacrilege in Louis XIV's France* (University Park, PA, 2007), pp. 11–17.

56. Peck, *Leicester's Commonwealth*, pp. 82–3, 86; *Letters and Papers, Henry VIII 1536*, item 200 (Chapuys to Granvelle: 29 January 1536); Bellany, *Politics*, p. 147. On poison and Italy, see also Mariangela Tempera, "The Rhetoric of Poison in John Webster's Italianate Plays", in Michele Marrapodi et al. (eds), *Shakespeare's Italy: Functions of Italian Locations in Renaissance Drama* (Manchester, 1993); and Normand, "Venomous Words", pp. 122–9. For medieval images of the poisoner and the foreign Other, see Collard, *Crime of Poison*, pp. 40–1, 101–4, 248–51.

57. *Forerunner*, p. 16.

58. Guyon in Milles, *Treasurie*, p. 170; Ramesey, *Lifes Security*, p. 10; Harrison, "Literary Background", pp. 44–6, quotation from Theophrastus at p. 44; Tacitus, *Annals*, IV.8, XII.66.

59. *Cymbeline*, Act 1, scene 5, ll. 10–11, 21–6, 40–51; Act 5, scene 5, lines 60–2; Benjamin Schmidt (ed.), *The Discovery of Guiana by Sir Walter Ralegh*, (Boston and New York, 2008), pp. 85–6; Birch (ed.), *History of the Royal Society*, vol. II, pp. 43–4; Guyon in Milles, *Treasurie*, pp. 165, 171; Harrison, "Literary Background", pp. 47–8; Carey, "Political Economy"; Susan Scott Parrish, *American Curiosity: Cultures of Natural History in the Colonial British Atlantic World* (Chapel Hill, 2006), pp. 253–8, 262, 274–9, 288.

60. See e.g. Ramesey, *Lifes Security*, pp. 14–17, 26, 142–5, 166 ff; Paré, *Workes*, pp. 776, 781–2, 804; Guyon in Milles, *Treasurie*, pp. 165–7; Sennert, *Sixth Book*, pp. 46, 51; Harrison, "Literary Background", pp. 46–54.

61. Cheshire RO, MS CR 63/2/19, fo. 6r; Bellany, *Politics*, pp. 148–53; MacDonald and Murphy, *Sleepless Souls*, p. 226; Keith Thomas, *Religion and the Decline of Magic: Studies in Popular Belief in Sixteenth- and Seventeenth-Century England* (Harmondsworth, 1973), pp. 226, 520; Reginald Scot, *The Discoverie of Witchcraft*, ed. Montague Summers (New York, 1972), book VI.

62. *Laud*, pp. 154, 157; *Chamberlain*, II, p. 601 (to Carleton: 26 February 1625); Goodman, *Court*, II, p. 377 (Coventry and Heath to Buckingham: 24 February 1625); Bellany, "Lambe", p. 59.

63. *Forerunner*, pp. 4, 10, 12; Bellany, "Lambe", pp. 48–63; *PP1626*, IV, p. 335.

64. *Forerunner*, pp. 4–5.

Part 3 Prologue

1. KHLC U269/1, CP 16/2 (Brett to Middlesex: 19 March 1626); NA C115/N3/8538 (Herbert to Scudamore: 23 May 1626); C115/N24/7770 (Laud to Scudamore: 10 June 1626).

2. NLW MS 9061E/1410 (Owen to Sir John Wynn: 19 May 1626); NA SP 78/79/64 ([Conway] to Carlisle: 5 June 1626); *Scrinia*, II, p. 71.

3. Conrad Russell, *Parliaments and English Politics, 1621–1629* (Oxford, 1979), pp. 306, 316, 319. For other accounts of 1626, see S. R. Gardiner, *The History of England* (London, 1896), vol. VI, pp. 59–121; Lockyer, *Buckingham*, pp. 320, 323, 329; Harold Hulme, "The Leadership of Sir John Eliot in the Parliament of 1626", *Journal of Modern History* 4:3 (1932); J. N. Ball, "The Impeachment of the Duke of Buckingham in the Parliament of 1626", in *Mélanges Antonio Marongiu*, International Commission for the History of Representative and Parliamentary Institutions, 34 (Palermo, 1967); J. S. Flemion, "The Dissolution of Parliament in 1626", *EHR* 87:345 (1972); and Vernon Snow, "The Arundel Case, 1626", *The Historian* 26:3 (1964).

Chapter 8

1. *Scrinia*, II, p. 71; *PP1626*, IV, p. 335 (Browne to [anon.]: 20 May 1626).

2. NA SP 84/127, fo. 22r (Buckingham to Cecil: 4 May 1625); SP 78/73, fo. 401v (Buckingham to [Richelieu?]: [early 1625]).

3. NA SP 95/2, fo. 133v (Instructions to Buckingham and Holland for Sweden: 17 October 1625); *CSPV 1625–26*, p. 247 (5 December 1625).

4. NA SP 84/127, fo. 22r (Buckingham to Cecil: 4 May 1625); Anon., *Great Britaines Sorrow* (London, 1625). On reactions to the expedition, see *Mercure François*, XI, p. 1,051.

5. Michael Questier, *Catholicism and Community in Early Modern England* (Cambridge, 2006), pp. 428–31; Myron Noonkester, "Charles I and Shrieval Selection, 1625–26", *Historical Research* 64:155 (1991), pp. 305–11; and Barbara Donagan, "The York House Conference Revisited: Laymen, Calvinists and Arminians", *Historical Research* 54:155 (1991).

6. BL Harl. MS 2013, fo. 295r (account of Buckingham's entourage: spring 1625); Harvard Law School, LMS 1101, fo. 1v (Lightfoot's case notes); BL Add. MS 72331, no. 174 (Wolley to Trumbull: 17 June 1625). See also Randall Davies, "An Inventory of the Duke of Buckingham's Pictures", *Burlington Magazine* 10 (1907).

7. NA SP 78/73, fo. 401r (Buckingham to [Richelieu]: [early 1625]). See also Thomas Cogswell, "'The Warre of the Commons for the honour of King Charles': The Parliament-Men and the Reformation of the Lord Admiral in 1626", *Historical Research* 84:226 (2011); and Frederick C. Dietz, *English Public Finance, 1558–1641* (New York, 1964), pp. 219–22.

8. NA SP 16/7/71 (Hopton to Conway: 12 October 1625); SP 16/3/59 and 16/3/67 (Ogle to Conway: 12 and 14 June 1625); F. T. R. Edgar, *Sir Ralph Hopton* (Oxford, 1986), pp. 6–10.

9. NA SP 16/12/62 (Eliot to Conway: 22 December 1625); SP 63/242/203i (Hookes to Falkland: 22 December 1625); Charles Dalton, *The Life and Times of Edward Cecil, Viscount Wimbledon* (London, 1885), vol. II, pp. 83–152.

10. BL Stowe MS 176, fo. 268r (Delaware to Edmondes: 22 November 1625); Nottingham University Library, NeC 15406, pp. 417–19 (Cecil's Report: [1626]); *Cabala* (London, 1663), p. 413 (Cromwell to Buckingham: 8 September 1625).

11. [Randulph Mayeres], *Mayeres His Travels* (London, 1638), p. 39; NA SP 63/242/203i and ii (Butler to Buckingham: 25 December 1625); Dalton, *Wimbledon*, II, pp. 48–241.

12. KHLC U269/2, CP 25 (Carey to Middlesex: 27 October 1625); Suffolk RO (Ipswich) EE1/O1/1, fo. 8r (Aldborough Letterbook: [early 1626]).

13. Kings Lynn Borough Archives KL/C7/7, fo. 249r (Hall Book: 16 January 1626); Norfolk RO Y/C19/6, fo. 18r (Great Yarmouth Assembly Book: 11 March 1626). See also R. A. Stradling, *The Armada of Flanders: Spanish Maritime Policy and European War, 1568–1668* (Cambridge, 1992), pp. 44–5.

14. NA SP 16/11/64 (Coke to Conway: 14 December 1625); Thomas Cogswell, "Foreign Policy and Parliament: The Case of La Rochelle, 1625–1626", *EHR* 99: 391 (1984).

15. Cogswell, "Foreign Policy", pp. 241–67.

16. *PP1625*, pp. 395, 399–400, 403; *APC 1625–26*, pp. 28–30, 42–5 (orders for seamen and soldiers: 20 April and 5 May 1625).

17. *PP1625*, pp. 417, 460; Conrad Russell, *Parliaments and English Politics, 1621–1629* (Oxford, 1979), pp. 260–9.

18. *Scrinia*, II, pp. 14, 65; NA SP 75/6/219 (Buckingham to Christian IV: 1 December 1625).

19. *PP1625*, p. 438; CCA Urry MS 66, fo. 127v (Thomas Scott, *Canterburie Cittizens for the Parliament*).

20. NA SP 16/7/73 (Mildmay to Conway: 12 October 1625); HHStA Belgien Fasz. 62, fo. 437r (Della Faille to [anon]: 1 October 1625); HHStA Belgien Fasz. 61, unfoliated (X to [della Faille]: 13 and 28 June and 9 September 1625); SP 16/18/70 (Eliot to agent [abstract]: 16 January 1626). See also Paul Honeyball, "Sir John Eliot", *HOC*, IV, pp. 182–200.

21. Vernon Snow, *Essex the Rebel* (Lincoln, 1970), pp. 124–47; B. W. Quintrell (ed.), *The Maynard Lieutenancy Book, 1608–1639* (Chelmsford, 1993), vol. I, pp. xlix–lvii.

22. HHStA Belgien Fasz. 61, unfoliated (X: 15 April 1625); BL Harl. MS 1581, fo. 66v (Lorkin to Buckingham: 7 September 1625).

23. KHLC De L'Isle MSS, U1475/C60/1 (North to Leicester: 17 October 1625); HHStA Belgien Fasz. 61 (X to della Faille: 3 May [1625]); Thomas Cogswell, "The Return of 'The Deade Alive': The Earl of Bristol and Dr. Eglisham in the Parliament of 1626 and in Caroline Political Culture", *EHR* 128:532 (2013).

24. *Scrinia*, II, pp. 16–32, 70; NLW MS 9061E/1391(Owen to Sir John Wynn: 17 February 1626).

25. NA SP 16/1/25 (Eliot to Buckingham: 1 April 1625); SP 16/7/31, 16/10/35, 16/12/38, 16/12/95 (Eliot's letters: 6 October, 22 and 26 November, and 31 December 1625).

26. NA SP 16/12/38 (Eliot to Conway: 22 December 1625); SP 16/10/35 (Eliot to Coke: 26 November 1625); Anne Duffin, *Faction and Faith: Politics and Religion of the Cornish Gentry Before the Civil War* (Exeter, 1996), pp. 109–43; Mary Wolffe, *Gentry Leaders in Peace and War* (Exeter, 1997), pp. 47–67, 93–164.

27. *PP1625*, p. 417; NA SP 16/533/77 (Bagg to Buckingham: [March 1626]).

28. *PP1626*, II, pp. 16–18; BL Harl. MS 390, fo. 13v (Mead to Stuteville: 18 February [1626]); John Forster, *Sir John Eliot* (London, 1864), vol. I, pp. 446–73; Harold Hulme, *The Life of Sir John Eliot* (London, 1957), pp. 94–104.

29. Cornwall RO Port Eliot MSS, EL 655/2/13–18 ("Perticular misdemeanours of the Duke": [early 1626]); copies include BL Add. MS 4155, fos 143r–44v; Bod. MS Rawlinson C674, fos 22–24. See also Hulme, *Eliot*, p. 127 n.3.

30. BL Add. MS 4155, fo. 144v.

31. *LJ*, III, pp. 74–6, 78–86 (17, 19 and 24 April 1621); pp. 312–81 (20 April to 12 May 1624).

32. *PP1626*, I, pp. 413, 430, 469–70.

33. *LJ*, III, pp. 53–7, 344 (20 March 1621 and 7 May 1624); NLW MS 9061E/1395 (Owen to Sir John Wynn: 8 March 1626).

34. *PP1626*, II, pp. 294, 324, 392–3; *Scrinia*, II, p. 70.

35. *PP1626*, II, pp. 249–50, 262, 285.

36. *PP1626*, II, pp. 317, 393, 409, 412; NA SP 99/27/32 (Conway to Wake: 14 April 1626); Colin Tite, *Impeachment and Parliamentary Judicature in Early Stuart England* (London, 1974), p. 191.

37. *Scrinia*, I, pp. 17–18.

38. *PP1626*, I, pp. 180–1; KHLC U269/1, CP77 (Monmouth to Middlesex: [March 1626]); Oo92 (Willis to Middlesex: 14 March 1626); Oo63 (Rochford to Middlesex: [March 1626]); CP 105 (Herman to Middlesex: 13 March 1626).

39. KHLC U269/1, CP 16/2 (A. Brett to Middlesex: 19 and [30–31] March 1626); CP 17 (H. Brett to Middlesex: [early April 1626]); Menna Prestwich, *Cranfield: Politics and Profit under the Early Stuarts* (Oxford, 1966), pp. 469–92.

40. KHLC U269/1, CB 309 (Middlesex to Herman: 29 April 1626); and CB 105 [bundle #1] (Herman to Middlesex: 3 May 1626).

41. *Scrinia*, II, p. 70; NA 31/3/63, fos 61–4 (Mende to Richelieu: April 1626); Arundel Castle, Autograph Letters, 285 (Mainwaring to Arundel: 24 April 1626).

Chapter 9

1. KHLC U269/1, CB105 (Herman to Middlesex: 3 May 1626); CB309 (Middlesex to Herman [draft]: 29 April 1626). See also CB309 (Herman's abstract: 29 April 1626).

2. *PP1626*, III, pp. 37–51, 53–9.

3. *Wotton*, II, p. 295 (to Elizabeth of Bohemia: [1626]); Edward Hyde, *A Full Answer to an Infamous and Trayterous Pamphlet* (London, 1648), pp. 13–14; and *PP1626*, IV, pp. 334–7 (Gabriel Browne to anon.: 20 May 1626).

4. KHLC U269/1, CB105 (Herman to Middlesex: 2 May 1626); NLW MS 9061E/1402 (anon. newsletter: [2 May 1626]); *PP1626*, III, p. 160; BL Add. MS 17677L, fo. 204r (Joachimi to the States General: 4 May 1626); *CSPV 1625–26*, p. 416 (5 May 1626).

5. Hyde, *A Full Answer*, pp. 13–14; *Wotton*, II, p. 291, our emphasis; Cogswell, *Revolution*, pp. 22–4; Bellany, *Politics*, pp. 80–5, 107–8.

6. *Peake*, fo. 152v; *PP1626*, III, p. 38. See for example the committee on religion (established 10 February), *PP1626*, II, p. 13.

7. Bod. MS Rawlinson A346, fo. 226r (Digges to Hippesley: 8 January 1626). On the members, see *HOC*, IV, pp. 65–80 (Digges); IV, pp. 148–57 (Erle); IV, pp. 634–7 (Glanville); IV, pp. 735–47 (Hoby); V, pp. 264–78 (Marten); V, pp. 669–76 (Phelips); V, pp. 797–808 (Pym); VI, pp. 267–71 (Selden); VI, pp. 306–10 (Sherland); VI, pp. 671–4 (Wandesford); VI, pp. 746–8 (Whitby).

8. *PP1626*, III, pp. 53–6.

9. *Peake*, fo. 145v. See also the biography of Peake in *HOC*, V, pp. 625–6.

10. *Chamberlain*, I, p. 346 (to Carleton: 29 April 1612), and II, p. 482 (to Carleton: 8 March 1623); NA SP 14/66/100–101 (Atkins and Lister to Salisbury: [October 1611?]); William Munk, *The Roll of the Royal College of Physicians of London* (London, 1878).

11. NA SP 99/58/106, 154, 161, 163 and 176 (Lister to Salisbury: October–December 1610); *CSPD 1603–10*, p. 95 (warrant to Atkins: 14 April 1604).

12. NA SP 14/15/32 (Atkins to Salisbury: 21 August 1605); *Register PSC*, p. 655 (G. Primrose to J. Primrose: 21 May 1624); SP 14/214, p. 52 (Conway's Letterbook: 13 June 1623).

13. NA SP 14/40/56 ("Fees and wages", [1608?]); *HMC Salisbury*, XXIV, p. 211 (medical expenses: 3 March 1612).

14. *CSPD 1611–18*, pp. 230, 446 (grant to Atkins: 13 April 1614; grant to Chambers: 14 March 1617), and *CSPD 1619–23*, p. 103 (grant to Chambers: 11 December 1619); NA SP 16/103/30 and 30:1–3 (Chambers petition: 5 May 1628); SP 14/141, p. 11 (abstract of the patent rolls: 27 September 1609).

15. SP 15/42/41 (Digby to Buckingham: [late 1620]); *Chamberlain*, II, p. 326 (to Carleton: 4 November 1620).

16. Munk, *Roll,* I, p. 174; Margaret Pelling, *Medical Conflicts in Early Modern London: Patronage, Physicians, and Irregular Practitioners, 1550–1640* (Oxford, 2003), pp. 326–7; John Gee, *The Foot out of the Snare: With A Detection of Sundry Late Practices and Impostures of the Priests and Jesuites in England,* '4th Edition' (London, 1624), sig. X1r; D. Shanahan, "The Death of Thomas More, Secular Priest", *Recusant History* VII (1963–4), pp. 23–32; and *Holles*, II, p. 291 (to Gondomar: 24 August 1624).

17. BL Add. MS 12528, fos 6r, 15v; Bod. MS Tanner 73, fos 354–57 (Duchess to Duke of Buckingham: 12 August 1623); *Holles*, II, p. 326 (to Countess of Clare: 25 March 1626); NA SP 16/81/61 (Lewis to Nicholas: 16 October 1627); and SP 16/4/140 (Duchess of Buckingham to Mrs Porter: 28 July [1625?]).

18. NA SP 14/181/12 (Dodsworth to More: 3 January 1625); SP 16/55/26 (Mansfield to Buckingham: 27 February 1627); Menna Prestwich, *Cranfield: Politics and Profits under the Early Stuarts* (Oxford, 1966), pp. 473–5.

19. *Register PSC*, p. 655; Gilbert Burnet, *History of My Own Time*, ed. Osmund Airy (Oxford, 1897), vol. I, pp. 22–3; and Martin Greig, "Burnet, Gilbert (1643–1715)", *ODNB*.

20. NA SP 14/141, pp. 109, 313 (abstracts of the patent rolls: 5 November 1614 and 9 July 1621); John Henry, "Craig, John (d. 1620?)", *ODNB*.

21. *Register PSC*, pp. 187–8 (Charles's warrant: 22 October 1625); NA SP 16/92/29 (order of payment to Ramsey: 4 February 1628); and John Henry, "Craig, John (d. 1655)", *ODNB*; Frederick Devon (ed.), *Issues of the Exchequer* (London, 1836), p. 350 (gift to Harvey: 28 July 1626); *CSPD 1625–26*, p. 59 (Chambers's reappointment: 12 July 1625).

22. William Paddy's MS notes, *The Booke of Common Prayer* (London, 1615), St John's College, Oxford, Cpd.b.2.upper shelf.5.

23. *Forerunner*, pp. 19, 21–22; *CSPV 1625–26*, p. 416 (5 May 1626); BL Harl. MS 390, fo. 49r (letter to Mead: 28 April 1626); and NA 31/3/63, fo. 64r (Mende to d'Herbault: 29 April 1626).

24. *PP1626*, II, pp. 221, 241; III, p. 85.

25. *Peake*, fos 150v, 147v, 146v, 134v [reverse foliation]; *PP1626*, III, p. 57.

26. *Peake*, fos 148v, 142v; *PP1626*, III, p. 66.

27. *Peake*, fos 150v, 140v. On the date see Chambers's testimony, *PP1626*, III, p. 67.

28. *PP1626*, III, pp. 64, 67; *Peake*, fos 152v, 140v–139v, 137v.

29. *PP1626*, III, pp. 57, 64, 67, 74; *Peake*, fos 152v, 138v.

30. *Forerunner*, p. 21; *PP1626*, III, pp. 57, 68; *Peake*, fo. 137v.

31. *PP1626*, III, pp. 57–8, 64, 67, 68; *Peake*, fo. 140v.

32. *PP1626*, III, pp. 67, 68; *Peake*, fos 140v, 136v.

33. *PP1626*, III, p. 57; *Peake*, fos 150v, 149v, 147v.

34. *PP1626*, III, pp. 64, 67; *Peake*, fos 133v, 134v.

35. *PP1626*, III, p. 68; *Peake*, fos 150v, 147v.

36. *Peake*, fo. 133v; *PP1626*, III, pp. 67–8.

37. *PP1626*, III, p. 68; *Peake*, fo. 146v.

38. *PP1626*, III, pp. 67–8; *Peake*, fo. 136v.

39. *Peake*, fo. 139v.

40. *Peake*, fos 147v, 140v; *PP1626*, III, p. 57.

41. *PP1626*, III, pp. 57, 74; *Peake*, fo. 150v.

42. *PP1626*, III, pp. 67, 69, 74; *Peake*, fos 149v, 139v, 138v.

43. *Peake*, fo. 140v; *PP1626*, III, pp. 64, 68.

44. *PP1626*, III, pp. 68–9.

45. *PP1626*, III, p. 74; *Peake*, fo. 145v.

46. *PP1626*, III, pp. 66, 68–9; *Peake*, fo. 145v.

47. *PP1626*, III, p. 58; *Peake*, fos 140v, 145v, 148v, 149v.

48. The College of Physicians, *Pharmacopoea Londinensis* (London, 1618), pp. 75–6, 78–80; [Walter Baley], *A Discourse of the medicine called Mithridatium* (1585); Gilbert Watson, *Theriac and Mithridatium: A Study in Therapeutics* (London, 1966); Adrienne Mayor, *The Poison King: The Life and Legend of Mithradates, Rome's Deadliest Enemy* (Princeton, 2010), pp. 240–6; J. P. Griffin, "Venetian Treacle and the Foundation of Medicines Regulation", *British Journal of Clinical Pharmacology*, 58:3 (2004); David Gentilcore, *Healers and Healing in Early Modern Italy* (Manchester, 1998), pp. 113–15.

49. Baley, *Discourse*, sigs B5v, D3r ff; Nicholas Culpeper, *A Physicall Directory or A translation of the London Dispensatory Made by the College of Physicians* (London, 1649), pp. 91–2, 179–80, 183–4; Watson, *Theriac*, pp. 73–7; Paul Slack, *The Impact of Plague in Tudor and Stuart England*, rev ed. (Oxford, 1990), pp. 30–1; A. Lloyd Moote and Dorothy Moote, *The Great Plague: The Story of London's Most Deadly Year* (Baltimore, 2004), p. 105.

50. Baley, *Discourse*, sigs D4v, D6r; John Woodall, *The Surgions Mate* (London, 1617), pp. 84–5.

51. Culpeper, *Physicall Directory*, pp. 113–14; Lazarus Rivière, *The Practice of Physick, In Seventeen several Books . . . Being chiefly a Translation of The Works of that Learned and Renowned Doctor Lazarus Riverius* (London, 1672), pp. 582–4; *PP1626*, III, p. 57.

52. John Gerard, *The Herball or Generall Historie of Plantes . . . Very much Enlarged and Amended by Thomas Johnson Citizen and Apothecarye of London* (London, 1633), pp. 427–8, 457–8, 1,465; Culpeper, *Physicall Directory*, pp. 67, 104, 110; John Hall, *Select Observations on English Bodies of Eminent Persons in desperate Diseases. First written in Latin by Mr. John Hall, Physician: After Englished by James Cook, Author of the Marrow of Chirurgery* (London, 1679), pp. 18, 21, 56–7, 121, 126, 137–9, 144–5, 147, 150, 237, 260–1.

53. *PP1626*, III, p. 73.

54. *PP1626*, III, pp. 73–4.

55. Reconstruction based on *PP1626*, III, p. 68.

56. E.g. NA PC 2/30/131 (warrant: 14 May 1619); *CSPD 1625–6*, p. 536 (declaration: 18 May 1625); *CSPD 1626–28*, p. 136 (grant: 12 April 1627); NA SP 16/540, fo. 154r (Heath to Carr: 30 May 1631).

57. *PP1626*, III, p. 73.

58. NA 31/3/63, fo. 62v (Mende to Richelieu: late April 1626); Society of Antiquaries, MS 190E, fo. 29r (Buckingham to Mayor of Rochester: 27 April 1626); *APC 1625–26*, p. 450 (Privy Council warrants: 28 April 1626).

59. *CSPV 1625–26*, pp. 416–17 (5 May) and pp. 604–5 ("Relazione" on the state of England: 1626); NA SP 14/158/1 (examination of Ferdinando Kelly and Owen Doulen: 1 January 1624).

60. Jan Baptiste van Helmont, *Van Helmont's Works: Containing his most Excellent Philosophy, Physick, Chirurgery, Anatomy* (London, 1664), "The Plague-Grave", ch. 79 "Butler", sigs Ffff1r–Ggggggg3r.

61. Arne Jönsson (ed.), *Works and Correspondence of Axel Oxenstierna* (Stockholm, 2007), 2nd series, XIII, pp. 198–9 (Spens to Oxenstierna: 26 November 1626).

62. BL Harl. MS 6987, fo. 219r (Buckingham to James: undated).

63. NA 31/3/63, fos 62r, 66r (Mende to Richelieu: late April 1626).

64. *PP1626*, III, pp. 58, 64, 68.

65. *PP1626*, III, p. 58.
66. *PP1626*, III, pp. 64–5, 67; *Peake*, fos 137v–134v. Our emphasis.
67. *Salvetti*, p. 62 (5 May 1626).

Chapter 10

1. *CSPV 1625–26*, p. 425 (19 May 1626).
2. *PP1626*, II, pp. 405, 408–9, 412; NA SP 99/27 fo. 32v (Conway to Wake: 17 April 1626); BL Harl. MS 390, fo. 39r (anon. newsletter: 8 April 1626)
3. *Holles*, II, p. 29 (to Exeter: 1 May 1626).
4. *PP1626*, III, pp. 84–7.
5. *PP1626*, III, pp. 84–6.
6. *PP1626*, III, pp. 90–4.
7. *PP1626*, III, pp. 91, 93.
8. *PP1626*, III, pp. 91, 93–4; NLW MS 9061E/1406 (Owen to Sir John Wynn: 5 May 1626); Andrew Thrush, "Sir Robert Mansell", and Alan Davidson and Andrew Thrush, "Humphrey Newbery", *HOC*, V, pp. 248–9, 506–7.
9. *PP1626*, III, pp. 129–30.
10. *PP1626*, III, pp. 133, 140, 143, 146–7, 151; Karen Bishop and Simon Healey, "Sir Christopher Wandesford", *HOC*, VI, pp. 669–74.
11. *Holles*, II, p. 294 (to Exeter: 9 September 1626).
12. Cogswell, *Revolution*, pp. 172–3; Robert E. Ruigh, *The Parliament of 1624: Politics and Foreign Policy* (Cambridge, MA, 1971), pp. 162–5; Conrad Russell, *Parliaments and English Politics, 1621–1629* (Oxford, 1979), pp. 158–9.
13. BL Add. MS 72276, no. 114 (Castle to Trumbull: 7 May 1624); NA SP 15/43/156 and 159 (Bristol to Conway: 11 June and 3 July 1624). See also S. R. Gardiner (ed.), "The Earl of Bristol's Defence", *Camden Miscellany* 6 (London, 1870), p. xiv; and Thomas Cogswell, "The Return of 'The Deade Alive': The Earl of Bristol and Dr. Eglisham in the Parliament of 1626 and in Caroline Political Culture", *EHR* 128:532 (2013).
14. *PP1626*, I, p. 192; III, pp. 25–6.
15. *PP1626*, I, pp. 284–5, 295–6, 320–4; NLW MS 9061E/1402 (Henry to Sir John Wynn: [early May 1626]).
16. *PP1626*, I, pp. 329–31, 343.
17. *PP1626*, I, pp. 317, 337–9, 342–3, 367; BL Harl. MS 390, fo. 51v (anon. newsletter: 5 May 1626); *Salvetti*, p. 62 (5 May 1626).
18. *PP1626*, I, pp. 328–35, 345.
19. *PP1626*, I, pp. 367–8; *Forerunner*, p. 20.
20. BL Add. MS 72371, fo. 5r (Atye to Trumbull: 4 June 1625); Henri Lonchay (ed.), *Correspondance de la Cour d'Espagne* (Brussels, 1927), II, p. 246 (Philip to Isabella: 25 December 1625).
21. *PP1626*, I, pp. 380, 383–5, 388, 400, 404; III, pp. 190, 194, 202, 204, 206–7, 212.
22. *PP1626*, III, pp. 233, 238.
23. *Salvetti*, p. 64 (12 May 1626); NA 31/3/63, fo. 70r (Mende to d'Herbault: 13 May 1626).
24. *PP1626*, I, pp. 408–10; Kevin Sharpe, "A Commonwealth of Meanings", in *Politics and Ideas in Early Stuart England* (London and New York, 1989).
25. Holinshed, *Chronicles* (1589), 6:1257 http://www.english.ox.ac.uk/holinshed/texts.php?text1=1587_9078; Stephen Johnston, "Digges, Thomas (c. 1546–1595)", *ODNB*; Tycho Brahe, *Learned Tico Brahe his Astronomical Coniectur of the new and much Admired [star] Which Appered in the year 1572* (London, 1632); Keith Thomas, *Religion and the Decline of Magic* (London, 1971), pp. 104, 106, 396; Alexandra Walsham, *Providence in Early Modern England* (Oxford, 1999), p. 174.
26. *PP1626*, I, p. 409; III, p. 195.
27. *PP1626*, I, p. 410; III, p. 246.
28. *PP1626*, I, p. 473.
29. *PP1626*, III, pp. 90–2.

30. *PP1626*, III, pp. 89, 93–4 (but cf. p. 91). On treason and intent see Edward Coke, *The Third Part of the Institutes*, 4th ed. (London, 1670), p. 6.

31. *PP1626*, I, p. 460.

32. *PP1626*, I, pp. 457–8, and III, p. 472. The key statutes are 3 Hen.VIII c.11; 14&15 Hen. VIII c.5; 32 Hen.VIII c.40; and 1 Mary st.2 c.9.

33. 34&35 Hen.VIII c.8 (though, arguably, 1 Mary st2. c.9 might have overturned this law); 3 Hen.VIII c.11; 1 Mary st.2 c.9. On challenges to the College's regulatory and punitive powers, see Harold J. Cook, "Against Common Right and Reason: The College of Physicians Versus Dr. Thomas Bonham", *The American Journal of Legal History* 29 (1985); Edward Coke, "Report on Dr. Bonham's Case" in *The Reports of Sir Edward Coke* (London, 1826), 107a–121a, pp. 355ff.

34. *PP1626*, I, p. 458; see, too, Edward Coke, *The Fourth Part of the Institutes*, 5th ed. (London, 1671), p. 251.

35. *PP1626*, I, p. 459.

36. J. M. Kaye, "The Early History of Murder and Manslaughter", *Law Quarterly Review* 83 (1967), pp. 365–95 (part 1), pp. 569–601 (part 2); William Holdsworth, *History of English Law*, 3rd ed. (London, 1923), vol. III, pp. 313–15; J. H. Baker, *An Introduction to English Legal History*, 4th ed. (Oxford, 2007), pp. 529–31: Coke, *Third Part*, pp. 54–7.

37. *PP1626*, I, pp. 459–60; William Staunford, *Les Plees del coron* (London, 1583), Lib.1 cap. 9, "Homicide voluntairement fait", pp. 16v–17r; John Wilkinson, *A treatise collected out of the statutes of this kingdom* (London, 1620), sigs C2r–v; Coke, *Fourth Part*, pp. 251–2; Sollom Emlyn (ed.), *Historia Placitorum Coronae: The History of the Pleas of the Crown. By Sir Matthew Hale*, 2 vols (London, 1800), vol. I, p. 429; Baker, *Introduction*, p. 176.

38. *PP1626*, III, pp. 201–2, 209–12, 214.

39. Samuel E. Thorne (trans.), *Bracton on the Laws and Customs of England*, (Cambridge, MA, 1968), vol. II, pp. 340–2; Francis Morgan Nichols (ed. & trans.), *Britton: The French Text Carefully Revised With An English Translation Introduction and Notes* (Oxford, 1865), vol. I, pp. 34–5; Coke, *Fourth Part*, pp. 251–2; Wilkinson, *Treatise*, sigs A6r–v; Baker, *Introduction*, p. 176; and Cook, "Against Common Right", p. 304 and n.10. If Saye recorded Wandesford correctly (rather than mishearing Bracton for Britton), it is likely Wandesford was misled by Staunford's *Plees del coron*, which attributes the opinion to "BRACTON f.14". Emlyn, *Hale*, I, pp. 429–30, argues that the doctrine was "apocryphal".

40. *PP1626*, I, p. 460; Coke, *Fourth Part*, pp. 251–2; William Joseph Whittaker (ed.), *Mirror of Justices* (Selden Society Publications 7 (1893): London, 1895), p. 137; J. S. Cockburn, "Patterns of Violence in English Society: Homicide in Kent 1560–1985", *P&P* 130 (1991), pp. 90–3; Robert Parker Sorlien (ed.), *The Diary of John Manningham of the Middle Temple, 1602–1603* (Hanover, NH, 1976), p. 53; Baker, *Introduction*, ch. 23; Cook, "Against Common Right"; Coke, "Dr. Bonham's Case", 117a–b.

41. *PP1626*, I, pp. 458–9.

42. *PP1626*, III, pp. 221–2; John Forster, *Sir John Eliot* (London, 1864), vol. I, pp. 538, 541–2; Alexander B. Grosart (ed.), *An Apology for Socrates and Negotium Posterorum* (London, 1881); Markku Peltonen, *Rhetoric, Politics and Popularity in Pre-Revolutionary England* (Cambridge, 2012).

43. *PP1626*, III, pp. 220–2.

44. *PP1626*, III, p. 222; "M. Tulli Ciceroni pro P. Quinctio Oratio" (81 BCE), ch. 18, section 57. We follow here the translation by C. D. Yonge (London, 1903), rather than *PP1626*, III, p. 289 n.8.

45. *PP1626*, III, p. 223; *The Annales of Cornelius Tacitus*, trans. Richard Greenwey, (London, 1622), p. 89. See also Curtis Perry, *Literature and Favoritism in Early Modern England* (Cambridge, 2006), pp. 229–52.

46. *PP1626*, III, p. 223 (adapting *Annals*, IV:2).

47. *Annals*, IV:3, 8, 10–11; *Annales*, pp. 90–3.

48. *Annales*, p. 89; BL Add. MS 4155, fo. 143r; *PP1626*, I, p. 331.

49. *PP1626*, III, pp. 223–4.

Chapter 11

1. *Rous*, p. 3; BL Add. MSS 22959, 28640, 29304.

2. *Roe*, pp. 502, 505 (Conway to Roe: 20 April and 4 May 1626); BL Add. MS 64888, fo. 111r (Conway to Coke: 30 May 1626).

3. NA SP 16/30/75 (Naval Commissioners to Buckingham: 30 June 1626); *APC 1625–26*, p. 480 (17 May 1626); SP 16/30/84 (petition of the ship owners).

4. NA SP 75/7/108, 115 (Christian IV to Charles I: 6 and 13 May 1626); HHStA Belgien Fasz. 63, fo. 23r (Moine to [della Faille?] contemporary decipher: 8 April 1626). The other letters from Christian are SP 75/7/1, 10, 13, 30, 64, 86, 98, 102 and 104 (6, 14 and 25 January, 3 February, 8 March, 18 and 28 April, and 3 May 1626).

5. NA SP 16/26/20 ("Touching the Companies retourned from Cales": 3 May 1626); *APC 1625–26*, p. 465 (letter to Lord Lieutenant of Devon); SP 16/30/51, 51:1 (Mayor of Southampton to Hampshire Deputy Lieutenants: 26 June 1626).

6. NA SP 16/29/46 and 16/30/67 (Devon Commissioners to the Council: 8 and 29 June 1626).

7. NA SP 63/242/277 (Villiers to Irish Privy Council: 16 May 1626); SP 63/242/245 (Villiers's receipt to Corporation of Cork: 21 April 1626).

8. NA SP 63/242/288 and 300 (Council of Munster to Privy Council: 18 May 1626; and Falkland to same: 26 May 1626); HHStA Belgien Fasz. 63, fo. 23r (anon. newsletter: 18 April 1626).

9. *ESL*, Oi8.

10. NA SP 16/27/80 (Palmer to Nicholas: 28 May 1626); SP 16/30/44 (same to same: 22 June 1626).

11. NA SP 16/26/49, 49.1 (Elworthy to Conway and Elworthy's testimony: 5 May 1626).

12. Cheshire RO MS 63/2/19, fos 43r–57v; NA SP 16/26/57 (Crowe to Conway: 6 May 1626).

13. NA SP 16/27/10 (Palmer to Buckingham: 16 May 1626); SP 16/27/13 (Totnes to Buckingham: 17 May 1626); SP 16/27/13.1 (Buckingham to Totnes: 15 May 1626).

14. NA SP 16/29/25 (Ellzey to Nicholas: 6 June 1626); SP 16/29/17 (Willet to Nicholas: 4 June 1626).

15. NA 31/3/63, fo. 66r (Mende to Richelieu: 29 April 1626); *CSPV 1625–26*, p. 432 (19 May 1626).

16. *Scrinia*, II, p. 67.

17. *PP1626*, II, pp. 250, 258, 268; and NA SP 16/523/73 (Conway to Buckingham: 12 March 1626).

18. *PP1626*, II, pp. 285, 288–94.

19. *PP1626*, I, pp. 398–404; III, pp. 233, 255–6, 269; BL Harl. MS 390, fos 55v–56r (anon: 12 May 1626).

20. NA 31/3/63, fo. 74r (Mende to Richelieu: 15 May 1626).

21. NLW MS 9061E/1414 (Henry to Sir John Wynn: [mid-May 1626]); *PP1626*, III, pp. 237, 240–2.

22. NA SP 16/20/23 (Rudyerd to Nethersole, 3 February 1626); *Salvetti*, p. 66 (19 May 1626); *Laud*, p. 189. On the proxies see under Laud, Bridgewater, Conway, Denbigh, Dorset, Holland, Manchester and Rutland, *PP1626*, IV, pp. 10–12.

23. NA 31/3/63, fos 61v, 63v (Mende to Richelieu [April 1626]); and *PP1626*, I, pp. 71–3, 259–62.

24. *PP1626*, I, pp. 399–400, 404.

25. *PP1626*, I, pp. 441–2; Esther Cope, *The Life of a Public Man: Edward, First Baron of Montagu of Boughton, 1562–1644* (Philadelphia, 1981), pp. 113–19.

26. *PP1626*, I, pp. 479–80, 485.

27. *PP1626*, I, pp. 479–82.

28. *PP1626*, I, pp. 482–4; BL Harl. MS 390, fo. 65v (anon: 26 May 1626).

29. *PP1626*, I, pp. 482–4; NA 31/3/63, fo. 74v (Mende to Richelieu: 15 May 1626).

30. *PP1626*, I, pp. 482–4.

31. BL Harl. MS 390, fo. 60r (anon: 19 May 1626); *CSPV 1625–26*, pp. 431–2 (19 May 1626); *PP1626*, I, p. 486.

32. NA 31/3/63, fo. 77r (Mende to d'Herbault: 19 May 1626); *Scrinia*, I, p. 169.

33. BL Harl. MS 390, fos 60r, 65v (anon: 19 and 26 May 1626); *APC 1625–26*, p. 479 (15 May 1626); and *PP1626*, III, p. 266.

34. NA SP 16/27/17–18 ("Questions to be propounded to Sir John Elliott"; Eliot's examination: 18 May 1626).

35. *C&T Charles*, I, p. 101 (D'Ewes to Stuteville: 11 May 1626).

36. Quoted in Alan T. Bradford, "Stuart Absolutism and the 'Utility' of Tacitus", *HLQ* 46:2 (1983), p. 151. On early modern Tacitism, see Peter Burke, "Tacitism", in T. A. Dorey (ed.), *Tacitus* (New York, 1969); Curtis Perry, *Literature and Favoritism in Early Modern England* (Cambridge, 2006), ch. 7; J. H. M. Salmon, "Stoicism and Roman Example: Seneca and Tacitus in Jacobean England", *Journal of the History of Ideas* 50:2 (1989); Kevin Sharpe, "The Foundation of the Chairs of History at Oxford and Cambridge: An Episode in Jacobean Politics" (1982), reprinted in *Politics and Ideas in Early Stuart England: Essays and Studies* (London, 1989); R. Malcolm Smuts, "Court-Centred Politics and the Uses of Roman Historians, c. 1590–1630", and Blair Worden, "Ben Jonson among the Historians", both in Kevin Sharpe and Peter Lake (eds), *Culture and Politics in Early Stuart England* (Basingstoke, 1994).

37. *PP1626*, III, pp. 288–9, 290–1, 293–4.

38. *PP1626*, III, pp. 289, 291, 294–5, 297–8.

39. *PP1626*, III, pp. 289, 292, 295–6.

40. *PP1626*, III, p. 296.

41. Victoria & Albert Museum, Forster and Dyce Collection, F.48.G.26/4 (Bevil Greville to his wife: 20 May 1626).

42. BL Harl. MS 390, fo. 65r (anon. newsletter: 26 May 1626); *PP1626*, III, p. 312. A sampling of these rumours includes BL Harl. MS 390, fo. 60v (anon. newsletter: 19 May 1626); and reports in *CSPV 1625–26*, pp. 380, 384, 390, 429, 433 and 441.

43. NA 31/3/63, fos 72v, 84r (Mende to Richelieu: 14 May 1626; Mende to d'Herbault: 27 May 1626).

44. *CSPV 1625–26*, p. 448 (9 June 1626); NA 31/3/63, fo. 91r (Mende to d'Herbault: 14 June 1626); *Whiteway*, p. 82; BL Add. MS 18979, fo. 3r (F. Fairfax to T. Fairfax: 9 June 1626); *Cornwallis*, p. 150 (Meautys to Cornwallis: 8 June 1626); BL Harl. MS 390, fo. 73r (anon. newsletter: 9 June 1626).

45. *PP1626*, I, pp. 564–6, 574–5, 579, 581.

46. *PP1626*, I, pp. 578–9; BL Egerton MS 2544, fo. 28r (Nicholas); NA SP 16/27/25 (Laud).

47. *PP1626*, III, pp. 406, 416, 425–6.

48. *Forerunner*, p. 10; *PP1626*, III, pp. 436–41.

49. *PP1626*, III, pp. 445, 449.

50. NA SP 16/24/48 (Rudyerd to Nethersole: 6 April 1626).

51. *Rous*, pp. 3–4; Cheshire RO MS 63/2/19, fos 46v–57v.

Chapter 12

1. NA SP 16/31/93 (Morgan to Buckingham: 17 July 1626).

2. Winfried Schleiner, "A Plott to Have His Nose and Eares Cutt off"; Schoppe as seen by the Archbishop of Canterbury", *Renaissance and Reformation* XIX (1995), pp. 69–86; Ian Philip, *Dragon's Teeth* (Claremont, 1970), p. 16; *Wotton*, III, pp. 280–1 (to Calvert: 5 November 1623).

3. BL Egerton MS 2715, fo. 359r (Moundsford to Gawdy: 19 June [1626]); BL Harl. MS 390, fo. 70r (Mead to Stuteville: 17 June 1626); Charles R. Elrington (ed.), *The Whole Works of . . . James Ussher* (Dublin, 1864), XV, p. 339 (Ussher to Ward: 16 June 1626).

4. BL Add. MS 11044, fo. 11v (J. Scudamore to R. Scudamore: 22 June 1626); NA SP 84/132/18A (Misselden to Coke: 27 July 1626).

5. NLW MS 9061E/1417 (Owen to Sir John Wynn: 16 June 1626); HHStA Belgien Fasz. 63, fos 29r–v (X to [della Faille?] with contemporary deciphers: 23 June 1626).

6. NA SP 88/4 fos 131v–2r (Camerarius to Oxenstierna: 6 October 1626); NA 31/3/63, fo. 101v (Mende to Richelieu: 16 June 1626). See also NA SP 81/34/40, 80 and 92 (Elizabeth to Charles: 4 April and 16 June 1626; and Elizabeth to Conway: 30 August [1626]).

7. NA SP 16/31/114 (Palmer to Buckingham: 19 July 1626); SP 16/33/43 (Petition of Thomas Marsh: 5 August 1626).

8. BL Add. MS 64889, fo. 49r (Fleming and Downing to Coke: 18 July 1626); NA SP 16/31/112 (Norton to Council: 19 July 1626); and SP 16/31/80 (Devon commissioners to Council: 15 July 1626).

9. NA SP 75/7/160 and 176 (Anstruther to Conway: 8 July 1626; to Buckingham: 22 July 1626); and SP 78/78 fo. 68v ([Deleted text in draft], Holland and Carleton to Coke: 1 March 1626).

10. NA 31/3/63, fo. 87r (Mende to Richelieu: 1 June 1626); HHStA Belgien Fasz. 63, fo. 103v (Sterrell to [della Faille]: 14 September 1626).

11. NA SP 16/44/5 (Clifford to Buckingham: [summer 1626?]); SP 16/32/46 (Anticipations: 27 July 1626); and SP 16/31/28 (Coke to Archbishop Abbot et al.: 5 July 1626).

12. *CSPV 1625–26*, p. 508 (4 August 1626); HHStA Belgien Fasz. 63, fo. 33r (X [to della Faille]: [June 1626]). See also Richard Cust, *The Forced Loan and English Politics, 1626–1628* (Oxford, 1987).

13. NLW 9061E/1424 (Owen to Sir John Wynn: 12 July 1626); BL Add. MS 64889, fo. 37r (Coke to Brooke: [summer] 1626).

14. University of London Library MS 195, II, fo. 34v (1 January 1627). See also NLW MS 9061E/1424 (Owen to Sir John Wynn: 12 July 1626); and Thomas Cogswell, "'In the Power of the State': Mr. Anys and the Tobacco Colonies, 1626–1628", *EHR* 123:500 (2008).

15. *APC 1626*, pp. 44–9, 72–7, 87–90 (30 June, and 10 and 15 July 1626); A *Declaration of the True Causes which moved His Maiestie to assemble, and after inforced Him to dissolve the last two Meetings in Parliament* (London, 1626), p. 19. See also L. Boynton, *The Elizabethan Militia* (London, 1967), pp. 248–50; and Thomas Cogswell, *Home Divisions: Aristocracy, the State and Provincial Conflict* (Manchester, 1998), pp. 122–6.

16. NA 31/3/63, fo. 101r (Mende to Richelieu: 16 June 1626); and *Proclamations, Charles I*, II, pp. 98–9, 110–12. See also Cust, *Forced Loan*, pp. 13–39.

17. BL Harl. MS 383, fo. 35r (D'Ewes to Stuteville: 6 July 1626); NLW MS 9061E/1428 (anon. newsletter: 30 July 1626).

18. HHStA Belgien Fasz. 63, fo. 33r (fragment: [June 1626]); Bod. MS Carte 77, fo. 439v (Radcliffe to Huntington: 3 August 1626); NA SP 16/33/30 (Rudyerd to Nethersole: 3 August 1626). See also BL Harl. MS 383, fo. 32r (Pory to [anon.]: 5 July 1626).

19. *Holles*, II, p. 334 (to Saye: 12 September 1626); HHStA Belgien Fasz. 63, fo. 84r (contemporary decipher, X to [de la Faille?]: 16 August 1626).

20. NA 31/3/63, fo. 118r (Mende to d'Herbault: 26 July 1626); *CSPV 1625–26*, pp. 500, 512, 515 (28 July and 11 August 1626); Trinity College Cambridge MS 0.7.3, fo. 6v; *Salvetti*, p. 82 (21 July 1626). On Carlisle, see NLW MS 9061E, 1142 (Henry to Sir John Wynn: 2 November 1626); and Roy Schreiber, *The First Carlisle: Sir James Hay, First Earl of Carlisle* (Philadelphia, 1994), pp. 99–101.

21. NA SP 16/33/37 (Rudyerd to [Nethersole]: 3 August 1626); SP 16/32/91–92 (Conway's speech to the French retainers: 31 July 1626; and "A discoverie of practices of the Queenes French servantes": [31 July] 1626).

22. HHStA Belgien Fasz. 63, fo. 61r (anon. report: July 1626); *Roe*, p. 541 (Grandison to Roe: 1626); *CSPV 1625–26*, pp. 494–5, 498, 512, 520, 542, 583 (21 and 28 July, 11 and 18 August, 8 September and 13 October 1626); *Salvetti*, pp. 80, 82, 85 (14 July, 3 August, and 22 September 1626); and Lockyer, *Buckingham*, p. 335.

23. NA SP 16/32/51 (Beaumont to Buckingham: 27 July 1626); *CSPV 1625–26*, p. 453 (26 June 1626).

24. NA SP 14/214, fos 28r, 129r (14 June and 11 and 18 July 1626, Conway's Letterbook); NA C115/N5/8491 (Salvetti to Scudamore: 17 June 1626). See also Mary F. S. Hervey, *The Life, Correspondence and Collections of Thomas Howard, Earl of Arundel* (Cambridge, 1912), pp. 250–62.

25. NA SP 14/214, fo. 128r (16 June 1626: Conway's Letterbook); BL Egerton MS 2978, fo. 18r (Charles's warrant: 28 June 1626); NA SP 16/31/60 (Dolburie to Val: 12 July 1626).

26. BL Egerton MS 2715, fo. 359r (Moundsford to Gawdy: 19 June [1626]); BL Stowe MS 365, fos 77v–78v (Heath to Charles: 24 July 1626).

27. BL Stowe MS 365, fos 98v, 99v–100r, 111r (Bristol to Chief Justices: 19 October 1627; Bristol's draft submissions: February 1626; Bristol to Heath: 13 March 1628; and Heath to Bristol: 19 March 1628).

28. NA SP 16/36/37, fo. 58v (Bagg to Buckingham: 22 September 1626); BL Harl. MS 286, fo. 297r (Coventry's warrant: 8 July 1626); Surrey History Centre, Loseley Manuscripts, LM Corr. 4/57 (G. More to [anon.]: 29 August 1626); *Rous*, p. 7; and Alison Wall, "The Great Purge of 1625: 'the late Murraine amongst the Gentlemen of the Peace'", *Historical Research* 82:218 (2009).

29. *Rous*, p. 4; *Salvetti*, p. 76 (23 June 1626); *CSPV 1625–26*, p. 462 (23 June 1626). Existing secondary accounts of the scheme are incomplete: see e.g. John Forster, *Sir John Eliot* (London, 1864), vol. I, pp. 578–80; S. R. Gardiner, *History of England from the Accession of James I* (New York, 1965), vol. VI, pp. 123–4; Lockyer, *Buckingham*, p. 332.

30. Forster, *Eliot*, I, pp. 578–80; BL Egerton MS 2978, fos 14r–15r ("Questions delivered the 18th of June 1626 to divers members of the Commons house"); BL Egerton MS 3779, fo. 1r; NA SP 16/30/29 (Rudyerd to Nethersole: 19 June 1626) (*PP1626*, IV, p. 310).

31. BL Egerton MS 2978, fos 14–15; Egerton MS 3779, fos 3r, 7r; *PP1626*, IV, pp. 368–9.

32. *C&T Charles*, I, p. 116 (Mead to Stuteville: 26 June 1626; Letter to Mead: 30 June 1626); NA SP 16/31/107 ("Information exhibited in the Court of Star Chamber by Sir Robert Heath ... against George Duke of Buckingham": July 1626); *Rushworth*, I, p. 413; Bulstrode Whitelocke, *Memorials of English Affairs* (Oxford, 1853), vol. I, p. 19.

33. NLW, MS 9061E/1427 (Bangor to Sir J. Wynn: 22 July 1626); BL Add. MS 64889, fo. 36r (Coke to Brooke: [July 1626]); NA SP 16/31/30 (Instructions: [July 1626]).

34. NA SP 16/34/17:1 (Suffolk JPs to Council: 15 August 1626); SP 16/35/46 (Worcestershire JPs to Council: 8 September 1626).

35. NA SP 16/35/90 (Derbyshire loan commissioners to Council: 15 September 1626); SP 16/35/9 (Kent Deputy Lieutenants to Montgomery: 2 September 1626); Cust, *Forced Loan*, p. 96.

36. NA SP 75/7/214 (Anstruther to Charles: 16 September 1626). See also Peter Wilson, *The Thirty Years War* (Cambridge, 2009), pp. 409–16; Paul Douglas Lockhart, *Denmark 1513–1660* (Oxford, 2007), pp. 166–9.

37. NA SP 16/37/5 (Poulett to Buckingham: 1 October 1626); SP 16/37/52 (Drake to Nicholas: 7 October 1626); *Roe*, p. 557 (Conway to Roe: 20 September 1626); *Rushworth*, I, pp. 413, 626–7; Whitelocke, *Memorials*, I, p. 19; Cust, *Forced Loan*, ch. 3; and Mark Kishlansky, "Tyranny Denied: Charles I, Attorney General Heath and the Five Knights Case", *HJ* 41:1 (1999).

38. BL Harl. MS 390, fo. 51v (Meddus to Mead: 5 May 1626); *PP1626*, III, pp. 157, 160–3.

39. *Wotton*, II, pp. 291–2 ("The examination of the Lord of Oldebare's Daughter"); Rob McPherson, "Lyon, Sir Thomas (c. 1546–1608)", *ODNB*.

40. *Forerunner*, pp. 7, 19.

41. *Wotton*, II, pp. 292–3.

42. *Wotton*, II, pp. 290, 292–3, 296. For negative stereotypes of the London carman, see [Richard Verstegan], *Londons Looking-Glasse* ([St Omer]), 1621), sig. C4v.

43. *Wotton*, II, pp. 290, 292–3, 295–6.

44. NA SP 16/524/9 (Bolton to Buckingham: 28 May 1626).

45. NA SP 16/13/1 (Edmund Bolton[?], "The End of King JAMES his reign & the beginning of King CHARLES").

46. Alastair Bellany, "Libel", in Joad Raymond (ed.), *The Oxford History of Popular Print Culture: Cheap Print in Britain and Ireland to 1660* (Oxford, 2011), pp. 155–7.

47. See e.g. William F. Church, *Richelieu and Reason of State* (Princeton, 1972), part 2.

48. Sir Henry Wotton, *A Parallel betweene Robert late Earle of Essex and George late Duke of Buckingham* (London, 1641), pp. 10–11.

49. See e.g. Alastair Bellany, "Buckingham Engraved: Politics, Print Images and the Royal Favourite in the 1620s", in Michael Hunter (ed.), *Printed Images in Early Modern Britain* (Farnham, 2010); Thomas Cogswell, "Thomas Middleton and the Court, 1624: *A Game at Chess* in Context", *HLQ* 47 (1984); "The People's Love: The Duke of Buckingham and Popularity", in Thomas Cogswell, Richard Cust and Peter Lake (eds), *Politics, Religion*

and Popularity: Early Stuart Essays in Honour of Conrad Russell (Cambridge, 2002); "'Published by Authoritie': Newsbooks and the Duke of Buckingham's Expedition to the Ile de Ré", *HLQ* 67 (2004); and Thomas Cogswell and Peter Lake, "Buckingham Does the Globe: *Henry VIII* and the Politics of Popularity in the 1620s", *Shakespeare Quarterly* 60:3 (2009).

50. *Proclamations, Charles*, II, pp. 93–5, no. 44; *Rous*, p. 4; Trinity College, Cambridge, MS 0.7.3, fo. 5r (*PP1626*, IV, p. 343); *Whiteway*, p. 82; *CSPV 1625–26*, p. 462 (24 June 1626); *Salvetti*, p. 76 (24 June 1626).

51. *Declaration of the True Causes*, pp. 2–4, 14–15, 19–20, 27–8.

52. Trinity College, Cambridge, MS 0.7.3, fo. 7r (*PP1626*, IV, p. 347); *C&T Charles I*, I, pp. 123–4 (Letter to Mead: 7 July 1626).

53. NA SP 78/80/206 (Brickdale to Coke: 6 December 1626).

Part 4 Prologue

1. *ESL*, Oiii12.

2. The best study of the aftermath of the 1626 Parliament is Richard Cust, *The Forced Loan and English Politics* (Oxford, 1987).

3. On Buckingham and popularity, see Thomas Cogswell and Peter Lake, "Buckingham Does the Globe: *Henry VIII* and the Politics of Popularity", *Shakespeare Quarterly* 60 (2009); Thomas Cogswell, "'Published by Authoritie': Newsbooks and the Duke of Buckingham's Expedition to the Ile de Ré", *HLQ* 67 (2004), and "The People's Love: The Duke of Buckingham and Popularity", in Thomas Cogswell, Richard Cust and Peter Lake (eds), *Politics, Religion and Popularity* (Cambridge, 2002); and Alastair Bellany, "Buckingham Engraved: Politics, Print Images and the Royal Favourite in the 1620s", in Michael Hunter (ed.), *Printed Images in Early Modern England* (Farnham, 2010).

4. On the assassination see Thomas Cogswell, "John Felton, Popular Political Culture, and the Assassination of the Duke of Buckingham", *HJ* 49:2 (2006); Alastair Bellany, "Raylinge Rymes and Vaunting Verse: Libellous Politics in Early Stuart England" in Kevin Sharpe and Peter Lake (eds), *Culture and Politics in Early Stuart England* (Basingstoke, 1994), esp. pp. 297ff; "'The Brightnes of the Noble Leiutenants Action': An Intellectual Ponders Buckingham's Assassination", *EHR* 118:479 (2003); and James Holstun, *Ehud's Dagger: Class Struggle in the English Revolution* (New York and London, 2000), ch. 5.

Chapter 13

1. Ben Jonson, *The Staple of News*, ed. Anthony Parr (Manchester and New York, 1988), Act 1, scene 2, ll. 26–7, 35, 50–3, 59–60, 75–77; Act 1, scene 4, ll. 2–6; Act 1, scene 5, ll. 3–17; Act 3, scene 2, ll. 21–86, 110, 160–214.

2. Parr, "Introduction", p. 49; *Staple*, Act 3, scene 2, ll. 115–22, and "To the Readers" (pp. 152–3).

3. See e.g. *Staple*, Act 3, scene 2, l. 122. On Charles and "popularity", see esp. Richard Cust, *The Forced Loan and English Politics, 1626–1628* (Oxford, 1987); and Peter Lake, "Anti-Popery: The Structure of a Prejudice", in Richard Cust and Ann Hughes (eds), *Conflict in Early Stuart England* (London, 1989).

4. Cogswell, *Revolution*, prologue; Bellany, *Politics*, ch. 2; Peter Lake and Steve Pincus, "Rethinking the Public Sphere in Early Modern England", *JBS* 45:2 (2006); Alastair Bellany, "Railing Rhymes Revisited: Libels, Scandals, and Early Stuart Politics", *History Compass* 5:4 (2007), pp. 1,152–3.

5. For information management and assessment, see e.g. David Colclough, *Freedom of Speech in Early Stuart England* (Cambridge, 2004), ch. 4; Kevin Sharpe, *Reading Revolutions: The Politics of Reading in Early Modern England* (New Haven and London, 2000); David Randall, *Credibility in Elizabethan and Early Stuart Military News* (London, 2008); and Ann Blair, "Reading Strategies for Coping with Information Overload, ca. 1550–1700", *Journal of the History of Ideas* 64:1 (2003).

6. *PP1626*, IV, p. 300 (Herman to Middlesex: 2 May 1626).

7. For a parallel case, see Malcolm, *Reason*, ch. 4.

8. Robert Darnton, *The Literary Underground of the Old Regime* (Cambridge, MA, 1982); Bellany, "Rayling Rhymes Revisited", pp. 1,151–2.

9. Leona Rostenberg, *The Minority Press and the English Crown: A Study in Repression 1558–1625* (Nieuwkoop, 1971); Penry Williams, *The Tudor Regime* (Oxford, 1979), pp. 280–1; Paul Arblaster, *Antwerp & the World: Richard Verstegan and the International Culture of Catholic Reformation* (Leuven, 2004), pp. 50–1.

10. P. R. Harris (ed.), "The Reports of William Udall, Informer, 1605–1612", *Recusant History* 8:4–5 (1966), pp. 228, 238, 243, 258–9, 262; Rostenberg, *Minority Press*, p. 34.

11. Harris, "Udall Reports", p. 233; Rostenberg, *Minority Press*, pp. 35–6; *APC 1596–97*, p. 10; Bellany, "Libel", in Joad Raymond (ed.), *The Oxford History of Popular Print Culture: Cheap Print in Britain and Ireland to 1660* (Oxford, 2011), p. 153; and cf. NA SP Domestic 16/387/79.

12. *APC 1596–7*, p. 10; Harris, "Udall Reports", pp. 203–4, 256, 260, 281.

13. Harris, "Udall Reports", p. 237; Rostenberg, *Minority Press*, pp. 106, 144.

14. John Gee, *A Foot Out of the Snare* (London, 1624), sig. S4v.

15. Rostenberg, *Minority Press*, pp. 37, 106; Gee, *Foot*, sigs R4r–v, S1v–2r, S4v.

16. Gee, *Foot*, sigs T1r–v; Rostenberg *Minority Press*, pp. 98–104.

17. Gee, *Foot*, sigs D4v, R4r–S4r; Thomas Scott, *The Second Part of Vox Populi* (1624), sigs G3v–G4r, H2r; Lewis Owen, *The Running Register* (London, 1626), p. 14; Arblaster, *Antwerp & the World*, p. 51. On Puritan illicit book profits, see Bellany, "Libel", pp. 154–5; NA SP 16/346/58, 58:I; 16/349/52; Guildhall Library MS 9657, item 3, unfoliated.

18. Rostenberg, *Minority Press*, p. 31; Harris, "Udall Reports", p. 237.

19. Harris, "Udall Reports", pp. 233, 235, 237; *CSPV 1607–10*, p. 314 (28 July 1609).

20. Harris, "Udall Reports", pp. 233, 239, 257, 264–7.

21. See e.g. *HMC Salisbury*, XII, p. 312 (Bancroft to Cecil: 21 August 1602).

22. Harris, "Udall Reports", pp. 203–4, 244–6, 253, 260, 262, 264, 279; *CSPV 1607–10*, pp. 307, 313–14 (19 and 28 July 1609); Rostenberg, *Minority Press*, pp. 104–5.

23. Scott, *Second Part*, sigs G3v–4v; Gee, *Foot*, sig. T1r.

24. Guildhall Library MS 9657, item 3, unfoliated; Bellany, "Libel", pp. 154–5.

25. Harris, "Udall Reports", p. 264; Gee, *Foot*, sig. T1r; Rostenberg, *Minority Press*, pp. 100–1.

26. BL Harl. MS 390, fo. 51v (Meddus to Mead: 5 May 1626).

27. *C&T Charles*, I, p. 149; BL Harl. MS 390, fo. 123r (Mead to Stuteville: 16 September 1626); cf. Malcolm, *Reason*, pp. 64–5.

28. BL Add. MS 4106, fos 149v–157r; BL Add. MS 22591, fos 31r–39v; BL Egerton MS 2026, fos 51v–60v; BL Harl. MS 405, fos 72r–77v; BL Sloane MS 1779 [aka Add. 1779], fos 160r–188v; BL Stowe MS 182, fos 76r–84r; Bod. MS Rawlinson C573, 94r–126r; Bod. MS Rawlinson D 171, 26r–45v; Bod. MS Rawlinson D1062, fos 122r–160r; CUL MS Ee.2.32, fos 159r–182v; CUL MS Dd.14.28, part 2; CUL MS Gg.4.13, fos 137–45; Folger MS V.a.470; Folger MS X.d.236; NLS MS Acc.11944 (incomplete); Northumberland MSS, Alnwick Castle, MS 527; Surrey History Centre, Loseley MS LM/1327/10; TCD MS 731, fos 285r–317r; University of London MS 309, 103r–132v; West Yorkshire Archive Service, Leeds, MS WYL 230/2959; Wellcome MS 254; Wellcome MS 255 (missing); University of Kassel Library, 2⁰ Ms. Hist. 34 (see Peter Vogel [ed.] *Die Handschriften der Universitats-Bibliothek Kassel Landesbibliothek und Murhardsche Bibliothek der Stadt Kassel* [Wiesbaden, 2000], p. 33).

29. Alnwick Castle, Northumberland MS 527 (Percy); Surrey History Centre, Loseley MS LM/1327/10 (More); NLS MS Acc.11944 (Bacon); West Yorkshire Archive Service MS WYL 230/2959 (Ingilby); TCD MS 731, fos 285r–317r (Alexander); Louis A. Knafla, "More, Sir George (1553–1632)", *ODNB*; J. T. Cliffe, *The Yorkshire Gentry from the Reformation to the Civil War* (London, 1969), pp. 13–14, 296, 334, 343, 373–4; and Peter Beal, *In Praise of Scribes: Manuscripts and their Makers in Seventeenth-Century England* (Oxford, 1998), p. 222 (appendix II, item 17A).

30. Folger MS V.a.470 and MS X.d.236 (Le Neve); BL Sloane MS 1779 (Sloane). The work remained of antiquarian interest—Thomas Baker (1656–1740) made a copy of part of

Eglisham early in the eighteenth century from an earlier scribal version in the Bishop of Ely's library: see CUL MS Mm.1.43, item 5 (Baker copy) and MS Ee.ii.32, item 17, fos 159r–182v (Baker's source).

31. E.g. Wellcome MS 254 (folio); BL Sloane MS 1779, fos 160r–188v (4°); and BL Harl. MS 405, fos 72r–77v (8°).

32. E.g. Loseley MS LM/1327/10; Wellcome MS 254.

33. E.g. BL Add. MS 4106, fos 149v–157r, part of a seventeenth-century series of copies (fos 130r–157r), bound up into a compilation of materials by Thomas Birch in the eighteenth century; University of London MS 309, fos 105r–134v, a compilation of early Stuart materials in several hands and formats.

34. Folger MS V.a.470, fo. 5v (signature); University of London MS 309, fo. 105r (title page emphases); BL Add. MS 22591, fos 31r–39v (engraved border).

35. Harold Love, *Scribal Publication in Seventeenth-Century England* (Oxford, 1993), esp. chs 1–3, pp. 79–83. For a plebeian user-publisher, see Paul Seaver, *Wallington's World: A Puritan Artisan in Seventeenth-Century London* (Stanford, 1985).

36. See Love, *Scribal Publication*; and Bellany, *Politics*, pp. 85–114.

37. Harris, "Udall Reports", p. 264.

38. BL Add. MS 28640, fos 8–16; NA SP 14/118/102 (information for Sir George Calvert).

39. NA SP 16/49/16 (Bushy examination: 12 January 1627); *C&T Charles*, I, p. 188 (Mead to Stuteville: 16 January 1627), reports the arrest of a schoolmaster "for receiving or writing some book against the Duke". Cf. Malcolm, *Reason*, pp. 67–70.

40. On Starkey see Beal, *Praise of Scribes*, pp. 86ff; Louis A. Knafla, "Starkey, Ralph (d. 1628)", *ODNB*.

41. On the tension see Beal, *Praise of Scribes*, ch. 1, p. 88 and n.27.

42. NA C115/108/8575 (Starkey to Scudamore: 11 February 1626); Beal, *Praise of Scribes*, pp. 86ff.

43. NA C115/108/8575 (Starkey to Scudamore: 11 February 1626). Starkey's next letter included copies of some of the speeches he had promised, see NA C115/108/8576. On Scudamore see Ian Atherton, "'The Itch grown a Disease': Manuscript Transmission of News in the Seventeenth Century", in Joad Raymond (ed.), *News, Newspapers, and Society in Early Modern Britain* (London, 1999), esp. pp. 41, 45, 47, 51, 58.

44. NA C115/108/8577 (Starkey to Scudamore: 1 October 1626). Starkey charged Scudamore a similar amount for a scribal *Altera secretissima instructio*, see Malcolm, *Reason*, pp. 66–7.

45. Beal, *Praise of Scribes*, appendix III, p. 273, item 84 and n.13; Folger MS V.a.470.

46. E. H. Phelps Brown and Sheila V. Hoskins, "Seven Centuries of Building Wages", reprinted in E. M. Carus-Wilson (ed.), *Essays in Economic History* (London, 1962), vol. II, p. 177.

47. "Rekeningen der boeken geleverd door Balthasar Moretus aan P. P. Rubens", in *Bulletin-Rubens: Annales de la Commission Officielle Instituée par le Conseil Communal de la ville d'Anvers pour la publication des documents relatifs à la vie et aux oeuvres de Rubens* (Antwerp and Brussels, 1883), vol. II, p. 200; Prosper Arents et al. (eds), *De bibliotheek van Pieter Pauwel Rubens: een reconstructie*, p. 176.

48. *C&T Charles*, I, pp. 107–9, 118; Trinity College, Cambridge MS O.7.3, fo. 4v (printed *PP1626*, IV, p. 343); Alexandra Walsham, "*Vox Piscis: Or The Book-Fish*: Providence and the Uses of the Reformation Past in Caroline Cambridge", *EHR* 114:457 (1999), pp. 587–90.

49. See e.g. BL Sloane MS 1779, fos 160r–188v (incomplete); NLS MS Acc. 11944 (petition to Charles with variants and cuts to verses); West Yorkshire Archive Service MS WYL 230/2959, fos 2v–3v (cut verses); and Surrey History Centre, Loseley MS LM/1327/10, fos 2v, 5v (verses placed before the text).

50. Bod. MS Ashmole 749, III, fos 16v–21r. Four other summarized items precede the Eglisham copy in the same hand, fos 2r–13r.

51. Bod. Ashmole MS 749, III, fo. 17v.

52. See e.g. Bod. Ashmole MS 749, III, fo. 18v, cutting material from *Forerunner*, pp. 10–11.

53. Bod. MS Ashmole 749, III, fo. 19r.

54. Bod. MS Ashmole 749, III, fos 18r, 20r.

55. Bod. MS Ashmole 749, III, fo. 17r; *Forerunner*, p. 3.
56. Bod. MS Ashmole 749, III, fos 18v, 20r.
57. Bod. MS Ashmole 749, III, fos 16v–17v, 18v, 20r.
58. Bod. MS Ashmole 749, III, fos 19r–v.
59. Bod. MS Ashmole 749, III, fos 20r–21r.
60. Surrey History Centre, Loseley MS LM/1327/10 (our foliation).
61. Loseley MS LM/1327/10, fos 2v (transcript), 5v (keyed location).
62. Loseley MS LM/1327/10, fos 7v–8r.
63. Folger MS V.a.339, fos 30v–31r; Leeds University, Brotherton Library, MS Lt31, fos 10r–v.
64. *Forerunner*, pp. 5, 7; Loseley MS LM/1327/10, fo. 7v.
65. Bod. MS Wood D18, fos 88r–97r.
66. Bod. MS Wood D18, fo. 93r; *Forerunner*, p. 12.
67. Bod. MS Wood D18, fos 90r–v.
68. Bod. MS Wood D18, fos 88v, 91r; *Prodromus*, sigs A2v, B3v; *Forerunner*, pp. 3, 8.
69. Bod. MS Wood D18, fo. 92r; *Prodromus*, sig. C3r; *Forerunner*, pp. 10–11.
70. Bod. MS Wood D18, fo. 90v; *Prodromus*, sig. B2v ("Marchio Hamiltonius & Doctor Eglisham ut embametur"); *Forerunner*, p. 7.
71. Bod. MS Wood D18, fo. 96r; *Prodromus*, sigs E3r–v; *Forerunner*, p. 17.

Chapter 14

1. NA C115/108, no. 8577 (Starkey to Scudamore: 1 October 1626).
2. Bernard Mellor (ed.), *The Poems of Sir Francis Hubert* (Hong Kong, 1961), pp. xi–xxii, 175, 280, 286–9. Extant scribal versions include BL Harl. MS 558 (linked to Starkey); BL Harl. MS 2393, fos 1–44 (Elizabethan), and fos 45–117 (Jacobean); BL Add. MS 34316 (Jacobean); BL Add. MS 28021 (Jacobean and heavily annotated). All quotations (given by stanza number) are taken from the 1628 pirate edition, Francis Hubert, *The Deplorable Life and Death of Edward the Second, King of England* (London, 1628). See too Curtis Perry, *Literature and Favoritism in Early Modern England* (Cambridge, 2006), pp. 202–16.
3. E.g. Hubert, *Deplorable Life*, stanzas 1, 19–21, 428–40.
4. E.g. on dissimulation, Hubert, *Deplorable Life*, stanzas 78, 426.
5. Hubert, *Deplorable Life*, stanza 182.
6. Hubert, *Deplorable Life*, stanzas 37–41, 44–5, 48–9, 67, 69, 92, 107.
7. Hubert, *Deplorable Life*, stanzas 81, 146, 155–6, 237, 241, 243, 248–9.
8. Hubert, *Deplorable Life*, stanzas 257, 303–4. Stanzas 259–60 insist that Hubert was not drawing parallels between Edward and the early Stuart kings.
9. Hubert, *Deplorable Life*, stanzas 355–62. See too the critique of resistance sermons, stanzas 404–5, 414.
10. *PP1626*, IV, p. 293 (Meddus to Mead: 16 June 1626).
11. *C&T Charles*, I, pp. 113–14 (Mead to Stuteville: 17 June 1626); John Stow and Edmond Howes, *Annals* (London, 1631), p. 1,042; Cheshire RO CR 63/2/19 (Commonplace Book of William Davenport), fo. 46r; *HMC Twelfth Report, Appendix, Part IV, The Manuscripts of his Grace the Duke of Rutland* (London, 1888), vol. I, p. 477 (Henry Wicliffe to George Falcon: 15 June 1626); *PP1626*, IV, p. 293; *Rushworth*, I, p. 393. The tempest attracted attention beyond England, see Paul Arblaster, "Posts, Newsletters, Newspapers: England in a European System of Communications", *Media History* 11:1/2 (2005), pp. 30–1.
12. *C&T Charles*, I, pp. 113–14 (Mead to Stuteville: 17 June 1626); *Rushworth*, I, p. 393.
13. Trinity College, Cambridge MS O.7.3, fo. 4v (*PP 1626*, IV, p. 343); *PP1626*, IV, p. 293 (Meddus to Mead: 16 June 1626); Cheshire RO CR 63/2/19, fo. 46r; *C&T Charles*, I, pp. 113–15 (Mead to Stuteville: 17 and 24 June 1626).
14. We follow here *C&T Charles*, I, pp. 113–14, 117 (Mead to Stuteville: 17 June, 1 July 1626), with supplementary details from Cheshire RO CR 63/2/19, fo. 46r.
15. Cheshire RO CR 63/2/19, fo. 46r.
16. *C&T Charles*, I, pp. 113–14, 117.

17. *C&T Charles*, I, pp. 114–15; Trinity College, Cambridge, MS 0.7.3, fos 5v–6r; Jeremiah Dyke, *A Sermon Preached At the Publike Fast* (London, 1628), pp. 7, 22; Alexandra Walsham, "*Vox Piscis: Or The Book-Fish*: Providence and the Uses of the Reformation Past in Caroline Cambridge", *EHR* 114:457 (1999), *passim* and p. 585–6.

18. Cheshire RO CR 63/2/19, fo. 46r; Trinity College, Cambridge MS 0.7.3, fo. 4v (*PP1626*, IV, p. 343).

19. F. S. Boas (ed.), *The Diary of Thomas Crosfield* (London, 1935), p. 3; *HMC Rutland*, I, p. 477.

20. Trinity College, Cambridge MS 0.7.3, fo. 5r (*PP1626*, IV, pp. 343–4, with omissions); *Rushworth*, I, p. 393.

21. *C&T Charles*, I, p. 169 (Mead to Stuteville: 11 November 1626); *CSPV 1625–1626*, p. 521 (8 August 1626); Bellany, "Lambe", pp. 60–1.

22. *ESL*, Oi10.

23. NA SP 16/32/27 (information of Edmund Willett and Roger Dade); 16/33/60 (Edward Nuttall to Edward Nicholas: 8 August 1626); and 16/38/20 (Samuel Ward to Edward Nicholas: 19 October 1626).

24. NA SP 16/39/40–1 (examinations of Dorothy and Henry Manners: 9 November 1626); 16/52/57 (undated interrogatories for Brediman); PC Registers, 2 November 1626.

25. NA SP 16/39/41; 16/52/57.

26. *C&T Charles*, I, pp. 141–2, 158 (Pory to Mead: 17 August 1626; Letter to Mead: 13 October 1626; Mead to Stuteville: 14 October 1626); *Salvetti*, p. 89 (13 October 1626); *CSPV 1625–1626*, p. 587 (13 October 1626).

27. *C&T Charles*, I, pp. 176–8 (Pory to Mead and letters from London: 26 November 1626); *Salvetti*, pp. 98–99 (1 and 8 December 1626); *CSPV 1626–1628*, pp. 55, 63 (1 and 8 December 1626).

28. See e.g. *CSPV 1626–1628*, p. 63 (8 December 1626).

29. *C&T Charles*, I, pp. 189, 191, 193, 194 (Letter to Mead: 2 February 1627; letter from London: 2 February 1627; letter to Mead: 9 February 1627; Mead to Stuteville: 10 February 1627); *CSPV 1626–1628* (2 February 1627); *Salvetti*, p. 109 (9 February 1627).

30. *C&T Charles*, I, pp. 165, 167–8, 178, 182 (Letters to Mead: 4 and 10 November 1626; London letter: late November 1626; Mead to Stuteville: 9 December 1626).

31. NA SP 16/55/67 (Brediman to Conway: [n.d.] February 1627); Minutes, Conway Letter Book, SP 14/214, fo. 145 (Letter to Coke: 4 September 1627).

32. E.g. NA SP 16/25/65, 65:I, 66 (Mayor and aldermen of Barnstaple to the Council: 25 April 1626; examinations of Edward Heywood, Edward Poyntz and Nicholas Voysey; certificate of Humphrey Venner).

33. *C&T Charles*, I, pp. 169, 191 (Mead to Stuteville: 11 November 1626 and 3 February 1627).

34. NRS GD 406/1/8187 (Hamilton to Buckingham: 16 March 1628); NLS MS 79, no. 81 (Hamilton to Morton: c. 1625–26); John J. Scally, "Hamilton, James, First Duke of Hamilton (1606–1649)", *ODNB*.

35. NRS GD 406/1/582 (Charles to Hamilton: 6 December 1627); 406/1/8177 (Carlisle to Hamilton: 23 April 1627 or 1628); 406/1/93–94 (Charles to Hamilton: 11 February 1628; Hamilton to Buckingham: c. 1626–8); Allan MacInnes, *Charles I and the Making of the Covenanting Movement, 1625–1641* (Edinburgh, 1991), pp. 49–101; Maurice Lee, Jr., *The Road to Revolution: Scotland Under Charles I, 1625–37* (Urbana and Chicago, 1985), ch. 1.

36. NRS GD 406/1/8204 (Murray to Hamilton: 2 May [1627?]); 406/1/8230 (Buckingham to Hamilton: [1628]); 406/1/8228 (Buckingham to Hamilton: 1627 or 1628); 406/1/18 (Charles to Hamilton: 22 December 1626).

37. NRS GD 406/1/91/1–2 (Murray to Hamilton: 5 March and 25 February 1628). See also GD 406/1/81–8 (Roxburgh to Hamilton: 1627); and 406/1/98 and 100–2 (Mar to Hamilton: 15 and 21 July and 7 August 1628).

38. NRS GD 406/1/96 (Arran to Buckingham: 24 March 1628); GD 406/1/8187 (Hamilton to Buckingham: 16 March 1628); NLS MS 79, no. 75 (Hamilton to Morton: 1 October 1627).

39. *C&T Charles*, I, pp. 159–61, 166 (Letter to Mead: 27 October 1626; Letters from London: 20 October and 4 November 1626); *CSPV 1625–1626*, p. 594 (20 October 1626); *Salvetti*, p. 91 (27 October 1626).

40. *CSPV 1626–1628*, pp. 5–6 (27 October 1626); Trinity College, Cambridge, MS 0.7.3, fo. 9r (*PP1626*, IV, p. 349); *Whiteway*, p. 85.

41. *CSPV 1625–1626*, pp. 490, 500 (14 and 28 July 1626); *CSPV 1626–1628*, pp. 5–6, 78, 86–7 (27 October and 22 December 1626; and 8 January 1627); *C&T Charles*, I, p. 132 (Mead to Stuteville: 24 July 1626); Cf. *Salvetti*, pp. 102, 104 (22 December 1626 and 5 January 1627).

42. *C&T Charles*, I, pp. 415, 419 (Beaulieu to Puckering: 30 October 1628; Mead to Stuteville: 1 November 1628); Scally, "Hamilton, James".

43. *Forerunner*, p. 18; Lee, *Road to Revolution*, p. x. For later rumours on Hamilton's loyalty, see Boas, *Diary*, p. 8; Scally, "Hamilton, James"; Lee, *Road to Revolution*, pp. 88–9.

44. *Mercure François* XII (1626), p. 258.

45. Anon, *Le Favorit d'Angleterre, Dediè A Monseigneur le Duc de Buckingam*, (A Paris: Iouxte la Copie imprimée 1626); *Mercure François* XII (Paris, 1626), p. 258; J. H. M. Salmon, *Society in Crisis: France in the Sixteenth Century* (London, 1979), p. 241; Julia Briggs, "Marlowe's *Massacre at Paris*: A Reconsideration", *The Review of English Studies*, NS 34: 135 (1983), p. 264 and n.21; Katherine B. Crawford, "Love, Sodomy, and Scandal: Controlling the Sexual Reputation of Henry III", *Journal of the History of Sexuality* 12:4 (2003), p. 541 and n.121.

46. Jean Boucher, *Histoire Tragique et Memorable, de Pierre de Gaverston Gentil-homme gascon iadis le mignon d'Edouard 2. Roy d'Angleterre .... Dediée a Monseigneur le Duc D'Espernon*, (Paris, 1588), sig. A2v.

47. On surviving Catholic elements see Anon, *Le Favorit*, p. 20, but cf. Boucher, *Histoire Tragique*, sig. A3r and pp. 51–2.

48. Anon, *Le Favorit*, pp. 3–4, 6–10, 15.

49. Anon, *Le Favorit*, p. 13.

50. Anon, *Le Favorit*, pp. 16–20.

51. Anon, *Le Favorit*, pp. 9 and 20; Boucher, *Histoire Tragique*, pp. 50–1. On the politics of the original images see Crawford, "Love, Sodomy and Scandal".

Chapter 15

1. NA C115/108 no. 8578 (Starkey to Scudamore: May 1627); BL Add. MS 64892, fos 59, 87; Malcolm, *Reason*, pp. 67–71.

2. Malcolm, *Reason*, pp. 17, 46, 53–8, 63–70.

3. Malcolm, *Reason*, pp. 30–4, 45–6ff.

4. See e.g. NA SP 81/34/81 (Elizabeth to Conway: 30 May 1626).

5. Malcolm, *Reason*, pp. 168, 172.

6. Malcolm, *Reason*, pp. 132–8.

7. Malcolm, *Reason*, pp. 134, 138.

8. Malcolm, *Reason*, pp. 134, 144.

9. Malcolm, *Reason*, p. 180.

10. Malcolm, *Reason*, p. 48.

11. *ESL*, Oi16.

12. *ESL*, Oii5.

13. *ESL*, Oii12.

14. I. R., *The Spy, Discovering the Danger of Arminian Heresie and Spanish Trecherie* ("Strasburgh", 1628), sigs F4v–G1r; Guildhall Library MS 9657, item 3.

15. *ESL*, Oiii5; A. Lloyd Moote, *Louis XIII: The Just* (Berkeley, 1989), pp. 92–5; and Roland Mousnier, *The Assassination of Henry IV*, trans. Joan Spencer (New York, 1973), chs 2–3.

16. P. M. [Pierre Matthieu], *The Powerfull Favorite or, The life of Ælius Seianus* ("Paris", 1628), STC 17664 (complete), STC 17665 (abridged). Quotations are taken from the longer version. Matthieu's original appeared in Paris in 1617, was reprinted in Rouen

(1618, 1635, 1642) and Lyon (1619, 1622), and translated into Spanish (1621) and Italian (1627). An alternative English translation, attributed to Sir Thomas Hawkins, appeared in London in 1632 and 1639, see *Unhappy Prosperitie Expressed in the histories of Ælius Seianus and Philippa the Catanian*. See too J. H. Elliott, "Introduction", in J. H. Elliott and L. W. B. Brockliss (eds), *The World of the Favourite* (New Haven and London, 1999), p. 9 n.8; Sharpe, *Image Wars*, pp. 271–2.

17. See Pierre Matthieu, *La Conjuration de Conchine* (Paris, 1618); Moote, *Louis XIII*, pp. 89ff; Silje Normand, "Venomous Words and Political Poisons: Languages of Exclusion in Early Modern France", in Melissa Caларesu et al. (eds), *Exploring Cultural History: Essays in Honour of Peter Burke* (Farnham, 2010), pp. 125–6.

18. P. M., *Powerfull Favorite*, sig. A2r.

19. P. M., *Powerfull Favorite*, sigs A3v–B1r, B2v, E4r, H1v, L1r.

20. P. M., *Powerfull Favorite*, sigs B3r–C1v, D1v, D3v, E4r.

21. P. M., *Powerfull Favorite*, sigs H2r–H3v.

22. NA SP 16/103/40 (Melvin's examination: 6 May 1628); 16/106/27 (Conway to Buckingham: 4 June 1628); 16/107/96 (letter of Robert Heath: 21 June 1628); 16/107/104 (Heath memorandum); 16/108/38 (Heath to Conway: 27 June 1628); 16/110/13 (Melvin to Buckingham: 15 July 1628).

23. NA SP 16/107/96; *PP1628*, IV, pp. 311ff; *C&T Charles*, I, p. 362 (Mead to Stuteville: 15 June 1628); Bellany, "Lambe".

24. BL Harl. MS 390, fo. 420r (Pory copy); *C&T Charles*, I, pp. 372–3 (Mead to Stuteville: 5 July 1628); NA SP 16/119/56 (Susanna Prince's examination: 28 October 1628); BL Sloane MS 826, fos 119v–120r; Yale Osborn MS fb165, pp. 421–2; and Yale Osborn MS fb189, pp. 388–9; *Rushworth*, I, p. 627.

25. BL Harl. MS 390, fo. 420r (Pory copy); *C&T Charles*, I, pp. 371–3. We quote from this Pory/Mead version and indicate significant variants in the notes.

26. The Pory/Mead copy specifies Jesuits and Scots; others, e.g. BL Sloane MS 826, fo. 119v, Yale Osborn fb165, p. 421, and Yale Osborn fb189, pp. 388–9, imply the men are Scottish Jesuits, or Jesuited Scots; *Rushworth*, I, p. 627, refers to "certain Jesuites, Scotch-men".

27. BL Sloane MS 826, fo. 119v, estimates "6000 foote and 1200 horse", while Yale Osborn fb189, p. 389, claims "16000 foote 12000 horse". Yale Osborn fb165, p. 421, and the copy in *Rushworth*, I, p. 627, agree with the Mead/Pory version numbers.

28. Note omissions here in Yale Osborn MS fb165 and fb189, and in *Rushworth*, I, p. 627.

29. Yale Osborn MSS fb165 and fb189 break this article into two (articles 6 and 7); Patricia Crawford, "Charles Stuart, that Man of Blood", *JBS* 16:2 (1977); Bellany, *Politics*, ch. 5.

30. Bellany, *Politics*, ch. 4.

31. D'Ewes, *Autobiography*, I, p. 91; NA SP 16/26/49:I (statement of William Wraxthall: 5 May 1626); see too *C&T James*, II, pp. 354–5 (letters to Mead: 3 and 18 January 1623); *Chamberlain*, II, p. 474 (to Carleton: 25 January 1623); *Whiteway*, p. 50; D'Ewes, *Diary*, p. 112; BL Add. MS 28640, fo. 153v.

32. BL Harl. MS 390, fo. 420r; *C&T Charles*, I, p. 372; NA SP 16/108/38 (Heath to Conway: 27 June 1628).

33. *Holles*, III, p. 383 (to Lord Vere: 2 July 1628); *C&T Charles*, I, pp. 375, 377 (Mead to Stuteville: 12 and 19 July 1628). The compiler of BL Sloane MS 826, fo. 119v, thought Melvin "had his tryall at the Kings bench, werof he wa[s] acquitted by a iury".

34. *C&T Charles*, I, pp. 375, 377; NA SP 16/110/13 (Melvin to Buckingham: 15 July 1628).

35. NA SP 16/119/54 (Bankworth to Nicholas Coote: October 1628) [virtually illegible]; 16/119/56 (Examinations of Susanna Prince, Dionisia Grant and Edward Grant: 28 October 1628). Our emphasis.

36. Henry Foley (ed.), *Records of the English Province of the Society of Jesus* (London, 1877), vol. I, pp. 98ff, 117–18.

37. Noah Millstone, "Seeing Like a Statesman in Early Stuart England", *P&P* 223 (2014), pp. 119–21.

38. "The Copie of the Letter sent from the Emperours Confessour", 8 April 1628, NLS, Deposit 175, Gordon-Cumming Papers, Box 80, Bundle 1, unfoliated; *Translaet uyt den*

Hooghduytschen, eene missive van den biecht-vader der roomsche keyserlijcke majesteyt, aen eenen voornemen iesuyt naer Hildisheym (np, 1628).

39. "Ane answer to a young Jesuits letter", NLS, Deposit 175, Gordon-Cumming Papers, Box 80, Bundle 1, pp. 1–2, 6.

40. "Ane answer", pp. 3–4.

41. "Ane answer", pp. 1, 3–4, 7.

42. NA SP 16/110/6 (Edward Cosowarth to Conway: 13 July 1628).

43. NA SP 16/110/41 (Council to assize justices: 20 July 1628). On rumour see Tamotsu Shibutani, *Improvised News: A Sociological Study of Rumor* (Indianapolis and New York, 1966); Adam Fox, *Oral and Literate Culture in England, 1500–1700* (Oxford, 2000), ch. 7, and esp. pp. 359–61; Ethan H. Shagan, "Rumours and Popular Politics in the Reign of Henry VIII", in Tim Harris (ed.), *Politics of the Excluded* (Basingstoke and New York, 2001); and James C. Scott, *Domination and the Arts of Resistance: Hidden Transcripts* (New Haven and London, 1990), p. 145.

44. NA SP 16/110/28 (Heath to Conway: 18 July 1628); 16/110/41; 16/110/42 (Council to Cosowarth and JPs: 20 July 1628).

45. NA SP 16/111/21:I & II (Browne and Emett examinations: 28 July 1628); Thomas Nicholas, *The History and Antiquities of Glamorganshire and its Families* (London, 1874), p. 158.

46. NA SP 16/114/23:I (examinations of Patrick Jones, John Howell, William ap Evan and Richard Morgan: 28 August 1628).

47. NA SP 16/114/23:I (examinations of John Howell, Patrick Jones, Griffith Bennett and Charles Davis: 28 August 1628).

48. Henry Wotton, *A Short View of the Life and Death of George Villers, Duke of Buckingham* (London, 1642), p. 24; *ESL* Pi1; NA SP 16/114/32 (George Willoughby's examination: 28 August 1628); 16/119/25 (examinations of Willoughby and Richard Harward: 24 October 1628); and 16/119/30 (Lawrence Naylor's examination: 25 October 1628). See also Thomas Cogswell, "John Felton, Popular Political Culture and the Assassination of the Duke of Buckingham", *HJ* 49:2 (2006); and Alastair Bellany, "Felton, John (d. 1628)", *ODNB*.

49. *PP1628*, IV, pp. 311ff; NA SP 16/116/101 (interview of John Felton: 11 September 1628).

50. NA SP 16/116/101; 16/118/16 (Elizabeth Josselyn's examination: 3 October 1628).

51. Wotton, *Short View*, pp. 22–3.

52. *ESL*, Pi22, Pi36, Pi37.

53. *ESL*, Pi17, Pi34.

54. *ESL*, Pi21, Pi30.

55. *ESL*, Pi31.

56. *ESL*, Pi24.

57. *ESL*, Pi32.

58. *ESL*, Pi18.

59. *ESL*, Pi25.

60. *ESL*, Pii4.

61. *ESL*, Pii20.

Chapter 16

1. KHLC, Z17, fo. 12v. On Scott, see Peter Clark, "Thomas Scott and the Growth of Urban Opposition to the Early Stuart Regime", *HJ* 21:1 (1978); Andrew Thrush, "Thomas Scott", *HOC*, VI, pp. 246–52; and Cesare Cuttica, "Thomas Scott of Canterbury (1566–1635): Patriot, Civic Radical, Puritan", *History of European Ideas* 34 (2008).

2. Thomas Scott, "Canterburie Cittizens for the Parliament", CCA U66, fos 18v, 27r, 74r, 77v, 98v; KHLC U951/Z17, fo. 243r.

3. CCA U66, fos 50v, 59v, 69v, 76r, 78v, 82–2v, 122v.

4. CCA U66, fos 51r, 87–8, 120r, and 130v.

5. CCA U66, fo. 120.

6. Thomas Scott, *A Discourse of Polletique and Civell Honor* printed in G. D. Scull, *Dorothea Scott* (Oxford, 1883), pp. 149, 151, 155, 170; KHLC U951/Z17, fos 57r, 129v, 131r, 210r.

7. KHLC U951/Z17, fos 38–8v, 49r, 75r, 78r, 89r, 119–20, 149r; Scott, *Discourse*, p. 158.
8. KHLC U951/Z17, fos 78r, 89r, 119–20, 147v, 149r.
9. KHLC U951/Z17, fos 60r, 92r, 208r, 245r; Thrush, "Thomas Scott", *HOC*, VI, p. 247.
10. KHLC U951/Z17, fos 59v–60r, 63r, 209r.
11. KHLC U951/Z16 (unfoliated), paragraphs 49, 59.
12. KHLC U951/Z17, fos 49r, 33v, 55v.
13. KHLC U951/Z16, paragraphs 29, 59, 72–4.
14. KHLC U951/Z17, fos 107v–8r, 110v, 112r.
15. KHLC U951/Z16, paragraphs 49, 58; and U951/Z17, fo. 23r.
16. KHLC U951/Z17, fos 67–70.
17. KHLC U951/Z17, fos 34r, 128v.
18. KHLC U951/Z17, fos 6–7, 26r, 98r, 120r. The meditation on the murders runs fos 1–122v.
19. KHLC U951/Z17, fos 8v, 27v.
20. F. M. Stenton, *Anglo-Saxon England* (Oxford, 1971), pp. 381–9, 394–9; Ann Williams, *Æthelred the Unready* (London, 2003), pp. 70–5, 112–17, 121–4, 132–7, 147; N. J. Higham, *The Death of Anglo-Saxon England* (Stroud, 1997), pp. 17, 24, 39–70; M. Swanton (ed.), *The Anglo-Saxon Chronicle* (New York, 1998), pp. 138, 145–54.
21. KHLC U951/Z17, fos 11r–12v, 19r, 26v.
22. KHLC U951/Z17, fos 27v and 58r.
23. KHLC U951/Z17, fos 17r, 20v.
24. KHLC U951/Z17, fos 7–8, 12r, 140v.
25. KHLC U951/Z17, fos 30v–31r, 34v.
26. KHLC U951/Z17, fos 30v–32r.
27. KHLC U951/Z17, fos 66r–67v.
28. KHLC U951/Z17, fos 8v, 9v.
29. KHLC U951/Z17, fos 37v–39r, 8v.
30. KHLC U951/Z17, fos 8–9v, 21r, 22v.
31. KHLC U951/Z17, fos 38–40.
32. KHLC U951/Z17, fos 39v–42r, 47v.
33. KHLC U951/Z17, fos 42v, 44v, 45v–46r.
34. KHLC U951/Z17, fos 117r, 118r.
35. KHLC U951/Z17, fos 48r, 49v–52r.
36. KHLC U951/Z17, fos 109r, 116v.
37. KHLC U951/Z17, fos 89r, 90r, 91r, 108v.
38. KHLC U951/Z17, fos 64v–65r.
39. KHLC U951/Z17, fos 111v–112r, 113r, 114r, 116v.
40. KHLC U951/Z17, fos 113r, 118–119v.
41. KHLC U951/Z17, fos 112r, 113r.

Part 5 Prologue

1. S. R. Gardiner, *History of England from the Accession of James I to the Outbreak of the Civil War, 1603–1642*, 10 vols (Reprint: New York, 1965), vol. X, p. 214; Michael Braddick, *God's Fury, England's Fire: A New History of the English Civil Wars* (London, 2008), pp. 216–17, 271; Austin Woolrych, *Britain in Revolution, 1625–1660* (Oxford, 2002), p. 247.
2. *CJ*, II, pp. 666–9; Vernon F. Snow and Anne Steele Young (eds), *The Private Journals of the Long Parliament*, 3 vols (New Haven and London, 1992), vol. III, pp. 201–5.
3. NA SP 16/491/78 (testimony of Richard Mumford, Richard Robertson and Thomas Ridley: 17 July 1642).
4. Key studies of the media revolution include Sharon Achinstein, *Milton and the Revolutionary Reader* (Princeton, 1994); Nigel Smith, *Literature and Revolution in England, 1640–1660* (New Haven and London, 1994); Joad Raymond, *Invention of the Newspaper: English Newsbooks, 1641–1649* (Oxford, 1996), and *Pamphlets and Pamphleteering in Early Modern Britain* (Cambridge, 2003); Dagmar Freist, *Governed by Opinion: Politics, Religion, and the Dynamics of Communication in Stuart London, 1637–1645* (London, 1997); David Zaret, *Origins of Democratic Culture: Printing,*

Petitions and the Public Sphere in Early Modern England (Princeton, 2000); Ann Hughes, *Gangraena and the Struggle for the English Revolution* (Oxford, 2004); Jason Peacey, *Politicians and Pamphleteers: Propaganda During the English Civil Wars and Interregnum* (Aldershot, 2004), and *Print and Public Politics in the English Revolution* (Cambridge, 2013); Jason McElligott, *Royalism, Print and Censorship in Revolutionary England* (Woodbridge, 2007); David Como, "Secret Printing, the Crisis of 1640, and the Origins of Civil War Radicalism", *P&P* 196 (2007), and "Print, Censorship, and Ideological Escalation in the English Civil War", *JBS* 51:4 (2012); and Helen Pierce, *Unseemly Pictures: Graphic Satire and Politics in Early Modern England* (New Haven and London, 2008). For recent studies that situate media culture at the heart of the revolutionary experience, see David Cressy, *England on Edge: Crisis and Revolution, 1640–1642* (Oxford, 2006); Braddick, *God's Fury*; and Sharpe, *Image Wars*.

Chapter 17

1. NA SP 16/158/60 (Eglisham to unknown Benedictine: 18 January 1630).
2. "The Relation of Sr Balthazar Gerbier", BL Add. MS 4181, fos 45v–48r; Balthazar Gerbier, *Les Effects Pernicieux de Meschants Favoris et Grands Ministres d'Estat Es Provinces Belgiques, en Lorraine, Germanie, France, Italie, Espagne, & Angleterre. Et Des-Abuzé d'Erreurs Populaires Sur le Subject de Iacques & Charles Stuart, Roys de la Grande Bretagne* (The Hague, 1653), sigs D2r–5r; *Progresses*, IV, p. 612 and n.2; Simon Healey, "Chaloner, Sir Thomas (?1564–1615)", *HOC*, III, pp. 485–8; John Westby-Gibson, rev. Kenneth L. Campbell, "Chaloner, Sir Thomas, the Younger (1563/4–1615)", *ODNB*; David Scott, "Chaloner, Thomas (1595–1660)" and "Chaloner, James (c. 1602–1660)", *ODNB*. See also Geoffrey Parker, *The Army of Flanders and the Spanish Road, 1567–1659*, 2nd ed. (Cambridge, 2004), pp. 52–3.
3. Gerbier, *Les Effects*, sigs D2v–3r.
4. "Relation", fo. 47r; Gerbier, *Les Effects*, sig. D3r.
5. "Relation", fo. 47r. On Gerbier's manoeuvring in the 1640s and 1650s, see Jason Peacey, "Print, Publicity, and Popularity: The Projecting of Sir Balthazar Gerbier, 1642–1662", *JBS* 51:2 (2012).
6. Gerbier, *Les Effects*, sig. D2v.
7. Gerbier, *Les Effects*, sigs D3r–v; "Relation", fo. 47r; *Dictionnaire de l'Académie francaise* (1694), in the ARTFL database "Dictionnaires d'autrefois".
8. NA SP 16/277/87, 16/278/12, 16/278/13, 16/283/74 (William King's declaration: 24 November 1634; William Eardley's examination: 4 December 1634; Christopher Clough's declaration: 4 December 1634; Christopher Clough's bond: 23 February 1635).
9. On active political readers and collectors, see Kevin Sharpe, *Reading Revolutions: the Politics of Reading in Early Modern England* (New Haven and London, 2000); Noah Millstone, *Plot's Commonwealth* (forthcoming); and Alastair Bellany, "Railing Rhymes Revisited: Libels, Scandals, and Early Stuart Politics", *History Compass* 5:4 (2007), pp. 1,149–50.
10. BL Add. MS 22591, fos 31r–39v; Cynthia Herrup, *A House in Gross Disorder: Sex, Law and the 2nd Earl of Castlehaven* (Oxford and New York, 1999).
11. BL Harl. MS 405, fos 72r–77v; BL Add. MS 4106, fos 130r–157r (Eglisham fos 149v–157r). The manuscript was assembled by Thomas Birch in the eighteenth century, but the compilation of separates that includes Eglisham and the parliamentary materials was put together in the seventeenth century.
12. BL Egerton MS 2026, fos 51v–60v, 64r–65r; *ESL*, Pi35, Pii8, Pii10.
13. BL Egerton MS 2026, fos 24r–25r, 48v–49v ("Observations concerning Sr Henry Yelvertons Charge"). On the "popular" Puritan, see e.g. Peter Lake, "Anti-Popery: The Structure of a Prejudice", in Richard Cust and Ann Hughes (eds), *Conflict in Early Stuart England: Studies in Religion and Politics* (London, 1989).
14. BL Egerton MS 2026, fos 50r–51r ("The Examinacion of Edward Hawley"); *ESL*, Nvi1; Victor Stater, "Vere, Henry de, Eighteenth Earl of Oxford (1593–1625)", *ODNB*.
15. D'Ewes, *Autobiography*, I, pp. 241, 258, 261–2.

16. D'Ewes, *Autobiography*, I, pp. 263–5, 292–3, 301, 380 (our emphasis).

17. Henry Wotton, *A Parallel between Robert late Earle of Essex, and George late Duke of Buckingham* (London, 1641), and *A Short View of the Life and Death of George Villers, Duke of Buckingham* (London, 1642), pp. 17–18; NA SP 16/277/87 (William King's examination: 24 November 1634); Alastair Bellany, "'The Enigma of the World': Memorializing and Remembering George Villiers, First Duke of Buckingham in the Aftermath of Assassination, c. 1628–1642", in Martin Wrede and Horst Carl (eds), *Zwischen Schande und Ehre. Errinerungsbrüche und die Kontinuität des Hauses* (Mainz, 2007), pp. 41–50.

18. Wotton, *Short View*, pp. 2, 13, 23.

19. Wotton, *Parallel*, pp. 4, 10–11.

20. BL Add. MS 4739, p. 2,010/fo. 409v; Thomas Thomson (ed.), *The History of the Kirk of Scotland. By Mr David Calderwood* (Edinburgh, 1845), vol. VII, pp. 630–1; Vaughan T. Wells, "Calderwood, David (c. 1575–1650)", *ODNB*. Note the signs of revision in BL Add. MS 4739, p. 2,010/fo. 409v (Hamilton), and pp. 2,011–13/fos 410r–11r (James).

21. BL Add. MS 4739, pp. 2,010–11/fo. 409v–10r; Calderwood, *History* (Thomson ed.), VII, pp. 632–3.

22. BL Add. MS 4739, pp. 2,011–13/fos 410r–11r; Calderwood, *History* (Thomson ed.), VII, pp. 634–8.

23. David Calderwood, *The True History of the Church of Scotland, from the beginning of the Reformation, unto the end of the Reigne of King James VI* (Edinburgh[?], 1678), pp. 814–16; Wells, "Calderwood, David", *ODNB*.

24. Siobhan Keenan and John Jowett (eds), "Introduction", *The Emperor's Favourite* (Malone Society 174: 2010), pp. xxiv–xxxiv; Keenan, "Staging Roman History, Stuart Politics, and the Duke of Buckingham: The Example of the Emperor's Favourite", *Early Theatre* 14 (2002); Curtis Perry, *Literature and Favoritism in Early Modern England* (Cambridge, 2006), pp. 249ff.

25. *Emperor's Favourite*, pp. 19–22, 27–8, 41, 44, 48, 52, 62–4, 85–8, 95.

26. *Emperor's Favourite*, pp. 51–3, 102–5.

27. *Emperor's Favourite*, Act 3, scene 1; pp. 77, 79–80.

28. *Emperor's Favourite*, pp. 20–1, 40, 90.

29. *Emperor's Favourite*, pp. 21–3, 35–6, 43, 105.

30. *Emperor's Favourite*, pp. 6, 10, 14–15, 17, 26, 49–50, 55–6, 65–7.

31. *Emperor's Favourite*, pp. 12–13, 60.

32. *Emperor's Favourite*, pp. 70, 105; Tacitus, *Annals*, XII:66–7, XIII:15–16; Suetonius (trans. Philemon Holland), *The Historie of Twelve Caesars, Emperours of Rome* (London, 1606), pp. 175–6, 195.

33. *Emperor's Favourite*, pp. 95–9, 109, 112–13, 115–19.

34. NA SP 16/277/87, 16/278/12, 16/283/74; Bellany, "'Enigma'", pp. 41–2.

Chapter 18

1. Devon RO, EQSOB 64, fo.15v; NA SP 16/491/187 (Richard Mumford's information: 17 July 1642); Mark Stoyle, *From Deliverance to Destruction: Rebellion and Civil War in an English City* (Exeter, 1996), pp. 177–8; Mark Stoyle, *Loyalty and Locality: Popular Allegiance in Devon during the English Civil War* (Exeter, 1994), pp. 37–42, 53.

2. Figures taken from the English Short Title Catalogue.

3. Vernon F. Snow and Anne Steele Young (eds), *The Private Journals of the Long Parliament*, 3 vols (New Haven and London, 1992), vol. III, pp. 341–4, 354, 357; John Walter, *Understanding Popular Violence in the English Revolution: The Colchester Plunderers* (Cambridge, 1999); S. R. Gardiner, *History of the Great Civil War*, 4 vols (London, 1886–91; reprint: London, 1987), vol. I, pp. 1–88; Austin Woolrych, *Britain in Revolution, 1625–1660* (Oxford, 2002), ch. 8; Michael Braddick, *God's Fury, England's Fire: A New History of the English Civil Wars* (London, 2008), ch. 8; Clarendon, *History*, II, pp. 292ff; and P. R. Newman, *Atlas of the English Civil War* (New York, 1985), pp. 20–1.

4. Anon., *King Iames His Iudgement of a King and of a Tyrant* (London, [9 September] 1642: TT E116/20), sigs A1r–2r, A3v; Anon., *King Charles His Defence Against some trayterous Observations upon King Iames His Judgement of a King and of a Tyrant*. (n.p, 1642), p. 2; J. P. Sommerville (ed.), *King James VI and I: Political Writings* (Cambridge, 1994), pp. 179 ff, esp. pp. 183, 295 and n.851.

5. Anon., *King James His Iudgement*, sigs A1r–v, A2r–3r. See too David Como, "Secret Printing, the Crisis of 1640, and the Origins of Civil War Radicalism", *P&P* 196 (2007), e.g. pp. 65–6, 79; and Braddick, *God's Fury*, pp. 108–10.

6. Anon., *King James His Iudgement*, sigs A2v–3v, A4v. On the letters to the pope, see BL Add. MS 28640, fos 149v–50v (1620s' copies); Anon., *Behold! Two Letters, The One Written by the Pope to the (then) Prince of Wales, now King of England: The Other, An Answere to the said Letter by the said Prince, now His Majesty of England* ([London], 1642); J. L., *A Just Apology for His Sacred Majestie or, An Answer to A Late Lying and Scandalous Pamphlet, Intituled, Behold Two Letters* (London, 1642).

7. D. F. McKenzie and Maureen Bell, *A Chronology and Calendar of Documents Relating to the London Book Trade, 1641–1670*, 3 vols (Oxford, 2005), vol. I, pp. 69, 71–2, 76–7; Snow and Young, *Private Journals*, III, p. 348.

8. Anon., *King Charles His Defence*, p. 2; NA SP 16/357/172 (Articles against Thomas Purslowe, Gregory Dexter and William Taylor: May? 1637); 16/371/102 (William Taylor's testimony: 14 November 1637); McKenzie and Bell, *Chronology*, I, p. 77; David Como, "Print, Censorship, and Ideological Escalation in the English Civil War", *JBS* 51:4 (2012), pp. 829–30ff; and Como, "Secret Printing".

9. Anon., *King Charles His Defence*, pp. 3–8 (alluding to 2 Samuel 16:5–8).

10. *Rous*, pp. 3, 124.

11. BL TT E.119/15; Bod. Wood 614(51).

12. (1) Thomason version: BL TT E.119/15; other copies include Trinity College, Cambridge X.9.105[7] and Beinecke Library, Yale, By 35 4 7; (2) Variant 1: copies include: Union Theological Seminary, New York, Wing E265cA; BL 100.C.72; Indiana University, Lilly Library, DA 391.E32; Bod. C.14.1.Linc (38); Bod. Firth e35(3); (3) Variant 2: copies examined include: New York Academy of Medicine (Wing E256cA); Beinecke Library, Yale, Z 45 90 3; Bod. Ashmole 735(17); Bod. Godw. Pamph. 1524(1).

13. Copies include: Huntington Library (Wing E256); BL G.2022(1); BL 1093.b.110; NLS Ry II.e.52.

14. (1) Copies include: Folger Library E256; New York Public Library, *KC 1642; Trinity College Cambridge (partially uncut); Bod. Wood 614(51); (2) NLS Crawford.ET.s. 1642/274.

15. Jason Peacey, "'Fiery Spirits' and Political Propaganda: Uncovering a Radical Press Campaign of 1642", *Publishing History* 55 (2004).

16. Charles I, *His Maiesties Last Message, September 11. 1642* (London, 1642); Clarendon, *History*, II, pp. 321, 327–9; A. H., *A Speedy Post From Heaven to the King of England* (London, [5 October] 1642: TT E.121/6), pp. 4–5; *CJ*, II, p. 795.

17. A. H., *A Speedy Post*, p. 1.

18. Mark Stoyle, *The Black Legend of Prince Rupert's Dog: Witchcraft and Propaganda during the English Civil War* (Exeter, 2011), pp. 36–42, 190 n.56.

19. D. F. McKenzie, *Stationers' Company Apprentices, 1605–1640* (Charlottesville, 1961), p. 43. Aston's 1641 output includes: *The ivdges jvdgement a speech penn'd in the beginning of the Parliament against the iudges*; *The petition of the citizens of London to both Houses of Parliament wherein is a demonstration of their grievances, together with their desires for justice to bee executed upon the Earle of Strafford, and other delinquents*; *Mr. Pymmes speech in answer to Thomas Lord Straffords defence at the barre, the 13 of April, 1641*; *Sir Thomas Roe his speech in Parliament wherein he sheweth the cause of the decay of coine and trade in this land*; *Densell Hollis Esq; his speech at the delivery of the protestation to the Lords of the upper House of Parliament. 4. May, 1641*; *A petition delivered in to the Lords Spirituall and Temporall, by Sir Thomas Aston, Baronet, from the county palatine of Chester concerning episcopacy*; Aston, *A remonstrance, against presbitery. Exhibited by divers of the nobilitie, gentrie, ministers and inhabitants of the county palatine. of Chester*.

20. McKenzie and Bell, *Chronology*, I, p. 13; Anon., *A preamble with the protestation made by the whole House of Commons the 3. of May, 1641*; *Two speeches made by Sr. Thomas*

Wentworth: now Earle of Strafford, in the Parliament holden at VVestminster. 1628 (London, 1641).

21. John Digby, Earl of Bristol, *Articles Drawn up By the now Iohn Earle of Bristoll and presented to the Parliament, against George late Duke of Buckingham, in the yeare 1626* (London, [5 November] 1642: TT E.126/20), tp, p. 8; Clarendon, *History*, II, p. 327.

22. George Eglisham, *Strange Apparitions, or The Ghost of King Iames, With a late conference between the ghost of that good King, the Marquesse Hameltons, and George Eglishams, Doctor of Physic, unto which appeared the Ghost of the late Duke of Buckingham concerning the death and poysoning of King Iames and the rest* (London, [21 October] 1642: TT E.123/23). It is possible that there were two different printings: some copies have a blemish in the ornamental tailpiece (e.g. TT E.123/23; BL G.2022[2]; Union Theological Seminary); others have no blemish (e.g. Beinecke Library, Yale By 38 35j).

23. Eglisham, *Strange Apparitions*, pp. 4–5.

24. Eglisham, *Strange Apparitions*, pp. 3–8.

25. Eglisham, *Strange Apparitions*, pp. 2–3, 7; *Forerunner*, p. 20; Anon., *A Briefe and True Relation of the Murther of Mr Thomas Scott, Preacher of God's Word and Batchelor of Divinitie* (London, 1628).

26. Eglisham, *Strange Apparitions*, pp. 3, 7.

27. [Edward Hyde], *A Full Answere to an Infamous and Trayterous Pamphlet* (London, 1648), p. 15.

28. Henry Wotton, *A Parallell betweene Robert late Earle of Essex, and George late Duke of Buckingham* (London, 1641: TT E.164/20), pp. 10–11.

29. Henry Wotton, *A Short View of the Life and Death of George Villers, Duke of Buckingham* (London, [22 October] 1642: TT E.124/1), pp. 17–18, 23; Alastair Bellany, "Buckingham Engraved: Politics, Print Images and the Royal Favourite in the 1620s", in Michael Hunter (ed.), *Printed Images in Early Modern Britain: Essays in Interpretation* (Farnham, 2010), pp. 219–23.

30. Warwickshire RO Feilding of Newnham Paddox MSS, CR 2017/C1/152; Ann Hughes, "Feilding, Basil, Second Earl of Denbigh (c. 1608–1675)", *ODNB*.

Chapter 19

1. TT E.276/2, fos 1r–2r, endorsed "Aprill 1st 1645"; Hyder Rollins (ed.), *Cavalier and Puritan: Ballads Illustrating the Period of the Great Rebellion, 1640–1660* (New York, 1923), pp. 150–3, reads "Pockets", but the initial letter is more like an "S" than a "P". On Lostwithiel, see P. R. Newman, *Atlas of the English Civil War* (New York 1985), p. 59; Mark Stoyle, *Soldiers and Strangers: An Ethnic History of the English Civil War* (New Haven and London, 2005), pp. 50–2; and Michael Braddick, *God's Fury, England's Fire: A New History of the English Civil Wars* (London, 2008), p. 332.

2. Anon., *A Declaration* (London, 1642: TT E.118/36); Anon., *A Discoverie of Treason* (London, 1642: TT E.124/30); Anon., *Foure Wonderfull, Bloudy and Dangerous plots* (London, 1642: TT E.147/1); Anon., *The Plots Revealed* (London, 1643: TT E.63/20); Anon., *Plots, Conspiracies and Attempts* (London, 1642: TT E.121/29).

3. Gregory Thims, *The Protestant Informer* (London, 1643: TT E.91/17), p. 2; Anon., *The English Pope* (London, 1643: TT E.56/13), p. 24.

4. Anon., *A New Invention, or a Paire of Cristall Spectacles* (London, 1644: TT E.50/20), p. 1; Anon., *Thankes to Parliament* (London, 1642: TT 669.f.6/30); Anon., *A Damnable Treason, By a Contagious Plaster of a Plague-Sore* (London, 1641: TT E.173/23); Mark Stoyle, *The Black Legend of Prince Rupert's Dog: Witchcraft and Propaganda during the English Civil War* (Exeter, 2011), pp. 85–6, 201 n.98; Braddick, *God's Fury*, pp. 160–1.

5. Caroline M. Hibbard, *Charles I and the Popish Plot* (Chapel Hill, 1983), pp. 157–62, 239–42; William M. Lamont, *Marginal Prynne, 1600–1669* (London and Toronto, 1963), ch. 6; Alastair Bellany, "Libels in Action: Ritual, Subversion and the English Literary Underground, 1603–42", in Tim Harris (ed.), *The Politics of the Excluded, c. 1500–1850* (Basingstoke, 2001), pp. 110–16.

6. William Prynne, *Romes Master-peece. Or, The Grand Conspiracy of the Pope and his Iesuited Instruments, to extirpate the Protestant Religion* (London, [8 August] 1643: TT E.249/32), tp; Austin Woolrych, *Britain in Revolution, 1625–1660* (Oxford, 2002), pp. 263–5, 270–3; J. H. Hexter, *The Reign of King Pym* (Cambridge, MA, 1941), chs 6–7.

7. Prynne, *Romes Master-peece*, pp. 18–19 (an "Indian nut" was the common name for a coconut); Hibbard, *Charles I*, pp. 157, 270 n.60; G. Davies, "Life of Sir William Boswell", in G. Davies (ed.), *Autobiography of Thomas Raymond and Memoirs of the Family of Guise of Elmore, Gloucestershire*, Camden Society, 3rd Series, 28 (London, 1917), pp. 69–80.

8. Prynne, *Romes Master-peece*, pp. 18–19, 34.

9. Prynne, *Romes Master-peece*, pp. 24, 33. Prynne also elaborated a portrait of Buckingham as Jesuited favourite in *The Popish Royall Favourite: Or, A full Discovery of His Majesties Extraordinary Favours to, and Protections of notorious Papists, Priests, Jesuits* (London, 1643), p. 56.

10. Prynne, *Romes Master-peece*, pp. 16, 28–9, 31. On the plot's "royalism" see Hibbard, *Charles I*, p. 162, and Lamont, *Marginal Prynne*, p. 138.

11. Prynne, *Romes Master-peece*, pp. 35–6.

12. William Prynne, *The fourth part of The soveraigne power of parliaments and kingdomes* (London, 1643), p. 188.

13. Prynne, *Popish Royall Favourite*, p. 59; William Prynne, *Hidden Workes of Darkenes Brought to Publike Light. Or, A Necessary Introduction to the History of the Archbishop of Canterburies Triall* (London, 1645), p. 172.

14. William Prynne, *Canterburies Doome, or, The first part of a compleat history of the commitment, charge, tryall, condemnation, execution of William Laud* (London, 1646), pp. 420–1, 459–60.

15. Lamont, *Marginal Prynne*, pp. 124, 126–7; William Laud, *The Works of the Most Reverend Father in God, William Laud, D.D. Sometime Lord Archbishop of Canterbury* (Oxford, 1853), vol. 4, pp. 325–6, 499, 501; Henry Burton, *A full and satisfactory answere to the Arch-bishop of Canterburies speech* (London, 1645), sig. B1r.

16. John Vicars, *Prodigies & Apparitions or Englands Warning Pieces* (London, 1643), pp. 3, 12–20; Julia Gasper, "Vicars, John (1580–1652)", *ODNB*.

17. Dudley Digges, *A Speech Delivered in Parliament, By Sir D.D. Knight* (London, [27 December] 1643: TT E.79/13), tp, p. 7.

18. George Eglisham, *Een moordadich, schrickelijck, ende heel wonderbaer Secreet, in Engelandt ontdeckt. Waer in wordt verthoont 't groot ghevaer, daer des selfs konincklijcke huys in ghestelt is, Leest, Schrickt, en Beest! In 't Engels beschreven Door Joris Eglisham, der Mediciinen Doctor, ende een van de Medciin-meesters, weghen den Persoon sijns koninckl. Majestyts van Groot Brittannien, etc, meer als den tijdt van thien jaren* (18 Februarij, Anno 1644), sig. A1v.

19. Richard Baker, *A Chronicle of the Kings of England* (London, 1643), pp. 155–6; G. H. Martin, "Baker, Sir Richard (c. 1568–1645)", *ODNB*.

20. A. N. B. Cotton, "John Dillingham, Journalist of the Middle Group", *EHR* 93 (1978); Joyce Macadam, "Mercurius Britanicus on Charles I: An Exercise in Civil War Journalism and High Politics, August 1643 to May 1646", *Historical Research* 84 (2011); Jason Peacey, "The Struggle for *Mercurius Britanicus*: Factional Politics and the Parliamentarian Press, 1643–1646", *HLQ* 68 (2005).

21. *Mercurius Britanicus*, no. 29 (25 March 1642), p. 223.

22. Anon., *A True and Faithfull Journall*, no. 2 (10 April 1644), p. 12; Woolrych, *Britain in Revolution*, pp. 273–95.

23. Anon., *The Second Part of the Spectacles* (London, [5 June] 1644: TT E.53/21), pp. 3, 6–7.

24. Anon., *A Prognosticall Prediction of Admirable Events* (London, [13 July] 1644: TT E.2/2), p. 6.

25. Anon., *A Satyre against the Cavaliers* (London 1643); Thims, *Protestant Informer*, p. 6.

26. John Booker, *No Mercurius Aquaticus, But A Cable-Rope, Double twisted for Iohn Tayler, The Water-Poet; who escaping drowning in a Paper-Wherry-Voyage, is reserved for another day* (London, [19 July] 1644: TT E.2/22); Bernard Capp, "Booker, John (1602–1667)", *ODNB*. The other texts in the 1644 feud are John Booker, *Mercurius Coelicus: Or, A Caveat To all people of the Kingdome* (24 January); "George Naworth" (George

Wharton), *Mercurio-Coelico Mastix* (before 4 March); John Booker, "Timotheus Philo-Bookerus", *Mercurius Vapulans, or Naworth Stript and Whipt* (4 March); John Booker, *A Rope for a Parret* (6 March); John Taylor, *No Mercurius Aulicus* (before 10 July); John Taylor, *Iohn Taylor Being yet unhanged, sends greeting, to Iohn Booker* (after 19 July, before 27 September); and John Booker, *A Rope Treble-twisted, for John Tayler the Water-poet* (27 September).

27. Booker, *No Mercurius*, pp. 2, 4, 6–8; Taylor, *Iohn Taylor Being yet unhanged*.

28. Anon., *A Dog's Elegy, or Rupert's Tears, For the late Defeat given him at Marston-moore* (London, [27 July] 1644: TT E.3/17), esp. pp. 6–8; Stoyle, *Black Legend*, esp. pp. 137–41.

29. Anon., *Parliaments Kalender of Black Saints* (London, [24 August] 1644: TT E.7/9), pp. 3–4; Anon., *A Nest of Perfidious Vipers, or the Second Part of the Parliaments Kalendar* (London, [21 September] 1644 TT E.9/9), p. 7.

30. Anon., *Hell's Hurlie-burlie* (London, [5 October] 1644: TT E.11/4), pp. 6–7.

31. His other tracts include *The Eye Clear'd* (London, [25 June] 1644: TT E.52/11); *The Earl of Straffords Ghost* (London, [22 August] 1644: TT E.6/33); *A New Mercury* (London, [9 September] 1644: TT E.8/17); *Speculum Impietatis* (London, 1644: TT E.6/31); and Paul Baynes, *The Diocesans Trial* (London, 1644).

32. *Mercurius Aulico-Mastix*, no. 1 (12 April 1644: TT E.12/15), p. 3.

33. George Wither, *The Two Incomparable Generalissimos of the World* (London, 1644: TT 669.f.10/5).

34. Anon., *A Survey of Monarchie* (London, [2 August] 1644: TT E.4/8), pp. 2, 13.

35. Christopher Love, *Englands Distemper, Having Division and Error, as its Cause: Wanting Peace and Truth for its Cure* (London, [21 March] 1645: TT E.274/15), pp. 4, 7, 16, 20–3, 30–8. Love delivered two versions of the sermon, and according to his marginal note, the allusion to James's death only appeared in the Windsor version. For context and Royalist reaction, see *Mercurius Aulicus* (2 February 1645), pp. 1,361–2; E. C. Vernon, "Love, Christopher (1618–1651)", *ODNB*; Woolrych, *Britain in Revolution*, pp. 296–305.

Chapter 20

1. Anon., *An Antidote Against An Infectious Aire* (London, [14 February] 1648: TT E.427/18), sigs A2v–3v.

2. *Kingdomes Weekly Intelligencer*, no. 247 (15 February 1648), p. 840; *Mercurius Bellicus*, no. 3 (14 February 1648), p. 4[6]; and *Mercurius Aulicus*, no. 3 (17 February 1648), sig. C2. See also *Mercurius Melancholicus*, no. 23 (19 February 1648), pp. 145–6 [erratic pagination]; *Moderate Intelligencer*, no. 152 (17 February 1648), pp. 1,168–71; *Mercure Anglois*, no. 31 (17 February 1648), pp. 232–4; *A Perfect Diurnall*, no. 237 (14 February 1648), pp. 1,905, 1,911; and *Kingdomes Weekly Post*, no. 7 (16 February 1648), pp. 52–4.

3. Anon., *White-hall Fayre* (London, [30 April] 1648: TT E.434/16), p. 8; Anon., *Troy-Novant Must Not Be Burnt* (London, [8 May] 1648: TT 669.f.12/21); Anon., *Treasons Anatomie or The duty of a loyall subject* ([London], [19 February] 1648: TT E.427/24), p. 4; *Mercurius Bellicus*, no. 3 (14 February 1648), p. 6.

4. Anon., *The Anarchie* (London, [11 January] 1648: TT 669.f.11/14); *Mercurius Poeticus*, no. 1 (13 May 1648), p. 2.

5. Anon., *A Letter to the Earle of Pembroke* (London 1648), p. 10; *Mercurius Pragmaticus*, no. 22 (15 February 1648), sigs Y1v–2r.

6. J. G. Fotheringham (ed.), *The Diplomatic Correspondence of Jean de Montereul* (Edinburgh, 1898), vol. I, p. 209 (Bacon to Montereul: 11 June 1646); Bod. MS Clarendon 29/2460, 2530 (newsletters: 4 March and 10 June 1647); O. Ogle and W. H. Bliss (eds), *Calendar of the Clarendon State Papers* (Oxford, 1872), vol. I, pp. 364–5; and John R. MacCormack, *Revolutionary Politics in the Long Parliament* (Cambridge, MA, 1973), pp. 127, 168.

7. *CJ*, V, pp. 416–17; David Underdown (ed.), "The Parliamentary Diary of John Boys, 1647–8", *BIHR* 39:100 (1966), p. 155; *Mercurius Pragmaticus*, no. 17 (11 January 1648), sigs R1v–R2; *The Kingdomes Weekly Post*, no. 1 (5 January 1648), p. 8; *Mercurius Dogmaticus*, no. 1 (13 January 1648), p. 7; S. R. Gardiner, *History of the Great Civil War* (London, 1987), vol. IV, pp. 50–1, 56–8; David Underdown, *Pride's Purge: Politics in the*

Puritan Revolution (London, 1971, 1985), p. 88. Gardiner and Underdown still offer the most compelling interpretations of the parliamentary politics of this period.

8. Underdown, *Pride's Purge*, appendix A; Blair Worden, *The Rump Parliament* (Cambridge, 1974), appendix A; Marc L. Schwarz, "Fiennes, Nathaniel (1607/8–1669)", and George Yerby, "Pierrepont, William (1607/8–1678)", *ODNB*; Valerie Pearl, "The Royal Independents in the English Civil War", *TRHS*, 5th Series, 18 (1968), p. 90 and n.3; C. H. Firth (ed.), *The Memoirs of Edmund Ludlow* (Oxford, 1894), vol. I, p. 162; S. R. Gardiner (ed.), *Hamilton Papers. Addenda* (Camden Society Misc. 9: London, 1893), p. 8.

9. *Mercurius Pragmaticus*, no. 17 (11 January 1648), sigs R1–2; and no. 18 (18 January 1648), sig. S1.

10. Thomas Fairfax, *A Declaration From His Excellency Sir Tho: Fairfax* (London, [12 January] 1648), p. 7; *LJ*, IX, p. 662; Clarendon, *History*, IV, pp. 281–3; *Mercurius Pragmaticus*, no. 22 (15 February 1648), sigs Y1v–2r; [Clement Walker], *Relations and Observations, Historical and Politick* (*The History of Independency*) (London, 1648), pt. 1, p. 73; Gardiner, *Great Civil War*, IV, pp. 52–3; Austin Woolrych, *Britain in Revolution, 1625–1660* (Oxford, 2002), p. 401; Robert Ashton, *Counter-Revolution: The Second Civil War and its Origins* (New Haven and London, 1994), pp. 38–9.

11. *Perfect Occurrences*, no. 55 (21 January 1648), p. 379; *CJ*, V, p. 446; *Mercurius Melancholicus*, no. 34 (15 January 1648), p. 116; Fairfax, *Declaration From His Excellency*, p. 7; *Mercurius Elencticus*, no. 8 (19 January), p. 54 *Mercurius Pragmaticus*, no.18 (18 January 1648), sig. 5.

12. *CSPV 1647–52*, docs 94 and 101; S. R. Gardiner (ed.), *The Hamilton Papers: Being Selections From Original Letters In the Possession of His Grace the Duke of Hamilton and Brandon. Relating to the Years 1638–1650* (Camden Society NS 27: London, 1880), p. 153.

13. *CJ*, V, p. 457; *Perfect Occurrences*, no. 58 (11 February 1648), p. 406; *Kingdomes Weekly Intelligencer*, no. 247 (15 February, 1648), p. 833. One other clause was recommitted that day. Royalists alleged that the "first rude catalogue" of Charles's crimes, prepared by the parliamentary Army, had also charged the king "with the death of his elder brother Prince Henry": see [George Bate], *The Regall Apology: Or, The Declaration of the Commons, Feb. 11. 1647 Canvassed*, ([London], [19 April] 1648: TT E.436/5), p. 26. For another Royalist report, see *Hamilton Papers Addenda*, pp. 7–8.

14. *CJ*, V, p. 457; and *Perfect Occurrences*, no. 58 (11 February 1648), p. 407.

15. *CJ*, V, p. 471; *Kingdomes Weekly Intelligencer*, no. 247 (15 February 1648), p. 837; and *Perfect Occurrences*, no. 58 (11 February 1648), p. 410.

16. Bod. MS Clarendon 30/2723, 2724 (newsletters: 13 and 14 February 1648); W. C. Abbott (ed.), *The Writing and Speeches of Oliver Cromwell* (Cambridge, MA, 1937), vol. I, pp. 583–4; John Morrill and Philip Baker, "Oliver Cromwell, the Regicide and the Sons of Zeruiah", in Jason Peacey (ed.), *The Regicides and the Execution of Charles I* (Basingstoke and New York, 2001), pp. 23–4; Gardiner, *Great Civil War*, IV, pp. 61–2; *Hamilton Papers Addenda*, p. 9.

17. *CJ*, V, p. 462; Bod. MS Clarendon 30/2724 (newsletter: 14 February 1648); NA SP 16/516/30 (Receipt: 14–17 February 1648).

18. *A Declaration of the Commons of England In Parliament assembled; Expressing Their Reasons and Grounds of passing the late Resolutions touching No farther Address or Application to be made to the King* (London, [15 February] 1648: TT E.427/9), pp. 7–12, 18–19.

19. *Declaration*, pp. 13–18; *Clarendon State Papers*, II, Appendix, p. xlv (Letter of Intelligence: 17 February 1648); Abbott, *Writing and Speeches*, I, pp. 583–4.

20. Clarendon, *History*, IV, pp. 281–5; Anon., *Great Britans Vote: Or, God save King Charles* (London, [13 March] 1648: TT E.431/26), p. 8; *Hamilton Papers*, pp. 153, 162.

21. *CJ*, V, pp. 471, 494; *Perfect Occurrences*, no. 61 (3 March 1648), p. 500; [Walker], *Independency*, p. 74; *Calendar of the Clarendon State Papers*, I, p. 364, no. 2455 (misfiled under February/March 1647).

22. Anon., *The Returne of the People of England: Tendred to the Speaker of the House of Commons* ([London], [15 November] 1648: TT E.472[7]), p. 1; *Perfect Occurrences*, nos 57–58 (11 February 1648), pp. 402, 406–10; and no. 59 (18 February 1648), pp. 413–15; *The Kingdomes Weekly Intelligencer*, no. 247 (15 February 1648); *The Kingdoms*

Weekly Account, no. 6 (16 February 1648); *The Moderate Intelligencer*, no. 152 (17 February 1648).

23. Bod. Clarendon MS 30/2722 (newsletter: 10 February 1648); George Eglisham, *A Declaration to the Kingdome of England, Concerning the poysoning of King James of happy memory, King of Great Brittain* (London, [14 February) 1648: TT E.427/5), pp. 1–2, adapting *Forerunner*, p. 9. On Horton see *A New Declaration from Eight Regiments* (London, 1647: TT E.416/35); Anon., *The Humble Remonstrance and Desires of . . . Divers Officers* (London, 1647: TT E.413/6); *The Kings Maiesties Last Message . . . to Fairfax* (London 1647: TT E.374/8); and *England's Remonstrance* (London [17 February] 1648: TT E.427/20).

24. Eglisham, *Declaration*, tp, pp. 2–6; *Forerunner*, pp. 15, 20–2.

25. *The Kingdoms Weekly Account*, no. 7 (23 February 1648), p. 53; *Perfect Occurrences*, nos 60–1 (25 February and 3 March 1648), pp. 422, 500–1; [Du Mornay], *Vindiciae Contra Tyrannos: A Defence of Liberty against Tyrants . . . Being a Treatise written in Latin and French by Junius Brutus* (London, 1648: TT E.430[2]).

26. Anon., *The Humble Petition . . . of Taunton* (London, [17 February] 1648: TT E.427/21), p. 4; and Anon., *The Humble Petition . . . of Buckingham* (London, [15 March] 1648: TT E.432/12), p. 4.

27. *Mercurius Aulicus*, no. 3 (17 February 1648), sigs C2r–v.

28. Anon., *The Declaration . . . of Hampeshire* (London, [14 June] 1648: TT E.447/18), sigs A2r, A3r; Anon., *The Sad and Bloody Fight at Westminster* (London, [18 May] 1648: TT E.443/17); Anon., *The Petition . . . of Essex* (London, [4 April] 1648: TT E.434/22); Anon., *A Declaration . . . of Surrey* (London, [18 May] 1648: TT E.443/8); Anon., *The Humble Petition of divers citizens of the city of London* (London [29 May] 1648: TT 669.f.12/38); Underdown, *Pride's Purge*, pp. 90–105.

29. Anon., *Antidote*, sig. A2r; Anon., *Great Britans Vote*, pp. 27–8; *Mercurius Aulicus*, no. 3 (17 February 1648), sig. A2v.

30. *CJ*, V, p. 427; *CSPD 1648–49*, p. 19 (19 February 1648); *Calendar of Clarendon State Papers*, I, p. 415, no. 2738; *Perfect Occurrences*, nos 53–4 (7 and 14 January 1648), pp. 369, 373, 377; no. 58 (11 February 1648), p. 410; no. 60 (25 February 1648), p. 421; and no. 61 (3 March 1648), pp. 500–1; Anon., *Great Britans Vote*, pp. 7–8, 27, 47–8; Gardiner, *Great Civil War*, IV, p. 46; Jason Peacey, *Politicians and Pamphleteers: Propaganda During the English Civil Wars and Interregnum* (Aldershot, 2004), ch. 4.

31. *Mercurius Elencticus*, nos 6–8 (5, 12 and 19 January 1648), pp. 41–2, 50–1, 53–4; no. 10 (2 February 1648), p. 76; and no. 14 (1 March 1648), p. 105; *Perfect Occurrences*, no. 63 (17 March 1648), p. 517.

32. Clarendon, *History*, IV, p. 286.

33. BL Add. MS 78194, fos 68r, 72r, 74–5 (Nicholas to Browne: 20 March, 10 April, 1 and 4 May, 1648).

34. Anon., *Antidote*, sigs A2r–v; Anon., *Great Britans Vote*, pp. 28–32.

35. Anon., *Treasons Anatomie*, pp. 4–7;

36. *Mercurius Bellicus*, no. 4 (20 February 1648), p. 2; *Mercurius Elencticus*, no. 11 (9 February 1648), p. 81; *Mercurius Aulicus*, no. 3 (17 February 1648), sigs A2v–3r.

37. *Mercurius Pragmaticus*, nos 22–23 (15 and 22 February 1648), sigs Y1v–2r, Z3r; Anon., *Treasons Anatomie*, p. 7.

38. *Mercurius Pragmaticus*, no. 23 (22 February 1648), sig. Z2v; *Mercurius Melancholicus*, no. 25 (19 February 1648), p. 145; *Mercurius Aulicus*, no. 3 (17 February 1648), sig. A3r (C3r); and cf. *Mercurius Elencticus*, no. 9 (26 January 1648), pp. 65–6. On Royalist scatology see David Underdown, *A Freeborn People: Politics and the Nation in Seventeenth-Century England* (Oxford, 1996), ch. 5.

39. [Bate], *Regall Apology*, p. 25. On Marten see too *Mercurius Elencticus*, nos 6–7, 9–10 (29 December–2 February 1647/8), pp. 46, 48, 64, 71–2; Anon., *Great Britans Vote*, p. 6.

40. Anon., *The Kingdomes Briefe Answer, to the Late Declaration* (London, [7 March] 1648: TT E.431/9), pp. 1, 18.

41. Anon., *White-hall Fayre*, tp, p. 8.

42. BL Add. MS 78194, fo. 69r (Nicholas to Browne: 6 April 1648).

43. *Mercurius Elencticus* no. 19 (5 April 1648), pp. 141, 143–5.

44. Eglisham, *Declaration*, pp. 4–5.
45. On Palmer see *HOC*, V, pp. 587–8.
46. BL Add. MS 78194, fos 73–5 (Nicholas to Browne: 17, 24 April and 1 May 1648); Theophraste Renaudot, *Recueil des Gazettes Nouvelles Ordinaires et Extraordinaires* (Paris, 1649), no. 73 (10 May 1648), pp. 625–9; Anon., *Waerachtich Bewys Vande onnooselheydt des Drancks ende Plaesters: Door middel des Hertogen van Buckingham aen den Coninck Jacobus* (1648), sigs A2r–3r. For a scribal copy see Folger MS V.a.402, fos 68v–70v.
47. [Bate], *Regall Apology*, pp. 20–5; Christopher Wirtzung, *The General Practise of Physicke* (London, 1617), p. 624.
48. [Bate], *Regall Apology*, pp. 22–5. Bate was a fellow of the College of Physicians.
49. [Edward Nicholas], *The Royall Apologie; or An Answer to the Declaration* (London, [24 April] 1648: TT E.522/21), pp. 11–12; [Edward Hyde, Earl of Clarendon], *State Papers Collected by Edward, Earl of Clarendon* (Oxford, 1773), vol. II, pp. 391–7 (compare [Nicholas], *Royall Apologie*, pp. 10–13); BL Add MS. 78194, fo. 68r (Nicholas to Browne: 20 March 1648). Thomason attributed the tract to Sir Kenelm Digby.
50. [Nicholas], *Royall Apologie*, pp. 11–13.
51. Anon., *The Declaration Declared Or an Examination of the Declaration in the name of the house of Commons the 11. of February 1647* (1648), pp. 6–8, 14.
52. Anon., *Troy-Novant Must Not Be Burnt* (London, [8 May] 1648: TT 669.f.12/21); Anon., *A Satyrical Catechisme* (London, [20 June] 1648: TT E.449/1), sig. A2r.
53. [Edward Hyde], *An Answer To a Pamphlet, Entitled, A Declaration of the Commons of England* ([London], [3 May] 1648: TT E.438/3), p. 9.
54. [Edward Hyde], *A Full Answer to An Infamous and Trayterous Pamphlet* (London, [28 July] 1648: TT E.455/5); [Edward Hyde], *Plenum Responsum ad Famosum et Proditorium Libellum* (London 1648); Clarendon, *History*, IV, p. 286 fn.1; Paul Seaward, "Hyde, Edward, First Earl of Clarendon (1609–1674)", *ODNB*.
55. [Hyde], *Full Answer*, pp. 13–14.
56. [Hyde], *Full Answer*, pp. 15–16. Hyde dates these events to the period after the early January 1642 attempt on the five members, but we have found no corroborating evidence of these factional manoeuvres or of an Eglisham republication before September.
57. [Hyde], *An Answer*, p. 9; [Hyde], *Full Answer*, pp. 13, 16–17.
58. Anon., *A True Coppy of two severall Letters Sent by Mr. Richard Osborne (late Attendant on his Majesty in Carisbrooke Castle,) touching a designe to poyson his Majesty* (London, [21 June] 1648: TT E.449/6); Anon., *Two Letters Sent by Mr. Richard Osburn . . . touching a Design to poyson or make away his Majesty . . . With an Answer to the said Letters, and a Narrative of the whole Designe* (London, [22 June] 1648: TT E.449/14).
59. Anon., *True Coppy*, p. 4.
60. At least twenty-one printed publications were produced. From late August they focused on the fall-out of the failed prosecution of Edmund Rolfe: see Anon., *The Case of Major Edmond Rolphe* (London, [28 August] 1648: TT 669 f.13/8); Anon., *The Grave and Learned Speech of Serjeant-Wilde* (London, [31 August] 1648: TT E.461/25); and Edmond Rolfe, *The humble Petition and Remonstrance of Edmond Rolph* (London, [5 September] 1648: TT 669 f.13/12).
61. The fullest version of the Royalist case is Anon., *The Independent's Loyalty. Or, The most Barbarous Plot (to Murther his sacred Majestie)* (London, [13 July] 1648: TT E.452/25). See too Anon., *A Discovery of the Intentions of the Army* (London, [11 July] 1648: TT 669 f.12/75).
62. Anon., *An Answer To a scandalous Letter Written by Hammond* (London, [12 July] 1648: TT E.452/8), p. 2; and Anon., *The Resolution, Vow, and Covenant of 4736 Persons* (London, [30 June] 1648: TT 669 f.12/62).
63. Anon., *Independent's Loyalty*, pp. 17, 22; Anon., *An Allarme To the City of London* (London, [29 August] 1648: TT E.461/19), p. 7.
64. Anon., *Independent's Loyalty*, pp. 20–1.
65. Charles I (attrib.), *The Kings Declaration* (London, [8 February] 1648: TT E.426/5); see similar images in *Mercurius Elencticus*, nos 6, 9, 10, pp. 48, 68, 72. On the reconstruction

of the royal image see Ashton, *Counter-Revolution*, pp. 205–15; and Sharpe, *Image Wars*, pp. 284, 289–90, 292–3, 302–3, 374.

66. [Bate], *Regall Apology*, pp. 25–6; Philip A. Knachel (ed.), *Eikon Basilike: The Portraiture of His Sacred Majesty in His Solitudes and Sufferings* (Ithaca, 1966), p. 171.

67. *Hamilton Letters*, p. 158; Clarendon, *History*, IV, pp. 384–5; George Villiers, 2nd Duke of Buckingham, *The Declaration of the Right Honourable The Duke of Buckingham, and the Earles of Holland, and Peterborough* (London, [8 July] 1648: TT E.451), pp. 2–3; Lewis Awdeley, *A True Relation . . . of the Great Victory of the Parliaments Forces* (London, [8 July] 1648: TT E.451/30), p. 6; John Aubrey, *The Natural History and Antiquities of the County of Surrey* (London, 1719), vol. I, pp. 46–7; Gardiner, *Great Civil War*, IV, pp. 160–1; R. Malcolm Smuts, "Rich, Henry, First Earl of Holland (bap. 1590, d. 1649)", *ODNB*; Bruce Yardley, "Villiers, George, Second Duke of Buckingham (1628–1687)", *ODNB*; Nigel Smith (ed.), *The Poems of Andrew Marvell* (Harlow, 2007), pp. 11–17.

Chapter 21

1. *Mercurius Pragmaticus*, no. 36–7 (12 December 1648), sig. CCC3–3v; *Kingdomes Weekly Intelligencer*, no. 289 (12 December 1648), p. 1,178; *Mercurius Elencticus*, no. 55 (12 December 1648), pp. 526–8; Anon., *A True and Ful Relation* (London, [13 December] 1648: TT E.476/14), pp. 3–4; Anon., *The Staffe Set at the Parliaments Owne Doore* (London, [8 December] 1648: TT E.475/29), pp. 7–8.

2. William Prynne, *The Substance of a Speech* (London, [25 January] 1649: TT E.539/11), p. 114; William Prynne, *Mr. Prynnes Demand of his Liberty* (London, 1648: TT 669.f.13/63); Edward Massey, *A Short Declaration* (London, 1648: TT E.541/7), p. 6; Anon., *The Parliament under the Power of the Sword* ([London, 1648]: TT 669.f.13/52); *Mercurius Elencticus*, no. 55 (12 December 1648), p. 527; Charles I (attrib.), *His Maiesties Declaration . . . concerning his restraint under the Power of the Sword* (London, 1648: TT E.477/28), tp.

3. "The Humble Petition of . . . Col. Inglesbyes Regiment", in *The Moderate*, no. 17 (7 November 1648), sig. R3r; Anon., *The True Informer* (London 1648: TT E.526/28), p. 16.

4. *The Moderate*, no. 8 (5 September 1648), sig. H1v; no. 10 (19 September 1648), sig. K1r; no. 12 (3 October 1648), sig. M3r; no. 14 (17 October 1648), sigs O3r–O3v; and no. 17 (7 November 1648), sig. R3r.

5. *Mercurius Militaris*, no. 2 (17 October 1648), pp. 13–14; Anon., *A New Marriage* (London 1648: TT E.526/34), p. 4.

6. Anon., *The Returne of the People of England: Tendred to the Speaker of the House of Commons; in Answer . . . to their Declaration of the 11 of February, 1647* ([15 November] 1648: TT E.472/7), pp. 10–11, 29–31.

7. Anon., *A Letter from Head-quarters* (London, 1648: TT E.470/34), pp. 6, 8; *The Humble Petition of Thousands well-affected persons inhabiting in . . . London*, in *The Moderate*, no. 9 (12 September 1648), sig. I4r.

8. Anon., *The True Copie of a Petition* (London, 1648: TT E.468/18), pp. 5–6; Anon., *A Copie of two letters, sent from divers officers of the army in the north* (London, 1648: TT 669.f.13/27).

9. Anon., *The Independent's Loyalty. Or, The most Barbarous Plot (to Murther his sacred Majestie)* (London, 1648: TT E 452[25]), p. 14; [Henry Ireton], *A Remonstrance of His Excellency Thomas Lord Fairfax* (London, [22 November] 1648: TT E.473/11); Anon., *The Articles and Charge of the Army, Exhibited in Parliament against the Kings Majesty, the Prince of Wales, and the Duke of York; Read in both Houses yesterday, Novemb. 21. 1648* (London, [22 November] 1648: TT E.473/14); [Henry Ireton], *An Abridgment Of the late Remonstrance of the Army* (London, [27 December] 1648: TT E.536/8).

10. [Ireton], *Remonstrance*, pp. 47, 52, 64 and *passim* (our emphasis). The *Remonstrance's* commitment to regicide has been questioned by Sean Kelsey, "The Death of Charles I", *HJ* 45:4 (2002), pp. 730–1; and "Politics and Procedure in the Trial of Charles I", *Law*

and History Review 22 (2004), pp. 4–5; and reaffirmed by Clive Holmes, "The Trial and Execution of Charles I", *HJ* 53:2 (2010), pp. 305–9.

11. Anon., *The Declarations and Humble Representations of the Officers and Soldiers* (London, 1648: TT E.475/24), p. 4.
12. Anon., *The Humble Petition, or Remonstrance . . . of Rutland* (London, [24 November 1648]: TT 669.f.13/47) (our emphasis).
13. "Petition of Pride's Regiment", in *The Moderate Intelligencer*, no. 195 (14 December 1648), sig. Lllllllll2.
14. *A Declaration*, no. 3 (20 October 1648), p. 20; *Mercurius Pragmaticus*, no. 38 (12–19 December 1648), sig. Ddd.
15. *Mercurius Pragmaticus*, nos 38–9 (19 and 26 December 1648), sigs Ddd, Ddd2v, Eee, Eee2; *Mercurius Elencticus*, no. 55 (12 December 1648), sig. Hhh2v.
16. *Mercurius Pragmaticus*, no. 38 (19 December 1648), sig. Ddd3; *CJ*, VI, 7, 13–14 and 19 December 1648; Anon., *A Declaration of the Commons* (London, 1649: TT E.538[23]), pp. 5, 8, 12; and *Mercurius Elencticus*, no. 57 (26 December 1648), sig. Kkk2v.
17. *CJ*, 13, 23 and 28 December 1648; *Mercurius Elencticus*, no. 31 (2 January 1649), p. 554.
18. Anon., *Heads of the Charge Against the King, Drawn up by The Generall Councell of the Armie* (London, [24 December] 1648: TT E.477/25), pp. 4–6; Anon., *Articles Exhibited against the King, and The Charge of the Army, against His Majesty* (London, [29 December] 1648: TT E.536/21), pp. 1–2; Charles I (attrib.), *His Majesties Declaration Concerning The Charge of the Army* (London, [1 January] 1649: TT E.536/25), p. 4; Anon., *A New-years Gift: Presented by Tho. Lord Fairfax, And the General-councel of Officers* (London, [1 January] 1649: TT E.536/24), p. 8.
19. Anon., *The Resolution Of His Excellency the Lord General Fairfax . . . Also, The dangerous Articles of Impeachment against the King; and the Charge of the Army* (London, [14 December] 1648: TT E.476/19), pp. 1–3; Holmes, "Trial and Execution", p. 313 and n.133.
20. Anon., *The People Informed of their Oppressors and Oppressions* (London, [28 December?] 1648: TT E.536/17), esp. pp. 3–6.
21. Anon., *The Charge of the Army, and Counsel of War Against the King. With a brief Answer thereunto by some of the Loyall Party* ([29 December] 1648: TT E.536/20), p. 3. Kelsey, "Politics and Procedure", pp. 9–10, discusses the tract but not its Royalist agenda.
22. Patricia Crawford, "'Charles Stuart, That Man of Blood'", *JBS* 16:2 (1977), pp. 41–61.
23. Anon., *Charge of the Army*, pp. 5–7.
24. *The manner of the Deposition of Charles Stewart, King of England, by the Parliament, and Generall Councell of the Armie* ([4 January] 1649: TT E.537/4), pp. 1–2.
25. Eleutherius Philodemius, *The Armies Vindication* (London, [11 January] 1648: TT E.538/3), pp. 20–1.
26. *Mercurius Elencticus*, no. 59 (9 January 1649), sigs Mmmv, Mmm2v; *Mercurius Pragmaticus*, nos 40–41 (26 December 1648–9 January 1649), sig. Fff3v; *Perfect Occurrences*, no. 106 (12 January 1649), p. 791; *LJ*, 2 January 1649; *CJ*, VI, 3–4 January 1649.
27. "The Charge Against the King", in S. R. Gardiner (ed.), *The Constitutional Documents of the Puritan Revolution, 1625–1660* (Oxford, 1906), pp. 371–4.
28. *Perfect Occurrences*, no. 107 (19 January 1649), pp. 801, 803; *Kingdomes Weekly Intelligencer*, no. 295 (23 January 1649), pp. 1,226–7; Anon., *An Exact and most Impartial Accompt Of the Indictment, Arraignment, Trial, and Judgment . . . of nine and twenty Regicides* (London, 1660), p. 119.
29. *Exact and most Impartial Accompt*, pp. 44, 54v. Harrison later insisted that "I abhorred the doing of any thing touching the Blackning of the King".
30. For a stimulating debate on these issues see Kelsey, "Death of Charles I" and "Politics and Procedure", and Holmes, "Trial and Execution".
31. John Cook, *King Charls his Case: Or, An Appeal To all Rational Men, Concerning His Tryal At the High Court of Justice* (London, [9 February] 1649: TT E.542/3), tp; Jason Peacey, "Reporting a Revolution: A Failed Propaganda Campaign", in Peacey (ed.), *The Regicides and the Execution of Charles I* (Basingstoke and New York, 2001).

Geoffrey Robertson, *The Tyrannicide Brief: The Story of the Man Who Sent Charles I to the Scaffold* (New York, 2005), pp. 190–4, 206–7, gives a revealingly bifurcated account of Cook's pamphlet, praising the forward-thinking legal arguments, but dismissing the interpolated "inflammatory material" on James's death and other matters as a "weakness".

32. Cook, *King Charls*, pp. 6, 8, 10–11; "The Charge against the King", pp. 371–2.

33. Cook, *King Charls*, pp. 11–12.

34. Cook, *King Charls*, pp. 12–13.

35. Cook, *King Charls*, pp. 39–40.

36. [William Lilly?], *The Prophecy of the White King Explained* (London, [26 January] 1648/9: TT E.540/4), pp. 1–6.

37. *The Kingdomes Weekly Intelligencer*, no. 297 (6 February 1649), p. 1,244; cf. *The Moderate Intelligencer*, no. 203 (8 February 1648), sig. Ttttttttv.

38. Anon, *A Perfect Cure for Atheists, Papists, Arminians and all other Rebels and Traytors* ([19 June] 1649: TT 669.f.14/44).

39. House of Commons, *A Declaration of the Parliament of England, Expressing the Grounds of their late Proceedings, And of Setling the present Government In the way of A Free State* (London, 22 March 1649: TT E.613/2), pp. 6–9, 13, 15. For a Royalist critique, see Anon., *Traytors Deciphered in an Answeare to a Shamelesse Pamphlet* (London [31 May 1650]: TT E.777/7), p. 10.

40. Anon, *The Charge Against the King discharged: or, The King cleared by the people of England, from the severall Accusations in the Charge, delivered in against him at Westminster-Hall Saturday last, Jan. 20. by that high Court of Justice erected by the Army-Parliament* ([13 February] 1649: TT E.542/10), tp, pp. 10–11.

41. [James Howell], *An Inquisition After Blood* ([17 July] 1649: TT E.531/23), pp. 11–12 (reprinted in *Some of Mr Howel's Minor Works, Reflecting upon the Times Upon Emergent Occasions* (1654)); Daniel Woolf, "Conscience, Constancy, and Ambition in the Career and Writings of James Howell", in John Morrill, Paul Slack and Daniel Woolf (eds), *Public Duty and Private Conscience in Seventeenth-Century England: Essays Presented to G. E. Aylmer* (Oxford, 1993).

42. Samuel Butler, *The Plagiary Exposed: Or An Old Answer to a Newly revived Calumny Against the Memory of King Charles I* (London, 1691), pp. 13–18. Butler's eighteenth-century editor had seen a manuscript of the tract in Butler's hand and accepted it as a genuine work from the era of the regicide: see Robert Thyer (ed.), *The Genuine Remains of Samuel Butler*, 2 vols (London, 1822), vol. I, p. 333; Hugh de Quehen, "Butler, Samuel (bap. 1613, d. 1680)", *ODNB*.

43. Anon., *The Royall Legacies of Charles the First* (London [29 May] 1649: TT E.557/1), p. 43.

44. Anon., *Eikon Alethine* (London, [16 August] 1649: TT E.569/16), pp. 37, 47. A jumbled aside compares the denial of justice in 1626 to other occasions including perhaps the Overbury affair.

45. Anon., *Eikon e Piste* (London, [11 September] 1649: TT E.573/11), pp. 32, 40.

46. John Milton, *Eikonoklastes* (London, [6 October] 1649: TT E.578/5), pp. 1–2; Philip A. Knachel (ed.), *Eikon Basilike* (Ithaca, 1966), p. 3.

47. Anon., *A Serious and Faithfull Representation* (London, 1648), pp. 2–3, 7, 9, 12; John Price, *Clerico-Classicum* (London, [19 February] 1649: TT E.544/1), pp. 9, 11, 31; Anon., *A Parallel between the Ministerial Integrity of the Forty Seven London Ministers* (London, [26 February] 1649: TT E.545/8), p. 7; Jordan Downs, "The Curse of Meroz and the English Civil War", *HJ* 57:2 (2014).

48. [Christopher Love], *A Modest and Clear Vindication* (London, 1649: TT E.549/10), pp. 15–16, 43–4.

49. *The Several Speeches of the Duke of Hamilton*, printed in *King Charls His Trial* (London, 1649), pp. 89–90, 92; *Digitus Dei . . . The Life and Death of the late James Duke of Hamilton* (London, 1649: TT E.550/6), p. 27; and Hilary L. Rubenstein, *Captain Luckless* (Totowa, 1976), pp. 21–3, 60–1 and 231–7.

Part 6 Prologue

1. Ruth Spalding (ed.), *The Diary of Bulstrode Whitelocke, 1605–1675* (Oxford, 1990), pp. 312, 325, 337; Henry Reeve (ed.), *A Journal of The Swedish Embassy in the Years 1653 and 1654 Impartially Written by the Ambassador Bulstrode Whitelocke*, 2 vols (London, 1855); Ruth Spalding, "Whitelocke, Bulstrode (1605–1675)", *ODNB*; Blair Worden, "Review Article: "The 'Diary' of Bulstrode Whitelocke", *EHR* 108:426 (1993); Geoff Baldwin, "Ascham, Anthony (bap. 1614, d. 1650)", *ODNB*; Margo Todd, "Dorislaus, Isaac (1595–1649)", *ODNB*.
2. Whitelocke, *Diary*, pp. 316–20; Reeve, *Journal*, I, pp. 247–69.
3. Reeve, *Journal*, I, pp. 272–3; Whitelocke, *Diary*, pp. 53–4, 320.
4. Spalding, "Whitelocke, Bulstrode"; Veronica Buckley, *Christina Queen of Sweden: The Restless Life of a European Eccentric* (New York, 2004), e-book, p. 77.
5. On post-revolutionary legitimation see Sean Kelsey, *Inventing a Republic: The Political Culture of the English Commonwealth, 1649–53* (Stanford, 1997); Sharpe, *Image Wars*; Jason Peacey, *Politicians and Pamphleteers: Propaganda During the English Civil Wars and Interregnum* (Aldershot, 2004); Quentin Skinner, "Conquest and Consent: Thomas Hobbes and the Engagement Controversy", in G. E. Aylmer (ed.), *The Interregnum: The Quest for Settlement* (London, 1972); Quentin Skinner, *Hobbes and Republican Liberty* (Cambridge, 2008); Blair Worden, *Literature and Politics in Cromwellian England* (Oxford, 2007); and Blair Worden, "Providence and Politics in Cromwellian England", *P&P* 109 (1985), pp. 55–99.

Chapter 22

1. Anon., *Truth Brought to light and discovered by Time or A discourse and Historicall Narration of the first XIII yeares of King Iames Reigne* (London, 1651), sig. A1v. See too Anon., *A True and Historical Relation Of the Poysoning of Sir Thomas Overbury* (London, 1651); Anon., *Cabala: Sive Scrinia Sacra* (London, 1654); and Bellany, *Politics*, pp. 262–6.
2. Anon., *Somnium Cantabrigiense, Or A Poem Upon the death of the late King brought to London* (London, [20 March] 1650: TT E.596/5), pp. 1, 6–11; John Quarles, *Regale Lectum Miseriae: Or A Kingly Bed of Miserie* (np, 1649), p. 42; Philemon Holland, trans., *The Romane Historie Written by T. Livius of Padua* (London, 1600), p. 34.
3. Anon., *Somnium*, p. 1.
4. *Mercurius Pragmaticus*, no. 53 (1 May 1649), sig. Rrr; *Mercurius Politicus*, no. 1 (13 June 1650), pp. 1–2, 7, 13, 16.
5. Austin Woolrych, *Britain in Revolution, 1625–1660* (Oxford, 2002), pp. 480ff.
6. Anon., *A Declaration by the Kings Majesty* (London [27 June] 1650: TT E.1030/8), pp. 1–2; Anon., *The Answer of the Parliament* (London [20 September] 1650: TT E.613/2), p. 12.
7. *Mercurius Politicus*, nos 11–12 (22 and 29 August 1650), pp. 162, 180.
8. *Mercurius Politicus*, no. 14 (12 September 1650), pp. 209–11. This indictment of the royal family also appeared verbatim in A.B., *Mutatus Polemo* (London, [2 September] 1650: TT E.612/2), p. 30, note A.
9. [Henry Parker], *The True Portraiture of the Kings of England* (London, [7 August] 1650: TT E.609/2). Parker signed the preface but claimed the author "is unknown to me" (A4v). Michael Mendle makes the case for Parker's authorship in *Henry Parker and the English Civil War: The Political Thought of the Public's "Privado"* (Cambridge, 1995), pp. 166–8.
10. [Parker], *True Portraiture*, sigs A2r–v, pp. 4–5, 12, 15–16, 37–42.
11. Anthony Weldon, *The Court and Character of King James* (London, 1650); Bellany, *Politics*, p. 266. For the Wright-Ibbitson 1650 editions, see ESTC R209127; R204065; R186354 may well prove a ghost. For the Ibbitson-Collins 1651 editions, see T301136, R229346 and R34738.
12. John Morrill and Philip Baker, "The case of the armie truly re-stated", in Michael Mendle (ed.), *The Putney Debates of 1647: The Army, The Levellers, and the English State*

(Cambridge, 2001), p. 110; Henry R. Plomer, *A Dictionary of the Booksellers and Printers Who Were at Work in England, Scotland and Ireland From 1641 to 1667* (London, 1907), pp. 105–6; Zachary Lesser, *Renaissance Drama and the Politics of Publication: Readings in the English Book Trade* (Cambridge, 2004), pp. 33–4; D. F. McKenzie and Maureen Bell, *A Chronology and Calendar of Documents Relating to the London Book Trade, 1641–1670* (Oxford, 2005), vol. I, pp. 265, 277; Jason Peacey, *Politicians and Pamphleteers: Propaganda During the English Civil Wars and Interregnum* (Aldershot, 2004), p. 297 n.123. Ibbitson's regicide publications include *Collections of notes taken at the Kings tryall* (with Henry Walker) and *The kings last farewell to the world* (London, 1649: TT 669.f.13/77). For his collaborations with Peter Stent, see Alexander Globe, *Peter Stent, London Printseller* (Vancouver, 1985), p. 34.

13. Weldon, *Court and Character* (1650 ed.), sigs A2r–3r; Plomer, *Dictionary*, pp. 197–8.
14. Weldon, *Court and Character* (1651 ed.), preface.
15. Weldon, *Court and Character* (1651 ed.), pp. 48–9, 94, 172–3.
16. Weldon, *Court and Character* (1651 ed.), pp. 7, 82–4, 114, 119, 124, 127; Bellany, *Politics*, pp. 266–9.
17. Weldon, *Court and Character* (1651 ed.), pp. 138–41, 144–9.
18. Weldon, *Court and Character* (1651 ed.), pp. 160–3.
19. Anon., *The None-such Charles His Character* (London, [6 January] 1651: TT E.1345/2), pp. 1–2, 13, 21, 193. The two books were paired in later Royalist critiques, see e.g. Anon., *The Court and Kitchin of Elizabeth, Commonly called Joan Cromwel* (London, 1664), sig. A6r.
20. Anon., *None-such*, pp. 12, 42–3, 111–14, 127, 135ff., 154.
21. See George P. Warner (ed.), *The Nicholas Papers* (Camden Society NS 40: London, 1886), vol. I, p. 310 (Nicholas to Hyde, 10 October 1652); and BL Add. MS 4181, which contains a number of stories later presented in a radically distorted ideological form in the *None-such*. On Gerbier and Ibbitson, see Jason Peacey, "Print, Publicity, and Popularity: The Projecting of Sir Balthazar Gerbier, 1642–1662", *JBS* 51:2 (2012), esp. pp. 297–303; Jeremy Wood, "Gerbier, Sir Balthazar (1592–1663/67)", *ODNB*. Ibbitson printed Gerbier's *The Art of Speaking Well* (London 1650) and several other tracts.
22. Anon., *None-such*, pp. 85, 128ff, 168, 170–1, 183.
23. Anon., *None-such*, pp. 13–17, 20–34.
24. Anon., *None-such*, pp. 3, 33–4, 99–100.
25. Weldon, *Court and Character* (1651 ed.), pp. 177–81; Anon., *None-such*, p. 133. The promised additional volume may be related to the history of Charles's reign abortively serialized in an Ibbitson newsbook: see *Severall Proceedings in Parliament*, nos 143–5 (June–July 1652).
26. Anon., *The True Manner of the Crowning of Charles the Second King of Scotland, on the First day of January, 1650* (London, 1651). Ibbitson would publish another broadside noting James's murder in 1652; see Anon., *A List of the Princes, Dukes, Earls, Lords . . . of the Scots Party Slaine* (London: [October] 1652: TT 669.f16/29).
27. John Milton, *Pro Populo Anglicano Defensio*, in Martin Dzelzainis (ed.), *John Milton: Political Writings* (Cambridge, 1991), pp. 103–4, 137, 176. The tally of editions is available on ESTC.
28. John Hall, *The Grounds and Reasons of Monarchy Considered in a Review of the Scotch Story* (Edinburgh, 1651), pp. 14–15, 42–8.
29. *Mercurius Politicus*, nos 49–50 (15 and 22 May 1651), pp. 784, 797, 799–801.
30. *Mercurius Politicus*, nos 51, 53 (29 May and 12 June 1651), pp. 815–16, 831–2.
31. William Lilly, *Monarchy or No Monarchy* (London, [6 August] 1651: TT E.638/17), pp. 74, 81, 84–5, 118–19; and Patrick Curry, "Lilly, William (1602–1681)", *ODNB*.
32. Anon., *The Life and Reigne of King Charls; or the Pseudo-Martyr Discovered* (London, [29 January 1652] 1651: TT E.1338/2), sigs A8, *A3, *A5; *Mercurius Politicus*, no. 67 (18 September 1651), p. 1,076. The three editions are ESTC R179718, R483057 and R12978.
33. Anon., *Life and Reigne*, pp. 11–13.
34. John Philipps, *Joannis Philippi Angli Responsio* (London, [24 December] 1652: TT E.1385/1), translated in Don M. Wolfe (ed.), *Complete Prose Works of John Milton* (New Haven 1966), vol. IV, pp. 945–6.

35. John Nickolls (ed.), *Original Letters and Papers ... Addressed to Oliver Cromwell* (London 1743), p. 50 (Bishop to Cromwell: 14 January [1651]).

36. Arthur Wilson's "Autobiography", in Francis Peck (ed.), *Desiderata Curiosa*, 2 vols (London, 1779), vol. II, pp. 460–83, quotations at pp. 470, 472; Anthony A. Wood, *Athenae Oxoniensis*, ed. Philip Bliss (London, 1817), vol. III, pp. 318–23.

37. Arthur Wilson, *The History of Great Britain, Being the Life and Reign of King Iames the First* (London, 1653), proeme, "The Authors Picture", p. 291; "Autobiography", p. 470.

38. Wilson, *History*, pp. 172–3, 184, 275.

39. Wilson, *History*, pp. 289–90.

40. Wilson, *History*, pp. 257–8, 284–5.

41. Wilson, *History*, pp. 285–8; but cf. "Autobiography", pp. 476–7, on witchcraft.

42. Wilson, *History*, pp. 272, 287.

43. [Marchamont Nedham?], *A Cat May Look Upon a King* (London, [10 January] 1652/3?: TT E.1408/2). Thomason usually corrected dates to conform to the old-style new year, which would suggest that he got his copy on January 10, 1652/3. However, *Severall Proceedings in Parliament*, no. 143 (17 June 1652), supplemental insert p. 4, refers to "a booke called *A Cat may looke at a King*", which suggests either that Thomason's copy was bought in January 1652 (and he did not correct the date on the title page to "1651"), or that there may have been a now-lost edition of the book available by the summer of 1652, or simply that Thomason bought his copy months after its first appearance. On its authorship, see Blair Worden, "'Wit in a Roundhead': The Dilemma of Marchamont Nedham", in Susan Amussen and Mark Kishlansky (eds), *Political Culture and Cultural Politics in Early Modern England* (Manchester, 1995), p. 331 n.73.

44. [Nedham?], *Cat*, pp. 15, 20, 26, 28, 33–4; cf. [Parker], *True Portraiture*, pp. 16–37; Christopher Hill, "The Norman Yoke", in *Puritanism and Revolution* (London, 1958), pp. 28–9.

45. [Nedham?], *Cat*, pp. 78–80.

46. [Nedham?], *Cat*, pp. 2, 37–8, 40, 54–9, 86–91, 97, 105.

47. Edward Peyton, *The Divine Catastrophe of The Kingly Family of the House of Stuarts, or A Short History of the Rise, Reign, and Ruine Thereof* (London, [24 April] 1652: TT E.1291/1), p. 57; *A Discourse concerning ... Bread and Wine* (London, 1642: TT E.136/10), pp. 6–7; Peyton, *The High-Way to Peace* (London, 1647: TT E.411/12); *PP1626*, III, p. 68; Andrew Thrush, "Sir Edward Peyton", *HOC*, V, pp. 665–71.

48. BL Harl. MS 3364, fos 20r, 29r–v, 30v, 32v.

49. Peyton, *Divine Catastrophe*, sigs A3v–A4r, p. 12.

50. Peyton, *Divine Catastrophe*, pp. 14–17, 21–2, 27–8, 30–1.

51. Peyton, *Divine Catastrophe*, pp. 28–9, 31, 33–4, 36, 46.

52. Peyton, *Divine Catastrophe*, pp. 31, 42–3, 47, 56, 69–70, 128.

53. Peyton, *Divine Catastrophe*, pp. 2–3, 6–7, 59.

54. Peyton, *Divine Catastrophe*, pp. 37–41; *PP1626*, III, p. 68.

55. Peyton, *Divine Catastrophe*, pp. 37–41.

56. Peyton, *Divine Catastrophe*, pp. 27–8.

57. Peyton, *Divine Catastrophe*, pp. 7, 53, 79–81, 86, 90–1, 121–5. On wheels and "revolution", see Christopher Hill, "The Word 'Revolution'", in *A Nation of Change and Novelty: Radical Politics, Religion and Literature in Seventeenth-Century England* (London, 1990).

58. Thomason's copy of *Life and Reigne*, TT E.1338/2; George F. Warner (ed.), *The Nicholas Papers* (Camden Society NS 50: London, 1892), vol. II, p. 55 (Nicholas to Hyde: January 1654); Joad Raymond, *The Invention of the Newspaper: English Newsbooks, 1641–1649* (Oxford, 1996), pp. 69–79.

59. [Joseph Jane], *The Image Unbroaken* ([London?], 1651), pp. 60–1; Anon., *Reliquiae Sacrae Carolinae* (The Hague, 1651), p. 271.

60. [William Sanderson], *Aulicus Coquinariae: Or A Vindication in answer to a pamphlet, Entitled the Court and Character of King James* (London, [18 March] 1651: TT E.1356/2).

61. [Sanderson], *Aulicus Coquinariae*, pp. 192–5.

62. Anon., *Life and Reigne*, sigs *A4v, *A7v.

63. Balthazar Gerbier, *Les Effects Pernicieux de Meschants Favoris et Grands Ministres d'Estat Es Provinces Belgiques, en Lorraine, Germanie, France, Italie, Espagne, & Angleterre. Et Des-Abuzé d'Erreurs Populaires Sur le Subject de Iacques & Charles Stuart, Roys de la Grande Bretagne* (The Hague, 1653).

64. "The Relation", BL Add. MS 4181, fos 3r, 4r–5r, 46r–48r.

65. *Les Effects*, esp. sigs D2r–5r; BL Add. MS 4181, fo 47r; Peacey, "Print, Publicity", pp. 288–90.

66. Blair Worden, *Literature and Politics in Cromwellian England* (Oxford, 2007), pp. 54–81; Joad Raymond, "Hall, John (bap. 1627–d. 1656)", *ODNB*.

67. William Sanderson, *A Compleat History of the lives and reigns of Mary Queen of Scotland, and of her son . . . James* (London, 1656), pt II, proeme.

Chapter 23

1. James Parry, *Two Horrid Murthers* (London, 1661), pp. 2–3, 8–11; Roland Mousnier, *The Assassination of Henry IV*, trans. Joan Spencer (New York, 1973); Michel Foucault, *Discipline and Punish: The Birth of the Prison*, trans. Alan Sheridan (London, 1977), part 1.

2. R. P. [Richard Perrinchef], *Nuntius a Mortuis* (London and Paris, 1657), and *Nuntius e Mortuis; or a Messenger from the Dead* (Paris, 1657); Anon., *A Messenger from the Dead* (London, 1657: TT E.936/4), pp. 5–8, 10 and 18–19.

3. J. T. Rutt (ed.), *The Diary of Thomas Burton* (London, 1828), vol. II, p. 382; C. H. Firth and Sean Kelsey, "Scott, Thomas (d. 1660)", *ODNB*.

4. James Howell, "To the Author", in William Sanderson, *A Compleat History of the Life and Raigne of King Charles* (London, 1658), sig. A2r

5. Fuller, *Church*, "To the Reader"; Goodman, *Court*, I, p. 4; *Scrinia*, I, pp. 8, 224–6.

6. Goodman, *Court*, I, pp. 396, 399, 409–11; Geoffrey Soden, *Godfrey Goodman* (London, 1953), pp. 417–18.

7. *Scrinia*, I, pp. 222–3; Brian Quintrell, "Hacket, John (1592–1670)", *ODNB*.

8. Fuller, *Church*, "To the Reader", and part 10, p. 113; W. B. Patterson, "Fuller, Thomas (1607/8–1661)", *ODNB*.

9. William Prynne, *The First and Second Part of A Seasonable, Legal, and Historical Vindication*, 2nd ed. (London, 1655), sigs D2r–v; William Lamont, *Marginal Prynne, 1600–1669* (London and Toronto, 1963), pp. 138ff.

10. [William Sanderson], *Aulicus Coquinariae* (London, 1650: TT E.1356/2), p. 205.

11. James Howell, "To the Author", in Sanderson, *Compleat History . . . King Charles*, sigs A2r–v; William Sanderson, *A compleat history of the lives and reigns of, Mary Queen of Scotland, and of her son and successor, James* (London, 1656), tp, and Proeme to part 2; [Hamon L'Estrange], *The Reign of King Charles* (London, 1655).

12. Sanderson, *Compleat History . . . James*, pp. 255–8, 560, 562–3, 590–1.

13. Sanderson, *Compleat History . . . James*, pp. 591–2; Anthony Weldon, *The Court and Character of King James* (London, 1650), p. 174.

14. Sanderson, *Compleat History . . . James*, pp. 592–3.

15. Sanderson, *Compleat History . . . James*, p. 593.

16. Sanderson, *Compleat History . . . James*, p. 593.

17. Sanderson, *Compleat History . . . King Charles*, pp. 35, 1,038–9.

18. See e.g. Sanderson's debates with Carew Ralegh and Peter Heylin: [Carew Ralegh], *Observations upon . . . A Compleat History* (London, 1656); William Sanderson, *An Answer to a Scurrilous Pamphlet* (London, 1656), p. 21; Peter Heylin, *Respondet Petrus* (London, 1658); William Sanderson, *Peter Pursued, or Dr. Heylin Overtaken* (London, 1658).

19. Lambert van den Bos, *Florus Anglicus* (London, 1656), p. 228; Richard Baker, *A Chronicle of the Kings of England*, 2nd ed. (London, 1653), p. 616.

20. John Gadbury, *The Nativity of the late King Charls* (London, 1658), p. 23.

21. Richard Brathwait, *An Excellent Piece of Concepted Poesy* (London 1658), pp. 239–40.

22. [Richard Brathwait], *Panthalia: Or the Royal Romance* (London, 1659), pp. 76–7, 92–3, 96–7.

23. E. S. De Beers (ed.), *The Diary of John Evelyn* (Oxford, 1959), pp. 394–5; Anon., *A Conference Held between the Old Lord Protector and . . . Hugh Peters* (London, [19 March] 1660: TT E.1017/24), p. 3.

24. Anon., *The Court & Kitchin of Elizabeth, Commonly called Joan Cromwell* (London, 1664), sigs A6r–v; Anon., *An Eye-Salve for the English Armie* (London, 1660), pp. 2, 5; [Roger L'Estrange], *Physician Cure Thy Self* (London, [27 April] 1660: TT E.1021/15), p. 1; Anon., *Plain English to . . . General Monck* (London, 1660), pp. 2–4.

25. [Roger L'Estrange?], *Treason Arraigned in Answer to Plain English* (London, [3 April] 1660: TT E.1019/14), pp. 18–20.

26. Anon., *A Third Conference between O. Cromwell and Hugh Peters* (London, [17 May] 1660: TT E.1025/3), pp. 2–4, 9, 13.

27. *Rushworth*, "Epistle Dedicatory", pp. 159, 164, 639; Joad Raymond, "Rushworth, John (c. 1612–1690)", *ODNB*.

28. 2 Kings, 2:8, 11–12, and Malachi 4:5 (King James translation); W. S., *A Compleat Collection of the Lives . . . of Those Persons Lately Executed* (London, 1661), p. 142.

29. Anon., *The Game Is Up* (London [15 November] 1659: TT E.1005/12), p. 8.

30. Anon., *The Arraignment of the Anabaptists good old cause* (London, [22 March] 1660: TT E.1017/32), p. 15.

31. W. S., *Compleat Collection*, pp. 26, 157; Edmund Ludlow, *A Voyce from the Watch Tower*, ed. A. B. Worden, (Camden Society 4th Series 21: London, 1978), pp. 150, 154; Anon., *Certain News of Lambert's Being Taken* (London [23 April] 1660: TT E.138/13); C. H., *A True Narrative . . . of the Apprehension of . . . Thomas Scot* (London, [4 October] 1660: TT E.1046/1); Anon., *Englands Object* (London 1660).

32. W. S., *Compleat Collection*, pp. 131, 143; Ludlow, *Voyce*, pp. 212, 221–2, 244.

33. W. S., *Compleat Collection*, pp. 15, 54; Ludlow, *Voyce*, pp. 214, 240; and Ian Gentles, "Harrison, Thomas (1616–1660)", *ODNB*.

34. W. S., *Compleat Collection*, pp. 31, 64, 142 and 167.

35. R. C. Latham and W. Matthews (eds), *The Diary of Samuel Pepys* (London, 1971, 1995), vol. I, pp. 265, 268 (13 and 18 October 1660); *Mercurius Publicus*, no. 42 (11–18 October 1660), pp. 660, 671; De Beers, *Diary of John Evelyn* (17 October 1660), p. 412.

36. "A Bonfire Caroll", in Anon., *A Private Conference between Mr. L. Robinson and Mr. T. Scott* (London, 1660), pp. 10–12.

37. Anon., *Private Conference*, p. 2.

38. James Raine (ed.), *Depositions from the Castle of York Relating to Offences Committed in The Northern Counties in the Seventeenth Century* (Surtees Society 40: Durham, 1861), pp. 83–4, 88, 94.

39. Raine (ed.), *Depositions*, p. 84.

40. NA SP 29/86/36–7 (examinations of William Vigures, Jane Vigures and James Allen: 18 December 1663).

41. NA SP 29/86/34 (Trelawney to Williamson: 20 December 1661).

Epilogue

1. Edward Hyde, Earl of Clarendon, *The History of the Rebellion and Civil Wars in England* (Oxford, 1702), vol. I; Blair Worden, *Roundhead Reputations: The English Civil Wars and the Passions of Posterity* (London and New York, 2001), p. 39 and chs 1–6, *passim*; Paul Seaward, "Hyde, Edward, First Earl of Clarendon (1609–1674)", *ODNB*.

2. We use the modern edition, Clarendon, *History*, I, pp. 4–54. The last forty-four pages of this section were originally part of the *Life* drafted in the late 1660s, see p. 10 n.1.

3. Clarendon, *History*, I, pp. 42, 51.

4. Clarendon, *History*, I, pp. 8–10, 29–30.

5. Lucy Hutchinson, *Memoirs of the Life of Colonel Hutchinson* (London and New York, 1908), pp. 67–9; David Norbrook, "Hutchinson [née Apsley], Lucy (1620–1681)", *ODNB*.

6. R. C. Latham and W. Matthews (eds), *The Diary of Samuel Pepys* (London, 1971, 1995), vol. IV, p. 417 (13 December 1663), and vol. VI, pp. 10, 33 (15 January and 10 February 1665).

7. Pepys, *Diary*, III, p. 93 (26 May 1662), V, pp. 172–3 (6 June 1664).

8. Alan Marshall, "Oates, Titus (1649–1705)", *ODNB*; J. P. Kenyon, *The Popish Plot* (London, 1972).

9. Anon., *The Grand Designs of the Papists, In the Reign of our late Sovereign Charles the I. And now carried on against His Present Majesty* (London, 1678) [imprimatur 2 November 1678], p. 21; Anon., *A True Relation of the Popish-Plot Against King Charles I. And The Protestant Religion* (London, 1679); Henry Care, *The History of the Damnable Popish Plot In its various Branches & Progress* (London, 1680), p. 61.

10. Titus Oates, *A True Narrative of the Horrid Plot and Conspiracy of the Popish Party Against the Life of His Sacred Majestie, the Government, and the Protestant Religion* (Dublin, 1679), sig. A2v.

11. Roger L'Estrange, *A Brief History of the Times, &c. Shewing the Pretended Popish Plot to have been quite another Thing then it has been taken for*, Part II (London, 1688), pp. 57, 59, 60–71, 73, 75ff.

12. Worden, *Roundhead Reputations*, pp. 33–6.

13. Anon., *A Letter from Major General Ludlow To Sir E.S. Comparing the Tyranny of the first four Years of King Charles the Martyr, with the Tyranny of the the [sic] four Years Reign of the Late Abdicated King* (Amsterdam, 1691).

14. Worden, *Roundhead Reputations*, p. 32.

15. Anon., *A Letter*, pp. 21, 24, 27.

16. Anon., *A Letter*, pp. 5, 22–3.

17. [Edmund Elys], *An Earnest Call To the People of England, To Beware of the Temptations of the Regicide Ludlow* (1692), pp. 2–3. Elys's second response did not discuss James's murder: see *The Letter Torn in Pieces: Or, A Full Confutation of Ludlow's Suggestions, That King Charles I was An Enemy to the State* (London, 1692).

18. Richard Hollingworth, *A Defence of King Charles I. Occasion'd by the Lyes & Scandals of Many Bad Men of this Age* (London, 1692); *A Second Defence of King Charles I. By Way of Reply to an Infamous Libel, Called Ludlow's Letter to Dr. Hollingworth* (London, 1692); and *The Character of King Charles I* (London, 1692). The "Ludlow" responses include Anon., *A Letter from General Ludlow to Dr. Hollingworth* (Amsterdam, 1692); and [Slingsby Bethel?], *Ludlow no Lyar, Or a Detection of Dr. Hollingworth's Disingenuity in his Second Defence of King Charles I* (Amsterdam, 1692).

19. [Bethel?], *Ludlow no Lyar*, pp. 61–2. See too Anon., *A Letter from General Ludlow to Dr. Hollingworth*, p. 6.

20. Walter Scott (ed.), *Secret History of the Court of James I*, 2 vols (Edinburgh, 1811).

21. Henry Parker, ed., *The True Portraiture of the Kings of England* (London, 1688), pp. 38, 40–8. Anthony Weldon, *The Court and Character of K. James. Written and taken by Sir A.W. being an Eye, and Ear Witness* (London, 1689); [Marchamont Nedham?], *A Cat May Look Upon a King* (Amsterdam, 1714), pp. 50, 54.

22. Worden, *Roundhead Reputations*, p. 192.

23. Anon., *The Secret History of K. James I and K. Charls I. Compleating the Reigns of the Four last Monarchs* (London, 1690), pp. 90–3, reprinted in 1691's *Secret History of the Four Last Monarchs*.

24. For a more complex recent account see Rebecca Bullard, *The Politics of Disclosure, 1674–1725: Secret History Narratives* (London, 2009), ch. 2.

25. Roger Coke, *A Detection of the Court and State of England During the Four Last Reigns*, 3rd ed. (London, 1697), vol. I, pp. 3–5, 147; John Callow, "Coke, Roger (c. 1628–1704x7)", *ODNB*.

26. David Jones, *The Tragical History of the Stuarts. From The First Rise of that Family, in the Year 1086, down to the Death of Her Late Majesty Queen MARY* (London, 1697), pp. 316–24. See too the account, stitched together with bits from Weldon and Wilson, in [John Somers], *The True Secret History of the Lives and Reigns Of All The Kings and Queens of England* (London, 1702), pp. 387–8.

27. White Kennett et al., *A complete history of England: with the lives of all the kings and queens thereof* (London, 1706), vol. II. Sentences from Wilson's account of the death of James I were also appropriated by a satirical pamphlet, published early in April 1689, reporting the supposed death of James II: see Anon., *A Full and True Relation of the Death of K. James. Who Departed this Life, the 27th of March* (London, 1689), p. 3.

28. Hugh Trevor-Roper, "Our First Whig Historian: Paul de Rapin-Thoyras", in *From Counter-Reformation to Glorious Revolution* (Chicago, 1992), p. 261.

29. Paul de Rapin-Thoyras, *The History of England As Well Ecclesiastical as Civil. By Mr De Rapin Thoyras*, 15 vols (London, 1729), vol. IX, pp. 606–7. The note, added by N. Tindal, cited material from Wilson and from Gilbert Burnet.

30. Laurence Echard, *The History of England. From the First Entrance of Julius Caesar and the Romans, To the End of the Reign of King James the First* (London, 1707), p. 978.

31. David Hume, *The History of England, From The Invasion of Julius Caesar to The Revolution in 1688*, 8 vols (London, 1767; new edition), vol. VI, pp. 96, 152–3. Note too Hume's absolute scepticism (based on the autopsy reports) about claims that Prince Henry was "carried off by poison" (p. 2).

32. [Oliver Goldsmith], *A History of England, In a Series of Letters from a Nobleman to his Son*, 2 vols (London, 1772), vol. II, p. 6. One of Goldsmith's readers, the young Jane Austen, alas had nothing to say on the subject of James I's death in her own *History of England* (1791).

33. Osmund Airy (ed.), *Burnet's History of My Own Time*, 2 vols (Oxford, 1897), vol. I, pp. 12–16, 19, 22–4; Gilbert Burnet, *Bishop Burnet's History of His Own Time. Vol. 1. From the Restoration of King Charles II To the Settlement of King William and Queen Mary at the Revolution: To which is prefix'd A Summary Recapitulation of Affairs in Church and State from King James I to the Restoration in the Year 1660* (London, 1724), pp. 16–17.

34. Kennett et al., *A complete history of England*, I, Preface, and II, pp. 790–1.

35. W. S. Lewis et al. (eds), *The Yale Edition of Horace Walpole's Correspondence* (New Haven, 1937 and 1948), vol. I, pp. 61–2, and vol. XIV, p. 133; Paget Toynbee et al. (eds), *Correspondence of Thomas Gray* (Oxford, 1971), vol. II, p. 834.

36. Francis Cogan, *Proposals for Printing by Subscription A Second Collection of Scarce and Valuable Tracts on the Most Interesting and Entertaining Subjects* (1 March 1748/9), sig. A3v; Anon., *A Second Collection of Scarce and Valuable Tracts, On the Most Interesting and Entertaining Subjects* (London, 1750), vol. II, pp. 129–33.

37. Anon., *The Harleian Miscellany: Or, A Collection of Scarce, Curious, and Entertaining Tracts* (London, 1744–45), vol. II, pp. 61–71, and vol. IV, pp. 501–4.

38. Anon., "The Death of King James the First. From a most rare and curious Print by Hollar, in the Collection of William Beckford, Esquire", British Museum, London. The broadside is undated. The Museum acquired its copy in 1849, but there was a version in circulation by February 1835, at the very latest, when the image was reproduced in *The Mirror of Literature, Amusement, and Instruction* 708 (28 February 1835), p. 137. Beckford was almost certainly William Beckford (d. 1844), and the broadside also notes a recent publication of an image of John Lambe by the print-dealer John Thane (d. 1818).

39. See e.g. *Burlington Fine Arts Club 1875 Exhibition of a Selection from the Work of Wenceslaus Hollar* (London, 1875), no. 84, p. 29.

40. Anon., *The Devil upon Dun: Or The Downfall of the Upstart Chymist* (London, 1672); Richard Pennington, *A descriptive catalogue of the etched work of Wenceslaus Hollar, 1607–1677* (Cambridge, 1982), no. 468, p. 69, "Satire against chemists".

41. For another early nineteenth-century image of Lambe, see Roy Porter, *Quacks: Fakers & Charlatans in English Medicine* (Stroud, 2000), p. 169.

42. Gustav Parthey, *Wenzel Hollar. Beschreibendes Verzeichniss Seiner Kupferstiche* (Berlin, 1853), no. 468, pp. 90–1; *Burlington Fine Arts Club*, p. 29. George Vertue, *A Description of the Works of the Ingenious Delineator and Engraver Wenceslaus Hollar* (London, 1745), p. 10, listed it as "A Satyr upon Chemical Medicines, a Man lying in his Bed, a Coffin covered with a Pall".

43. *Catalogue of A Collection of Engraved Portraits . . . Now on Sale . . . By Edward Evans Book and Print Seller* (London, nd), tp and p. 185; Huntington Rare Books, 143487 (available on EEBO).

44. For one particularly long-lived early nineteenth-century discussion, see "The Slow Poisoners" in Charles Mackay, *Memoirs of Extraordinary Popular Delusions*, 2nd ed. (London, 1852), vol. II.

45. Walter Scott (rev. and ed.), *A Collection of Scarce and Valuable Tracts* (London, 1811), vol. V, pp. 437–44. Scott was apparently aware of the complete version of Eglisham in the *Harleian Miscellany* (see his compilation *The Secret History of the Court of James I* [1811]), and would at some point own a copy of the 1626 English edition of *The Forerunner*. He makes no mention of the complete version in his notes on the radically truncated edition here.

46. George Brodie, *A History of the British Empire, From the Accession of Chares I to the Restoration*, 4 vols (Edinburgh, 1822), vol. II, pp. 126–30; Francis Espinasse, rev. H. C. G. Matthew, "Brodie, George (1786?–1867)", *ODNB*. Brodie did not believe that Charles played any role in his father's murder.

47. Thomas Babington Macaulay, *The History of England From the Accession of James II* (1848) 3 vols (London, 1906), vol. I, pp. 339–40.

48. See esp. Ian Burney, *Poison, Detection and the Victorian Imagination* (Manchester, 2006).

49. Norman Chevers, *Did James the First of England Die From the Effects of Poison, or From Natural Causes?* (Calcutta and London, 1862), pp. 1, 3–4.

50. Ivan A. D'Cruz and Robert A. Miller, "Norman Chevers: A Description of Congenital Absence of Pulmonary Valves and Supravalvular Aortic Stenosis in the Eighteen-Forties", *British Heart Journal* 26 (1964), pp. 723–5; Norman Chevers, *A Manual of Medical Jurisprudence for Bengal and the North-Western Provinces* (Calcutta, 1856), esp. pp. 5ff; Edward W. Said, *Orientalism* (New York, 1978).

51. Chevers, *James I*, pp. 30–1, 43–5.

52. Chevers, *James I*, p. 66.

53. Chevers, *James I*, pp. 6–10, 12–13, 17–18, 20, 23. He accepts Sanderson's account of the posset's ingredients.

54. Chevers, *James I*, pp. 36, 38–40. He does note (p. 15) that the newsletter report of James's swollen tongue might be read by modern forensic science to indicate mercury sublimate poisoning. He believed, however, that the report was incorrect.

55. S. R. Gardiner, *History of England from the Accession of James I*, 10 vols (New York, 1965), vol. V, p. 314 n.1.

56. Chevers, *James I*, pp. 1, 32, 49–58, 61–5.

Conclusion

1. NA E317/Herts/26 ("Theobalds House in Countie Hert": April 1650: transcript by the Edmonton Hundred Historical Society, Hertfordshire Archives and Library Service, 942.587CHE), pp. 9, 26, 48; *CJ*, VI (8 May, 30 June and 13 July 1649).

2. BL Add. MS 12528, fos 18v–19r.

3. On Charles's political mentality, see esp. Richard Cust, *The Forced Loan and English Politics, 1626–1628* (Oxford, 1987), and *Charles I: A Political Life* (London, 2005).

4. Maximin Deloche, *Autour de la Plume de Cardinal du Richelieu* (Paris, 1920); William F. Church, *Richelieu and Reason of State* (Princeton, 1972); J. K. Sawyer, *Printed Poison: Pamphlet Propaganda, Faction Politics, and the Public Sphere in Early Seventeenth-Century France* (Berkeley, 1991); and Helene Duccini, *Faire voir, faire croire: L'Opinion publique sous Louis XIII* (Champ Vallon, 2003).

5. BL Add. MS 78194, fo. 68r (Nicholas to Browne: 20 March 1648).

6. For a recent study emphasizing these interconnections back into prehistory, see Barry Cunliffe, *Britain Begins* (Oxford, 2013).

7. For an interesting recent example, see Paul Arblaster, *Antwerp & the World: Richard Verstegan and the International Culture of Catholic Reformation* (Leuven, 2004).

8. See e.g. Malcolm, *Reason*; Paul Arblaster, "Posts, Newsletters, Newspapers: England in a European System of Communications", *Media History* 11:1/2 (2005); Paul Arblaster, "Antwerp and Brussels as Inter-European Spaces in News Exchange", in Brendan Dooley (ed.), *Dissemination of News and the Emergence of Contemporaneity in Early Modern Europe* (Farnham and Burlington, 2010); Helmer Helmers, *The Royalist Republic: Literature, Politics and Religion in the Anglo-Dutch Public Sphere, 1639–1660* (Cambridge,

2015); and forthcoming transnational research projects by literary historians Joad Raymond, Nigel Smith and Alan Stewart.

9. See Peter Lake's Ford Lectures, delivered in 2011 under the title "Bad Queen Bess: Libelous Politics and Secret Histories in an Age of Confessional Conflict".

10. Marc Bloch, *The Royal Touch: Monarchy and Miracles in France and England* (1924), trans. J. E. Anderson (New York, 1989), p. 5. The key recent works in this vein have come from scholars of several different academic generations, including David Como, David Cressy, Richard Cust, Ann Hughes, Peter Lake, Noah Millstone, Jason Peacey, Curtis Perry, Joad Raymond, John Walter, and the late Kevin Sharpe and David Underdown.

11. *Forerunner*, p. 4.

12. Norman Chevers, *Did James the First of England Die From the Effects of Poison, or From Natural Causes?* (Calcutta and London, 1862), p. 1.

INDEX

(Illustrations indicated by italics)